THE NEW YORK TIMES ON
GAY AND LESBIAN ISSUES

SUSAN BURGESS

◉SAGE | **CQPRESS**

Los Angeles | London | New Delhi
Singapore | Washington DC

CQ Press
2300 N Street, NW, Suite 800
Washington, DC 20037

Phone: 202-729-1900; toll-free, 1-866-4CQ-PRESS (1-866-427-7737)
Web: www.cqpress.com

Cover design: Matthew Simmons, www.MyselfIncluded.com
Composition: C&M Digitals (P) Ltd.

♾ The paper used in this publication exceeds the requirements of the American National Standard for Information Sciences–Permanence of Paper for Printed Library Materials, ANSI Z39.48-1992.

Printed and bound in the United States of America

15 14 13 12 11   1 2 3 4 5

Library of Congress Cataloging-in-Publication Data

Burgess, Susan
    The New York times on gay and lesbian issues / Susan Burgess.
       p. cm. — (TimesReference from CQ Press)
    Includes bibliographical references and index.
    ISBN 978-1-60426-593-4 (alk. paper)
    1. Gays—United States—Press coverage. 2. Lesbians—United States—Press coverage. 3. New York times. I. Title. II. Series.

    HQ76.3.U5B87 2011
    306.76'60973—dc22

                                                                                    2011012923

For Kate

OTHER TITLES FROM

TimesReference from CQ Press

2008

The New York Times on the Presidency, 1853–2008

The New York Times on the Supreme Court, 1857–2008

2009

The New York Times on Critical Elections, 1854–2008

The New York Times on Emerging Democracies in Eastern Europe

CONTENTS

ABOUT TimesReference
from CQ Press

The books in the TimesReference from CQ Press series present unique documentary histories on a range of topics. The lens through which the histories are viewed is the original reporting of *The New York Times* and its many generations of legendary reporters.

Each book consists of documents selected from *The New York Times* newspaper accompanied by original narrative written by a scholar or content expert that provides context and analysis. The documents are primarily news articles, but also include editorials, op ed essays, letters to the editor, columns, and news analyses. Some are presented with full text; others, because of length, have been excerpted. Ellipses indicate omitted text. Using the headline and date as search criteria, readers can find the full text of all articles in *The Times'* online archive at nytimes.com, which includes all of *The Times'* articles since the newspaper began publication in 1851.

The Internet age has revolutionized the way news is delivered, which means that there is no longer only one version of a story. Today, breaking news articles that appear on *The Times'* Web site are written to provide up-to-the-minute coverage of an event and therefore may differ from the article that is published in the print edition. Content could also differ between early and late editions of the day's printed paper. As such, some discrepancies between versions may be present in these volumes.

The books are illustrated with photographs and other types of images. While most of these appeared in the print or online edition of the paper, not all were created by *The Times,* which, like many newspapers, relies on wire services for photographs.

There are also editorial features in these books that did not appear in *The Times*—they were created or selected by CQ Press to enhance the documentary history being told. For example, in *The New York Times on Critical Elections, 1854-2008,* electoral and popular vote return boxes help readers crunch the numbers as they read about the highlights of each election.

Readers will note that many articles are introduced by several levels of headlines—especially in pieces from the paper's early years. This was done to emphasize the importance of the article. For very important stories, banner headlines stretch across the front page's many columns; every attempt has been made to include these with the relevant articles. Over the years, *The Times* added datelines and bylines at the beginning of articles.

Typographical and punctuation errors are the bane of every publisher's existence. Because all of the documents included in this book were re-typeset, CQ Press approached these problems in several different ways. Archaic spellings from the paper's early days appear just as they did in the original documents (for example, "employe" rather than "employee"). CQ Press corrected minor typographical errors that appeared in the original articles to assist readers' comprehension. In some cases, factual or other errors have been marked [*sic*]; where the meaning would be distorted, corrections have been made in brackets where possible.

ABOUT THE AUTHOR

Susan Burgess is professor of political science and professor of women's and gender studies at Ohio University. She is the author of *The Founding Fathers, Pop Culture and Constitutional Law: Who's Your Daddy?* (Ashgate, 2008) and *Contest for Constitutional Authority: The Abortion and War Powers Debates* (University Press of Kansas, 1992), as well as articles in various journals. Her work in the profession includes serving on the governing council of the American Political Science Association (APSA) as well as chair of its LGBT Caucus. She is also active in the Western Political Science Association (WPSA) and has sat on its Executive Council and served several times as program organizer for its Politics and Sexuality section. Burgess is the recipient of several departmental and university-wide teaching awards.

ACKNOWLEDGMENTS

I am grateful to Ohio University's Department of Political Science as well as its Program in Women's and Gender Studies for providing a work environment in which research on sexuality and politics is not only tolerated but also valued. Thanks in particular to Judith Grant, Ron Hunt, Vince Jungkunz, Lynette Peck, Nicole Reynolds, Kathleen Sullivan, Barry Tadlock, and Julie White for taking time away from their own work to discuss LGBT politics with me. Thanks also to friends and colleagues in the Sexuality and Politics and the Law and Courts sections of the APSA and WPSA, as well as those in the Feminist Political Theory Group in the WPSA. This book would have been impossible without their input and support. Very special thanks to Kate Leeman for her assistance with this project, which was, as always, invaluable.

INTRODUCTION

This book explores *The New York Times* coverage of lesbian, gay, bisexual, and transgender (LGBT) issues, from 1851 to 2010, focusing primarily on events in the United States. Reporting on these issues has changed considerably over time, ranging from little to no coverage in the mid- to late 1800s; to coverage of sensational trials focused on the censorship of gay- and lesbian-themed written work, purges of gay workers from the federal government, and panicked warnings about startling new levels of sexual perversity in New York in the period following World War II; to growing coverage of the LGBT movement as it emerged and then came to address a range of issues from the late 1960s to the present. During this latter period *The Times* coverage of LGBT issues increased significantly, documenting significant shifts in medical, psychological, legal, moral, and religious understandings of homosexuality. These shifts came to form the basis of a growing public tolerance of LGBT people and an increased awareness of the movement's struggle to gain equal rights and liberties. While there is by no means political consensus on issues such as same-sex marriage or gays in the military, it is now generally accepted that these issues, as well as other topics relating to LGBT sexuality, form an important part of public debate and thus are worthy of sustained news coverage.

The Stonewall Rebellion

The book begins with the first chapter's exploration of events surrounding a multinight riot that took place at the Stonewall Inn in New York City's Greenwich Village in June 1969, during which LGBT people resisted routine police efforts to shut down a gay bar and arrest its patrons. Typically understood as the beginning of the modern LGBT movement, *The Times* coverage of the events surrounding the Stonewall Rebellion offers a baseline that helps to assess how gays and lesbians were treated in the periods before, during, and after the event.

Prior to Stonewall, homosexuality was regarded by many as a criminal offense, a moral perversion, and a psychological disorder. Many states and localities had laws that prohibited homosexuals from meeting or working in state-licensed places. LGBT people were routinely arrested merely for socializing in bars. Such arrests often led to the loss of jobs, family support, and religious communities and in some cases institutionalization or suicide.

The work of researchers in the post–World War II period helped the public to understand that same-sex behavior was more common than had previously been imagined. Several prominent members of Congress had argued that homosexuals who worked for the government, especially those in the State Department, would have to hide a homosexual identity, thus making them vulnerable to communist and fascist blackmail and thereby endangering national security. Repeated purges of these employees, many of whom were longstanding federal workers, led to what is thought to be the first public protest on behalf of homosexual rights at the White House in 1965. These protests were nonviolent and orderly; participants were well dressed and nonconfrontational during the demonstration.

While other protests on behalf of homosexual rights took place in various cities across the country, the resistance to police harassment that occurred at the Stonewall Inn in the summer of 1969 is often said to be the catalyst for a dramatic new demand for equal treatment for the gay community. Rather than passively accepting yet another police raid and the arrests that came with it, the patrons of the Stonewall Inn fought back, calling for an end to such discriminatory practices and changing the way that the gay community understood itself, as well as the way that the public understood the gay community. For example, the language in which nonheterosexual identity was discussed changed. Rather than continuing to refer to themselves as "homosexuals," a term that for many connoted a clinical and deviant medical disorder (see discussion of the third chapter, "Sexuality, Gender, and Science" below), homosexuals instead substituted the less negative term "gay" and referred to the drive for equal rights as "the gay rights movement." As a result, greater numbers of people began to publicly proclaim their sexuality to their families, work colleagues, and congregations by "coming out" to them (see discussion of "Coming Out, Outing, and the Closet" below). The movement adopted the tagline "Gay is good," signifying a rejection of the condemnation and shame long associated with homosexuality that had led many to think of it as an illness, a criminal offense, and a moral perversion.

This new pride in being gay was reflected in annual parades held in cities across the country to publicly commemorate the 1969 Stonewall Rebellion. These "pride parades," as they came to be known, celebrated the diversity and political potency of the gay community. Pride in gay sexuality also led to a proliferation of organizations designed to promote gay rights. Organizations such as the Gay Activists Alliance and the Gay Liberation Front provided new forums in which gays could socialize, organize politically, and educate the public about the emerging LGBT movement.

A Word on Language

The New York Times did not officially adopt the use of the term "gay" in place of "homosexual" until the 1980s, during a turnover in senior management that occurred in the midst of coverage of the AIDS crisis (see discussion of the next chapter, "AIDs," below). This book attempts to reflect the changing language of the movement and *The Times* coverage as it evolved over time, sometimes resulting in the overlapping use of the terms.

It has been said that gays are the only group that includes members from all parts of society, regardless of race, gender, socioeconomic status, religion, or other demographic indicators. As the movement for gay rights gained strength, tensions emerged between more radical and reformist participants, between gay men and lesbians, and between gay people of color and white gays, who often had different political visions that were expressed in varying styles of organization and protest. For example, even though people of color and transgender people had played a central role in the Stonewall Rebellion, this was often left undiscussed. They were sometimes excluded or marginalized by less radical organizers, who assumed that most gays were white or that the "flamboyance" associated with cross-dressing would undercut demands for equal rights, which they often saw as being based on a claim that gay people were as mainstream as white middle-class straight people, apart from their sexuality. Bisexuals were also frequently excluded or marginalized, often dismissed as uncommitted or afraid to come out as gay. While recognizing that these tensions remain in the movement, this book typically will use the inclusive language of "lesbian, gay, bisexual, and transgender" (LGBT) when referring to the movement, except when *The Times* articles being referred to demand otherwise.

CIVIL RIGHTS LAWS

The second chapter, "Gay Civil Rights Laws and the Emerging LGTB Community," explores *The New York Times* coverage of the passage of many new civil rights laws that protected gays and lesbians from discrimination in housing, employment, and public accommodations, beginning with the college towns of East Lansing and Ann Arbor, Michigan, in 1972. In addition, a national civil rights bill to protect against discrimination based on sexual orientation was introduced into Congress for the first time in 1974. Over time a backlash emerged against some localities that had adopted these sorts of civil rights protections, perhaps most famously in Dade County (Miami), Florida, which became the first locality to repeal its civil rights protections for gays (in 1977) following a high-profile campaign led by Anita Bryant, a popular singer and evangelical Christian. Several other cities followed suit, including St. Paul, Minnesota; Eugene, Oregon; and Wichita, Kansas. Although these developments were obviously a setback for gay and lesbian rights, they did serve to consolidate the LGBT community at national and local levels. Owing in part to the work of these newly emerging groups, in late 1978 Californians rejected a statewide initiative that would have led to the firing of homosexual teachers or any teachers advocating homosexuality. In 1982 Wisconsin became the first state to pass a law making discrimination on the basis of sexual orientation illegal, as various localities across the country continued to adopt such measures throughout the 1980s.

In the early 1990s constitutional amendments appeared on the ballot in Oregon and Colorado that proposed to prohibit local governments from passing civil rights protections for homosexuals. While such a referendum successfully passed in Colorado, it was ultimately struck down by the U.S. Supreme Court, which said that it denied gays and lesbians equal protection under the law, unconstitutionally making them second-class citizens. The ruling, *Romer v. Evans* (1996), was the biggest legal victory for the LGBT movement up to that time.

SCIENCE

The next chapter, "Sexuality, Gender, and Science," explores *The Times* coverage of sexuality, gender, and science. Various unfounded assumptions about sexuality and gender needed to be debunked scientifically before additional movement could be made with respect to equal rights for LGBT people. For example, the American Psychological Association (APA) had long classified homosexuals as psychopaths in its *Diagnostic and Statistical Manual* (DSM). Although many considered such medical classification more humane than criminal or moral condemnation, the fact remained that such a medical characterization implied a condition with a cure, and this often had negative consequences for homosexuals in a wide variety of areas including employment, immigration, child custody, and military service. In addition, leading psychiatrists during this period regularly blamed homosexuality on dysfunctional parenting, as documented in several lengthy articles that appeared in *The Times*

Magazine, further entrenching the isolation and shame of families with gay and lesbian adult children.

In 1973, after years of efforts by gay advocates and path-breaking new studies by leading psychologists such as Dr. Evelyn Hooker, the APA reversed its position on this issue, declaring the average homosexual to be as well adjusted as the average heterosexual, removing a longstanding basis for gay stigmatization and exclusion. Now that the evidence suggested that parents were no longer to blame for homosexuality, *The Times* turned its attention to the scientific community's exploration of various other biological, cultural, and hybrid explanations.

Transgender issues also received attention in the science coverage of *The Times,* ranging from rather sensationalistic discussions of Christine Jorgensen's sex change operation in the 1950s, to the controversy over male-to-female (MTF) transsexual Renee Richards being allowed to play in the women's draw of the U.S. Open in the 1970s, to a tuberculosis outbreak in transgender communities in New York City and Baltimore in the 1990s, to a female-to-male (FTM) transsexual carrying a baby to term in the 2000s.

AIDS

Of all the scientific issues pertaining to sexuality and gender covered by *The New York Times,* none received more coverage than AIDS. Accordingly, the fourth chapter focuses exclusively on AIDS, exploring its discovery, the response of the government as well as the gay community, and its impact on the civil rights and liberties of people with AIDS. While gays are certainly not the only people affected by AIDS, the high rate of mortality in the gay community served to change the style and substance of LGBT movement activism. It is hard to overestimate the import of the emergence of AIDS for the LGBT community, as the movement's focus in the early 1980s turned away from civil and political rights to the delivery of adequate medical treatment and more responsive health care policy. Many of those afflicted by the disease who had previously been closeted were suddenly politicized as they fought for a more effective government response to the disease.

When the disease was first discovered in 1981, it was called gay-related immune deficiency (GRID), reflecting the early (and mistaken) understanding, even in the scientific community, that the disease afflicted only homosexual men. Even the Center for Disease Control (later, Centers for Disease Control and Prevention; CDC) initially stated that the disease posed no danger to heterosexuals. By 1983 the scientific community changed the name of the disease to acquired immune deficiency syndrome (AIDS), reflecting the growing understanding that the disease could affect heterosexuals as well as homosexuals. In a highly competitive atmosphere, both French and American scientists claimed to have found the cause of the disease as early as 1984. The urgency of this work grew as nearly 10,000 cases and 5,000 deaths had been reported by 1985. Procedures were developed to screen the blood supply, and new drugs such as AZT were tested. By 1987 French and American scientists agreed to share credit for finding the cause of AIDS, which they called human immunodeficiency virus (HIV). They also agreed to share the profits accruing from related testing.

Early uncertainty regarding the transmission and cause of AIDS, along with its high mortality rate, fueled public fears about the disease, which sometimes threatened the civil rights and liberties of people with AIDS. For a time high-profile politicians and journalists and a significant portion of the population seriously entertained tattooing and quarantining people with AIDS, as well as prohibiting them from having sex, ostensibly as a means of containing the epidemic. People with AIDS were evicted from their apartments, fired from their jobs, and prevented from attending public and private schools. Coverage of the high-profile case of young Ryan White's exclusion from school brought greater public attention and empathy to these issues.

These difficulties were perhaps exacerbated by the federal government's slow response to the disease. President Ronald Reagan did not address the disease in a major speech until 1987, six years after news of it had broken. By this time over 25,000 Americans had died of AIDS. Tensions arose in the Reagan administration when Surgeon General C. Everett Koop argued that a scientific approach required frank talk about sex and condom usage, while Secretary of Education William Bennett urged the administration to take a values-based approach that would advocate abstinence for teens and monogamy for adults. Congress also grappled with these issues as Sen. Jesse Helms (R-NC) successfully prevented the allocation of funds to groups advocating Koop's approach.

The LGBT community responded to the disease, and to federal inaction, with a combination of grass-roots social service and activism. New groups were formed such as Gay Men's Health Crisis (GMHC) and AIDS Coalition to Unleash Power, better known as ACT UP, to provide care for people with AIDS and to challenge the government's tepid response to the crisis. Creative political actions at diverse locations, including Wall Street, the National Institutes of Health (NIH), St. Patrick's Cathedral, and New York Mets baseball games, played an important role in hastening the development of accessible and affordable drugs to fight the disease. Owing in part to these actions, drugs that made it possible to live with HIV increasingly became available, particularly to more affluent populations, as the 1990s wore down. However, the number of HIV-positive people continued to grow worldwide, disproportionately affecting groups such as black women in the United States and, on a worldwide scale, those in sub-Saharan Africa.

Some have suggested that the AIDS crisis prompted *The Times* itself to reconsider its understanding of the gay community, including the language used to describe it. *The Times* had long declined to use the word "gay" unless in a direct quotation or to describe the name of a specific group. In 1986 the paper slowly began to use appellations such as "gay" and "lesbian" in place of the previous designation of "homosexual." Some speculated that this change in policy was not only the result of a change in executive editors and a desire to reach a wider readership but also due to a change in consciousness at *The Times* as a result of a beloved assistant editor coming out as HIV positive. One indication of a changing consciousness in the newsroom occurred on March 26, 1987, when *The Times* corrected a caption on a picture that had originally described arrests at a Manhattan demonstration as "Homosexuals Arrested at AIDS Drug Protest." The correction stated: "Although homosexual rights groups took part in the protest, those arrested—for crossing police barricades and blocking traffic—were not identified by sexual orientation." While gay rights groups were still called homosexual, the correction did seem to indicate a deepened understanding of the complicated nature of identifying sexual orientation.

COMING OUT

Coming out, the focus of the chapter "Coming Out, Outing, and the Closet," has been a central focus of the LGBT movement at least since Stonewall. Because children are typically not raised to be gay, they publicly acquire the identity, usually as teens or adults, through a process that has become known as coming out (of the closet). This involves accepting an LGBT identity and declaring it to some portion of family, friends, colleagues, or others while discarding the shame that is associated with hiding one's sexuality. Coming out is thought to be personally and politically empowering. Greater visibility is associated with increased tolerance in the private sphere, which in turn translates into greater political equality in the public sphere. While LGBT people began to come out in increasing numbers in the 1970s and 1980s, it was still risky for many to do so, for fear of losing their jobs, friends, and families. Coming out remains difficult for some, particularly vulnerable populations such as teachers (owing to persistent myths that gay people prey on youths), teens (who are typically still economically and emotionally dependent on their families or guardians), and bisexuals and transgender people (who are sometimes marginalized even within the LGBT community).

The move toward greater numbers of LGBT people coming out was slowly reflected in popular culture. Although gays and lesbians were portrayed in a largely negative light or used as the butt of humor early on in the 1960s and 1970s, gradually they came to be portrayed more sympathetically in television shows such as *Ellen,* whose presumably straight central character came out as a lesbian near the end of the show's run. By 2003, the same year as the pathbreaking gay rights case *Lawrence v. Texas* (see discussion of the following chapter), gay men were giving advice to straight men about how to conduct their lives more effectively on cable television's *Queer Eye for the Straight Guy.* Transgender people gained more visibility in the movies in the 1990s through several feature films that performed well at the box office, such as 1994's *The Adventures of Priscilla, Queen of the Desert,* while network television's *Dirty Sexy Money* offered the first recurring portrayal of a transgender person in 2007.

Although coming out had long been thought of largely as a voluntary or chosen act, the practice of publicly outing politicians and celebrities that emerged in the 1990s challenged that assumption. During the AIDS crisis, journalists working at alternative newspapers began to question the informal norm in mainstream media sources (such as *The New York Times)* that allowed high-profile gay men to remain in the closet, even while numerous other aspects of their lives were widely discussed. These journalists were particularly concerned with public figures (for example, Assistant Secretary of Defense Pete Williams) who supported policies that restricted open participation of gays in public life, such as the military's "Don't Ask, Don't Tell," or who failed to advocate for stronger governmental intervention in the area of AIDS. They began to out the sexuality of such figures, to underscore the inconsistency between their private lives and their public policy positions. Some criticized the practice of outing as a breach of privacy. Nonetheless, this new practice led many politicians and celebrities, such as Rep. Barney Frank (D-MA), to come out preemptively, for fear that if they did not, the alternative media would do it for them.

Privacy

As long as homosexual sex remained a felony, the rights of LGBT people were at risk in a number of other areas such as employment and child custody. The sixth chapter, "The Right to Privacy and the Decriminalization of Sodomy," explores the slow decriminalization of sodomy as growing numbers of people began to believe that various forms of sexual intimacy, including same-sex sexual expression, should be private and beyond the reach of state. Britain took the lead in 1957, issuing a now famous document known as the Wolfenden Report, which recommended that sodomy be decriminalized, and the American Law Institute followed suit in 1960. Shortly thereafter, individual states began to repeal their antisodomy laws, beginning with Illinois in 1961. By 1985 only twenty-five states still had antisodomy laws on the books. Despite this trend toward decriminalization, the Supreme Court reaffirmed the right of any state to continue to criminalize sodomy in a close 5–4 1986 decision, handing the LGBT movement one of its biggest defeats. The ruling in this case, *Bowers v. Hardwick,* stood for seventeen years, until 2003, when the 6–3 ruling of the Supreme Court in *Lawrence v. Texas* declared antisodomy laws unconstitutional breaches of the constitutional right to privacy. Declaring that

Bowers was wrongly decided, the Court said that the Constitution protected both homosexual and heterosexual intimacy. Supporters as well as opponents regarded the *Lawrence* case as the single most important decision in the history of the LGBT movement in the United States, with many on both sides of the issue predicting that its recognition of gay rights would lead to the legalization of same-sex marriage in the not-too-distant future. When Massachusetts became the first state in the Union to decide to recognize gay marriage several months later, it seemed to many that this prediction had been affirmed (see "Same-Sex Marriage and the Family" below).

MILITARY

While LGBT people have always served in the military, they have typically not been allowed to do so openly. The chapter "Gays in the Military" explores changing public policy on this issue over time, with a focus on the development and eventual repeal of the Don't Ask, Don't Tell policy, which has received an enormous amount of coverage in *The Times.* Since 1919 periodic purges have been conducted at various military bases and in the federal government, leading to discharges of LGBT service members and defense employees, particularly women and people of color. While such discharges have periodically been challenged by individual members of the military, such as Leonard Matlovich in the 1970s, in 1992 Bill Clinton became the first president to advocate lifting the ban on gay military service. His proposal, however, met with stiff resistance, particularly from the military leadership and members of Congress.

Rather than issuing an executive order, as President Harry Truman had done to end racial segregation in the military, President Clinton chose to negotiate with his opponents, resulting in the Don't Ask, Don't Tell policy of 1993. Advocates of the policy said that it represented a compromise, offering decreased military investigations of sexuality in return for military members' silence on the matter. It soon became clear, however, that neither end of the compromise would be upheld, since the military continued to vigorously investigate members' sexuality and since members of the military continued to come out as gay. As a consequence, the rate of discharge increased significantly under the new policy, even in the face of the enormous recruitment needs later generated by two ongoing wars.

Like Clinton, Barack Obama also promised to lift the ban while campaigning for president. By the time of Obama's election, the demand for troops had risen even further, and several retired generals, including a former chair of the Joint Chiefs of Staff, declared that they were now in favor of allowing gays and lesbians to serve openly, despite previous statements to the contrary. Public opinion had also shifted as a popular majority now supported ending the ban, including a majority of Republicans and regular churchgoers. In 2010 President Obama announced that he and the Congress had agreed to repeal Don't Ask, Don't Tell, allowing LGBT people to serve openly in the military, pending the results of a Pentagon study designed to determine whether such a move might affect military readiness. In July 2010, when the Pentagon commissioned a survey asking troops how they would react to homosexuals serving openly in the military, some gay advocacy groups objected to its repeated use of the term "homosexual," arguing that it is a derogatory way to refer to gay people and hence that the survey was biased. A *New York Times*/CBS News poll conducted earlier, in February 2010, supported this claim, finding that respondents who were asked whether they favored letting "homosexuals" serve in the military were 11 percent less likely to answer the question favorably than those who were asked whether they favored letting "gay men and lesbians" serve. Despite these concerns, when the Pentagon released the results of the survey in November 2010, 70 percent of those serving in combat and noncombat positions said they believed that the impact of lifting the ban on gays in the military would have a positive, mixed, or inconsequential impact on their units. In December 2010, Congress repealed Don't Ask, Don't Tell on the basis of bipartisan votes in both the House (250–175) and the Senate (63–33), providing legal sanction for gays and lesbians to serve openly in the armed forces for the first time in American history.

YOUTH

While acceptance of and support for LGBT youth have improved over time, young people with alternative gender and sexual orientation still face greater difficulties than their heterosexual counterparts. Both developments have been tracked by The Times, as discussed in the chapter "Youth and Education." Many LGBT children experience regular teasing and bullying in school, particularly transgender youth. Often regarded as outsiders not only in society but also in their own families, LGBT kids are at greater risk for being beaten and sexually abused within their own homes. Some are institutionalized by their families or put into programs that are designed to "convert" them to heterosexuality, while others run away from home. Experts have estimated that over 30 percent of homeless teens are LGBT and have suggested that LGBT youth more generally experience lower self-esteem as well as higher rates of depression and are at greater risk to abuse substances, to drop out of school, and to contemplate or commit suicide than are non-LGBT youth.

Efforts at elementary and high schools to address these risks by creating a more inclusive curriculum or by offering support groups such as Gay-Straight Alliances have been resisted in some areas, even when they were part of larger efforts to diversify the curriculum or to broaden club access for all students, with controversy often focusing on the appropriateness of allowing the discussion of sexual content of any sort in the schools. Even at the college level, for many years traditional practices strongly discouraged gay students from coming out, sometimes leading to such tragic results as the suicides associated with the infamous 1920 homosexual purge at Harvard. As society became more accepting of sexual privacy and freedom in the 1960s and 1970s, many colleges offered more supportive environments in which LGBT students could more safely come out. As the culture wars heated up in the 1980s, some conservative student groups challenged the morality of these developments as well as the legitimacy of LGBT studies programs and antidiscrimination policies, several of which began to include transgender students in late 1990s and early 2000s.

Extracurricular activities also raised questions of inclusion and morality, as, for example, in the high-profile case of James Dale and the Boy Scouts of America. Although the founder of the Scouts is thought by some to have himself been gay, the Boy Scouts revoked the membership of Rutgers student James Dale, an Eagle Scout in good standing and Assistant Scoutmaster of a troop in New Jersey, after learning that he was gay, arguing that homosexuality was incompatible with the Scouts' oath to be morally straight and clean. While the Scouts won the case at the U.S. Supreme Court level and were permitted to bar Dale and other gays from access to their organization, they lost a significant number of members and financial support in the wake of the case, because many viewed the Scouts' decision to exclude gays as discriminatory.

VIOLENCE

The chapter "Violence against LGBT People" discusses the alarmingly high rate of attacks against those in the LGBT community, a subject that received extensive coverage in The Times. A 1984 study of 2,000 subjects living in six cities found that 44 percent of LGBT people had been threatened with violence, while 19 percent had actually been assaulted. This high incidence of violence tends to instill fear in the LGBT community, even among those who have not personally been attacked. Murderous attacks on LGBT people often exhibit "overkill," or a use of force that significantly exceeds that which is necessary to kill a person, leading experts to categorize such attacks as hate crimes, since they seem to be rooted in hatred of those who do not conform to mainstream sex or gender norms, or homophobia. *The New York Times* is thought to be the first major newspaper to address this issue, beginning with a piece by William Greer in 1986, in which such violence was recognized as a unique category of crime.

The justice system has an uneven record in dealing with violence against LGBT people, with reports sometimes being ignored, charges being filed slowly or lessened, and cases being dismissed or given light sentencing. In addition, LGBT distrust of police is often quite high, due in part to a history of poor treatment at the hands of police stemming from the time before Stonewall. To address these issues, police in many cities have been given training on LGBT issues and LGBT advocacy groups have endeavored to better communicate with police, providing information about harassment and violence in the community. Despite these efforts, and the enormous media attention given to the 1998 murder of Matthew Shepard (including extensive coverage in *The Times*), efforts to pass hate crime bills in the wake of the incident failed at the federal level as well as in Wyoming, where the crime took place.

Ultimately, the Matthew Shepard and James Byrd Hate Crimes Prevention Act was passed by Congress and signed by President Obama in 2009; however, the rate of violence against LGBT people remains high. Transgender people are particularly at risk for severe violence, as evidenced by the 1993 murder of Brandon Teena, a female-to-male transgender person who was raped and murdered after police revealed to others in Teena's town that he was born a woman. Teena's story became well known to the public in 1999 through a Hollywood feature film titled *Boys Don't Cry*. Another, more recent case that received attention in *The Times* was that of Angie Zapata, who was beaten to death by a boyfriend when he discovered that she had male genitalia. Designed to memorialize those murdered and to raise public awareness, "Remembering Our Dead" events are held each year on November 20, the day that Rita Hester was brutally stabbed to death in Allston, Massachusetts, in 1998.

MARRIAGE

Of all the issues covered in this volume, same-sex marriage and family issues have received the greatest amount of coverage in *The Times*. Gay and lesbian couples have been seeking marriage recognition from the state at least since the early 1970s, as part of the more general drive for equal rights and as a means to secure hospital visitation of spouses, coadoption of children, joint property and inheritance rights, and a host of other benefits. *The Times* coverage of these developments was relatively spare in the 1970s and 1980s; however, as illustrated in the chapter "Same-Sex Marriage and the Family," that changed in the early 1990s, when national attention turned to Hawaii, which was poised to become the first state in the Union to legalize same-sex marriage. Ultimately, the Hawaii effort to legalize same-sex marriage failed; the federal government and several states passed laws that clearly declined to recognize same-sex marriages that might be performed in Hawaii or any other state, despite the longstanding practice of states recognizing marriages performed in other states with different marriage requirements (such as age, lack of family relation, and the like).

The Times again devoted a great amount of coverage to the issue when in 1999 the Vermont Supreme Court ordered the state legislature to devise a plan that would make equal benefits available to gay and straight couples alike. The legislature ultimately decided to offer civil unions as an alternative. Although this move fell short of marriage, it nevertheless prompted a new wave of states to ban same-sex marriage, with thirty-seven states doing so by

2003, the same year that the U.S. Supreme Court issued a monumental decision, in *Lawrence v. Texas,* preventing states from criminalizing sodomy, a huge victory for the LGBT rights movement (see "The Right to Privacy . . . "). Just a few months later the Massachusetts Supreme Judicial Court declared that its state constitution required equal marriage rights for both gay and straight couples. This decision may well have affected the outcome of the 2004 presidential campaign, leading to the election of George W. Bush, a staunch opponent of same-sex marriage (see discussion of the following chapter).

In response to President Bush's public opposition to same-sex marriage, Mayor Gavin Newsom allowed gay and lesbian couples to get married in San Francisco in February 2004 until a court halted the proceedings one month later. In a blockbuster ruling that rivaled the Massachusetts decision in its enormity, the California Supreme Court said that its constitution required the state to recognize same-sex marriage, a decision that stood until it was overturned by popular referendum (Proposition 8) during the 2008 presidential election, shifting the momentum in the debate back to those who oppose same-sex marriage. When Iowa legalized gay marriage the following year, the momentum shifted again as few expected a state in the heartland of America to embrace equality for gays and lesbians. However, after a popular vote in the largely liberal New England state of Maine rescinded the same-sex marriage rights that had earlier been granted by that state's legislature and governor, the future direction of the debate became decidedly uncertain. When a federal district court declared Proposition 8 unconstitutional in the summer of 2010, it appeared that the momentum had again swung in favor of same-sex marriage supporters. As of this writing, a ruling on the appeal of that decision is pending. In late 2010 Illinois became the tenth state to either offer civil unions or recognize same-sex domestic partnerships. Five states and the District of Columbia recognize gay marriage as the controversy continues.

RELIGION

"The Intersection of Religion with Gay and Lesbian Issues" addresses many of the ways that religion comes into play with LGBT issues, including congregation membership and the ordination of clergy. Religious groups have also played a major role in several highly charged political debates external to the church, such as same-sex marriage. Outright exclusion of LGBT people from the membership of mainstream congregations, as well as subtle or not-so-subtle suggestions that gay members could retain religious affiliation if they remained closeted, led to the 1968 creation of the Metropolitan Community Church (MCC), which welcomes all members regardless of sexual orientation. However, as more LGBT people began to come out of the closet in the wake of Stonewall, many congregations started to reconsider their exclusionary policies, welcoming gays and lesbians as members and clergy. By the 1970s many mainstream religious groups began to question the longstanding view that homosexuality is a moral failing; however, as *The Times* coverage indicates, some churches resisted these developments, leading to conflict among members and leadership about the meaning of their beliefs in practice.

Perhaps the most visible example of this conflict occurred when the Episcopal Church decided to install Rev. Eugene Robinson as a bishop in 2003. Because Robinson was openly gay and in a committed gay partnership, his selection stirred great controversy in some sectors of the global Episcopal Communion, leading a handful of congregations in the United States to align with more conservative Episcopal congregations in Africa. Also in 2003, same-sex marriage became legal for the first time in the United States as the state of Massachusetts joined France, Belgium, and Germany, with Britain and Canada soon to follow. Although religious congregations had long been a part of both sides of the political discussion regarding equal rights for LGBT people, many congregations felt a new urgency to declare their beliefs about whether gay and lesbian marriages should be celebrated within their bodies, owing to these developments. Beliefs ran so strong that many experts claimed that anti–same sex marriage initiatives on the ballots in several states during the 2004 presidential elections tipped the election in favor of George W. Bush owing to conservative "value voters," many of whom were regular churchgoers. President Obama's 2008 selection of both Bishop Robinson and the conservative, antigay Rev. Rick Warren to lead prayers at his inauguration celebrations reflects the ongoing conflict on these issues within religious congregations in the United States.

EMPLOYMENT

As discussed in the final chapter, "Sexuality and Gender in the Workforce," many experts anticipate the federal government will soon pass employment protections for LGBT workers. Although a federal civil rights bill addressing discrimination in housing, public accommodations, and employment was first introduced into Congress in 1974, it has yet to pass. A more specific bill addressing discrimination in the context of employment was first introduced in 1994. Known as the Employment Non-Discrimination Act (ENDA), the bill aims to protect against discrimination on the basis of sexual orientation and gender identity in the workplace. It has failed to pass as yet, coming within one vote in the Senate in 1996 and gaining a bipartisan majority in the House for the first time in 2007. Controversy arose at that time because this broad-based coalition came together only after gender identity was omitted from the bill. Although some workplaces now have antidiscrimination policies in place that include sexual orientation and gender identity, as well as domestic partner benefits, supporters of ENDA argue that the protection it would provide is necessary because of ongoing discrimination against LGBT people in many workplaces. A lack of legal protection leaves LGBT employees in many jurisdictions at risk, as documented by several of *The Times* stories included in this chapter that discuss LGBT workers who have been fired for no reason other than their sexual or gender identity. While the Obama administration has begun to offer some limited domestic partner benefits to federal workers (not including health care benefits) and has added gender identity to its antidiscrimination hiring policies, it remains to be seen whether ENDA will pass soon.

The Times coverage of LGBT issues from 1851 to 2010 reveals a great deal of change in attitudes, language, and policy. Homosexuality is no longer classified as a mental disorder or a felony, and most Americans no longer consider it a moral perversion. LGBT people continue to come out in greater numbers, although numbers are much lower in vulnerable populations. In addition, results are still mixed with respect to the movement's goal of gaining equal rights for LGBT people. Sodomy has been decriminalized, and Congress has passed legislation that allows gays and lesbians to serve openly in the military. While many local governments, nonprofits, educational institutions, and businesses have adopted antidiscrimination polices that protect against discrimination on the basis of sexual orientation and gender identity, the federal government has yet to pass the Employment Non-Discrimination Act. The federal government and many states have passed hate crimes legislation that addresses violence perpetrated because of sexuality and gender identity; however, LGBT people are still victimized in shockingly brutal and mutilating attacks. And while gays and lesbians may now legally wed in five states and Washington, D.C., such marriages are not recognized by the federal government or by forty-one other states. Mixed evidence such as this led noted *Times* columnist Frank Rich to comment that forty years after Stonewall gay Americans are often still treated as if they are second-class citizens.

BIBLIOGRAPHY

Ball, Carlos. *From the Closet to the Courtroom: Five LGBT Rights Lawsuits That Have Changed Our Nation.* Boston: Beacon Press, 2010.

Carter, David. *Stonewall: The Riots That Sparked the Gay Revolution.* New York: St. Martin's Press, 2010.

FROM *THE NEW YORK TIMES*

AP. "Rights Groups Object to Pentagon Survey on Gays." July 12, 2010.

Blow, Charles. "Gay? Whatever, Dude." June 4, 2010.

Rich, Frank. "40 Years Later, Still Second-Class Americans." June 28, 2009.

Unsigned. "Editor's Note." March 26, 2010.

THE STONEWALL UPRISING AND ITS AFTERMATH

● ●

The modern struggle for lesbian, gay, bisexual, and transgender (LGBT) rights is often said to have started with the riots at New York City's Stonewall Inn on June 27–29, 1969. How did a routine police raid on a gay bar become the basis for a new civil rights movement? Prior to this time there had been many instances of gay bar raids, arrests, police violence, and entrapment in New York and across the country. However, the uprising at the Stonewall Inn in Greenwich Village marks the beginning of sustained resistance to such harassment. Previously hidden from mainstream view, homosexuals post-Stonewall began to demand cultural, social, and political equality, including the right to get married, obtain suitable housing, pursue a career, and simply congregate with friends without fear of arrest. A watershed moment for the modern LGBT movement, the impact of the rioting Stonewall patrons is often compared to the impact on the black civil rights movement of Rosa Parks's refusal to move to the back of the bus. A retrospective *Times* report issued on March 27, 1994, called Stonewall, "The Raid Heard Around the World," an obvious play on Ralph Waldo Emerson's phrase "the shot heard 'round the world," a reference to the beginning of the American Revolution. While contemporaneous *Times* coverage of Stonewall may not be as extensive as an event of this magnitude seems to warrant, at the time it may well have appeared to be just another bar raid, albeit one that had gotten a bit out of control.

In 1969 homosexuals had few safe options for public socializing. Respectable institutions typically did not cater to openly gay people. Further, many states and localities, including New York, had passed laws making it illegal for homosexuals to meet or work in state-licensed venues, including bars and restaurants. The few institutions that did cater primarily to gay populations, such as the Stonewall Inn, were typically controlled by organized crime and functioned by paying off the police in lieu of obtaining formal liquor licenses. Because of their scarcity, gay bars often demanded higher cover charges and served watered-down drinks at prices well above the going rate in straight establishments.

The Stonewall Inn was dingy and dimly lit, with black walls and few windows. It was located in Greenwich Village, an area frequented by gay populations, at least since the turn of the twentieth century, and its patrons were a diverse group, including many drag queens, homeless street youth, and hustlers. Even though the Village had a reputation for being relatively friendly to gays, the treatment they received was by no means equal to heterosexuals. Bouncers viewed prospective patrons through a peephole prior to entry, and many were turned away. The police often raided these bars on the grounds that liquor was being sold illegally. While bar owners were usually tipped off in advance (and back in business by the end of the night), these raids had serious consequences for bar patrons. They were typically arrested and their names were subsequently published with the charges of homosexuality in the morning newspaper. Because homosexuality was thought to be deviant and immoral, this publicity often led to the loss of jobs, family, and friends. Some cases resulted in longer-term imprisonment, institutionalization, electroshock therapy, or even suicide.

When the police arrived at the Stonewall Inn on Saturday night, June 28, they undoubtedly thought of it as a routine event. Police had raided several bars in the area over the last two weeks and the Stonewall as recently as the previous Tuesday with little fuss. It is unclear what exactly triggered the resistance that night, but the crowd at the Stonewall Inn was in no mood to go quietly. Approximately 200 LGBT patrons actively resisted the police, and they were joined by an additional crowd of 200–800 who had gathered outside of the inn. Rather than passively capitulating to arrest, bar patrons and onlookers threw pennies at the police, mocking their corrupt relationship with the mob bar owners. They hurled bricks, bottles, and garbage, resulting in the injury of four officers. Protesters also used a parking meter as a battering ram in an attempt to regain entry to the bar. Resistance was so unexpected and fierce that the police called for reinforcements, fearful of losing control of the situation. Over the course of the evening, the police eventually restored order, arresting thirteen.

The Stonewall Inn, a West Village bar frequented by gay men and transgender people, a week after the infamous 1969 police raids that would kick-start the movement for LGBT rights.

*Source: Larry Morris/*The New York Times

On the following evening angry crowds once again rioted in the area of the Stonewall, protesting the raid that had been conducted the night before and, more generally, police harassment of LGBT people. Rioters chanted slogans such as "Support Gay Power" and "Legalize Gay Bars"—truly outrageous suggestions at this time. Similar to the previous night, the group's strength and persistence made it necessary for the police to call in reinforcements, and even with this extra help, the crowds proved difficult to control. Three more were arrested.

The Stonewall Rebellion is significant because prior to this time gay people had offered little resistance, typically accepting their unequal treatment as inevitable. There were other instances of LGBT people angrily rising up during this period, such as challenges to the arrests of both gay and straight people who were openly associating at the ball to benefit the Council on Homosexuality and Religion in San Francisco in 1965 and the 1966 Compton Cafeteria riots led by transgender people who were refused service and harassed by the police in Los Angeles. But Stonewall

continues to be thought of as the genesis of the modern LGBT movement. Unlike the previous skirmishes, the Stonewall riot spawned numerous gay political groups and organized efforts such as Pride Parades that increased the visibility of the LGBT community, creating new demands for equal rights and liberties regardless of sexual orientation.

The rebels at Stonewall and the LGBT movement that followed in its wake were generally fighting for liberation from traditional societal norms. As a result both are sometimes thought of as part of the sexual revolution, which was characterized by a new, more open set of sexual attitudes and behaviors, including increased acceptance of premarital sex, open relationships inside and outside of marriage, the use of the birth control pill, and the legalization of abortion. The LGBT movement also parallels other movements prominent in the 1960s, such as the antiwar movement, the black civil rights movement, and the women's movement, each of which challenged important mainstream institutions and norms that had previously been taken for granted.

Before Stonewall

Distinct and sometimes relatively open homosexual subcultures existed since the late 1800s and through the 1930s in New York City and other major cities such as Berlin. However, they typically did not receive much attention in the mainstream press. When homosexuality did receive press coverage, the focus was largely on gay men, and they were regularly stereotyped as perverted, dangerous, deviant, laughable, or pathological.

The press occasionally referred to homosexuality in the context of high profile legal trials, as for example when the literary figure Oscar Wilde (1854–1900) was convicted of gross indecency with other men in London. Although *The Times'* account of the trial does not explicitly mention homosexuality, it quotes at length Wilde's famous defense of pederasty, which he offered in response to the prosecutor's question about the "love that dares not speak its name." In a subsequent trial Wilde was found guilty and sentenced to two years of hard labor, ruining his literary career. On November 9, 1913, and July 1, 1905, *The Times* accounts report that he had been sighted alive and well after his documented death, suggesting that his celebrity remained enormous despite his infamy, perhaps paralleling the periodic Elvis sightings reported in our own time.

In 1928 Radclyffe Hall (1880–1943) was charged with obscenity for writing *The Well of Loneliness,* a novel featuring the masculine lesbian Stephen Gordon. A London court found the book more "corruptive than anything ever written," and copies were seized and destroyed in the United Kingdom. However, the book was subsequently cleared in a U.S. court, as noted by a *New York Times* report on April 20, 1929. Similarly, Lillian Hellman's play *The Children's Hour* was banned in both Boston and London as indecent because it focuses on a potential lesbian relationship between two headmistresses at a girls' boarding school. A December 15, 1935, *Times* report notes that a central theme of the play is homosexuality, offering an unusually direct discussion of this theme for this era. By contrast, the motion picture industry's guidelines banned all overt references to homosexuality in mainstream movies at this time.

In general the 1930s ushered in a long period of stricter legal, political, and social regulation of homosexuality worldwide, in part because libertine sexual habits were blamed for the economic crisis ushered in by the Great Depression. It was during this time that New York City passed laws forbidding homosexuals from meeting in or being employed by state-licensed places, such as bars and restaurants. It also became illegal for one man to ask another man to have sex.

During the period before Stonewall, most authorities considered homosexuality a criminal behavior, a moral perversion, or a psychological illness. As a consequence, many gays and lesbians regularly hid their sexual identities, owing to a fear of persecution and retribution from police, employers, families, and friends. Openly gay people were often arrested and imprisoned, fired from their jobs, ostracized in their communities, and subject to invasive treatments at mental institutions, such as electroshock therapy. These threats were further exacerbated by Sen. Joseph McCarthy's claim that homosexuals in government were a threat to national security, leading to the firing of thousands of gay and allegedly gay federal employees in the 1950s and 1960s. This drive to rid the government of homosexuals may have been inadvertently fueled by the findings of the 1948 Alfred Kinsey report *Sexual Behavior in the Human Male.* Extensive interviews with 5,200 men that were conducted by Professor Alfred Kinsey (1894–1956) revealed that 37 percent of them had had at least one homosexual experience. Kinsey was trying to break the taboo surrounding so-called deviant sexuality by demonstrating that such practices were more common than people typically thought. This provided homosexuals with a measure of hope as they came to understand that they were not idiosyncratic or freakish but rather a significant portion of the population. However, as *The Times* reported on March 31 and April 1, 1948, many found Kinsey's findings shocking and inappropriate, leading a well-established professor at Columbia University to call for a law against undertaking research on sexuality. McCarthy-era worries about communist infiltration and related security risks fueled fears that homosexuals working in the State Department would be particularly vulnerable to blackmail, leading to the firing of many gay people in this period. In response, some of the first LGBT groups emerged in the United States during the 1950s. Known as homophile organizations, newly emerging groups such as the Mattachine Society and the Daughters of Bilitis provided the general public with a more positive understanding of homosexuality, generally adopting an orderly and low-key approach. As reported by *The Times* on May 30, 1965, the Mattachine Society staged nonviolent events at the White House and at Philadelphia's Independence Hall, protesting the federal government's purging of homosexuals.

During the pre-Stonewall period there were many instances of bars refusing to serve homosexuals, gay bar raids, arrests, and entrapment. For example, a *Times* report on April 26, 1966, chronicled the New York State Liquor

IN FOCUS

Dr. Magnus Hirschfeld (1868–1935)

Pioneering sex researcher Dr. Magnus Hirschfeld is notable for his early and outspoken advocacy on behalf of homosexuals. Born in Germany in 1868, Hirschfeld hypothesized that all humans were a mixture of male and female and that homosexuals were an intermediate or third sex. In 1897 he founded what is thought to be the world's first gay rights organization, the Scientific Humanitarian Committee, and in 1919 he established the Institute for Sexual Science in Berlin. Hirschfeld was an early opponent of Paragraph 175, a part of the German legal code that criminalized homosexual acts, and he is credited with coining the term "transvestism." He was also instrumental in the creation of a registry that legalized public cross-dressing in Germany as long as the individual's actual gender was appropriately identified.

The radical nature of Hirschfeld's views caused significant hardship during his lifetime. In 1919 stink bombs and live mice were released in some German theaters, protesting a film that attempted to popularize his views on homosexuality and the need for increased tolerance. The following year, Hirschfeld was briefly hospitalized and initially reported dead after he and his long-term partner, Karl Giese, were attacked by a Munich mob. Later, he was persecuted by the Nazis, and books from the library of the Institute for Sexual Science were burned as "Un-German in spirit." His transvestite registry was also misused by the Nazis in order to identify "moral deviates," to be sent to concentration camps. Hirschfeld died in exile in 1935, and, following the custom of the time, his May 17 *Times* obituary did not name his partner, cite the groundbreaking work he performed related to same-sex sexuality, or acknowledge that his Jewish heritage was only a partial explanation for the mistreatment he received from the Nazis.

In 2007 the Hirschfeld-Eddy Foundation for the Human Rights of Lesbians, Gays, Bisexuals and Transgender People was founded in Berlin. Named in honor of Dr. Magnus Hirschfeld and Ms. Fannyann Eddy, a murdered lesbian activist from Sierra Leone, the foundation aims to foster respect, provide advocacy and support, promote awareness, and dismantle prejudices related to lesbian, gay, bisexual, and transgender people throughout the world.

From *The New York Times*

O'Conner, John J. 'Different from Others,' Film on Homosexuality. June 27, 1986.
Smith, Dinitia. Books on Health; On Being Male, Female, Neither or Both. October 29, 2002.
Unsigned. "Kill Dr. M. Hirschfeld; Well-Known German Scientist Victim of a Munich Mob." October 12, 1920.
———. "Deny Professor Hirschfeld Is Dead." October 15, 1920.
———. "Dr. Hirschfeld, 67, Psychologist, Dies; Noted German Writer on Sex Problems Succumbs During His Exile in France." May 17, 1935.

Authority's decision to not take action against bars that refused to serve homosexuals. Police often practiced entrapment, posing as homosexuals in an effort to lure men into having sex with them. Gay sex was illegal even in private settings at this time. Officials regularly denied such practices, despite growing public concern. Entrapment made homosexuals vulnerable to blackmail, such as the nationwide ring that was uncovered in 1966 in which criminals posed as detectives and extorted large sums of money from prominent professionals in exchange for not revealing their homosexuality. Rampant harassment of this sort eventually drove gay people to resist continued persecution. The angry uprising at the Stonewall Inn would come to be seen as the first salvo in the modern fight for LGBT rights.

After Stonewall

Although it would be inaccurate to say that homosexuals simply accepted unequal treatment prior to the Stonewall riot, it is certainly the case that the LGBT community advocated for equal rights much more vocally and publicly in the wake of this event. A more cohesive gay community emerged, characterized by a newfound pride regarding LGBT identity, along with what was then considered militancy with respect to equal rights. After Stonewall the community was seen as "more assertive and less willing to hide" as a *New York Times* headline of November 17, 1969, announced. This led to important changes in the LGBT community's self-understanding, which in turn affected the image it portrayed to the general public. For example, while some in the medical profession continued to view homosexuality as an illness, the LGBT community began to reject such marginalization, asserting instead, "Gay is good."

Another consequence of Stonewall was a nationwide proliferation of new organizations dedicated to gay rights. A June 25, 1989, *Times* report reflecting back on the growth of the LGBT movement noted that while 50 such groups existed prior to Stonewall, there were 800 by 1979 and over 3,000 by the twentieth anniversary in 1989. Two of the most important groups that emerged shortly after Stonewall were the Gay Liberation Front (GLF) founded in July 1969 and the Gay Activists Alliance (GAA) founded in December 1969. These groups organized the LGBT community to combat unequal treatment under the law, offered regular social events to address the pervasive isolation of gays and lesbians, and educated the general public about issues related to homosexuality.

The new LGBT movement paralleled other prominent political movements that had come to the fore in the 1960s, such as the black civil rights movement and the women's movement. While mainstream society tended to view all LGBT organizations as militant, there were important differences within the movement. More radical organizations such as the GLF saw all civil rights efforts as part of one united struggle for liberation from oppressive societal norms. They anticipated large-scale political revolution and sought to work with other groups to rebuild a new society free from discrimination based on sexuality, gender, race, and class. Working across groups was not always easy, as evidenced by the emergence of the Lavender Menace, which was founded to protest discriminatory treatment of lesbians within the women's movement. However, when successful, such collaborations provided important points of cohesion within the political left, as indicated by a *New York Times* report of December 18, 1970, that documented public support for lesbians from key leaders of the women's movement.

Organizations such as the GAA focused primarily on gay issues, more interested in reforming society to accept gays and lesbians rather than advocating its radical transformation through full-scale revolution. Accordingly, they concentrated their efforts on gaining equal treatment for gays and lesbians. GAA members welcomed the relaxation of rules that prohibited homosexuals from eating, drinking, or being employed in public places, using it as an occasion to press for passage of a more general civil rights bill that would prohibit discrimination in housing, employment, and public accommodations. The GAA also obtained the first ever public support for gay rights from candidates running for senator and governor in New York state, suggesting the LGBT community's growing political importance. Two years later, five homosexuals made history by becoming the first openly gay Democratic National Convention delegate candidates from New York state, as noted in a *Times* report of June 16, 1972.

Commemorating Stonewall

The Stonewall Rebellion came to be commemorated in annual Pride Parade celebrations, signifying the importance of the event in challenging the shame LGBT community members have traditionally felt in relation to their sexual identity. Participation in these parades has numbered in the thousands since their establishment on the first anniversary of Stonewall and has increased dramatically, reaching more than 700,000 in recent years. Pride Parades have multiple aims, including the commemoration of the Stonewall riots, celebration of the LGBT community in all its diversity, protestation of discrimination based on sexuality, and demonstration of the growing strength of this relatively new political constituency.

Since 1970 LGBT communities in New York City, Chicago, and other cities across the nation have organized annual parades in June. Initially called Gay Liberation Marches or Gay Freedom Marches, the first Pride Parade was held in New York City on June 28, 1970, and was seen as a direct outgrowth of the "new militancy" that had emerged in the wake of Stonewall. Participants numbered in the thousands, extending fifteen city blocks and including members of the Gay Liberation Front and the Gay Activists Alliance as well as various other homosexual organizations. These parades would eventually include not only LGBT groups but also groups composed primarily of heterosexual allies, such as PFLAG (Parents, Families, and Friends of Lesbians and Gays). For several years thereafter the numbers of participants doubled each year, as reported in *The Times* on June

IN FOCUS

Historic Stonewall Site Generates Tourism and Controversy

• •

Although the original bar closed within months of the riots, the Stonewall Inn continues to be recognized as a symbol of the struggle for lesbian, gay, bisexual, and transgender (LGBT) civil rights. The building site at 51–53 Christopher Street, a nearby park, and the surrounding blocks were entered into the National Register of Historic Places in 1999 and designated as a National Historic Landmark the following year, as discussed in a *New York Times* article of April 2, 2000. In coordination with the fortieth anniversary of the Stonewall riots, New York City tourism officials kicked off a $1.9 million marketing campaign titled Rainbow Pilgrimage, promoting a visit to New York City as a "rite of passage" for gays and lesbians. As noted in an April 8, 2009, *Times* piece, the campaign included special travel packages, a new Web site, and a variety of advertising strategies targeting both American and European tourists.

Despite recognition at the national and citywide level, Christopher Street's reputation within the LGBT community has not always been embraced by local residents. As described in a March 31, 2002, *Times* article, the area became home to upscale shops and million-dollar town houses in the 1990s, as much of the gay scene shifted to the less expensive Chelsea neighborhood. However, Christopher Street continued to attract "pier kids"—gay black and Latino youth, often homeless, who see this neighborhood as a refuge from heterosexual norms. "Where I come from, you can't be black and gay," said 19-year-old Darnell, "so we call this our home."

In response to what they described as an increase in public sex, harassment, drunkenness, and urination, some living in the area organized under the name Residents in Distress, or RID. According to RID founder Jessica Berk, "The people who are coming to my neighborhood—black or white, gay or straight, transgendered or not—they are not treating the community with respect. They are treating it as a toilet." Others argued that community conditions had actually improved but that the tolerance of straight people living in the area had decreased. In any case the waterfront area that once served as "a 24-hour playground of sexual trysts" was fenced off and a police-enforced "zero-tolerance corridor" was established from Washington Square Park to the Christopher Street Piers. Said Melissa Sklarz, a transsexual member of Community Board 2: "It's easy to pick on the black tranny kids, but where will it stop? Where are the queer kids supposed to go?"

From *The New York Times*

Chan, Sewell. "Stonewall Uprising Given Role in Tourism Campaign." April 8, 2009.
Lee, Denny. "Street Fight." March 31, 2002.
Wade, Betsy. "Travel Advisory; Landmark Status for Stonewall." April 2, 2000.

• •

28, 1971, and June 26, 1972. *The Times* reported crowd estimates of 100,000 on the tenth anniversary in 1979, 250,000 at the twentieth anniversary in 1989, and 700,000 at the thirtieth anniversary in 1999.

In many cities Pride Parades are now held as the culmination of Gay Pride Week, a series of events designed to celebrate and mobilize the LGBT community. Although Pride

Parades had been held in other cities from the start, *The Times* coverage of them did not appear until 1977, focusing for the first time on the parades in San Francisco and Barcelona in addition to the annual event in New York City. As reported in *The Times* on June 17, 1994, the twenty-fifth anniversary festivities in New York also featured broad international participation and included the Gay Games, a weeklong, multievent sporting competition in which gay athletes from around the world participated.

Pride Parades typically highlight the diversity of the gay community, as, for example, in various reports that reference social workers, gospel singers, drag queens, the Human Rights Campaign, the Log Cabin Republicans, residents of Harlem, veterans, clergy, Catholic laypeople, the AIDS Prevention League, firefighters, the Gay (police) Officers Action League, the Lambda Legal Defense and Education Fund, FBI agents, and parents of gays and lesbians. A *Times* report on June 28, 1971, suggested that about one-third of the participants were women. As is sometimes the case in large social and political movements, tension often exists between the more radical or "flamboyant" groups, who seek liberation from mainstream sexual norms, and the more reformist "middle of the road" groups, who seek inclusion in mainstream society. Opponents of gay rights hailing from the political and religious right sometimes seek to exploit this tension, fostering fear and hatred in the general population.

Many developments surrounding annual Pride Parades indicate a growing integration of the LGBT movement into mainstream society. Prominent politicians, such as Hillary Clinton and Rudy Giuliani, regularly march in New York's parade, suggesting the growing political clout of the LGBT community. Just prior to the twentieth anniversary, on June 22, 1989, *The Times* reported that the United States Post Office issued a special cancellation to commemorate Stonewall, offering mainstream recognition of the LGBT movement and its origins. Similarly, a June 29, 1999, *Times* report on the thirtieth anniversary noted that the Stonewall Inn had been listed in the National Register of Historic Places. An April 8, 2009, *Times* story notes that in recognition of the fortieth anniversary, New York had initiated a new gay-focused tourism campaign called Rainbow Pilgrimage, named after the rainbow flag, which has come to symbolize the LGBT movement. In June 2009 *The Times* reported that President Barack Obama invited several gay groups to the White House to celebrate the fortieth anniversary of Stonewall.

BIBLIOGRAPHY

Chauncey, George. *Gay New York: Gender, Urban Culture, and the Making of the Gay Male World, 1890–1940*. New York: Basic Books, 1994.

Duberman, Martin. *Stonewall*. New York: Plume, 1994.

Faderman, Lillian. *Odd Girls and Twilight Lovers*. New York: Columbia University Press, 1991.

Kaiser, Charles. *The Gay Metropolis: 1940–1996*. New York: Houghton-Mifflin, 1997.

Stryker, Susan. *Transgender History*. Berkeley, CA: Seal Press. 2008.

FROM *THE NEW YORK TIMES*

"Is Wilde Alive?" July 1, 1905.

"No One Found Who Saw Wilde Dead." November 9, 1913.

"Deny Professor Hirschfeld Is Dead." October 15, 1920.

"*Well of Loneliness* Cleared in Court Here." April 20, 1929.

"Nazi Students Raid Institute on Sex." May 7, 1933.

"Nazi Book-Burning Fails to Stir Berlin." May 11, 1933.

"Dr. Hirschfeld, 67, Psychologist, Dies: Noted German Writer on Sex Problems Succumbs During His Exile in France." May 17, 1935.

"'Children's Hour' Banned in Boston." December 15, 1935.

"Speakers Assail Kinsey on Report." March 31, 1948.

"Effects Weighed of Kinsey Report." April 1, 1948.

"Homosexuals Stage Protest in Capital." May 30, 1965.

"S.L.A. Won't Act Against Bars Refusing Service to Deviates." April 26, 1966.

"The Woman Homosexual: More Assertive, Less Willing to Hide." November 17, 1969.

"The Lesbian Issue and Women's Lib." December 18, 1970.

"5,000 Homosexuals March to Central Park for a Rally." June 28, 1971.

"5 Gay Candidates Are in State Contests." June 16, 1972.

"March Is Staged by Homosexuals." June 26, 1972.

"Homosexuals Parade Marks 10th Year of Rights Drive." June 25, 1979.

"Postal Service to Mark Riot by Homosexuals." June 22, 1989.

"Rally Opens Weekend for Homosexual Pride." June 24, 1989.

"Homosexuals See 2 Decades of Gains, but Fear Setbacks." June 25, 1989.

"The Raid Heard Around the World." March 27, 1994.

"Let the Games, and the Lobbying, Begin; Thousands Gather for Gay Sports Festival and 25th Anniversary of Stonewall Uprising." June 17, 1994.

"30 Years After Stonewall, Diversity Is Shown in Gay Pride Parade." June 28, 1999.

"Stonewall, Then and Now." June 29, 1999.

"Stonewall Uprising Given Role in Tourism Campaign." April 8, 2009.

"Obama Invites Gay Rights Advocates to the White House." June 22, 2009.

HOMOSEXUALS PROTEST POLICE TREATMENT AT NEW YORK'S STONEWALL INN

At about 3 A.M. on the night of June 28, 1969, police raided the Stonewall Inn, a Greenwich Village bar patronized by a largely gay clientele. Police were investigating reports that the Stonewall was illegally selling liquor without a license. An estimated 200 bar patrons actively resisted arrest, throwing bricks, bottles, garbage, and coins at the police. As the police evicted the patrons from the bar, an additional 200–800 people congregated, joining the melee. Police called for reinforcements, who restored order after thirteen were arrested and four police officers were injured. Police said that this was the third raid that had occurred in the Village during the past two weeks.

JUNE 29, 1969
4 POLICEMEN HURT IN 'VILLAGE' RAID
Melee Near Sheridan Square Follows Action at Bar

Hundreds of young men went on a rampage in Greenwich Village shortly after 3 A.M. yesterday after a force of plainclothes men raided a bar that the police said was well known for its homosexual clientele. Thirteen persons were arrested and four policemen injured.

The young men threw bricks, bottles, garbage, pennies and a parking meter at the policemen, who had a search warrant authorizing them to investigate reports that liquor was sold illegally at the bar, the Stonewall Inn, 53 Christopher Street, just off Sheridan Square.

Deputy Inspector Seymour Pine said that a large crowd formed in the square after being evicted from the bar. Police reinforcements were sent to the area to hold off the crowd.

Plainclothes men and detectives confiscated cases of liquor from the bar, which Inspector Pine said was operating without a liquor license.

The police estimated that 200 young men had been expelled from the bar. The crowd grew to close to 400 during the melee, which lasted about 45 minutes, they said.

Arrested in the melee was Dave Van Ronk, 33 years old, of 15 Sheridan Square, a well-known folk singer. He was accused of having thrown a heavy object at a patrolman and later paroled in his own recognizance.

The raid was one of three held on Village bars in the last two weeks, Inspector Pine said.

Charges against the 13 who were arrested ranged from harassment and resisting arrest to disorderly conduct. A patrolman suffered a broken wrist, the police said.

Throngs of young men congregated outside the inn last night, reading aloud condemnations of the police.

A sign on the door said, "This is a private club. Members only." Only soft drinks were being served.

RIOTS CONTINUE AT THE STONEWALL INN

The night after the police raided the Stonewall, a bar frequented by homosexuals, a crowd again formed outside the inn in Greenwich Village at 2 A.M. to protest police harassment of homosexuals, offering slogans such as "Support gay power" and "Legalize gay bars." Crowds of young protesters linked arms and swept through Sheridan Square, throwing stones and bottles while others started fires, as the Tactical Patrol Force proved unable to control the crowd. The police beat several of the protesters with clubs. Three were arrested as police restored order after about two hours of mayhem.

JUNE 30, 1969
POLICE AGAIN ROUT 'VILLAGE' YOUTHS

Outbreak by 400 Follows a Near-Riot Over Raid.

Heavy police reinforcements cleared the Sheridan Square area of Greenwich Village again yesterday morning when large crowds of young men, angered by a police raid on an inn frequented by homosexuals, swept through the area.

Tactical Patrol Force units assigned to the East Village poured into the area about 2:15 A.M. after units from the Charles Street station house were unable to control a crowd of about 400 youths, some of whom were throwing bottles and lighting small fires.

Their arms linked, a row of helmeted policemen stretching across the width of the street made several sweeps up and down Christopher Street between the Avenue of the Americas and Seventh Avenue South.

The crowd retreated before them, but many groups fled into the numerous small side streets and re-formed behind the police line. The police were not withdrawn until 4 A.M.

A number of people who did not retreat fast enough were pushed and shoved along, and at least two men were clubbed to the ground.

Stones and bottles were thrown at the police lines, and the police twice broke ranks and charged into the crowd.

Three persons were arrested on charges of harassment and disorderly conduct.

The crowd had gathered in the evening across the street from the Stonewall Inn at 53 Christopher Street, where the police staged a raid early Saturday. The police were denounced by last night's crowd for allegedly harassing homosexuals. Graffiti on the boarded-up windows of the inn included: "Support gay power" and "Legalize gay bars."

Saturday's raid took place when about 200 people were in the bar. Plainclothes men, with a warrant authorizing a search for illegal sales of alcohol, confiscated cases of liquor and beer.

A melee involving about 400 youths ensued, a partial riot mobilization was ordered by Police Headquarters, and 13 persons were arrested on a number of charges. Four policemen were injured, one suffering a broken wrist. Among those arrested was Dave Van Ronk, a folk singer.

Homosexuality Seen as Threat to Public Safety

As this article attests, in the period before Stonewall homosexuality was primarily seen as a mental illness, a moral failing, or a crime. Accordingly, homosexuals are portrayed as a threat to the city, justifying regular police raids on gay bars, many of which were controlled by organized crime.

DECEMBER 17, 1963
GROWTH OF OVERT HOMOSEXUALITY IN CITY PROVOKES WIDE CONCERN

By ROBERT C. DOTY

The problem of homosexuality in New York became the focus yesterday of increased attention by the State Liquor Authority and the Police Department

The liquor authority announced the revocation of the liquor licenses of two more homosexual haunts that had been repeatedly raided by the police. The places were the Fawn, at 795 Washington Street near Jane Street, and the Heights Supper Club at 80 Montague Street, Brooklyn.

The city's most sensitive open secret—the presence of what is probably the greatest homosexual population

in the world and its increasing openness—has become the subject of growing concern of psychiatrists, religious leaders and the police.

One division of the organized crime syndicate controls bars and restaurants that cater to the homosexual trade. Commenting yesterday on the situation, Police Commissioner Michael J. Murphy said:

"Homosexuality is another one of the many problems confronting law enforcement in this city. However, the underlying factors in homosexuality are not criminal but rather medical and sociological in nature.

"The police jurisdiction in this area is limited. But when persons of this type become a source of public scandal, or violate the laws, or place themselves in a position where they become the victims of crime they do come within our jurisdiction.

"This matter is of constant concern to us in our efforts to preserve the peace and protect the rights of all the people. It has been given, and will continue to be given, special attention."

The two latest places to be put out of business by the liquor authority were described by Donald S. Hostetter, authority chairman, as "notorious congregating points for homosexuals and degenerates."

Mr. Hostetter said the Heights Supper Club had a signal-light system that "warned the boys to stop dancing with one another" when a newcomer was suspected of being a policeman.

The Fawn has a back room to which an admission was charged and where as many as 70 to 80 deviates had parties on Friday and Saturday nights. Most of the patrons were males, but on occasion police found women dancing with women.

There were 19 police visits this year resulting in summonses and complaints of a noisy jukebox, disorderly premises, insufficient lighting and dancing without a cabaret license, and an arrest for degeneracy.

Both places were so wary about nonmembers of the "fraternity" that the police used specialists known in the department as "actors" to get evidence.

Oscar Wilde Tried for Homosexuality

During Oscar Wilde's trial for gross indecency, Wilde pleaded with the court to find him not guilty, offering an eloquent speech about homosexuality without directly mentioning it. Noting that numerous stories of intense, even spiritual, affection between older and younger men can be found in the Bible, as well as the works of Plato and Shakespeare, he argued that such love had been greatly misunderstood in his own time. Despite society's attempts to deal punitively with such relationships, Wilde explained their appeal, namely that in such relationships the older man has intellectual gifts to offer, while the younger man has joy, hope, and glamour.

MAY 2, 1895
OSCAR WILDE'S GUILT DOUBTED
Acquittal on Conspiracy Charges and Disagreement on Others.
LONDON, MAY 1—

Several newspapers say that Wilde's speech may have saved him from a verdict of guilty. They quote as the most eloquent part of his plea the following phrases:

"It is such a great affection of the elder for the younger man as existed between David and Jonathan; such as Plato made the very basis of his philosophy; such as we find in the sonnets of Michael Angelo and Shakespeare. It is that deep spiritual affection which is as pure as it is perfect, and dictates great works of art like those of Shakespeare and Angelo and these two letters of mine, such as they are.

"This love is misunderstood in the present century—so misunderstood that on account of it I am placed where I now am. It is beautiful; it is fine; it is the noblest form of affection. It is intellectual and has existed repeatedly between an elder and a younger man when the elder has the intellect and the younger has all the joy and hope and glamour of life. That it should be so the world does not understand. The world mocks at it and sometimes puts one in the pillory for it."

LESBIAN NOVEL FOUND INDECENT

Despite having the support of various prominent literary figures, Radclyffe Hall's novel *The Well of Loneliness* was found to be indecent by a London appeals court, which ordered police to seize and destroy all extant copies. After the book had been banned in England, new copies had appeared from France. Although George Bernard Shaw, H. G. Wells, and others were prepared to defend the book, they were never called as witnesses. The attorney general argued that the book was the most immoral book ever written.

DECEMBER 14, 1928
PUBLISHERS LOSE APPEAL

British Court Upholds Seizure of Radclyffe Hall's Novel
Wireless to The New York Times.

LONDON, Dec. 14.—Jonathan Cape, Ltd., the publishers of Miss Radclyffe Hall's novel, "The Well of Loneliness," lost their appeal today against the decision that all copies of the book must be seized and destroyed by the police.

Sitting in the crowded court room was Rudyard Kipling, who was apparently prepared to testify for the government in favor of the book's suppression. Previously George Bernard Shaw, H. G Wells, but not Mr. Kipling, had strongly disapproved of the censorship of the book. Forty literary witnesses were in the court at the previous hearing prepared to defend Miss Hall's much discussed novel.

At the time they were not allowed to testify and today Mr. Kipling was likewise not called upon for evidence.

The Attorney General, Sir Thomas Inskip, declared the book was "more subtle, demoralizing, corrosive and corruptive than anything ever written. The fact that the author did not intend it to be obscene does not matter," he said. "The book seeks to glorify vice or to produce a plea of toleration of people who practice it. It is propaganda."

The book was withdrawn from circulation in England at the request of the Home Secretary, but later it made its appearance in France and copies were brought back across the Channel.

• •

PRE-STONEWALL GAY HISTORY IS COMPLEX

On the occasion of the twenty-fifth anniversary of the Stonewall Rebellion, widely understood to be the event that initiated the modern LGBT movement, this piece notes that the mainstream press ignored much of gay life prior to Stonewall and attempts to remedy that omission, presenting a complex story of gay life in the twentieth century. Although pre-Stonewall gay men are usually thought of as closeted and passive, gay culture was vibrant in various parts of New York City, including the Bowery, Greenwich Village, and Harlem up until the early 1930s, for example, drag balls and Broadway performances featuring transvestites. The period after 1930 was characterized by much greater repression of homosexuality. During the latter period it became illegal for actors to discuss homosexuality on stage and for one man to invite another man to have sex. Federal employees suspected of being homosexuals were dismissed from their jobs because Sen. Joseph McCarthy claimed they were a threat to national security. In light of these dire consequences, homosexuals began to closet themselves, in marked contrast to the relative tolerance that homosexuals enjoyed during the early twentieth century.

JUNE 26, 1994
A GAY WORLD, VIBRANT AND FORGOTTEN

By GEORGE CHAUNCEY

It would have been unthinkable 25 years ago for thousands of openly gay fans to cheer openly gay athletes at Yankee Stadium, for openly gay artists to perform to the acclaim of openly gay audiences at Carnegie Hall, or for the mainstream media to provide extensive and sympathetic coverage of it all. Today's march and the Gay Games and Cultural Festival are testimony to the legacy of the Stonewall rebellion of June 28, 1969—when a police assault on a Greenwich Village gay bar turned a small civil rights campaign into a mass liberation movement.

But the enshrinement of Stonewall as the genesis of gay culture threatens to deny the richness and resiliency of gay and lesbian life before the late 60's and to obscure the long history of gay resistance that made the gay-rights movement possible.

Pre-Stonewall lesbians and gay men are often held up as passive victims of social hatred who lived solitary lives (in the "closet") that kept them vulnerable to anti-gay ideology. Many gay people blame previous generations for not having had the courage to come out of the closet. Or they condescendingly imagine that their predecessors internalized society's hatred of homosexuality and became self-loathing.

But the systematic suppression of the gay community was not due to some age-old, unchanging social antipathy, nor was it a sign of passivity and acquiescence by gay people. Anti-gay forces created the closet in response to the openness and assertiveness of gay men and lesbians in the early 20th century.

Beginning in the 1890's, an extensive gay world took shape in the streets, cafeterias, saloons and apartments of New York City, and gay people played an integral role in the social life of many neighborhoods. Openly gay men drank with sailors and other working men at waterfront dives and entertained them at Bowery saloons; well-known gay people casually mixed with other patrons at Harlem's basement cabarets; lesbians ran speakeasies where Greenwich Village bohemians—straight and gay—gathered to read their verse.

These men and women, who saw themselves as part of a visible, largely working-class gay world, forged a culture with its own language, customs, folk histories, heroes and heroines. In the 1920's and early 30's, gay impresarios organized drag balls attracting thousands of gay dancers and straight spectators. Gay writers, actors and musicians produced a distinctive gay literature and performance style. This cultural outpouring was so popular by the late 20's that gay performers moved from the margins of the city and briefly became the darlings of Broadway.

This flourishing gay world has been forgotten. It was wiped into historical oblivion by a fierce backlash in the 30's—part of a wider Depression-era condemnation of the cultural experimentation of the 20's, which many blamed for the economic collapse. With millions of male breadwinners losing their jobs, people were fearful of any additional threats to traditional family hierarchies.

In New York, laws were enacted prohibiting homosexuals from gathering in any state-licensed public place. Bars, restaurants and cabarets were threatened with loss of their liquor licenses if they employed homosexuals, allowed them to gather on the premises or served them drinks—and the State Liquor Authority closed hundreds of establishments for tolerating a gay presence. This continued for decades: nearly every gay bar in the city was closed in the winter of 1959–60 in response to an anti-gay campaign by the newspaper columnist Lee Mortimer, and again in 1964 in a pre-World's Fair "cleanup."

The public discussion of gay issues was also censored. In the early 30's, after a generation of films had dealt with gay images, the new Hollywood production code prohibited gay characters and even talk of homosexuality in films. In the theater, the backlash had started even before the Depression: after the appearance of a lesbian drama on Broadway and Mae West's threat to stage a farce about transvestites called "The Drag" in 1927, a state law was passed prohibiting the representation or discussion of homosexuality on the stage.

In the 30's, the New York City police, using a 1923 state law that made it a criminal act for one man to invite another to have sex, began sending good-looking plain-clothes officers into gay bars to strike up conversations with men, lead them on and arrest them if the victims suggested going home. (Between 1923 and 1967, when gay activists persuaded Mayor John V. Lindsay to end most entrapment, more than 50,000 men had been arrested on this charge.)

Anti-gay policing around the country intensified in the 40's and especially the 50's, when Senator Joseph McCarthy claimed that homosexuals in the State Department threatened national security. Thousands of gay Federal employees were dismissed. Equally without substance, police departments and newspapers around the country began to demonize homosexuals as child molesters; arrest rates increased dramatically.

The degree to which gay men had to fear arrest—and the subsequent exposure of their homosexuality to their families and employers—is almost impossible to understand today. Although New York's gay world grew in the post-war years, gay life became less visible and gay meeting places more segregated and carefully hidden from the straight public. The state built the closet in the 30's, and the isolation of homosexuals made it easier for them to be demonized.

Still, some gay people fought for their rights. In the 1930's, gay bars challenged the prohibitions against them in the courts (unsuccessfully), and in the 1950's a handful of courageous souls organized political groups, such as the Mattachine Society and the Daughters of Bilitis, to advocate the homosexual cause. Although most did not speak out so openly, taking this as evidence that they accepted the laws against them misinterprets silence as acquiescence. It construes resistance in the narrowest of terms—as only the organization of formal political groups or protests.

Threatened with police raids, harassment and the loss of their jobs, families and reputations, most people hid their participation in gay life from their straight associates. But this did not necessarily keep them hidden from one other. They developed a sophisticated system of subcultural codes of dress, speech and style that enabled them to recognize one another and to carry on covert conversations. "Gay" itself was such a word until the 60's, when its homosexual connotations began to be known to nongay New Yorkers.

The tactics gay people devised for communicating, claiming space and affirming their self-worth did not directly challenge anti-gay repression in the way the post-Stonewall movement would, but they allowed many gay people to form a supportive community despite the larger society's injunction against their doing so. This enabled many lesbians and gay men to build happy, self-confident, loving lives.

That the openness of gay life in the early 20th century was brought to an end after a few decades, and that the memory of it was systematically suppressed, reminds us that the growth of tolerance in recent years cannot be taken for granted. Then as now, increased gay visibility produced a powerful reaction.

But the relative tolerance of homosexuality in the early 20th century also shows that America has not been monolithically and inevitably homophobic, and that social conventions of sexuality are no more natural or timeless than those of race or gender. Attacks on gay men and lesbians have often resulted from broader anxieties in American culture as much as from fears about homosexuality itself. Above all, the last century shows us that attitudes toward gay people can change—and can be changed.

HOMOSEXUALS DISMISSED FROM STATE DEPARTMENT

Deputy Undersecretary for Administration Carlisle Humelsine reported that the State Department had discharged 126 homosexuals in an ongoing effort to rid the department of security risks. He stated that the department hoped to have resolved the problem by the following year.

MARCH 26, 1952
126 PERVERTS DISCHARGED
State Department Reports Total Ousted Since Jan. 1, 1951

WASHINGTON, March 25 (UP)—The State Department has discharged 126 homosexuals since Jan. 1, 1951, and is determined to remove any others from the department.

Carlisle H. Humelsine, Deputy Under Secretary for Administration, made the report for the department during recent testimony before a House Appropriations subcommittee.

"There is no doubt in our minds that homosexuals are security risks," and "we have resolved that we are going to clean them up," Mr. Humelsine said in the testimony released today.

"I hope that next year will show that we have broken . . . this particular problem," Mr. Humelsine commented.

. . . .

Entrapment of Gays Addressed in New York City

Chief Inspector Garelik of the New York City Police Department urged the public to report instances of police entrapping homosexuals by luring them into breaking the law. The New York Civil Liberties Union said entrapment was widespread, particularly in the wake of highly publicized cleanup campaigns in Greenwich Village and Times Square, both popular meeting places for homosexuals. Police guidelines and Garelik explicitly condemned entrapment, even as an unnamed high-ranking officer said that the police do not encourage people to commit crimes they would not otherwise commit, a statement suggesting that entrapment may have been condoned in practice. The Civil Liberties Union called Garelik's approach naïve, charging that the police department may have abridged homosexuals' rights. The Mattachine Society, a gay advocacy group of more than 1,000 members, argued that Garelik's approach was futile, suggesting that homosexuals would not be inclined to complain, owing to a fear of reprisal. Garelik insisted that he was simply enforcing law on the books.

APRIL 2, 1966
GARELIK URGES PUBLIC TO REPORT TRAPPINGS OF HOMOSEXUALS
By ERIC PACE

Chief Inspector Sanford D. Garelik said yesterday that he hoped the public would report cases in which policemen lure homosexuals into breaking the law and then arrest them.

Chief Garelik's appeal, made in an interview, followed similar remarks that he made Thursday night at a neighborhood meeting held under the auspices of the Judson Memorial Church, on Washington Square South.

The chief appeared there to discuss the police cleanup campaign in Greenwich Village and Times Square. Both areas are gathering points for homosexuals.

The New York Civil Liberties Union has charged that the practice of luring homosexuals into breaking the law, known as entrapment, is widespread. However, a high police officer contended yesterday that "we don't encourage people to commit a crime that they weren't going to commit."

Chief Garelik declined to appraise the extent, if any, of such actions, but said that "I'm very severe in my condemnation of entrapment."

The chief said he hoped the public would report entrapment incidents as they would crimes. A Police Department rule stipulates that "members of the force . . . shall not use practices known as 'entrapment' to obtain evidence."

The question of how policemen should treat homosexuals has become increasingly controversial during recent years as growing tolerance by the general community has made it easier for homosexuals to assert themselves in public. The police crackdown, which is directed at illegal and disorderly behavior in general, prompted the Civil Liberties Union last month to protest that it seemed aimed at infringing on homosexuals' rights.

A spokesman for the group said yesterday that Chief Garelik's appeal "shows a certain naïveté."

"It's alarming to think that the chief inspector doesn't know that a large number of police spend their duty hours dressed in tight pants, sneakers and polo sweaters . . . to bring about solicitations," the spokesman added.

A provision of the State Penal Law makes it an offense if "any person, with intent to provoke a breach of the peace or whereby a breach of the peace may be occasioned . . . frequents or loiters about any public place soliciting men for the purpose of committing a crime against nature or other lewdness."

A spokesman for the Mattachine Society, Inc., of New York, an organization that provides legal and medical aid for homosexuals and information about them, questioned the worth of Chief Garelik's appeal.

"The last thing homosexuals are going to do is complain about something," the society spokesman said, "They'll just sit there like a possum, they're so afraid of their families' finding out or losing their jobs."

The New York society, which reports a membership of 1,000, is an offshoot of the Mattachine Society of San Francisco, which was founded 15 years ago.

In moving against homosexuals, Chief Garelik said, "We are not carrying out a vendetta against social behavior. . . . We are only enforcing the law, and until such time as the law is changed, we have to accept our responsibility."

He said that plainclothes men in general dressed to fit their surroundings and that offenses by homosexuals were of only minor concern to them.

He also asserted that the homosexual problem was a minor problem in Greenwich Village, compared with the total problem of narcotics, crowd control and other matters.

· ·

GAYS VICTIMIZED BY BOGUS POLICE IN NATIONWIDE SCAM

For ten years a nationwide ring operated to extort money from prominent homosexuals in exchange for a bogus promise not to arrest them or to disclose their sexuality. Victims included deans of universities, theater personalities, and military officers. Decoys would lead victims to hotels and begin to have sex, when a bogus police officer would enter and threaten the victim with arrest and public disclosure unless he was paid off. Alternatively, decoys would assault the victim, stealing his money and credentials, which would then be used by bogus police to shake the victim down for cash. More than a thousand victims had paid millions of dollars to phony police officers over the ten-year period, and at least one victim, a highly ranked military officer, committed suicide.

MARCH 3, 1966
NATIONWIDE RING PREYING ON PROMINENT DEVIATES.
Bogus Policemen Victimize Theatrical Figures—Even Reach Into Pentagon
By JACK ROTH

Eminent educators, including at least two deans of Eastern universities, prominent theatrical personalities and officers of the armed services—all homosexual—have been the victims of an extortion ring that has operated throughout the nation for nearly 10 years.

So brazen is the operation that in one instance two gang members, posing as New York City detectives, walked into the Pentagon and walked out with a high officer in the armed services.

The man, whom they shook down for several thousand dollars, committed suicide the night before he was scheduled to testify before a New York County grand jury.

This was learned yesterday from the police and sources in the District Attorney's office. It was also learned that more than a thousand victims had paid millions of dollars in extortion, with some individuals paying more than $20,000 to ring members posing as policemen. Only a small number of persons have been willing to sign complaints.

District Attorney Frank S. Hogan announced last Feb. 17 the indictment of 17 defendants on charges of extortion from homosexuals and reported that nine were in custody. At the time, he said the victims who had made complaints had given $15,529 to the gang.

It came to light yesterday, however, that the report on the extent of the ring's operation had only touched the surface.

With about 25 members, the ring worked with what are called decoys, or "chickens," and phony policemen. The decoy would lure the victim to a hotel room, usually from a midtown bar, and get him into a compromising situation. Then one of two things would follow.

A bogus policeman would break in and threaten the victim with arrest and disclosure unless he [was] paid off or the decoy would assault the victim and steal his money and credentials. The credentials would then be sent to bogus policemen who would shake down the victim at a later date.

Mr. Hogan has said that the police in cities in various parts of the country have been asked to apprehend several of the men who had been indicted.

Antihomosexual Arguments Challenged

This op-ed piece was written by the president of the New York chapter of the Mattachine Society, a gay advocacy group. It debunks three major fallacies associated with homosexuality, namely: homosexuality is unnatural, homosexuality is immoral, and homosexuality is an illness. Noting that what is considered natural, moral, and pathological varies across time and between cultures, the author relied on prominent scientists such as Margaret Mead and Alfred Kinsey, as well as practices from other cultures such as that of Great Britain, to back up his claims.

FEBRUARY 19, 1971
HOMOSEXUAL MILITANCE
By MICHAEL KOTIS

To many people, the recent demonstrations and confrontations concerning homosexuals' civil rights might seem to be just another of those liberation movements which are so popular at present. There may be a minor element of truth in this view, but the gay liberation movement is primarily concerned with profound issues—a few of which will be mentioned here—involving the very basis of man's psychological and physical relationship to man.

Cutting through the ancient rhetoric of antihomosexual militants, who have existed infinitely longer than the homosexual militants, one discovers the sources of all prejudice against us: our difference and our refusal to conform. An elaborate structure has been built upon this untenable foundation to justify centuries of polemics, purges, and "scapegoatism," but science and truth are now exposing it as fallacious.

Fallacy I—Homosexuality Is Unnatural. The pitfalls in defining varying forms of behavior as "natural" and "unnatural" are obvious. What is natural at one time and in one place is unnatural at another time and in another place, i.e., polygamy, human sacrifice, abortion. Such scientists as Margaret Mead, Ruth Benedict, Alfred Kinsey and Frank Beach have shown us that homosexual behavior has existed throughout man's history, in many diverse societies and among many animal species. Many cultures accept and/or require homosexual activity as part of their socialization process. Yet it is called unnatural in our own country.

In reality, such terminology is merely camouflage for an early tribal need for workers, hunters and warriors. Essentially, it is the glorification of reproduction as the sole purpose of sexual relationships. Few intelligent people would accept this idea today, but it remains a persuasive factor in justifying antihomosexual theory. The real issue, masked in verbal cliché, is the justification of majority behavior and the proscription or elimination of minority behavior.

Fallacy II—Homosexuality is Immoral. Again, the semantic problem is evident. "Moral" and "immoral" are judgmental terms relative to time, place, and the needs of the majority. For example, various societies and eras have defined anti-Semitism and antiblack pogroms as moral while others have not. The basic problem is to establish a durable definition of moral and immoral which applies to all times and to all places. Joseph Fletcher and Norman Pittenger, among others, suggest such definitions: Any behavior or attitude manifesting selfless loving concern for another person is moral, and any behavior or attitude bringing physical or mental harm to another person is immoral.

There are two overriding considerations which must be borne in mind: 1) homosexual relations between consenting individuals bring joy, not harm, and are therefore moral; 2) individual man must not be manipulated by government, church, or society to fulfill goals inimical to the happiness of individual citizens when their happiness does not infringe upon the rights of other individual citizens.

Fallacy III—Homosexuality Is an Illness. This currently popular theory is a glaring example of the contemporary mania for calling tastes, habits and behavior which differ from one's own "sick." The famed Wolfenden Commission in Great Britain and the "Kinsey Institute" in the United States have exposed the fallacy of these views. Dr. Kinsey's research found that one-third of the adult male population has had a homosexual experience to the point of orgasm while one-half of that same population is capable of homosexual response. (The discrepancy between the two figures is the result of societal pressures favoring a heterosexual "norm" and suppressing an individual's homosexual desires, a fact which has been detrimental to families and jobs when the clash between homosexual desires and antihomosexual pressures became too great.) The consequence of Kinsey's findings is that one-third to one-half of the male population is either "sick" to some degree or that something is basically wrong with the majority's "illness theory."

The essential questions are clear. Are meaningful expressions of emotion only valid between members of opposite sexes? Is the sole purpose of intense human relationships mechanical reproduction? Is the strength of a society founded upon its sameness rather than its diversity?

Perhaps Henry David Thoreau provided the answer when he wrote "Let every man mind his own business and endeavor to be what he was made." The time has come for the homosexual to be what he was made, not the grotesque outcast which the heterosexual population would have him be.

—

Michael Kotis is president of New York Mattachine and the editor of a forthcoming book on homosexuality.

Gays More Visible After Stonewall

Homosexuals were becoming more visible at this time, working in a wide variety of careers, ranging from Wall Street brokerage to social work. Along with this greater visibility came vulnerability, since known homosexuals could be fired from their jobs. Despite this risk homosexuals continued to come out in greater numbers, taking pride in their identity and challenging oppression based on sexuality. Adopting slogans such as "Out of the closets and into the streets," and "Gay is good," LGBT organizations demanding equal rights for gays had proliferated in the wake of Stonewall. Noting that the Kinsey Report suggested that 10 percent of the population is gay, the president of the Mattachine Society argued that "the philosophical ideals on which this country was founded have yet to be realized."

AUGUST 24, 1970
HOMOSEXUALS IN REVOLT
By STEVEN V. ROBERTS

Steve Gerrie wears a well-trimmed mustache, works as an accountant in a Wall Street brokerage and lives with his lover in a neat but threadbare apartment in the West Village here. His roommate, Jack Waluska, is a former welfare case worker now studying for a master's degree in sociology.

One evening recently a friend asked Mr. Gerrie if he would publicly identify himself as a homosexual. Mr. Gerrie said he would, and the friend worried that he might lose his job.

"I don't give a damn," Mr. Gerrie almost shouted. "If it means all that much to my employer, I don't want the job."

Steve Gerrie's reaction reflects a new mood now taking hold among the nation's homosexuals. In growing numbers they are publicly identifying themselves as homosexuals, taking a measure of pride in that identity and seeking militantly to end what they see as society's persecution of them.

Their feelings could be summed up by two of their popular slogans. One is "Out of the closets and into the streets," an allusion to the "closet queen" who passes for "straight" and conceals his homosexuality. The other says, "Gay is good."

[. . .]

Hundred Organizations

Three years ago there were only about 25 organizations serving this community. Today there are more than a hundred, ranging from old line "homophile" groups that concentrate on legal reform to self-proclaimed "revolutionaries" who have adopted the style and rhetoric of the New Left.

Some include only men, some only women, a few both sexes.

Probably the major new force in the homosexual community is the Gay Liberation Front, which started last year in San Francisco and now has about 60 loosely connected chapters from Billings, Mont., to St. Louis to Tallahassee, Fla.

It was the front that organized parades of homosexuals in New York and Los Angeles last June 28, and for the first time made the public fully aware of what had been happening in the "gay" community.

The parade commemorated the first anniversary of the "Stonewall incident," the Boston Tea Party of the "gay revolution." On that occasion the police raided a homosexual bar in Greenwich Village and the patrons, for the first time within anyone's memory, fought back, throwing bricks through the bar's windows and forcing the police to call for reinforcements.

CANDIDATES ENDORSE GAY RIGHTS FOR THE FIRST TIME

Three major statewide candidates running for governor of New York and the U.S. Senate issued statements in support of gay civil rights, marking the first time that any political candidate was known to have taken an official position on the matter.

OCTOBER 27, 1970
3 CANDIDATES SUPPORT RIGHTS OF HOMOSEXUALS

Three of the major statewide candidates have issued statements in support of the Gay Activists Alliance platform on homosexual civil rights.

Arthur J. Goldberg, the Democratic-Liberal candidate for Governor, Senator Charles E. Goodell, the Republican-Liberal incumbent for the United States Senate, and his Democratic opponent, Representative Richard L. Ottinger, have issued similar statements calling for an end to discriminatory laws and practices against homosexuals.

According to Mark Rubin, a spokesman for the alliance, this is the first time that any political candidate has taken an official position on homosexual rights.

NEW YORK CITY REVERSES PROHIBITIONS ON HOMOSEXUALS

As part of Mayor Lindsay's policy of relaxing rules that arbitrarily oppressed citizens of New York, the Department of Consumer Affairs proposed rescinding a regulation that prohibited homosexuals from working in or patronizing restaurants, bars, and dance halls. Under the regulation establishments allowing entry to known homosexuals could have lost their licenses. Stating that the regulation was impossible to enforce and therefore a vehicle for corruption, an official in the Department stated that "homosexuals have a right to congregate in places of accommodation. They have a right to a drink." Under the new rules, transvestites were still prohibited from entering teenage cabarets. Gay Activists Alliance members lauded the action as a first step toward adopting a gay civil rights bill that would prohibit discrimination against homosexuals citywide.

OCTOBER 12, 1971
CITY ACTS TO LET HOMOSEXUALS MEET AND WORK IN CABARETS
By ALFONSO A. NARVAEZ

A relaxation of regulations governing cabarets, dance halls and food-catering establishments to allow them to be frequented by homosexuals has been proposed by the city's Department of Consumer Affairs.

The proposed changes in the regulations, published in The City Record, the city's official journal, would delete sections that prohibit homosexuals of either sex from frequenting cabarets, dance halls and food-catering establishments and would allow homosexuals, lesbians or persons pretending to be such to be employed in cabarets.

Currently the regulations prohibit homosexuals from remaining in or being employed in cabarets and prohibit them from making a rendezvous of dance halls. The regulations also prohibit persons who are homosexuals or pretend to be such from entering or remaining in food-catering places.

995 Places Licensed

The Department of Consumer Affairs licenses 771 cabarets, 79 dance halls and 145 catering establishments. Under existing regulations, these establishments could lose their licenses if homosexuals were found to be frequenting them. Although there are various bars in the city where homosexuals meet and sometimes dance they are said to be harassed constantly by the police.

"The laws are impossible to enforce and have simply been a vehicle for corruption and oppression," said Henry J. Stern, first deputy commissioner of the Department of Consumer Affairs. "Homosexuals have a right to congregate in places of public accommodation. They have a right to a drink."

Mr. Stern said that no changes were contemplated in regulations that prohibit criminals, gangsters, racketeers, prostitutes, pimps, procurers or degenerates from frequenting these establishments of public accommodation.

He added that the intention of the department was to drop all restrictions on homosexuals in places of public accommodation except for one regulation that prohibits transvestites in teen-age cabarets.

A spokesman for Mayor Lindsay said the proposed changes in regulations "appear to be consistent with administration policy of broadening safeguards for citizens against all forms of arbitrary victimization."

Members of the Gay Activists Alliance hailed the proposed changes and noted that for months they had been pressing for passage of a bill in the City Council that would prohibit discrimination against homosexuals in employment or housing because of their sexual orientation or choice of sexual partners.

The council's Committee on General Welfare is scheduled to hold a public hearing on the bill next Monday.

Publication of the relaxation of the regulations governing homosexuals was printed in The City Record to elicit comment from the public on the proposed changes. Barring strong adverse comment the Department is expected to adopt the changes in December.

First Gay Pride March Held in New York City

A crowd estimated at 3,000–20,000 in size and stretching fifteen city blocks marched from Greenwich Village to Central Park in New York City, displaying the newly emerging militancy and strength of the gay community in the wake of the Stonewall Rebellion, a protest against police discrimination that had occurred in June of the previous year. Drawn from cities and towns across the East and Midwest, the crowd protested discriminatory laws aimed to prohibit homosexual behavior in public and private. Several leaders of the LGBT community commented on the parade, calling it "an affirmation of our new pride" and "a notice to every politician in the state and nation that homosexuals are not going to hide any more." Another leader concluded: "We're different, but we're not inferior."

JUNE 29, 1970
THOUSANDS OF HOMOSEXUALS HOLD A PROTEST RALLY AT CENTRAL PARK
By LACEY FOSBURGH

Thousands of young men and women homosexuals from all over the Northeast marched from Greenwich Village to the Sheep Meadow in Central Park yesterday, proclaiming "the new strength and pride of the gay people."

From Washington, Boston and Cleveland, from Ivy League colleges, from Harlem, the East Side and the suburbs, they gathered to protest laws that make homosexual acts between consenting adults illegal and social conditions that often make it impossible for them to display affection in public, maintain jobs or rent apartments.

As the group gathered in Sheridan Square before marching up the Avenue of the Americas to hold what the participants described as a "gay-in" in the Sheep Meadow, one of the organizers said a new militancy was developing among homosexuals.

"We're probably the most harassed, persecuted minority group in history, but we'll never have the freedom and civil rights we deserve as human beings unless we stop hiding in closets and in the shelter of anonymity," said 29-year-old Michael Brown. He is a founder of the Gay Liberation Front, an activist homosexual organization that has held small demonstrations in Greenwich Village in the past year.

"We have to come out into the open and stop being ashamed, or else people will go on treating us as freaks. This march," he went on, "is an affirmation and declaration of our new pride."

Then, chanting, "Say it loud, gay is proud," the marchers held bright red, green, purple and yellow silk banners high in the warm afternoon air and began to move up the avenue.

At the head of the line, which extended for 15 blocks, were about 200 members of the Gay Activists Alliance. They were followed by people representing the Mattachine Society, women's liberation groups, the Queens and 14 other homosexual organizations.

Crowd Estimates Vary

Estimates of the size of the demonstration ranged from that by one police officer, who said casually there were "over a thousand," to organizers who said variously 3,000 and 5,000 and even 20,000.

"We've never had a demonstration like this," said Martin Robinson, 27, a carpenter who is in charge of political affairs for the Gay Activists Alliance. He walked with the others past crowds of people standing in silence on the sidewalks.

"It serves notice on every politician in the state and nation that homosexuals are not going to hide any more. We're becoming militant, and we won't be harassed and degraded any more," Mr. Robinson said.

Throughout the demonstration, first along the Avenue of the Americas and later in the park, where the group sat together, laughing, talking and waving their banners, hundreds of on-lookers gathered.

Some eagerly clicked their cameras, others tittered, many were obviously startled by the scene. There was little open animosity, and some bystanders applauded when a tall, pretty girl carrying a sign, "I am a Lesbian," walked by.

Michael Kotis, president of the Mattachine Society, which has about 1,000 members around the country, said that "the gay people have discovered their potential strength and gained a new pride" since a battle on June 29, 1969, between a crowd of homosexuals and policemen who raided the Stonewall Inn, a place frequented by homosexuals at 53 Christopher Street.

"The main thing we have to understand," he added, holding a yellow silk banner high in the air, "is that we're different, but we're not inferior."

- -

GAY PRIDE MARCH RESPONDS TO MIAMI REPEAL

In the largest homosexual demonstration held of its time, tens of thousands of gay men and women marched up Fifth Avenue in New York City, commemorating the seventh anniversary of the beginning of the modern LGBT movement at the Stonewall Inn and demanding equal rights regardless of sexuality. Noted gay rights opponent Anita Bryant was singled out for particular scorn, owing to her efforts to repeal an established gay rights law in the Miami area. Parallel rallies were held in other major cities including Miami, Chicago, Seattle, and Atlanta. In San Francisco marchers memorialized a city gardener who was killed by four men who shouted "faggot" as they stabbed him to death, while police in Barcelona fired rubber bullets to disperse a crowd of 4,000.

JUNE 27, 1977
HOMOSEXUALS MARCH FOR EQUAL RIGHTS
Thousands Parade in New York and Other Cities Across U.S.

Waving placards and chanting rallying cries, a vast sea of homosexual men and women marched up Fifth Avenue under bobbing banners of liberation yesterday in what many called the largest homosexual rights demonstration ever held in New York City.

It was one of numerous huge demonstrations organized by homosexuals over the weekend in cities throughout the United States, including San Francisco, Miami, Los Angeles, Chicago, Atlanta, Kansas City, Seattle and Providence.

The sponsors attributed much of their success to spreading resentment caused by the efforts of Anita Bryant, the singer, who recently led a successful campaign to repeal Miami's ordinance prohibiting discrimination against homosexuals.

Paraders Jam Fifth Avenue

In New York, where tens of thousands joined the line of march from Greenwich Village to Central Park, the paraders jammed Fifth Avenue from curb to curb, chanting and shouting slogans for equal rights. The police did not interfere with the march—which was staged without a parade permit—and the afternoon was peaceful, if boisterous.

Along the route, spectators variously cheered, booed, waved, hissed, smiled, jeered and occasionally spoke sympathetically to the marchers, who carried red, white, blue, green and orange placards and shouted:

"Out of the closet and into the street."

"Anita, we would rather fight than switch."

"Two, four, six, eight; being gay is better than straight."

Some Parents Participate

About a dozen men and women carried signs proclaiming they were proud to be the parents of homosexuals.

"I am a proud gay parent," read one sign held aloft by Richard and Marsha Ashworth of Bronxville. "I am proud of my son—I don't care whether he is gay or straight."

A flatbed trailer carried lesbian mothers and their children.

The line of marchers stretched for 27 blocks up Fifth Avenue. Many of the protesters said they had come from the metropolitan area and New England regions. Many embraced each other as they marched, and hundreds wore buttons bearing Lambda, the Greek letter, which has become a symbol of the homosexual-rights movement.

Some of the slogans and placards were muted; others were defiantly explicit, particularly in denunciation of Miss Bryant. A myriad of views were cited—that women excel as heads of households, that homosexual men do not rape, abuse or murder women.

"Human rights for all," read one placard. Others proclaimed: "No more Miamis," "Pass New York City gay rights law now," "Down with antigay, antiblack, antipoor Supreme Court," and "We are your children."

The march began at Christopher Street and Seventh Avenue in Greenwich Village, a short distance from the site of the old Stonewall Inn. Many homosexuals have viewed the site as a symbol of resistance to oppression since 1969, when a riot broke out as the police moved in to raid and close the tavern. Since then, annual demonstrations have marked the riot and have renewed demands for passage of equal-rights ordinances by the city and state.

Shortly after the march began, a dispute arose over who would lead the parade—members of the Lesbian Feminist Liberation or a group of New York City politicians that included Tony Olivieri, Democratic candidate for the Manhattan Councilman at Large; Councilman Theodore Weiss; Ronnie Eldridge, candidate for Manhattan Borough President; Ruth Messinger, candidate for City Council, and John Laciero, a Greenwich Village district leader.

The politicians lost the argument and dropped out.

As the march continued uptown, loud boos erupted as the throngs passed St. Patrick's Cathedral at 50th Street, apparently expressing opposition to the Roman Catholic Church's official position that homosexuality is wrong.

At 79th Street, the marchers moved into Central Park for three more hours of music and speeches.

In San Francisco, the site of one of the largest weekend demonstrations, interest in the parade was spurred by the slaying of a city gardener outside his home by four young men who were said to have stabbed him more than 15 times as they shouted, "faggot."

SPAIN DISPERSES DEMONSTRATORS

BARCELONA, Spain, June 26 (UPI)—Policemen firing rubber bullets dispersed a homosexual rights demonstration by 4,000 people today in honor of a "World Day of Gay Pride."

The demonstration, sponsored by the Gay Liberation Front of Catalonia, was supported by various political and labor groups.

- -

THE TIMES COMMEMORATES STONEWALL WITH AN ENDORSEMENT

This opinion piece, published twenty-five years after the Stonewall riots, noted that the riots showed gay men and lesbians that they had to organize in order to make political gains. The piece went on to say that gay rights opponents had also learned that lesson and had mounted various antigay efforts in states and localities across the nation. Inaccurately portraying gay rights as "special rights," and exploiting prejudices about cross-dressers, these groups used distortion and fear to turn voters against gay rights. Calling *special rights* manipulative code words that voters should be able to see through, *The Times* editors stated that while cross-dressers have always been controversial, "the measure of a just society is not how it treats people in business clothes. A just society must offer the same protections to men in leather and chains as to those who wear Brooks Brothers suits." Accordingly, *The Times* supported federal protection of gay rights in the newly proposed Employment Non-Discrimination Act.

JUNE 26, 1994
AFTER STONEWALL: PRIDE AND PREJUDICE

The gay rights movement began in earnest 25 years ago, when police raided the Stonewall Inn, a cross-dressers' bar in Greenwich Village. The raid led to a small but fierce riot—prominently featuring men in drag—followed by three days of civil disobedience in the streets.

Stonewall showed gay men and lesbians that they needed to organize for political action and demonstrations, like the march today in New York that commemorates that evening 25 years ago.

Unfortunately, the enemies of gay rights have taken the same message to heart and are doing their own organizing. According to the Human Rights Campaign Fund, the religious right and others are mounting campaigns in seven states to block or repeal laws that forbid discrimination against gay men and lesbians. Among the states with gay-bashing referendums pending, four—Arizona, Ohio, Michigan and Missouri—will have hotly contested Senate races, fertile ground for demagoguery and fearmongering by the anti-gay movement.

In most places extremists will try to persuade voters that to protect gay people against discrimination in housing and employment would be to create "special rights." Thoughtful voters will see through those code words. These referendums aren't about "special rights" at all. They are about voiding reasonable protections under the law that gay people have won through hard political struggle in many cities and towns. They aim to render gay people without rights.

The cross-dressers who sparked the Stonewall event remain an issue in the gay rights struggle today. The religious right uses them to fan fear and hatred. Gay moderates and conservatives, even organizers of the Stonewall parade, seem to feel a constant obligation to divorce themselves from gay flamboyance, to assure the country that the vast majority of gay people are "regular" people just like the folks next door.

The fact that gay people are fixating on folks-next-doorness is understandable, given how they have been demonized. But the measure of a just society is not how it treats people who dress in business clothes. A just society must offer the same protections to men in leather and chains as to those who wear Brooks Brothers suits.

One step toward that ideal would be for Congress to extend Federal protections to gay men and lesbians. A bill that would help in one key area, the Employment Nondiscrimination Act, has just been introduced in Congress with wide support in both houses.

Today's march commemorates the event that energized the gay struggle for equal rights under the law. The backlash prevalent in many states is a reminder that the battle is far from won.

GAY CIVIL RIGHTS LAWS AND THE EMERGING LGBT COMMUNITY

● ●

EARLY CIVIL RIGHTS LAWS

The drive for gay civil rights gained steam after the Stonewall Rebellion. As communities across the country debated gay rights, the lesbian, gay, bisexual, and transgender (LGBT) community became more visible and well organized, fostering the development of a national LGBT movement. This chapter explores debates at the local, state, and federal levels through a detailed examination of the struggle for gay rights in various localities including New York City, Miami, Oregon, and Colorado.

Since the modern LGBT movement began in Greenwich Village, one might have expected New York City to be among the first to pass a gay civil rights law. However, two midwestern college towns shared this honor in 1972, when both East Lansing (home of Michigan State University) and Ann Arbor (home of the University of Michigan) successfully adopted legislation to protect the rights of homosexuals. A number of cities and counties in various regions of the country followed suit, including communities with both traditionally progressive and conservative political cultures. As documented by *The New York Times* in a report on April 19, 1974, these cities included Columbus, Ohio; Berkeley, California; San Francisco; Boulder, Colorado; Seattle; Detroit; Minneapolis, Minnesota; and Washington, D.C. Typically, these cities amended preexisting civil rights laws by adding the category of sexual orientation onto the list of protected categories (such as race, religion, and sex), protecting homosexuals from discrimination in the areas of employment, public accommodations, and housing.

Although a gay civil rights bill had been introduced to the New York City Council as early as 1971 with Mayor John Lindsay's endorsement, the Council did not adopt such a law until 1986. A protracted discussion, which followed the introduction of the bill, contained arguments that would shape debate for many years to come. Opponents were concerned that the bill would permit transvestism (crossdressing) in the workplace and that the police, fire, and education departments would have to hire or retain avowed homosexuals. They also argued that sexuality is a private matter that falls outside the reach of public law. Advocates of gay rights countered that known homosexuals often are discriminated against when they try to rent apartments, book hotel rooms, and apply for jobs, particularly for positions as teachers, police, or firefighters. They added that the issue of transvestism is separate from gay civil rights. Finally, they claimed that those who opposed the bill did so out of bigotry and cowardice.

As reported by *The Times,* the original New York bill died in committee by a 7–5 vote. One day prior to the vote, the police arrested seventeen members of the Gay Activists Alliance (GAA). Labeled "militant" in a *Times* report of January 28, 1972, the activists chained themselves to a brass railing outside Mayor Lindsay's office, claiming that he had provided lip service rather than strong support for the bill. One Council member said that he decided to vote against the bill because of the disruptive tactics of the GAA. As noted in a *Times* report on February 8, 1972, Mayor Lindsay soon issued a directive to protect homosexuals from discrimination in city government hiring and promotion practices, instructing city agency and department heads not to consider private sexual behavior when making such decisions. He also pledged to continue to work with the Council to pass a gay civil rights law that would apply to the entire city. Calling it "the weakest thing that the Mayor could do," GAA leader Rich Wandel said it was nevertheless "a step in the right direction."

The New York bill was revived five times over a three-and-one-half-year period before the General Welfare Committee approved a floor vote in 1974. According to a *Times* report of April 19, 1974, this development occurred owing to a new amendment that clarified that the bill was about sexual orientation, not transvestism. Controversy regarding transgender people persists to this day, as evidenced by the struggle over their inclusion in the Employment Non-Discrimination Act (see discussion in the final chapter). While observers expected the bill to pass through the Council at its next meeting, the

The first Gay Liberation Day Parade took place in 1970 in New York City, considered by many to be the birthplace of gay rights advocacy.

*Source: Mike Lein/*The New York Times

politically influential Catholic Archdiocese of New York asked the Council to defeat the bill and effectively stalled its passage, as documented in a *Times* report of April 28, 1974. Calling homosexuality "a menace to family life" that would compel landlords to accept homosexual renters in two-family dwellings and force employers to hire homosexuals into "sensitive" teaching and counseling positions, the Catholic Church claimed that the bill would "afford unrestricted opportunities to propagandize deviant forms of sexuality." Orthodox Jewish groups also formed a key part of the religious opposition. The Council rejected the bill by a 22–19 vote, with many politicians citing the opposition of the Catholic Church as a critical factor in the defeat. As reported in *The Times* on July 13, 1975, disappointed gay activists quickly organized a demonstration at St. Patrick's Cathedral with support from the Episcopal Diocese, the lieutenant governor of New York, and former vice president Hubert Humphrey.

The bill was rejected several more times, until the New York City Council finally passed it in 1986 by a 21–14 vote, joining over sixty localities that at the time protected homosexuals from discrimination in housing, public accommodations, and employment. Although Council opponents promised to pursue a public referendum to repeal the law in the manner of the Miami campaign (see below), this never came to pass.

NATIONAL

The LGBT community was working to heighten its profile nationally as well as locally. At about the same time that various localities began to consider protections for homosexuals, Rep. Bella Abzug (D-NY) introduced the first national gay rights bill to Congress in 1974, on the fifth anniversary of the Stonewall Rebellion. Like the local laws discussed above, the national bill was designed to protect homosexuals from discrimination in housing, employment, and public accommodations. *The Times* coverage of the bill began in 1975, in a story about the annual meeting of the Gay Academic

Union, which convened in New York City to discuss Abzug's bill and other issues of import to the growing national LGBT community. At this time the bill had been reintroduced on four separate occasions and had been assigned to the House Judicial Committee. By 2007 the House had passed a bill prohibiting discrimination based on sexual orientation, but it stalled in the Senate.

President Jimmy Carter made human rights a central focus of his administration. Although he opposed including a gay rights plank in the Democratic Party platform in 1976, Carter stated during his campaign that he was personally opposed to discrimination on the basis of sexual orientation. In 1977 a mid-level presidential aide named Margaret "Midge" Costanza invited several LGBT activists to the White House for the first known meeting between gay leaders and a representative of the president. Costanza, who was serving as presidential assistant for public liaison, took a great deal of political heat for issuing the invitation. One of her most vocal critics was singer-celebrity Anita Bryant, who was then spearheading a drive to repeal a Miami area gay civil rights ordinance. While Bryant argued that the meeting gave presidential approval to an abnormal lifestyle, the White House maintained that all Americans share the basic right to redress.

In another sign that the LGBT community was gaining national visibility, the LGBT community held its first March on Washington in 1979. While some LGBT leaders were originally skeptical about the march, concerned in part that it would not draw an adequate crowd, an estimated 75,000–125,000 people turned out for the event. Attendees from cities and towns across the country highlighted the movement's growing national profile with the slogan "We Are Everywhere." Marchers themselves even seemed surprised by the strength of their numbers, arguing that the march would unify the national movement, break the isolation of gays and lesbians who remained closeted, and send a message that the LGBT community would continue to press for gay civil rights laws at both the national and local levels despite successful repeal efforts in Miami and elsewhere. Official demands included passing a comprehensive gay and lesbian rights bill in Congress, issuing a presidential order banning discrimination on the basis of sexual orientation in the federal government, repealing all antigay and antilesbian laws (such as laws that criminalized sodomy), ending discrimination in gay and lesbian custody cases, and protecting gay and lesbian youth from harassment. The LGBT community has organized four additional Washington marches since the 1979 march. Held in 1987, 1993, 2000, and 2009, these marches have served to highlight the national visibility of the movement and to foreground issues key to the community in each period.

MIAMI

While the emergence of local and national legislation to protect gay civil rights was important to the development of the emerging LGBT community, the struggle that occurred in Miami in 1977 had an effect like no other on the shape of the gay rights debate for years to come. Like many other localities in the late 1970s, the Dade County Commission passed a gay civil rights bill, protecting homosexuals from employment, public accommodation, and housing discrimination throughout the greater Miami area. Since many city and county governments were doing the same, this development was not especially eventful in and of itself. However, when Anita Bryant, the former beauty pageant queen turned religious and patriotic singer, began to lead the first movement in the country to repeal a gay civil rights law, her celebrity and the novelty of the repeal effort drew an enormous amount of national attention, including significant coverage in *The Times.*

Bryant became involved in opposing the Miami law protecting gay civil rights at the behest of her minister, Rev. William Chapman. Head of a large Baptist church in the area, Chapman was part of a growing wave of politically oriented Christian fundamentalists who opposed gay rights as well as equal rights for women. Once Dade County passed the law, Bryant became the face of the campaign for its repeal. This campaign, and the attention it attracted from national media, served to strengthen connections between LGBT communities across the country.

While opponents of gay rights had long argued that homosexuals should not be allowed to teach, Bryant brought a new fervency to the debate. Leading a group called Save Our Children, she claimed that homosexuals had to recruit converts from each new generation because they couldn't reproduce on their own. Playing off fears that parents would be endangering their children by approving gay civil rights laws, she argued that homosexuals were immoral and prone to pedophilia. Despite opponents' compelling evidence that most child molesters are heterosexual, Bryant's continued exploitation of this myth generated powerful support for her cause among fearful Miami residents.

The Times ran several stories during the four-month repeal campaign. While the paper defended Bryant's right to speak, a March 26, 1977, editorial titled "No, No, Anita!" made it clear that the editors did not support her position, calling her arguments "absurd." An additional *Times* report

IN FOCUS

Anita Bryant's Change of Heart

• •

Anita Bryant endured a series of professional and personal setbacks following her work on the Miami repeal. The LGBT community and its allies protested her singing appearances, raising security costs for promoters and discouraging potential attendees. A *Times* report of June 17, 1977, noted that a crowd of 3,000 held a candlelight march in opposition to Bryant's appearance at a lawyers' convention. Less than a year later she had lost her lucrative secular bookings and was literally passing the hat while singing at religious revivals, as *The Times* reported on February 21, 1978. A judge barred her Save Our Children group from continuing to use its name following a request from the Save the Children Foundation, a well-known nonprofit organization that raises money for poor children. As reported by *The Times* on July 16, 1977, the Foundation said that it was losing donations because people were confusing it with Bryant's effort.

On June 14, 1978, *The Times* reported that Bryant had lost her bid to be elected first vice president of the Southern Baptist Church because many members were concerned that she was too much of a one-issue candidate. She was also dropped from her role as regular Orange Bowl Parade commentator, and the Florida Citrus Commission dismissed her from a $100,000-a-year job as spokesperson for the state's orange juice industry. Less than two years after the Miami campaign, Bryant ended her 20-year marriage to Bob Green, her agent, manager, and co-coordinator of the repeal effort. On May 24, 1980, *The Times* reported that she asked the court for child support, stating that she was "without sufficient funds."

In the wake of these events, Bryant announced that her divorce had caused her to have a change of heart about homosexuals and that she was "more inclined to say 'live and let live,' just don't flaunt it or try to legalize it." Reflecting on the Miami campaign in a *Times* report of November 15, 1980, Anita Bryant concluded, "The answers don't seem so simple now. If I had to do it again I would, but not in the same way."

From *The New York Times*

"3,000 in Houston Protest Anita Bryant's Appearance." June 17, 1977.

"Anti-Homosexual Group Barred From Use of Name." July 16, 1977.

"Secular Bookings Off, Anita Bryant Sings at Revivals." February 21, 1978.

"Anita Bryant Sues to End 20-Year Marriage." May 24, 1980.

"Anita Bryant Says 'Live and Let Live.'" November 15, 1980.

• •

on May 31, 1977, highlighted the lack of Christian consensus on the issue, noting that some clergy were calling for tolerance of homosexuals and that each of the eleven biblical passages purported to condemn homosexuality are open to alternative interpretations. Bryant steadfastly maintained that opposition to gay rights was God's work, and her group's activism apparently affected the Florida legislature, which passed bills during the campaign that outlawed gay marriage and adoption, as noted in a *Times* report of May 31, 1977.

In June 1977, Miami-area residents voted to repeal their gay rights law by an overwhelming 2–1 margin, making Dade County the first locality in the nation to repeal a gay civil rights law. Although the loss was a significant blow, several LGBT leaders said that Anita Bryant had done gay men and lesbians a favor by uniting them in a national campaign against public prejudice and discrimination. In a *Times* report of December 28, 1977, titled "Miami Homosexuals See a Victory Despite Defeat of Anti-Bias Law," one leader stated, "Individuals who had never been involved publicly in gay rights, business and professional people, came out of the closet on this issue because of the bigotry and discrimination expressed by our opponents."

The impact of the Miami campaign was substantial. On the night of the Miami vote, an apparently spontaneous protest march emerged on the streets of New York City, with an estimated crowd of 5,000, while the White House received written protests from as far away as the Netherlands. Politicians across the country including Mayor George Moscone of San Francisco and Rep. Edward Koch of New York stated that they were disappointed in the Miami outcome, as did many national and local leaders of LGBT groups. Leaders on both sides of the issue presciently agreed that this was only the beginning of a larger national debate on gay rights that would continue for years to come.

Life for gay and lesbian Americans had become more complicated, a mix of increased tolerance with persistent exclusion. While a majority of people thought that homosexuals should have equal job opportunities, they also said that homosexuals should not be allowed to teach or serve in the clergy. Although LGBT subcultures were developing in major cities in all regions of the country, violence against gays persisted. This growing complexity was also reflected in various *Times* opinion pieces. A "Topics" piece published in *The Times* on June 13, 1977, argued that the results in Miami confirmed the need for tolerance, asserting that "respect for the rights of others is necessary precisely to the degree that the community fails to share their values." Further, in a June 9, 1977, piece politically conservative *Times* columnist William Safire applauded the results in Miami but called for Bryant not to spread her Save the Children campaign to other localities, characterizing her as a "bluenose moralizer" and urging her to stay out of private citizens' personal behavior.

Post–Miami Repeal Efforts

Miami's repeal of its gay civil rights law led to similar campaigns in several cities, even while others continued to pass new laws protecting the rights of homosexuals. St. Paul, Minnesota, and Eugene, Oregon, both voted to repeal their gay civil rights laws by a 2–1 margin, while Wichita, Kansas, did so by a whopping 5–1 margin. In a May 3, 1978, editorial, *The Times* noted that despite the events in Miami, more than forty other cities had gay civil rights laws in place at that time. Opposing the repeal efforts in St. Paul, Eugene, and Wichita, *The Times* argued that homosexuals "simply want a fair chance to find a job and a place to live." Repeal efforts failed in Seattle, which resoundingly supported its

gay rights law in a 63–37 percent vote. Twelve years later St. Paul passed a new gay civil rights ordinance that was again challenged through repeal, prompting an LGBT leader to comment in a *Times* report of September 24, 1991, "It's a consistent theme in the civil rights of gay people that we have to win twice. First we have to convince a legislature to protect our rights, then we have to stop the repeal efforts from overturning the legislative protection. The battle is never over."

States

During this time a variety of gay rights measures also began to emerge at the statewide level. One week after the Miami campaign concluded, California state senator John Briggs proposed a statewide anti–gay rights initiative. Proposition 6, or the Briggs Initiative, proposed the mandatory firing of all public school teachers who were homosexuals or who advocated homosexuality. Although this effort did not receive much coverage in *The Times,* the paper detailed arguments for and against in an "Issue and Debate" piece on June 24, 1977, titled "Should Professed Homosexuals Be Permitted to Teach School?" Notable conservative individuals (including Ronald Reagan) and groups (such as the John Birch Society) came out against the Briggs Initiative, which was resoundingly defeated by a 58–42 percent margin in the November 1978 elections. More recently, in 2008, the popular film *Milk* documented the role that San Francisco's supervisor Harvey Milk, the first openly gay elected official in a major city, played in defeating the Briggs Initiative and passing a gay civil rights law in San Francisco.

In 1982 Wisconsin became the first state to adopt a comprehensive law protecting gay rights by prohibiting discrimination against homosexuals in housing, public accommodations, and employment as well as in real estate and in credit and union practices. This development did not receive contemporaneous coverage in *The Times,* perhaps because the law gained passage largely by remaining outside of the limelight. However, *The Times* did cover Massachusetts' successful effort to become the second state to secure statewide gay rights protection in 1989. By this time more than eighty municipalities across the country had adopted laws prohibiting discrimination against homosexuals. While the Massachusetts bill had been introduced more than twenty-five years earlier and had long enjoyed majority support, opponents used parliamentary maneuvers to successfully block its passage. Supporters ended the stalemate by adding two key amendments that exempted religious organizations from coverage and clarified that the bill in no way recognized

IN FOCUS

"Abnormal, Wrong, Unnatural and Perverse"

• •

The following is the text of Oregon's Ballot Measure 9, described in an August 16, 1992, *Times* article as "the strongest anti-homosexual measure ever considered by a state."

> This state shall not recognize any categorical provision such as "sexual orientation," "sexual preference," and similar phrases that include homosexuality, pedophilia, sadism or masochism. Quotas, minority status, affirmative action, or any similar concepts, shall not apply to these forms of conduct, nor shall government promote these behaviors. State, regional and local governments and their properties and monies shall not be used to promote, encourage, or facilitate homosexuality, pedophilia, sadism or masochism. State, regional and local governments and their departments, agencies and other entities, including specifically the State Department of Higher Education and the public schools, shall assist in setting a standard for Oregon's youth that recognizes homosexuality, pedophilia, sadism and masochism as abnormal, wrong, unnatural, and perverse and that these behaviors are to be discouraged and avoided. It shall be considered that it is the intent of the people in enacting this section that if any part thereof is held unconstitutional, the remaining parts shall be held in force.

If it had passed, Ballot Measure 9 could have been interpreted as calling for the removal of books with homosexual characters from local libraries, the refusal of liquor licenses to gay bars, and the firing of gay men and lesbians from teaching positions and other government jobs. Although the measure failed, 44 percent of Oregon voters cast their ballots in favor of its passage.

From *The New York Times*

Egan, Timothy. "Oregon Measure Asks State to Repress Homosexuality." August 16, 1992.

• •

same-sex domestic partnerships. While opponents threatened repeal through referendum, this did not come to pass. As of this writing, twenty states now have some form of statewide gay civil rights protection, most often ensuring nondiscrimination in employment, which is the most commonly reported form of antigay discrimination.

Although often effective, orchestrating campaigns to repeal gay civil rights laws proved to be both time consuming and costly; therefore, opponents adopted a new strategy that focused on passing statewide laws that would prevent cities and towns from passing LGBT civil rights protections in the first place. In 1992 the states of Oregon and Colorado held referenda on two of the most stringent antigay proposals ever considered up to that time, Ballot Measure 9 and Amendment 2.

Ballot Measure 9 sought to amend the Oregon Constitution, legalizing discrimination against gays on the grounds that homosexuality is "abnormal, wrong, unnatural and perverse." Both supporters and opponents of Ballot Measure 9 agreed that if passed, its impact would be significant. Gays and lesbians could be legally evicted from their homes if they were renters, fired from their jobs if they worked for state or local government, or excluded from access to various public services, such as library usage. A *Times* report of October 4, 1992, notes that legal scholars argued that "the measure was so vaguely worded that the city could be seen as condoning homosexuality by allowing an openly lesbian officer to stay in the [police] department." This concerned the chief of police of Portland greatly, both professionally and personally, as many gay officers were serving on his force, including his lesbian daughter, who had been a patrol officer for nearly four years. The chief explained that while he was raised to believe all the stereotypes about gay people as child molesters and unnatural, he changed his mind when one of his best friends "a family man, came to me and said he was gay." He added, "I believe my daughter was born that way. In the same way I was born left-handed. But my parents tried to make me learn to be right-handed. As a result, I developed a stutter whenever I tried to write with my wrong hand."

Lon Mabon, chair of the Oregon Citizens Alliance and a leader of the right-wing forces in the state's Republican Party, offered several arguments in support of Ballot Measure 9. Adopting language that the political right had long circulated, he claimed that civil rights for homosexuals were really special rights that excluded the rest of population. In addition, he argued that homosexuals were not a politically disadvantaged minority group in need of special protection, contrary to claims made by advocates of cultural diversity. Traveling the state with the videotape *The Gay Agenda,* Mabon and his supporters played on popular fears about homosexuals, suggesting that homosexuals threatened the safety of children and that the entire state of Oregon would look like a gay pride parade unless voters passed the measure. Opponents of Ballot Measure 9 argued that civil rights are protections that all citizens are guaranteed under the law, rather than special rights accorded to a privileged few. They also provided evidence to show that heterosexuals are more likely to be child molesters than homosexuals. Despite the opposition's efforts to portray the most outlandish behavior as representative of the entire LGBT community, gay rights supporters argued that the community had always been quite diverse and encompassed people of all races, religions, and political persuasions, including urban singles and suburban couples with kids; buttoned-up preppies and fantastically dressed drag queens; Dykes on Bikes lesbian motorcyclists and politically conservative Log Cabin Republicans.

Various religious groups, including the Catholic Church, opposed passage of Ballot Measure 9, owing in part to a concern about growing violence against gays and lesbians. A *Times* report issued on November 1, 1992, documented a sharp increase in violence during the campaign. In addition, several major newspapers opposed the measure, including *The New York Times,* which called for moderate Republicans to stand up to religious extremists attempting to take over the party. In the end the public rejected Ballot Measure 9 in a 56–44 percent vote. After the measure failed, *The Times* reported in a November 14, 1992, story that Craig Berkman, the politically moderate chair of the state Republican Party, had become so frustrated with the culture war politics of the religious right that he threatened to join supporters of Ross Perot, an independent running for president at the time. Mabon stated, "We are the Republican Party. . . . If the Republican leadership had helped us, we would have won again against the homosexuals in Oregon."

Less than a year after the vote on Ballot Measure 9, four rural counties and two small towns in Oregon overwhelmingly approved referenda that barred their towns from passing any laws that would protect homosexuals from discrimination. In a *Times* report of July 1, 1993, Lon Mabon said, "We are in a mode of full-scale cultural war now, and we've just picked up a lot of momentum. . . . We're saying flat out: Don't even try to pass something to protect homosexuals." LGBT leaders argued that this development showed the need for a national civil rights law to protect gay citizens. Gregory King of the Human Rights Campaign Fund, the nation's largest gay and lesbian group, said that "people should not have to fight 50,000 local ordinances across the country just to have their basic rights." By October 11, 1995, *The Times* reported that voters in twenty-nine towns in Oregon had approved similar measures that blocked gay rights laws.

Oregon rejected Ballot Measure 9 in the same election cycle that Colorado passed Amendment 2, which prohibited local governments within the state from adopting gay civil rights laws and rendered void gay civil rights laws already in effect in Denver, Aspen, and Boulder. Fifty-three percent of the Colorado electorate voted in favor of Amendment 2. As in Oregon, opponents of legal protections for gays and lesbians in Colorado argued against special rights for homosexuals, while supporters of gay rights countered that they simply wanted the same protections afforded to other citizens. The Colorado debate also paralleled the Oregon campaign in that LGBT leaders worried that the passage of Amendment 2 would lead gay people to be evicted from their homes, fired from their jobs, and denied access to governmental services.

In response to Colorado's adoption of Amendment 2, LGBT leaders planned a national boycott of Colorado's $5 billion-a-year tourism industry. As reported in *The Times* on December 30, 1992, various celebrities who visit Aspen regularly, such as Jack Nicholson, scorned the boycott, while others such as Barbra Streisand supported it. In response, Thomas Stoddard, former executive director of the Lambda Legal Defense and Education Fund, said, "This is not about a few hundred decent people being inconvenienced. It is about guaranteeing basic human rights to American citizens." Noting that groups in seven other states were trying to get similar initiatives on the ballot in the next election cycle, Bill Rubenstein of the American Civil Liberties Union added, "People need to know that if they adopt measures that discriminate against gays they will be ostracized." *The Times* offered an editorial supporting the boycott, arguing that it could help turn the tide in Colorado and in other states preparing to consider similar measures.

The American Civil Liberties Union, the National Gay and Lesbian Task Force, the Lambda Legal Defense and Education Fund, and the cities of Aspen, Boulder, and Denver filed suit in federal court to prevent Amendment 2 from being implemented. As reported in *The Times* on January 16, 1993, a state judge in Denver blocked the law from taking effect until a trial could be held to determine whether Amendment 2 posed a "real, immediate and irreparable injury" to homosexuals in violation of the state or federal constitution. At the hearing various people testified that homosexuals need legal protection. Angela Romero, a lesbian police officer in Denver, said that she feared for her safety if the law was upheld, stating that "there are some officers who I think would jeopardize my life." John Miller, a professor at the University of Colorado in Denver, argued that the law would have a chilling effect on academic freedom. Paul Brown, a gay man working for the state who had been harassed to the point of contemplating suicide, said, "There has to be a clear message from someone in authority that this is not O.K." Several months later, the Colorado Supreme Court upheld the stay on Amendment 2, setting the stage for a full trial.

Meanwhile, as reported in *The Times* on April 13, 1993, Colorado had one of its best snow seasons ever that winter, drawing a record number of skiers to the state and significantly decreasing the effect of the boycott. While several conventions had been cancelled, experts said that the $35 million lost because of the boycott accounted for a small fraction of Colorado tourism dollars. Supporters of the boycott argued that its effects would extend well beyond Colorado to other states currently considering antigay laws. While Denver mayor Wellington Webb traveled to New York City to encourage people to come to Colorado to work against Amendment 2 rather than boycott the state, Robert Bray of the National Gay and Lesbian Task Force asked, "If the boycott hasn't had any effect in Colorado, then why is everybody there so agitated about it?"

When the trial was held in December, a state judge ruled that Amendment 2 violated the United States Constitution's guarantee of equal protection under the law. According to a *Times* report of December 15, 1993, Judge Jeffrey Bayless rejected the family values argument of the law's supporters, stating that "if one wished to promote family values, action would be taken that is pro-family rather than anti some other group." While gay rights supporters rejoiced, announcing a suspension of the boycott, supporters of Amendment 2 expressed frustration that a law approved by a majority of voters could be struck down in court. The Supreme Court of Colorado upheld this decision, setting the stage for a final

decision to be made at the United States Supreme Court. As reported by *The Times* on February 22, 1995, attorney Suzanne Goldberg of the Lambda Legal Defense and Education Fund said that "the boundaries on what the majority can do to a minority" were at stake in the case, creating the potential to make it "one of the pivotal civil rights cases of the 1990s."

Titled *Romer v. Evans,* the case did indeed turn out to be one of the most important civil rights cases of its time, as evidenced by the lengthy excerpt of the case that appeared in *The Times* on May 21, 1996. By a 6–3 vote, the United States Supreme Court struck down Colorado's Amendment 2 on the grounds that it violated equal protection as guaranteed by the federal Constitution. Writing for the majority of the Court, Justice Anthony Kennedy argued that Amendment 2 was based on irrational animus against homosexuals, who had been singled out as a group for special disadvantage. Stating that "a state cannot so deem a class of persons a stranger to its laws," Kennedy argued that it was outside of the nation's constitutional tradition to enact legislation of this nature. In response, Justice Antonin Scalia's strongly worded dissenting opinion argued that it was entirely reasonable for Colorado voters to uphold traditional sexual morality by prohibiting the passage of gay civil rights laws. He also argued that gay civil rights amounted to special rights, countering Kennedy's argument that protecting equal rights was not akin to granting special rights.

In a *Times* analysis of the case also published on May 21, 1996, Suzanne Goldberg of the Lambda Legal Defense and Education Fund highlighted the importance of the case: "This is the most important victory ever for lesbian and gay rights." Matt Coles of the American Civil Liberties Union agreed, stating that the ruling should prevent similar initiatives from emerging in other states. According to Coles, "For the first time the Supreme Court has said that the Government cannot justify discrimination simply out of hostility and fear." Both Goldberg and Coles accurately predicted that the battleground would now shift to different issues, such as sodomy laws, custody battles, and same-sex marriage.

In the course of the struggle over gay civil rights laws, the national LGBT movement had become a force to be reckoned with. At the same time, many individuals and communities throughout the nation demonstrated increased awareness of, and support for, LGBT issues. However, this was by no means the end of the battle. As Jay Sekulow of the conservative American Center for Law and Justice conceded after *Romer v. Evans* was announced, "There has been a shift of momentum towards the homosexual community." However, he vowed to fight on, saying, "This is the first case of many to come."

BIBLIOGRAPHY

Fejes, Fred. *Gay Rights and Moral Panic: The Origins of America's Debate on Homosexuality.* New York: Palgrave-Macmillan, 2008.

Ghaziani, Amin. *The Dividends of Dissent: How Conflict and Culture Work in Lesbian and Gay Marches on Washington.* Chicago: University of Chicago Press, 2008.

FILMOGRAPHY

The Times of Harvey Milk. 1985.
The Question of Equality. 4 parts. 1995.

FROM *THE NEW YORK TIMES*

"Homosexuals Bill Protecting Rights Is Killed by Council." January 28, 1972.

"New City Directive Bars Hiring Bias on Homosexuals." February 8, 1972.

"Homosexual Bill Gains in Council." April 19, 1974.

"Archdiocese Asks City Council to Defeat Bill on Homosexuals." April 28, 1974.

"Marchers Back Homosexual Bill." July 13, 1975.

"No, No, Anita!" March 26, 1977.

"Florida House Votes Homosexual Controls." May 31, 1977.

"Miami Homosexual Issue Dividing Clerics." May 31, 1977.

"Now Ease Up, Anita." June 9, 1977.

"Reprise." June 13, 1977.

"Should Professed Homosexuals Be Permitted to Teach School?" June 24, 1977.

"Miami Homosexuals See a Victory Despite Defeat of Anti-Bias Law." December 28, 1977.

"A Fair Chance for Homosexuals." May 3, 1978.

"Minnesota City Renews Gay Rights Fight." September 24, 1991.

"Chief of Police Becomes the Target in an Oregon Anti-Gay Campaign." October 4, 1992.

"Violent Backdrop for Anti-Gay Measure." November 1, 1992.

"Oregon G.O.P. Faces Schism Over the Agenda of Christian Right." November 14, 1992.

"Anger and Regret in Aspen as Boycott Grows." December 30, 1992.

"A Ban on Gay-Rights Laws Is Put on Hold in Colorado." January 16, 1993.

"Snow in Colorado Buries Tourism Boycott Threat." April 13, 1993.

"Voters in Oregon Back Local Anti-Gay Rules." July 1, 1993.

"Colorado Judge Overturns Initiative Banning Gay Rights Laws." December 15, 1993.

"Colorado Is Engine in Anti-Gay Uproar." October 11, 1995.

"The Gay Rights Ruling; Excerpts From Court's Decision on Colorado's Provision for Homosexuals." May 21, 1996.

"The Gay Rights Ruling: In Colorado, Ruling Signals More Fights to Come." May 21, 1996.

NEW YORK CITY INTRODUCES HOMOSEXUAL CIVIL RIGHTS BILL

In 1971 a civil rights bill that prohibited discrimination against homosexuals in employment and housing was introduced in the New York City Council, with the endorsement of Mayor John Lindsay. It was referred to the General Welfare Committee, and roughly twenty-five people testified during the meeting. The bill became stalled when some representatives expressed concern about transvestism and open homosexuality among educators, firefighters, and police. Other opponents claimed that homosexuality is private and thus falls outside the realm of public law. Supporters of the bill attempted to separate issues of transvestism from homosexuality, claiming that the bill did not address the former.

The hearing was conducted in the midst of considerable disorder. One opponent used a slur while asserting that she did not want homosexuals to teach her children, which was met with shouting and stomping from the gallery. Other supporters used obscenities to refer to representatives who opposed the bill. One witness testified to discrimination that compelled him to remain closeted at work, while another described differential allocation of resources at Columbia University.

NOVEMBER 16, 1971
HOMOSEXUAL BILL ARGUED IN COUNCIL
Hearing on Discrimination Erupts Into a Debate
By EDWARD RANZAL

A bill to prohibit discrimination against homosexuals in employment and housing was reported yesterday to be in trouble in the City Council's 15-man Committee on General Welfare.

Councilman Theodore S. Weiss, one of the sponsors of the local legislation, which is backed by the Lindsay administration, said that unexpected opposition had "surfaced" and that proponents might have difficulty getting a majority of eight votes to send the bill to the Council floor.

The committee . . . [chair?]man Saul S. Sharison, threatened time and again to adjourn a raucous day-long hearing in the Council's chamber. About 150 persons, mostly in favor of the bill, attended.

Opposition within the committee stemmed from a reluctance to open employment rolls to homosexuals in the Board of Education, and the Police and Fire Departments.

Mr. Sharison said he had requested that representatives of the three agencies testify at a future public meeting as to their hiring practices regarding homosexuals.

The hearing at one point flared into a shouting session when a committee member mentioned that he had observed a transvestite entering the women's restroom. Two males dressed as females, who had been sitting in the balcony, rushed to the Council floor while spectators shouted "heterosexual bastards!" at committee members.

'Nub of the Problem'

"That's the nub of the problem–transvestitism," Mr. Sharison said.

The witness at the time, Richard Ammato, who had described himself as a homosexual, a former high school teacher and an elected Democratic committeeman from Babylon, L.I., immediately charged that the committee was attempting to confuse the issue.

Mr. Ammato said the bill before the committee pertained only to ending discrimination against homosexuals. He insisted that transvestitism was a separate issue and to protect the rights of these people would require additional legislation. He said that not all transvestites were homosexuals.

Another witness, a nurse, who said she had five adopted children, said she strongly opposed the bill and did not want a "homo" as a teacher for her children.

Spectators began shouting derisively at the witness and stamping their feet. It was finally determined that there was a strong objection to the word "homo," which, it was explained, was considered derogatory and debasing.

A witness who said he had deliberately given a false name, described his work as an assistant caseworker on welfare cases. He said he wanted to remain in social service work after gradating from college this year and had applied to a governmental agency. He had wanted to list himself as a homosexual, he said, but was advised by a superior not to do so.

Another illustration of alleged discrimination was given by Morty Manford, who said he was a member of the Columbia University Gay Activists Alliance. He said his group had requested that university officials give them a lounge for themselves. Although other minority groups were able to have lounges set aside for their particular group, he said, his organization had been denied such privileges.

The bill was opposed by two Staten Island women who contended that homosexuality was "a private affair," and should not be legislated into a public scandal. Their principal concern was the role of the homosexual as a teacher.

About 25 persons testified at the session, which began at 11 A.M. and ended at 5:45 P.M. A date for the next session was not set.

• •

NEW YORK GAY RIGHTS BILL FAILS AGAIN

Although a gay civil rights bill failed in the New York City Council at three earlier times, it was again given consideration in 1978, about a year after similar bills had been repealed in cities such as Miami; Boulder; St. Paul, Minnesota; Eugene, Oregon; and Wichita, Kansas. Despite strong support from high-profile celebrities such as Lauren Bacall, politicians such as Mayor Edward Koch, and various union and religious leaders, it was unclear whether the Committee on General Welfare would allow a vote on the bill. In addition, opponents promised a popular referendum if the bill passed. (On the following day it was voted down by the Committee.)

NOVEMBER 8, 1978
PUBLIC HEARING TO BE HELD TODAY ON HOMOSEXUAL RIGHTS MEASURE
By DENA KLEIMAN

The homosexual rights bill, narrowly defeated in the City Council four years ago, is scheduled to be opened to new public debate today amid uncertainty over whether this time its chances for passage are any better.

The hearing, before the Council's Committee on General Welfare, is expected to draw a long list of proponents and opponents of the measure, including prominent entertainers, politicians, union leaders, religious leaders and others.

Mayor Koch is scheduled to head the list of supporters. Others expected to speak in favor of the measure include the actress Lauren Bacall, City Council President Carol Bellamy, Victor Gottbaum, the municipal union leader, and Joseph Papp, the theatrical producer. A principal opponent is expected to be the Patrolmen's Benevolent Association.

Four Firm 'No' Votes

The emotionally-charged measure would amend the city's civil rights law and would bar "sexual orientation" as a ground for refusing housing, employment, or public accommodations. If approved by the nine-member committee, the bill could be considered by the entire Council next week. But, as lobbying continued down to the wire late yesterday, there appeared to be four firm "no" votes on the committee and perhaps as many as six.

It was unclear yesterday whether, following today's hearing—expected to last late into the evening—there would be a vote on the measure. Supporters have said that even if the bill is defeated or a vote postponed, they would attempt to take the measure directly to the entire Council for a vote.

People on both sides have suggested that even if the measure is eventually passed by the Council, opponents would force a public referendum on the issue. The bill, which was defeated 22 to 19 in May 1974, was re-introduced in the Council last April. Some supporters worked to delay consideration of the measure until after yesterday's election on the theory that a 1979 referendum would give the city a year or so to live with the new law before the public would be polled.

In other cities, such as Miami; Boulder, Colo.; St. Paul, Minn.; Eugene, Ore., and Wichita, Kan., similar referendums have overturned homosexual rights ordinances.

On his first day at City Hall, Mayor Koch announced that he would issue an order imposing a ban on discrimination against homosexuals. He did issue such an order, but it applied only to agencies under the Mayor's control. The Council proposal would have a much broader effect, applying to the city as a whole.

In recent days, in an effort to rally support for the measure, Mayor Koch spoke to individual Council members. In addition, he sent all Council members copies of "Consenting Adults," a novel by Laura Hobson that describes the relationship of a homosexual teen-ager with his parents. An accompanying letter requested that each of them read the book prior to today's hearing.

· ·

THE TIMES SUPPORTS GAY RIGHTS

In the following editorial *The Times* decries the New York City Council's failure to pass a gay civil rights bill, noting that the result was not surprising in the wake of Anita Bryant's successful campaign to repeal such a law in Miami. The board notes with approval California's rejection of a statewide proposal to ban homosexuals or advocates from teaching in the public schools, which was opposed by Governors Jerry Brown and Ronald Reagan as well as President Jimmy Carter. Noting that increasing numbers of homosexuals are coming out of the closet, the editorial attempts to separate protection against "senseless and cruel discrimination" from a more general endorsement of homosexuality.

NOVEMBER 10, 1978
BRINGING RIGHTS OUT OF THE CLOSET

For the fourth time in seven years, a bill to prohibit discrimination against homosexuals in employment, housing and public accommodations has been defeated in the New York City Council. The latest version was voted down Wednesday by the Council's General Welfare Committee despite a strong plea for it by Mayor Koch.

The result was not surprising. Similar measures have been defeated in other cities since Anita Bryant's successful campaign against homosexuals in Miami. In New York, the Patrolmen's Benevolent Association and some religious groups offered strong opposition.

A happier result came Tuesday in the nation's first statewide vote on homosexual rights, or lack of them. Californians rejected a proposition that would have permitted school boards to fire or refuse to hire anyone who engages in "homosexual conduct," broadly defined as the "advocating, soliciting, imposing, encouraging or promoting of public or private homosexual activity." It affronted a teacher's freedom of speech, as well as the right to be judged on his or her competence, and was opposed by Gov. Jerry Brown, former Gov. Ronald Reagan and President Carter.

If there is a lesson to be drawn from the propositions put forth in California and elsewhere, it is that most Americans have no wish to oppress homosexuals but many are uneasy about explicitly guaranteeing them rights, particularly in the classroom.

In part, this may be due to a misconception about the people who are homosexual. So a recent public television program, "Word Is Out," which permitted a score of such people to talk frankly about their lives, was particularly welcome. Although the producers were not always subtle in making their case, the experiences recounted by several of these men ad women were truly moving, bringing home the painful choices they face in seeking satisfactions that most of us take for granted.

The causes of homosexuality are far from clear but it is only too clear that a substantial number of Americans have been compelled for years to hide their deepest feelings for fear of losing a job or even a place to live. It is no endorsement of homosexuality to hold that they deserve protection against senseless and cruel discrimination. As long as people keep the peace and pay the rent, they should be able to live where they like. As long as they do their jobs satisfactorily, they should be left to do them without harassment.

• •

NEW YORK CITY APPROVES GAY RIGHTS BILL

After numerous attempts over a fifteen-year period, the City Council of New York City approved a gay civil rights bill by a 21–14 vote. In passing this legislation, the city of New York joined fifty cities, twelve counties, and the state of Wisconsin in banning such discrimination.

Although the margin of success was large, key opponents including the Catholic Church promised to challenge the law in court and through the referendum process, arguing that it amounted to an endorsement of the homosexual lifestyle. Opponents countered that the law would merely extend civil rights protections to homosexuals in the areas of housing, public accommodations, and employment. While the city code had long prohibited discrimination on the basis of race, religion, and sex, it would also do so on the basis of sexual orientation, covering heterosexuality, homosexuality, or bisexuality. Although the outcome had long been clear, unexpected drama emerged during the hearing. A group of forty men and women turned their backs on Councilman Dear as he spoke in opposition to the bill, emulating a group of Hasidic Jews who had turned their back on Mayor Koch as he supported it in a previous hearing. In addition, one council member asserted that the controversy had caused him to be emotionally and physically upset all week, while another cried before the vote.

MARCH 21, 1986
HOMOSEXUAL RIGHTS BILL IS PASSED BY CITY COUNCIL IN 21-TO-14 VOTE
Measure, Approved by Unexpectedly Big Margin, Blocks Discrimination in Housing and Jobs
By JOYCE PURNICK

The New York City Council ended an often intense and emotional 15-year battle last night and approved a homosexual rights bill by an unexpectedly wide margin of 21 to 14.

The Council vote, which came after a long and dramatic but unusually decorous Council hearing, was greeted by cheers and tears from supporters, their arms raised in jubilation or wrapped around each other.

Opponents were silent, or already absent from the crowded chamber on the second floor of City Hall, the same stately room where the Council last considered and defeated a similar bill 12 years ago.

History was not unfamiliar to the supporters. "God, I can't believe it, after all this time," Thomas B. Stoddard, executive director of the Lambda Legal Defense and Education Fund, said after the 35-member Council voted on the measure known as Intro. 2.

Mayor Koch left his office and came up to the second floor to say that he would soon sign the bill and to counsel: "The sky is not going to fall. There isn't going to be any dramatic change in the life of this city."

Opponents did not agree. Even before the meeting was over, Council members who had fought the legislation vowed to challenge it through legal means, in a lawsuit questioning the city's jurisdiction to pass such a law, and perhaps—though city lawyers deemed it an illegal approach—through a public referendum.

Discrimination Is Target

"We are going to go to the very end to see that this bill is defeated," said Councilman Noach Dear, the Brooklyn Democrat who headed the opposition.

The bill, which amends the administrative code of New York City, is intended to ban discrimination on the basis of sexual orientation in housing, employment and public accommodations. Supporters say it is basic civil-rights legislation; opponents contend that it puts an imprimatur of acceptance on homosexual life styles.

Supporters, while not ignoring the possibility of problems ahead for the legislation, were looking to a calmer future. "It's not revolutionary, but it's something that's going to bring a lot more peace to this city," said Andrew Humm, a leader of the Coalition for Lesbian and Gay Rights. "Now we can give more full attention to protecting our civil rights."

Statement From Archdiocese

In a statement last night, the Roman Catholic Archdiocese of New York, which had opposed the bill, said the passage of the bill "is contrary to the public interest and detrimental to our society." It said that "we will seek legal counsel to determine what steps may be taken to reverse this action."

Mr. Humm, Mr. Stoddard and 75 other supporters or opponents of the bill had listened quietly through the more-than-four-hour meeting, a session in marked contrast to the bitter, often vituperative Council hearings on homosexual rights bills in the past.

Perhaps because the bill's chance of passage was clear long before the meeting, and in part because, as many Council members indicated, the debate covered familiar ground, angry exchanges among Council members were at a minimum and outbursts from the spectators seated in the gallery above the Council floor were nonexistent.

The only protest came when Councilman Dear spoke. As he denounced the bill, at least 40 men and women stood silently in the gallery and turned their backs on him, emulating a group of Hasidic Jewish men who had turned their backs on Mayor Koch when he testified in favor of the bill at a committee hearing on March 11.

Yesterday's meeting, compared to the hearing 10 days ago, was calm—notable for its drama and surprise rather than for its hostility.

The surprises came from two Council members who were uncommitted on the bill, until they rose from their chairs to announce their votes. Councilman Wendell Foster of the Bronx, a minister with the United Church of Christ, had said for days that he was upset, emotionally and even physically, by the impending vote and he repeated that yesterday to his colleagues.

Then, Mr. Foster set many people in the gallery to cheering when he said: "In the spirit of Christ I must love my homosexual brothers and sisters, even though I don't understand them. They frighten me. They intimidate me. Yet, I have to live with myself."

Two hours after the bill had passed, Councilman Joseph F. Lisa of Queens, who had originally surprised his colleagues by voting for the bill, citing his role as chairman of a subcommittee on AIDS, came into the press room at City Hall and announced that he had sent a telegram to the City Clerk reversing his vote. But the Democratic majority leader, Peter F. Vallone, said Mr. Lisa's reversal did not count.

Chairman of AIDS Panel

Mr. Lisa emphasized during the Council meeting that he is chairman of the Council's subcommittee on AIDS. "I find that I must, in order to be able to justify my ability to represent this Council in this epidemic, vote in the affirmative," he said.

But later, he said he had made a mistake. "Emotionally I thought the bill was the vehicle I could use to end discrimination against AIDS, but it doesn't meet the legislative

criteria to accomplish that end." He said he would seek other legislation to do that.

With the outcome clear even to opponents by the time the meeting got under way at 1:39 P.M. yesterday, there was little evidence of intense lobbying during the meeting, other than colleagues speaking to each other. Samuel Horwitz of Brooklyn, the chairman of the Council committee that voted out the measure on March 11, had a long talk with Mr. Foster, for instance, and Mr. Dear cornered a number of his colleagues before the meeting started.

Momentum With the Bill

But afterward it was clear that the momentum was with the bill, and it stayed that way, through an unsuccessful vote to refer the measure back to committee and two unsuccessful votes on amendments Mr. Dear introduced.

The amendments, dealing with housing and religious institutions, may be considered as separate bills amending the measure approved yesterday by his committee, Mr. Horwitz said.

When it came time for the vote, a new member of the Council, Julia Harrison of Queens, cried before she cast her vote. "It's been very difficult for me," she said.

A few minutes later came the tie-breaking 18th vote, cast by a longtime backer of homosexual rights, Councilwoman Ruth W. Messinger of Manhattan. With her vote, supporters of the bill shouted and applauded.

The bill adopted yesterday essentially amends the city code to ban discrimination because of sexual orientation. The code already forbids discrimination on the basis of race, religion and sex. Sexual orientation is defined in the bill as heterosexuality, homosexuality or bisexuality. A victim of bias could file a complaint with the City Commission on Human Rights.

The bill provides exceptions for companies with fewer than four employees, owner-occupied dwellings of one or two families and religious organizations.

Fifty cities, 12 counties and the state of Wisconsin have already enacted homosexual rights legislation.

National Civil Rights Bill Covered in *The Times*

In 1974 Rep. Bella Abzug introduced the first federal gay rights bill to ban discrimination against homosexuals in housing, employment, and public accommodations. The first mention of this bill appeared in *The Times* in November 1975 in a story that covered the annual meeting of the Gay Academic Union in New York City. Attendees at that meeting, most of whom were students and younger professors, also discussed New York City's recently defeated gay civil rights bill, gay literature, the relationship between feminism and lesbianism, and the psychology of sexuality. As is common for new legislation, the measure had been reintroduced four times and had been assigned to the House Judicial Committee. This bill was an expansion of the Civil Rights Act of 1964, and leaders in the LGBT community hoped to have the bill introduced into the Senate.

NOVEMBER 30, 1975
MEETING BACKS U.S. HOMOSEXUAL RIGHTS MEASURE

More than 1,000 people at the third annual conference of the Gay Academic Union here yesterday were urged to support a Federal homosexual civil rights bill to ban discrimination against homosexuals in public accommodations and facilities, housing, education and Federal programs.

Supporters of the bill said that the measure faced a difficult battle for passage because of the failure of the Equal Rights Amendments to the New York and New Jersey State Constitutions earlier this month.

"It is the most effective legislation for battling discrimination, which strikes at the core of human dignity," said Mary L. Stevens, a law student at Rutgers University who has been active in organizing Lesbians in Law, as she stood before a mostly male meeting on "Legislation Affecting Gays."

The bill was first presented to the House of Representatives in January 1974. It has been re-introduced four times since then and is now in a subcommittee of the House Judicial Committee.

"We want to introduce the same type of legislation in the Senate to expand the Civil Rights Bill and the Fair Labor Standards Act," said Jean O'Leary, founder of Lesbians Feminist Liberation and a member of the advisory committee to the State Human Rights Commission.

New York City's homosexual civil rights bill, which would have barred discrimination against homosexuals in housing and employment, was defeated by the City Council in September, for the sixth time in four years.

The second day of the three-day conference, which drew mostly students and young professors, was held at Columbia University and included meetings on "Criticism of Gay Male Poetry," "Feminism and Lesbianism: Where Do We Want to Go?" and "Attitudes Toward Homosexuality in Judaism." Some of the meetings were restricted to men or women only.

John Money, author and professor of medical psychology and pediatrics at Johns Hopkins University, addressed a crowded auditorium in a general session about human sexuality.

"There has been a tendency to see behavior in terms of pathology instead of from its assets," he remarked. "And from the Greek times onwards, if you really wanted to get someone politically you called him a homosexual, which was like treason, heresy or crime."

Bisexuality and homosexuality were later classified under sickness," he said.

Dr. Money made references to scientific behavior studies of the sexual behavior of rats, hamsters and other animals and said it was found that "it is possible that the hormonal environment of the womb and the fetus might have something to do with the person being homosexual or heterosexual."

GAY AND LESBIAN ACTIVISTS GAIN FIRST MEETING IN WHITE HOUSE

The first ever meeting of gay and lesbian activists and White House officials was held in 1977 during the presidency of Jimmy Carter. *The Times* coverage of the event focused on Anita Bryant, a nationally known opponent of gay rights who was then leading efforts to repeal a civil rights law protecting homosexuals in the Miami area. Several gay and lesbian activists, including Jean O'Leary and Bruce Voeller, had met with presidential aide Margaret "Midge" Costanza at the White House to discuss laws discriminating against homosexuals. Bryant argued that the meeting inappropriately legitimated the human rights claims of the gay activists, transforming a moral issue into a political one. Stating that homosexuals were seeking approval from the office of the president for their "abnormal lifestyle," Bryant objected to the meeting. In response, President Carter's press secretary, Jody Powell, appeared on the *Face the Nation* news program and stated that the invitation to gay activists to discuss discrimination displayed "the essence of what America is all about," as organized groups who feel aggrieved have a right to appeal for redress.

MARCH 28, 1977
ANITA BRYANT SCORES WHITE HOUSE TALK WITH HOMOSEXUALS
Miami Beach, March 27 (UPI)

Anita Bryant, the singer who has been campaigning against a homosexual rights ordinance in the Miami area, was sharply critical of the White House today for holding a meeting with a group of homosexual activists.

"I protest the action of the White House staff in dignifying these activists for special privilege with a serious discussion of their alleged 'human rights,'" she said in a statement.

About two dozen homosexual rights activists met with a Presidential aide, Margaret Costanza, at the White House yesterday to lobby for repeal of laws discriminating against homosexuals.

Miss Bryant, who is best known in recent years for her television commercials advertising Florida orange juice, said that the issue of homosexual rights was a moral one and not political.

"Behind the high-sounding appeal against discrimination in jobs and housing, which is not a problem to the 'closet' homosexual, they are really asking to be blessed in their abnormal life style by the Office of the President of the United States," she said.

"What these people really want, hidden behind obscure legal phrases, is the legal right to propose to our children that there is an acceptable alternate way of life—that being homosexual or lesbian is not really wrong or illegal."

MIAMI PASSES GAY RIGHTS BILL

On January 18, 1977, Dade County, which contains the city of Miami, passed a civil rights ordinance that made it illegal to discriminate against homosexuals in the areas of housing, public accommodations, and employment. Following standard procedure, the County Commission passed the law twice, the first time unanimously and the second time with a more contested 5–3 result. A former beauty pageant queen turned popular singer who was known for stirring renditions of religious and patriotic songs, Anita Bryant emerged as the central leader of the opposition to the law. Setting the terms of the debate for years to come for those opposed to civil rights, she argued that homosexuality was immoral and a threat to children's safety. At the eleventh hour, the Catholic Archdiocese of Miami joined Bryant in opposition to the bill, fearful of the effect that it could have on hiring practices in church-affiliated schools.

JANUARY 19, 1977
BIAS AGAINST HOMOSEXUALS IS OUTLAWED IN MIAMI
Special to the New York Times

MIAMI, Jan. 18—The Dade County Commission today gave its final approval to an ordinance that prohibits discrimination against homosexuals in housing, public accommodation and employment. The law takes effect in 10 days.

The commission, which passed the controversial ordinance unanimously on the first reading last month, voted 5 to 3 this morning after an emotional two-hour public hearing.

A group of opponents of the measure, led by the singer Anita Bryant, filled the commission's chambers. "We're not going to take this sitting down," said Miss Bryant after the vote. "The ordinance condones immorality and discriminates against my children's right to grow up in a healthy, decent community."

In what some observers regarded as a surprise development, the Archdiocese of Miami, through its attorney, urged defeat of the ordinance, apparently on the grounds that it would affect parochial schools.

MIAMI GAY RIGHTS DEBATE GOES NATIONAL

After having collected six times the number of required signatures, Anita Bryant's group Save Our Children obtained a referendum (popular vote) on the months-old Dade County (Miami area) ordinance protecting homosexuals from discrimination in the area of housing, public accommodations, and employment. While early polls suggested that the law would be retained, the outcome was still an open question because of the uncertainty about undecided voters and the level of turnout at a special election.

The debate in Miami was perhaps the most visible example of an emerging national conversation about gay civil rights. By this time more than three dozen localities had adopted civil rights laws protecting homosexuals from discrimination, and national civil rights legislation had been introduced in Congress. The debate in Miami gained perhaps the greatest national attention owing to the celebrity of Anita Bryant, a former beauty pageant queen and popular religious and patriotic singer who was a leading opponent of gay rights. Ironically, the organizing and fund-raising in opposition to Bryant at the local and national level contributed to a strengthened national LGBT community, united around civil rights and determined to defeat its opponents, many of whom hailed from increasingly politicized fundamentalist religious groups in and outside of Dade County. Activists on both sides of the issue agreed that the vote in Miami would have implications for the direction of the debate nationwide for years to come.

The leading opponent of gay civil rights, Bryant, was a Southern Baptist and a mother of four. She argued that homosexuality was immoral and a threat to the safety of children, alleging that homosexuals would recruit and molest innocent children. Robert Kunst, the most visible leader of those in favor of retaining the gay civil rights law, countered that such arguments were grounded in homophobia, an irrational fear of gays and lesbians. Noting that most child molesters are heterosexual, not homosexual, he countered that gay rights are human rights. He welcomed the national visibility ushered in by Bryant's celebrity, hoping for a broader discussion of the issues.

In addition to the leadership of Bryant, opponents of gay civil rights gained an important endorsement from Florida's governor, Reubin Askew, who asserted that homosexuality was not a constitutional issue, while gay rights supporters were backed by Sgt. Leonard Matlovich, who had gained national attention when he challenged his discharge from the Air Force after disclosing his homosexuality (see "Gays in the Military"). While Matlovich had been on the cover of *Time,* a national news magazine, his notoriety could not compare with Bryant's.

Because Bryant was the national spokesperson for Florida orange juice, gay groups across the country organized boycotts asserting that a day without human rights is like a day without sunshine, an obvious reversal of the slogan that ended Bryant's commercials, "a day without orange juice is like a day without sunshine." Although the Florida Department of Citrus claimed that the boycott had no effect on sales, Bryant's concert bookings substantially decreased.

MAY 10, 1977
MIAMI DEBATE OVER RIGHTS OF HOMOSEXUALS DIRECTS WIDE ATTENTION TO A NATIONAL ISSUE

By B. DRUMMOND AYRES, JR.
Special to the New York Times

MIAMI, May 9—A dispute over rights for homosexuals, building locally for the last several months, is focusing attention on a national issue.

As far as the Miami area is concerned, the argument will be settled on June 7, when residents vote to repeal or uphold a county ordinance that bars discrimination against homosexuals in employment, housing and public accommodations.

But both sides in the fight have vowed to continue the struggle elsewhere in the country, whatever the outcome of the Miami referendum. National committees are being organized and fund drives are under way in "gay" bars and fundamentalist churches from here to San Francisco.

The Miami dispute is not the first of its kind. At least three dozen other communities have debated the issue, with varying results. Other national committees have also existed for some time, including several that are lobbying for Federal legislation and White House support.

But no other homosexual debate has caught the national attention like the Miami dispute. No other debate has involved so many people, resulted in so much spending, stirred so many editors, made so many talk shows or generated so many bumper stickers and emblazoned T-shirts. Why?

Personalities at Issue

The answer lies primarily in personalities and the particular twist of the Miami issue. The main figure in the dispute is Anita Bryant, the Miami television singer known nationwide for her sunny purveying of Florida orange juice and her devoutly patriotic rendering of "The Battle Hymn of the Republic." A fervent Southern Baptist, the 37-year-old mother of four school-age children heads Save Our Children Inc., the main anti-homosexual group.

"If homosexuality were the normal way, God would have made Adam and Bruce," she says. "This has become a national fight. I've spoken all around the country. We've gotten more than 20,000 letters and taken in about $40,000 from more than 40 states. It won't stop here in Florida. We're setting up to go nationally."

Save Our Children was organized a few months ago after Miami homosexuals persuaded the county commission to pass a homosexual rights ordinance. Miss Bryant's group contends that the ordinance would force schools to hire homosexual teachers and that the teachers would then proselytize and possibly molest children. It warns that similar laws are being considered in other cities around the country and on Capitol Hill.

"Those arguments are all just a lot of homophobia," counters Robert Kunst, a Miami homosexual who helped organize the Miami Victory Campaign, one of several groups trying to preserve the ordinance.

"We've heard from just as many people, taken in just as much money, been on just as many talk shows," he adds. "The truth is that Anita Bryant is the best thing that has ever happened to us. She's really stirred it good, gotten it in the national limelight once and for all with that trash about child molestation. This is a human rights fight and we're prepared to take it all over the country. She knows as well as we do that child molestation is usually heterosexual."

Right or wrong, the Save Our Children argument has proved potent. To force the commission-passed law onto the ballot for a referendum, Miss Bryant's group needed 10,000 petition signatures. It got 60,000, many by approaching parents in local churches.

In Charlotte, N.C., members of the Jesus Is Lord Club, a Bible study group, heard of the petition drive and mailed checks for $10 and $20. An Alabama woman sent $1,000.

"Support is coming in from everywhere," says Mike Thompson, a Miami advertising executive who helped organize Save Our Children. "One day I'm on the phone to Minnesota, talking to legislators there about how to defeat a gay rights bill. The next night I'm on the 'Tomorrow' show in New York. This thing is leap-frogging."

Askew Joins Fight

A few days ago, the anti-homosexual forces received an important boost from Gov. Reubin Askew of Florida, a man who shuns alcohol and tobacco and is sometimes referred to by critics and supporters alike as "Reubin the Good."

"I've never viewed the homosexual lifestyle as something that approached a constitutional right," Governor Askew said at a news conference. "So if I were in Miami, I would find no difficulty in voting to repeal the ordinance. I do not want a known homosexual teaching my child."

The pro-homosexual forces in Miami are split about how to preserve the ordinance. One group, the Coalition for Humanistic Rights of Gays, offered at one point to foot the $300,000 bill for the referendum, apparently fearing that otherwise the vote might not be called. The offer infuriated Robert Kunst and others, who split to form their own lobby, arguing that the county was responsible for referendum costs.

As matters now stand, the county will pick up the tab.

Bob Basker, the executive director of the coalition, says that the June 7 vote will be "a very strong precursor" of what may happen elsewhere in the country. He predicts that defeat would result in a national "witch hunt" against homosexuals.

To help Miami homosexuals head off defeat, a number of leading homosexual activists have visited the city, among them Leonard Matlovich, the Air Force sergeant who was discharged when he disclosed his homosexuality. Homosexuals in New York recently held a fund-raising rally at the Waldorf Astoria Hotel and are planning several other rallies.

In San Francisco, homosexuals have set up a "Miami Support Committee." The operators of several dozen "gay" bars have ordered a "gaycott" of Florida orange juice. Bumper stickers proclaim, "A day without human rights is like a day without sunshine," a twist of Miss Bryant's juice ad that says "A day without orange juice is like a day without sunshine."

Has the "gaycott" had any effect on sales of Florida juice or endangered Miss Bryant's $100,000-a-year television advertising contract with the Florida Department of Citrus?

"Sales are up," says Arthur Darling, a department spokesman. "There's no way of knowing about contracts at this point. Obviously, we'd have been better off if the whole thing had never come up. But as long as she doesn't get involved on our time or with our name, we have no right to deny her First Amendment rights to speak out."

Miss Bryant says that her bookings for entertainment not related to selling citrus are down about 70 percent. "But I have to carry on this fight," she adds.

One of her agents is Richard Shack, husband of Ruth Shack, the county commissioner who proposed the homosexual rights ordinance. He said he and Miss Bryant talk only business, not politics.

With the referendum vote a month away, most surveys give the homosexual forces a slight edge. However, a considerable number of voters remain undecided and turnout remains an imponderable in a community made up, in good part, of conservative churchgoers and retired liberals from the Northeast.

On neither side does anyone pretend to understand a bumper sticker that reads:

"A Day Without Gays is like a Day Without Anita."

MIAMI REPEALS GAY CIVIL RIGHTS PROTECTIONS

Only four months after its passage by the Dade County Commission, Miami-area residents voted by a resounding 2–1 margin to repeal a civil rights law that protected homosexuals from discrimination in housing, public accommodations, and employment. Although over 35 cities and counties across the country had passed such laws, Dade County was the first major metropolitan area to repeal one. Anita Bryant, the leader of the "Save Our Children" group that opposed civil rights protections for homosexuals, vowed to challenge similar laws across the country, claiming to be doing God's work by battling an immoral and dangerous lifestyle. Robert Kunst, a leading advocate of LGBT civil rights stated that the fight for human rights had just begun.

Jean O'Leary, the executive director of the National Gay Task Force, bemoaned the loss in Miami, but noted that the vote had raised the visibility of gay issues here and in Europe. The gay community became more cohesive in the course of the campaign, as the conflict in Miami became a focal point for gay politics due to the novelty of the referendum and the national attention resulting from Bryant's celebrity. Various gay rights supporters asserted that the increased visibility resulting from the Miami repeal made Bryant the best thing that ever happened to the LGBT community.

JUNE 8, 1977
MIAMI VOTES 2 TO 1 TO REPEAL LAW BARRING BIAS AGAINST HOMOSEXUALS
By B. DRUMMOND AYRES, JR.
Special to the New York Times

MIAMI, June 7—In a decision almost certain to have national impact, residents of the Miami area voted more than 2-to-1 today to repeal a law that protects homosexuals from discrimination in employment, housing and public accommodation.

The vote, a referendum on an ordinance enacted more than four months ago by the Dade County Commission, was the first of its kind in a major United States city. It came at the end of a heated campaign that focused national attention on the long-smoldering question of what legal and social status should be given the 5 to 10 percent of the nation's population that practices homosexuality....

Anita Bryant, the pop singer and television personality who led the repeal forces, celebrated the victory by dancing a jig at her Miami Beach home. Later she told newsmen that she established a national committee to fight homosexuality and added:

"All America and all the world will hear what the people have said, and with God's continued help, we will

prevail in our fight to repeal similar laws throughout the nation which attempt to legitimize a life style that is both perverse and dangerous."

Robert Kunst, a leading figure in the Miami homosexual community, contended that the vote was "not a disappointment."

"We started from ground zero and got around 100,000 people to support us," he sad. "This is just the beginning of the fight."

Jean O'Leary, an executive director of the National Gay Task Force, said after the vote: "The defeat for human rights in Dade County is all the evidence anyone could need of the extent and virulence of prejudice against lesbians and gay men in our society, and of the necessity to redouble our efforts to end such prejudice and the discrimination it inspires."

With the votes of 439 of Miami's 446 precincts tabulated, the referendum results were 202, 319 votes for repeal and 89, 562 for retention of the ordinance. Slightly more than 40 percent of eligible voters went to the polls, an unusually high turnout for a referendum.

John W. Campbell, another leading member of Miami's homosexual community, also attempted to view the defeat optimistically. At a "victory dance" at the Fontainebleu Hotel on Miami Beach, as hundreds of homosexuals chanted, "We Shall Overcome," he said:

"The campaign has motivated gay people politically, not merely in Florida but all across the nation and even in Europe. We're going national now. We've got more than $50,000 left over, more than any gay group has ever had before."

"For decades," he continued, "homosexuality was 'the love that dare not speak its name.' Now the whole world is talking about our cause. We are everywhere. We are not going to go away. And we are going to win. We didn't get the votes we expected. But we got one heck of a lot."

Ruth Shack, the county commissioner who originally proposed the ordinance, said the vote was "three times worse than I ever expected."

"They came out of the woodwork," she said of the law's opponents. "It was a huge step back nationally. We lost heavily among Jewish liberals in Miami Beach. My political future? I'll be back to work again tomorrow. Life goes on."

Jean O'Leary, an executive director of the National Gay Task Force, said after the vote: "The defeat for human rights in Dade County is all the evidence anyone could need of the extent and virulence of prejudice against lesbians and gay men in our society, and of the necessity to redouble our efforts to end such prejudice and the discrimination it inspires."

Miami's homosexual community was not particularly large or vocal before homosexual rights erupted as an issue. The community, situated in the Coconut Grove section of the city, just south of the business district, became a national focal point for homosexual politics mainly through the efforts of Miss Bryant.

Miss Bryant became an outspoken opponent of homosexuality early this year after the Dade council adopted the ordinance.

A number of smaller cities around the country have adopted similar bans in recent years as homosexuals, encouraged by the civil rights progress made by blacks, have begun to press their own case for legal and social recognition. But only in Miami did the extension of rights run into implacable opposition.

Miss Bryant, a devout Baptist, formed an anti-homosexual group that she named Save Our Children. She argued that the Miami ordinance was a religious abomination and license for homosexuals to recruit and molest children. She demanded that the ordinance be rescinded and persuaded 60,000 people—six times the required number—to sign petitions that subjected it to today's countywide referendum.

Using her national reputation and church ties, she helped Save Our Children raise almost $200,000 in campaign funds. Much of the money came from beyond Florida.

"If homosexuality were the normal way," she asserted time after time, "God would have made Adam and Bruce."

Miss Bryant's campaign cost her a number of entertainment engagements. It also infuriated and mobilized homosexuals all over the country.

To work for preservation of the ordinance, Miami homosexuals formed two groups, the Coalition for Human Rights and the Victory Campaign.

The two groups disagreed a bit over strategy, but they agreed totally on the ultimate goal and on Anita Bryant. "She's the best thing that ever happened to gays," they asserted repeatedly.

In San Francisco and New York, cities with large homosexual communities, thousands of dollars were raised for the Miami struggle.

Political organizers came from several other cities to help the homosexual cause. Using a war chest of some $300,000, they devised a campaign that relied heavily on television and newspaper advertisements. Most of the ads asserted that homosexuals were not child molesters and were being subjected to bigotry and a Nazi-style witch hunt.

Homosexuals March in New York

Word of the vote sparked a spontaneous demonstration by what the police said was at least 500 men and women in Greenwich Village last night. The demonstrators, many of whom were at bars that cater to homosexuals, paraded along Christopher Street from Sheridan Square to West Street, carrying candles and signs in support of homosexual rights.

NEW YORKERS MARCH TO PROTEST MIAMI REPEAL

In response to the news that Miami-area residents had voted to repeal a civil rights law protecting homosexuals from discrimination in housing, public accommodations, and employment, several thousand demonstrators marched in protest from Greenwich Village to Columbus Circle in New York City on June 8, 1977. Police estimated the crowds to be 5,000 strong. Rep. Bella Abzug (D-NY) and Rep. Edward Koch (D-NY), both sponsors of a federal gay civil rights bill, spoke to the crowd. Leaders of the LGBT community in the New York area bemoaned the result in Miami and vowed to redouble efforts to gain passage of a gay civil rights law in New York City. A law banning discrimination against homosexuals with respect to housing and employment was first introduced in the City Council in 1971 but had yet to pass.

JUNE 9, 1977
THOUSANDS BACKING HOMOSEXUALS MARCH UPTOWN TO COLUMBUS CIRCLE
By DENA KLEIMAN

Responding to the repeal Tuesday in Miami of a homosexual-rights law, several thousand demonstrators turned out in Sheridan Square in Greenwich Village last night and then marched uptown to Columbus Circle to declare a new fight to ban discrimination against homosexuals.

The demonstration, which had filled both Columbus Circle and Sheridan Square, appeared to be a grass-roots rally without any one focus or sponsor, but attracted men and women from throughout New York City as well as New Jersey.

At 10:45 P.M., the demonstrators headed north along the Avenue of the Americas, summoning spectators to join them. The police said the crowd grew to as many as 5,000.

As they moved, hoisting banners above their heads, the demonstrators chanted and cheered, but it was not until two hours later, when they reached Central Park South, that anyone seemed to take notice.

Bella Abzug was waiting in the street when the demonstrators reached Columbus Circle. She gave them words of encouragement, after which the rally began to break up.

From the start, there was no agreement on what was the best means to wage the fight for equality—within the system or in opposition to it.

"The traditional system failed," said Harvey Jackson, a vice president of the Gay Activists Alliance of New Jersey, explaining why some demonstrators had heckled Representative Edward I. Koch.

Mr. Koch, who appeared at the rally at 10:10 P.M., tried to encourage the demonstrators.

"The state has no business in the bedrooms of our nation," Mr. Koch said.

Earlier in the day leaders of the homosexual community in New York City made plans to get their own long-stalled antidiscrimination measure through the next City Council.

New York's measure, which would have barred discrimination against homosexuals in housing and employment by extending the city's Human Rights Law to include homosexuals, died in a City Council Committee in 1975 and has not been resubmitted.

It was introduced in 1971 by Councilman Carter Burden, Manhattan Democratic Liberal and was defeated by the City Council in 1974 by a 22 to 19 vote.

Mr. Burden, who is now running for Manhattan Borough President, said yesterday that he would be conferring with co-sponsors and homosexual leaders to decide "the most strategic moment" to bring the measure up again.

At least 500 demonstrators had gathered Tuesday night in Sheridan Square, at Grove and Christopher Streets, an area with numerous homosexual bars, to protest the results of the Miami vote.

Miami Repeal Sparks National Debate on Gay Rights

Miami-area residents' vote to repeal a gay civil rights law started a national debate on the issue. While Miami may have been the first major city to hold a referendum on the matter of gay rights, both proponents and opponents of such protections anticipated that the fight would continue in Miami and in localities across the country. The National Gay Task Force, a leading organization in the struggle for gay rights, planned to hold a major conference at its headquarters in New York City, while leaders of opposition forces planned to open a national office in Washington, D.C., to block federal and local gay civil rights laws. Anita Bryant, the most visible leader in the Miami campaign, planned to play a central role. Her public appearances had begun to attract demonstrations from groups advocating gay rights. Politicians such as Mayor George Moscone of San Francisco and Rep. Edward Koch (D-NY) bemoaned the results in Miami, as did national organizers such as Eleanor Smeal, executive director of the National Organization for Women (NOW), and Mike Sedberry, head of the Gay People's Union in the heartland area of Indianapolis. European groups contacted President Carter to protest the results; however, the president had been keeping a low profile on the issue, despite his strong advocacy of human rights.

JUNE 9, 1977
MIAMI VOTE INCREASES ACTIVISM ON HOMOSEXUAL RIGHTS
By B. DRUMMOND AYRES, JR.
Special to the New York Times

MIAMI, June 8—Though Miami area residents voted overwhelmingly yesterday to revoke broad legal protection for homosexuals, the argument over their status in society resumed full force today, not only in Miami but also in other parts of the country.

[In New York City, several thousand demonstrators gathered in Greenwich Village then marched straight through midtown Manhattan last night to declare the start of a new effort to end discrimination against homosexuals. D21.]

The homosexual rights referendum, the first of its kind in a major United States city, appeared to have started a noisy national debate on a question that previously had been discussed mainly in muted tones.

Both the winning and the losing sides in the vote, which overturned an ordinance that protected homosexuals from discrimination in employment, housing and public accommodation, began drawing up plans to continue the struggle here and elsewhere.

Local homosexual leaders threatened to take their cause to court and prepared to send representatives to New York this weekend for a major conference on homosexual rights at the headquarters of the National Gay Task Force, one of the country's largest homosexual organizations.

"It's unconstitutional to subject human rights to a referendum," said John W. Campbell, chairman of the Coalition for Human Rights, the main Miami homosexual group. "We may go to court. We got beaten so badly in the battle here, but the war is just beginning. We're coming out of Miami with national unity and momentum."

Exultant leaders of Miami's anti-homosexual forces offered advice and assistance to similar groups elsewhere and announced plans to establish a national office in Washington.

"We won 2 to 1, which is proof that the country sees homosexuals as child molesters and religious heretics," asserted Robert Brake, a top official of Save Our Children, the main anti-homosexual group here.

"We're going to set up in Washington next to fight 'gay' proposals before Congress," he said. "We'll advise and help any anti-gay group in the country that invites us in. Already we've heard from people in San Francisco, Los Angeles, D.C., Minneapolis, and San Antonio."

Mr. Brake said that Anita Bryant, the singer and television personality who served as chairman of Save Our Children, would continue to take part in the spreading dispute. She flew to Norfolk, Va., early today for an entertainment engagement before a religious convocation. The Norfolk Coalition for Human Rights, a group formed a few weeks ago as a result of interest stirred up by the Miami issue, picketed her appearance.

The Norfolk demonstration followed earlier demonstrations in San Francisco and New York, the American cities with the largest concentration of homosexuals. When the results of the Miami referendum reached those cities shortly before midnight yesterday, scores of homosexuals poured into the streets in noisy protest.

The San Francisco Mayor, George Moscone, said the results of the vote were "terribly wrong" and indicated that "some people have rights and others do not." Representative Edward I. Koch, a liberal Manhattan Democrat who is the sponsor of a homosexual rights measure before Congress, called the vote "regrettable."

In Indianapolis this morning the results of yesterday's referendum led Mike Sedberry, the leader of the Gay People's Union, to call a press conference on the steps of the Indiana State Capitol. "We expect violence," he said.

In Washington, Eleanor Smeal, who heads the National Organization for Women, said the Miami vote smacked of Nazi-style oppression and suggested that Save Our Children should be renamed "Save Some of Our Children—Discard the Rest."

The Miami vote also sparked some overseas comment. Two Dutch groups, the Free Friendship Rights Society and the Association for the Integration of Homosexuality, called the results "degrading" in a telegram sent to President Carter.

The President, a strong human rights advocate, has avoided significant personal involvement in the homosexual rights dispute. However, he did permit White House officials to meet a few weeks back with several leading homosexuals.

Several dozen small communities have enacted laws similar to the one repealed in Miami as the nation's homosexuals, estimated to be 5 to 10 percent of the population, have begun to follow the black lead in pushing for civil rights.

No other city has previously become embroiled in such a hot debate about homosexuality mainly because the issue elsewhere has never caught the attention of a person of Miss Bryant's national stature and influence.

Miss Bryant was instrumental in persuading two of every three persons who went to the polls that the issue was not a matter of legal rights, as homosexual leaders contended, but a matter of biblical morality and childhood molestation.

Miami homosexual leaders said the molestation assertion was "a totally false issue."

· ·

Gay Life Post-Miami: Tolerance and Backlash

In the wake of the repeal of the Miami-area gay civil rights law, life for gay people became increasingly complex. On the one hand, the repeal was a tremendous setback for gay rights. On the other hand, LGBT issues had become much more visible to the general population as a result of the struggle in Miami. Gallup polls conducted at this time suggested a growing tolerance toward homosexuals, including support for equal employment rights except in the area of education and religion. Fifty-six percent of those polled said that they thought homosexuals should have equal job opportunities, while 65 percent said that homosexuals should not be hired as elementary school teachers and 54 percent were against homosexuals serving as members of the clergy. Major cities had developed significant homosexual subcultures, which included gay political groups, community centers, newsletters, bars, baths, and other cultural institutions. Despite these developments, violence against gays and lesbians persisted. After four teenagers had beaten a 21-year-old gay male to death in Tucson, Arizona, a judge failed to charge them with murder and granted probation. However, this violence led the Tucson City

Council to pass a gay civil rights law, with no referenda for repeal on the horizon. While various cities such as Atlanta held gay pride parades, many of which featured demonstrations against Anita Bryant, the leader of the Miami repeal effort, the culture of such cities as Salt Lake City remained opposed to gay rights, largely owing to the influence of the Mormon Church.

JULY 17, 1977
HOMOSEXUALS ARE MOVING TOWARD OPEN WAY OF LIFE AS TOLERANCE RISES AMONG THE GENERAL POPULATION
By GRACE LICHTENSTEIN
Special to the New York Times

TUCSON, Ariz., July 12—On Saturday night the new Las Culture discotheque in the heart of town, its narrow-beamed lights flashing and soul beat thumping, was crowded with some 300 young men and women, most of them homosexuals.

"For the most part, you still have to spend your nights differently than your days," observed Bob Ellis, publisher of the weekly Arizona Gay News. "It's still a double life here, but things have loosened up in the past two years."

Tucson, a liberal university town in a very conservative state, is far from San Francisco or New York in terms of an active homosexual movement. But it reflects a growing national trend toward more organized homosexual groups, more open displays of homosexual life style and greater acceptance of homosexuals by the majority population.

Despite a successful anti-homosexual campaign in Miami that attracted nation-wide attention last month, a spot check this week by The New York Times indicated widespread outward tolerance of homosexuals, although some backlash generated by the Florida campaign was evident.

Poll Was After Florida Vote

These findings seemed to be supported by the most recent Gallup Poll, which shows that a slim majority of Americans approve of equal job rights for homosexuals.

But the poll is not altogether encouraging for homosexuals. A big majority of those sampled disapproved of homosexuals in specific professions such as the clergy and elementary school teaching.

The Gallup Poll was conducted among 1,513 adults in mid-June. That was after Dade County, as a result of a campaign led by Anita Bryant, the singer and orange juice promoter, repealed an ordinance that had banned discrimination in hiring because of a person's sexual orientation.

According to the Gallup findings, 56 percent of those questioned answered yes when asked, "In general, do you think homosexuals should or should not have equal rights in terms of job opportunities?" Thirty-three percent said no and 11 percent had no opinion.

When asked about selected jobs, however, 65 percent were against homosexuals as elementary school teachers, compared with 27 percent in favor and 8 percent with no opinion. Fifty-four percent of those polled were against homosexuals as members of the clergy, 36 percent for them and 10 percent had no opinion.

Those polls were split evenly on whether homosexuals should be physicians and 51 percent said they should be allowed in the armed forces. Sixty-eight percent approved of homosexuals as sales persons.

The poll also showed that the larger the city, the more tolerant the population was of this minority group. Residents of the Middle West and South were more apt to be against job rights for homosexuals, as were those who called themselves churchgoers and those older than 50.

The pattern of apparent tolerance is, nevertheless, complicated by much evidence of discrimination against homosexuals, state laws that make homosexual sex a criminal act and attitudes of certain religious groups, according to reports from 10 cities checked by The Times.

There is a thriving homosexual community in every city. Most have at least one men's bath, several bars catering to homosexual males, lesbians or both, and homosexual community centers, political groups and newsletters.

Tucson, for example, a rapidly growing Sunbelt city with a population of 330,000, supports all of these elements. In addition, the City Council unanimously passed in February an ordinance barring job discrimination on many groups, among them "sexual or affectional preference." There was no move to repeal it after the Dade County vote.

About 200 Tucson residents turned out for a "gay pride" picnic June 26, as thousands of marchers paraded in San Francisco and New York. There is no harassment of homosexuals by the Tucson police.

One Beaten to Death

However, a year ago a 21-year-old man named Richard Heakin was beaten to death outside a homosexual bar in Tucson by four teen-agers.

Despite objections, the youths were tried as juveniles. Thus they were not charged with murder in adult court. A local judge found the four "delinquent" and granted them all probation. The case outraged both homosexuals and heterosexuals. The judge was assailed in The Arizona Daily Star, the city's morning newspaper.

The case served as a rallying point for homosexuals on the civil rights issue, according to Michael Cebulski and Cathy Hemlar, leaders of the Tucson Gay Coalition.

But Phyllis Sugar, the assistant city attorney who drafted the anti-discrimination code, said of City Council members: "They didn't really know what they were doing when they passed it." Neither she nor the other civil libertarians interviewed would predict, if it were submitted to a public vote, that the ordinance would remain on the books.

Life is similarly complex for homosexuals in places such as Atlanta; Wichita, Kan.; Denver; Little Rock, Ark.; Salt Lake City; Jackson, Miss.; Boise, Idaho, and Portsmouth, N.H.

More than 100 Jackson residents went to New York and Washington for "Gay Pride Week." Others joined New Orleans demonstrators against Miss Bryant. But the Gay Alliance lost a four-year court fight recently to allow "gay counseling" and literature ads in the Mississippi State University newspaper.

In Atlanta, homosexuals have marched each June for seven years. But instead of labeling the occasions "Gay Pride Day," as he did last year, Mayor Maynard Jackson this year merely proclaimed the entire week "Civil Liberties Days."

In Denver, several hundred people marched in a "Gay Pride" demonstration. But across the Rockies in Salt Lake City, the Church of Jesus Christ of Latter-day Saints (the Mormon church) has waged an unremitting campaign against homosexuals.

Spencer W. Kimball, president of the church, has said that the reason for Western drought was the Mormons' tolerance of late of too much homosexuality.

Scandal in Boise

Meanwhile, The Deseret News, Salt Lake's afternoon newspaper, editorially praised Miss Bryant this week and condemned homosexual sex as "disgusting, repulsive, severely condemned by Almighty God." The paper is owned by the Mormon Church. The Hotel Utah, another church property, revoked the contract for the homosexual group that had booked a convention there in June.

Boise was the scene in 1955 of a scandal in which numerous men were sent to jail for consensual homosexual acts with youths. This year, the city has been shaken by a new scandal that began when six women were dismissed from the police department for alleged lesbian activity. None of the six have said they were lesbians but they have been unable to find work elsewhere. They are suing the police department for damages and reinstatement.

Wichita had its first "Gay Pride Week" this year. However, the city commissioners this month postponed action on a proposed ordinance that would have banned discrimination because of sexual preference, saying it was a "very emotional issue."

In Little Rock, the Arkansas legislature has passed a law making acts of homosexuality a misdemeanor, even though a criminal code passed two years ago eliminated a similar law. The Arkansas House of Representatives also passed, by voice vote, a resolution supporting Miss Bryant's campaign.

In New Hampshire, Gov. Meldrim Thomson Jr. has criticized homosexuals. His allies in the State Senate passed an antihomosexuality law but it was killed in the House.

Despite setbacks, homosexuals in every city said that more and more men and women were "coming out of the closet." Even before the Dade County vote, their political organizations were growing more vocal on issues such as job discrimination. Now, according to one leader in Minneapolis, among the most tolerant of cities, they are getting renewed support.

Steven Endean, a member of the board of directors of the National Gay Task Force, said: "Nongays understand that this is an important civil rights issue. I think we've gained more than lost by the Florida vote. Many gays who have never been political before now are eager to get involved with both time and money."

First National March for Gay Rights Held in D.C.

The repeal of the Miami area gay civil rights law in 1977 prompted several other cities to revisit the issue. While some other localities had repealed such laws, others sought to pass new laws that would protect the civil rights of homosexuals in their communities. St. Paul, Minnesota, and Eugene, Oregon, voted to overturn their ordinances by a 2–1 margin, while Wichita, Kansas, did so by a 5–1 margin. In addition, the state of California was considering a referendum that would prohibit homosexuals from teaching in public schools, which eventually failed to pass, as did a similar measure in Seattle. Other localities, such as Baltimore, Hartford, Richmond, and San Francisco, had already passed or were in the process of passing new laws to protect gay civil rights. The Miami repeal also led the gay community to organize nationally, conducting its first march on Washington, D.C., on October 14, 1978. Drawing at least 75,000 people from all across the nation, the march was designed to display the increased visibility of the LGBT community and to press Congress and the president to adopt civil rights protections for gays and lesbians at the federal level. Adopting the slogan "We Are Everywhere," marchers sent a message that the national LGBT community was not going to back down despite setbacks in Miami and other localities on civil rights issues. Marchers also urged recognition for gay and lesbian families, stating, "We are family." Meanwhile, several ministers met on Capitol Hill, asking God to deliver homosexuals from "lives of perversion" and calling homosexuality "an outright assault on the family."

OCTOBER 15, 1979
75,000 MARCH IN CAPITAL IN DRIVE TO SUPPORT HOMOSEXUAL RIGHTS
By JO THOMAS
Special to the New York Times

WASHINGTON, Oct. 14—An enthusiastic crowd of at least 75,000 people from around the country paraded through the capital today in a homosexual rights march and gathered afterward on the grounds of the Washington Monument to marvel at their own numbers and urge passage of legislation to protect the rights of homosexuals.

"Almost 30 years ago I thought I was the only gay person in the world," said the keynote speaker, Betty Santoro, of New York, as she looked over a sea of banners that proclaimed "Alaska," "Wyoming," "Gay Mormons United."

"There are still gay people who feel alone and isolated," she said. "We are here today because we refuse, we refuse to allow this kind of suffering to continue. Our message today is they need not be alone, not ever again.

Our very presence here is living proof we are, indeed, everywhere."

Most of the marchers were young, although all age groups were represented. Most were white, and it appeared that men slightly outnumbered women. Many of the marchers were parents and there was much talk about family.

'Sharing' and 'Flaunting'

"When a heterosexual person shows a picture of his family, it's called sharing," Robin Tyler, a lesbian feminist comedian told the crowd. "When we show a picture of our lover, it's called flaunting. We want to share."

"We are family," said Howard Wallace, a homosexual activist and candidate for city office in San Francisco. "A new day is coming. It will come so much sooner if we cast out the great authoritarian father figures housed in our minds; if we shed our self-hatred and shame; if we stop assuming that the President, the governor, the mayor, the official, knows better than we."

Estimates of the number of people in the crowd varied. The United States Park Police first put the number [at] 75,000 but later said between 25,000 and 50,000 showed up. Eric Rofes, an organizer of the march, said he thought there were "more than 100,000."

Speaker after speaker cited an estimate that there were more than 20 million homosexuals in the United States, a sizeable minority group.

The demonstrators and speakers called for legislation to amend the Civil Rights Act of 1964 to protect homosexuals against discrimination. They also have urged that President Carter sign an executive order banning discrimination in the military, civil service and among Government contractors.

While demonstration was under way, a coalition of ministers met on Capitol Hill to organize National Day of Prayer on Homosexuality to ask God "to deliver them from their lives of perversion," a spokesman for the group said.

The Rev. Richard Zone, executive director of the religious group Christian Voice, said that the coalition had asked 40,000 ministers to urge their congregations to petition the President to resist efforts to give homosexuals special consideration under the law.

"God didn't create Adam and Steve but Adam and Eve," said the Rev. Jerry Falwell, a television evangelist from Lynchburg, Va. He called homosexuality "an outright assault on the family."

MASSACHUSETTS ADOPTS STATEWIDE PROTECTIONS FOR GAYS AND LESBIANS

In 1982 Wisconsin became the first state to pass a comprehensive law prohibiting discrimination against homosexuals in housing, public accommodations, and employment as well as in real estate and in credit and union practices. Since then hundreds of gays and lesbians had brought complaints pursuant to the law. Although *The Times* did not cover this event contemporaneously, it did mention it in an article devoted to the second state to do so, Massachusetts, which passed a gay civil rights law in 1989. First introduced nearly twenty years before, in 1973, Massachusetts joined more than eighty municipalities that had passed similar laws up to that time. Despite the fact that the Massachusetts bill had long had majority support in the legislature, parliamentary maneuvers prevented it from coming to the floor for a vote up until 1989. The bill passed when supporters allowed it to be amended to exempt religious institutions and to clarify that it did not recognize homosexual partnerships. While some opponents promised to pursue repeal through the referendum process, most observers agreed that this was unlikely, and the threat did not, in fact, materialize.

NOVEMBER 1, 1989
A GAY RIGHTS LAW IS VOTED IN MASSACHUSETTS
Special to the New York Times

BOSTON, Oct. 31—After a legislative battle of almost two decades, Massachusetts is about to become the second state to pass a law prohibiting discrimination against homosexuals in employment, housing, credit and public accommodations.

The bill, first introduced in 1973, seeks to protect people from discrimination based on their sexual preferences, just as the state now prohibits discrimination based on race, religion, ethnicity, sex, handicap or age.

The State Senate approved the bill, 22 to 13, on Monday, a week after it passed the House, 79 to 73. Opponents in the Senate asked that the measure be reconsidered, a parliamentary maneuver that a sponsor of the bill, Senator Michael J. Barrett, said is virtually certain to be defeated.

"The chances are 95 to 5 that the Senate will not vote to reconsider and that by next Monday the bill will be sent to the Governor for his signature," Mr. Barrett said. Gov. Michael S. Dukakis has said he will sign the bill.

Eighty municipalities around the country now have measures prohibiting discrimination against homosexuals in some or all of the following categories: education, housing, credit, union practices, employment and public accommodations. Eleven states have executive orders or civil service rules that bar discrimination in public employment, according to the National Gay and Lesbian Task Force.

Wisconsin has been the only state to have a comprehensive law barring discrimination, said State Representative David Clarenbach, who sponsored the 1982 Wisconsin law and said hundreds of complaints have been investigated since then. Mr. Clarenbach said the vote in Massachusetts signals that the tide of conservatism that has dominated the country is ebbing.

Sue Hyde, a spokeswoman for the National Gay and Lesbian Task Force, said: "Most of the other New England states have made an attempt to introduce or enact a gay rights bill in recent years, and they will take heart from this. It's a crowning glory."

New York City adopted a homosexual rights bill in the 1980's after many years of debate, but the issue was not raised in the New York State Legislature this year.

Measures Debated Elsewhere

A bill came up for debate in Trenton but no action was taken. New Jersey relies on general anti-discrimination and civil rights laws meant to protect all citizens.

Similar legislation reached the floor of the Connecticut Legislature without coming up for passage.

The Massachusetts bill moved through after its backers agreed to amendments that some homosexuals found offensive. Among them are provisions stating that the state does not endorse homosexuality or recognize homosexual partnerships and exempting religious institutions.

But many gay people are jubilant, said Arline Isaacson, co-leader of the Massachusetts Gay and Lesbian Political Caucus. "Finally, we won't be second-class citizens," she said.

Opponents, like State Senator Edward P. Kirby, have vowed to fight for repeal through a referendum. "This is bad for society," he said.

Until this law was passed, the Massachusetts Commission Against Discrimination, the state agency that monitors compliance with anti-discrimination laws, had no jurisdiction over complaints based on sexual orientation, Senator Barrett said.

Supporters of the bill say a majority of legislators have supported it since about 1983, but it has been held up in committees or by filibusters. Last spring, the powerful Senate President, William Bulger, whose opposition had helped to block the bill for years, cut off debate and allowed the bill to come up for a vote. Senator Bulger declined to comment.

Senator Barrett said, "You can't sustain a blatantly undemocratic game of resistance forever."

Strict Anti—Gay Rights Measure under Consideration in Oregon

In 1992 Oregon held a referendum on the most stringent antihomosexual measure ever considered up to that time. The proposal, called Ballot Measure 9, would amend the Oregon Constitution in a manner that would legitimize discrimination against homosexuals and classify homosexuality as "abnormal, wrong, unnatural and perverse." While other states and localities had considered stripping homosexuals of civil rights protections, the Oregon measure went a step further and required the state to instruct that homosexuality is morally wrong and offensive, as well as to adopt policies and practices consistent with that viewpoint. Experts stated that the measure could lead to evictions, firings, and a loss of public library usage and other governmental services. Some experts argued it could affect freedom of speech not only of homosexuals but also of supporters of gay rights, while others countered that it was possible for the state to favor the viewpoint that homosexuality is immoral without denying the right for others to oppose that view.

Lon Mabon, the chair of the Oregon Citizens Alliance, named his campaign the "No Special Rights Committee" to foreground the view that gay civil rights are special protections beyond those that are secured for all other citizens. Opponents stated that they were not asking for special rights but simply the same civil rights protections that every citizen is entitled to under the law. The measure would overturn a local ordinance in Portland that protects gay and lesbian civil rights.

Similar to Anita Bryant in the Miami campaign, Mabon employed a strategy that played on public fear of homosexuals, especially when it comes to children, stating that he wanted to put a stop to cultural diversity curricula in the schools and the use of children's books that represent same-sex couples as parents, such as *Heather Has Two Mommies* and *Daddy's Roommate*. During the campaign he traveled across the state screening videotapes from gay pride parades and political rallies that portrayed men in drag, women without shirts on, and other acts that may have appeared outlandish to mainstream populations, suggesting that such behavior was representative of the entire LGBT community and thus a threat to the state. Asserting that "homosexuality is not a civil right, but an aberration," Mabon argued that cultural diversity curricula promoted the belief that homosexuals were a minority, which in turn would lead to civil rights protection.

During the campaign many prominent state politicians, major newspapers, and religious organizations stated that they opposed Ballot Measure 9. Several residents said that they recently observed an increase in public harassment and violence against gays. The Catholic Church, usually a staunch foe of gay rights, stated its opposition, on the grounds that the measure was likely to contribute to an increase in hate crimes, intolerance, and violence against homosexuals. Although the vote was expected to be close, the public rejected the measure by a substantial (56–44 percent) margin.

AUGUST 16, 1992
OREGON MEASURE ASKS STATE TO REPRESS HOMOSEXUALITY
By TIMOTHY EGAN
Special to the New York Times

WILSONVILLE, Ore., Aug.13—Using videos from gay pride marches and a children's book called "Heather Has Two Mommies" to stir the electorate, a conservative political group has forced a referendum on the strongest anti-homosexual measure ever considered by a state.

The proposal, which would classify homosexuality as "abnormal, wrong, unnatural and perverse" and allow discrimination against homosexuals in Oregon, is part of a burgeoning backlash against homosexuals and a theme that has flared, in a much less defined way, in the Presidential campaign.

In November, voters in Oregon and Colorado will decide on citizen-initiated measures that would remove legal protection for homosexuals. But Oregon's initiative is far more extreme. It would require the state government to actively discourage homosexuality, teaching that it is a moral offense similar to pedophilia, sadism and masochism.

The questions of whether homosexuals can serve in the military, in Presidential Cabinets and as foster parents have become part of the national debate in recent years. The issue has been a subtext in Vice President Dan Quayle's comments on the campaign trail on family values. But here in Oregon, the issue is much more overt.

"This is what we're fighting against," said Lon Mabon, waving a copy of a book called "Daddy's Roommate," which is intended to describe gay relationships to children. Mr. Mabon is the director of the conservative group sponsoring the initiative, Oregon Citizens Alliance.

"Cultural diversity is the buzzword being used to make homosexuals full-fledged minorities that require civil rights protection," he said. "Homosexuality is not a civil right, but an aberration."

Some legal scholars in the state say the measure could be used to remove homosexuals from teaching positions and state jobs, and as a basis to take books from libraries and deny parade permits and liquor licenses.

If the measure passes—and political experts give it a strong chance, based on previous support in the state for anti-gay measures—it could do for Oregon what David Duke did for Louisiana during his run for Governor last year. Similar to the problems raised in Louisiana when Mr. Duke, a former Ku Klux Klan leader, made his unsuccessful bid, some business and convention groups outside the state have threatened to boycott Oregon.

While Oregon has long been considered a bastion of tolerance and innovative social policy, its voters have also come out against gay rights in several recent elections. Poll takers say there is little sympathy among the general electorate for homosexuals if they can be portrayed, as the Oregon conservatives have successfully done in the past, as demanding special rights.

'Homosexuality Is Wrong'

"Most of society is willing to tolerate a subculture built around a homosexual life style," Mr. Mabon said. "What we want to do is establish a barrier. The state must ultimately say that homosexuality is wrong."

Mr. Mabon is using videotapes from gay pride marches and excerpts from alternative newspapers as part of his campaign to show that homosexuals have gone too far and should be condemned by the state. One video, an edited tape from a 1991 gay march in San Francisco and a 1987 rally in Washington, shows men and women in outlandish costumes simulating sex acts. Banners from the "Bay Area Sadomasochists," and "The North American Man/Boy Love Association," are prominently displayed.

The campaign, which largely plays on public fear of homosexuals, was used successfully by Mr. Mabon's group in May, when the Oregon town of Springfield voted, by 55 percent to 45 percent, to become the nation's first municipality to include anti-gay language in its city charter. The act bars Springfield from taking any steps that protect homosexuals and it says the town may not "promote, encourage or facilitate" homosexuality, sadism, masochism or pedophilia.

Four years ago, Mr. Mabon's group led a successful statewide campaign to overturn an executive order by the Governor of Oregon that had barred discrimination against homosexuals. The statewide vote against gay rights was approved by 53 percent of the voters in 1988.

'I No Longer Feel Entirely Safe'

Passage of the Springfield measure has led to more brazen harassment of homosexuals, some homosexuals in the city said.

"I was walking out of a supermarket the other day when a man came up to me and spat in my face and called me a queer," said Jean Marchant, a lesbian who lives in Springfield and is chairwoman of that town's human rights commission.

"I no longer feel entirely safe or welcome here," Ms. Marchant said. "It seems that it is now acceptable to call someone a faggot and spit on them. That's not the Oregon I grew up knowing."

Ms. Marchant said her partner, whom she did not name, is a teacher who would be forced out of her job if the new ballot measure passes in November.

In designing the statewide anti-gay proposal, called Ballot Measure 9, Mr. Mabon went one step further than he did in Springfield, adding the provision that "all levels of government" must work to teach that homosexuality is wrong. His group gathered 115,629 voter signatures to qualify for the Nov. 3 ballot.

The question voters will read at the polls is "Shall Constitution be amended to require that all governments discourage homosexuality, other listed 'behaviors,' and not facilitate or recognize them?" The proposed amendment lists the other "behaviors" as pedophilia, sadism or masochism.

Fearing a Witch Hunt

If the measure passes, opponents say, it could only be enforced by a vast bureaucracy of investigators to find and root out people who speak favorably of homosexuals in state and local government. "What you would have is thought police and peeping Toms crawling all over Oregon looking for homosexuals," said Sherry Oeser, chairwoman of the No On 9 Committee.

But Mr. Mabon said the intent of the measure was not to have a witch hunt of homosexuals, but rather, "to simply state that it is the government's position that homosexuality is abnormal and wrong."

But he admits that the measure would allow discrimination against homosexuals, giving landlords the right to evict gay tenants, or employers the right to dismiss homosexuals. The city of Portland's ordinance protects homosexuals from such discrimination, but it would be overturned by the state measure.

Many legal scholars here say the measure poses a clear violation of constitutional protections of free speech. It would not only single out homosexuals, but people who support them.

"It's censorship, it's guilt-by-association and it's against the First Amendment," Ms. Oeser said.

In his advertisements and public appearances, Mr. Mabon quotes from an opinion, which he obtained for a fee, from a prominent conservative legal scholar to counter the claim that the measure violates the right of free speech. Bruce Fein, a former high-ranking member of the Reagan Administration's Justice Department who was also a visiting scholar at the conservative research organization the Heritage Foundation, says the ballot measure would not take away someone's right to speak or march.

"I don't see what's wrong, in constitutional terms, with the state teaching that lying is bad, for example," he said. "The Supreme Court has ruled that you can teach that childbirth is better than abortion. It's not wrong-headed for the state to side with one idea."

Most of this state's political establishment, as well as the major newspapers and religious organizations, have come out strongly against Ballot Measure 9. The Catholic Church, which has generally opposed gay rights legislation, has joined in this fight.

"Given the increase in the number of hate crimes in our society, particularly those directed at homosexuals, this proposed constitutional amendment may contribute to attitudes of intolerance and hostility," the Oregon Catholic Conference said in a statement that has been sent to parish priests.

Campaign Against Measure

The campaign against the measure is relying on support from gay-rights groups around the country, appearances by celebrities and fund-raising events with rock bands.

The Colorado measure would amend the state constitution to prohibit "protected status based on homosexual, lesbian or bisexual orientation." It would invalidate local ordinances that protect homosexuals from discrimination in Denver, Boulder and Aspen.

Tony Marco, the founder of Colorado for Family Values, said he was troubled by the extreme provisions of the Oregon measure.

"We have taken a strong stand against gay-bashing," he said. "We're simply saying that certain behavior should not have protected status. What got us going was an attempt by gay activists in this state to make it a crime to criticize gay life styles."

Both Colorado and Oregon have liberal political traditions and are considered likely to vote Democratic in the Presidential election this year; Oregon was one of only two states in the West to vote against George Bush in 1988. But with gay rights, the voters do not follow traditional conservative-liberal lines, some political experts say.

"We find in our polling that homosexuals are not the most sympathetic group in society, and that's not a value judgment on my part but a statement of fact," said Tim Hibbitts, an Oregon poll taker. "People hold a lot of misconceptions about homosexuals, making voters very easy prey for a manipulative type campaign such as the one we're seeing in Oregon now."

Although there are no recent polls on Ballot Measure 9, Mr. Hibbitts said he believed the vote would be very close. "If the message from Lon Mabon's group is, 'We're just trying to keep these people from having special rights,' then the measure will likely pass," he said.

In fact, Mr. Mabon has named his group the No Special Rights Committee. They operate out of an unmarked building in a business park just off the freeway in this small town, 35 miles south of Portland. From this base, Mr. Mabon hopes one day to take his campaign to the rest of the nation, he said.

The Times Opposes Bigotry in Oregon

In an editorial written just prior to the referendum, *The New York Times* came out against Oregon's Ballot Measure 9, the most stringent antigay proposal of its time. A constitutional amendment that would have trumped local civil rights laws protecting homosexuals in Portland and other localities in the state, Ballot Measure 9 proposed to legitimize discrimination against homosexuals, classifying them as "abnormal, wrong, unnatural and perverse" and instructing state officials to promote that viewpoint. Taking note of two other discriminatory measures that would be on the ballot in Portland, Maine (to repeal a recently passed gay civil rights law), and in Colorado (to trump gay civil rights laws passed in localities such as Aspen, Boulder, and Denver), *The Times* emphasized that all three campaigns had received strong backing from fundamentalist Christian groups. The editorial singles out Oregon's measure, however, as the most stringent, noting that possible effects could include the firing of gay teachers and police, denying gay people licenses necessary to practice law or medicine, or even denying gay Oregonians access to basic state services such as library privileges. While the editors seemed certain that such a measure would ultimately be held unconstitutional, they noted that its passage could nevertheless harm many in the meantime. At the time of this editorial, Ballot Measure 9 was trailing badly in the polls and expected not to pass. *The Times* called for a strong vote against all three antigay proposals, noting that a clean sweep would send a powerful message of tolerance that might encourage moderate Republicans to become more vocal in resisting the religious right.

OCTOBER 29, 1992
THE OREGON TRAIL OF HATE

Bigotry is on the ballot next Tuesday in Oregon, Colorado and in Portland, Me. Voters in those states will consider initiatives that would legitimize discrimination against homosexuals.

All three campaigns originated with fundamentalist Christian groups that portray legal protections for gays as undeserved "special rights." The Oregon and Colorado measures have received strong backing from Pat Robertson's Christian Coalition, which has been organizing furiously this fall in local races across the nation.

The measure in Portland would repeal the city's five-month-old ordinance prohibiting discrimination against homosexuals. Colorado's Amendment 2 would bar communities from passing such laws.

These measures are mild compared with Oregon's Ballot Measure 9. It would amend the State Constitution to classify homosexuality as "abnormal, wrong, unnatural or perverse," and bar government from doing anything that might be seen to promote it. That's a broad mandate for discrimination that could hurt many people before eventually being declared unconstitutional.

Ballot Measure 9 might, for example, be used to justify firing openly gay teachers or police officers, or to deny homosexuals licenses to practice medicine or law. Librarians might be pressured to purge their shelves of works that portray homosexuality in a favorable light.

Most of Oregon's business, religious and political leaders have denounced Ballot Measure 9, which is trailing badly in the latest polls. But some leading Republicans have ducked—including President Bush, who has sidestepped the issue in keeping with his surrender to the antigay rhetoric of Mr. Robertson and Patrick Buchanan at the Republican National Convention in August.

A strong vote against the anti-gay initiatives in all three states would send a powerful national message of tolerance. It might also finally embolden moderate and fair-minded conservative Republicans to exert themselves to prevent the growing threat to their party by religious extremists.

Colorado Adopts Anti–Gay Rights Constitutional Amendment

During the 1992 election cycle in which Oregon soundly rejected a statewide antigay law, Colorado voters adopted one. While seven states and numerous localities had by this time adopted gay civil rights laws, 53 percent of the Colorado electorate approved Amendment 2, a change to the state constitution that repealed gay civil rights laws in Denver, Aspen, and Boulder. Amendment 2 also prevented other localities from ever passing laws that would protect homosexuals from discrimination. Its passage surprised many because Bill Clinton, widely perceived to be a progay candidate, was easily elected president. In addition, Colorado's culture has long been thought to be tolerant of difference. However, more recently Colorado had also become a stronghold of the increasingly powerful religious right. During the same election cycle Colorado voters outlawed hunting for bears in the spring, leading some to suggest that bears were worthy of greater protection than homosexuals in Colorado.

Led by the group Colorado for Family Values, proponents of Amendment 2 stated that they were opposed to "special rights" for homosexuals. The group campaigned widely in Christian churches across the state, gaining visibility from the strong endorsement of popular University of Colorado football coach Bill McCartney. Calling homosexuality "an abomination," McCartney served as a member of the group's board of directors during the campaign.

Opponents of Amendment 2 countered that they simply wanted the same rights as other citizens. While gay groups worried that the law would lead to rampant discrimination in housing and employment, Gov. Roy Romer, an opponent of Amendment 2, vowed that he would fire anyone working in state government who discriminated against homosexuals. Leaders in the LGBT community feared increased violence, citing several murders that had occurred earlier in the year. The National Gay and Lesbian Task Force predicted that the approval of Amendment 2 in Colorado would lead conservative groups to place Colorado-style initiatives on the ballot in other states. LGBT leaders planned a boycott of the state of Colorado, which has a strong tourist industry.

NOVEMBER 8, 1992
COLORADO HOMOSEXUALS FEEL BETRAYED
By DIRK JOHNSON
Special to The New York Times

DENVER, Nov. 7—They sat around a cafe table two days after the election, but nobody felt much like eating. It seemed like they had just been on trial. And the verdict was not pleasant.

"I feel like I've been kicked in the stomach," said Lawrence Pacheco, a 23-year-old gay man. "Do they really hate us that much?"

In a state usually known for its live-and-let-live spirit, gay men and lesbians in Colorado searched for a meaning behind the anti-homosexual-rights measure passed by Colorado voters.

The measure prohibits the Legislature and every city from passing anti-discrimination protection for homosexuals. It repeals gay-rights ordinances in Denver, Boulder and

Aspen, and officials in those cities have vowed to challenge the measure in Federal Court under the 14th Amendment to the Constitution, which guarantees equal protection under the law.

Taking Business Elsewhere

Some gay business groups have canceled trips and conventions in the state. For instance, the American Association of Physicians for Human Rights, a group of gay doctors, says it will move its convention, originally scheduled for next August in Denver. "It's inconceivable to us to spend our money in a state that endorses discrimination against us," said Benjamin Schatz, the group's executive director.

Backers of the anti-gay-rights measure, which was led by a group called Colorado for Family Values, said they did not endorse discrimination against homosexuals. "Our objectives have never been to discriminate," said Will Perkins, the leader of the group. "Our position is that sexual orientation is not an acceptable criterion for special rights."

Robert Bray, a spokesman for the National Gay and Lesbian Task Force, predicted that right-wing groups would "try to export the Colorado measure to other states." He pointed to Oregon, where a much harsher measure that would have required the state to "discourage" homosexuality was soundly defeated, and noted that Lon Mabon, who led the anti-gay measure in Oregon, vowed to return with a "Colorado-style" measure.

Polls Were Deceiving

Seven states (California, Connecticut, Hawaii, Massachusetts, New Jersey, Vermont and Wisconsin) have measures banning discrimination in jobs or housing on the basis of sexual orientation. Dozens of cities and counties around the country have similar provisions.

Polls had indicated that the Colorado measure would be defeated, and it was rejected soundly in Denver, Boulder and Aspen. But it passed in most suburbs and rural communities, and the overall results suggest that some people told poll takers one thing and did another in the voting booth.

Gov. Roy Romer, a Democrat who joined homosexuals in a protest march late Tuesday after the vote, has vowed to dismiss anyone in state government who discriminates against homosexuals.

Gay-rights groups expressed concern that the measure would spur violent attacks on homosexuals and lead to discrimination in housing and jobs.

A Feeling of Peril

Earlier this year, gay men were victims in three separate slayings. And one man was shot to death at a convenience store after attackers, believing that he was homosexual, shouted slurs. The man was heterosexual. As he was being gunned down, his pregnant wife was waiting in a parked car.

"I can tell you, our community does not feel safe," said Susan E. Anderson, the executive director of the Gay and Lesbian Community Center in Denver.

For many gay people around the country, the past week was a time for celebration. The election of Bill Clinton, who has vowed to lift the ban on homosexuals in the military, had spurred hope for an increasing tolerance.

"We finally have a President who can at least say the words—gay and lesbian," Ms. Anderson said.

But the Colorado vote spoiled the Election Day parties in the homosexual community here. Nearly 2,000 gay people had gathered in a community center here to watch the returns, confident that the anti-gay-rights measure would be defeated.

The Celebration That Wasn't

Frank Brown, who calls himself a sentimental patriot, was in charge of the victory celebration. He had arranged for 100 red, white and blue balloons to be released at the moment of victory.

Early election night, spirits were high. Mr. Clinton was headed for an easy victory. The Oregon anti-gay measure was failing. And the Colorado measure was expected to be rejected, too. Mr. Brown said the evening seemed to be restoring his faith in American values.

As Mr. Brown talked in the cafe about the celebration that never came, his voice began to shake and his eyes filled with tears. "These people talk about a hidden agenda," he said. "You know what I want? I want to go to my job. I want to have a home. I want to save my money. And I want to go on vacation. What kind of hidden agenda are they talking about?"

Michael Hayes, a stockbroker who voted for the anti-gay-rights measure, said he was swayed by the "special rights" argument. "I don't have any problems with them, per se," he said, referring to homosexuals. "I just felt it was unfair to equate their interests with those of other minorities like Hispanics or blacks."

A Coach Weighs In

Colorado for Family Values, the anti-gay-rights group, campaigned vigorously in churches. A member of the group's board is Bill McCartney, the coach of the University of Colorado football team, who has called homosexuality "an abomination."

Organizations that work with people with AIDS say clients have been calling with fears about losing insurance or being evicted from their homes. But beyond the legal meaning of the measure, gay people said what hurt most was the knowledge of scorn from so many neighbors and co-workers.

"I don't think the voters understand how painful this is—to be told that you're inferior, a second-class citizen," said Glenda Russell, a psychologist who is a lesbian.

While voters were passing the anti-gay measure, they extended state protection to bears by passing a measure that outlaws the spring bear hunt.

With a bit of gallows humor, some gay people here have complained, only half in jest, that bears seem more deserving of protection in Colorado than gay people. A cartoon in The Rocky Mountain News depicted two hunters near a bear. "Don't, Frank," one hunter tells another, who has a gun aimed at a bear. "Black bears are protected in Colorado." The other hunter, who holds a finger on the trigger, responds, "Not if he's gay!"

Enduring the Stereotypes

As they gathered for solace this week, gay people spoke of the awful stereotypes they endure. "I'm a human being, not some kind of deviant," said Mr. Pacheco, who was pummeled with a brick in a sidewalk attack in Washington two years ago. He needed reconstructive surgery on his right ear.

Tim Robinson, a 30-year-old case manager for AIDS clients, took his early morning stroll on Wednesday past the state Capitol. A graduate of Brigham Young University who cast his first vote for Ronald Reagan in 1980, Mr. Robinson said the gold-domed Capitol suddenly looked very different.

"First I am told that my church has no place for me, and now my state has lost its belief in me," he said. "I walked up the Capitol steps and looked into the distance. And I thought about all of the people out there who hate me."

THE TIMES CALLS FOR COLORADO BOYCOTT

In the month following Colorado's passage of Amendment 2, an antigay change to the state constitution that would prohibit localities from passing gay civil rights laws, The Times wrote an editorial supporting the LGBT community's boycott of Colorado's tourism and convention industry. Stating that Amendment 2 "amounts to an aggressive statewide policy to allow discrimination and blocks attempts to mitigate it," the editors argued that a successful boycott could lead Colorado to overturn the law, while warning that the Christian Coalition had targeted eight other states for similar antigay initiatives. While many celebrities seemed lukewarm about disrupting their vacation plans, mayors of several major cities across the nation endorsed the boycott. Wellington Webb, the mayor of Denver, called the Christian Right's strategy a stealth campaign that portrayed basic civil rights for gays as "special rights." The Times argued that a boycott was "a legitimate weapon in a democratic society" that could "help reverse the tide."

DECEMBER 21, 1992
THE CASE FOR THE COLORADO BOYCOTT

Deciding where to go for a skiing vacation ordinarily poses no moral dilemma. But this winter it surely does. Colorado, site of some of the finest ski areas in the nation, adopted a bigoted anti-gay initiative last month, shattering the state's reputation for tolerance. Gay groups and others are urging a boycott; their call deserves to be heeded.

Admittedly, an economic boycott is not a precision weapon. Targeting Colorado's $5 billion tourist industry stands to hurt not just the unenlightened, but also the progressive towns of Denver, Aspen, and Boulder, where most voters opposed the anti-gay amendment.

But that is no reason to let Colorado off the hook. A successful boycott can help energize the most progressive Coloradans to overturn their new law. And it would send a potent warning to other states that may soon consider similar measures.

When it takes effect next month, Colorado's Amendment 2 will void existing civil rights protections in jobs and housing for gay men and lesbians in Denver, Aspen and Boulder and will bar other localities from passing such ordinances. That puts Colorado a big step behind even states like New York, which has no statewide gay rights law but allows cities and towns to enact their own protective ordinances. The Colorado law amounts to an aggressive statewide policy to allow discrimination and block attempts to mitigate it.

Legal challenges to Amendment 2 are under way. Meanwhile, homosexual Coloradans live in fear, with gay-bashing incidents rising steeply. And forces of intolerance aligned with Pat Robertson's Christian Coalition are already working to put Colorado-style initiatives on the ballot by 1994 in at least eight other states: California, Idaho, Maine, Minnesota, Missouri, Ohio, Oregon and Washington.

The boycott's prospects are uncertain. Barbra Streisand's vocal support has ignited a civil war in the Hollywood film community—leaving the impression that some top entertainers care a lot about civil rights, except when it interferes with their Aspen vacation plans.

But momentum appears to be building. Several big-city mayors, including those of New York City, Los Angeles, Chicago, Philadelphia and Atlanta, have now endorsed the boycott, and the U.S. Conference of Mayors has just pulled its annual meeting from Colorado Springs next June.

Mayor Wellington Webb of Denver, a longtime supporter of gay rights who opposes the boycott, pleads that Colorado is merely the first "casualty" of a broader assault by the Christian right. He warns that the clever stealth strategy used in Colorado—depicting basic anti-discrimination protections for homosexuals in housing and employment as unjustified "special rights"—is likely to have even greater appeal in other states with less tolerant traditions.

It's easy to sympathize with Mr. Webb's plight. But a successful boycott could help reverse the tide. The boycott is a legitimate weapon in a democratic society and, historically, one of the most effective.

SUPREME COURT OVERTURNS COLORADO ANTIGAY LAW

In *Romer v. Evans,* the most important gay rights case of its time, the United States Supreme Court struck down Colorado's Amendment 2, finding it contrary to the U.S. Constitution's guarantee of equal protection under the law. Amendment 2, which had been approved by 53 percent of the Colorado electorate, prohibited any gay civil rights protections in the state of Colorado, voiding existing laws in Denver, Aspen, and Boulder and preventing any other Colorado localities from passing laws that would protect homosexuals from discrimination at any time in the future. By a 6–3 margin, the U.S. Supreme Court said that Amendment 2 lacked a legitimate government purpose and was based on irrational prejudice, an unconstitutional basis for any law.

Writing for the majority of the Court, Justice Anthony Kennedy, a conservative appointed by President Ronald Reagan, spoke for a largely conservative court, stating that "it is not within our constitutional tradition to enact laws of this sort." He added, "A state cannot so deem a class of persons a stranger to its laws." He was joined in his opinion by Justices Stevens, O'Connor, Souter, Ginsburg, and Breyer.

Justice Antonin Scalia wrote a scathing dissent in response, arguing that Amendment 2 was legitimate because a majority of voters in Colorado had approved it. Characterizing Amendment 2 as a victory in a culture war, he contended that it was reasonable for the voters to protect traditional sexual morality by passing a measure that prohibits local governments from adopting laws that protect gay rights. Adopting the language of supporters of Amendment 2, Scalia said that gay civil rights amount to "special rights," which the voters were free to reject. Noting that it was constitutional for states to criminalize sodomy (see "The Right to Privacy . . . "), he argued that they should be able to reject special civil rights protections for homosexuals as well. Scalia was joined in his dissent by Justices Rehnquist and Thomas.

Rejecting Scalia's framing of the issues in the case, Kennedy responded that granting equal rights to homosexuals was not the same as offering special rights and that Amendment 2 inappropriately singled out gays and lesbians for special disability. Asserting that most people take civil rights for granted, he argued that antidiscrimination laws are necessary when the rights of some groups, such as homosexuals, are not being protected for reasons of animus.

Conservative supporters of Amendment 2 railed against the Court, claiming that it had overstepped its legitimate authority by overturning a democratically passed law. Gov. Roy Romer, a long-standing opponent of Amendment 2, said he was anxious to return home and unify Coloradoans under the Court's decision, stating, "Let's stop litigating and see if we can bring people together."

MAY 21, 1996
THE GAY RIGHTS RULING: THE RULING; GAY RIGHTS LAWS CAN'T BE BANNED, HIGH COURT RULES
By LINDA GREENHOUSE

WASHINGTON, May 20—In a significant victory for gay rights, the Supreme Court today struck down a provision of the Colorado Constitution that not only nullified existing civil rights protections for homosexuals in the state but also barred the passage of new anti-discrimination laws.

"A state cannot so deem a class of persons a stranger to its laws," Justice Anthony M. Kennedy said in a forceful opinion for a 6-to-3 majority. He said the Colorado provision, known as Amendment 2, had placed the state's homosexuals "in a solitary class," singling them out in violation of the Constitution's equal protection guarantee for a legal disability so sweeping as to be inexplicable on any basis other than "animus."

It is not within our constitutional tradition to enact laws of this sort," Justice Kennedy said in an opinion joined by Justices John Paul Stevens, Sandra Day O'Connor, David H. Souter, Ruth Bader Ginsburg, and Stephen G. Breyer.

Justice Antonin Scalia filed an equally forceful dissent, accusing the majority of taking sides in "the culture wars" through "an act not of judicial judgment but of political will." The process by which Colorado's voters adopted Amendment 2, by 53 percent to 47 percent in 1992, was the "most democratic of procedures," Justice Scalia said.

While no other state has such a provision in its constitution, petitions to place a similar referendum on the November ballot are now circulating in Idaho, Oregon and

Washington. Voters in Maine defeated a similar proposal last year. Local governments in Florida, Oregon and Ohio have taken the same approach through local ordinances. A Federal appeals court last year upheld a Cincinnati ordinance that stripped homosexuals of civil rights protections in a case that is now on appeal to the Supreme Court.

Chief Justice William H. Rehnquist and Justice Clarence Thomas joined Justice Scalia's dissenting opinion today, accusing the majority of "inventing a novel and extravagant constitutional doctrine to take the victory away from traditional forces." The Colorado amendment, Justice Scalia wrote, was an "eminently reasonable" means of preventing the "piecemeal deterioration of the sexual morality favored by a majority of Coloradans."

The decision, Romer v. Evans, No. 94–1039, does not necessarily portend victory for homosexuals in other cases working their way through the legal system, including the constitutional challenge to the current policy on homosexuals in the military or—much farther down the road—the question of homosexual marriage. Nor does the ruling provide affirmative rights for gay people; a constitutional shield rather than a sword, it does not require states to offer new civil rights protections.

Nonetheless, the decision was a strong statement, coming from a conservative member of a basically conservative Court, that prejudice is not a valid justification for a policy that singles out gay people for special burdens not placed on others.

Justice Kennedy said the Colorado amendment did not meet even the lowest level of scrutiny accorded an official action that is challenged as a violation of the constitutional guarantee of equal protection. Under that test, as Justice Kennedy described it, "a law must bear a rational relationship to a legitimate governmental purpose, and Amendment 2 does not."

He said the provision "is a status-based enactment divorced from any factual context from which we could discern a relationship to legitimate state interests; it is a classification of persons undertaken for its own sake, something the Equal Protection Clause does not permit."

Suzanne B. Goldberg, a lawyer for the Lambda Legal Defense and Education Fund, who worked on the case, said the decision marked "a historic shift in the Court's response to anti-gay discrimination." Ms. Goldberg said the Court had rejected "gay-bashing by referendum" while making it clear that "discrimination is discrimination and that anti-gay sentiment is not a justification for discrimination by government."

Many of those who responded to the decision today noted that it came 10 years after the Court refused in Bowers v. Hardwick to overturn state laws that criminalized homosexual sex. The majority opinion did not refer to that decision, although Justice Scalia did so at length, arguing that if it was constitutionally permissible for a state to make homosexual conduct a crime, it was certainly permissible to adopt a provision "merely prohibiting all levels of state government from bestowing special protections upon homosexual conduct."

In defense of Amendment 2, Colorado had argued that it did not amount to discrimination but rather a removal of special protections, ordinances that had been adopted in Aspen, Boulder, and Denver to extend civil rights protections to homosexuals. Amendment 2 nullified these laws, as well as a range of statewide policies, and barred their re-enactment unless a new majority of Coloradans voted to amend the state constitution again.

In many respects, the "equal rights" versus "special rights" debate was the crux of the case; the Cincinnati organization that successfully sponsored the similar referendum there is in fact called Equal Rights, Not Special Rights, Inc. Justice Kennedy's majority opinion strongly rejected the characterization of Amendment 2 as only taking away "special rights."

"We cannot accept the view that Amendment 2's prohibition on specific legal protections does no more than deprive homosexuals of special rights," Justice Kennedy said. "To the contrary, the amendment imposes a special disability upon those persons alone."

Justice Kennedy added: "We find nothing special in the protections Amendment 2 withholds. These are protections taken for granted by most people either because they already have them or do not need them."

Matt Coles, director of the Lesbian and Gay Rights Project of the American Civil Liberties Union, said the Court appeared to "go out of its way to take on the 'special rights' rhetoric." Mr. Coles said the Court's conclusion that "anti-discrimination protections are not special rights, they are equal rights, has enormous implications because the Court speaks not only to the parties in this case but to the entire country about what's right in a democratic society."

Gov. Roy Romer of Colorado, who opposed the amendment but defended it in court, said in an interview today that the Court had given the "right answer" and that he would "do everything I can to get Colorado to accept that answer."

"Let's stop litigating and legislating and see if we can bring people together," Mr. Romer said.

Reaction from groups that have been active in support of the amendment and similar proposals was as sharp as the reaction on the gay rights side was exultant. Gary L. Bauer, president of the Family Research Council, said the decision was the product of "an out-of-control unelected judiciary" and "should send chills down the back of anyone who cares whether the people of this nation any longer have the power of self-rule."

Tom Minnery, vice president of Focus on the Family, said the effect of the ruling was to "disparage the moral views of the people of Colorado." Once again, he said, judicial activism has imposed itself upon the Constitution and the democratic process."

The decision upheld a 1994 ruling by the Supreme Court of Colorado, but its analysis was substantially different. The state court analyzed the amendment as violating the fundamental right of "equal protection in the political process." That was a tenuous argument to sustain before the United States Supreme Court, because the precedents on which it was based were arguably limited to measures that had stripped civil rights protections from black people. Justice Kennedy took a different approach, adopting a line of argument proposed in a brief filed by Prof. Laurence H. Tribe of Harvard Law School and several other constitutional scholars. That brief had suggested that "Amendment 2 is a rare example of a per se violation of the Equal Protection Clause," without much other analysis being needed. Today Justice Kennedy said: "A law declaring that in general it shall be more difficult for one group of citizens than for all others to seek aid from the government is itself a denial of equal protection of the laws in the most literal sense."

Professor Tribe, who argued the losing side in Bowers v. Hardwick 10 years ago, said in an interview today that while the Court then "seemed incapable of applying its normal approach to the law where gays were involved," that was no longer the case.

In his dissenting opinion, Justice Scalia seemed at times torn between belittling the ruling—he called it "terminal silliness" at one point and declared that "the Court has mistaken a Kulturkampf," German for "culture war," "for a fit of spite"—and describing it as a mistake of profound significance. He described homosexuals as a group with "high disposable income" and "disproportionate political power" with "enormous influence in American media and politics."

The decision could prove to be important beyond the area of gay rights, lending force to constitutional arguments against proposals to keep the children of illegal aliens out of public school, for example, as an instance of singling out a particular population for a special burden.

SEXUALITY, GENDER, AND SCIENCE

Is Homosexuality a Disease?

Although the lesbian, gay, bisexual, and transgender (LGBT) movement made significant advances toward securing equal rights in the period immediately following the Stonewall riots, progress was limited by the continued classification of homosexuality as an illness. Many initially believed that it was more progressive and humane to treat homosexuality as an involuntary psychological problem to be treated rather than as a willful crime or sin that should be punished. For example, a *Times* report of November 19, 1965, notes that the Jewish women's group National Federation of Temple Sisterhoods supported the liberalization of laws regarding homosexuality (as well as birth control and abortion), adding that "today enlightened men understand that homosexuality may be symptomatic of psychiatric disturbances which require sympathetic understanding and psychiatric evaluation."

The distinction between punishment and treatment, however, was not always clear. Psychiatrists often employed painful behavior modification techniques aimed at converting homosexuals to heterosexuality, as a *Times* piece of June 4, 1967, graphically describes: "A 35 year-old homosexual man sits in a darkened room with an electrode strapped to his calf. A picture of a nude man is illuminated before him, while a steady painful shock is applied to his calf; after a short while the picture goes dark, a different picture—of a nude woman—is lit up, and the electric shock stops. The hope is that the homosexual stimulus will be associated with, and hence inhibited by, the painful shock, while the heterosexual stimulus will be rewardingly associated with the pleasurable cessation of the pain. This, it is hoped, will turn the patient into a heterosexual."

Although psychiatric treatment sometimes led people to change their sexual behavior, results were mixed. A *Times* report of February 28, 1971, titled "More Homosexuals Aided to Become Heterosexual," lauded the "conversion therapy" undertaken at the famous Masters and Johnson Institute but reported that only 25 to 50 percent of homosexual subjects successfully transitioned to heterosexual behavior. In addition, whether such treatment was able to change

sexual orientation as well as behavior remains a matter of great controversy (see In Focus, page 429).

Characterizing homosexuality as a mental disorder also had serious political and legal consequences in a variety of areas including employment, immigration, child custody, and military service. (See chapters "Gays in the Military" and "Sexuality and Gender Identity in the Workplace"). A particularly severe example from this period involved Clive Michael Boutilier, an émigré from Canada. Boutilier was deported in 1967 when the Supreme Court found that Congress's Immigration and Nationality Act, passed in 1952 during the Red Scare, included homosexuals within the category of immigrants to be refused entry to the United States owing to their "psychopathic personalities." While attempting to obtain U.S. citizenship, Boutilier admitted to being arrested four years earlier on a charge of sodomy in New York, and although these charges were later dropped, his admission of "sexual deviate behavior" was deemed sufficient cause for deportation.

The American Psychiatric Association (APA) supported defining homosexuality as a mental illness, listing it in its *Diagnostic and Statistical Manual of Mental Disorders* (DSM) for nearly a century. This went virtually unquestioned for many years, and leading psychiatrists such as Dr. Charles Socarides stated categorically: "The homosexual is ill, and anything that tends to hide that fact reduces his chances of seeking and obtaining treatment." Similarly, Dr. Irving Bieber encouraged homosexuals to follow the example of Alcoholics Anonymous, which is founded on the "recognition that alcoholism is a disease and the determination to do something about it." Other experts in the field described homosexuals as unable to accept the responsibilities of adult relationships and parenting, with one comparing lesbians to "virginal girls" playing with "life dolls."

As LGBT people became more visible in mainstream society, psychiatric experts, gay and lesbian organizations, and a wide variety of other groups began to challenge these assumptions, asserting that homosexuality was not an illness but simply an alternative form of sexual expression. Some pointed out that the illness hypothesis was based on research done exclusively with homosexual subjects who had sought psychoanalytic treatment, a potentially skewed sample. As

IN FOCUS

Evelyn Hooker (1907–1996)

• •

Evelyn Hooker was an unlikely academic. At a time when few women attended college, she financed her education by working as a maid and successfully achieved her Ph.D. in psychology at Johns Hopkins University in 1932. As noted in *The Times* on November 22, 1996, Dr. Hooker credited her decision to make "her life count in helping to correct social injustice" to her experience of Nazism while on fellowship in Berlin in the 1930s. Hooker was hired by the University of California at Los Angeles in 1939, where she befriended a gay student named Sam From, who introduced her to several of his gay friends and encouraged them to speak candidly with her about their lives. From reportedly told her, "We have let you see us as we are, and now, it is your scientific duty to make a study of people like us." At the height of the politically and socially conservative McCarthy era, Hooker successfully applied for a grant in 1953 from the National Institute of Mental Health to study homosexual men.

Hooker's most influential research involved administering three standard personality tests to sixty men matched for intelligence, age, and education, half of whom were homosexuals and half heterosexuals. Without being told which participants were gay, three experienced clinicians were asked to evaluate their social adjustment based on the test results. Not only were they unable to distinguish between the heterosexuals and homosexuals, but all three experts also agreed that two-thirds of the gay men were at least as well adjusted as the average citizen. These results may in part be explained by Hooker's method for identifying her subjects. Unlike previous studies that focused on homosexuals seeking psychiatric treatment, she obtained her sample from the membership of homophile groups such as the Mattachine Society.

Published in 1957, Hooker's results provided the fledgling gay rights movement with its first scientific support and, according to Cornell University professor of clinical psychiatry Dr. Richard A. Isay, a "framework within which the American Psychiatric Association could rethink its viewpoint." In 1992 Hooker received the APA's award for distinguished contribution to psychology in the public interest for her "revolutionary study" that "supported the radical idea then emerging that homosexuality is within the normal range of human behavior." During an interview in the 1990s, Hooker commented, "They talk about all this courage I'm supposed to have had. I don't get that. Curiosity and empathy were what compelled me to do my study."

From *The New York Times*

Dunlap, David W. "Evelyn Hooker, 89, Is Dead; Recast the View of Gay Men." November 22, 1996.

• •

early as 1957, Dr. Evelyn Hooker wrote a paper that broke new ground in this area, "The Adjustment of the Overt Male Homosexual." She administered a battery of mainstream psychological tests to both heterosexuals and homosexuals and then asked three distinguished psychologists if they could identify who were the homosexual subjects based on the results. When none of them could, Hooker concluded that homosexuals were no less well adjusted than heterosexuals. These findings led some psychologists to assert that homosexuality is simply a different way of loving and that the view that it is pathological might be the result of societal prejudice.

Homophile groups began to use this research to further the cause of gay rights. In 1964 the lesbian group Daughters of Bilitis invited two leading psychotherapists to their biennial meeting to offer alternatives to the prevailing view of homosexuality as an illness. Barbara Gittings, other activists in the Gay Activists Alliance (GAA), and members of other gay and lesbian groups also began to attend the APA's annual meeting, offering exhibits displaying healthy homosexuals. By October 25, 1971, the author of a *Times* book review related to the history of homosexuality declared that only members of the "extreme fringes" would be outraged by his conclusion that homosexuals are not sick but are nevertheless dysfunctional because of their inability to relate sexually to the opposite sex. The controversy and stigma surrounding this issue was powerful enough that a gay psychiatrist felt it necessary to wear a mask to hide his identity while participating on the 1972 APA panel "Psychology: Friend or Foe to the Homosexual?"

In February 1973 an APA committee began to formally study whether homosexuality should continue to be listed as a mental disorder in the DSM. Dr. Henry Brill, chair of the committee, indicated a shift in professional opinion when he noted that such listings tend to foster prejudice against homosexuals. Dr. Judd Marmor, vice president of the APA, added that he believed homosexuality was not an illness but rather an alternative form of sexual expression, albeit one that engendered much societal disapproval. A few months later a *Times* report of May 10 noted that the APA's stand had led to detrimental "social and legal consequences" for homosexuals. Referencing the outdated medical belief in masturbation as evidence of serious medical disturbance, Marmon suggested that the APA classification of homosexuality as an illness "rests chiefly on the fact that society disapproves of this behavior" and that psychiatrists who continue to hold this belief are "merely acting as agents of such cultural value systems." At the same meeting Ronald Gold, an officer in the GAA, called for the APA to stop labeling homosexuality a mental illness, urging the organization's 20,000 members to "take the damning label of sickness away from us." Others present, such as noted psychiatrist Irving Bieber, argued that even if homosexuality should no longer be classified as a disease, it would be equally inappropriate to consider it normal. Said Bieber, "The notion that it is [normal] is a myth promulgated largely by the militant homosexual organizations."

On December 15, 1973, the Board of Trustees of the APA finally declared that homosexuality is not a mental illness, stating, "We will no longer insist upon a label of sickness for individuals who insist that they are well and demonstrate no generalized impairment in social effectiveness." This development occasioned a tongue-in-cheek comment from lesbian activist Barbara Gittings, who joked that gays and lesbians went to bed sick one day and woke up cured the next thanks to the pronouncement of the APA. At the same meeting the organization also voted to support gay civil rights and the decriminalization of sodomy, suggesting a linkage between the repeal of the illness hypothesis and progress toward equal rights for gays and lesbians. Subsequently, the entire membership voted to cease describing homosexuality as a mental illness in a 5,854–3,810 vote, as reported in a *Times* article of May 19, 1974.

The decision remained controversial for some time. As a December 23, 1973, op-ed exchange in *The Times* suggested, "The Issue is Subtle, The Debate Still On." This piece pitted Bieber, who argued that "a homosexual adult is a person whose heterosexual function is crippled like the legs of a polio victim," against Dr. Robert Spitzer, who countered that "psychiatry, which once was regarded as in the vanguard of the movement to liberate people from their troubles, is now viewed by many, and with some justification, as being an agent of social control." Spitzer further clarified that the members of the APA who voted for removal of homosexuality from the DSM "are not saying that it is normal or that it is as valuable as heterosexuality" but simply that homosexuality does not qualify as a psychiatric disorder. As reported in *The Times* on May 26, 1974, eight prominent psychiatrists called for a new vote on the issue, claiming that the earlier vote was inappropriately influenced by gay activists. One supporter of a new vote was Socarides, who argued that saying homosexuality was not a mental illness "sacrificed our scientific knowledge," akin to the way that Soviet scientists manipulated longstanding laws of genetics to serve political purposes during the rule of Joseph Stalin. While the APA did not vote on the issue again, almost ten years later psychiatrists continued to debate the matter, as noted in a *Times* article of January 26, 1982, titled "Psychiatrists on Homosexuality: Vigorous Discord Voiced at Meeting."

Although the APA never voted on the mental health status of bisexuals, psychiatrists engaged in similar discussions about whether this orientation constitutes a healthy and normal lifestyle, as documented in a March 24, 1974, article by Jane Brody that summarizes both viewpoints in the emerging debate. However, scientific questions related to bisexuality did not receive as much *Times* coverage, perhaps because psychologists sometimes question its validity as an independent sexual category, as evidenced by a surprisingly recent *Times* report of July 5, 2005, with the rather provocative title "Straight, Gay or Lying? Bisexuality Revisited." As a July 12, 2005, letter to the editor noted, the headline "is not only disrespectful, but also unprofessional in its insinuation." The letter writer added, "Those of us living outside the boxes of gay and straight are not 'lying,' thank you very much! Many of us have struggled to stay open to ourselves in an increasingly, and oppressively, black-and-white, reductionist world."

The political and legal impact of the APA decision to declassify homosexuality as an illness was significant but slow. For example, the surgeon general did not direct his staff to stop classifying homosexuality as a mental illness until 1979, as noted in a *Times* report of August 3, 1979. Further, although this change in policy ended the role of U.S. Public Health Service doctors in screening immigrants suspected of being homosexual, it did not end the controversy surrounding gay immigration. As noted in a December 27, 1979, report in *The Times*, immigrants who admitted that they were homosexuals could still be denied entry to the United States, since the Immigration and Naturalization Service (INS) continued to enforce the 1952 Immigration and Nationality Act excluding homosexuals as psychopathic personalities. Now that the Public Health Service would no longer assess whether an immigrant was a psychopathic homosexual, immigration officials with no particular medical training made the determination. As reported in a June 18, 1982, *Times* article, this rule was not overturned until a federal judge found it unconstitutional, stating that the INS "has asserted no legitimate governmental or public interest in its policy of excluding homosexual aliens on the sole grounds that they are homosexuals." He added that "homosexuals pose no threat to national security merely because they are homosexuals. Nor do they pose a threat to the health, safety, and welfare of the American public." When the ruling was appealed, a federal court held that the law against homosexual immigration was constitutional but that a doctor's certification would be necessary for it to be enforced. Although the INS continued to maintain that a doctor's certificate was not necessary, the law long went unenforced, until 1990, when rumors circulated that activists attending the 6th International AIDS Conference in San Francisco planned to challenge the rule by declaring their homosexuality at the border. According to a June 3, 1990, *Times* report, immigration and public health officials reluctantly prepared to enforce the law. However, no activists challenged the ruling and, as described in an October 26 *Times* article, the controversial provision was

formally removed from the law as part of the Immigration Act of 1990.

Similarly, even after the APA declared that homosexuality was not an illness, many psychiatrists continued to offer conversion, or reparative, therapy in an effort to transform gays and lesbians into heterosexuals. These included pioneering sex researchers Masters and Johnson, who claimed to be able to reverse homosexuality in a two-week course of intensive therapy. In an April 17, 1979, *Times* piece, Dr. William Masters expressed disappointment with the high failure rate of 35 percent, although he hastened to add that these results far outpaced those of other facilities offering such treatment. As noted in a letter to the editor that appeared in *The Times* on February 19, 1989, the APA session "Toward a Further Understanding of Homosexual Men" presented evidence suggesting that conversion therapy was ineffective and outdated. Nevertheless, several leading therapists continued to offer such treatment, including former homosexuality defender Dr. Spitzer, whose practice is discussed in a *Times* report of May 9, 2001. Gay rights groups have criticized Spitzer's efforts to cure homosexuality, noting that the practice is often linked to politically conservative groups and fundamentalist Christian ministries and therefore is typically based on a moral rather than scientific understanding of sexuality.

A *Times* report of August 6, 2009, noted that the governing council of the APA had recently adopted a resolution that constituted "its most comprehensive repudiation of so-called reparative therapy, a concept espoused by a small but persistent group of therapists, often allied with religious conservatives, who maintain that gay men and lesbians can change." The council voted overwhelmingly in favor of the resolution, with 125 in favor and only 4 opposed, and issued a report along with the vote. Based on a review of eighty-three studies of sexual orientation change conducted since 1960, the report indicated that no solid evidence supported the practice of attempting to alter sexual orientation through therapy. Instead of trying to change gay and lesbian clients, the panel recommended that therapists help clients explore a variety of options for negotiating the conflict between their sexual orientation and their religious faith, including changing churches or practicing celibacy. The chair of the review panel, Dr. Judith Glassgold, commented: "Both sides have to educate themselves better. The religious therapists have to open up their eyes to the potential positive aspects of being gay or lesbian. Secular therapists have to recognize that some people will choose faith over their sexuality" (see "The Intersection of Religion. . . "). The controversy over conversion therapy is frequently linked to another topic of scientific exploration—the role of nature versus nurture in the development of homosexuality.

THE NATURE-OR-NURTURE DEBATE

Is homosexuality caused by psychological factors such as upbringing? Or is it a matter of biological determinants such as specific genes? Over the years, science has provided a wide variety of evidence that supports both positions, leading some to conclude that sexual orientation is determined by experience and choice, while others maintain that it is programmed into a person's genes. Most recently, some researchers have begun to argue that a combination of environmental and biological factors is likely at play.

Prior to the 1970s psychiatrists regularly argued that poor parenting and dysfunctional family background were the primary cause of homosexuality. For example, Bieber argued in 1964 that male homosexuality is the result of both overly protective, possessive mothers who feminize their sons and distant, unaffectionate fathers. Similarly, hypercritical mothers who fail to teach their daughters appropriate feminine behaviors and possessive or rejecting fathers were thought to lead girls to become lesbians. Emphasizing the crucial role of fathers in this process, a lengthy piece in The Times' Sunday Magazine of May 26, 1968, again cited Bieber, this time asserting that "a constructive, supportive, warmly related father precludes the possibility of a homosexual son: he acts as a neutralizing, protective agent should the mother make seductive or close-binding attempts."

Accordingly, psychiatrists regularly offered parents advice about how to avoid raising a homosexual, which could be accomplished, if "detected early enough," as noted in a Times review of a television program featuring Bieber and printed on May 21, 1966. Although these parenting theories were offered by esteemed authorities in the field, hindsight suggests many of these theories were based in unfounded assumptions and unproven anecdotes about gender and sexuality. For example, Bieber counseled fathers to spend time with their sons because "you don't find many homosexuals whose fathers took them on camping trips or to baseball games." He concluded that such advice would help parents to address the "problem of homosexuality," so their children could grow up healthy.

This view, however, soon came to be challenged by other psychiatrists, as evidenced by a Sunday Magazine piece on sex research appearing in The Times on April 20, 1969, and asserting that the theory that homosexuality was rooted in a child's relation to his or her parents was "no

longer accepted unquestioningly." Arguing that newer theories drew on a number of factors such as endocrinological and chromosomal variations, the piece suggested that the older theories may have inadvertently harmed homosexuals: "What is important is that homosexuals have existed in every known culture since the dawn of history, that they exist in substantial numbers now, that few are cured or changed or appear to want a cure or change and that to a considerable degree their emotional problems can be traced to their virtual exclusion from heterosexual society and the extraordinary difficulty put in the way of their achieving a measure of self-acceptance."

Beginning in the 1970s, research began to suggest that dysfunctional parenting was unlikely to be the sole determinant of sexual orientation. In a 1971 study of more than 1,000 subjects, Dr. Lawrence Hatterer found that homosexual men came from a wide variety of familial types, including "every combination and variation of parental history that you can imagine," leading scientists to theorize that boys' effeminate behavior might be a cause rather than an effect of atypical parental treatment. This supposition was supported by the findings of a 1981 Kinsey Institute study of more than 1,500 subjects that also found no substantial linkage between family type and homosexuality. Instead, researchers found early gender nonconformity to be predictive of homosexual orientation. This includes boys preferring activities normally associated with femininity (wearing dresses, for example) and girls behaving in ways typically associated with masculinity (participating in contact sports). Researchers speculated that the root of such norm-challenging behavior was probably biological in origin. These findings were supported by subsequent research undertaken by Dr. Richard Green, director of the Program in Psychiatry, Law and Human Sexuality at UCLA. Commenting on Green's work in a December 16, 1986, Times article, Dr. Alan Bell of the Kinsey Institute concluded that "the pendulum is swinging back to biology."

It is perhaps not surprising that many parents of gay and lesbian children welcomed the turn toward biological factors in scientific research about the causes of homosexuality. In a Times report of August 26, 1985, the president of the group Parents and Friends of Lesbians and Gays (P-FLAG) said, "We have learned that there is no choice. No one chooses to be gay. We believe our children were born that way, that homosexuality, like heterosexuality, is innate." She added that parents in her group have come to realize that their children "do not have a problem, that the problem is with a misinformed society," and that this realization has paved the way for most families to report "a richer and more loving relationship."

Once familial explanations had been challenged, scientists also began to consider the possibility that a wide variety of biological factors might influence sexual orientation, including variations in hormones, brain structure, chromosomes, and aural sensitivity. Perhaps the most famous among these were twin studies and so-called gay gene studies. In 1991 researchers at Northwestern University in Chicago studied identical, fraternal, and adopted brothers. They found that 52 percent of identical twin brothers were both gay compared with only 22 percent of fraternal twins and 11 percent of adopted brothers, suggesting a genetic basis for sexual orientation. Shortly thereafter, Dr. Dean Hamer of the National Cancer Institute studied pairs of gay brothers and found that a gene on the X chromosome could play a role in predisposing some men toward homosexuality. Although he carefully noted that this did not amount to finding a "gay gene," that phrase was quickly adopted by many in the media (not including *The Times)* when Hamer's results were disseminated to the general public. Despite this study being subsequently replicated by Hamer, *The Times* published a report on April 23, 1999, stating that other scientists had been unable to replicate the "gay gene" study.

Nevertheless, findings about the genetic basis of homosexuality, along with studies of gay brains and lesbian ears and other instances of significant biological variation between gay and straight people, occasioned a more general discussion about the political consequences of such scientific research, as noted in two *Times* reports by Natalie Angier. The first, a September 1, 1991, piece, noted that some believed that evidence of biological determinants was a positive development for gays and lesbians because it might definitively show that homosexuality is not a product of bad upbringing or a perverse desire to flout mainstream norms, but rather a result of deepseated, unchangeable biological factors. Others argued that the new findings could be misused in a homophobic manner, such as aborting homosexual fetuses or transforming them into heterosexual fetuses by administering some sort of hormonal cocktail. In the second report, on July 18, 1993, Professor Lillian Faderman of Cal State–Fresno added, "As a historian, I know that whenever the cause of homosexuality has been questioned, a cure is looked for."

Still others suggested that a preoccupation with the causes of homosexuality distracted from the more important issue of the social and political reactions to gays and lesbians. In the 1991 Angier piece, David Barr of the Gay Men's Health Crisis (an AIDS service organization in New York City; see the following chapter) said, "It doesn't really matter why people are gay or not gay. What's really important is how they're treated." Opponents of gay rights also argued that the new scientific findings would not fundamentally change the tenor of the political debate. In the 1993 report Lon Mabon, chair of the Oregon Citizens Alliance, a conservative political organization working against gay rights, contended, "Some people have said there's a genetic link to alcoholism, but that does not excuse the drunk." In an apparent attempt to signal the limitations of such arguments, a tongue-in-cheek letter to the editor titled "Republicanism Can Be Cured" appeared in *The Times* on July 26, 1993, stating that scientists had announced in the (nonexistent) journal *Nurture* that affiliation with the Republican Party was genetically determined, shocking the "medical, political, and golfing communities."

Scientists continued to explore the genetic roots of sexual orientation, even as arguments about the political and social consequences of this work persisted. For example, a *Times* report of October 25, 2003, titled "Gay at Birth?" discussed a new study of the connection between homosexuality and blinking rates as well as various other research on the relationship of sexual orientation to chromosomes, brain anatomy, hormones, and finger size, arguing that the accumulating evidence should not be ignored. By April 10, 2007, a *Times* report concluded, "Desire between the sexes is not a matter of choice." Dr. Marc Breedlove, a neuroscientist at Michigan State University, argued that "most of the scientists working on these questions are convinced that the antecedents of sexual orientation in males are happening early in life, probably before birth." He added that while some females "are probably born to become gay, clearly some get there quite late in life." Commenting on this phenomenon in a January 2, 2001, interview in *The Times,* Dr. Anne Fausto-Sterling, a professor of biology and women's studies at Brown University, said, "I think that lesbians have more of a sense of the cultural component in making us who we are. If you look at many lesbians' life histories, you will often find extensive heterosexual experiences. They often feel they've made a choice." Stating she believes that sexual orientation is a combination of nature (biology) and nurture (culture), she noted that it is "not a popular position to take in today's academic environment, but it is the one that makes the most sense."

TRANSGENDER ISSUES

Although this concept continues to evolve, the term *transgender* is generally used to describe people who wish to move away from, or transcend, a given gender, which is typically a product of the anatomical sex assigned at birth by parents and physicians. Thus babies born with male genitalia are generally classified as of the male sex and expected to behave according to masculine gender norms, while babies born with female genitalia are typically classified as of the female sex and expected to fulfill feminine gender norms. However, as noted in a September 24, 2006, *Times* report, in up to .05 percent of cases, sexing babies by their genitalia is not as straightforward as has often been assumed. Transgender people challenge sex and gender categories in a variety of ways. Some believe they have been born into a body that does not correspond with their gender and seek to have their sex reassigned through surgery. Others identify as the opposite gender of their birth but do not surgically alter their anatomy at all or choose to modify some sex characteristics but not others. Some have been born with both male and female sex characteristics, but do not necessarily identify with one gender or the other. Still others question the idea that there are only two varieties of sex (male and female) and gender (masculine and feminine), arguing instead that there are multiple ways to enact sex and gender identity, and that it is possible for one individual to occupy various versions of such identities.

In 1952 U.S. citizen Christine Jorgensen traveled to Denmark for the first widely publicized sex reassignment surgery. Although she was certainly not the first person to undergo surgery to move from a male to female (MTF) identity, her procedure received an enormous amount of press coverage. Professor Susan Stryker, author of *Transgender History,* claims that the Jorgensen story received more press coverage that year than the coronation of Queen Elizabeth II, the testing of hydrogen bombs in the Pacific Ocean, the Korean War, or Dr. Jonas Salk's invention of a polio vaccine. Stryker contends that "part of the intense fascination with Jorgensen undoubtedly had to do with the fact that she was young, pretty, gracious, and dignified—but another part of it surely had to do with the mid-twentieth-century awe for scientific technology, which now could not only split atoms but also, apparently, turn a man into a woman."

Formerly George Jorgensen, Christine underwent a two-year course of treatment that included hormonal therapy and culminated in a number of surgeries. A U.S. Army veteran, Jorgensen was later denied a marriage license when a city clerk said that she lacked adequate proof of being female. As *The Times* reported on April 4, 1959, despite the extensive medical treatment she had received in Denmark, Jorgensen's birth certificate still listed her as male. Since she wished to marry a male, Howard Knox, her request for a license was denied, same-sex marriage being prohibited at that time

throughout the United States. Legal problems such as this persist in many localities to this day because some states allow postsurgical transgender people to change the sex on their birth certificates, while others do not. As a *Times* report of April 19, 1966 notes, states refusing to make such changes often argue that a birth certificate should "reflect the facts at birth." In addition, relationships that involve transgender people are often penalized in a variety of other ways, as, for example, when Jorgensen's fiancé lost his job when their plans to marry became known.

Jorgensen remained a public figure years after her operation, as evidenced by an incident instigated by Vice President Spiro Agnew's reference to a senator as "the Christine Jorgensen of the Republican Party," attempting to equate a change in the senator's political position with Jorgensen's sex change. As reported in *The Times* on October 11, 1970, Jorgensen sent Agnew a telegram stating that the "blatant use of my name in connection with your political feud with Senator Charles Goodell is not only unfair, but totally unjustified."

In 1966 Johns Hopkins became the first hospital in the United States to formally endorse sex reassignment surgery. While European hospitals had been performing such surgeries for years, the endorsement of a prestigious university hospital in the United States opened the door for many others to consider performing what was then an extremely controversial surgery. Most of the candidates for surgery at Johns Hopkins were males seeking to become female; however, around 10 percent were females seeking to become males (FTM). In an October 29, 2002, *Times* book review titled "On Being Male, Female, Neither or Both," Dr. Harry Benjamin was identified as "a pioneer in sex-change treatment." An endocrinologist who had studied transgender people for more than a decade, Benjamin referred many of his clients to Johns Hopkins. The work of both Benjamin and Johns Hopkins researchers gained financial support from Reed Erickson, a wealthy FTM engineer who had been a patient of Benjamin's.

As reported in *The Times* on November 20, 1972, by that time, only six years after the Hopkins announcement, more than 500 people had undergone sex reassignment surgery, with transgender people beginning to become more visible to the public eye. As with homosexuals, some psychiatrists at the University of Mississippi reported that they had cured a transsexual through behavior modification that included electric shocks. A *Times* article of April 21, 1973, documents the response of Dr. John Money of Johns Hopkins, who dismissed such work, stating that "one case doesn't prove anything. Show me 20 consecutive cases and

IN FOCUS

Intersex Treatment Controversy

• •

Previously referred to as hermaphrodites, intersex individuals are born with ambiguous genitals. Both male and female structures may be present, or the proportions may simply fall outside defined norms. By medical convention, baby boys are expected to have a penis that measures no less than 2.5 centimeters (1 inch) and baby girls a clitoris no larger than 1 centimeter (0.4 inch). Estimates of the frequency of intersex births vary from 1 in 2,000 to 1 in 4,500 births.

Until recently, the vast majority of doctors followed the "optimal gender of rearing" protocol established by Dr. John Money, founder of the Johns Hopkins Gender Identity Clinic. The genitals of intersex infants were surgically altered to resemble the assigned gender (usually female, since it is easier to construct a vagina than a penis), and the parents were encouraged to permanently conceal the procedure and its cause from their intersex child.

Cheryl Chase, founder of the Intersex Society of North America, learned of her own intersex status and early genital surgery only after she was an adult. She has been working since the mid-1990s to discourage such surgeries, which, in addition to sometimes resulting in a loss of sexual function, have not been shown to improve quality of life for intersex adults. Chase believes that parents should receive counseling to help them accept their child's ambiguous sex and that surgical decisions should not be made until the child is old enough to give informed consent. In large part because of Chase's efforts, the journal *Pediatrics* published a paper in 2006 on the management of intersex disorders. Signed by fifty international experts, this new protocol encourages the provisional designation of gender at birth but recommends that doctors discourage parents from immediate surgical intervention.

Nevertheless, when interviewed by Katrina Karkazis, a medical anthropologist at Stanford's Center for Biomedical Ethics, a majority of parents with intersex children as well as experts in the field still believe early surgery is a good idea. Said one mother of her daughter's surgery: "We felt that she would have a better self-image if she did not have a 'phallic structure' and 'scrotum.'" Similarly, Larry Basking, chief of pediatric urology at the University of California, San Francisco, argues that being intersex is a congenital anomaly that should be corrected like any other. "If you have a child born with a cleft lip or cleft palate or an extra digit or a webbed neck, I don't know any family that wouldn't want that repaired."

From *The New York Times*

Weil, Elizabeth. "What If It's (Sort of) a Boy and (Sort of) a Girl?" September 24, 2006.

• •

then I'll listen." In 1979 Johns Hopkins stopped offering sex reassignment surgery, but by that time various major medical centers across the country had adopted the practice, leading to more than 4,000 surgeries in the United States alone, as noted in a *Times* report of October 2, 1979.

A highly visible controversy regarding the scientific basis of sex and gender erupted in 1977 when a court ruled that MTF Renee Richards had a right to participate in the U.S. Open Tennis Tournament as a woman even though she had failed to pass a chromosome test used to screen Olympic participants. As noted in a *Times* report of August 31, 1976, Richards questioned the validity of the test and asserted that, physically and psychologically, she was a woman. Noting that her passport and license to practice medicine recognized her new sex, she argued: "In the eyes of the law, I am female." The judge agreed, ruling that the evidence

Thomas Beatie, born a woman, underwent gender reassignment surgery in 2002, but kept his reproductive organs in hopes of having a child. His first child, Susan, was born in 2008, and as of early 2011, he and his wife Nancy have had two other children, Jensen and Austin.

Source: AP Images/Hermann J. Knippertz

supported Richards's claim. He added that the United States Tennis Association had inappropriately adopted the test solely to exclude Richards from play. By 2001 sex reassignment surgery was included in health care benefits for employees of the city of San Francisco as noted in a *Times* report of February 18. However, such coverage is by no means the norm as of this writing.

As noted by Professor Judith Halberstam, an expert in gender issues, "Medical innovations have expanded the possibilities for body modification." Advances in reproductive technology have recently increased the options available to an FTM transgender person interested in conceiving and delivering a baby. In 2008 this issue received enormous media attention when Thomas Beatie carried a child to term. Born a woman, Beatie had undergone hormone therapy to develop male secondary sex characteristics, as well as surgery to alter his chest and clitoris, though he opted against adding a penis. Halberstam noted: "Not a lot of transmen get what's called 'bottom' or 'lower' surgery."

Because Beatie did not have his ovaries removed, he was able to use a sperm donation to conceive a child. While he was surely not the first to use science to make this sort of a reproductive breakthrough, like Christine Jorgensen's, Beatie's case was frequently characterized as unique, perhaps because such circumstances were new to many in the general public. As Professor Eve Sedgwick noted, many people "experience gender very differently and some have really individual and imaginative uses of it." She added: "That's an important thing for people to wrap their minds around." A sophisticated understanding of these issues is increasingly necessary on college campuses, where transgender students and allies have begun to lobby for accommodations such as all-gender bathrooms and showers, as well as housing and sports teams not designated by gender. According to a *Times* report of March 7, 2004, such accommodations have been made at several universities, including Brown and Wesleyan, as well as Sarah Lawrence and Smith, both women's colleges.

HEALTH CARE ISSUES

Various studies have suggested that specific health practices and issues can have a unique impact on LGBT populations. After years of being largely ignored by the mainstream medical establishment, lesbian health began to receive attention from the federal government in the mid-1990s, including two large-scale studies funded by the National Institutes of Health. A study of more than 13,000 women undertaken by Dr. Katherine O'Hanlan in 1995 found that lesbians tend to have less frequent medical checkups than straight women, owing in part to discriminatory treatment from their physicians. As noted in a January 11, 1998, *Times* report, even high-achieving and career-oriented lesbians often find physician visits to be a difficult experience, fraught with misunderstanding between patient and doctor. Joyce Hunter, an AIDS researcher with a Ph.D. in social welfare, admitted that "there was no way I felt comfortable revealing my sexual orientation." An interviewee in a March 30, 1999, *Times* report explains further: "When they ask, 'Are you having intercourse?' And you say, 'No.' Then they ask, 'So you're not sexually active?' And you say, 'I didn't say that.' Then they ask, 'Well, what do you do?' And you have to decide whether to lie or whether to come out." Thus lesbian patients often find themselves in a health care catch-22. If patients lie, they may not get the information they need, but if they come out, their physician may suddenly become uncomfortable with them. Faced with this dilemma, many lesbians choose to avoid regular medical examinations.

Irregular visits put lesbians at higher risk for developing forms of cervical and breast cancer as well as heart disease that may not be detected until advanced and untreatable stages. To address these issues, the American Medical Association reminded physicians to adopt a nonjudgmental attitude toward their patients. Additionally, several practices were opened to address the health care needs of lesbians, such as the Gay Women's Focus in New York City, which serves more than 3,000 male and female patients, 30 percent of whom are lesbians. Such practices tend to be more aware of the specific health concerns of LGBT populations, such as higher risk of breast cancer among lesbians owing to lower birth rates, the need for MTF transsexuals to continue to have their prostates checked, and the heightened risk of heart disease among FTM transsexuals. Dr. H. Joan Waitkevicz, the director of Gay Women's Focus said, "I hope that we can make ourselves obsolete. I hope that there will be a time when every doctor will approach everyone who walks in the door with the right questions and information."

When lesbians do become ill, they often encounter additional obstacles to nondiscriminatory treatment. A November 23, 1999, *Times* article reported that lesbians in long-term relationships can be denied access to their partners who are hospitalized or the right to make crucial health decisions for a severely ill partner. Kathleen DeBold, the executive director of the Mautner Project for Lesbians With Cancer, said that she "had a client who couldn't get into the intensive care unit to see her lover except by posing as her sister. When the woman's family came, they said, 'That's not her sister,' and the hospital threw her out. This is the kind of thing people go through all the time." She added that while doctors, researchers, and insurers all discriminate, cancer does not.

Concerning gay men's health, AIDS was given primary attention through the 1980s and well into 1990s, as will be discussed in detail in the next chapter. By the end of the 1990s, however, work began to emerge suggesting that HIV status could no longer be the sole measure of gay men's health. For example, a study of 2,600 gay and bisexual men indicated that gay men are almost twice as likely to smoke, significantly increasing their health risk for a variety of illnesses. Relatedly, an August 14, 2001, *Times* report noted that powerful drug combinations have lowered the death rates associated with AIDS, freeing researchers concerned with gay men's health to explore other concerns such as hepatitis, chronic fatigue syndrome, prostate cancer, substance abuse, and depression.

In the spring of 2000, the Centers for Disease Control and Prevention announced that an outbreak of tuberculosis (TB) had emerged in black transgender communities in New York City and Baltimore. The outbreak was concentrated among transgender people living in "houses" that compete against each other in drag balls across the East Coast, and well over half of those affected also tested positive for HIV. People living in these houses had become known to the mainstream through a documentary film that became a hit in 1990, *Paris is Burning,* which detailed the lives of various drag queens in New York City. Although the total number of people involved was relatively small, this TB outbreak highlights the unique health issues that may be faced by people of color in the LGBT community.

BIBLIOGRAPHY

Fausto-Sterling, Anne. *Myths of Gender: Biological Theories about Women and Men.* New York: Basic Books, 1995.

LeVay, Simon. *Queer Science: The Use and Abuse of Research into Homosexuality.* Cambridge, MA: MIT Press, 1996.

Stryker, Susan. *Transgender History*. Berkeley, CA: Seal Press, 2008.

FROM *THE NEW YORK TIMES*

Angier, Natalie. "Ideas & Trends; The Biology of What It Means to Be Gay." September 1, 1991.

———. "Study of Sex Orientation Doesn't Neatly Fit Mold." July 18, 1993.

Associated Press. "Psychologists Reject Gay 'Therapy.'" August 6, 2009.

Bernstein, Fred A. "On Campus, Rethinking Biology 101." March 7, 2004.

Blakeslee, Sandra. "Panelists Cite Biological Roots of Homosexuality." August 26, 1985.

Brody, Jane. "More Homosexuals Aided to Become Heterosexual." February 28, 1971.

———. "500 in the U.S. Change Sex in Six Years with Surgery." November 20, 1972.

———. "Doctors Report Transsexual Cure." April 21, 1973.

———. "Bisexual Life-Style Appears to Be Spreading and Not Necessarily Among 'Swingers.'" March 24, 1974

———. "Aid for Problems of Homosexuals Reported by Masters and Johnson." April 17, 1979.

———. "Benefits of Transsexual Surgery Disputed As Leading Hospital Halts the Procedure." October 2, 1979.

———. "Psychiatrists on Homosexuality: Vigorous Discord Voiced at Meeting." January 26, 1982.

———. "Boyhood Effeminacy and Later Homosexuality." December 16, 1986.

Buckley, Tom. "All They Talk About Is Sex, Sex, Sex." April 20, 1969.

Burns, Paul. "Gauging Bisexuality." July 12, 2005.

Carey, Benedict. "Straight, Gay or Lying? Bisexuality Revisited." July 5, 2005.

Dreifus, Claudia. "A Conversation with—Anne Fausto-Sterling; Exploring What Makes Us Male or Female." January 2, 2001.

Friedman, Richard C. "Understanding Homosexuality" (Letter to the Editor). February 19, 1989.

Goode, Erica. "Study Questions Gene Influence on Male Homosexuality." April 23, 1999.

———. "Study Says Gays Can Shift Sexual Orientation." May 9, 2001.

Gould, Jack. "Channel 13 Presents a Homosexual Study." May 21, 1966.

Grady, Denise. "Lesbians Find Cancer Support without Excuses." November 23, 1999.

Herman, Robin. "Issue and Debate: Controversy Over Renee Richards Adds Dimension to Sex Role in Sports." August 31, 1976.

Hilts, Phillip J. "Agency to Use Dormant Law to Bar Homosexuals from U.S." June 3, 1990.

Hunt, Morton. "Freudians Are Wrong, The Behavioralists Say—A Neurosis Is 'Just' a Bad Habit." June 4, 1967.

Kihss, Peter. "A New Study Urges Homosexuals to Speak Out." May 19, 1974.

———. "8 Psychiatrists Are Seeking New Vote on Homosexuality as Mental Illness." May 26, 1974.

Kristof, Nicholas D. "Gay at Birth?" October 25, 2003.

Lehmann-Haupt, Christopher. "An Audacious History of Sex." October 25, 1971.

Lewine, Edward. 1998. "Neighborhood Report: Union Square; A Health Center for Lesbians." January 11, 1998.

Mendelsohn, Daniel. "Republicanism Can Be Cured." July 26, 1993.

Pear, Robert. "Ban Is Affirmed on Homosexuals Entering Nation." December 27, 1979.

Roberts, Steven V. "Man Asks Change in His Sex Listing. Cites Recent Operation—City Fighting Request." April 19, 1966.

Smith, Dinita. "Books on Health; On Being Male, Female, Neither or Both." October 29, 2002.

Thompson, Ginger. "New Clinics Let Lesbian Patients Be Themselves; An Effort to Help a Group That Often Shuns Doctors." March 30, 1999.

Tuller, David. "For Gay Men, Health Care Concerns Move beyond the Threat of AIDS." August 14, 2001.

Unsigned. "Bars Marriage Permit. Clerk Rejects Proof of Sex of Christine Jorgensen." April 4, 1959.

———. "Jewish Women Urge Eased Moral Laws." November 19, 1965.

———. "Miss Jorgensen Asks Agnew for an Apology." October 11, 1970.

———. "Doctors Urged Not to Call Homosexuality Illness." May 10, 1973.

———. "The A.P.A. Ruling on Homosexuality: The Issue Is Subtle: The Debate Still On." December 23, 1973.

———. "U.S. Lifts Ban on Aliens Who Are Homosexuals." August 3, 1979.

———. "Judge Ends Immigration Rule." June 18, 1982.

———. "National News Briefs; San Francisco Workers Get Sex-Change Coverage." February 18, 2001.

Wade, Nicholas. "Pad de Deux of Sexuality Is Written in the Genes." April 10, 2007.

Weil, Elizabeth. "What if It's (Sort of) a Boy and (Sort of) a Girl. September 24, 2006.

Wyden, Peter, and Barbara Wyden. "Growing up Straight: The Father's Role." May 26, 1968.

· ·

PSYCHOANALYTIC ASSOCIATION ADDRESSES FEMALE HOMOSEXUALITY FOR THE FIRST TIME

During the 1961 annual meeting of the American Psychoanalytic Association, noted New York analyst Dr. Charles Socarides characterized female homosexuality as a growing problem. He suggested this increase may be the byproduct of "a disordered and confused society" or a "compensating drive" in response to an increase in male homosexuality. Asserting that child rearing was a unique problem for the female homosexual, psychoanalyst Judith S. Kestenberg described all lesbians as "young virginal girls at heart," enacting the mother-daughter relationship in homosexual relationships and playing with "life dolls." Kestenberg also commented on society's permissive attitude toward lesbians, concluding that "we adults look upon them with indulgence, pity and amused smilings." Since the 1961 meeting of the American Psychoanalytic Association, professional as well as societal views on homosexuality have drastically changed, perhaps most dramatically with the removal of homosexuality from the *Diagnostic and Statistical Manual of Mental Disorders* (DSM) in 1973. More recently, lesbian parents received accolades from the psychological community when the 2010 study *US National Longitudinal Lesbian Family Study: Psychological Adjustment in 17-Year-Old Adolescents* suggested that children raised by lesbians tended to be as well or better adjusted than those raised by heterosexual couples.

DECEMBER 11, 1961
WOMEN DEVIATES HELD INCREASING
Problem of Homosexuality Found Largely Ignored
By EMMA HARRISON

The problem of homosexuality in women is increasing, a psychologist said here yesterday.

Yet, said Dr. Charles Socarides, the New York analyst, this psychic problem of women has been largely ignored both by psychiatry and by society in general.

Even the legal injunctions imposed by some societies on overt male homosexuality do not pertain to the female, he observed. The attitude probably rests in the "archaic unconscious morality of men," he said.

Part of the rise in female homosexuality may be accounted for, he said, in the increase of the problem among men. Although figures are scanty in the field, he said that the fact that male homosexuality had risen some 600 per cent in England since World War II indicated the possibility of some compensating drive in women. Also, he observed, such aberration is often a consequence of a disordered and confused society.

Symposium on Subject

Acknowledgement of the extent of the problem was indicated by the fact that the American Psychoanalytic Association held its first symposium on overt female homosexuality before its annual session ended yesterday at the Baltimore Hotel. Dr. Socarides participated in the panel discussion and summarized the findings of the group.

The problem of child-rearing plays a distinct role in female homosexuality, according to Dr. Judith S. Kestenberg of Sands Point, L.I. The homosexual woman "wastes nothing except, of course, her motherliness," she said. In the homosexual relationship, women "play out the mother-child relationship," she said.

There is no better description of these women, she said, than that of the poet Sappho whom she quoted as saying "I shall remain eternally maiden." All homosexual women, Dr. Kestenberg said, "are young virginal girls at heart." They play, she said, with "life dolls."

She, too, commented on the role that society played in the kind of permissive attitude toward this form of sexual deviation. "We adults," she said, "look upon them with indulgence, pity and amused smilings."

Dr. David Beres, a New York psychoanalyst, was named president-elect of the association at the final business session.

* *

Medical Community Rejects Homosexual Claims of Normality

Claiming to be the first study of homosexuality by an authoritative body representing all branches of medicine, a report issued in 1964 by the New York Academy of Medicine's Committee on Public Health asserted that homosexuality was an illness and that the homosexual was "an emotionally disturbed individual" who lacked the ability to accept the adult responsibilities of marriage and parenting. The report also asserted that parental neglect and abuse are the root causes of homosexuality and that the problem may be successfully treated but was "more easily dealt with by early preventative measures." Maintaining that their findings applied "to homosexuals everywhere," the researchers linked their results to two other committee studies on the spread of salacious literature and venereal disease, both of which implicated homosexuals. This report challenged the claims of gay advocacy groups such as the Mattachine Society, then known as homophile groups, which argued that homosexuality is simply an acceptable difference, rather than an illness in need of correction. The gay community would be forced to deal with attitudes similar to those expressed in this study for much of the twentieth century. While the characterization of homosexuality as an illness changed in the 1970s, the morality of homosexuality and homosexual relationships still remains controversial among some segments of American culture.

MAY 19, 1964
HOMOSEXUALS PROUD OF DEVIANCY, MEDICAL ACADEMY STUDY FINDS
By ROBERT TRUMBULL

Homosexuals have gone beyond the plane of defensiveness and now argue that their deviancy is "a desirable, noble, preferable way of life," according to a report issued yesterday by the Committee on Public Health of the New York Academy of Medicine.

The report is the first authoritative study of homosexuality by a recognized organization representing all branches of medicine, a spokesman for the committee said. Public comment on sexual variance has been confined heretofore to the psychiatric branch of the profession, he declared.

Homosexuality is an "illness" that can be treated successfully in "some case" but is more easily dealt with by early preventive measures, the report concludes.

The study takes strong issue with the contention of spokesmen for homosexuals that their aberration makes them merely "a different kind of people leading an acceptable way of life."

Organized homosexuals now go even further than this, the committee found.

"They would have it believed that homosexuality is not just an acceptable way of life but rather a desirable, noble, preferable way of life," the report goes on. "For one thing, they claim that it is the perfect answer to the problem of the population explosion."

The committee's findings were said to apply to homosexuals everywhere, not just in New York. Various authorities have estimated the number of sexual deviants in this city at between 100,000 and 600,000.

"There is . . . an impression that at the present time the practice of homosexuality is increasing among the population at large," the report says. "Certainly, if there is not more homosexuality than in the past, it appears to be more open and obtrusive.

"More plays and books are having homosexual characters, and more homosexuals seem to have taken to writing autobiographies. Furthermore the homosexuals seem to have become more formally organized, with a central office and a magazine of their own."

Allusion to Organization

This was apparently an allusion to the Mattachine Society, a national organization of homosexuals with headquarters in San Francisco and branch offices in New York and other cities. The group publishes a monthly magazine, Mattachine Review, devoted to problems of sex inverts.

"These developments," the report continues, "stand out in sharp contrast with the situation which existed in New York 30 years ago, when the subject was less frequently and less openly presented and its votaries rallied once a year to hold their well-known Fairy Ball."

The study on homosexuality was a by-product of the committee's investigations of two other public health problems—the increases in salacious literature and venereal disease. The committee found that "a substantial portion" of the objectionable publications were of a homosexual nature and that homosexuals were apparently "playing a larger role in transmitting" venereal disease.

'Indeed an Illness'

Society, including the medical profession, "has not really confronted" the problem of homosexuality, the report asserts.

"The Committee on Public Health believes that of all groups the medical profession should state clearly its position," the report says. "It should declare what homosexuality is and what can be done about it."

"Homosexuality is indeed an illness," the medical committee declared. "The homosexual is an emotionally disturbed individual who has not acquired a normal capacity to develop satisfying heterosexual relationships.

"Consequently overt homosexuality may be an expression of fear of the opposite sex and of inability to accept adult responsibility, such as marriage and parenthood."

In other words, the report says, the homosexual is a victim of "arrested development."

As main factors in early environmental life leading to deviation from customary sexual behavior, the report lists "neglect, rejection, overprotection, overindulgence" by parents.

Homosexual inclinations begin earlier in life than is generally realized, and their appearance is often motivated by defective parental relationships, the report states.

Psychotherapy Urged

Recognition of deviant tendencies may be difficult, the committee found. Personal mannerisms and characteristics can be deceptive.

"Although treatment is difficult and prognosis is guarded, it can be successful and of value," the report continues. "Psychotherapy offers the greatest probability of benefit. There is little valid evidence that other treatment is effective."

Treatment works better the earlier it is started, the report states, and it is a prerequisite to success that the deviant possess a genuine desire to correct his condition.

"There is a widespread need and desire for proper and authoritative sex education," the report goes on. "But here the reaction of society manifests an interesting ambivalence."

This ambivalence is illustrated by a prevailing "superficial, immature and artificial attitude toward sex" in the midst of general "preoccupation with sex as a symbol," the report says.

"The argument most commonly advanced is that sex education belongs in the home. But if the home is not providing that education, where will it be found?" the report asks.

The medical committee recommended that sex education in the United States be "examined realistically."

CONFLICTING MEDICAL VIEWS OF HOMOSEXUALITY

In the 1960s, viewing homosexuality as a treatable illness, as opposed to a criminal offense, was considered enlightened. Although many medical authorities continued to regard homosexuality as pathological in the early 1970s, others began to question this view at the time, pointing out that past research was based exclusively on homosexuals who sought psychoanalytic treatment. When studies by psychologist Dr. Evelyn Hooker revealed no "demonstrable pathology" differentiating gays from heterosexuals, many medical authorities began to argue that homosexuality is a "way of loving, not a pathology" and that the majority of mental health issues stem from anxiety related to discovery and potential criminal prosecution. Dr. Lawrence LeShan argued in a *New York Times* editorial that therapists should resist societal prejudice and help homosexual individuals to cope with cultural resistance, stating that "the Gay Liberation movement is the best therapy the homosexual has had in years."

FEBRUARY 28, 1971
THE CHANGING VIEW OF HOMOSEXUALITY

A decade ago, the concept of homosexuality as an illness to be treated medically was considered an enlightened view in a society that regarded homosexuals as criminals to be punished for acting on their sexual inclinations.

Today, a sharp debate is going on within the medical community as to whether homosexuality, practiced by millions of Americans, is really an illness or merely a form of behavior at one extreme of the continuum of normal human sexuality.

In recent years, the debate has been fed by the vocal segment of the homosexual population—such groups as the Gay Liberation Front, the Mattachine Society and the Daughters of Bilitis. Proclaiming their behavior to be within the range of normal, these groups maintain that the "sickness" one finds in the homosexual community is largely a result of society's "sick attitude toward this form of sexual expression.

The kinds of sexual acts performed by homosexuals are still illegal in 48 states and the District of Columbia (illegal for heterosexuals, too, but the laws are not enforced against them). As a National Institute of Mental Health study group on homosexuality noted, the threat of discovery is anxiety-producing, and laws against homosexuals hardly contribute to their mental health.

Irving Bieber, a New York psychoanalyst who has evaluated many hundreds of homosexuals, and many of his colleagues regard homosexuality as "pathological." Dr. May E. Romm, a Beverly Hills analyst, says that the label "gay" is "a defense mechanism against the emptiness, the coldness, and the futility" of the homosexual life.

All Seeking Therapy

However, Dr. Judd Marmor, director of psychiatry at Cedars-Sinai Medical Center in Los Angeles, points out that "the concepts of psychoanalysts are all derived from the study of homosexuals who have sought psychoanalytic therapy."

Dr. Evelyn Hooker, a Los Angeles psychoanalyst who is chairman of the National Institute's study group, reports that many of the homosexuals she has studied reveal, on psychological testing, no "demonstrable pathology" that would differentiate them in any way from a group of relatively normal heterosexuals.

Lawrence LeShan, a New York psychologist, views homosexuality as "a way of loving, not a pathology. The therapist's job is not to go along with the prejudices of the culture, but to help a person adjust to himself so that he can deal adequately with the culture."

"The Gay Liberation movement," he says, "is the best therapy the homosexual has had in years."

PSYCHOTHERAPISTS BEGIN TO CHALLENGE VIEW THAT HOMOSEXUALITY IS AN ILLNESS

In 1964, speaking at the two-day biennial meeting of the Daughters of Bilitis, a national organization of lesbians, psychotherapist Dr. Ernest van den Haag argued that homosexuality is "to some extent, a matter of choice conditioned by early emotional experiences." Both he and fellow speaker Dr. Wardell Pomeroy (coauthor of the Kinsey Report) argued against the prevailing medical opinion that homosexuality is a disease. Presumably owing to the controversial nature of the topic at the time, the New York affiliate of ABC-TV was ordered by its legal department to cancel a proposed panel discussion on lesbianism.

JUNE 21, 1964
HOMOSEXUAL WOMEN HEAR PSYCHOLOGISTS

The Daughters of Bilitis, a national organization of homosexual women, heard two psychologists take issue yesterday with the prevailing medical view that homosexuality is a disease.

This counter opinion was expressed by Dr. Wardell B. Pomeroy, co-author with the late Dr. Alfred Kinsey of "Sexual Behavior in the Human Female," and Dr. Ernest van den Haag. Both men are psychotherapists here.

About 100 persons, including representatives of male homosexual organizations, attended the opening session of a two-day biennial convention at the Barbizon-Plaza Hotel. Today's meeting will be limited to members of Bilitis, which takes its name from a fictional daughter of Sappho.

Dr. Pomeroy said that Western culture, in contrast with the majority of world cultures, was more lenient toward female homosexuality than male deviation.

Dr. van den Haag said that, to some extent, homosexuality was a matter of choice, conditioned by early emotional experiences.

A panel discussion of lesbianism that was to have been presented Friday night on the Les Crane television show on WABC-TV was ordered canceled by the station's legal department. A spokesman for the show said that no reason had been given.

• •

PSYCHIATRISTS CONSIDER CHANGING CLASSIFICATION OF HOMOSEXUALITY IN DSM

In early 1973 an American Psychiatric Association (APA) committee began to review whether homosexuality should continue to be listed in its *Diagnostic and Statistical Manual of Mental Disorders* as a form of mental illness and disorder. Dr. Henry Brill, chair of the committee, said that such a classification fosters discrimination against homosexuals, leading many to think that all homosexuals are "dangerous or sex fiends or untrustworthy or some other part of a stereotype." Members of the Gay Activists Alliance presented studies suggesting that homosexuals are as well adjusted as heterosexuals. Supporting the proposal to remove it as a diagnostic category, Dr. Judd Marmor, vice president of the APA, said that homosexuality is not a mental illness, but rather an alternative form of sexual expression of which society disapproves. Others noted that Sigmund Freud himself argued that homosexuals should not be excluded from training as analysts. As a result of this review, homosexuality was removed from the DSM as a mental disorder, paving the way for further progress in the gay rights movement.

FEBRUARY 9, 1973
PSYCHIATRISTS REVIEW STAND ON HOMOSEXUALS

By BOYCE RENSBERGER

A committee of the American Psychiatric Association yesterday began deliberating whether homosexuality should be considered a form of mental illness and whether it ought to be stricken from the association's official catalog of mental disorders.

Gay organizations have contended that psychiatry's continued recognition of homosexuality as a mental disorder lends support to efforts to discriminate against homosexuals in business and government.

In a closed meeting at Columbia University's Psychiatric Institute the association's eight-member Committee on Nomenclature, which recommends revisions in the catalog, heard members of the Gay Activists Alliance present the findings of nearly a score of medical studies showing that many homosexuals are as well adjusted mentally as most heterosexuals.

Although the "Diagnostic & Statistical Manual [of] Mental Disorders" still classifies homosexuality as a "sexual deviation" along with fetishism, sadism and masochism, a growing number of individual psychiatrists are voicing a contrary opinion.

One of the most prominent is Dr. Judd Marmor, vice president of the A.P.A. and professor of psychiatry at the University of Southern California.

"Homosexuality in itself," Dr. Marmor said, "merely represents a variant sexual preference which our society disapproves of but which does not constitute a mental illness."

Dr. Marmor, who is also president elect of the prestigious Group for the Advancement of Psychiatry, said he supports the movement to eliminate homosexuality as a diagnostic category.

'Term Misused'

A new edition of the manual is not due to be published until 1978. In the meantime the organization of homosexuals is seeking a statement from the A.P.A. disavowing the implications of the old classification.

Dr. Henry Brill, director of Pilgrim State Hospital and Chairman of the Nomenclature Committee, said after the meeting that his group hoped to draw up a statement in time to be considered by the A.P.A. at its annual meeting in May in Honolulu.

"There's no doubt this label [homosexuality] has been used in a discriminatory way," Dr. Brill said. "We were all agreed on that."

Dr. Brill said the committee also agreed that whether a person prefers to have sexual relations with a member of the same or of the opposite sex was, in itself, not an indicator of a mental disorder.

"This term has been misused by the public at large," Dr. Brill said. "The public assumes that all homosexuals are dangerous or sex fiends or untrustworthy or some other part of a stereotype. This, of course, isn't so. We know of many successful, well adjusted people in various professions who are homosexual."

Dr. Brill added, however, that some members of the committee felt that in some cases homosexuality was the central feature of a psychiatric problem.

"What are we going to do about the homosexual who comes to us and says he's miserable, that he doesn't like the homosexual way of life and he wants to change?" Dr. Brill asked. "Very often these people have very clear psychiatric problems."

Statement to Be Drafted

Dr. Brill said the statement his committee expected to draft would express the points he summarized.

In its memorandum to the committee the Gay Activists Alliance contended that "the 'illness' model of homosexuality is unwarranted" and that, "on the contrary, there is a significant body of research data which supports the contention that a sizable number of homosexual persons are sufficiently well adjusted as to be indistinguishable from a control group of heterosexual peers."

Among the various excerpts from psychiatric reports supporting the homosexual position was one from Freud in which he responded to a question as to whether a homosexual candidate should be accepted for training as an analyst.

"We cannot," Freud wrote in a letter, "exclude such persons without other sufficient reasons, as we cannot agree with their legal prosecution. We feel that a decision in such cases should depend on a thorough examination of the other qualities of the candidate."

The delegation that presented the homosexuals' case before the committee comprised Charles Silverstein and Bernice Goodman, directors of the Institute for Human Identity; Ray Prada, a psychologist; Jean O'Leary, chairwoman of the Lesbian Liberation Committee of the Gay Activists Alliance and Ronald Gold, G.A.A. News and Media Relations chairman.

American Psychiatric Association Declares Homosexuality Is Not a Mental Illness

In 1973 the board of trustees of the American Psychiatric Association announced that the organization would no longer consider homosexuality a mental illness, stating that individuals who exhibit no sign of social impairment should not be labeled sick. From this point on, people who requested treatment because of dissatisfaction with their same-sex attraction would be classified as having "sexual orientation disturbance." Leaders in the organization argued that the change was independent of any judgment about whether or not homosexuality was normal or abnormal. However, they argued that the change would enable more homosexuals to seek treatment for other issues, confident that psychiatrists would not seek to treat them by attempting to convert them to heterosexuality. Noting that the organization's previous classification of homosexuality as a mental illness may have served to legitimize discrimination against homosexuals, the trustees also adopted resolutions that opposed laws criminalizing sodomy and supported gay civil rights laws in the area of housing, employment, and licensing.

DECEMBER 16, 1973
PSYCHIATRISTS, IN A SHIFT, DECLARE HOMOSEXUALITY NO MENTAL ILLNESS
By RICHARD D. LYONS
Special to the New York Times

WASHINGTON, Dec. 15.—The American Psychiatric Association, altering a position it has held for nearly a century, decided today that homosexuality is not a mental disorder.

The board of trustees of the 20,000-member group approved a resolution that said in part, "by itself, homosexuality does not meet the criteria for being a psychiatric disorder."

Persons who are troubled by their homosexuality, the trustees said, will be classified as having a "sexual orientation disturbance" should they come to a psychiatrist for help.

"We will no longer insist on a label of sickness for individuals who insist that they are well and demonstrate no generalized impairment in social effectiveness," the trustees said.

The trustees defined "sexual orientation disturbance" as a category for "individuals whose sexual interests are directed toward people of their own sex and who are either disturbed by, in conflict with or wish to change their sexual orientation."

The semantics of the resolution and exactly how it differed from the association's previous position were challenged by reporters during a news conference at A.P.A. headquarters. But association leaders insisted they had not given in to pressure from homosexual groups and that the difference in position was indeed real, rather than imaginary despite the apparent vagueness of their resolution.

Dr. Robert L. Spitzer, who is a psychiatrist at the Columbia College of Physicians and Surgeons, explained that "we're not saying that homosexuality is either 'normal' or 'abnormal'" . . . [missing text]. . . psychiatrists on notice that some homosexuals—the exact number is not known—have adjusted to their sexual status and do not wish to change.

According to Dr. Spitzer, this would mean that many more homosexuals who need psychiatric help for reasons other than homosexuality would seek professional help because the homosexuals would know that the psychiatrists would not necessarily try to "cure" them by converting them to heterosexuality.

Deplore Discrimination

In a related action, the association's trustees adopted a resolution deploring discrimination against homosexuals in the fields of housing, employment and licensing.

Further, the board of trustees said it "supports and urges the enactment of civil rights legislation at local, state, and Federal levels that would insure homosexual citizens the same protections now guaranteed to others."

In addition, the board said, "The A.P.A. supports and urges the repeal of all legislation making criminal offense of sexual acts performed by consenting adults in private."

Such laws exist in 42 states and the District of Columbia, according to the National Gay Task Force, a New York-based homosexual activist group.

The group hailed the association's action as "the greatest gay victory," adding, "The diagnosis of homosexuality as an illness has been the cornerstone of oppression for a tenth of our population." The fraction has been set far lower by other estimates.

Self-Appraisal

The group said in a statement that linking homosexuality to mental illness "has forced many gay women and men to think of themselves as freaks."

"It has been used as a tool of discrimination in the private sector, and in the civil service, military, Immigration and Naturalization Service, health services, adoption and child-custody courts," the statement added.

Dr. Alfred M. Freedman, president of the A.P.A., noted that the association's official list of mental disorders had classed homosexuality as a "sexual deviation" along with fetishism, voyeurism, pedophilia, exhibitionism, and others.

He said that whether homosexuality belonged there had been the subject of increasing debate, "fanned by the organized homosexual community, which has vigorously protested the prejudice that derives from classifying their condition as a mental illness."

PARENTS BLAMED FOR HOMOSEXUALITY

In 1964, noting that then-modern scientific research suggested parents could be influential in preventing the development of homosexuality, psychiatrist Dr. Irving Bieber offered families guidance on "immunizing" children against the "human misery" and frustration of homosexual relationships. According to Bieber, homosexuality was caused by a failure to develop "natural sex identification" and a fear of stable, long-term heterosexual relationships. As a result, mothers should avoid being overly protective, possessive, or intimate with their sons and take care not to discourage an interest in girls or the development of normal masculine behaviors.

Research was cited to suggest that homosexual men were raised by mothers who demanded too much attention, dominated and minimized their husbands or deliberately tried to make "sissies" out of their boys. In turn, the father of a homosexual man was said to tend to have been unaffectionate, indifferent or hostile to his son, depriving the young man of "a masculine image with whom he [could] can identify." To prevent this, fathers were encouraged to spend more time with their boys as "you don't find many homosexuals whose fathers took them on camping trips or to baseball games."

Although Bieber admitted scientific knowledge of the causes of female homosexuality was limited, in his words, "present evidence indicates that this condition, too, is caused by destructive psychological conditions within the family." In addition to being hypercritical and competitive with their daughters, many mothers of female homosexuals were said to fail to dress them "becomingly" or teach them appropriate feminine behavior such as cooking, sewing and other homemaking activities. Fathers of female homosexuals were said to reject their daughters completely or to have behaved in overly possessive or even seductive manner towards them. According to Dr. Bieber, parents owed it to their children "to use our constantly developing insight into the problem [of homosexuality] so that in the future they may fulfill their roles as healthy men and women." Until 1973 when homosexuality was removed from the DSM, Dr. Bieber's study would be a defining work on male homosexuality. His research and his Triadic Family Model continue to be influential in conversion therapy.

AUGUST 23, 1964
SPEAKING FRANKLY ON A ONCE TABOO SUBJECT
By IRVING BIEBER

Until recently, homosexuality was a taboo subject in most households. In many families, it still is—just as cancer was only a short time ago. As a practicing psychiatrist, I am glad that the discussion of homosexuality is moving more and more from the old hush-hush atmosphere into the open. This increasing candor benefits everybody. For, uncomfortable as many people feel when the problem is talked about, nothing less than our self-interest as parents and enlightened citizens demands it. Our children can be helped by such discussion, and I believe we owe it to them to use our constantly developing insight into the problem so that in the future they may fulfill their roles as healthy men and women.

The discussion has been hampered by something even more basic than our discomfort. There still is much that science doesn't know about homosexuality; that is, continuing erotic activity between members of the same sex. Even the number of homosexuals in the United States is unknown. At a guess, there are about two million. What is far more important is that many—perhaps most—are desperately unhappy about it. Fortunately, new research indicates that homosexuality can, in many instances, be headed off during childhood and adolescence. And it is parents who are usually in the best possible position to prevent homosexual tendencies from developing in their youngsters in the first place.

Few parents know how to go about this, yet science today can give them guidelines to help relieve much human misery. . . .

Second, again contrary to common belief, homosexuality is not a trait that develops because of individual choice. Essentially, it comes about because homosexuals have been conditioned, from early life, to be afraid of long-term romantic relationships with the opposite sex. They avoid normal sexual activity because they have developed overwhelming fears of their sexual capability and enjoyment with members of the opposite sex. Having been thus cut off from the normal channels for romantic and sexual gratification, homosexuals seek it with members of their own sex. Nevertheless, although basic sexual urges may thus be fulfilled to varying degrees, a feeling of complete attainment of romantic longings probably never occurs. This is one important reason why nearly all homosexual relationships turn out to be frustrating.

To prevent childhood homosexual symptoms from developing—or possibly even to "immunize" youngsters against them—it is necessary to consider the behavior of parents.

We know, for instance, that mothers of male homosexuals usually behave in characteristic and abnormal ways. They are also excessively possessive, over-protective and inclined to discourage the son's masculine ways. In families with more than one child, the mother generally favors the prehomosexual son. One mother of a patient who showed clear signs of homosexuality by the age of 6, had begun quite deliberately, as far back as his birth, to make a "sissy" out of him simply because she already had one son and had badly wanted her second child to be a girl.

Such a mother spends an inordinate amount of time with the favored son and demands that he be unusually attentive to her. She may encourage an alliance with him against his father and often openly prefers the son to her husband.

There is more to this unhealthy pattern. Mothers of homosexuals frequently make their sons the principal confidants, sometimes even in sexual matters. They interfere with the boy's heterosexual interests in childhood and adolescence, often by discouraging their sons from dating. If the sons show interest in girls, the mothers quickly find fault with them and usually succeed in disrupting the relationships ("You can't trust women; all they want is a meal ticket"). Typically, these mothers baby their sons by being excessively concerned about illness and injuries and tend to discourage participation in sports and other boyhood activities, presumably out of concern for their sons' welfare.

A boy with prehomosexual tendencies responds to this kind of mothering by becoming submissive. Typically, he is likely to worry excessively about displeasing his mother or hurting her feelings. That this is a very big worry indeed to such a boy is not at all surprising. After all, his whole life has led him to believe that his mother is the center of his world, and usually he loves and admires her out of all proportion. He turns to his mother—and only rarely to his father—for protection against his many fears.

Mothers of homosexuals, incidentally, are usually inadequate wives. They tend to dominate and minimize their husbands and frequently hold them more or less openly in contempt. The plain fact is that, unconsciously, these mothers are engaged in romances with their sons. Sometimes this shows itself in seductive behavior toward prehomosexual boys.

We have come to learn that fathers of most homosexuals also tend to behave in typical ways. They are usually unaffectionate and spend little time with their boys. You don't find many homosexuals whose fathers took them on camping trips or to baseball games. The prehomosexual son reacts to his father's indifference or hostility with fear, lack of respect and sometimes even hatred. Perhaps most damaging of all, he does not see in his father a masculine image with whom he can identify. In fact, he tries to be as much unlike his father as possible. It stands to reason, therefore, that homosexual sons (or heterosexual sons with severe homosexual problems) are most likely to develop in families where mothers are close-binding, intimate and seductive toward their sons and at the same time dominate their husbands who are detached or hostile as fathers. . . .

Our knowledge of prehomosexual girls is more limited. Detailed studies of sufficiently large samples of female homosexuals have not yet been reported, but present evidence indicates that this condition, too, is caused by destructive psychological conditions within the family. Again, certain telltale patterns exist. Mothers of female homosexuals are usually hostile and extremely competitive with these daughters. These girls are rarely taught feminine behavior by learning how to cook, sew or perform other homemaking functions. They may not even be permitted in the kitchen while Mama presides over the stove and exercises her role as Queen Bee. Of course, tailored suits without frills and ribbons are not necessarily unfeminine. And homosexual girls do not necessarily wear severe clothes. Many, however, are not *becomingly* dressed by their mothers.

The mother of the prehomosexual girl is unconsciously envious and openly critical of her daughter. She is likely to ignore evidence of the girl's grace, but she will be eager to criticize any show of clumsiness. With such mothers, beautiful girls learn to underestimate their own attractiveness; and plain girls come to consider themselves ugly ducklings.

Fathers may behave in an openly possessive or seductive manner toward their daughters or may reject them completely. These fathers commonly side with their wives against their daughters in family disputes. They usually fail to be protective whenever the mothers are treating their daughters unfairly or destructively.

Thus, one parent (and usually both) interferes with the child's natural sex identification and in a romantic interest in the opposite sex. . . .

Homosexuals Come from a Variety of Families

Although parents are said to play a substantial role in shaping their children's development, studies published in the 1970s suggested that homosexuals hailed from a wide variety of families. This called into question earlier claims that homosexuality was caused by dysfunctional families, specifically aggressive, hypercritical mothers and rejecting or emasculating fathers. According to Dr. Lawrence J. Hatterer, a psychiatrist who evaluated more than 1,000 homosexuals, these men came from "every combination and variation of parental history that you can imagine." It remained unclear what allowed one boy to "resist strong homosexualizing influences" while another "succumbed" despite limited encouragement. For the first time in a *Times* report, a young boy's effeminate behavior was suggested as the possible cause, rather than the result, of how his parents treated him.

FEBRUARY 10, 1971
HOMOSEXUALITY: PARENTS AREN'T ALWAYS TO BLAME
By JANE E. BRODY

Scrawled in large black letters on a subway wall:

"My mother made me a homosexual."

And beneath it, in a somewhat more timid hand:

"If I get her the wool, will she make me one, too?"

The graffiti have long since been erased by whitewash, but mother remains in the public mind as the butt of the not-very-funny homosexual joke. Among professionals, however, more careful studies of the roots of homosexuality are beginning to take mother—and father—somewhat off the hook.

While a child's parents obviously play a substantial role in whatever kind of person he eventually becomes, a number of experts now say that to give parents the sole blame—or credit—for his sexual development is simplistic and misleading.

"With perhaps 20 million American men who practice some form of homosexuality," says Dr. Lawrence J. Hatterer, psychiatrist at New York Hospital's Payne Whitney Clinic, "it's inconceivable that all should have emerged from the same set of causes—the stereotype of the domineering, overprotective, feminizing mother and the weak or absent father."

Dr. Hatterer has evaluated more than 1,000 homosexual men and treated more than 200 of them in the last 15 years. He says:

"I've heard well over 10,000 life stories of homosexuals, with every combination and variation of parental history—from the most hostile, aggressive, hypercritical mother and rejecting, emasculating father to the dominating, loving, attentive father and the gentle, almost too submissive mother."

Eda LeShan, New York psychologist and expert on child rearing, believes that the psychoanalytic emphasis on how parents affect their child's sexuality has made many parents "self-conscious and uneasy."

"I have seen mothers who are hysterical with fear when their perfectly normal 4-year-old sons wanted to wear high heels, and affectionate fathers who are ashamed that they like to have their children climb into bed with them on a Sunday morning," Mrs. LeShan relates in her book, "Natural Parenthood."

"It is important to remember," she continues, "that for every aggressively seductive mother and passive or emotionally absent father whose son turns out to be a homosexual, there are other mothers and fathers with exactly the same qualities who get to be grandmas and grandpas in the traditional fashion."

Psychiatrists agree that it is by no means easy to turn a child into a homosexual, and most children seem able to resist even the worst combination of influences.

David D. is a case in point. His mother was an overpowering, overprotective, emasculating woman who clearly wore the pants in the family. His father, although physically "there," played almost no role in the boy's upbringing. The parents had frequent violent arguments.

The boy himself was pretty, overweight, clumsy, always lagging behind in physical activities, and often ridiculed by his playmates for ineptness.

Yet, through all this, his masculine self-image remained intact. Today, at the age of 26 after a number of heterosexual affairs, he is about to be married to a lovely, feminine girl.

Since cases like David's rarely come to psychiatric attention, professionals really know very little about what enables one youngster to resist strong homosexualizing influences while another succumbs to relatively innocuous forces.

At least one study indicates that a young boy's effeminate behavior (which sometimes but not always evolves into homosexuality) may be the cause, not the result, of how his parents treat him.

In a long term study of boys, most of whom first showed effeminate characteristics as early as age 2, 3 or 4, Dr. Bernard Zuger, child psychiatrist at Greenwich Hospital in Connecticut, found that the effeminate boys were no more likely than noneffeminate boys to have dominant mothers, their parents were no more likely to have wished for a girl, they were just as likely to be affectionate toward the child and there was no greater incidence of marital conflict.

Two important differences did emerge however. While the noneffeminate boy solicited his mother's attention and sympathy, the effeminate boy aligned himself with her interests and activities. He had no interest in his father's activities. In fact, a careful analysis of the family relationships indicated that it wasn't the father who rejected his son, it was the son who rejected his father.

In many cases that Dr. Hatterer and others have investigated, the parents of homosexuals have not been such bad folks, but other members of the family—such as a brother or sister the boy repeatedly lost out to or who continually bullied him, or an older relative, male or female, who consistently exploited the boy sexually—might have "homosexualized" him.

Dr. Martin Hoffman, psychiatrist at Mount Zion Medical Center in San Francisco, who summarized his study of homosexuals in a book, "The Gay World," also deplores the emphasis on parental influences.

While parent-child interactions are a "crucial factor" in the development of sexual feelings, he says, "a full explanation of any given adult's sexual patterns must take into account the vital years between the beginning of schooling and the end of adolescence. It is during these years that the individual learns a great deal about who he is, what he can and cannot do, and how his age-mates will respond to his actions."

Dr. Hoffman recalls the case of a 47-year-old business executive who had a "happy childhood," a close, satisfactory relationship with his father and a passive mother who was devoted to her husband. . . .

Gender Nonconformity Seen as Strong Predictor of Homosexuality

In the 1980s, Kinsey Institute researchers challenged traditional notions that parental role is the central cause of homosexuality, countering that sexual orientation comes from a variety of factors, including a fundamental predisposition that is probably biological in origin. After interviewing nearly 1,500 people, the scientists found no aspect of family life that appeared central to either homosexual or heterosexual development. For men, gender nonconformity (a childhood preference for girls' activities, a dislike of traditional boys' activities, and other evidence of gender nonconformity) was identified as most predictive of future homosexuality. For lesbians, gender nonconformity was the second most predictive factor, surpassed only by adolescent homosexual experience. Said project director Dr. Alan Bell, "I expect the study to be condemned from both sides—by the radical gays for even looking into the subject and by the analysts who may say we're trying to paint a glowing picture of homosexuality." Studies conducted by Dr. Bell on the topic of homosexuality would be among the first to suggest a biological basis for homosexuality, rather than a dysfunction in family life.

AUGUST 23, 1981
KINSEY STUDY FINDS HOMOSEXUALS SHOW EARLY PREDISPOSITION
By JANE E. BRODY

A major new study of homosexual men and women by the Kinsey Institute for Sex Research has found little or no support for most of the traditional theories about the origins of homosexuality.

In particular, the study of nearly 1,500 people indicates that the parents' role in a child's sexual orientation has been "grossly exaggerated," as have theories that homosexuality results from a lack of heterosexual opportunities or from traumatic heterosexual experiences.

Rather, the researchers conclude that a homosexual orientation usually seems to emerge from a fundamental predisposition, possibly biological in origin, that first appears as a failure to conform to society's stereotype of what it means to be a boy or a girl.

Research Method an Issue

The report, to be published as a book, is likely to arouse controversy not only because of its findings, which the authors expect to anger both the psychoanalytic and the homosexual communities, but also because it relies on the memories of those interviewed and on a statistical technique called path analysis that is subject to misuse and can only explore existing notions, not create new ones.

"I expect the study to be condemned from both sides—by the radical gays for even looking into the subject and by the analysts who may say we're trying to paint a glowing picture of homosexuality," said Dr. Alan Bell of the Alfred C. Kinsey Institute for Sex Research at Indiana University, who directed the project. "But we are reporting what people say, and it's all very consistent."

The institute was founded by the late Dr. Kinsey, a pioneer in sex research. Dr. John DeCecco, a psychologist at San Francisco State University who is editor of The Journal of Homosexuality, called the report "very dubious on a theoretical basis and on the basis of how reliable and valid is asking people about their childhood."

Nonetheless, others in the field, who have not yet read the report, said it was likely to be important and provocative, if only for the numbers of people interviewed and for the researchers' use of an analytical method that, its proponents say, discards spurious correlations and instead indicates what factors are likely to be truly important.

Dr. Lawrence Hatterer, a New York psychiatrist who has studied the life histories of many homosexuals, said he agreed with the Kinsey findings that sexual orientation was the result of a combination of many factors.

Path analysis, a method used to study events in natural settings where individual variables cannot be controlled, permits researchers to examine the importance of any one of a sequence of possible factors while taking all the others into account. The analysis can then show whether a particular factor is important per se or if it only works through its connections to other, more significant factors.

"No particular phenomenon of family life can be singled out, on the basis of our findings, as especially consequential for either homosexual or heterosexual development," the researchers state. "What we seem to have identified is a pattern of feelings and reactions within the child that cannot be traced back to a single social or psychological root; indeed, homosexuality may arise from a biological precursor that parents cannot control."

For homosexual men, the study showed, "gender nonconformity," which is a childhood preference for girls' activities, a dislike of boys' activities and a feeling that they were not very masculine, was the single most important factor in predicting their eventual sexual orientation. For homosexual women, gender nonconformity was the second most important predictive factor, surpassed only by homosexual involvements in adolescence.

No 'Guarantee' for Parents

"You may supply your sons with footballs and your daughters with dolls," the researchers pointed out, "but no one can guarantee that they will enjoy them. In short, to concerned parents we cannot recommend anything beyond the care, sympathy and devotion that good parents presumably lavish on all their children anyway."

They noted that gender nonconformity did not necessarily signal future homosexuality. One-fourth of the heterosexual men in the study were nonconforming as youngsters, and only a third of the heterosexual women described themselves as "highly feminine" in childhood.

The researchers concluded that "homosexuality is as deeply ingrained as heterosexuality" and that behavioral and social differences between prehomosexual and preheterosexual boys and girls "reflect or express, rather than cause," their eventual sexual preference.

Most existing ideas about the origins of homosexuality are derived from psychoanalytic and sociological theories and from studies of people who sought psychotherapy. Such patients are widely believed to represent a "biased" group that might be expected to have had abnormal childhood experiences and disturbed parental relationships.

200 Questions Asked

The new study will be published in November by Indiana University Press as "Sexual Preference: Its Development in Men and Women." The study involved interviews of three to five hours with 979 homosexuals and 477 heterosexuals living in the San Francisco Bay Area in 1969 and 1970. The participants answered 200 questions about their childhood and adolescent experiences.

The authors of the report, Dr. Bell and two sociologists, Martin S. Weinberg and Sue Kiefer Hammersmith, concede that the information they obtained may represent distorted or faulty memories of some or all of those interviewed. However, they insist that the data are closer to reality than statements made by a limited sample of patients in psychotherapy.

The findings from this retrospective study agree with those of a study that followed up boys with "gender identity disorder," meaning they are dissatisfied with being boys and prefer girls' activities and friendship. According to Dr. Richard Green, psychiatrist at State University of New York at Stony Brook, the prospective study, which he conducted, showed that such boys were more likely to become bisexual or homosexual adults than were boys with conventional boyhood behaviors.

Contrary to popular belief, the Kinsey study found that boys who grew up with dominant mothers and weak, inadequate fathers were no more likely to become homosexual than if they had had an "ideal" family setting. And although lesbians were more likely to have been raised by rejecting mothers and detached or hostile fathers, daughter-parent relationships were found to have only a weak connection to a girl's eventual sexual preference.

Small Role for Mother-Son Link

Further, the researchers found no evidence that a seductive mother-son relationship had any bearing on the development of sexual preference. An unusually close relationship between mother and son was shown to be the least important of the 15 factors found in the study to be of any significance in the development of homosexuality. And

homosexual men were as likely as heterosexuals to have identified with their mothers, the study showed.

"Our findings suggest that a mother's influences on her son's psychosexual development are not only of small magnitude, and thus much exaggerated in psychoanalytic theory, but also dependent on other, subsequent experiences if they are to have any effect at all," the researchers concluded.

A boy's relationship with his father was found to have somewhat more, but also limited, significance. Though homosexual men reported that as children they had poorer relationships with the father than did heterosexuals, this was not found to have much effect on their chances of becoming homosexuals unless many other experiences also intervened.

Dr. Irving Bieber, a New York psychoanalyst who studied the family backgrounds of 106 male homosexuals and interviewed more than a thousand others in psychiatric consultation, said the Kinsey findings were "totally disparate with the extensive experience I've had." He said that every one of the homosexuals he had interviewed had had "a disturbed relationship with his father."

Therapy May Effect Views

However, Dr. Judd Marmor, a psychiatrist at the University of Southern California in Los Angeles, said, "A rejecting and cold father is likely to produce a son who is neurotic and in need of help, regardless of whether he is homosexual or heterosexual. Overprotective, dominant mothers and distant or rejecting fathers may make neurotic sons, but they don't in themselves determine sexual preference."

In the Kinsey analysis, homosexual men who had been in psychotherapy were more likely than those who had never had therapy to describe the father as cold, detached or hostile and the mother as dominant and close-binding. The researchers suggested that therapists may "teach" their homosexual patients to view their parents in a way that conforms to existing analytic theories. However, in an interview, Dr. Bell conceded that those who have had psychotherapy may have more insights into their relationships with their parents.

In analyzing their data, the authors looked at all the variables they could find that had been prominently linked in the psychiatric and sociological literature to the development of a homosexuality. Superficially, the data seemed to support many of the existing theories. But when subjected to the more sophisticated statistical technique of path analysis, most of the apparent correlations proved to be of little or no significance in predicting the child's eventual sexual preference.

Applying path analysis to the Kinsey data, the researchers discovered these things about the emergence of a homosexual orientation in men and women:

- When compared with heterosexuals, those who became exclusive homosexuals did not have fewer heterosexual dating experiences, nor were they more likely to have been traumatized by an early heterosexual experience or seduced by an older homosexual. The main difference was that the homosexuals were less likely to have enjoyed their youthful heterosexual encounters.
- Though homosexual men tended to be less involved socially with other boys their age when they were young, isolation from peers had no independent causal connection to the development of a homosexual orientation. Rather, it seemed to reflect the fact that the prehomosexual boys felt and acted "different" from other boys.

- Homosexual males classified as effeminate, 44 percent of the sample, were far more likely to have failed to identify with their fathers than were noneffeminate homosexuals. Yet, even the noneffeminate homosexuals reported disliking boys' activities.
- Homosexual feelings almost always preceded homosexual activity by several years. For males in particular, sexual orientation was seen to evolve early in life, often before the teen years.

Pitfalls of path analysis include "the possibility that the wrong path, or sequence of factors, may be used and result in spurious correlations, and that an important variable may fail to be considered and thus be overlooked," noted Albert Klassen, a sociologist at the University of North Dakota who developed refinements on the statistical technique. However, the authors of the Kinsey study say that every conceivable factor was run through a series of preliminary analyses to determine whether it had any possible causal effects that warranted its inclusion in the final path analysis.

HORMONES SEEN AS CAUSE OF HOMOSEXUALITY

It was found in the 1970s by researchers at the Masters and Johnson Institute that gay college students had substantially lower blood levels of the male sex hormone testosterone than their heterosexual classmates. Although scientists could not conclusively say whether such differences were a cause or an effect of sexual orientation, they stated that their work indicated that homosexuality should no longer be thought of as simply a product of one's environment. They also stated that previous attempts to treat homosexuality by increasing testosterone levels were not successful, having simply increased patients' sexual drive rather than "changed its direction," the same reaction that would be expected from a similar increase of testosterone level in heterosexual men.

NOVEMBER 18, 1971
HOMOSEXUALITY LINKED TO HORMONE LEVEL
By BOYCE RENSBERGER

Researchers at the Masters and Johnson sex research institute in St. Louis have found that young men who are predominantly or exclusively homosexual generally have lower levels of the male sex hormone testosterone in their blood than do young heterosexual men.

The scientists said it could not be determined from the findings whether the hormone differences were a cause or an effect of homosexuality.

But, they agreed, the finding adds strong new evidence to a small but growing body of recent research challenging the traditional view that sexual orientation is a purely social and psychological matter.

Until recent improvements in biochemical assay methods, repeated attempts to find physiological differences between heterosexuals and homosexuals failed. Now, however, a few differences are coming to light.

The latest report, which appears in the current issue of The New England Journal of Medicine, is by Dr. Robert C. Kolodny, Julie Hendryx, and Dr. Gelson Toro, all of the Reproductive Biology Research Foundation. Dr. William H. Masters, director of the St. Louis-based foundation, also contributed to the research.

Comparison of Samplings

The findings are based on a sample of 30 male homosexual college students who were interviewed and classified according to a standard scale of the degree of homosexuality devised years ago by a pioneer sex researcher, Alfred Kinsey. They were compared with findings in a group of 50 heterosexual males of the same age.

The homosexuals were rated according to the following five-group Kinsey scale system:

- Predominantly heterosexual but more than incidentally homosexual
- Equally hetero- and homosexual
- Predominantly homosexual but more than incidentally heterosexual
- Predominantly homosexual but only incidentally heterosexual
- Exclusively homosexual.

The average concentration of testosterone in the blood of the heterosexuals was found to be 689-billionth of a gram per 100 cubic centimeters of blood.

By comparison, men who were judged to have been exclusively homosexual throughout their lives had an average of about 40 per cent as much testosterone in their blood. Men who were predominantly homosexual but who had incidental heterosexual experiences had hormone levels about 54 per cent of the heterosexual average.

Dr. Kolodny said these differences were large enough to be statistically significant.

A number of the homosexuals whose sex lives were less consistently homosexual had slightly lower than normal testosterone levels but the differences were not large enough to be significant. These groups included men who, though predominantly homosexual, had some continuing heterosexual relations and men whose orientation was equally strong in both directions.

Nine of the 15 homosexuals in the two most extreme groups also had below-normal sperm counts. Of the nine, four were totally unable to produce sperm.

"I think these findings clearly show that we can no longer think of homosexuality as purely a behavioral condition," Dr. Kolodny said. "If our work is confirmed by other researchers, then I think we can begin to look at homosexuality from a much stronger scientific basis than we have had."

Both Dr. Kolodny and Dr. Masters emphasized in an interview that their findings did not mean that hormone imbalances cause homosexuality. It may be, they said, that homosexual behavior in some way causes changes in hormone level.

They also noted that past attempts to "cure" homosexuality by administering testosterone had only increased the sex drive of the patient, not changed its direction. The hormone has the same effect on heterosexuals.

In the last year a handful of other studies have also turned up hormonal differences between homosexuals and heterosexuals.

Notable among them were a British report last November that hormonal differences were detected in the urine of three male and four female homosexuals, and a Los Angeles study last April showing subtle differences in the breakdown products of testosterone in urine of 14 homosexuals.

Although some researchers frankly concede that they are working on the hypothesis that there is a chemical cause of homosexuality, a theory advanced as far back as 1892 by the German psychiatrist Richard von Krafft-Ebing, Dr. Masters said:

"We're not suggesting this is a cause [of homosexuality], and we're not presenting a cure."

Dr. Masters said his research foundation considered homosexuality to be "a natural sexual function." He said the foundation's clinic has treated both homosexuals who wanted "to convert" to heterosexuality and homosexuals who wanted to achieve satisfactory homosexual relations.

BIOLOGY MAY PLAY ROLE IN HOMOSEXUAL DEVELOPMENT

A study conducted at State University of New York at Stony Brook in 1981 found that the hormonal response of gay men to a form of estrogen (a female hormone) landed between responses found in heterosexual men and women, indicating that homosexual and heterosexual men processed the female hormone differently. Levels of testosterone (a male hormone) initially decreased in both groups of males, but heterosexual males returned to normal rates more quickly than did homosexuals. While the results at the time still lacked corroboration through larger-scale studies, these initial findings suggested that biology may play an important role in homosexual development. However, researchers cautioned against concluding that homosexuality could be chemically corrected based on this research.

SEPTEMBER 24, 1984
HOMOSEXUAL STUDY CITES HORMONE LINK
By JANE E. BRODY

A group of homosexual men has been found to have a hormone-response pattern midway between that of heterosexual men and heterosexual women, according to a study published yesterday. The pattern suggests, but does not prove, that a biological factor may play a role in the development of homosexuality in some men.

The finding is consistent with previous research indicating that prenatal hormonal influences in mammals can affect later sexual orientation. In these earlier studies, the fetal hormone exposure led to lifelong changes in physiology and behavior.

However, since the current research was done with adults, it is not possible to tell exactly what influences throughout life may be responsible for the observed differences.

The new study, conducted at the State University of New York at Stony Brook, L.I., and reported in the current issue of the journal Science, examined the hormonal responses to the drug Premarin, a potent form of the female hormone estrogen that is often used to treat women with menopausal symptoms and uterine bleeding. Normal women given this drug early in the menstrual cycle experienced a characteristic change in the level of luteinizing hormone, or LH. Initially, the LH level in the blood fell, then rose to about double the original baseline level. In men, a different pattern was seen. An initial drop in LH occurs, followed by a gradual return to baseline.

Different Pattern in Homosexuals

However, in the homosexual men studied, an intermediate response pattern was observed. Following an initial decline in LH, there was a rise to a level about 35 percent higher than baseline. The 35 percent increase occurred in 9 of the 14 exclusively homosexual men studied, but in none of the 17 exclusively heterosexual men given the same treatment.

In the remaining five homosexual men, LH release in response to Premarin was similar to that of the heterosexual men. In none of the homosexual men was the LH response anywhere nearly as dramatic as that in the women studied.

The level of the male sex hormone, testosterone, dropped in both the heterosexual and homosexual men after the Premarin treatment. Although in both groups this level gradually returned to normal, the return to the baseline took longer in the homosexual men, probably because production of testosterone was suppressed by the higher levels of LH in this group.

Dr. Brian A. Gladue, director of the study who now heads psychoendocrinology research at North Dakota State University, said the findings indicated that "most of the homosexual men in our study are processing the estrogen differently from heterosexual men."

A Word of Caution

He cautioned, however, that such a finding, if corroborated by future research, does not mean that there is "a correctable chemical difference in the brain or else-where that makes a man gay or straight." Nor does it mean that such a hormonal response occurs in homo-sexuals under ordinary circumstances, since men are rarely exposed to potent estrogens like the one used in the study.

Dr. Gladue and his co-authors, Dr. Richard Green, a psychiatrist and expert on sexual development at Stony Brook, and Dr. Ronald E. Hellman of the South Beach Psychiatric Center in Brooklyn, also cautioned that their finding may not apply to most or even many homosexuals.

The men they studied were at the extreme of homosexual orientation: Since puberty, their sexual fantasies and activities had involved only other men. The heterosexual men were at the opposite end of the spectrum: Their fantasies and activities had been exclusively heterosexual since puberty.

"Whether a differential neuroendocrine response is present in men of less exclusive homosexual orientation is an open question," wrote the researchers, who said there was a need for future studies involving larger groups of homosexual and heterosexual men and women.

- -

Homosexual and Heterosexual Brains Found to Be Different

Research into the biology of homosexuality continued as the twentieth century came to a close. In 1991 scientists at the Salk Institute in La Jolla, California, found significant differences between heterosexual and homosexual men's hypothalamus, a region of the brain that is thought to effect sexual behavior. Specifically, Dr. Simon LeVay found that a portion of this structure in gay men is only one quarter to one half the size of the same region in heterosexual men. This discovery further reinforced scientific evidence suggesting that biological as well as environmental forces may influence sexual orientation. Noting that brain tissues from only forty-one people were examined, scientists said that if the findings were corroborated in larger studies, they would be the first to identify a distinct pattern in the brain that could help explain the cause of homosexuality. This finding could lend support to the view that homosexuality is an innate trait rather than a perverse reaction to bad upbringing, potentially leading mainstream society to greater acceptance of homosexuals. Scientists also cautioned, however, that "biology is clearly not destiny" and that both genetics and environment likely play a role in determining sexual orientation.

AUGUST 30, 1991
ZONE OF BRAIN LINKED TO MEN'S SEXUAL ORIENTATION
By NATALIE ANGIER

The brains of homosexual men are structurally different from those of heterosexual men in a region thought to influence male sexual behavior, a scientist says he has found.

The discovery, if confirmed, would be the first detection of a distinct pattern in the brain that could help explain sexual preference among men.

"The main result of this research is to show that it is possible to study sexual orientation at the biological

level," said Dr. Simon LeVay, a neurobiologist at the Salk Institute in La Jolla, Calif. "It's not just the province of the psychologists and the psychoanalysts anymore."

In the new work, Dr. LeVay reports that in homosexual men, one segment of the hypothalamus, an important structure in the forebrain, is only a quarter to a half the size of the same region in heterosexual men. Dr. LeVay's study appears in today's issue of the journal Science, which relies on evaluations of independent researchers before publication.

"It's quite a striking observation, and as far as I know it's unprecedented," said Dr. Thomas R. Insel, a behavioral neuroscientist at the National Institute of Mental Health in Rockville, Md. "Simon LeVay is a top-notch, world-class neuroanatomist, and this is a very provocative paper."

But other researchers warned that the findings are highly preliminary, and that they involve only a small number of brain tissue samples. They said the results by no means prove homosexuality is caused by a particular variation in the brain, or anywhere else in the body for that matter.

"This just points in a possible research direction," said Dr. Richard Nakamura, chief of the cognitive and behavioral neuroscience research branch at the National Institute of Mental Health. "Biology is clearly not destiny, and this shouldn't be taken to mean that you're automatically homosexual if you have a structure of one size versus a structure of another size."

Many scientists argued that even with biological differences, environment was likely to play a role in shaping and refining one's sexuality.

"The consensus in the scientific community is that it's likely to be a combination" of inborn factors and environmental influence, said Dr. Nakamura. "I think most of us hope that not too much is made of this or any single finding."

Gay Men, Heterosexual Women

The size of the region studied by Dr. LeVay is roughly equal in gay men to that in heterosexual women, and in each case the area is often so tiny as to be essentially non-existent.

Dr. LeVay proposes that the hypothalamic segment could be responsible for inspiring males to seek females, and that its absence in men would be one possible element predisposing them toward homosexuality.

In studies of male rats and monkeys, researchers have found that injury to this portion of the brain causes males to lose interest in females while continuing to express sexual vigor by such activities as masturbation.

But Dr. LeVay and many other researchers emphasize that the results remain to be confirmed in follow-up studies. And even if definitively proved, they said the brain discrepancy is likely to be only a small part of the story of how male sexuality unfolds.

"I think this work is very interesting and very important," said Dr. Sandra F. Witelson, a behavioral neuroscientist at McMaster University in Hamilton, Ontario. "But it doesn't mean that other anatomical differences aren't also present. I'm sure additional biological factors, perhaps related to hormones, will also be found."

Dr. LeVay also said it was not yet known if the difference arises during the development of the brain, or whether a man's homosexual preferences could somehow influence the contours of certain neural pathways later in life. If that were the case, he said, his finding would be a mere consequence of homosexuality, rather than one of its possible causes.

"It's axiomatic that sexual orientation is going to be represented in the brain somewhere," said Dr. John Money, a professor emeritus at Johns Hopkins School of Medicine in Baltimore who has long studied the origins of sexual behavior. "The really interesting questions are when did it happen and how did it get there?"

Dr. LeVay believes the variation in hypothalamic size probably arises during the growth of the fetus. But whether that alteration is caused by genetic programming that is hardwired into the baby's DNA, he said, or by fluctuations during pregnancy of critical hormones known to affect fetal brain development, remains a mystery.

AIDS Question Raised

Other caveats of the new report abound. The gay men whose brain samples were examined all died of AIDS, a disease that infiltrates the central nervous system. But Dr. LeVay said that factor was unlikely to account for the discrepancy observed in the hypothalamus because six of the men presumed to have been heterosexual also died of AIDS, contracted as a result of intravenous drug use. Nevertheless, these men had hypothalamic structures several times the size of those in gay men, he said.

In December researchers from Amsterdam reported that they had found differences between homosexual and heterosexual men in a part of the brain, the superchiasmic antenucleus, that is near the region examined by Dr. LeVay. In that finding the scientists said the area was twice as large in the homosexual brains.

But other scientists said it was unlikely that the structural discrepancy previously reported could explain sexual orientation because the superchiasmic antenucleus controls circadian rhythms—telling the body what time it is—rather than sexual behavior.

Although nobody can predict the political and socio-logical implications of the recent discoveries if they are confirmed, Dr. LeVay and others said that if homosexuality is viewed as something innate, rather than, say, a perverted reaction to a bad upbringing, then homosexuals may be more easily accepted by mainstream society.

"The gay community has worked very hard and long to persuade psychiatrists that this shouldn't fall into the category of a mental illness," said Dr. Ingeborg L. Ward, professor of psychology at Villanova University, near Philadelphia. "This would provide possible scientific basis for that viewpoint."

"They say their sexual personality is something very deeply ingrained in them," he said, "so they're not surprised to be told there are structural differences in the brain."

In the new research, Dr. LeVay examined thin slices of autopsied brain tissue from 19 homosexual men, 16 presumed heterosexual men and six women also thought to have been heterosexual. The average age at the time of death for all three groups was about 40, and thus the brains had not yet undergone the profound changes known to be associated with age.

He focused on a particular segment of the hypothalamus known as the third interstitial nucleus of the anterior hypothalamus, which previous studies had shown to differ significantly between men and women.

Confirming the results of that study, Dr. LeVay measured the volume of cells in that region of the brain and found that in the heterosexual men it averaged about the size of a large grain of sand, while in the women it was almost indetectable. In the new study he found that in gay men, as in women, the region was almost nonexistent.

"Perhaps there are a few cells lying around, but there's nothing like a recognizable cluster," he said.

Although the region is tiny, the discrepancy between heterosexuals and homosexuals is significant.

"Most of us who look at the influence of the brain on behavior work at the molecular level," said Dr. Insel. "But this is a rather gross anatomical difference, and that's a dramatic finding."

Dr. Ward said the finding fits in logically with what is known about the development of the central nervous system. The brain is thought to be basically female, and to require the influence of the male hormone, testosterone, generated by a male fetus's testes, to develop a masculine structure. With a masculinized brain, the animal will later display standard behavior, including a lust for ovulating females.

Male rats that are exposed to testosterone blockers during fetal development will emerge from the womb with characteristically feminine brains, including in the region that corresponds to the anterior hypothalamus in humans. The affected animals fail to engage in rough and tumble play as pups, and as adults they refuse to mount either females or other males, as ordinary male rats will do routinely.

Whether or not homosexuality in men is caused by fluctuating testosterone concentrations during fetal development remains unknown.

In follow-up studies, Dr. LeVay plans to see whether the anterior hypothalamus differs between heterosexual women and lesbians. If the theory is correct that the region sparks an innate attraction for women, he said, then the hypothalamic structure should be as large in lesbians as it is in heterosexual men.

- -

Twin Studies Suggest Genetic Basis for Homosexuality

A study of gay identical twins conducted at Northwestern University provided strong evidence for the view that homosexuality has a genetic basis. Researchers studied 167 sets of twins, finding that 52 percent of identical twin brothers of gay men were also gay, while 22 percent of fraternal twins were both gay, and only 11 percent of adopted brothers were both gay, a pattern that supports the view that genetics plays a role in sexual orientation. Noting that other factors such as social conditioning also could be important, researchers estimated that genetics could account for up to 70 percent of sexual orientation. While earlier studies had suggested a genetic component to sexual orientation, Dr. Gregory Carey at the University of Colorado claimed that this work "really sort of clinches it."

DECEMBER 17, 1991
GAY MEN IN TWIN STUDY

A new study of twins provides the strongest evidence yet that homosexuality has a genetic basis, researchers say, though they say other factors like social conditioning may be important.

The study, published in the December issue of The Archives of General Psychiatry, adds to evidence that sexual orientation does not result from a maladjustment or moral defect, one author said.

"We found 52 percent of identical twin brothers of gay men also were gay, compared with 22 percent of fraternal twins, compared with 11 percent of genetically unrelated brothers," said J. Michael Bailey, an assistant professor of psychology at Northwestern University in Evanston, "which is exactly the kind of pattern you would want to see if something genetic were going on." By "unrelated," Dr. Bailey was referring to brothers by adoption.

"The genetically most similar brothers were also the ones most likely to be gay, by a large margin," he added.

The study examined 56 identical twins, 54 fraternal twins and 57 adoptive brothers recruited through advertisements in gay-interest publications.

Identical twins are genetic clones, having developed in the womb from a single egg that split after being fertilized by a single sperm. Fraternal twins develop simultaneously from two separate eggs fertilized by two separate sperm cells, making them only as similar as non-twin siblings.

"This is the first real genetic study of sexual orientation in about 40 years," said Dr. Bailey, whose co-author was Dr. Richard C. Pillard, a psychiatry professor at Boston University School of Medicine.

Dr. Bailey estimated that the degree of the genetic contribution to homosexuality could range from 30 percent to more than 70 percent, depending on varying assumptions about the prevalence of homosexuality and how well the sample represents twins in the general population.

Gregory Carey, an assistant professor of psychology at the University of Colorado, called the work very important. "I'm not terribly surprised at the conclusions," he said. "I think they're very well founded. Some of the earlier evidence suggested there was genetic effect, but the studies were not well done. This is something that really sort of clinches it."

• •

IS THERE A GAY GENE?

A study published in the influential journal Science in 1993 found that a gene or set of genes on one part of the X chromosome could play a role in predisposing some men toward homosexuality. Forty pairs of gay brothers were studied, 33 of whom had identical chromosomal markers on the end of the X chromosome, well more than statistical probability would suggest. Noting the complexity of sexual orientation, researchers cautioned that they had not found a "gay gene" that would singularly predict sexuality, arguing that homosexuality was likely the result of the interaction of a number of factors including genes, the brain, and environment. While some scientists lauded the report's cautionary tone, Dr. Simon LeVay, chairman of the Institute of Gay and Lesbian Education, stated that it was the most important study about sexual orientation to date, saying "For so long people have been thinking there is some genetic element for sexual orientation and this is by far and away the most direct evidence there has been."

Some legal experts suggested that evidence that sexual orientation is innate might lead courts to overturn laws that discriminate against gays. However, others cautioned that the research could be used by some to attempt to cure or eliminate homosexuality through genetic therapy or selection. Ironically, since a child's X chromosome is provided by the female parent, this research lends some credibility to early claims that mothers are the cause of homosexuality, albeit genetically rather than as the result of a particular style of parenting.

JULY 16, 1993
REPORT SUGGESTS HOMOSEXUALITY IS LINKED TO GENES

By NATALIE ANGIER

Ushering the politically explosive study of the origins of sexual orientation into a new and perhaps more scientifically rigorous phase, researchers report that they have linked male homosexuality to a small region of one human chromosome.

The results have yet to be confirmed by other laboratories, and the chromosomal region implicated, if it holds up under further scrutiny, is almost surely just a single chapter in the intricate story of sexual orientation and behavior. Nevertheless, scientists said the work suggests that one or several genes located on the bottom half of the sausage-shaped X chromosome may play a role in predisposing some men toward homosexuality. (The researchers have begun a similar study looking at the chromosomes of lesbians.)

The findings, which appear today in the journal Science, indicate that sexual orientation often is at least partly inborn, rather than being solely a matter of choice. But researchers warn against overinterpreting the work, or in taking it to mean anything as simplistic as that the "gay gene" had been found.

The researchers emphasized that they do not yet have a gene isolated, but merely know the rough location of where the gene or genes may sit amid the vast welter of human DNA. Until they have the gene proper, scientists said they had no way of knowing how it contributes to sexual orientation, how many people carry it, or how often carriers are likely to become gay as a result of bearing the gene.

And even when they do have this gene on the X chromosome pinpointed, scientists said they will continue to search for other genes on other chromosomes that may be involved in sexual orientation.

"Sexual orientation is too complex to be determined by a single gene," said Dr. Dean H. Hamer of the National Cancer Institute in Bethesda, Md., the lead author on the new report. "The main value of this work is that it opens a window into understanding how genes, the brain and the environment interact to mold human behavior."

In the new work, the scientists studied the genetic material from 40 pairs of gay brothers and found that in 33 of the pairs, the brothers had identical pieces of the end tip of the X chromosome. Under ordinary circumstances ruled by chance alone, only half of the pairs should have shared that chromosomal neighborhood in common, a region designated Xq28. The odds of Dr. Hamer's results turning up randomly are less than half a percent, indicating that the chromosomal tip likely harbors a genetic sequence linked to the onset of the brothers' homosexuality.

Passed Through Maternal Line

In men, the X chromosome pairs with the Y chromosome to form the so-called sex chromosomes, the final set of the 23 pairs of chromosomes found in all cells of the human body. A man's X chromosome is always inherited from the mother, who bestows on her son a reshuffled version of one of her two copies of the X chromosome. The latest results indicate that the newly reported genetic factor is passed through the maternal line, a curious twist given that in the past psychiatry has held women at least partly responsible for fostering their sons' homosexuality.

The gene could work by directly influencing sexual proclivity, perhaps by shaping parts of the brain that orchestrate sexual behavior. Or it might affect temperament in a way that predisposes a boy toward homosexuality. At the moment, researchers said, all scenarios are mere speculation.

Despite the cautionary notes, the latest study is likely to add fuel to the debate over gay rights in the military and civilian realms.

If homosexuality is shown to be largely inborn, a number of legal experts say, then policies that in any way discriminate against homosexuals are likely to be shot down in the courts.

"We think this study is very important," said Gregory J. King, a spokesman for the Human Rights Campaign Fund in Washington, the largest national lesbian and gay lobbying group. "Fundamentally it increases our understanding of the origins of sexual orientation, and at the same time we believe it will help increase public support for lesbian and gay rights."

Not all gay rights leaders have a sanguine view of the work. Some denounce it as yet another attempt to draw a reductionist and implacable line between homosexuality and heterosexuality, while others see in it the dangers of attempts to "fix" homosexuality, perhaps through gene therapy.

"I don't think it's an interesting study," said Darrell Yates Rist, co-founder of the Gay and Lesbian Alliance Against Defamation. "Intellectually, what do we gain by finding out there's a homosexual gene? Nothing, except an attempt to identify those people who have it and then open them up to all sorts of experimentation to change them."

The study appears in the same journal that two years ago unleashed a furious debate when it published a report asserting to have found an anatomical difference between the brains of gay and straight men. Other recent reports have also weighed in on the possible biological basis of homosexuality in both men and women, and all have been subjected to volleys of scientific and political attack.

Other attempts to make a genetic link to behavior, like alcoholism, manic depression and schizophrenia, have thus far all been disappointing. By contrast, today's study is considered to be impressive science even by many who denounced the previous studies.

'Merits Being Followed Up'

"It's a good piece of work," said Dr. Anne Fausto-Sterling of Brown University, a geneticist who has been one of the most outspoken critics of the genetic studies of human behavior. "Hamer is appropriately cautious about the meanings you can glean from it, and he admits that there may be more than one path to the endpoint of homosexuality."

Dr. Eric Lander of the Whitehead Institute for Biomedical Research in Cambridge, Mass., said, "From a geneticist's point of view, if you strip away the nonscientific considerations, it's an interesting finding that merits being followed up in a larger sample."

Dr. Simon LeVay, chairman of the Institute of Gay and Lesbian Studies in West Hollywood, Calif., who did the 1991 study comparing gay and heterosexual brains, was considerably more ecstatic in his appraisal of the latest report.

"For so long people have been thinking there is some genetic element for sexual orientation and this is by far and away the most direct evidence there has been," Dr. LeVay said. "It's the most important scientific finding ever made in sexual orientation."

In the latest experiments, the researchers began by taking the family histories of 114 men who identified themselves as homosexual. Much to their surprise, the researchers discovered a higher than expected number of gay men among the men's maternal uncles and male cousins who were the sons of their mothers' sisters. The ratio was far higher than for men in the general population, suggesting a gene or genes that are passed through the maternal line and thus through the X chromosome.

The scientists then focused on gay brothers, on the assumption that if two boys in a family are homosexual, they were more likely to be so for genetic reasons than were those homosexual men without gay brothers. Using a well-known genetic technique called linkage mapping, they scrutinized the X chromosome in the brothers and other relatives by the application of DNA markers, tiny bits of genetic material that can distinguish between chromosomes from different people. The researchers found that more than three-quarters of the brothers had inherited identical DNA markers on the Xq28 region of the chromosome.

"I was surprised at how easy this was to detect," Dr. Hamer said. "Part of that ease was because we were working with the X chromosome," the most extensively studied chromosome in the human genetic blueprint. So far the study has been limited to men who said they were gay, eliminating the ambiguity that would come from considering the genes of men who called themselves heterosexual.

Nonetheless, the region is about four million bases, or DNA building blocks long, and hence holds hundreds of genes, meaning the scientists have much work ahead of them to sort out which gene or genes are relevant. The researchers are also trying to perform a similar linkage study on lesbian sisters, but so far they have not managed to find a chromosomal region that is consistently passed along in families.

Is There a Lesbian Ear?

A study published in *The Proceedings of the National Academy of Sciences* found that the cochlea, or inner ear, of lesbians works more like that of men than of straight women, suggesting a biological difference between heterosexual and homosexual women. Research participants were broken down into four groups; lesbians, gay men, heterosexual men, and heterosexual women. Although the women were generally found to be more sensitive to very soft sounds than were the men, the lesbian participants demonstrated less ability to respond to these sounds than did heterosexual women. Because androgens affect the development of the inner ear before birth, scientists theorize that, in addition to "masculinizing" lesbians' cochlea, they may also alter the region of the brain related to sexual orientation.

MARCH 3, 1998
LINK TO LESBIANISM FOUND

Researchers say they have found the first strong evidence of a physical difference between lesbians and heterosexual women, a finding that the inner ears of gay women work more like those of men.

In the study to be published on Tuesday in The Proceedings of the National Academy of Sciences, researchers at the University of Texas, Austin, said they measured the function of the cochlea, a key sound amplifier in the inner ear, said Dr. Dennis McFadden, a professor of experimental psychology. Lesbians had less sensitive cochlea amplifiers than heterosexual women. But women over all have a better ability to detect very soft sounds than men.

Development of the inner ear is affected before birth by androgens. "Their auditory centers have been masculinized and the presumption is that so have the sites in the brain that direct sexual preference," said Dr. McFadden, the lead author of the study. Androgens, he said, may also "alter the brain centers that produce sexual orientation."

To test for differences between the sexes, the researchers studied more than 200 adults divided into four groups: lesbians, gay men, and heterosexual women and men.

Johns Hopkins Becomes First American Hospital to Endorse Sex Reassignment Surgery

At a time when many hospital boards refused to allow sex reassignment surgeries on moral and ethical grounds, Johns Hopkins Hospital performed two of these operations in 1966 and established a gender identity clinic to screen additional prospective candidates for surgery. Such procedures had been performed in Europe for many years and occasionally in the United States, but Johns Hopkins was the first American hospital to officially endorse the controversial surgery. This endorsement by a prestigious institution led other hospitals to make similar changes to their policies. Identified as transsexuals, individuals requesting this surgery were often described as feeling like women trapped in men's bodies or men trapped in women's bodies as distinguished from transvestites, who enjoy wearing the clothes of the opposite sex but do not wish to change their gender. To be considered for surgery, an individual must be deemed mentally stable, demonstrate an understanding of the transsexual condition, be currently living as a member of the opposite sex and receiving appropriate hormone therapy. The

Johns Hopkins clinic screens two patients a month and reports a long waiting list. Roughly 10 percent of the 100 or so applicants for surgery are women seeking to become men.

Of the over 2,000 sex reassignment surgeries performed throughout the world until this time, roughly 500 involved U.S. citizens, with Christine Jorgensen being perhaps the most famous. Named George Jorgensen Jr. at birth, the 26-year-old American citizen traveled to Denmark in the early 1950s to undergo a two-year course of treatment involving hormone therapy and surgery. The Harry Benjamin Foundation has referred many of the surgery candidates to the Hopkins program. Dr. Benjamin was an endocrinologist who studied and treated transsexuals for fifteen years, persistently arguing that transsexualism is a distinct medical phenomenon. His work was supported by the Erickson Educational Foundation, which also underwrote the cost of transsexual research at Johns Hopkins and which was founded by Reed Erickson, an independently wealthy consulting engineer.

Experienced psychiatrists described transsexuals at that time as "shockingly normal except for that one area," and none of the surgical subjects expressed postprocedure regrets. Some, but not all, were able to obtain birth certificates with their new sex status, thus obviating the danger of arrest for cross-dressing, an illegal behavior in many localities at the time. After surgery, most were able to experience sexual pleasure, some to the point of orgasm, although surgeons remained unable to create functioning male genitals.

NOVEMBER 21, 1966
A CHANGING OF SEX BY SURGERY AT JOHNS HOPKINS
By THOMAS BUCKLEY

The Johns Hopkins Hospital has quietly begun performing sex change surgery.

The Baltimore hospital, one of the most eminent teaching and research institutions in the country, has also established a "gender identity clinic," staffed by a special committee of psychiatrists, surgeons and other specialists, to screen applicants for the operation.

Although the controversial surgery has been performed in many European countries in the last 15 years and by a few surgeons in this country, Johns Hopkins is the first American hospital to give it official support.

Two operations approved by the committee of specialists have already been performed, the first last September and the second last month. Both subjects were males, one white and one Negro, in their 20's. They are said to be recovering satisfactorily.

In the male-to-female operation, which takes three and a half to four hours, the external genitals are removed and a vaginal passage created.

Female hormone treatments before and after surgery gradually reduce secondary male sexual characteristics such as body hair and enhance feminine appearance through breast development and the widening of the hips.

About 10 per cent of the 100 applications received by the hospital have been from women, on whom a transformation operation can also be performed.

The men and women who seek sex change surgery are called transsexuals. They are almost always physically normal, but they have a total aversion to their biological sex that dates from early childhood. They have the apparently unshakeable conviction that they are either female beings trapped in a male body or males trapped in a female body.

Desire Is for Acceptance

The overriding desire in the case of men is to be accepted as women. For this reason, psychiatrists believe, they are often sexually inactive before surgery because of their distaste for homosexual relationships.

Although transsexuals frequently assume the identity of the opposite sex without surgery, they are distinguished from transvestites, who derive pleasure from wearing the clothing of the opposite sex but have no desire for a sex change.

While opinion is not unanimous, many leading psychiatrists and psychoanalysts who have examined transsexuals believe that they cannot be helped by psychotherapy. Such persons, moreover, are regarded as prone to mental breakdown and depression, suicide and, occasionally, self-mutilation.

Dr. John E. Hoopes, a plastic surgeon who is chairman of the Johns Hopkins committee, said last week:

"After exhaustively reviewing the available literature and discussing the problem with people knowledgeable in this area, I arrived at the unavoidable conclusion that these people need and deserve help."

Transsexualism is thought to be relatively rare and far more frequent in men than in women. Dr. Hoopes said transsexuals in this country probably numbered in the thousands.

2,000 Have Operation

About 2,000 persons have undergone sex change surgery. Of these, perhaps 500 are from the United States. The best known is probably Christine Jorgensen, formerly George Jorgensen, who was operated on in Copenhagen, Denmark, in 1952 and has since become a night-club performer and actress.

Virtually all the operations have been performed in Europe, Morocco, Japan and Mexico. A few surgeons have performed the operation in this country, probably not more than a dozen times in all, but many hospital boards have refused to permit it.

Experts in the field believe that the Johns Hopkins decision that the surgery does not violate legal restrictions on mutilation or ethical or moral codes will lead to its being performed at other hospitals in the United States.

The Johns Hopkins committee was formed a year ago. After preliminary studies, it began accepting applications for surgery in July. Most of its patients have been referred to it by the Harry Benjamin Foundation here.

The foundation is headed by Dr. Harry Benjamin, an endocrinologist, who has been studying and treating transsexuals, often without charge, for the last 15 years.

Benjamin Leads Fight

Dr. Benjamin has led the fight to have these persons regarded as a distinct medical phenomenon and coined

the term transsexual to describe them. Earlier this year he published a book, "The Transsexual Phenomenon."

His work is supported by the Erickson Educational Foundation of Baton Rouge, La., which also pays the cost of transsexual research at Johns Hopkins. The foundation, headed by Reed Erickson, also supports research in air pollution and human resources. Mr. Erickson is a consulting engineer of independent wealth.

The Johns Hopkins clinic examines only two patients a month. There already is a long waiting list. Applicants receive a thorough physical and mental examination from the committee, which costs $100. Only those who show no signs of psychosis and appear to have a degree of insight into their condition are accepted.

To reduce the chance of poor adjustment to the new sex after surgery, the committee considers only subjects who are already living entirely as women and receiving female hormones.

A number of psychiatrists familiar with the subject regard the majority of transsexuals as emotionally normal except for their gender confusion, which leads to intense feelings of frustration.

"It flies in the face of everything I believed when I began," said a Los Angeles psychiatrist-psychoanalyst, who has done considerable research in the field. "They are shockingly normal except for that one area."

After surgery and about two weeks of hospital care, the overall cost of which averages about $1,500, the patient is asked to be available for further study at the hospital. Also, for a former male, for example, to retain external female characteristics, he must continue receiving female hormones.

"This program, including the surgery, is investigational," Dr. Hoopes said. "The most important result of our efforts will be to determine precisely what constitutes a transsexual and what makes him remain that way.

"Medicine needs a sound means of alleviating the problems of gender identification and of fostering public understanding of these extremely unfortunate individuals. It is too early in the program to be either optimistic or pessimistic."

Origins Uncertain

The origins of transsexualism are not yet certain. No organic basis for the condition has been found, but research is continuing into the possibility that it may be at least partly due to heredity or abnormal glandular functions before birth.

Psychiatrists believe that transsexualism is caused by prolonged conditioning early in life, perhaps within the first three years. Some cases, in which a mother wanted a daughter instead of a son and raised her child accordingly, seem obvious, but the origin of others is obscure.

By means of the family histories that it takes from transsexuals, the Johns Hopkins committee, as well as the Benjamin Foundation, hopes to shed new light on the problem. Similar investigations, although without surgery, are also being carried on at the University of California at Los Angeles Medical Center.

There appear to be no known cases in which the subject of sex transformation surgery has expressed regrets later. Nor do there seem to be many cases of serious postoperative complications. Relatively few subjects of the surgery, such as Miss Jorgensen, become well known; most seem content to disappear into the general population.

"The adjustment that most of them make is truly amazing," said Dr. Benjamin, who has studied more than 60 subjects of the surgery.

"They find useful jobs, many for the first time, and abject misery is transformed into happiness. Others require psychological guidance and counseling."

Many males who were operated on have obtained new birth certificates giving their sex as female, thus freeing themselves from the possibility of arrest as transvestites. State laws and procedures, however, differ widely.

A large number have also married, in some cases to men who are unaware of their previous life. The use of the sensitive skin of the penis to line the vaginal passage permits the subjects to have ostensibly normal sexual relations, although they cannot have children.

Some have reported experiencing orgasms. In the case of women who wish to become men, the transformation surgery includes a hysterectomy and breast removal. Attempts to create functioning male genitals have not yet been successful.

The members of the Johns Hopkins committee, in addition to Dr. Hoopes, are Dr. Milton T. Edgerton, professor and plastic surgeon-in-charge; Dr. Howard W. Jones Jr., associate professor of gynecology and obstetrics; Dr. Norman J. Knorr, assistant professor of psychiatry and plastic surgery, and Dr. Claude J. Migeon, associate professor of pediatrics.

Also, Dr. John W. Money, associate professor of medical psychology and pediatrics; Dr. Eugene Meyer, professor of psychiatry; Dr. Horst K. Schirmer, associate professor of urology, and Dr. Sanford Wolf, instructor in psychiatry.

· ·

COURT RULES MALE-TO-FEMALE TRANSSEXUAL CAN PLAY IN U.S. OPEN TENNIS TOURNAMENT

A court ruled that male-to-female transsexual Renee Richards had the right to attempt to qualify for the 1977 U.S. Open tennis championships as a woman, despite failing to pass a sex chromosome test. The chromosome test, called the Barr test, has been a medical requirement for females competing in the Olympics since 1968, but it was adopted by the U.S. Open only after Richards applied to play in the tournament last year. Citing overwhelming evidence that Richards is now a female and ruling under the New York State Human Rights Law, Judge Alfred Ascione said that it would be "grossly unfair, discriminatory, and inequitable" to use a test adopted solely to exclude Richards from play. The United States Tennis Association and the World Tennis Association countered that they adopted the test to prevent fraud, or men posing as women unfairly competing against women. Richards, an ophthalmologist formerly known as Richard Raskind, underwent sex reassignment surgery in 1975.

AUGUST 17, 1977
RENEE RICHARDS RULED ELIGIBLE FOR U.S. OPEN
By NEIL AMDUR

Dr. Renee Richards has won the right to qualify for the United States Open tennis championships without passing a sex chromosome test.

State Supreme Court Justice Alfred M. Ascione issued a preliminary injunction yesterday barring the United States Tennis Association, the United States Open Tennis Championship Committee and the Women's Tennis Association from excluding the 42-year-old transsexual from the world's richest tournament because of her inability to pass the Barr body test.

In a 13-page decision that could become a landmark, Ascione said the requirement that Dr. Richards pass the test in order to become eligible for the United States Open was "grossly unfair, discriminatory and inequitable, and violative of her rights under the Human Rights Law of this state."

Ascione also criticized the defendants for adopting the sex test for women players last year after Dr. Richards had filed an entry for the United States Open.

"It seems clear that defendants knowingly instituted this test for the sole purpose of preventing plaintiff from participating in the tournament," he wrote. "The only justification for using a sex-determination test in athletic competition is to prevent fraud, i.e., men masquerading as women competing against women."

Lawyers for the U.S.T.A. and the W.T.A. said they would review the decision before deciding whether to file an appeal. The women's qualifying event for the United States Open will begin Aug. 25.

Sources close to the U.S.T.A. believe the association may not contest Dr. Richards's right to play this year and then appeal yesterday's court decision at a later date. The U.S.T.A. concern, according to sources, is more over the long-range implications of transsexuals in women's tennis than the threat of a player who is probably past her prime as a professional.

The ruling capped a year-long struggle for acceptance by Dr. Richards, a New York ophthalmologist who, as Richard Raskind, underwent a sex-change operation in 1975. Ascione made reference to this in a section of his decision, which was unusually long for a preliminary injunction.

"When an individual such as plaintiff, a successful, physician, a husband and father, finds it necessary for his own mental sanity to undergo a sex reassignment," Ascione wrote, "the unfounded fears and misconceptions of defendants must give way to the overwhelming medical evidence that this person is now female."

"I feel ecstatic, I can't believe it," Dr. Richards said when informed of the ruling. "It's really a vindication of everything I've tried to prove in the last year. Whether I win the tournament doesn't mean anything in the long run."

PREGNANT MAN BLURS GENDER ROLES

Being an expectant father is not usually considered newsworthy, but a media frenzy erupted around Thomas Beatie because he was the one who was about to give birth. Born a woman, Mr. Beatie has had his chest and clitoris surgically altered as well as bimonthly testosterone shots to stimulate the development of male secondary sex characteristics (such as beard growth). Like many transmen, however, he does not have a penis and did not choose to have his female reproductive organs removed. As a result, once he ceased receiving hormone therapy, Mr. Beatie was able to use frozen sperm to conceive a baby girl and carry her to term.

According to Mara Kiesling, director of the National Center for Transgender Equality, "There's nothing really remarkable" about this situation, which drew attention to the increasingly fluid nature of gender made possible by changes in law, social mores, and technology.

For Eve Kosofsky Sedgwick, a professor at the City University of New York who has written extensively on gender, Beatie's decision to go public with the details of his story publicized the reality that anatomy isn't necessarily what defines a man or woman and that changing one's sex "isn't about getting a penis or losing a penis." Web postings related to the Beatie pregnancy suggested that many people remained confused and fearful about transgender issues and, according to Sedgwick, may need to go through various stages before they are able to accept and understand. She argued, "People experience gender very differently and some have really individual and imaginative uses to make of it. That's an important thing for people to wrap their minds around."

JUNE 22, 2008
HE'S PREGNANT, YOU'RE SPEECHLESS
By GUY TREBAY

When Thomas Beatie gives birth in the next few weeks to a baby girl, the blessed event will mark both a personal milestone and a strange and wondrous crossroads in the evolution of American pop culture.

Mr. Beatie—as anyone who has turned on a television, linked to a blog or picked up a tabloid in the last few months is aware—is a married 34-year-old man, born a woman, who managed to impregnate himself last year using frozen sperm and who went public this spring as the nation's first "pregnant father."

That this story attracted attention around the world was hardly surprising. Who, after all, could resist the image of a shirtless Madonna, with a ripe belly on a body lacking breasts and with a square jaw unmistakably fringed by a beard? For a time, clips of Mr. Beatie's appearance on "Oprah," where he was filmed undergoing ultrasound, as well as shirtless images of him from an autobiographical feature in the Advocate magazine, were everywhere, and they were impossible to look away from.

Partly a carnival sideshow and partly a glimpse at shifting sexual tectonics, his image and story powered past traditional definitions of gender and exposed a realm that seemed more than passing strange to some observers—and altogether natural to those who inhabit it.

"This is just a neat human-interest story about a particular couple using the reproductive capabilities they have," said Mara Kiesling, director of the National Center for Transgender Equality in Washington. "There's really nothing remarkable" about the Beatie pregnancy, she said.

Yet as the first pregnant transman to go public, Mr. Beatie has exposed a mass audience to alterations in the outlines of gender that may be outpacing our comprehension. In the discussions that followed his announcement, what became poignantly clear is that there is no good language yet to discuss his situation, words like an all-purpose pronoun to describe an idea as complex as a pregnant man.

"When there's a lot of fascination around a figure like Thomas Beatie," said Judith Halberstam, a professor of English and gender studies at the University of Southern California, "it points to other changes already happening elsewhere in the culture."

Among the changes Ms. Halberstam noted are medical innovations that have expanded the possibilities for body modification. There are also studies that indicate, as Ms. Halberstam noted, that women respond sexually to the individual, before differentiating by sex. And the broadening legal scope of marriage has also had its effects on people like Mr. Beatie, who says of himself, "I am transgender, legally male, and legally married to Nancy," but who might have trouble holding on to some of those assertions if he did something as simple as moving from Oregon.

Americans, Ms. Halberstam said, have long been fascinated by narratives of sexual transformation, at least since the era of Christine Jorgensen, an early male-to-female transsexual (born George Jorgensen Jr. in the Bronx) whose sex change, performed by doctors in Denmark, prompted The Daily News to run a front page story under the headline "Ex-GI Becomes Blonde Beauty" and made Miss Jorgensen as tabloid-notorious then as Mr. Beatie is, the man who "went abroad and came back a broad."

The Jorgensen case in 1951 was treated as groundbreaking, just as Mr. Beatie's was on "Oprah," despite the well-established fact that physicians at the German Institute of Sexual Science had performed successful sexual reassignment surgeries decades before. If Miss Jorgensen's story prefigured Mr. Beatie's, it also pointed toward a future in which gender continues to change in response to changing laws and mores and, as important, new technology.

"The Beatie case seems like a way of having some of the Trans 101 discussions publicly, giving them one kind of a face and doing it in a way that's not asking anybody for anything," said Eve Kosofsky Sedgwick, a professor at the City University of New York graduate school of English who has written extensively on gender. "He's pregnant, he seems happy. It's not happening in any kind of a judicial, let alone criminal, context so it's not a matter of claiming a right. It's a matter of exercising one."

By bringing his story to the public and disclosing the particulars of his anatomical journey, Ms. Sedgwick added, Mr. Beatie is "making visible the fact that a lot of people's experience of making these decisions isn't about getting a penis or losing a penis." For many transgender people, she said, "genital surgery is not what defines gender, and that will be news for lots and lots of Americans," who may have trouble comprehending the idea that for some, anatomy does not define woman or man.

Mr. Beatie does not have a penis; his clitoris was surgically reconfigured to mimic a phallus. And the person born in Hawaii in 1974 as Tracy Lagondino also altered his body with chest reconstruction surgery, took bimonthly testosterone injections for years to suppress feminine sex characteristics, grew a beard and saw his hairline change. Like many transmen, he chose not to remove his female reproductive organs. And so, when it was clear that his wife could not have another child (she has two grown daughters from a previous relationship), Mr. Beatie stopped hormone therapy until he could conceive.

"Not a lot of transmen get what's called 'bottom' or 'lower' surgery," Ms. Halberstam explained, referring to procedures like the one Mr. Beatie had, and to yet more radical interventions like hysterectomy. "If they want a penis, they don't want a micro-penis," she said. If what they want is to be men, she added, they see no reason why that goal is compromised by keeping their ovaries.

Issues like these have made Mr. Beatie's story so compelling; the sense that trans identity in the Webster sense of the prefix signifies some threshold state of being— "across" or "beyond" or "through."

Ms. Sedgwick said that if you look at postings on Web sites like Oprah Winfrey's and The Huffington Post, "It seems as though there are lots and lots of comments saying: 'That's not a man having a baby. That's a woman having a baby.' "

Partly that reaction results from what Ms. Sedgwick calls a phobic response to changes in identities that for most people seem God-given and settled at birth. Partly it is a matter "of people having to go through the stages of figuring things out," she said.

As Ms. Kiesling, of the National Center for Transgender Equality, noted: "The long-term benefit of this story is not 'Pregnant Man Trims Hedge,' " referring to a widely circulated photo of a bearded and pregnant Mr. Beatie wielding a power tool. "The Beatie story raises questions we're all looking at now, in a lot of contexts," about the welter of new possibilities produced by a landscape in which legalized same-sex partnerships reshape traditional ideas about husband and wife and mom and dad.

Contacted at home in Bend, Ore., Mr. Beatie declined to comment for this article. He was resting, he said, and would reserve further comment until after the baby is born. A book that he was contracted to write has been shelved, according to his publishers, St. Martin's Press. And so once the "pregnant father" delivers, he can return to being the person his neighbors refer to as "a quiet, regular guy."

By then his story may have served its purpose, Ms. Sedgwick said. It will have showed us that: "People experience gender very differently and some have really individual and imaginative uses to make of it. That's an important thing for people to wrap their minds around."

PHYSICIAN BIAS AFFECTS LESBIAN HEALTH CARE

A study published in 1995 suggested that insensitive treatment and flagrant prejudice from doctors lead lesbians to have less frequent check-ups and screenings than other women, placing them at risk for less treatable forms of cervical and breast cancer as well as heart disease. The author of the study, Dr. Katherine O'Hanlan, argued that her findings paralleled other studies focusing on the health care of gay men, blacks, and other minority groups. An earlier study found that 54 percent of gay and lesbian doctors saw colleagues denying or offering substandard care to gay and lesbian patients, with 88% saying they had heard colleagues joke about gay and lesbian patients.

Based on health surveys completed by 13,543 women, O'Hanlan found that 72 percent of lesbian patients report that their physicians have made derogatory comments or otherwise behaved in ways that cause 84 percent to be reluctant to return for additional treatment. As a result, lesbians became more likely to consult alternative medicine practitioners and less likely to receive basic screening tests, including Pap smears, mammograms, and cholesterol tests, than heterosexual women. According to Dr. O'Hanlan, lesbians allow three times as much time to elapse between Pap tests, and 10 percent have not been screened for cervical cancer in over 10 years, if ever. In addition, lesbians tend to be at greater risk for breast cancer as they are less likely to conceive children and more likely to be obese.

Pressure from gay and lesbian doctors led the American Medical Association to urge physicians to be aware that the sexuality of their patients may vary, and to adopt a nonjudgmental attitude when providing care. In addition, the American College of Obstetricians and Gynecologists updated brochures to include information on lesbian health. Further, two large-scale studies on lesbian health were conducted at Harvard and at the National Institutes of Health to explore the degree to which lesbians are at higher risk for illnesses such as breast cancer and heart disease. Findings showed that lesbians faced a different set of health risks and concerns than heterosexual women. Lesbians tended to have a higher body mass index than heterosexual women and were more likely to smoke, thus putting them more at risk for heart disease, the number one killer of women in America.

OCTOBER 11, 1995
BIAS IN DOCTORS' OFFICES MAY HARM GAY WOMEN'S HEALTH, STUDY FINDS
By SUSAN GILBERT

The trouble often begins with a woman's initial visit to a doctor. The doctor asks, "Are you sexually active?"

Patient: "Yes."

Doctor: "What form of birth control do you use?"

Patient: "None."

The doctor, looking shocked, proceeds to lecture the woman on the importance of preventing unintended pregnancy until the patient reveals that she is a lesbian.

What may seem like little more than an awkward moment is typical of the ways in which many doctors alienate lesbian patients and may ultimately jeopardize their health, a recent study concluded.

Because of insensitive treatment as well as flagrant prejudice from doctors, lesbians have fewer checkups than they should, fail to get important screening tests like Pap smears, mammograms and cholesterol tests, and are therefore less likely than other women to have cancer and heart disease diagnosed in the early, most treatable stages, says Dr. Katherine A. O'Hanlan, author of the study, which was published last month in Current Problems in Obstetrics, Gynecology and Fertility.

"It was a sad surprise to find out how prejudiced doctors are toward lesbians," said Dr. O'Hanlan, a gynecological cancer surgeon at Stanford University Medical Center and a former president of the Gay and Lesbian Medical Association.

Dr. O'Hanlan says the medical profession's bias against lesbians is comparable to that documented against gay men, blacks and other minority groups. It is widely recognized, she said, that groups that face discrimination are more likely than the general population to suffer from cancer and heart disease and to die from those illnesses because they do not see doctors as often.

Her study does not prove that lesbians die sooner than heterosexual women, or that they have a higher incidence of serious illnesses. This information is unavailable, she says, because there have been very few studies on lesbian health—just four have appeared in peer-reviewed obstetric and gynecological journals since 1966. She believes the lack of such research is itself evidence of bias against lesbians.

What her study does is identify risk factors that lesbians face for serious illnesses. It is the first broad review of research on lesbian health, incorporating data on 13,543 women who participated in seven health surveys.

A 1994 survey cited in Dr. O'Hanlan's study outlines the scope of the problem. In the survey, 54 percent of 710 gay and lesbian doctors said they had seen colleagues either deny care to gay and lesbian patients or give them substandard care. For example, some doctors erroneously told lesbians that they did not need Pap smears. In addition, 88 percent of the respondents had heard colleagues joke about gay and lesbian patients.

In another survey included in Dr. O'Hanlan's study, 72 percent of lesbian patients said their doctors had made derogatory remarks about them or ostracized them in some way. As a result 84 percent of the women said they hesitated to return to their doctors for treatment of new ailments. Instead, Dr. O'Hanlan found, many lesbians flock to chiropractors and practitioners of alternative medicine, whom they find more personable, even if their remedies are not scientifically proven.

Dr. O'Hanlan points to evidence that the alienation of lesbians from the medical establishment may increase their risk of cervical cancer and breast cancer. For one thing, lesbians let three times as much time go by between Pap smears as heterosexual women do, and as many as 10 percent of lesbians either have never had a Pap smear or have had just one in the previous 10 years.

The American College of Obstetricians recommends that all women initially have one Pap smear annually for three years. If these tests are negative, the college leaves it up to a woman's doctor to set a schedule for future Pap smears based on the patient's risk factors for cervical cancer, which include intercourse with multiple partners and smoking. The lack of routine Pap smears, Dr. O'Hanlan wrote in the study, "may delay diagnosis of cervix carcinoma in lesbians, increasing both the morbidity and mortality in this population."

Lesbians may also stand a greater chance than heterosexual women of getting breast cancer. For one thing, they have more risk factors: they are less likely to conceive children and more likely to be obese, Dr. O'Hanlan says. These risk factors make regular breast examinations especially crucial, and yet the study found that lesbians were less likely to get mammograms or perform breast self-examination than heterosexual women.

Despite the bad news, Dr. O'Hanlan and other doctors see signs of hope. After pressure by gay and lesbian doctors, the American Medical Association issued a policy statement last year urging doctors to be more sensitive toward gay patients. When discussing sexuality, for example, the association says doctors should ask women whether they are sexual with men, women, both or neither, and that they should have a "nonjudgmental attitude."

Dr. Richard Corlin, a spokesman for the association, said: "I suspect that gays and lesbians may really receive inferior care when they reveal their sexual orientation. But physicians are more aware than they once were of the need to make patients feel comfortable and to be aware of their sexuality as it pertains to their health."

With that goal in mind, the American College of Obstetricians and Gynecologists is updating its brochures to patients and doctors to include information on lesbian health. And this fall, the American Academy of Family Physicians is sponsoring its second forum for doctors on gay and lesbian health issues. Dr. F. Jay Ach, a family doctor in suburban Cincinnati who is organizing the forum, said, "last year's forum was so well attended that the academy wanted to do it again."

Two large studies are expected to have significant implications for care of lesbian patients. The Harvard Nurses Study and the Women's Health Initiative of the National Institutes of Health will soon collect data on lesbian participants in the hope of finding whether lesbians are actually at exceptionally high risk of certain illnesses and what preventive measures they can take. "Substantial strides are being made," Dr. O'Hanlan said.

Gay Men More Likely to Smoke

A study of 2,600 gay and bisexual men conducted in 1999 at the University of California at San Francisco found that gay men were almost twice as likely to smoke as the general male population. Among gay men, smoking rates were found to be highest in those aged 18 to 24, and researchers suggested that these increased rates may be related to drinking heavily, frequenting gay bars, and being personally affected by AIDS.

DECEMBER 21, 1999
VITAL SIGNS: BEHAVIOR
Antismoking Campaigns Elude Gay Men
By ERIC NAGOURNEY

Gay men are almost twice as likely to smoke cigarettes as men over all, a new study finds.

The study, by researchers at the University of California at San Francisco, looked at 2,600 men who described themselves as gay or bisexual. About 48 percent reported smoking, compared with about 27 percent of all American men.

Researchers said they were not sure how to account for the disparity. They looked at a variety of factors, including heavy drinking, frequenting gay bars and being personally affected by AIDS, and found that this seemed to explain some of the higher incidence of smoking.

Whatever the cause, they said, the study suggests a need for antismoking programs that are more effective with gays.

The lead author, Dr. Ron Stall, pointed out that the smoking rate was highest among younger gay men—50 percent for those 18 to 24. That, he said, suggests a health danger that could last for years.

The study, published in The American Journal of Public Health, found that although higher educational level was associated with a lower incidence of smoking, gay men at all educational levels smoked more than the general male population. Among older gay men, the smoking rate was lowest.

Tuberculosis Cases Emerge in Black Transgender Communities

The Centers for Disease Control and Prevention found twenty-six active cases of tuberculosis (TB) in black transgender communities in New York City and Baltimore between 1998 and 2000, which led to four deaths. The outbreak occurred among transgender people living in "houses," social groups that compete against each other in drag balls and other fashion- and dance-related contests in various cities along the East Coast. More than two-thirds of those with TB also tested positive for human immunodeficiency virus (HIV). Because house members travel regularly to compete, public health workers in cities such as Atlanta, Boston, Philadelphia, and Washington were alerted.

APRIL 21, 2000
OUTBREAK OF TB AFFLICTS TRANSGENDER PEOPLE
By JENNIFER STEINHAUER

The Centers for Disease Control and Prevention has identified an outbreak of H.I.V.-related tuberculosis among young transgender people in New York and Baltimore. The first cases turned up in Baltimore in the summer of 1998, and 26 cases in the two cities have since been diagnosed. Four of those infected have died.

The disease appears to have made its way throughout communities of young black males who identify themselves as transgender. The term encompasses cross-dressers, those who have undergone sex-change procedures or are planning to do so, and those who live full time in the gender opposite from that of their birth without surgery.

The people infected with this TB strain belong to social groups, known as houses, that participate in drag balls and travel along the eastern seaboard to take part in fashion and dance contests.

Health care workers in Baltimore discovered that those who tested positive for TB, as well as 37 others with dormant cases, were carrying the same strain, said Dr. Peter McElroy, an epidemiologist at the disease control center, in Atlanta.

Of the seven cases identified in New York, one stemmed from Jersey City.

All of those who contracted the disease were black. More than two-thirds also tested positive for H.I.V., which made them more vulnerable to TB.

Because this group tends to travel frequently, C.D.C. officials are concerned that the strain may migrate to other cities, and they have contacted public health workers in Atlanta, Baltimore, Boston, Philadelphia, Washington and New York to help them determine if there are more cases.

New York City Health Department workers have been working with community centers and groups that work on transgender concerns.

The Lesbian and Gay Community Services Center in Manhattan directed health care workers to some of the dance contests and helped refine language in some of the outreach pamphlets, said Rosalyne Blumenstein, the director of the community center's gender identity project.

AIDS

● ●

While AIDS is by no means an exclusively gay disease, it did initially emerge among gay men and affect substantial numbers of homosexuals, significantly altering the shape of the gay community in the years following its first discovery. The 1970s was a period of unprecedented openness and sexual freedom for gay men in particular, as evidenced by the development of the thriving network of discos and gay baths discussed in a retrospective *Times* report of June 16, 1983. After years of oppression and closeting prior to the Stonewall uprising in 1969 (see the first chapter), many embraced the notion, radical at the time, that sex between consenting adults does not need to be legitimized by monogamy or long-term commitment. This libertine attitude was a natural outgrowth of the sexual revolution and the questioning of authority that was characteristic of the 1960s.

The emergence of AIDS in 1981 caused many in the gay community to reexamine their attitudes about sex. While some came to question the views and practices embraced during the previous decade, others became even more committed to a radical sexual politics and fought hard to maintain their newfound freedom. Many seemed to feel they had nothing left to lose after being diagnosed with a disease that amounted, at that time, to a death sentence. Others who had been closeted through the 1970s, even many conservatives, came out as gay and became politically active in response to the federal government's apparent indifference to the plight of gay people with AIDS.

DISCOVERY

It is now well known that AIDS (acquired immune deficiency syndrome) is the late stage of an infection caused by HIV (human immunodeficiency virus) that is transmitted through contact with the bodily fluids of those already infected, primarily through sexual contact, through shared needles, or from infected pregnant women to their fetuses. However, when physicians and researchers first began to become aware of the disease in July 1981, they knew very little about the illness or its causes. It took over thirty months, forty-one cases, and eight deaths before the Centers for Disease Control (later, Centers for Disease Control and Prevention;

CDC) discussed the outbreak in its "Morbidity and Mortality Weekly Report." The report noted that all forty-one cases involved homosexual men from either New York City or San Francisco who had exhibited symptoms of Kaposi's sarcoma, a form of cancer that is rare in the United States. Published on July 3, 1981, the first *Times* report on the disease noted that Dr. Alvin Friedman of the New York University Medical Center characterized the outbreak as "rather devastating."

This early report reveals how little researchers knew about the disease at the time of its discovery. For example, although it was known that those afflicted typically had problems with their immune systems, researchers could not say whether this was related to the disease or to other factors related to the patients' lifestyle. While conceding that not all of those affected had been interviewed, researchers emphasized that most of the victims had "multiple and frequent" sexual encounters many nights of the week, often while using stimulants or psychedelic drugs. On the basis of these cases, Dr. James Curran of the CDC said that there was no apparent danger to heterosexuals.

Because scientists initially believed the disease affected only gay men, it was originally known as gay-related immune deficiency (GRID). By the summer of 1982 the CDC announced that the disease had reached epidemic proportions, with 335 people known to be infected and 136 dead. At this point, scientists had successfully identified the illness's major symptoms, which included swollen glands, weight loss, fever, and diarrhea. They had also discovered that the disease could lay dormant for some time, fueling concerns that "tens of thousands" could already be infected, including some heterosexuals. Although the cause of the disease remained unknown at this time, researchers strongly suspected that it was not spread by casual contact, and some theorized that the introduction of semen into the bloodstream during sex might be an important point of transmission. However, the line between scientific knowledge and moralistic assumptions was not always clear. Some physicians inaccurately concluded that anonymous sex was inherently more risky than sex with a known partner. This was not necessarily the case, as having contact with the infectious agent was the crucial element in contracting the disease, not the frequency or intimacy of sexual interactions. Nonetheless, some physicians such as Dr. Lawrence Mass concluded that "gay people whose life style consists of anonymous sexual encounters are going to have to do some serious rethinking." As other, more cautious researchers noted in a subsequent *Times* report of June 18, 1982, "Sexual contact with patients with GRID syndrome does not lead directly to the breakdown of the immunological system, 'but simply indicates a certain style of life.'" During a conference held in January 1983, CDC scientists and other major researchers decided to call the disease AIDS rather than GRID, to clarify that it was not solely associated with the gay community.

Over time, the disease became more visible and troubling to the general population, as evidenced by a lengthy *Times* Sunday Magazine article published on February 6, 1983, and titled "AIDS: A New Disease's Deadly Odyssey." The report noted that 365 of the 958 people known to have the disease had already died, an alarming mortality rate of 38 percent. As for the cases reported before June 1981, 75 percent were now dead. This piece called AIDS "the century's most virulent epidemic," explaining that it led to "the near-total collapse of the body's immune system, leaving the victim prey to cancers and opportunistic infections that the body is unable to defend against." Most of the conclusive cases tracked by the CDC still involved homosexuals, intravenous (IV) drug users such as heroin addicts, hemophiliacs, and Haitians, leading some at the CDC to use the somewhat callous shorthand term "4-H" to refer to those affected.

Subsequent research determined that AIDS could be transmitted through sexual contact between heterosexual men and women. A study published in *The New England Journal of Medicine* in May 1983 focused on seven long-term female partners of heterosexual men with AIDS. Although none fell within the four major risk categories for the disease (homosexual, Haitian, IV drug user, or hemophiliac), six of the seven were found to have either AIDS or compromised immune systems, suggesting that they had contracted AIDS through heterosexual sex. The validity of the four risk categories soon came under further attack, as demonstrated in a *Times* report of July 31, 1983. This article explored whether residents of Haiti and Haitians in the United States had been unfairly categorized as having an increased risk for AIDS. In New York City, public health officials had already removed Haitian Americans from their list of groups at risk for the disease, on the grounds that the small number of cases that had been found did not justify their inclusion. In addition, officials said that Haitian Americans who were infected were subsequently identified as members of one or several of the

other at-risk groups. In addition to stigmatizing Haitians, the tendency of AIDS researchers to initially focus their attention on those first infected may have delayed recognition of the disproportionate effect AIDS was having on African Americans. Publishing its first piece devoted to this topic on October 23, 1985, *The Times* noted that African Americans accounted for roughly 25 percent of the cases at that time, while they composed only about 12 percent of the population.

Earlier reports, such as a May 1, 1983, *Times* article, hinted at the growing competition among AIDS researchers, noting their reluctance to openly share findings and data as they raced to discover the cause of the disease. In April 1984 the CDC announced that a team of French scientists led by Dr. Luc Montagnier of the Pasteur Institute in Paris had discovered the cause of AIDS, a retrovirus that the French named lymphadenopathy-associated virus (LAV). The announcement created new optimism about the development of improved strategies for preventing, detecting, and treating the disease, which by this time had claimed 1,758 lives among a total of 4,087 cases. Dr. Robert Gallo of the U.S. National Cancer Institute quickly claimed to have identified an alternative cause of AIDS, a retrovirus he called human T-cell lymphotropic virus (HTLV-3). A *Times* report of April 26, 1984, titled "A Viral Competition over AIDS," provided various details about the conflict and quoted the secretary of Health and Human Services, Margaret Heckler. Heckler stated that she believed the French and the American viruses would "prove to be the same" and that "today we add another miracle to the long honor roll of American medicine and science." The controversy regarding who would be given credit for the discovery of the AIDS virus was resolved three years later, as noted in a *Times* report of April 1, 1987, which announced that researchers from both France and the United States would share the credit for the discovery; the Pasteur Institute and the U.S. government would co-own the patents for lucrative blood tests developed based on their joint findings, with 80 percent of the royalties being devoted to new international research on AIDS. An independent committee renamed the virus HIV.

Less than a year after the initial discovery of the cause, Secretary Heckler announced that a test had been developed to detect the presence of HIV in blood and blood products. The test was designed to screen the blood supply, long a matter of concern given that 113 AIDS victims were thought to have contracted the disease through blood or blood products containing HIV. However, officials cautioned that a positive result would not necessarily amount to a diagnosis of AIDS, as an estimated 17 percent of the positive tests would ultimately be found to not contain AIDS antibodies. To discourage those testing positive from being further stigmatized, Heckler recommended that all test results be kept confidential.

The first International AIDS Conference was held in Atlanta in April 1985, as covered in *The Times* reports of April 16 and 23, 1985. Sponsored by the U.S. federal government, the World Health Organization (WHO), and Emory University, the conference was larger than any previously held on the topic of AIDS; it included 392 panels, many of which commanded standing-room-only crowds. By this time, 9,760 cases of AIDS had been reported in the United States, with 4,760 deaths. Researchers attending the conference expressed cautious optimism regarding a range of new drugs to treat AIDS that they had recently begun to test. In the April 23 report, Dr. Martin Hirsch of Massachusetts General Hospital in Boston commented, "We have a long way to go before AIDS is preventable or treatable, but the first steps have been taken, and we are on our way."

This stance was also reflected in a major, four-part series published in *The Times* on March 16–19, 1987. The March 17 report, "AIDS Drugs Offer Hope but Cure Remains Distant," anticipated the approval of the drug azidothymidine (AZT), noting that the evidence suggested that it had prolonged the lives of many of the more than 5,000 patients who had used it up to that time. While not able to prevent or kill the AIDS virus, AZT significantly impeded its ability to reproduce. The clinical trials for AZT began in the spring of 1986 with two similar groups of AIDS patients, one receiving the drug and the other a placebo. However, scientists discontinued the placebo group ahead of schedule and placed all research participants on AZT when they discovered that only one patient out of 145 receiving AZT had died, compared with 19 of those receiving the placebo. Nevertheless, researchers cautioned that the drug appeared to have the potential for significant side effects, including a tendency to cause problems with patients' bone marrow, a vital component of a healthy immune system.

As anticipated, the Food and Drug Administration (FDA) soon approved AZT for use, and it was produced as a drug called Retrovir by the Burroughs Wellcome Company. At first only limited quantities were available at an extremely costly rate, creating great controversy among those with AIDS, including many in the gay community who demanded greater availability and affordability. Similar concerns would arise with the discovery of each promising new drug, such as the development of a multipill "cocktail" of protease inhibitors in the mid-1990s, as detailed in a February 6, 1996, *Times* report, "New AIDS Therapies Arise, but Who Can Afford the Bill?" As recently as 2006, a July 13 *Times* report noted that the FDA had approved the once-a-day pill Atripla but that it would wholesale at a cost prohibitive for most, $1,150 a month.

To date, a vaccine that would immunize people against HIV has yet to be discovered. The March 18 installment of *The Times'* 1987 four-part series on AIDS included a lengthy discussion of the prospects for such a vaccine. It concluded that although many experimental vaccines were about to be tested, scientists were extremely cautious about the outcome. Dr. Frank Young, commissioner of the FDA correctly predicted: "The prospects of a licensed AIDS vaccine in the immediate future are very slim." The report soberly noted that researchers "are not even sure whether it will be possible to develop a vaccine against the AIDS virus." As noted in a *Times* report of February 24, 2003, the first large-scale test of an AIDS vaccine failed, although it did have the effect of lowering the infection rate among African Americans and other non-Hispanic minorities, a result that scientists were not able to explain. A subsequent large-scale test also failed, but two second-generation vaccine candidates are currently being tested by the CDC. While work in this area continues, a vaccine has yet to be approved for public distribution.

FEDERAL RESPONSE

AIDS emerged during the administration of President Ronald Reagan, whose conservative political, social, and economic stances did not bode well for an early and active governmental response to the epidemic. While the administration often asserted the importance of combating AIDS, others, including many in the gay community, argued that such rhetoric was typically not accompanied by adequate funding or public health information. This was especially noteworthy in the early years of the outbreak, a crucial time for the effective control of a health crisis of epidemic proportions. For example, announcing the funding of six new grants for AIDS research, Dr. Edward Brandt, an assistant secretary of Health and Human Services (HHS), asserted that AIDS was "the No. 1 priority of the U.S. Public Health Service," as early as May 25, 1983, as noted in *The Times*. However, the executive director of the National Gay and Lesbian Task Force, Virginia Apuzzo, questioned the administration's rhetoric of commitment, arguing that it had neglected the disease because it had originated mainly among homosexuals. She added, "The entire agency is conducting business as usual insofar as this particular health crisis is concerned. It is inexcusable that a supplemental budget request has not been submitted to Congress." As reported in *The Times* on August 3, 1983, Reagan administration officials denied that prejudice against homosexuals had slowed their response to the disease. Another report on August 18, 1983, noted that HHS secretary Margaret Heckler said that she would request $40 million from Congress, doubling the outlay for AIDS research at that time.

A similar dynamic emerged when Heckler spoke at the first International AIDS Conference in 1985. She reasserted that AIDS was the Reagan administration's top health priority and added that her department was fighting an all-out war against the disease. Yet, a May 4, 1985, letter to the editor in *The Times* written by Dr. Marcus Conant, director of the AIDS Clinical Research Center of the University of San Francisco, questioned her assertion. While he agreed that a war on the new disease was necessary, he asked "where her armies are deployed, what her funds are for supplies and armaments, what her targets and strategies are?" In addition, he noted that Reagan had yet to speak publicly about the issue, causing him to wonder whether the president "is even aware that the Public Health Service has declared this war," particularly since the administration seemed "unwilling to commit the resources to win the battle."

According to *The Times,* the first time that Reagan publicly addressed AIDS was in response to a reporter's question at a press conference on September 18, 1985. When asked if he would support "a massive government research program against AIDS, like the program that President Nixon had launched against cancer," Reagan repeated that supporting AIDS research was a "top priority" for the administration. Confronted by the fact that Dr. Robert Gallo—said to be the best-known AIDS researcher in the country—had argued that what was needed was "a minor moon shot program to attack this AIDS epidemic," Reagan denied that more money was necessary. He claimed that his administration had provided $500 million for research, including $126 million for the following year, a figure he characterized as a "vital contribution" given "our budgetary restraints."

As reported in *The Times* on February 6, 1986, Reagan subsequently asked the surgeon general, Dr. C. Everett Koop, to prepare a report on AIDS, while reiterating the administration's commitment to finding a cure. Rep. Henry Waxman (D-CA), a leader in the effort to gain more funds for AIDS research, responded by questioning the sincerity of Reagan's rhetoric, calling it "outrageous" and "a shell game," and noting that the administration's proposed budget included a 22 percent reduction in spending for AIDS research. In October 1986 the National Academy of Sciences, a prestigious private organization chartered by Congress to provide advice to

the federal government on various issues, released a major report charging that the administration's response to AIDS was dangerously inadequate given the enormity of the risk posed by the continued spread of the disease. A co-chair of the report, Dr. David Baltimore of MIT, argued that the national health crisis posed by AIDS is "of a magnitude that requires Presidential leadership to bring together all of the elements of society to deal with the problem." Dr. Robert Windom, an HHS assistant secretary, responded to the report by saying that "there has been a conscientious effort to do a good job."

Surgeon General Koop's report on AIDS turned out to be a political bombshell. As noted in a supportive *Times* editorial of October 25, 1986, the report argued that silence about AIDS needed to end and that frank, age-appropriate discussions about sex needed to be instituted "at the lowest grade possible." The report urged greater condom usage, as well as clean needle usage for drug addicts. It also opposed compulsory blood testing to identify those with the disease, as well as quarantining of those found to have it. Concluding that "we are fighting a disease—not people," the report argued that "it is time to put self-defeating attitudes aside."

Koop's report was met with strong resistance by others in the Reagan administration, perhaps most notably Education Secretary William Bennett, as mentioned in a *Times* report of January 24, 1987. Arguing for "value-based" education, Bennett favored focusing on abstinence as the only certain method to prevent AIDS, rather than providing information about condom use and other practices designed to make sex safer, which he characterized as "morally ambiguous." Koop and Bennett subsequently attempted to downplay their differences, as evidenced by a *Times* report of January 31, 1987, in which they said that they agreed young people should be taught that abstinence is the safest practice "until it is possible to establish a mutually faithful monogamous relationship." As noted in a *Times* report of February 11, 1987, just a few weeks later Koop appeared to reignite the controversy, calling for television stations to accept advertisements for condoms because they provided the best protection for those disinclined "to practice abstinence or monogamy."

In response to this controversy, President Reagan announced that he would support a campaign to educate the public about AIDS by sending out informational materials to every household in the United States, with the caveat that the materials should stress "responsible sexual behavior" within marriage and abstinence for children. *The Times* reported on February 26, 1987, that this was the "first indication that the President has been engaging in strategy to combat the AIDS epidemic after months of criticism that he has been inactive on the issue." Shortly thereafter, the president gave his first major speech on AIDS. As a *Times* report of April 2, 1987, noted, prior to this time "the President had made only limited comments on AIDS." As Randy Shilts said in his book about AIDS titled *And the Band Played On* (1987), "by the time that President Reagan gave his first major speech on the crisis, more than 25,000 Americans had died of AIDS." For his part Dr. Koop defended himself against his conservative critics, stating, "When you walk into a health job, you make pronouncements about health based on the facts." He added, "You can't educate anybody about AIDS unless they know about sex."

Public education efforts about AIDS were further constrained by Congress. Under pressure from Sen. Jesse Helms, a Republican from North Carolina, a 1988 appropriations bill was amended to prohibit federal funding for any programs that "promote, encourage, or condone homosexuality." Although this rhetoric was subsequently modified, the end result was that the CDC created a policy prohibiting federally funded AIDS education materials likely to be deemed "offensive" by "a majority of adults." The materials that originally sparked Helms's response were designed to teach people how to practice safer sex and included sexually explicit language as well as graphic illustrations. They were produced by the Gay Men's Health Crisis (GMHC), a nonprofit group devoted to addressing the AIDS crisis. Lauding the efforts of groups such as the GMHC, Mayor Ed Koch of New York City wrote an opinion piece published in *The Times* on November 7, 1987. Koch dismissed Helms's initiative as "homophobic hysteria" likely to serve only to limit the ability of the government to educate the public adequately about AIDS. Several years later the CDC policy was overturned by a federal district court judge, who found it "unconstitutionally vague" and lacking "meaning that can reasonably be understood by a person of ordinary intelligence," as reported in *The Times* on May 12, 1992. "This decision will save lives," said Center for Constitutional Rights lawyer David Cole, adding that it will enable organizations to create the most effective education materials without worrying over "some government agent's subjective determination about what will be 'offensive' in Peoria, Illinois."

CIVIL RIGHTS AND LIBERTIES

As the American people became aware of AIDS, anxiety about the disease and its effects grew. Uncertainty about the cause and transmission of the disease, coupled with its frightening symptoms and alarming mortality rates, fueled fear and panic in the gay community as well as in the public at large.

As early as August 8, 1982, *The Times* published a story about the AIDS crisis in New York City, "A Disease's Spread Provokes Anxiety." Commenting on the situation in New York, Larry Kramer, a founder of the Gay Men's Health Crisis, said, "I don't think there is a thinking person in this town who isn't literally scared to death." Alarmed by threats to close gay bars and to declare homosexual conduct a public health risk, homosexuals began to fear that the disease would become an excuse for further stigmatizing the gay community. With physicians openly wondering whether AIDS was God's way of punishing homosexuals, some in the gay community began to "fear not only the disease itself but also possible erosion of their civil rights under the guise of preventing the spread of an epidemic."

As it turned out, the gay community, people with AIDS (PWAs), and those associated with either had much to fear. It would be difficult to exaggerate the range of threats to equal treatment suggested and/or imposed during the early days of the AIDS crisis, many of which were covered in *The Times*. As reported on October 17, 1983, police officers in Jersey City refused to drive a prisoner with AIDS to a hospital because they were afraid of contracting the disease, and, as reported on May 22 of the same year, San Francisco police were instructed to wear special masks and gloves when dealing with "a suspected AIDS patient." Some hospital workers refused to treat AIDS patients, despite a well-publicized study conducted at the University of California in San Francisco and discussed in *The Times* on September 22, 1983, that found "no scientific reason why health care personnel who are reluctant to treat victims of AIDS should be excused from doing so." Some localities, such as the state of Colorado, had begun to keep a list of people who tested positive for the virus, despite challenges from the American Civil Liberties Union, as noted in an August 24, 1985, *Times* report, and an October 26 piece later that year reported that New York state had begun to allow public health officials to close places where "high-risk sexual activities take place," such as gay bathhouses. In one particularly outrageous incident reported in *The Times* on October 26, 1985, the Republican challenger to the Democratic incumbent mayor in Houston said that one of his plans for combating AIDS was to "shoot the queers."

Basic needs—such as shelter—became challenges for some AIDS patients. On May 22, 1983, *The Times* reported that some landlords in San Francisco had begun to evict tenants with AIDS, and in a June 25, 1984, *Times* article, a housing consultant for the American Baptist Church said that many PWAs, especially the indigent, had difficulty finding housing "because of all the prejudices and misconceptions

IN FOCUS

Rock Hudson and Magic Johnson

· ·

As described in his *Times* obituary on October 3, 1985, Rock Hudson's handsome face and six-foot four-inch physique combined with masterful comedic timing to make him one of the most popular romantic actors of the 1950s and 1960s. When a spokesperson announced that he had AIDS in July 1985, Hudson became the first major public figure to openly acknowledge having the disease, and this revelation has since been described as a turning point in the public perception of AIDS. In addition to stimulating an almost immediate increase in sympathy for those infected, news of Hudson's illness seemed to dramatically affect many people's awareness of their own risk. As reported in a July 7, 1985, *Times* article, New York AIDS hotlines saw calls double and even triple in the days following the announcement of Hudson's illness. A few weeks before his death, on October 2, 1985, at age 59, Rock Hudson sent a telegram to an AIDS benefit he was too sick to attend. It read in part, "I'm not happy that I have AIDS. But if that is helping others, I can at least know that my own misfortune has had some positive worth."

In November 1991 professional basketball player Magic Johnson held a press conference to announce that he had tested positive for HIV and to encourage young people to practice safe sex, saying, "I think sometimes we think, well, only gay people can get it—'It's not going to happen to me.' And here I am saying that it can happen to anybody, even me, Magic Johnson." At the time, the 32-year-old Johnson was an extremely popular point guard for the Los Angeles Lakers who had led his team to five league championships and landed high-profile endorsement deals for products such as Diet Pepsi and Converse. "From a public health standpoint, this is the most important event for African Americans since the AIDS epidemic began," said Belinda Rochelle of the AIDS Action Council regarding Johnson's announcement. "The stigma of drugs and homosexuality have been too powerful to overcome. If any person can do it, it will be Magic." Johnson subsequently founded the Magic Johnson Foundation and has featured prominently in public service campaigns on HIV prevention and treatment. As Johnson said when announcing his diagnosis, "Life is going to go on for me, and I'm going to be a happy man." Magic Johnson has since founded his own for-profit consulting/management company, Magic Johnson Enterprises, and in 2009 he published a memoir cowritten with his long-time basketball rival, Larry Bird.

From *The New York Times*

Anderson, Susan Heller, and David W. Dunlap. "New York Day by Day; AIDS Hot Lines Get More Calls." July 27, 1985.
Berger, Joseph. "Rock Hudson, Screen Idol, Dies at 59." October 3, 1985.
Specter, Michael. "Basketball; Magic's Loud Message for Young Black Men." November 8, 1991.
Stevenson, Richard W. "Basketball; Magic Johnson Ends His Career, Saying He Has AIDS Infection." November 8, 1991.

· ·

connected with the disease." An October 1, 1983, *Times* report documented the attempted eviction of a physician who merely treated AIDS patients, on the grounds that his practice would lower property values.

An Indiana seventh grader who contracted HIV through blood products, Ryan White, was the most widely publicized example of the unique hysteria generated by parents fearful of their children contracting AIDS at school. Although many parents and administrators fought against his enrollment and successfully prevented him from attending classes for a time, a judge eventually ordered that Ryan must be allowed to attend school, saying that there were no legal grounds for his exclusion, as documented in a *Times* piece of April 11, 1986. Similarly, a September 10, 1985, *Times* report noted that parents of 11,000 students in Queens kept their children home for the first day of the 1985 school year, protesting the decision to allow a second grader with AIDS to attend classes. Another *Times* report of August 31, 1985, noted that parents of students attending a Catholic grade school on the Upper West Side forced the archdiocese to withdraw a plan to open an AIDS shelter in a former convent next door to the school by threatening to withdraw their children if plans for the shelter moved forward.

Perhaps the most limiting and controversial proposal of all was the suggestion that people with AIDS should be quarantined. Despite the fact that it was well documented that AIDS could not be transmitted through casual contact, as noted in a September 13, 1985, *Times* report titled "Fears on AIDS Termed Largely without Cause," a poll discussed in a December 20, 1985, *Times* report found that 51 percent of respondents supported a quarantine of AIDS patients, 48 percent approved of identity cards for those screened to have the AIDS virus, and 15 percent supported mandatory tattooing of individuals infected with HIV. Fifty-one percent also said that they favored a law "making it a crime for an AIDS patient to have sex with another person." In 1986 noted conservative political writer William F. Buckley outlined what he took to be the arguments for and against various restrictions on people with AIDS. While he advocated tattooing homosexuals and intravenous drug users on the buttocks and upper arms, he was not willing to support quarantining, though he held it out as a possible option for the future. As a subsequent *Times* report of January 21, 1986, made clear, public fear about AIDS had indeed increased bias and violence against homosexuals. Other *Times* reports, however, also suggest that public health officials faced a legitimate struggle in their efforts to find unbiased ways to protect public health without compromising the civil rights of PWAs.

Gay Community Response

Because gay men were the first group to be categorized as at risk for AIDS, the lesbian, gay, bisexual, and transgender (LGBT) community responded to the crisis early. Two of the most important organizations to emerge were the GMHC and the AIDS Coalition to Unleash Power (ACT UP). Founded in

1982, the GMHC is a nonprofit organization founded to provide a wide variety of services and support, including information, counseling, legal assistance, volunteer support, shared meals, and social opportunities for New York City's gay men with AIDS, many of whom had been ostracized, fired from their jobs, and evicted from their apartments, as noted in a December 5, 1983, *Times* story. This article, by noted columnist Maureen Dowd, has been called by some the first sympathetic story about AIDS to appear in *The Times*. Explaining that the genesis of the organization was six gay men who had lost friends to the disease and were worried about the lack of social services for AIDS victims, the piece offered a detailed look at the way the GMHC recruited volunteers, called "buddies," to shop for groceries, run errands, and make hospital visits, combating the isolation and neglect often experienced by people living with AIDS. Dowd noted that in two years, the GMHC grew into an organization with twelve paid staff members and a budget of $900,000, offering twenty therapy groups, a twenty-four-hour hotline that received 1,200 calls each week, and a variety of other services, including a vast volunteer network with a value estimated at $16 million.

The outpouring of energy and commitment represented by the GMHC's volunteer program also gave many hope that AIDS might not destroy the gay community but rather transform it into a more caring, connected group of people willing to work together to help each other cope with the disease. Many were astonished at the gay community's active response to the AIDS crisis, which has since often been characterized as the first time that those affected by an epidemic provided the services necessary to cope with the disease. Others in the gay community responded to AIDS with horror and anger, as the numbers of gay males dying from the disease continued to increase astronomically. They were enraged at the weak government response, which they attributed to hostility toward homosexuals. In 1987 Larry Kramer, one of the original founders of the GMHC, left the group to create a more politically oriented alternative, which came to be known as the AIDS Coalition to Unleash Power, or ACT UP. As Professor George Annas at Boston University School of Public Health noted in a *Times* report of March 11, 1990, "There never was a politically savvy group of sick people before."

ACT UP was purposefully designed as a leaderless organization, its up to 700 ACT UP members meeting weekly to discuss various problems associated with AIDS, such as the slow approval process and high cost of AIDS drugs. Affinity groups composed of those interested in a particular issue would then strategize about how to gain political and media attention, often resulting in creative demonstrations, such as "die-ins," and employing sophisticated graphic design to concisely convey powerful messages and calls to action. Most memorably, the group paired the pink triangle (a symbol used in Nazi concentration camps to identify gay prisoners) with thought-provoking slogans such as "silence = death." A March 21, 1997, *Times* retrospective notes that when ACT UP interrupted trading on the floor of the New York Stock Exchange in March 1987, the National Institutes of Health (NIH) budget for AIDS research was about $290 million and AZT was the only antiviral drug that the FDA had approved. Additional Wall Street demonstrations followed, along with the occupation of an office at the NIH in 1990 during which eighty-two were arrested. As early as January 3, 1990, a *Times* report noted that Dr. Stephen Joseph, a former New York City health commissioner, had said of ACT UP: "There's no doubt that they've had an enormous effect. We've basically changed the way we make drugs available." Numerous ACT UP chapters were founded not only across the nation but also in other countries. By 1997 the federal budget for AIDS research was roughly $1.5 billion and there were ten

antiviral drugs, leading *The Times* to report that ACT UP had "accomplished its bedrock goal" of increasing consciousness about AIDS in the general public through "nervy tactics [that] became a staple of television news."

ACT UP also undertook political actions at unlikely venues. As reported in *The Times* on July 22, 1988, several hundred ACT UP members attended a Mets game at Shea Stadium as a group, affording them the opportunity to have the scoreboard flash "ACT UP" and "Women's AIDS Day" while they unfurled huge banners visible to the crowd that read "Men Wear Condoms" and "AIDS Kills Women." In 1991 during the first Persian Gulf War, ACT UP members ran through the studios where the CBS Evening News and PBS' McNeil/Lehrer News Hour were being broadcast live, shouting "Fight AIDS, not Arabs" and "Fight AIDS, not Iraq," as reported in *The Times* on January 23.

Perhaps the most famous political action of ACT UP occurred in 1989 when an estimated 4,500 protesters disrupted the sermon of John Cardinal O'Connor during a Mass at St. Patrick's Cathedral in New York City to protest the

Seventeen protesters were arrested at a 1987 rally on Wall Street. Those assembled demanded faster government approval of drugs that could help those infected by HIV.

Source: John Sotomayer/The New York Times

Catholic Church's stance on AIDS education and condom use as well as O'Connor's frequent characterization of homosexuality as a sin. As noted in a *Times* report of December 11, 1989, several protesters shouted, chained themselves to pews, and lay in the aisles, resulting in 1,100 arrests and widespread controversy over the reported desecration of a communion wafer during the protest. "The church claims to be prolife and their policies are killing people," said one protester. O'Connor led parishioners in prayer to drown out the protesters. As reported in *The Times* on April 21, 1991, President Bush later denounced this type of action as "an excess of free speech."

ACT UP and the GMHC were not the only vehicles through which the gay community expressed public concern about AIDS. Perhaps the most visible of the others was the AIDS Quilt, a massive compilation of over 3,000 three-by-six-foot fabric panels, each representing the life of someone who had died of AIDS. Initially presented at the Washington Mall during the 1987 March on Washington for Gay and Lesbian Rights, the AIDS Quilt provided a moving, portable memorial powerfully symbolizing the enormous toll that AIDS had wrought on a wide variety of people across the country. At the march more than 200,000 protesters called for more federal money for AIDS research and for an end to discrimination against gays and lesbians, constituting the biggest gay rights march of its time, as noted in a *Times* report of October 12, 1987.

Numerous tactics were used by a wide variety of groups to address the AIDS crisis, including everything from testifying before the New York City Council against a bill that would ban PWAs from the public schools to raising hundreds of thousands of dollars for AIDS research at a celebrity-studded fund-raiser. At times, continued prejudice served as an impediment to creative protest, as when an AIDS-themed art show at the Henry Street Settlement House was cancelled allegedly because it was to include an apparently controversial banner by the Gran Fury group that read "All People with AIDS Are Innocent."

Conclusion

By the end of the 1980s, most Americans understood that AIDS was not a homosexual disease. As the March 16, 1987, installment of a lengthy four-part *Times* series noted, while 80 percent of cases in the United States could be attributed to homosexual men in the early days of the outbreak, by 1987 gay men accounted for only about half the cases, with indigent minorities at an increasingly disproportionate risk.

By 1990 AIDS had become the leading cause of death among black women aged 15 to 44, according to a *Times* report of July 11, 1990. In addition, *The Times* noted that the number of women with AIDS overall also was rising, with cases resulting from heterosexual sex up by nearly 40 percent in one year, as reported on December 28, 1990. On June 29, 1998, *The Times* issued a special report titled "Epidemic of Silence: Eyes Shut, Black America Is Being Ravaged by AIDS," which noted that African Americans account for 57 percent of all new HIV infections.

Despite these increases, public attention seemed to turn away from the AIDS crisis during the 1990s, as evidenced by the lengthy November 28, 1993, article "Whatever Happened to AIDS?" Written by Jeffrey Schmaltz, a *Times* editor who had died of AIDS three weeks earlier, this piece begins with a powerful narrative in which the author noted his own low T-cell count as an indicator that he was likely to die soon. Looking back to the days of the discovery of the disease, he notes that "AIDS was once a hot topic in America—promising treatments on the horizon, intense media interest, a political battlefield." He contrasts that with the situation twelve years later in which "AIDS has become normalized, part of the landscape. It is at once everywhere and nowhere, the leading cause of death among young men nationwide, but little threat to the core of American political power, the white heterosexual suburbanite."

Noted neoconservative columnist Andrew Sullivan, who is HIV positive, reflected on the AIDS epidemic in the article "When Plagues End." While conceding that the epidemic is not technically over in the sense that many will continue to contract AIDS, that Blacks and Latinos will continue to die at a disproportionate rate, and that the poor will not be able to afford treatment, he argued that, for some, the discovery of protease inhibitor treatment transformed AIDS from a certain death sentence into an illness.

Perhaps because of the shift in perspective that both Schmaltz and Sullivan discussed, public interest in AIDS waned and donations to research and related causes decreased, as noted in a *Times* report of January 13, 1999. The GMHC and many other organizations that address AIDS struggled as they tried to adapt to the new situation, addressing their traditional client base of primarily white gay men as well as additional groups more recently affected in larger numbers, such as women, minorities, intravenous drug users, and the poor. In addition, while new drugs such as protease inhibitors have dramatically extended the longevity of people with AIDS, many long-term survivors seem to be prone to medical problems typically experienced by people who are their seniors

IN FOCUS

Philadelphia, Tom Hanks and Mark Sorensen

• •

Released in 1993, the movie *Philadelphia* tells the story of a closeted gay lawyer who sues his upscale law firm for wrongful dismissal after being fired when his AIDS diagnosis is discovered. This was not the first drama to deal with the issue of AIDS. Television, live theater, and independent cinema had all produced critically acclaimed stories and documentaries prior to this time, including *An Early Frost* (1985), *The Normal Heart* (1985), *Tongues Untied* (1989), *Common Threads* (1990), *Our Sons* (1991), and *Angels in America* (1992). Neither was *Philadelphia* universally acclaimed for its skillful handling of this difficult topic. In a January 23, 1994, *Times* opinion piece, Frank Rich described the film as a "cautious effort" that "underestimates" the audience's intelligence by presenting a collection of characters that, with the exception of the conflicted lawyer played by Denzel Washington, are simplistically portrayed as either saints or villains.

Despite its limitations, *Philadelphia* is worthy of being remembered as the first mainstream Hollywood movie about AIDS. When it was filmed, Tom Hanks was at the height of his career as an A-list male lead starring in family-oriented blockbusters such as *Splash, Big, A League of Their Own,* and *Sleepless in Seattle.* His decision to accept a lead role as a gay man dying of AIDS was considered to be extremely risky at the time. In addition, director Jonathan Demme took the unusual step of casting fifty-three people who had AIDS or were HIV-positive as activists, as courtroom extras, and in other small roles throughout the film.

As described in a January 1, 1995, *Times* article, one of these actors, Mark Sorensen, chose not to conceal the Kaposi's sarcoma lesions on his face with makeup because, said his mother, "he wanted people to see how it really was." When the movie was in the final stage of production, Demme learned that Sorensen was critically ill. Although Sorensen appeared on screen for only three seconds, the director had one of his assistants hand deliver an unedited videotape of the movie to the dying man's home. The bedridden Sorensen was carried to the living room to watch the film with his family and died the following day.

Philadelphia became one of the most successful dramas of 1993, earning $125 million at the box office as well as both the Golden Globe and Oscar awards for Best Actor for Tom Hanks. During his Golden Globe acceptance speech, Hanks mentioned Mark Sorensen by name and paid tribute to his courage and humanity. By the end of 1994, all but ten of the actors with HIV or AIDS who appeared in the film were dead.

From *The New York Times*

Rich, Frank. "Journal; The Other Quake." January 23, 1994.
Rothman, Clifford. Film. "*Philadelphia*: Oscar Gives Way to Elegy." January 1, 1995.

• •

by twenty-five years or more, owing to irreparable damage to the immune system and the toxicity of many of the treatments.

Finally, despite significant advances for relatively affluent patients in the developed world, AIDS has grown into a worldwide pandemic, and over 33 million people were estimated to be HIV positive as of November 2007. Although this estimate represents a decrease from earlier predictions of nearly 40 million, such a number would have been

President Obama signs a bill in October 2009 to extend the Ryan White HIV/AIDS program, which offers medical services to those affected by the disease. The bill is named for Ryan White, a child who became infected with HIV in the early 1980s through blood products used to treat his hemophilia.

*Source: Doug Mills/*The New York Times

unthinkable during the years when AIDS was first being discovered. While the numbers no longer seem to be increasing at astronomical rates, researchers estimate that 2.5 million additional infections will be discovered annually, while approximately 2 million die from the disease each year, primarily in sub-Saharan Africa. Although *The Times* noted in an editorial that the pandemic appears to have stabilized, it nevertheless "remains one of the world's greatest scourges, requiring a strong campaign to bring it under control."

Bibliography

Altman, Dennis. *AIDS in the Mind of America.* Garden City, NY: Anchor Books, 1987.

Cohen, Cathy J. *The Boundaries of Blackness.* Chicago: University of Chicago Press, 1999.

Shilts, Randy. *And the Band Played On: Politics, People and the AIDS Epidemic.* New York: St. Martin's Press, 1987.

Treichler, Paula A. *How to Have Theory in an Epidemic: Cultural Chronicles of AIDS.* Durham, NC: Duke University Press, 1999.

From *The New York Times*

Altman, Lawrence K. "Clue Found on Homosexuals Precancer Syndrome." June 18, 1982.

———. "Rare Virus May Have Link with Immunological Illness." May 1, 1983.

———. "Debate Grows on U.S. Listing of Haitians in AIDS Category." July 31, 1983.

———. "The Doctor's World; AIDS Data Pour In, as Studies Proliferate." April 23, 1985.

———. "Test on Humans Near in AIDS Vaccine Hunt." March 18, 1987.

———. "U.S. and France End Rift on AIDS." April 1, 1987.

AP. "Top Health Official Refute Bias Charge in Combating AIDS." August 3, 1983.

———. "Panel Finds No Valid Excuse for Not Treating AIDS Case." September 22, 1983.

———. "Conference on AIDS Begins in Atlanta." April 16, 1985.

———. "Colorado Lists Those Exposed to AIDS Virus." August 24, 1985.

———. "Poll Indicates Majority Favor Quarantine for AIDS Victims." December 20, 1985.

———. "Bush Assails Tactics Used by AIDS Lobby." April 21, 1991.

Boffey, Phillip M. "Blacks Alerted on Risks of AIDS." October 23, 1985.

———. Philip M. "Reagan to Back AIDS Plan Urging Youths to Avoid Sex." February 26, 1987.

Boyd, Gerald M. "Reagan Urges Abstinence for Young to Avoid AIDS." April 2, 1987.

Bruni, Frank. "A Decade-Old Activism of Unmitigated Gall Is Fading." March 21, 1997.

Carroll, Maurice. "State Permits Closing of Bathhouses to Cut AIDS." October 26, 1985.

Conant, Marcus. "Where Is U.S. Fighting the War on AIDS?" May 4, 1985.

DeParle, Jason. "111 Held in St. Patrick's AIDS Protest." December 11, 1989.

———. "Rude, Rash, Effective, ACT-UP Shifts AIDS Policy." January 3, 1990.

Dowd, Maureen. "For Victims of AIDS, Support in a Lonely Siege." December 5, 1983.

Eckholm, Erik. "Fears on AIDS Termed Largely Without Causes." September 13, 1985.

Herman, Robin. "A Disease's Spread Provokes Anxiety." August 8, 1982.

Howe, Marvine. "For People with AIDS, Housing Is Hard to Find." June 25, 1984.

Koch, Edward I. "Senator Helms's Callousness toward AIDS Victims." November 7, 1987.

Kolata, Gina. "Ideas & Trends; Advocates' Tactics on AIDS Issues Provoking Warnings of a Backlash." March 11, 1990.

Lambert, Bruce. "AIDS in Black Women Seen as Leading Killer." July 11, 1990.

Marantz Henig, Robin. "AIDS: A New Disease's Deadly Odyssey." February 6, 1983.

McFadden, Robert. "Judge Overturns U.S. Rule Blocking 'Offensive' Educational Material on AIDS." May 12, 1992.

Meislin, Richard J. "AIDS Said to Increase Bias Against Homosexuals." January 21, 1986.

Morgan, Thomas. "Mainstream Strategy for AIDS Group." July 22, 1988.

Navarro, Mireya. "AIDS in Women Rising, but Many Ignore the Threat." December 28, 1990.

Norman, Michael. "Homosexuals Confronting a Time of Change." June 16, 1983.

Pear, Robert. "Health Chief Calls AIDS Battle 'No.1 Priority.'" May 25, 1983.

Pollack, Andrew. "F.D.A. Backs AIDS Pill to Be Taken Once a Day." July 13, 2006.

Pollack, Andrew, and Lawrence K. Altman. "Large Trial Finds AIDS Vaccine Fails to Stop Infection." February 24, 2003.

Richardson, Lynda. "AIDS Is Still Here, but Donors Drift Off; As Disease Lingers, Public Interest Wanes and Service Groups Falter." January 13, 1999.

Rohter, Larry. "11,000 Boycott Start of Classes in AIDS Protest." September 10, 1985.

Schmalz, Jeffrey. "Whatever Happened to AIDS?" November 28, 1993.

Schmeck, Harold M., Jr. "AIDS Drugs Offer Hope but Cure Remains Distant." March 17, 1987.

Shenon, Phillip. "A Move to Evict AIDS Physician Fought by State." October 1, 1983.

Shipp. E.R. "Concern over Spread of AIDS Generates a Spate of New Laws Nationwide." October 26, 1985.

Stolberg, Sheryl Gay. "Epidemic of Silence: A special report; Eyes Shut, Black America Is Being Ravaged by AIDS." June 29, 1998.

Sullivan, Andrew. "When Plagues End." November 10, 1996.

Sullivan, Ronald. "Parishioners Block Archdiocese's AIDS Shelter." August 31, 1985.

Unsigned. "San Francisco Seeks to Combat Fear of AIDS." May 22, 1983.

———. "Mrs. Heckler Asks for More AIDS Funds." August 18, 1983.

———. "Ideas & Trends: A Symposium on Science, Sociology and Disease: Attitudes That Shape the Fight against AIDS." June 2, 1985.

———. "Dr. Koop's Decent AIDS Dissent." October 25, 1986.

———. "AIDS: The Next Phase; An Ever-Widening Epidemic Tears at the City's Life and Spirit." March 16, 1987.

———. "AIDS Protesters Enter Sets of 2 Newscasts." January 23, 1991.

UPI. "The Region; 2 Officers Cited in AIDS Incident." October 17, 1983.

———. "Indiana Judge Allows AIDS Victim Back in
    School." April 11, 1986.
Weinraub, Bernard. "Reagan Orders AIDS Report,
    Giving High Priority to Work for Cure." February 6,
    1986.
Werner Maitland, Leslie. "Reagan Officials Debate AIDS
    Education Policy." January 24, 1987.

———. "2 Administration Leaders Agree on AIDS
    Education." January 31, 1987.
———. "Koop Urges TV Condom Ads to Fight AIDS."
    February 11, 1987.
Williams, Lena. "200,000 March in Capital to Seek
    Gay Rights and Money for AIDS." October 12,
    1987.

Doctors Puzzled by Cancer Outbreak among Gay Men

Between 1979 and 1981, forty-one cases of Kaposi's sarcoma were diagnosed in homosexual men in New York and California. Although more common in equatorial Africa, this cancer is rare in the United States and typically strikes men over the age of fifty who often live with the illness for up to ten years. This outbreak struck men as young as twenty-six and killed eight within twenty-four months of their diagnosis.

The cause of the outbreak was then unknown and was not believed to be contagious or to present any danger to "nonhomosexuals." All known cases involved homosexual men, most of whom reported frequent sexual activity with multiple partners, previous viral and parasitic infections, and the use of drugs such as amyl nitrate and LSD during sex. Dr. Friedman-Kien of the New York University Medical Center tested nine victims and found them to have severe problems with their immune systems, but he was unable to say if this was a causal factor or the by-product of infection or drug use. A research team investigated the possibility of a link to previous cytomegalovirus (herpes) infection.

Kaposi's sarcoma causes violet-colored spots or lumps on the victim's skin and is often accompanied by swollen glands. Doctors who regularly treated homosexuals were notified in an effort to identify additional cases and to ensure speedy access to chemotherapy. The federal CDC published a description of the outbreak based on twenty-six cases.

JULY 3, 1981
RARE CANCER SEEN IN 41 HOMOSEXUALS
By LAWRENCE K. ALTMAN

Doctors in New York and California have diagnosed among homosexual men 41 cases of a rare and often rapidly fatal form of cancer. Eight of the victims died less than 24 months after the diagnosis was made.

The cause of the outbreak is unknown, and there is as yet no evidence of contagion. But the doctors who have made the diagnoses, mostly in New York City and the San Francisco Bay area, are alerting other physicians who treat large numbers of homosexual men to the problem in an effort to help identify more cases and to reduce the delay in offering chemotherapy treatment.

The sudden appearance of the cancer, called Kaposi's Sarcoma, has prompted a medical investigation that experts say could have as much scientific as public health importance because of what it may teach about determining the causes of more common types of cancer.

First Appears in Spots

Doctors have been taught in the past that the cancer usually appeared first in spots on the legs and that the disease took a slow course of up to 10 years. But these recent cases have shown that it appears in one or more violet-colored spots anywhere on the body. The spots generally do not itch or cause other symptoms, often can be mistaken for bruises, sometimes appear as lumps and can turn brown after a period of time. The cancer often causes swollen lymph glands, and then kills by spreading throughout the body.

Doctors investigating the outbreak believe that many cases have gone undetected because of the rarity of the condition and the difficulty even dermatologists may have in diagnosing it.

In a letter alerting other physicians to the problem, Dr. Alvin E. Friedman-Kien of New York University Medical Center, one of the investigators, described the appearance of the outbreak as "rather devastating."

Dr. Friedman-Kien said in an interview yesterday that he knew of 41 cases collated in the last five weeks, with the cases themselves dating to the past 30 months. The Federal Centers for Disease Control in Atlanta is expected to publish the first description of the outbreak in its weekly report today, according to a spokesman, Dr. James Curran. The report notes 26 of the cases—20 in New York and six in California.

There is no national registry of cancer victims, but the nationwide incidence of Kaposi's Sarcoma in the past had been estimated by the Centers for Disease Control to be less than six-one-hundredths of a case per 100,000 people annually, or about two cases in every three million people. However, the disease accounts for up to 9 percent of all cancers in a belt across equatorial Africa, where it commonly affects children and young adults.

In the United States, it has primarily affected men older than 50 years. But in the recent cases, doctors at nine medical centers in New York and seven hospitals in California have been diagnosing the condition among younger men, all of whom said in the course of standard diagnostic interviews that they were homosexual. Although the ages of the patients have ranged from 26 to 51 years, many have been under 40, with the mean at 39.

Nine of the 41 cases known to Dr. Friedman-Kien were diagnosed in California, and several of those victims reported that they had been in New York in the period preceding the diagnosis. Dr. Friedman-Kien said that his colleagues were checking on reports of two victims diagnosed in Copenhagen, one of whom had visited New York.

Viral Infections Indicated

No one medical investigator has yet interviewed all the victims, Dr. Curran said. According to Dr. Friedman-Kien, the reporting doctors said that most cases had involved homosexual men who have had multiple and frequent sexual encounters with different partners, as many as 10 sexual encounters each night up to four times a week.

Many of the patients have also been treated for viral infections such as herpes, cytomegalovirus, and hepatitis B as well as parasitic infections such as amebiasis and giardiasis. Many patients also reported that they had used drugs such as amyl nitrite and LSD to heighten sexual pleasure.

Cancer is not believed to be contagious, but conditions that might precipitate it, such as particular viruses or environmental factors, might account for an outbreak among a single group.

The medical investigators say some indirect evidence actually points away from contagion as a cause. None of the patients knew each other, although the theoretical possibility that some may have had sexual contact with a person with Kaposi's Sarcoma at some point in the past could not be excluded, Dr. Friedman-Kien said.

Dr. Curran said there was no apparent danger to nonhomosexuals from contagion. "The best evidence against contagion," he said, "is that no cases have been reported to date outside the homosexual community or in women."

Dr. Friedman-Kien said he had tested nine of the victims and found severe defects in their immunological systems. The patients had serious malfunctions of two types of cells called T and B cell lymphocytes, which have important roles in fighting infections and cancer.

But Dr. Friedman-Kien emphasized that the researchers did not know whether the immunological defects were the underlying problem or had developed secondarily to the infections or drug use.

The research team is testing various hypotheses, one of which is a possible link between past infection with cytomegalovirus and development of Kaposi's Sarcoma.

CDC Raises Alarm about Gay-Related Immune Deficiency

The Centers for Disease Control announced that gay-related immune deficiency reached epidemic proportions in 1982, with 335 people infected and 136 dead. Further, initial research at the time suggested that the illness may lay dormant for an unknown period of time, implying that "tens of thousands" more homosexuals may have been unknowingly infected. In addition, some heterosexual men (primarily intravenous drug users) as well as 13 heterosexual women were known to have contracted the disease. The human toll of this illness was compounded by the financial impact, with hospital care that cost upwards of $64,000 per patient. As Dr. Bruce A. Chabner of the National Cancer Institute stated at a recent congressional hearing, this disease was "of concern to all Americans."

What was then known as GRID destroys the immune system, leaving its victims prone to a wide variety of illnesses and infections. Common symptoms include swollen glands, weight loss, and fever. The cause was unknown, but the fact that it had not spread to researchers, hospital workers, or victims' family members suggested that it was not spread person to person like the flu. Based on CDC comparisons of infected and noninfected homosexual men, researchers investigated the possibility that GRID might have been related to the use of nitrite drugs or the introduction of semen into the blood stream during sex. Dr. Lawrence Mass, a New York City physician, commented that "gay people whose life style consists of anonymous sexual encounters are going to have to do some serious rethinking." With the cause and transmission methods of this mysterious new disease then unknown, and no effective treatment or cure in sight, negative attitudes and discrimination toward gay men and others likely to be infected with AIDS were prevalent.

MAY 11, 1982
NEW HOMOSEXUAL DISORDER WORRIES HEALTH OFFICIALS
By LAWRENCE K. ALTMAN

A serious disorder of the immune system that has been known to doctors for less than a year—a disorder that appears to affect primarily male homosexuals—has now afflicted at least 335 people, of whom it has killed 136, officials of the Centers for Disease Control in Atlanta said yesterday. Federal health officials are concerned that tens of thousands more homosexual men may be silently affected and therefore vulnerable to potentially grave ailments.

Moreover, this immune-system breakdown, which has been implicated in a rare type of cancer, called Kaposi's sarcoma, and seems to invite in its wake a wide variety of serious infections and other disorders, has developed among some heterosexual women and bisexual and heterosexual men.

At a recent Congressional hearing, Dr. Bruce A. Chabner of the National Cancer Institute said that the growing problem was now "of concern to all Americans."

The cause of the disorder is unknown. Researchers call it A.I.D., for acquired immunodeficiency disease, or GRID, for gay-related immunodeficiency. It has been reported in 20 states and seven countries. But the overwhelming majority of cases have been in New York City (158), elsewhere in New York State (10), New Jersey (14) and California (71).

Thirteen of those affected have been heterosexual women. Some male victims are believed to have been heterosexual, and to have been chiefly users of heroin and other drugs by injection into their veins. But most cases have occurred among homosexual men, in particular those who have had numerous sexual partners, often anonymous partners whose identity remains unknown.

According to both the Centers for Disease Control and the National Cancer Institute in Bethesda, Md., GRID has reached epidemic proportions and the current totals probably represent "just the tip of the iceberg." Preliminary results of immunological tests have led some Federal health officials to fear that tens of thousands of homosexual men may have the acquired immune dysfunction and be at risk for developing complications such as Kaposi's cancer, infections and other disorders at some future date.

GRID is "a matter of urgent public health and scientific importance," Dr. James W. Curran, a Federal epidemiologist who coordinates the Centers for Disease Control's task force on Kaposi's sarcoma and opportunistic infections, told the Congressional hearing. Opportunistic infections are those that rarely cause illness except in those whose immunological resistance has been lowered by drugs or disease.

More than human suffering is involved. Hospital costs have reached more than $64,000 per patient, and Dr. Curran said that if such costs are typical, "the first 300 cases account for an estimated $18 million in hospital expenses alone."

Experts currently think of GRID as a sort of immunological time bomb. Once it develops, it may stay silent for an unknown period, and then, at a later date, go on to produce Kaposi's sarcoma, an opportunistic infection, a so-called auto-immune disorder, or any combination of these.

Further, no one is certain that the immune disorder can be reversed. Many patients have survived a bout of pneumonia or other illness, only to succumb to another or to go on to develop Kaposi's sarcoma or some other fatal cancer.

'Natural' Immunity Suppressor

GRID resembles the failures of the immunological system that complicate the treatment of many chronic disorders with steroid and other drugs that suppress the immune system. The same problem occurs among recipients of transplanted kidneys and other organs who take the immunosuppressive drugs to help prevent rejection of the organ. With immunity suppressed, the body becomes vulnerable to a variety of problems, chiefly infections by organisms that otherwise rarely cause disease.

GRID, however, is the first naturally occurring outbreak of immune suppression to affect a community of free-living people, in contrast, for example, to an epidemic in a hospital. The degree of immunological suppression is

extraordinary, far greater than usually observed in patients treated with immunosuppressive drugs, according to articles in medical journals and interviews with experts.

Those experts are now reporting finding a wider range of disorders than were associated with GRID when it first came to public attention last summer. These include eye damage, lupus, I.T.P. (idiopathic thrombocytopenic purpura), certain types of anemia, and other cancers, including Burkitt's lymphoma and cancers of the tongue and anus.

Doctors are also seeing many cases of a generalized lymph gland swelling throughout the body, together with weight loss, fever and thrush, a fungal infection often found in the mouth and throat.

So far, epidemiologists have found no evidence that the condition is spread from person to person like influenza or measles. Therefore, they say, the general public need not fear an epidemic.

Many Causes Are Likely

Rather, Dr. Arthur S. Levine of the National Cancer Institute said, development of the syndrome seems to result from an accumulation of risk factors. Most experts say that if there is an infectious cause, it is not a single organism, but an organism acting together with another factor or factors, perhaps a drug.

Epidemiologists from the Centers for Disease Control have done studies among homosexual men with and without the immune disorder but matched in age, background and other characteristics. After testing for more than 130 potential risk factors, they found that the median number of lifetime male sexual partners for affected homosexual men was 1,160, compared to 524 for male homosexual men who did not have the syndrome. The study also found more use of sexual stimulants and illicit drugs among the GRID patients.

As further evidence against simple contagious spread, epidemiologists note that the syndrome has not spread to other family members, hospital workers or researchers on the disease. . . .

Why Now and Not Before?

Given the fact that homosexuality is not new, the most puzzling question is why the outbreak is occurring now, and not sometime in the past.

Scientific investigations are wide ranging, although most are focused on viruses, other organisms, drugs, or a combination of such factors.

Because homosexuals affected by GRID have reported using nitrite drugs more frequently than homosexuals who have not, some studies have focused on this class of drugs, which have come into widespread street use since the 1960's.

But although epidemiological studies have not "totally exonerated nitrites, the scientific evidence to implicate them is quite shaky," according to Dr. Curran.

Some experts theorize that the immunological disorder may be triggered by the introduction of sperm or seminal fluid into the blood through sexual contact, though infection and drug reaction are still also candidates.

In studies on mice at the National Cancer Institute, Dr. Ursula Hurtenbach and Dr. Gene M. Shearer have reported that a single injection of mouse sperm into the veins of male mice produced a profound and long-lasting suppression of certain immune functions.

Dr. Lawrence D. Mass, a New York City physician, said that "gay people whose life style consists of anonymous sexual encounters are going to have to do some serious rethinking."

The urgent need to discover the cause of the immune system disorder and to prevent the problems it creates has been underscored by Dr. Linda Laubenstein of New York University Medical Center. Dr. Laubenstein, who said she has treated 62 such patients in the last year and who is a leading investigator of the syndrome, summarized it by saying: "This problem certainly is not going away."

● ●

STUDY SUGGESTS AIDS MAY BE TRANSMITTED THROUGH HETEROSEXUAL INTERCOURSE

Dr. Carol Harris and a team of physicians from the Albert Einstein College of Medicine completed a study in 1983 that suggested AIDS may have been sexually transmitted to six women by their male partners. In addition to homosexuals, Haitians, and intravenous drug users, a small percentage of AIDS cases were linked to blood transfusions and the blood products used by hemophiliacs. Because of this, researchers suspected that the syndrome may be caused by a virus or other transmissible agent. To further investigate this possibility, Dr. Harris's team examined seven long-term sexual partners of heterosexual men with AIDS. One was found to have the disease, one appeared to be developing it, four had related abnormalities, and one was healthy. All six denied using intravenous drugs, and none had any other risk factors for the disease. Dr. James Curran, a researcher working on AIDS with the CDC, suggested that the transmission of the disorder may be similar to hepatitis B and cautioned that these women may have contracted it through sharing razors or some other contact besides sexual intercourse.

Intensive research was being carried out during this time to find the cause of the disease. Work by Robert Gallo and Luc Montagnier established a connection between HIV and AIDS. Further advances allowed for the testing of donated blood in 1985 for the virus, but not before thousands of people were potentially exposed through blood transfusions.

MAY 19, 1983
RESEARCH TRACES AIDS IN 6 OF 7 FEMALE PARTNERS
By LAWRENCE K. ALTMAN

A study of seven female sexual partners of men with acquired immune deficiency syndrome, or AIDS, suggests that the disease may be sexually transmitted between heterosexual men and women, according to its authors.

Of the seven women in the study, which was reported in today's issue of The New England Journal of Medicine, one developed the disorder, another appeared to be in early stages of developing it, four had abnormalities linked to the syndrome and one was healthy.

Several other similarly suggestive but inconclusive cases have been identified by Federal epidemiologists at the Centers for Disease Control in Atlanta, the head of the AIDS research group there said yesterday.

An epidemic affecting at least 1,410 people has developed since 1980. The cause of the disease is unknown and as of May 9, 541 victims have died, according to the Atlanta center.

Four Groups Are at Risk

Most cases have involved male homosexuals, intravenous drug users and people from Haiti. A few cases have occurred among people receiving blood transfusions and hemophiliacs who have received blood products.

Because the transmission of the disease appears to have resulted occasionally from blood products, many researchers have strongly suspected that the syndrome may be caused by a virus or some other transmissible agent.

For that reason, a team of physicians headed by Dr. Carol Harris from the Albert Einstein College of Medicine studied the regular female sexual partners of the 17 heterosexual male patients with the syndrome who were treated at Montefiore Medical Center, North Central Bronx Hospital and the Bronx Municipal Hospital Center.

Dr. Harris's team learned that the 17 men had 12 regular female sexual partners. Seven female partners agreed to cooperate in the study; four could not be found and one refused to participate.

None Sought Doctors' Help

None of the seven women had sought medical attention. All said that their sexual relations were only with men and all denied using intravenous drugs or inhalants such as cocaine.

Six of the seven male partners of these females had injected heroin or cocaine; the seventh inhaled cocaine without injecting it. Six of the males were strictly heterosexual; the seventh had had homosexual encounters two to four years before becoming ill.

None of the women had any of the known risk factors. None were Haitian and none had hemophilia. They were 23 to 39 years old. "The only common risk factor we could identify was prolonged monogamous contact" with a male AIDS patient, Dr. Harris's team reported.

The study presented limited evidence that the scope of the syndrome may extend beyond the previously suspected groups of victims.

Comparison to Hepatitis B

Speaking of the findings, Dr. James Curran, the head of the group working on the syndrome at the Atlanta centers, said it was possible that the transmission of the disorder was similar to hepatitis B. This common liver infection can be spread by heterosexual contact as well as by blood and other ways.

Dr. Curran cautioned that the new findings did not necessarily mean that the seven women were infected specifically by sexual contact. Dr. Curran said: "They could have gotten it by sharing razors or something else. It is known that wives and husbands of hepatitis B carriers have higher rates of hepatitis B infection than other family members do. This may be something like that."

GUARDED OPTIMISM FOLLOWING POSSIBLE DISCOVERY OF AIDS VIRUS

In 1984 Dr. James O. Mason, head of the federal Centers for Disease Control, announced his belief that French scientists had discovered the virus that causes AIDS and that this then-new information would eventually lead to diagnostic tests, procedures for screening the blood supply, new treatments for patients, and the development of an AIDS vaccine. Despite the need for additional research to confirm the findings, Dr. Mason stated that "we have to move forward on the assumption that this virus is the cause in order to speed up trials of possible new therapies for the patients who are dying from AIDS."

Dr. Luc Montagnier and a team of French scientists at the Pasteur Institute in Paris discovered the retrovirus they believed was the cause of AIDS in 1983 and named it lymphadenopathy-associated virus (LAV). Dr. Robert Gallo at the National Cancer Institute also identified a retrovirus as a possible cause of AIDS, and he dubbed it human T-cell lymphotropic virus (HTLV-3). Dr. Gallo could not then be reached for comment. Dr. Mason expressed his belief that LAV and HTLV-3 were the same virus or closely related variants. This was confirmed shortly after this discovery, and the retrovirus was thereafter known as the human immunodeficiency virus, or HIV.

APRIL 22, 1984
FEDERAL OFFICIAL SAYS HE BELIEVES CAUSE OF AIDS HAS BEEN FOUND
By LAWRENCE K. ALTMAN
Special to the New York Times

Dr. James O. Mason, head of the Federal Centers for Disease Control, said today that he believed a virus discovered in France was the cause of acquired immune deficiency syndrome, or AIDS.

"I believe we have the cause of AIDS, and it is an exciting discovery," Dr. Mason, who is a virologist, said in an interview here. "The public needs to know that this is a breakthrough and that it is significant."

The French virus is called LAV, for lymphadenopathy-associated virus. It is a member of the retrovirus family, which over the past year has been the leading candidate as the cause of AIDS.

New Findings in Paris

Dr. Mason said he based his opinion on findings made in recent weeks by the researchers who discovered the virus at the Pasteur Institute in Paris last year. Dr. Mason said his opinion was also based on additional findings made by scientists at the disease centers here and at the National Institutes of Health in Bethesda, Md.

He stressed, however, the need for additional research to confirm the findings.

"We cannot know for sure now that the LAV virus is the agent that causes AIDS, but the pattern it follows in the human body makes us believe it is," Dr. Mason said.

AIDS, which was first recognized in 1981, is a fatal disorder that destroys the body's immune system. According to the Centers for Disease Control, 4,087 cases were reported in the United States as of Monday, and 1,758 patients have died.

More than two-thirds of the victims have been homosexual men; most of the others have been users of intravenous drugs or hemophiliacs who require frequent blood transfusions. A number of cases have been reported among people of Haitian descent who do not seem to fall into those categories, although there is controversy among medical authorities over their inclusion among the "risk groups."

Dr. Mason predicted that in time the new findings would lead to development of a diagnostic test for AIDS as well as a test to help in prevention. For one thing, he said a test might be developed to screen out AIDS-contaminated blood before it was transfused to patients.

Tests could also open up the possibility of developing a vaccine against AIDS.

Dr. Mason expressed confidence that methods would quickly be found to grow large amounts of the virus in cells in the laboratory.

Dr. Mason said he did not foresee any insurmountable obstacles to development of a vaccine, although the process could take many years. He said that when the time came for testing a vaccine, he doubted it would be difficult to recruit human volunteers.

Meanwhile, information derived from a diagnostic test might help researchers determine if there were other means of temporarily correcting the abnormalities of the immune system resulting from the syndrome.

Possible Treatment Mentioned

One possible treatment that is being discussed only in theory was mentioned by Dr. Mason. It would be to transfuse AIDS patients with gamma globulin from people who had developed some immunity to the disorder and who had not developed a full- blown case. Gamma globulin is the portion of the blood that contains the antibodies that humans normally form to protect against infections.

One reason for believing that the virus is the cause of AIDS, Dr. Mason said, is that tests first done in France have shown that the LAV attacks the same white blood cells, called OKT4, or helper T-cells, that are destroyed by the disease.

The centers' director said that the inability thus far to infect animals with the LAV virus had enormously increased the difficulty of proving the causal relationship between the virus and AIDS.

If the LAV virus is not confirmed or validated as the cause of the disease in months to come, Dr. Mason said he recognized that the Government agency might have a credibility problem.

Nevertheless, Dr. Mason said he was speaking out because of the urgency of the AIDS epidemic.

"We have to move forward on the assumption that this virus is the cause in order to speed up trials of possible new therapies for the patients who are dying from AIDS," Dr. Mason said.

Federal health officials have scheduled a news conference in Washington for 1 P.M. Monday, presumably to discuss findings made by an AIDS researcher, Dr. Robert Gallo, and his colleagues at the National Cancer Institute concerning a retrovirus they have reportedly called HTLV-3, for human T-cell lymphotropic virus. It is believed to be different from another retrovirus called HTLV-1 that had been a focus of research into AIDS.

A report by Dr. Gallo's group is scheduled to be published soon in the journal Science.

Dr. Gallo could not be reached for comment.

Dr. Mason and other scientists familiar with the research said that they presumed HTLV-3, LAV and a third virus known as IDAV were different names given to the same virus. But tests have not yet been made to determine whether the viruses are the same or not.

"Logic would lead you to believe that we are dealing with one agent with perhaps some closely related variants," Dr. Mason said. . . .

- -

TEST LICENSED TO SAFEGUARD BLOOD SUPPLY

In March 1985, Margaret M. Heckler, secretary of Health and Human Services, announced the imminent availability of a test to protect blood transfusion recipients from contracting AIDS. This test would allow blood banks, plasma centers, and laboratories to screen potential donors for antibodies to the virus believed to cause the disease. Of the 8,495 AIDS cases in the United States in 1985, 113 were thought to have resulted from contaminated blood or blood products. The test was licensed for commercial production and was expected to cost about $6 per person to administer. Up to $12 million in government funding would be provided to pay for the test.

The article raises concerns about false-positive results and the importance of confidentiality in testing. There was also hope expressed at the time that the new test would help to reduce blood supply shortages by encouraging fearful donors to resume giving blood. Since 1983, men who have sex with men have been barred by the FDA from donating blood. While reviews of the policy in 2000 and 2006 yielded no change, there was growing sentiment in 2010 to reverse the policy.

MARCH 3, 1985
AIDS BLOOD TEST TO BE AVAILABLE IN 2 TO 6 WEEKS
By ROBERT PEAR

Federal health officials say that a blood test to screen for acquired immune deficiency syndrome, or AIDS, licensed today for commercial production, will be widely available in the United States in two to six weeks.

Margaret M. Heckler, Secretary of Health and Human Services, announced approval of the test at a news conference here. She said that if the test indicated a person had antibodies to the virus suspected of causing the disorder he would not be allowed to donate blood.

Health officials said that thus far 113 cases of AIDS had been linked to blood or blood products. As of Feb. 18, the Centers for Disease Control reported the United States had 8,495 cases of AIDS, an illness that breaks down the body's ability to fight off the disorder.

More than 4,000 AIDS victims, most of them homosexual men, drug abusers or hemophiliacs, have died. The illness seems to be transmitted mainly through sexual contact or through blood from a person who has the disorder.

Abbott Laboratories Licensed

The Food and Drug Administration licensed Abbott Laboratories of North Chicago to make and distribute the test kits to 2,300 blood banks, plasma centers and laboratories. Four other companies have applied for licenses. Mrs. Heckler said she believed they would be approved soon.

In announcing approval of the test today, the Secretary said: "This test will simply reveal the presence in the blood of antibodies to the virus that causes AIDS. A positive result, in and of itself, does not mean that a person has AIDS. The test we are licensing today is not meant as a diagnostic tool for AIDS. It is designed to screen blood."

When a person is infected by a virus, the body's white blood cells normally begin to fight the infection by producing substances called antibodies. But, according to the Public Health Service, "Not everyone who is infected with the virus will have antibodies." And some people with antibodies will not develop the disorder caused by the virus.

Dr. Frank E. Young, the Commissioner of Food and Drugs, said the new test was not perfect. Out of 100 blood samples that produce positive test results in the initial screening, he said, about 17 will not, in fact, contain antibodies to the AIDS virus.

Cost of Test Put at $6

Dr. Young said blood banks should repeat the antibody test and use other laboratory techniques to confirm the results before notifying the donor, but he estimated that with the new test "we will be able to prevent 50 to 150 cases per year" of AIDS.

Federal officials said the new test would have to be used each time a person donated blood and would cost about $6 each time it was administered.

"The Government will provide the funding for those who wish to take the test and are not able to pay for the test themselves," Mrs. Heckler said, adding that up to $12 million in Federal funds would be available.

The antibody test may alleviate shortages of blood in some parts of the country that began in 1983, when concern and misunderstanding of the AIDS problem led many people to stop donating blood.

Red Cross Official Pleased

Richard F. Schubert, president of the American Red Cross, the nation's largest collector and processor of blood and blood products, said he was pleased with today's action. "Testing for the antibody," he said, "will help blood collection agencies to further improve the safety of the blood supply in the United States."

Each year, about 12 million pints of whole blood is collected to meet the needs of patients, and four million patients receive blood.

Some physicians and some groups representing homosexuals have expressed concern that positive test results, whether accurate or inaccurate, might be used unfairly to stigmatize blood donors.

The Government said it was important for physicians and laboratory personnel to maintain the confidentiality of test results indicating that a person had antibodies to the HTLV-III virus identified as the cause of AIDS.

* *

New AIDS Drug Stirs Hope and Controversy

Although hope for a cure for AIDS was dim in the early days of the endemic, the drug azidothymidine (AZT) was approved for use by the Food and Drug Administration in 1987 and offered "a shred of hope" to some patients, particularly those suffering from *Pneumocystis carinii* pneumonia.

Rather than actually killing the HIV virus, AZT impedes its ability to reproduce. The drug caused serious side effects in some but extended the lives of others by months. Produced by the Burroughs Wellcome Company under the name Retrovir, the drug was made available only in limited quantities initially and the cost—over $8,000 per year for a single patient—proved controversial.

The approval of AZT as an effective drug in combating the HIV virus was a breakthrough in treatment. In the 1990s more treatments were tested and brought to market, including drug "cocktails" that not only slowed down the progression of the disease but also delayed drug resistance. The quest for an AIDS vaccine and cure continues into the postmillennial era, but with treatment, those infected with HIV today can expect a much longer lifespan than ever before.

MARCH 22, 1987
THE NATION: AIDS TREATMENT WINS THE APPROVAL OF FEDERAL AGENCY
By MARTHA A. MILES AND CAROLINE RAND HERRON

Deciding that the promise of prolonging the lives of some AIDS patients outweighs serious side effects, the Food and Drug Administration last week approved the use of the drug azidothymidine, or AZT. A cure for acquired immune deficiency syndrome is not in sight, but AZT may offer many victims a shred of hope.

While AZT does not kill the AIDS virus, it impedes its ability to reproduce. While some AIDS patients have been harmed by the drug, tests have shown that months have been added to the lives of some of those suffering from a disease called pneumocystis carinii pneumonia.

Other categories of patients also have been helped by AZT, and doctors hope clinical trials will further extend its reach.

At first the drug, which is available from the Burroughs Wellcome Company under the name Retrovir, will be in short supply and prescriptions limited to those who seem most likely to benefit. But by the end of the year, it is expected to become more widely available. It has been estimated that treatment will cost each patient more than $8,000 a year, and the high price has become a matter of controversy. . . .

· ·

PRESIDENT REAGAN'S FIRST PUBLIC STATEMENTS ABOUT AIDS

President Reagan publicly responded to the AIDS crisis for the first time while answering news conference questions. In response to criticism of his administration's funding for AIDS research, the president cited budget restraints and defended his record of providing approximately $500 million since in 1981. This includes $126 million requested for next year's budget as well as funding increases proposed by Congress in each of the last three budget cycles.

When asked whether he would send a young child of his own to school with a classmate suffering from AIDS, Reagan expressed both compassion for children ostracized because of their illness and understanding for parents worried about safety issues. He acknowledged that the virus was generally believed to be transmitted through sexual contact, needles, and transfusions but also stated that until scientists conclusively determined that AIDS could not be transmitted by children at school, "I think we just have to do the best we can with this problem."

SEPTEMBER 18, 1985
REAGAN DEFENDS FINANCING FOR AIDS

By PHILIP BOFFEY

Special to the New York Times

President Reagan, who has been accused of public indifference to the AIDS crisis by groups representing victims of the deadly disease, said last night that his Administration was already making a "vital contribution" to research on the disease within the limits imposed by "budgetary restraints."

Mr. Reagan was asked at his news conference if he could support "a massive Government research program against AIDS like the program that President Nixon launched against cancer," in which Mr. Nixon called in 1971 for a "total national commitment" to "conquering this dread disease." Mr. Reagan said that he had been supporting research into AIDS, acquired immune deficiency syndrome, for the last four years and that the effort was a "top priority" for the Administration.

The President also expressed sympathy for both sides in the controversy over whether children suffering from AIDS should be permitted to attend school with healthy children.

His remarks appeared to be the first time he has publicly addressed the issue of the lethal disease that has claimed thousands of victims, primarily among male homosexuals, intravenous drug addicts and hemophiliacs whose condition requires frequent blood transfusions. Although the Department of Health and Human Services has declared AIDS its "number one priority," Mr. Reagan himself has been criticized by groups calling for more Government action on the disease. . . .

Mr. Reagan resisted the suggestion that more money was needed. He said that AIDS had been "one of the top priorities with us" and that the Administration had provided or appropriated some half a billion dollars for research on AIDS since he took office in 1981. He included in that figure the $126 million that the Administration is seeking for the next budget year. "So this is a top priority with us," he said. "Yes, there's no question about the seriousness of this, and the need to find an answer."

When told that the top AIDS scientist had said the Administration's budgets were "not nearly enough at this stage to go forward and really attack the problem," Mr. Reagan replied: "I think with our budgetary restraints and all it seems to me that $126 million in a single year for research has got to be something of a vital contribution."

Albert R. Brashear, a White House spokesman, said that Mr. Reagan intended to suggest that current spending levels, which have been increasing steadily, were enough.

However, a House appropriations subcommittee recently voted to boost the Administration's proposed budget for AIDS research at the National Institutes of Health next year by $70 million, which would double the amount of research proposed at that agency by the Administration. Congress has increased the Administration's proposed spending levels for AIDS research in each of the last three budgets. Total health research spending by the Federal Government was estimated at $4.96 billion in the fiscal year 1985 and is to rise to $5.20 billion in the fiscal year 1986 which begins Oct. 1.

On the issue of schools, Mr. Reagan was asked, "If you had younger children, would you send them to a school with a child who had AIDS?"

He said he was "glad I'm not faced with that problem today." He said he could "well understand" the plight of parents worried about the safety of their children and had compassion for children suffering from AIDS who might be made outcasts.

Mr. Reagan said "it is true that some medical sources" say that AIDS cannot be transmitted in ways that involve a child in school. The known routes of transmission, according to health experts, are sexual intercourse and exchanges of contaminated blood through needles or transfusions. "And yet medicine has not come forth unequivocally and said, this we know for a fact that it is safe," the President said. "And until they do, I think we just have to do the best we can with this problem. I can understand both sides of it."

STUDY FINDS GOVERNMENT AIDS EFFORT INADEQUATE

Calling into question claims that AIDS was the United States' top health priority, a 390-page report released in 1986 by the National Academy of Sciences stated that the federal government's response to the crisis had been inadequately funded and poorly coordinated. Public education and vaccine development efforts were singled out as particular areas of concern. Compiled by a team of public health experts and scientists, the report was touted by the Academy as "the most comprehensive study of the AIDS epidemic to date." Regarding the report's call for an annual AIDS investment of $2 billion, contributor Dr. James Chin of the University of California at Berkeley clarified that this figure covers only the cost of education and research necessary to manage the epidemic, not health care for its victims, which could require an additional $16 billion.

Dr. Robert E. Windom, assistant secretary of Health and Human Services, stated that the government was already increasing public education efforts but that he did not know if annual AIDS spending of $2 billion by 1990 could be justified. Unofficial estimates placed U.S. government expenditures for AIDS at a few hundred million dollars for fiscal year 1986.

By the 2000s the U.S. government had dramatically increased funding for AIDS programs. In the 2006 fiscal year, the federal government budgeted an estimated $19.7 billion dollars toward AIDS programs, up from an estimated $10 million in 1983.

OCTOBER 30, 1986
FEDERAL EFFORTS ON AIDS CRITICIZED AS GRAVELY WEAK
By PHILIP M. BOFFEY
Special to the New York Times

The National Academy of Sciences charged yesterday that the Federal Government's response to the AIDS epidemic had been dangerously inadequate and called for a $2 billion-a-year educational and research effort to avert a medical catastrophe.

The Academy said in a report that the AIDS problem was becoming so urgent that it required "perhaps the most wide-ranging and intensive efforts ever made against an infectious disease."

Dr. David Baltimore of the Massachusetts Institute of Technology, co-chairman of the report committee, said at a news conference in Washington that the Academy was "quite honestly frightened" by the AIDS virus's potential to spread.

'A National Health Crisis'

"This is a national health crisis," he said, "of a magnitude that requires Presidential leadership to bring together all elements of society to deal with the problem."

"If the spread of the virus is not checked, the present epidemic could become a catastrophe," the report warned. "The situation demands both immediate action to stem the spread of infection and a long-term national commitment to produce a vaccine and therapeutic drugs."

Dr. Robert E. Windom, an Assistant Secretary of Health and Human Services, took issue with the report. "I would say there has been a conscientious effort to do a good job," he said.

Acquired immune deficiency syndrome is a deadly disease that cripples the body's defenses against infection. More than 25,000 Americans have contracted the ailment; about half have died.

Team of Experts Assembled

The views of the Academy, generally considered the nation's most prestigious scientific organization, were set forth in a 390-page report, "Confronting AIDS," which was prepared by a large team of public health experts and scientists assembled by the Academy and its principal health unit, the Institute of Medicine. The report was described by the Academy as "the most comprehensive study of the AIDS epidemic to date."

The report was notable for its authoritative endorsement of the gravity of the AIDS epidemic and its polite but firm criticism of current efforts to deal with the problem as inadequate.

Despite the Federal Government's insistence that AIDS is its No. 1 health priority, the report concluded that the nation's response to the AIDS epidemic has been inadequate in many key aspects. The Academy team expressed "major concern" over "lack of cohesiveness" in planning the attack on AIDS and charged, "There has been inadequate Federal coordination of vaccine development." It complained that Federal programs to educate the public about how to avoid AIDS had been "woefully inadequate."

In an interview, Dr. Windom of the Department of Health and Human Services said the Government was already increasing its efforts to educate people about AIDS. He said he did not know whether the Government would be justified in spending $2 billion a year on AIDS by 1990, as the Academy recommended.

In Rapid City, S.D., Albert R. Brashear, a White House spokesman traveling with President Reagan, said, "We would have to wait and take a look at the Academy's report before we comment."

The Academy's judgments carry weight because of its reputation and function. Although it is a private organization, it has been chartered by Congress to provide advice to the Federal Government on a wide range of technical issues.

Some Echoes of Surgeon General

The Academy's report echoed some of the advice issued last week by the Surgeon General, C. Everett Koop, in a 36-page report on the need for explicit public education to stop the spread of AIDS. But the Academy panel went far beyond the Surgeon General's proposals in calling for a major infusion of new Federal funds to carry out a coordinated program of education, public health and research that would cost an estimated $2 billion a year by 1990.

According to unofficial estimates, only a few hundred million dollars were spent on such activities in the fiscal year 1986, which ended Sept. 30.

"The $2 billion yearly expenditure proposed for responding to the epidemic is a small fraction of the billions of dollars for care that the epidemic is sure to cost, especially if it is not rapidly curbed," the Academy said.

Dr. James Chin of the University of California at Berkeley, a member of the report committee, emphasized at the news conference yesterday, however, that the amount was proposed "for control" of the epidemic, not health care for its victims. Health care may cost up to $16 billion, he said. . . .

"Beginning in 1990," warned Dr. Frank Press, president of the Academy, "we will lose as many Americans each year to AIDS as we lost in the entire Vietnam War." About 58,000 Americans died in the war. . . .

SURGEON GENERAL CRITICIZED FOR AIDS RESPONSE

According to then surgeon general Dr. C. Everett Coop in 1987, "When you walk into a health job, you make pronouncements about health based on the facts." His focus on science over values led the 70-year-old surgeon to deal with the AIDS crisis in ways that angered many of his conservative colleagues and former supporters. In an effort to prevent an escalation of the epidemic, Dr. Koop advocated for straightforward sex education starting in kindergarten and "tasteful" television advertisements for condoms. In addition, he opposed calls for mandatory testing as an abridgment of individual rights. For these positions, Koop was lauded as a hero by many Democrats, including California representative Henry Waxman. However, he faced a lack of support from the White House and ongoing criticism from various members of the Republican Party, including Secretary of Education William J. Bennett and California representative William E. Dannemeyer. In defense of his position, Koop argued, "You can't educate anybody about AIDS unless they know about sex."

APRIL 6, 1987
WASHINGTON TALK: THE SURGEON GENERAL;

Dr. Koop Defends His Crusade on AIDS

By MAUREEN DOWD

The morning that Dr. C. Everett Koop went to Congress to testify in favor of condom advertising, his wife sent him off with these words: "Well, I'm glad your mother's dead."

"And you know," the Surgeon General said, smiling behind his Captain Ahab beard, "I know what she meant."

His mother, a sheltered housewife from Brooklyn, would never have understood.

For that matter, many people in Washington do not understand Dr. Koop's extraordinary shift in image from someone who was regarded at the time of his appointment as a "right winger" and a fervent opponent of abortion to someone who is now so graphically outspoken on an issue like AIDS.

A Hero or a Failure?

Many of the liberals who once criticized Dr. Koop now praise him. Representative Henry Waxman, a California Democrat who heads the Health subcommittee of the Energy and Commerce Committee, used to find the Surgeon General "scary." Now he calls him "a man of heroic proportions."

On the other side, Howard Phillips, the chairman of the Conservative Caucus who pushed for Dr. Koop's confirmation six years ago, now says that he has "failed in moral courage."

While President Reagan and most of his top officials either avoid the issue of AIDS or speak brightly of the virtues of sexual abstinence, the 70-year-old Dr. Koop spreads the graphic gospel of AIDS prevention, in forums ranging from radio and television talk shows to college commencements.

"Advertising condoms in a tasteful way is a lot different than throwing them from a Mardi Gras float in New Orleans," he said, sitting in his office the other morning and wearing the gold-braided military-style uniform that has made him a familiar figure around town.

"Kids aren't dumb—they know about these things," he added, with exasperation. "If you go to a drugstore to get a pack of gum, you'll see a box of condoms next to it."

Acquired immune deficiency syndrome, a fatal viral disease that is spread through intercourse with an infected person or through exchanges of blood, as in shared hypodermic needles, has killed thousands of male homosexuals and intravenous drug users in this country.

Dr. Koop fiercely wants to strip AIDS of its stigma and stop people from dying. To that end, he talks baldly about the proper way to use condoms, about making an animated educational video that would feature two condoms "with little eyes on them" chatting, and about the need for "gentle, nonmystifying" sex education for students, starting in kindergarten.

He even has a box of anatomically correct dolls in his office that someone has sent along, boys with prophylactics in their back pockets and girls with babies inside.

"I don't remember if I was embarrassed the first time I talked about these sort of things," he said. "But I'm sure not now."

An Award Is Rescinded

Dr. Koop's vivid emphasis on science rather than values, and his defense of individual rights and confidentiality in opposing mandatory testing for the disease, have stunned and enraged many of his former supporters on the right.

Nellie Gray, the chairman of the March for Life, last week rescinded an annual award her anti-abortion group had given Dr. Koop, notifying thousands of people on her mailing list that he was retroactively undeserving.

The doctor has become a lightning rod for one of the most sensitive moral issues in the country: How do you talk about sex in a way that is explicit enough to give health information without seeming to condone certain practices?

Representative William E. Dannemeyer, a conservative California Republican, thinks the Surgeon General may have to "be replaced."

"Dr. Koop's October report to the nation about AIDS could just as well have been directed to the farmers of America about a cattle population inflicted with a disease," Mr. Dannemeyer said. "There was no connection between human sexuality and morality."

On any given day, Dr. Koop says good-naturedly, a conservative Republican calls to hector him.

"You've changed," they say, accusingly. "I haven't," he replies. "You have," they insist.

"And it keeps going like that for a while, 'You have,' 'I haven't,'" he said.

He rebuts all such calls with the same answer. "I am not afforded the luxury of bringing ideology or morals into my job, especially with the sort of threat we have with AIDS," he said. "When you walk into a lab to do a sterile technique, you do a sterile technique. When you walk into a health job, you make pronouncements about health based on the facts.

"We're not talking about measles here," he added. "You can't give people a false sense of security. And you can't educate anybody about AIDS unless they know about sex."

Secretary of Education William J. Bennett has taken public issue with Dr. Koop, saying that schools should teach about sex only as part of marriage. And White House officials recently confirmed to NBC News that the President has never talked to his Surgeon General about AIDS nor read the report Dr. Koop sent him last October.

Dr. Koop is keenly aware of the irony of his situation. "The world has flip-flopped and it's bittersweet," he said. "Obviously, it's gratifying to have people like Senator Edward Kennedy and Henry Waxman saying I have integrity. But it's bitter to have people who liked me thinking that I've slipped the traces." . . .

• •

Mayor Koch Condemns AIDS Amendment

New York City mayor Ed Koch praised the work of the Gay Men's Health Crisis, a New York nonprofit organization that provides care for those with AIDS and public education to limit the spread of this deadly disease. Owing in large part to the efforts of this group, the rate of healthy gay men contracting AIDS had been reduced to 1 percent per year by 1987, compared with 8 percent among intravenous drug users. Mayor Koch also sternly rebuked Sen. Jesse Helms, who was offended by the Gay Men's Health Crisis's sexually graphic educational materials and proposed an amendment to a 1988 appropriations bill that would prohibit federal funding for AIDS programs that "promote, encourage or condone homosexual activity." Koch dismissed the amendment as "homophobic hysteria" and predicted that it would limit the effectiveness of future public education efforts and contribute to increased infection rates among heterosexual adults and children. In 1987 the measure passed both the House and Senate by wide margins; however, in 1992 a federal district court judge struck down the ban as unconstitutional.

NOVEMBER 7, 1987
SENATOR HELMS'S CALLOUSNESS TOWARD AIDS VICTIMS
By EDWARD I. KOCH

"We have got to call a spade a spade," said Senator Jesse Helms in offering an amendment to the fiscal 1988 appropriations bill for the Departments of Labor, Health and Human Services, and Education, "and a perverted human being a perverted human being." Ironic comments, indeed, given the profound perversity of the policy his amendment advances.

It prohibits the Federal Centers for Disease Control from funding AIDS programs that "promote, encourage or condone homosexual activities." The Senate passed it,

96 to 2. Only 47 House members had the good sense and common decency to resist homophobic hysteria and oppose the amendment.

Mr. Helms introduced it because he's upset with New York's Gay Men's Health Crisis. The organization has established a brilliant reputation in caring for and counseling those with AIDS and in educating others on how to prevent the spread of AIDS.

It serves gay men—Mr. Helms's "perverts"—because they're a primary AIDS risk group. Gays comprise about 10 percent of the United States' adult population, or 20 million people. If only half are male, 10 million men are at risk and in need of education and counseling on how to cut the risk. That's why the Gay Men's Health Crisis and organizations like it around the country exist.

The amendment, protests Senator Edward M. Kennedy, is "toothless" and "a foolish exercise." Then why did he vote to make it the law of the land, particularly since it ignores the proved effectiveness of AIDS education efforts and severely impedes our ability to expand them?

To date, New York has had 11,513 AIDS cases reported; of these, 6,605 have died. Of the total cases, 55 percent are homosexual or bisexual men. Among these, the Gay Men's Health Crisis and city educational efforts have helped contribute to a decline in the seroconversion rate to 1 percent annually. In nonscientific terms, this means that if you took blood samples from homosexual or bisexual men one year and found them not infected with the AIDS virus, there's only a 1 percent chance that samples from the same men would be infected the next year.

Among intravenous drug users there's an 8 percent seroconversion rate. Obviously, education changes behavior among those whose faculties aren't impaired and enslaved by needles and drugs.

Gay Men's Health Crisis materials, complains Senator Helms, use blunt words and sexually graphic illustration that "perpetuate the AIDS problem." But those the materials reach aren't innocents who'll be shocked by such literature. They already practice sex; they want to know how to practice it more safely. The organization tells them and thereby helps save lives.

If we're shy with one risk group, we'll probably make the same mistake with others. Today, AIDS is found principally among men who engage in homosexual or bisexual practices or intravenous drug abuse. By 1991, some 40,000 people in New York and 270,000 nationally may have AIDS. Some will be heterosexuals who've had intercourse with a bisexual man or a drug user. If they don't know how to protect themselves, how will they? Cutting off Federal funds to organizations like the Gay Men's Health Crisis may only help spread the disease, causing the deaths of not only homosexuals but heterosexuals of both sexes and, most tragic of all, innocent infants.

Senator Helms may not like homosexuals. But he and those who voted for the amendment should remember that homosexuals—and intravenous drug users—are the sons and daughters of families who love them. They too deserve protection against the gravest public health threat our nation faces.

Regrettably, lousy politics overwhelmed good public health policy. Apparently fearing an adverse reaction that a homophobic demagogue might inflame in their home state or districts, members of Congress gave in to homophobic hysteria. Only a few had the courage to vote against this foolish amendment. I commend Senators Daniel Patrick Moynihan and Lowell Weicker and members of New York's House delegation who joined the honor roll: Gary L. Ackerman, Bill Green, Major R. Owens, James H. Scheuer and Ted Weiss. They hold the moral high ground.

The amendment is a fait accompli. The blot on the Congress can't be erased. But what can't be undone can be uncovered. That alone may insure that future Congressional action on AIDS ignores the homophobes by supporting programs and policies that have proved so effective in fighting this tragic disease.

- -

RULE PROHIBITING "OFFENSIVE" AIDS MATERIALS FOUND UNCONSTITUTIONAL

A federal rule barring the Centers for Disease Control from funding AIDS organizations that distribute educational materials considered "offensive" to "a majority of adults" was declared "unconstitutionally vague." In 1992 federal district judge Shirley Wohl Kram stated that the rule had "no core meaning that can reasonably be understood by a person of ordinary intelligence."

Sen. Jesse Helms (R-NC) introduced the offensiveness guideline in 1986. It originally banned funding for programs that "promote, encourage or condone homosexual activity," but this language was later revised to modify its scope. In its present form the rule requires that organizations receiving federal AIDS education funding establish program review panels to evaluate the offensiveness of proposed posters, brochures, and other publications. The broad language of the bill left it open to diverse interpretations, and review boards had occasionally rejected material for racial and political content as well as sexual explicitness. According to Judge Kram, this had forced AIDS organizations to either self-censor or seek alternative funding sources. In 1988 the Center for Constitutional Rights and the AIDS Project of the American Civil Liberties Union challenged the rule on behalf of the Gay Men's Health Crisis and other organizations. David Cole, a lawyer for the Center for Constitutional Rights, said, "This decision will save lives."

MAY 12, 1992
JUDGE OVERTURNS U.S. RULE BLOCKING 'OFFENSIVE' EDUCATIONAL MATERIAL ON AIDS
By ROBERT D. MCFADDEN

A Federal rule barring Government financing for any AIDS educational materials deemed "offensive" to "a majority of adults" was declared unconstitutional yesterday by a Federal judge in New York. The decision was expected to have a nationwide impact on the content of posters, brochures and writings prepared to educate Americans to the dangers of the disease.

The rule that was struck down—part of the guidelines used by the Federal Centers for Disease Control for awarding $200 million a year to states and to thousands of AIDS education groups—has been described by critics as a tool of censors that has been used for years to block sexually explicit educational information. The critics argue that the rule has sacrificed lives to arbitrary moral standards.

In a 63-page ruling, Judge Shirley Wohl Kram of Federal District Court in Manhattan declared that the Centers for Disease Control exceeded its statutory authority in promulgating the restriction on "offensive" materials and that the rule itself was unconstitutionally vague.

"Can educational material be offensive simply because it mentions homosexuality?" the judge wrote. "Because it depicts an interracial couple? Can a proposed education project be offensive because it traps a captive audience, such as subway riders, and forces them to look at a condom?"

Pressure from Senator Helms

Judge Kram said the rule, written in 1986 under pressure from Senator Jesse Helms, a North Carolina Republican, and other conservatives in Congress, and later revised to narrow its scope, nevertheless had "no core meaning that can reasonably be understood by a person of ordinary intelligence."

The rule did not prohibit specific expressions or depictions, but was so broadly phrased that it was often interpreted in ways that found racial and political content, as well as sexually explicit language, offensive, the judge said.

Don Berreth, a spokesman for the Centers for Disease Control in Atlanta, declined to comment on the decision last night, saying officials of the agency had not had a chance to read it. He noted that any decision on a possible appeal would be made by the Justice Department.

But lawyers for the Center for Constitutional Rights, a public interest law firm in Manhattan, and the AIDS Project of the American Civil Liberties Union, which filed the suit in 1988 on behalf of the Gay Men's Health Crisis and other organizations, applauded the ruling.

"This decision will save lives," said David Cole, a lawyer for the Center for Constitutional Rights. "It allows organizations receiving Federal funds for AIDS education to create the most effective education materials possible, without being hampered by some government agent's subjective determination about what will be 'offensive' in Peoria, Illinois."

Ruth Harlow, a lawyer for the A.C.L.U.'s AIDS Project, said: "Finally, clear and supportive AIDS education can reach all the communities that desperately need it. This decision strongly reaffirms that the public health and the Constitution are more important than some vague notion of squeamishness about explicit H.I.V. prevention materials."

Under complex guidelines written by the Centers for Disease Control, the so-called offensiveness rule said the AIDS educational materials financed by the Government "should not include terms, descriptions or displays which will be offensive to a majority of the intended audience or to a majority of adults outside the intended audience."

In 1987, Senator Helms and other Congressional conservatives attached a rider to an appropriations bill that made the rule even harsher by prohibiting the centers from funding any programs that "promote, encourage or condone homosexual activities." The amendment was watered down and then dropped in later appropriations measures.

The guidelines required states and private organizations receiving funds for AIDS education to set up "program review panels" to judge whether posters, brochures, writings and other materials would meet the offensiveness standard. Judge Kram said the Federal rule had a chilling effect on the producers of AIDS education materials since what was offensive was so unclear.

"Organizations dependent upon C.D.C. funding cannot afford to waste resources and time using a trial-and-error approach to review," the judge declared. "They must self-censor to guarantee approval. For some organizations, the deterrent effect of the grant terms is so strong they avoid seeking C.D.C. funding."

Mr. Cole said the review panels had rendered thousands of largely arbitrary decisions. A panel in Los Angeles, for example, refused to approve a poster showing a black man and a white man sitting together, he said, while another in North Carolina rejected a poster of two men wrapped in an American flag and holding condoms.

Ms. Harlow said, "These rules had a harsher impact on organizations trying to serve the gay community or adolescents or particular racial minorities, because effective education tools may not be things that are commonplace for the majority of adults beyond the target audience."

Over the years, she said, the Federal rule has "tended to homogenize H.I.V. education and prevention materials to the lowest common denominator," instead of being designed specifically for gay men, racial minorities, older people and other groups that need the information.

Ms. Harlow added, "This is a terrific victory for public health in this country because our Federal H.I.V. prevention dollars can now be used most effectively."

· ·

AIDS Panic Grips Nation

The combination of AIDS's high fatality rate, agonizing physical symptoms, and uncertain means of transmission led to increasing panic and blame among both homosexuals and heterosexuals in the early years of the pandemic. As Larry Kramer, one of the founders of New York's Gay Men's Health Crisis, said in 1983, "I don't think there is a thinking person in this town who isn't literally scared to death." Some localities are attempting to enact laws that would close homosexual bars and declare homosexual conduct a health hazard. Some community leaders persisted in referring to the disease as the "gay plague," while others suggested that it was God's punishment of homosexuals for engaging in perverse behavior. Finally, despite widespread scientific belief that AIDS is spread through sexual contact, infected needles, and contaminated blood, even many within the medical community still feared catching the disease through casual contact and were reluctant to touch, bathe, or clean up after AIDS patients for fear of contracting the deadly illness.

JUNE 17, 1983
AIDS SPREADS PAIN AND FEAR AMONG ILL AND HEALTHY ALIKE

By DUDLEY CLENDINEN

As public awareness of the disease known as AIDS has grown in the last few months, a picture has begun to emerge of the emotional and physical agony of those afflicted and of the fear, among homosexuals and about homosexuals, that has spread around the country at a rate much faster than the disease itself.

In New York, a restaurant owner reflects on the way his lover, shunned by hospitals and airlines and then by undertakers, died this winter of the ailment, acquired immune deficiency syndrome.

In Denver, a woman calls to ask how she should fumigate an apartment she bought from a homosexual. In Houston, some people refuse to donate blood lest they contract AIDS from the needles at the blood bank. In New Orleans, a club owner sees a turn toward monogamy, a retreat from the casual, anonymous sex that has characterized "the gay life style" for many homosexuals.

In Washington, as the number of cases nationwide mounts beyond 1,500 and the number of deaths nears 600, Government officials are proclaiming AIDS the nation's No. 1 health priority, though they emphasize their belief that the vast majority of people are not in danger of contracting the deadly disease. . . .

As the AIDS caseload grows, homosexuals are faced with two prospects: a disease that burns in their own community like a fire in a barrel and a backlash that can be seen forming in places where tolerance held recent sway.

In New Orleans, a doctor wonders to a colleague if this is God's punishment, saying that if it is, it is not harsh enough. In Texas, preachers are calling for the closing of homosexual bars as health hazards. And in New York City, Bruce Mailman, the owner of a homosexual nightclub and a bathhouse, has nightmares about a "stalking fascism," fearing that the disease "opens the door to the most conventional and biased fears that people have" about homosexuals. . . .

The uncertainty has induced a sexual panic in New York and San Francisco, with their large homosexual populations. "I don't think there is a thinking person in this town who isn't literally scared to death," says Larry Kramer, the screenwriter and producer of the movie "Women in Love,"

a founder of the Gay Men's Health Crisis, a support group for victims in New York.

"I made love the other night for the first time in five months, with someone who checked out, so to speak," Mr. Kramer said. "But I couldn't get out of the back of my mind: Is this the one that will kill me?"

Dr. George A. Pankey, head of the infectious diseases section at the Ochsner Medical Institutions in New Orleans, says that hysteria about AIDS is not justified. "Considering the sexual habits of many homosexuals, there have to be tens of thousands exposed, and there's still under 2,000 sure cases," he said.

Some With the Disease Are Treated Like Lepers

Compounding the fear, and the ravages of the disease, is the fact that some victims have been treated like lepers. Ron Doud, the interior designer of the New York disco Studio 54, died of AIDS Feb. 17 at the age of 34 after five months of medical care that his lover of 10 years, Richard Ruskay, says cost "probably $300,000."

What the insurance did not cover was paid by Mr. Ruskay, a restaurant and bar owner, and his memories of the reluctance of medical, transportation and funeral service personnel to handle the case are graphic.

Principal among a range of infections that left Mr. Doud incontinent and incoherent, Mr. Ruskay said, was Pneumocystis carinii pneumonia, which seems to be the largest and perhaps the quickest single killer among the cluster of diseases that afflict AIDS victims, and which doctors treat as perhaps the most infectious.

Fear of Handling Body

At Lenox Hill Hospital, Mr. Ruskay said, "He was paying $420 a day for a hospital room, and I couldn't get the porter to clean the room. I had to clean the bath myself." A public affairs official at Lenox Hill said, after talking with Mr. Doud's doctor, that she could not speak to this specific instance. She said that the hospital was aware of fear of AIDS among its employees.

When Mr. Ruskay moved Mr. Doud to Phoenix, his mother's home, at her request, "the pilot wanted to throw him off the plane," Mr. Ruskay said. At St. Joseph's Medical

Center in Phoenix, "they really were very afraid to handle him," Mr. Ruskay said. "They weren't even washing him."

Finally, when Mr. Doud died, the hospital staff simply "wrapped him in the sheets he was in and put him in a plastic bag," Mr. Ruskay said. And the undertakers at the funeral home, "because of their fear, all they did was to pour embalming fluid on top of the sheets he was in, and closed the plastic bag and put him in the casket."

In San Francisco, where the public health authorities have now posted warning signs about AIDS in homosexual bars and bathhouses, where landlords have begun evicting homosexual tenants, and where the police chief issued vinyl gloves and masks to 250 officers fearful of contracting AIDS from policing the city's concentrated homosexual community, Chuck Morris is still alive at the age of 40, but his life has shrunk.

'The Enormous Horror Of All This Hit Me'

Three years ago, when he was diagnosed as having AIDS, Mr. Morris was publisher of The Sentinel, a newspaper for homosexuals. Now, he says, he has more than 30 active symptoms, has had three brain seizures in six months, is unable to work and is abandoned by friends of years' standing. Twice he has been forced out of his apartments, both times while in the hospital.

The second eviction, he said, took the form of a phone call from one of his roommates, who called to tell Mr. Morris that he would kill him if he moved back. He moved out.

"I was standing on Castro and 18th Street with a little plastic bag with all my possessions that I could grab, and all of a sudden the enormous horror of all this hit me," he says. "At that point I had been working for 25 years, and I felt that the year before I was a reasonably wealthy man. I had my own newspaper, and now here I was, standing on the street, homeless and broke, and I had no idea where I was going to stay. It was the first time that I realized that this had caused my whole world to crumble around me." . . .

Reaction and Fear Evident Around Country

At this point, the concern within the homosexual community about outside reaction appears to be more advanced than the reaction itself. "We are preparing a public position paper on the subject now," said Ronald S. Godwin, executive vice president of the Moral Majority in Lynchburg, Va.

"We feel the deepest sympathy for AIDS victims," he said, "but I'm upset that the Government is not spending more money to protect the general public from the gay plague." He was using what was at first a common term for the mysterious malady. Homosexuals, Mr. Godwin said, should be banned from giving blood by requiring them to identify themselves "on pain of law for giving false information."

"What I see," he said, "is a commitment to spend our tax dollars on research to allow these diseased homosexuals to go back to their perverted practices without any standards of accountability." . . .

'Can I Touch This Person?'

Fourteen cases of AIDS have been confirmed in Colorado, and "whenever a case is diagnosed in a Colorado hospital, people get a little freaked out," says Dr. David Cohn of the Denver Metro Health Clinic. "They ask, 'Can I touch this person,' and so forth. But with proper education, some become less paranoid, and once they understand the disease doesn't spread through the air, they calm down."

In Houston, where the City Health Department reports "an emerging epidemic" of 25 cases, blood donations are down by more than a fourth since January. "We're starting to get people who say they won't give blood because they're afraid of getting AIDS," says Bill Teague, executive director of the Gulf Coast Regional Blood Center, explaining that a myth has sprung up that the center uses only one needle.

Fundamentalist preachers in Houston have been calling on the health authorities to close homosexual bars and to declare homosexual conduct a health hazard. In Austin, the Texas Legislature adjourned without acting on a bill that would ban homosexual conduct by reinstituting a law recently struck down as unconstitutional by a Federal district judge. And in Dallas, a group of about 30 doctors and lawyers have formed "Dallas Doctors Against AIDS," with the goal of helping to appeal the court's decision.

But Support Is Growing As the Disorder Spreads

But around the nation, lines of governmental and volunteer support are growing in the face of an emergent medical crisis. In San Francisco, the city government has budgeted $4.1 million for medical and social services for AIDS victims.

Mayor Dianne Feinstein of San Francisco heads a group named by the United States Conference of Mayors to alert the nation to the growing danger of AIDS. The other members are the Mayors of New York, Los Angeles, Miami, Newark, Chicago, Houston, Philadelphia, Atlanta, Boston and Washington.

In Seattle, City Councilman Jack Richards is sponsoring a resolution of the Dorian Group, a predominantly homosexual political society, asking the city to declare AIDS a public health emergency, allocating funds for citywide surveillance, diagnosis and support services and requesting additional Federal funding for research.

Unity is Forged.

But, mainly, the effort to organize in support of the victims has come from those most affected: homosexuals themselves. And repeatedly, in city after city, those involved say that the human toll being exacted by AIDS is forging homosexuals into a community as nothing has before, even bringing bankers, doctors and others out of the closet. . . .

- -

Buckley Calls for Forced Sterilization and Mandatory Tattoos

Proposing to outline the arguments for and against strict efforts to contain the AIDS virus, author and editor William F. Buckley in 1986 labeled the extreme position on each side as School A and School B. School A resists efforts to identify and segregate AIDS carriers, fearing that concerns about public safety will be used as an excuse to roll back recent civil rights gains by homosexuals. While tending to "disapprove forcefully of homosexuality," School B is primarily focused on the seriousness of the epidemic and its catastrophic potential to spread to the general population. Based on this second position, Buckley advocated mandatory testing prior to marriage, insurance coverage, or other unspecified life events from "infancy to maturity." For those who tested positive, he recommended forced sterilization of potential spouses as well as tattoos on the upper arm and buttocks to alert intravenous drug users and homosexuals. While he conceded that quarantining AIDS victims was not necessary at the time, he argued that it should be considered if future research indicated the disease was transmitted through casual contact. Against those who would argue that he was suggesting a modern-day version of the visible punishment for adultery worn by Hawthorne's heroine in *The Scarlet Letter,* Buckley argued that his recommendations were designed to provide personal protection, not public shame.

MARCH 18, 1986
CRUCIAL STEPS IN COMBATING THE AIDS EPIDEMIC: IDENTIFY ALL THE CARRIERS
By WILLIAM F. BUCKLEY JR.

I have read and listened, and I think now that I can convincingly crystallize the thoughts chasing about in the minds of, first, those whose concern with AIDS victims is based primarily on a concern for them and for the maintenance of the most rigid standards of civil liberties and personal privacy, and, second, those whose anxiety to protect the public impels them to give subordinate attention to the civil amenities of those who suffer from AIDS and primary attention to the safety of those who do not.

Arguments used by both sides are sometimes utilitarian, sometimes moral, sometimes a little of each—and almost always a little elusive. Most readers will locate their own inclinations and priorities somewhere other than in the polar positions here put forward by design.

School A suspects, in the array of arguments of School B, a venture in ethical opportunism. Look, they say, we have made enormous headway in the matter of civil rights for all, dislodging the straight-laced from mummified positions they inherited through eclectic superstitions ranging from the Bible's to Freud's. A generation ago, homosexuals lived mostly in the closet. Nowadays they take over cities and parade on Halloween and demand equal rights for themselves qua homosexuals, not merely as apparently disinterested civil libertarians.

Along comes AIDS, School A continues, and even though it is well known that the virus can be communicated by infected needles, known also that heterosexuals can transmit the virus, still it is both a fact and the popular perception that AIDS is the special curse of the homosexual, transmitted through anal sex between males. And if you look hard, you will discern that little smirk on the face of the man oh-so-concerned about public health. He is looking for ways to safeguard the public, sure, but he is by no means reluctant, in the course of doing so, to sound an invidious tocsin whose clamor is a call to undo all the understanding so painfully cultivated over a generation by those who have fought for the privacy of their bedroom. What School B is really complaining about is the extension of civil rights to homosexuals.

School A will not say all that in words quite so jut-jawed, but it plainly feels that no laws or regulations should be passed that have the effect of identifying the AIDS carrier. It isn't, School A concedes, as if AIDS were transmitted via public drinking fountains. But any attempt to segregate the AIDS carrier is primarily an act of moral ostracism.

School B does in fact tend to disapprove forcefully of homosexuality, but tends to approach the problem of AIDS empirically. It argues that acquired immune deficiency syndrome is potentially the most serious epidemic to have shown its face in this century. Summarizing currently accepted statistics, the Economist recently raised the possibility "that the AIDS virus will have killed more than 250,000 Americans in eight years' time." Moreover, if the epidemic extended to that point, it would burst through existing boundaries. There would then be "no guarantee that the disease will remain largely confined to groups at special risk, such as homosexuals, hemophiliacs and people who inject drugs intravenously. If AIDS were to spread through the general population, it would become a catastrophe." Accordingly, School B says, we face a utilitarian imperative, and this requires absolutely nothing less than the identification of the million-odd people who,

the doctors estimate, are carriers. How? Well, the military has taken the first concrete step. Two million soldiers will be given the blood test, and those who have AIDS will be discreetly discharged. Discreetly, you say!

Hold on. I'm coming to that. You have the military making the first massive move designed to identify AIDS sufferers—and, bear in mind, an AIDS carrier today is an AIDS carrier on the day of his death, which day, depending on the viral strain, will be two years from now or when he is threescore and 10. The next logical step would be to require of anyone who seeks a marriage license that he present himself not only with a Wassermann test but also an AIDS test.

But if he has AIDS, should he then be free to marry?

Only after the intended spouse is advised that her intended husband has AIDS, and agrees to sterilization. We know already of children born with the disease, transmitted by the mother, who contracted it from the father.

What then would School B suggest for those who are not in the military and who do not set out to get a marriage license? Universal testing?

Yes, in stages. But in rapid stages. The next logical enforcer is the insurance company. Blue Cross, for instance, can reasonably require of those who wish to join it a physical examination that requires tests. Almost every American, making his way from infancy to maturity, needs to pass by one or another institutional turnstile. Here the lady will spring out, her right hand on a needle, her left on a computer, to capture a blood specimen.

Is it then proposed by School B that AIDS carriers should be publicly identified as such?

The evidence is not completely in as to the communicability of the disease. But while much has been said that is reassuring, the moment has not yet come when men and women of science are unanimously agreed that AIDS cannot be casually communicated. Let us be patient on that score, pending any tilt in the evidence: If the news is progressively reassuring, public identification would not be necessary. If it turns in the other direction and AIDS develops among, say, children who have merely roughhoused with other children who suffer from AIDS, then more drastic segregation measures would be called for.

But if the time has not come, and may never come, for public identification, what then of private identification?

Everyone detected with AIDS should be tattooed in the upper forearm, to protect common-needle users, and on the buttocks, to prevent the victimization of other homosexuals.

You have got to be kidding! That's exactly what we suspected all along! You are calling for the return of the Scarlet Letter, but only for homosexuals!

Answer: The Scarlet Letter was designed to stimulate public obloquy. The AIDS tattoo is designed for private protection. And the whole point of this is that we are not talking about a kidding matter. Our society is generally threatened, and in order to fight AIDS, we need the civil equivalent of universal military training.

William F. Buckley Jr., editor of the National Review, is author, most recently, of "Right Reason." His syndicated column appears locally in The New York Daily News.

· ·

STATES STRUGGLE TO PROTECT PUBLIC HEALTH WITHOUT COMPROMISING CIVIL RIGHTS

Cases like that of Stephanie Smith raised difficult questions about how to balance public health protection and the civil rights of people with AIDS. An HIV-positive drug addict with a history of prostitution, Smith had stated that she continued to have sex and use intravenous drugs without taking precautions to prevent transmission of the virus to others. As local health official Marilyn Mitchell said, "There's talk about quarantine, but you quarantine someone until they're no longer infectious and AIDS lasts for life."

Some states passed laws that made it a crime to knowingly transmit the AIDS virus. Nine states updated old laws in light of the crisis or passed new ones allowing some patients with AIDS to be quarantined. These laws varied with respect to who is covered, the steps necessary for enforcement, and the potential ramifications for those found to be noncompliant. Some states also required AIDS cases to be reported to local health authorities, with varying levels of protection for patient confidentiality. Many civil rights advocates, public health officials, and gay rights groups argued that these efforts were primarily designed to win votes and that increased support for those with AIDS—such as providing Smith with an alternative source of income besides prostitution—would do more to protect the public health.

OCTOBER 14, 1987
RIGHTS OF CITIZENS AND SOCIETY RAISE LEGAL MUDDLE ON AIDS
By TAMAR LEWIN

States around the nation are finding themselves in a legal muddle about how to control the spread of AIDS, and specifically how to balance the civil rights of people with AIDS against the goal of protecting public health.

For despite health officials' repeated statements that acquired immune deficiency syndrome cannot be caught through casual contact, there is continuing debate about when, and on what terms, certain AIDS sufferers should be isolated from the rest of society.

The case of Stephanie Smith, a drug addict and occasional prostitute in California, illustrates some hard questions that state legislators face. Last spring, when word got around that Ms. Smith was infected with the AIDS virus, she was shunned by people in her drug treatment program in Fresno, Calif. Ms. Smith decided there was no point in fighting her addiction if she was dying, and dropped out of the program.

A Troubling Situation

In Fresno, everyone who tests positive for the AIDS virus is reported to local health officials. Marilyn Mitchell, the health official counseling Ms. Smith, found her on the streets. "She told me she wasn't taking precautions sexually and she wasn't cleaning her needles," Ms. Mitchell said. "I didn't feel that I could let that continue."

So Ms. Mitchell called the police. They found Ms. Smith soliciting a truck driver and arrested her. She pleaded guilty to prostitution, entered and left another drug treatment program, and is now in jail for violating probation.

But she will be out soon, and "we will be right back to Square 1," said Ms. Mitchell. "California needs to decide what we're going to do with these people. There's talk about quarantine, but you quarantine someone until they're no longer infectious and AIDS lasts for life. And where are they going to put her? She doesn't even have a place to live."

The debate over whether people like Ms. Smith should be given supportive social services, quarantined by the health authorities or jailed on criminal charges of endangering the lives of others is symbolic of the nation's indecision about how to treat AIDS: as a disease, calling forth compassion and support, or a moral issue, a plague whose victims are pariahs.

Emotions figure strongly in almost every discussion about segregating people with AIDS, from the refusal by a school in Arcadia, Fla., to allow three brothers infected with the virus into the classroom to Northwest Airlines' refusing to sell a ticket to a passenger with AIDS. Most Americans deeply fear the disease and are not entirely convinced that casual contact with AIDS carriers is as safe as health experts say it is.

One sign of the times is that some people now speak in terms of quarantine, a charged word conjuring up frightening images of mass roundups and leper colonies. Senator Jesse Helms and Pat Robertson, the former television evangelist who is running for President, have suggested that quarantines may become necessary, although neither specified what he had in mind.

'Climate Has Turned Nasty'

Cuba has imposed a mass quarantine and has isolated 108 people carrying the virus on a farm outside Havana. But with an estimated 1.5 million Americans now carrying the AIDS virus, HIV, experts say mass quarantine in this country would be not only unnecessary and unconstitutional but also impossible.

Public health experts, civil liberties groups and gay rights groups say they are distressed to find the idea of quarantine gaining any currency at all.

"The social climate has turned nasty and the idea is being taken seriously," said Lawrence Gostin, executive director of the American Society of Law and Medicine. But he and others also said AIDS did not fit the pattern of diseases for which quarantine makes sense: it is not easily transmitted, it remains infectious for life, and because there is no cure, society would have to be prepared to confine people for the rest of their lives.

Since 1985, nine states have amended their old quarantine laws or passed new ones empowering health officials to isolate certain people with AIDS who endanger other people's health, but only as a last resort. . . .

* *

AIDS LEADS TO CHANGES IN THE GAY COMMUNITY

Since surfacing in 1981, AIDS greatly altered the lives of New York City's gay men. By 1985 it was the city's leading cause of death for men between the ages of 25 and 44, and over half of those infected were gay or bisexual. The Gay Men's Health Crisis, a nonprofit organization in Manhattan that provides support for AIDS patients, had 900 clients and 1,100 volunteers in 1985.

Author Larry Kramer said that he stopped counting the number of friends who had died when he reached 50—and that was in 1983. Although Kramer saw little cause for hope, others took a more a balanced view. Richard Dunne, executive director of the Gay Men's Health Crisis, argued that the devastating loss of life had resulted in an increased sense of community among gay men. Individuals reconnected with old friends and, in some cases, got involved in volunteering as a strategy for managing their fear.

For many, AIDS led to increased alienation from nonhomosexuals. The initial panicked response of the heterosexual community eventually died down, and by the mid-1980s it was no longer common to hear people expressing fear that they would contract AIDS from a hairdresser or waiter. However, many gay men became increasingly resentful at what was perceived to be an inadequate government investment in AIDS support services, education, and research. The motives assigned to this lack of commitment included "government inertia, hostility toward homosexuals, and outright conspiracy."

Regarding sexual behavior, Dr. Emery S. Hetrick, New York University Medical Center professor and member of the State Task Force on Gay and Lesbian Issues, stated that great diversity existed in the gay community before the AIDS crisis, from long-term committed relationships to extreme promiscuity, but that in light of the pandemic many were choosing to be monogamous, practicing safe sex, and/or avoiding drugs that might reduce inhibitions to engage in high-risk sex. However, Dr. Hetrick acknowledged that some would choose to not modify their behavior, despite educational efforts regarding the risks. The problem may be denial or that, as one 32-year-old New Yorker commented, "safe sex is boring sex."

In response to frustration about public attitudes toward the disease and government inaction, some turned away from the advocacy stressed by such groups as the Gay Man's Health Crisis and instead became more confrontational. Larry Kramer, for example, one of the original founders of the Gay Man's Health Crisis, went on to form a more militant group known as ACT UP (AIDS Coalition to Unleash Power). The group led dramatic protests on Wall Street, in New York's St. Patrick's Cathedral, and at the National Institutes of Health to bring attention to AIDS-related issues.

JULY 22, 1985
IMPACT OF AIDS: PATTERNS OF HOMOSEXUAL LIFE CHANGING
By GLENN COLLINS

Four years since the public first became aware of AIDS, the lethal viral disease has brought profound changes to the lives of homosexual men in New York.

It has had a pervasive effect on homosexual life styles, relationships, sexual patterns and self-images. Many believe the changes to be permanent, and some feel that the disease has led to a redefinition of contemporary homosexual life.

Successive stages of panic and apathy about AIDS have seized homosexuals since 1981. The years have taken their toll. "I think the gay community is still reeling from the devastation of this disease," said Dr. Stuart E. Nichols Jr., a psychiatrist at Beth Israel Medical Center who has treated and studied AIDS patients since 1981. "It's

a personal disease for any gay man, and the ability to deny is not there anymore for the majority of gays."

Death at an Early Age

For many, it has entailed the emotional cost of repeatedly coming to terms with death at an early age. "A man I know said to me today, 'I know 150 people who've died of AIDS'—150 people!" said Larry Kramer, author of "The Normal Heart," an Off Broadway play about AIDS.

"Most soldiers in Vietnam didn't know 150 people who died," Mr. Kramer said. "My mother is 86, and she doesn't know 150 people who've died. I counted 50 people I knew who died by 1983, and then I stopped counting." Currently AIDS, acquired immune deficiency syndrome, is the leading cause of death among men aged 25 to 44 in New York City, supplanting the usual causes in this age group such as suicide, accident and homicide. According to the City Health Department, 3,926 cases of AIDS have been reported in the city, 59 percent of them among homosexual or bisexual men; most of the rest come from a variety of risk groups, including intravenous drug users and the sex partners or children of those who have AIDS. Since 1978, 2,033 of the AIDS victims in the city have died—52 percent of the reported cases.

'Best of Times, Worst of Times'

Some of those interviewed, like Mr. Kramer, are despairing when asked for their overview of attitudes among the city's homosexuals in the wake of AIDS. Other assessments are more measured. "To paraphrase Dickens, it's the best of times and the worst of times," said Richard Dunne, executive director of the Gay Men's Health Crisis, a nonprofit social-service agency in Manhattan that provides support services for AIDS patients.

He explained: "It's the worst of times because so many people are dying before their time, or living in fear of dying. But it's the best of times because so many people in the gay community have coalesced. I find people touching more and calling up people they haven't talked to in a long time—sometimes with a sense of dread, I'll tell you."

Changes in Sexual Activity

Many of those interviewed agreed that AIDS has led to change in several areas, including modifications in sexual activity, a trend toward long-term relationships and a realignment in relation to the nonhomosexual part of the community. However, such changes have been complex, said Dr. Emery S. Hetrick, an assistant professor of clinical psychiatry at New York University Medical Center. He is a member of the State Task Force on Gay and Lesbian Issues appointed by Governor Cuomo.

It is hard to generalize about "extremely diverse" people, he said, noting that the impact of AIDS is only one aspect of life among homosexuals of different ages, social class and ethnicity.

"Many people have limited having sex to one's life partner, or are practicing 'safe sex,'" said Dr. Hetrick. He was referring to techniques such as limiting the number of sexual partners; using prophylactics and avoiding exchanges of body fluids that have been linked with transmission of the virus that is believed to cause AIDS; getting

regular physicians' checkups, and avoiding drugs that suppress the body's immune system or reduce inhibitions about high-risk sexual behavior.

Dr. Hetrick emphasized, though, that sexual patterns were varied before the advent of AIDS. "A number of men were extremely sexually promiscuous, and a proportion engaged in acts that could be dangerous," he said. "But a sizable number had been in stable relationships, and were not at risk at all. Some others were in primarily stable relationships, with perhaps an occasional trip to the baths."

Both public health experts and homosexuals have reported that the level of casual or promiscuous sex has declined, though few reliable statistics are available. "My sense is that fear has been a real stimulus in causing a change in sexual behavior," said Dr. David J. Sencer, the City Health Commissioner. He added that the rate of sexually transmitted disease in the homosexual population seems to have declined.

"Three of 12 bathhouses have closed since a year ago—we assume due to lack of attendance," said Marvin Bogner, an assistant health commissioner. Many of the remaining baths distribute prophylactics and "safe sex" guidelines to patrons.

But knowledge of such guidelines has not led to universal compliance. "Even with the best of education, we'll still have that group that will say, 'I don't care,'" said Dr. Hetrick. "It's fatalistic, a form of denial. There are some who have the illness and go to the baths anyway, knowing they're infecting others. These are people whose emotional investment in sexuality is such an important part of their identity that they feel hopeless despair about modifying their behavior."

Doubts About Promiscuity

Although sexual freedom was an important tenet of homosexual life before AIDS, promiscuity no longer seems socially acceptable to many of those interviewed. "I know people who live their lives as if AIDS doesn't exist, and they scare me," said a 36-year-old salesman who lives in Brooklyn and, like some others who were interviewed, requested anonymity. "They say, 'I got my motorcycle, my Batman comic books, I go to the gym and I go to the baths, and that's all I ever want to do.' "

"The problem is that safe sex is boring sex," said a 32-year-old art director who lives in Westchester and works on Madison Avenue. "Sure, lots of people are re-examining their life style, while at the same time they're wondering, how can I get away with doing what I used to do?"

Some homosexuals have reacted with resignation. Others have found active ways to cope with feelings of anxiety. "It's important for people who are afraid of AIDS to harness the energy of the fear they feel and direct that energy into positive community service of some type," said Tony Papp, who has been volunteering for the last year at the Gay Men's Health Crisis office in Manhattan.

Center Has 1,100 Volunteers

"Volunteering certainly has helped me," said Mr. Papp, who is 23 years old, "although I think there's so much more that I could be doing."

There are 1,100 volunteers at the agency, which is at 254 West 18th Street. Financed by private contributions as well by the state and city, the agency has 900 clients now and has had a total of 1,800 since it began. "That basically parallels the AIDS fatality numbers," Mr. Dunne said.

All those interviewed said that the widely reported panic that crested in 1983 has abated, and that it is no longer common for nonhomosexuals to express fear that hairdressers or waiters will give them AIDS. But even for many not directly affected by AIDS or involved in volunteer efforts, the disease has meant a basic rethinking with respect to people who are not homosexual.

One cause of alienation has been an angry belief among many homosexuals that government should be devoting more resources to caring for AIDS victims, to seeking a cure and to educating the public about prevention. This perceived inaction is variously ascribed to government inertia, hostility toward homosexuals or outright conspiracy.

Some feel that AIDS has provided a strong motive for a number of homosexuals to disclose their sexual orientation publicly as a gesture of solidarity with other homosexuals. But others say it is harder, after AIDS, to admit homosexuality.

Larry Kramer, seen here in 2004, is a playwright and activist. He helped to found the Gay Men's Health Crisis, a New York organization created to provide support and outreach to gay men infected with HIV and raise awareness about AIDS. He went on to found ACT UP, a group that would gain national attention for its high-profile, and sometimes controversial, protests that sought to raise awareness on a number of AIDS-related issues.

*Source: Sara Krulwich/*The New York Times

"These days you're not just coming out of the closet," said a 42-year-old editor who works in Manhattan, "but you're dragging a skeleton out of the closet with you. You're not only asking friends and relatives to accept someone who is gay, but also to accept someone who may be a carrier." . . .

ACT UP PROTESTERS ACCUSE THE NIH OF GENOCIDE

In May 1990, surrounded by colorful smoke bombs, 500 demonstrators protested outside the National Institutes of Health wearing costumes, carrying signs, and chanting "NIH, you can't hide; we charge you with genocide." Twenty-one people briefly occupied the office of the director of the AIDS division of the National Institute of Allergies and Infectious Diseases, and 81 people were arrested, mostly for trespassing.

Most of those protesting were members of the AIDS Coalition to Unleash Power (ACT UP), and the demonstration focused on the lack of effective drug treatments for AIDS patients and the length of time required to get drugs to those in need. Further, an ACT UP report distributed at the event complained that few drugs being tested fight the infections related to AIDS and that testing was rarely done in the regions where AIDS spread fastest, namely, poor, inner-city neighborhoods. Dr. Anthony Fauci, director of the National Institute of Allergies and Infectious Diseases, expressed surprise at these "irrational" statements. He stated that AZT is the most effective antiviral ever and was brought to market faster than any previous drug. However, he conceded that problems exist and that steps were taken to address the protesters' concerns, which included shifting drug research to focus on combating AIDS-related infections and increasing the number of women and minorities included within drug trials.

MAY 22, 1990
82 HELD IN PROTEST ON PACE OF AIDS RESEARCH
By PHILIP J. HILTS
Special to the New York Times

More than 500 demonstrators gathered here today at the National Institutes of Health, accusing the agency of being too slow in finding and testing drugs to treat AIDS. Eighty-two of the protesters were arrested, mostly on trespassing charges. Almost all were fined $50 and released.

Twenty-one of the demonstrators briefly occupied the office of Dr. Daniel Hoth, director of the AIDS division at the National Institute of Allergies and Infectious Disease. All were arrested, fined and released without incident, the police said.

Amid brightly colored smoke bombs and costumes both grim and humorous, the demonstrators declared that officials of the institutes were among the chief enemies in the fight against AIDS. Most of the protesters were members of the AIDS Coalition to Unleash Power, or Act Up. Some carried signs reading "N.I.H.: Neglectful Institute of Death," and crowds standing outside the administration building chanted, 'N.I.H., you can't hide; we charge you with genocide.'

Mark Harrington, a leader of Act Up, said, "Publicly funded AIDS research has been murderously irrelevant to the lives of people with AIDS." He said that too few drugs were being tested and that it took too long to get drugs to those who were sick, even though a billion dollars had been spent in the effort.

Dr. Anthony Fauci, director of the National Institute of Allergies and Infectious Diseases, the leading AIDS research agency in the Government, spoke in his office as demonstrators shouted a block away. He said he knew the leaders of the protest well and was surprised to hear "irrational" language on the street from people he had worked with in meetings.

"From the time an organism has been identified as a cause of disease to the time we have an effective drug for it, this is by far the fastest ever," he said, referring to the drug AZT, which slows the progress of AIDS, although it is not a cure. "And this drug is the most effective against viruses we've had." . . .

Act Up charged in a report handed out at the demonstration that few drugs had been tested to treat the infections related to AIDS, and that few of the clinical tests of drugs had been conducted in the poor, inner-city communities where the disease is spreading fastest.

Dr. Fauci said serious problems still had to be worked on, and he said the institutes were taking steps to increase the number of women and minorities in the drug trials. In addition, he said, the number of drugs being tested to fight AIDS-related infections would increase. He said in the next year 12 studies of those drugs were scheduled, as compared with only 5 studies on drugs that attack the virus itself, in a reversal of the previous priorities.

AIDS QUILT OFFERS STARK REMINDER OF THOSE LOST

The Names Project coordinated the creation of a giant quilt in 1987 made from nearly 3,000 3-by-6-foot panels, each of which represented an individual who had died from AIDS. Panels were made by family, friends, and coworkers, and many incorporated images or objects that represented the victim. As part of the October 11, 1987, National March on Washington for Lesbian and Gay Rights, 1,920 panels were stitched together and displayed on the Washington Mall. The quilt was to measure 150 by 500 feet, and organizers hoped it would provide a powerful visual reminder of the impact of AIDS. Cleve Jones, executive director of the Names Project, came up with the idea for the quilt and saw it as a way to mourn the loss of his best friend to the deadly illness. Said Sally Meiser of her friend Stephen's piece of the quilt: "We made his panel red with sequins. He was a quiet person, but he always wanted his name in lights."

OCTOBER 5, 1987
DENYING AIDS ITS STING: A QUILT FOR LIFE
By KATHERINE BISHOP
Special for the New York Times

Entering the storefront headquarters of the Names Project here, visitors are struck by the colorful fabric panels that cover the walls and floors: red velvet, pale-blue cotton, hot-pink satin, plain denim, rich brocade, ordinary felt, plaid wool. For just a moment, the visual impact masks the reality that each panel—there are thousands of them—represents a life lost to AIDS.

The Names Project is a campaign to provide memorials to those lives by creating a huge quilt made up of individual panels, each 3 by 6 feet, that have been made by the families, friends and co-workers of those who died. Each of the nearly 3,000 panels, which have come from all over the country, bears the name of a victim of acquired immune deficiency syndrome.

March on Washington

Of the panels in hand, 1,920 are being sewn together by volunteers working 12 hours a day to make a quilt that will be displayed at the Mall in Washington on Oct. 11 as part of the National March on Washington for Lesbian and Gay Rights.

Many panels depict aspects of the life of the person who died. Thus, some are made from shirts belonging to victims, others have teddy bears sewn onto them and one has an appliqué of a white chef's hat.

"I get overwhelmed by the number of people this represents," said Sally Meiser, a volunteer with the project. "But it's a juxtaposition of deep sadness with joyful creation."

While the final creation will simply be stitched together and not padded and cross-stitched, or quilted, it is referred to as a quilt because it is being made in the folk-art tradition of patchwork quilts, which were created in sewing bees.

Project organizers believe that the quilt, which will measure 150 by 500 feet, will be a striking visualization of a portion of the deaths from AIDS, which reached more than 24,000 nationwide as of September. Health officials expect the toll to reach 179,000 within three years. The organizers also hope to raise funds to take the quilt on a 35-city tour next year.

Mourning Friends

The Names Project's executive director is Cleve Jones, who helped found the San Francisco AIDS Foundation, a major resource and information center since the early years of the health crisis.

Mr. Jones said he conceived the quilt idea during a memorial march in 1986 for Harvey Milk, a homosexual who was a member of the city's Board of Supervisors and who was shot to death in his City Hall office in 1978. Marchers carried placards with the names of those who had died of AIDS.

For Mr. Jones, who is 32 years old, the project is also a way to mourn the death from AIDS last year of his best friend for 14 years.

"I went through a period of real despair," he said. "My past has been wiped out. I've lost all my friends from my youth."

Ms. Meiser worked with a group of friends to make a panel for another young man who died of AIDS. They worked on it for eight nights and spent the time designing and sewing and talking about their friend.

"It was a celebration of Stephen," Ms. Meiser said. "We made his panel red with sequins. He was a quiet person, but he always wanted his name up in lights." . . .

- -

Fashion Gala Raises $500,000 for AIDS Research

In one night the fashion, makeup, and fragrance industries raised an estimated $500,000 at a fund-raiser for the American Foundation for AIDS Research (AmFAR). Photographer Gordon Munro staged the "World's Largest Photo Session," posing celebrities with AIDS patients for the public service advertising campaign "To Care Is to Cure." Those in attendance included cohosts Calvin Klein and Elizabeth Taylor as well as nearly every top name in American fashion. At least 2,000 ticket holders paid $150 each to attend the event, which was held in the Crystal Palace entrance hall of the Jacob K. Javits Convention Center.

APRIL 30, 1986
FASHION INDUSTRY TURNS OUT IN FORCE FOR AIDS BENEFIT
By MICHAEL GROSS

Ultimately it was the deaths of friends and colleagues—horrible, sometimes lonely deaths from a disease most people were afraid to acknowledge—that brought the fashion, fragrance and cosmetics industries into the battle against acquired immune deficiency syndrome.

"Losing your friends, people you work with, the ramifications become apparent," said Donna Karan, one of the first fashion designers to become publicly involved in the cause. "I'm a mother," she said. "That more than anything is my inspiration. AIDS must be dealt with."

"It's time they brought this out of the closet," said Frank Masandrea, another designer.

Last night, a step toward finding a cure was taken when designers, retailers, fashion, makeup and fragrance manufacturers and the journalists who cover them joined entertainment luminaries at a glittering fund-raising benefit on behalf of the American Foundation for AIDS Research (Amfar). Organizers estimated that the evening would gross $500,000. At least 2,000 ticket holders paid $150 each to attend.

The event was held on two floors of the monumental Crystal Palace entrance hall of the Jacob K. Javits Convention Center. It was billed as the "World's Largest Photo Session"—and with reason. Group photographs of celebrities with AIDS patients, by Gordon Munro, will run in space donated by national publications as a public service advertising campaign. Its headline was the evening's theme: "To Care Is to Cure."

"Our concern is to involve everybody," said Dr. Mathilde Krim, an AIDS researcher and co-chairman of Amfar's board of directors.

Virtually every top name in the American fashion world was there, led by Calvin Klein, who arrived two hours after the party began with his co-host, Elizabeth Taylor. In a speech, Miss Taylor, holding Mr. Klein's hand, thanked "people who have the courage to care."

"These are the people who must lead," Dr. Krim said.

Many said it was Mr. Klein's presence that made the event a success, but the designer disagreed. "It's not me," he said. "It's Elizabeth Taylor. We're just helping her." Also in attendance were dozens of top-name designers, including Perry Ellis, Oscar de la Renta, Azzedine Alaia, who arrived with Kenzo, Carolina Herrera, Norma Kamali and Louis Dell'Olio. . . .

- -

Council Hearing on AIDS Leads to Demonstration and Conflicts

Numerous conflicts broke out on November 15, 1985, at a New York City Council hearing on issues related to AIDS. Scheduled for discussion were resolutions to close the city's bathhouses and to support a Council study of AIDS as well as legislation that would ban all who "have or 'carry' AIDS, including staff and students, from the public schools."

Outside City Hall, approximately 100 protesters carried signs and chanted, "Fight AIDS, Not Gays," protesting the arrest of a man with AIDS who claimed he was just trying to enter the building to testify. The police later claimed the man pushed and punched an officer. The demonstration ceased when the man was released about 30 minutes later.

During the hearing, discussion also grew heated. Rep. Ted Weiss of Manhattan stated that banning those with AIDS from the public schools "demonstrates the hysteria surrounding AIDS and the legal and civil-rights emergency generated by this unprecedented health crisis." Councilman Noach Dear, sponsor of the legislation, was hissed for suggesting that Rep. Weiss was more interested in helping the victims of AIDS than in stopping the spread of the disease. Gay activists also offered emotional testimony about the anger and fear generated by increased violence against homosexuals and the Council's continued failure to pass a bill to protect the civil rights of homosexuals.

Outside Council chambers, Paul Cameron, a psychologist who favored quarantining AIDS patients, also became involved in a heated argument with gay activists. A television camera arrived, and police officers were summoned to quell the disturbance.

NOVEMBER 16, 1985
A PROTEST ERUPTS OUTSIDE HEARING ON AN AIDS BILL
By JOYCE PURNICK

The frustration of many homosexuals over what they say is growing discrimination and hysteria generated by the fear of AIDS erupted at City Hall yesterday—at a demonstration outside and a hearing inside.

About 100 men and women, chanting "Fight AIDS, Not Gays" and carrying signs like ''1935—Juden Verboten, 1985—Homosexuals Verboten," protested outside after a man suffering from the disease was handcuffed and taken into custody as he tried to enter the building. They stopped only after the AIDS patient, David Summers, was released, about a half hour after he was arrested.

The protest was only one incident in a day of outbursts, impassioned testimony and expressions of frustration from homosexuals who said they had become the victims of a frightened public.

"Stop scapegoating in the name of providing medical solutions," David Rothenberg, a leading homosexual rights activist, told members of the City Council's Health Committee. "We're frightened, very frightened."

Violence Over AIDS Cited

He also said he wanted the lawmakers to understand that homosexuals were upset about seeing a homosexual-rights bill fail in the Council 14 years in a row.

David Wertheimer, head of a group founded to combat violence against homosexuals, testified that AIDS had led to increasing incidents of "homophobic violence" in the city.

"AIDS-related violence, a phenomenon as new to the city as the AIDS crisis, is a reality that the Council must consider as it ponders its own response to the current situation," said Mr. Wertheimer, executive director of the New York City Gay and Lesbian Anti-Violence Project.

The reason for the hearing, which is scheduled to continue Tuesday, was to consider proposed Council legislation and two resolutions related to AIDS, or acquired immune deficiency syndrome. But the legislation—which would ban all who have or "carry" AIDS, including staff and students, from the public schools—is given little chance of passage. The Koch administration and others contend it is unconstitutional.

A Plea for Help

While there was testimony relating to the bill and the resolutions—one to close bathhouses and similar places, the other supporting a study of AIDS by the Council—the hearing became a forum to vent opinions and concern.

"We have done our part and we will do more in years ahead," said Richard Dunne, executive director of the Gay Men's Health Crisis, a four-year-old organization founded to help people with AIDS. "We can't do it alone. We beseech you to help us. We are your children, your brothers and sisters, your nephews and nieces. We are persons with AIDS. We are care-givers to those with AIDS."

Councilman Noach Dear, Democrat of Brooklyn, a sponsor of the bill, called Intro. 1027, said: "I don't want anybody dying. That's why I'm here."

At one point, he set off a round of hisses when he said to one witness, Representative Ted Weiss of Manhattan, that "it was ironic that you want to help victims but you don't want to stop the spread of AIDS."

"I will take exception to that last comment," said Mr. Weiss, a Democrat from the West Side. "We all want to prevent the spread of AIDS."

He voiced "strenuous opposition" to the proposed bill. "The content of Intro. 1027 demonstrates the hysteria surrounding AIDS and the legal and civil-rights emergency generated by this unprecedented health crisis," he said.

Police Summoned

Other arguments broke out, including one outside the Council chambers between Paul Cameron, a psychologist who favors placing AIDS patients in quarantine, and a number of homosexuals who find his theories offensive.

God "will save this man," Mr. Cameron said, referring to Mr. Summers, the 33-year-old AIDS patient who by then had been released from custody and was standing next to him.

"How dare you?" Mr. Summers said. "I don't need saving." The encounter got heated, especially when a television camera arrived, and police officers were summoned. In an unusual display for City Hall, a phalanx of officers stood in front of the building during the demonstration.

Later, the police said Mr. Summers had pushed and punched a police officer, and he was charged with disorderly conduct. Mr. Summers said he was simply trying to enter the building to testify at the hearing.

- -

Controversial Banner Leads to Art Show Cancellation

Guest curator Humberto Chavez cancelled an AIDS-themed art show that was scheduled to open at the Henry Street Settlement House in December 1989. The cancellation stemmed from the Settlement House's refusal to display an 8-by-12-foot Gran Fury banner on the front of the building. Gran Fury was a group of artists and others who created and publicly displayed posters, banners, and billboards about AIDS. The banner was to read "All People with AIDS Are Innocent."

According to Chavez, he cancelled the show after Barbara Tate, chief administrator of the Henry Street Arts for Living Center, questioned the banner's status as art and raised concerns about potential community reactions owing to the political nature of the message. Tate denied making these statements and insisted that the Settlement House was committed to the show but had a policy against hanging banners on the front of the building. She stated, "We have had artworks on the front of the building, but this is the first request I've had for a banner that is considered a work of art."

According to Gran Fury member Robert Vasquez, another employee of Henry Street's gallery invited the group to submit work for the show and knew they were thinking about a banner for the front of the building but didn't raise concerns about policy until after the text for the banner was submitted. Vasquez stated he understood that "Henry Street has to deal with community reaction on a daily basis and we don't have to because as artists we go in, put up the work, and go away."

NOVEMBER 21, 1989
AIDS ART SHOW IS CANCELED OVER A BANNER
By MICHAEL KIMMELMAN

An art exhibition about AIDS that was to open at the Henry Street Settlement House on Dec. 1 has been withdrawn by its curator because of a dispute over the display of a banner on the building. The banner was proposed by Gran Fury, a group of artists and others that designs banners, posters, billboards and other works about AIDS for mass display. The 8-by-12-foot banner was to have carried the words, "All People With AIDS Are Innocent."

The guest curator of the show, Humberto Chavez, said yesterday that he was informed on Friday by Barbara Tate, chief administrator of the Arts for Living Center of the Henry Street Settlement, that the banner "was too political, that she was concerned about reactions from the community, that Gran Fury was not in her estimation a group of artists and that this was not a piece of art."

Ms. Tate said yesterday: "That's not what I said. The fact that we are doing the show demonstrates our commitment to the issue. We have a policy here that the facade of the building does not take banners. We have had artworks on the front of the building but this is the first request I've had for a banner that is considered a piece of artwork."

Ms. Tate had offered to display the banner in the gallery, but Mr. Chavez said that Gran Fury did not intend its works for galleries.

No Endowment Funds Involved

The arts program at the settlement receives funds from a variety of private and public sources, not including the National Endowment for the Arts. Mr. Chavez's show, which received no public financing, was to have been called "Images and Words: Artists Respond to AIDS" and included works by 47 artists and collectives, among them General Idea, Ann Meredith and Art Positive.

Robert Vazquez, a member of Gran Fury, said he had been asked by Susan Fleminger, the visual arts director at Henry Street, to submit a proposal in mid-October. "I told her we were thinking of putting a banner in the front of the building and she didn't seem to have any problem with that at the time, but she wanted to see something on paper," Mr. Vazquez said.

He said he was told by Ms. Fleminger last week that the facade was not a feasible location for the banner. "She gave me reasons that were fairly vague," he said. "She told me at first that it might be construed as advertising and she suggested other places for the banner, and it was clear that she wasn't familiar with the kind of work we do at Gran Fury. In fact this banner is the most innocuous thing the group has ever done. I think there were misunderstandings, and I also understand that Henry Street has to deal with community reaction on a daily basis and we don't have to because as artists we go in, put up the work and go away." . . .

AIDS' SHIFTING DEMOGRAPHICS CAUSES AGENCY CONFLICT

Like many AIDS organizations throughout the country in the 1990s, the Gay Men's Health Crisis struggled to manage an increasingly diverse client base. The nonprofit agency was founded in 1982 to provide services and support to those infected with AIDS and until the early 1990s had served primarily gay white men. However, because the rate of infection among homosexuals had sharply decreased and reported infections in people of color, heterosexual men and women, and IV drug users had increased, the profile of AIDS changed dramatically. The GMHC's 1993 caseload was 10 percent female, 22 percent IV drug users, and 44 percent nonwhite.

Although many expressed continued satisfaction with the agency and its services, others were beginning to complain. Many gay men were not comfortable mixing with drug users and were distressed by many of the new clients' homophobic attitudes and comments. Some female and heterosexual clients countered that the agency was still primarily geared to the needs of gay men and did not provide a full range of services to meet their needs. To meet this challenge, the GMHC partnered with other groups, trained staff and volunteers to deal with cultural differences, and offered new services such as day care, women's support groups, substance-abuse counseling, and legal services for immigrants.

Since suffering growing pains in the early 1990s, the GMHC has grown exponentially in both size and scope. It now includes several resources for a variety of groups affected by AIDS, including MyMethLife.com, launched in 2010, that serves as an aid for crystal meth users with the disease.

MAY 28, 1993
DIVERSITY BUT CONFLICT UNDER WIDER AIDS UMBRELLA
At the Gay Men's Health Crisis, a Struggle to Serve Competing Groups of Clients
By MIREYA NAVARRO
Correction Appended

Not long ago, a 29-year-old homosexual man struck up a conversation with another man and, finding him attractive, winked at him. Insulted, the second man, cursed the gay man and called him a "faggot."

Of the two, it was the gay man who said he was the one most surprised. After all, the confrontation took place at Gay Men's Health Crisis, the pioneering AIDS organization in New York City.

"I said, 'what are you doing here?'" the gay man recalled. "This is my place. This is for me and people like me."

Broadening Services

Gay Men's Health Crisis, as its name implies, is still primarily a nonprofit agency devoted to the needs of gay men sick with H.I.V. But as the virus has spread to infect heterosexuals, most of them users who inject drugs, and their children, gay clients are finding that the organization they have counted on to give them help and refuge is not theirs alone anymore.

Eleven years after the agency was founded by six gay men to cope with the "health crisis" among homosexuals, it has broadened its services to respond to the wider range of people who knock on its doors. But the organization has not found it an easy task: Its clients often have little more in common than the virus itself and grumblings can be heard from all quarters.

To be sure, there are still many satisfied clients. "This is the only agency in New York City that you can actually say is doing a good job," said a 37-year-old gay client from Queens recently as he ate a lunch of six kinds of salads and carrot juice in the organization's cafeteria, which serves 200 meals a day, free to its clients.

But many gay clients say that they do not feel comfortable mixing with drug users, some of whom heckle them even in the halls and the cafeteria. And they say some of their favorite programs are being discontinued. At the same time, female and heterosexual clients say that the agency still caters mostly to the needs of gay men and that they often have to go elsewhere for services.

The struggle at the agency between competing groups of AIDS sufferers is not unusual among AIDS organizations these days. In the last few years, many organizations that started out to serve gay people who suffered from AIDS have felt bound to make their programs available to all who need help.

Some are doing it simply because they believe it is the right action to take, while others are being swayed by public opinion and the possibility that they could lose financial support from both the government and private donors if they did not. Yet the organizations say that in trying to meet everyone's needs effectively they have no model to follow.

"There's no recipe for this," said Timothy J. Sweeney, 39, who ends a three-year term in July as executive director of Gay Men's Health Crisis. "There's always something new to learn."

The agency announced on Wednesday that 42-year-old Jeff Richardson, currently the Secretary of the Family and Social Services Administration for the State of Indiana, would take over the $135,000 job.

Officials at Gay Men's Health Crisis say the disgruntled are a minority, but they concede that the last few years have been a challenge. They say they are trying to improve the situation by teaching staff members and volunteers how to deal with issues arising from cultural and other differences.

Because they recognize that they cannot do it all well, they say they are forming partnerships with other groups to duplicate some of their trademark services like the "buddy" program that links volunteers to people with H.I.V. for moral support and help with daily chores and other needs.

The organization still regards homosexuals as its main constituency. But in a city with an estimated 235,000 people infected with H.I.V., and where homosexuals are experiencing the slowest growth in new reported cases of AIDS, those walking in to the agency to ask for its help have included more non-whites, women and heterosexuals. As a result, the agency's clients have shifted from almost exclusively white homosexual men to 10 percent female, 22 percent people with a history of intravenous drug use—of whom nearly a third are also gay, lesbian or bisexual—and 44 percent non-white.

The agency has responded by creating new programs like a day-care service for children, support groups for women and substance-abuse counseling, among others. But by tailoring some of its services to new clients it has antagonized some of its original constituents.

Some gay clients and workers complain that popular recreational programs like arts and crafts classes are given less attention now, and that lunches are no longer a social event but simply a meal program.

A 43-year-old client and volunteer who said he did not visit the agency as often as he used to said, "Part of the crisis at G.M.H.C. is that people like me, upper-middle-class gay males who were the soul of the organization, feel shunted aside as G.M.H.C. is getting away from gay."

But similar charges are heard from other groups. The organization, they say, is still very much set up for homosexuals.

Mary Beth Caschetta, who is a lesbian, was a staff member for three years until she left last January. She said that to serve women well the agency would have to offer specialized services including programs for women just released from jail and for those women with H.I.V. and their children who live in the other boroughs.

Ilka Tanya Payan, a lawyer who worked in the legal services division and who said she left the agency out of frustration last November, said it sometimes appeared mired in an identity crisis. She said she believed that there was an honest effort to provide legal services for immigrants, a project she directed. But she said she was discouraged by her supervisors from promoting the services or expanding them.

"I couldn't figure out if it was a real commitment or an effort to respond to criticism that we didn't serve these communities," she said. . . .

Older People with AIDS Face Daunting Medical Problems

Owing to a "cocktail" of antiretroviral drugs, many people with AIDS have lived decades longer than originally anticipated, but some are now prematurely facing a complex combination of medical problems more typically seen in the very elderly. John Holloway, a 59-year-old who was diagnosed with AIDS nearly twenty years ago, has more medical problems than his 84-year-old father, including "chronic obstructive pulmonary disease, diabetes, kidney failure, a bleeding ulcer, severe depression, rectal cancer and the lingering effects of a broken hip."

Because it took ten years to develop effective strategies for combating AIDS, few people who contracted HIV in the early days of the epidemic survived, and this has severely limited research efforts into the long-term impact of the disease. As a result, only small, inclusive studies have been performed, and it is not yet possible to definitively state that older people with AIDS face unique health problems. However, researchers theorize that many may have suffered irreversible damage to their immune system and organs prior to the advent of the antiretroviral drugs. Further, the toxicity of these drugs may have caused additional complications over time.

The impact of aging on AIDS is of growing concern, since one out of four Americans living with the disease is now age 50 or older, and the number of patients within this age group continues to rise nationwide. One study financed by the National Institutes of Health has tracked 2,000 subjects for the past twenty-five years and, over the next five years, plans to directly examine this issue to determine which health problems are the result of aging, which are the result of HIV, and what role, if any, prolonged use of antiretroviral drugs plays in the increased health problems of older people with AIDS.

JANUARY 6, 2008
AIDS PATIENTS FACE DOWNSIDE OF LIVING LONGER
By JANE GROSS

John Holloway received a diagnosis of AIDS nearly two decades ago, when the disease was a speedy death sentence and treatment a distant dream.

Yet at 59 he is alive, thanks to a cocktail of drugs that changed the course of an epidemic. But with longevity has come a host of unexpected medical conditions, which challenge the prevailing view of AIDS as a manageable, chronic disease.

Mr. Holloway, who lives in a housing complex designed for the frail elderly, suffers from complex health problems usually associated with advanced age: chronic obstructive pulmonary disease, diabetes, kidney failure, a bleeding ulcer, severe depression, rectal cancer and the lingering effects of a broken hip.

Those illnesses, more severe than his 84-year-old father's, are not what Mr. Holloway expected when life-saving antiretroviral drugs became the standard of care in the mid-1990s.

The drugs gave Mr. Holloway back his future.

But at what cost?

That is the question, heretical to some, that is now being voiced by scientists, doctors and patients encountering a constellation of ailments showing up prematurely or in disproportionate numbers among the first wave of AIDS survivors to reach late middle age.

There have been only small, inconclusive studies on the causes of aging-related health problems among AIDS patients.

Without definitive research, which has just begun, that second wave of suffering could be a coincidence, although it is hard to find anyone who thinks so.

Instead, experts are coming to believe that the immune system and organs of long-term survivors took an irreversible beating before the advent of lifesaving drugs and that those very drugs then produced additional complications because of their toxicity—a one-two punch.

"The sum total of illnesses can become overwhelming," said Charles A. Emlet, an associate professor at the University of Washington at Tacoma and a leading H.I.V. and aging researcher, who sees new collaborations between specialists that will improve care.

"AIDS is a very serious disease, but longtime survivors have come to grips with it," Dr. Emlet continued, explaining that while some patients experienced unpleasant side effects from the antiretrovirals, a vast majority found a cocktail they could tolerate. "Then all of a sudden they are bombarded with a whole new round of insults, which complicate their medical regime and have the potential of being life threatening. That undermines their sense of stability and makes it much more difficult to adjust."

The graying of the AIDS epidemic has increased interest in the connection between AIDS and cardiovascular disease, certain cancers, diabetes, osteoporosis and depression. The number of people 50 and older living with H.I.V., the virus that causes AIDS, has increased 77 percent from 2001 to 2005, according to the federal Centers for Disease Control, and they now represent more than a quarter of all cases in the United States.

The most comprehensive research has come from the AIDS Community Research Initiative of America, which has studied 1,000 long-term survivors in New York City, and the Multi-Site AIDS Cohort Study, financed by the National Institutes of Health, which has followed 2,000 subjects nationwide for the past 25 years.

The Acria study, published in 2006, examined psychological, not medical, issues and found unusual rates of depression and isolation among older people with AIDS.

The Multi-Site AIDS Cohort Study, or MACS, will directly examine the intersection of AIDS and aging over the next five years. Dr. John Phair, a principal investigator for the study, which has health data from both infected and uninfected men, said "prolonged survival" coupled with the "naturally occurring health issues" of old age raised pressing research questions: "Which health issues are a direct result of aging, which are a direct result of H.I.V. and what role do H.I.V. meds play?"

The MACS investigators, and other researchers, defend the slow pace of research as a function of numbers. The first generation of AIDS patients, in the mid-1980s, had no effective treatments for a decade, and died in overwhelming numbers, leaving few survivors to study.

Those survivors, like Mr. Holloway, gaunt from chemotherapy and radiation and mostly housebound, lurch from crisis to crisis. Mr. Holloway says his adjustment strategy is simple: "Deal with it." Still he notes, ruefully, that his father has no medical complaints other than arthritis, failing eyesight and slight hearing loss.

"I look at how gracefully he's aged, and I wish I understood what was happening to my body," Mr. Holloway said during a recent home visit from his case manager at the Howard Brown Health Center here, a gay, lesbian and transgender organization. The case manager, Lisa Katona, could soothe but not inform him. "Nobody's sure what causes what," Ms. Katona told Mr. Holloway. "You folks are the first to go through this and we're learning as we go."

Mr. Holloway is uncomplaining even in the face of pneumonia and a 40-pound weight loss, both associated with his cancer treatment. Has the cost been too high? He says it has not, "considering the alternatives." . . .

Glimmers of Hope as Epidemic Stabilizes

On November 23, 2007, UNAIDS, the United Nations' AIDS-fighting agency, and the World Health Organization announced a sharp reduction in their estimate of the number of people infected with the AIDS virus worldwide, from 39.5 million to 33.2 million. In addition, they forecast an additional 2.5 million new infections per year, far fewer than previously anticipated. Although some epidemiologists claimed the previous estimates were purposefully inflated to generate increased funding, the monitoring organizations pointed to better surveillance, improved methodology, and an increased understanding of the dynamics of the epidemic as responsible for the newer, more accurate numbers.

While the number of new infections and AIDS-related deaths had both declined, the total number of those infected continued to rise worldwide, and 2 million people die from the disease each year, primarily in sub-Saharan Africa, where eight countries have infection rates of 15 percent or higher. The global AIDS pandemic is no longer spiraling out of control; however, AIDS "remains one of the world's greatest scourges, requiring a strong campaign to bring it under control."

NOVEMBER 23, 2007
EDITORIAL
New Numbers on AIDS

It looks as if the global AIDS pandemic may not be spiraling out of control after all. Instead, the devastation is stabilizing at an unacceptably high level.

The United Nations' AIDS-fighting agency and the World Health Organization ate a lot of crow this week for previously overestimating the number of people infected with the virus. As a result of improved methodologies, better surveillance and new understanding of the dynamics of the epidemic, they sharply reduced their estimate—to 33.2 million worldwide from 39.5 million. They now peg the number of new infections per year at 2.5 million, much lower than past estimates.

A few epidemiologists have long charged that the United Nations numbers were wrong, and possibly designed to generate more contributions to battle the disease. We see no sign of any conspiracy. And make no mistake, even with the revised estimates, the AIDS epidemic remains one of the world's greatest scourges, requiring a strong campaign to bring it under control.

There are, thankfully, glimmers of hope that the epidemic is beginning to wane. The number of new infections peaked in the late 1990s, and the number of people dying from AIDS-related illnesses has declined in the last two years, in part thanks to life-prolonging drug treatments. Officials also point to a reduction in risky sexual practices in some regions of the world.

But it's hard to rejoice too much when the number of people living with AIDS infections is still rising, more than two million people—mostly in sub-Saharan Africa—are still dying from the disease each year, and eight countries in southern Africa have more than 15 percent of their populations infected, a devastating blow to their societies and economies. The revised numbers cannot be used as an excuse to relax the campaign against AIDS.

COMING OUT, OUTING, AND THE CLOSET

. . . .

INTRODUCTION

Coming out, outing, and *the closet* are all terms associated with the complex processes surrounding acquiring a publicly gay sexual identity. According to historian George Chauncey, the term *coming out* was originally a play on women's debutante balls. Just as young women traditionally "came out" into society at lavish parties, gay men in the 1930s held coming out balls in which they would dress in drag and hence "come out" into the gay world. The addition of the term *the closet* (as in "coming out of the closet") became common in the early 1970s, following the famous Stonewall Rebellion (see the first chapter) and is thought to be derived from the phrase *skeletons in the closet,* which more generally connotes hiding something shameful from public view.

Coming out has long been a central narrative of gay and lesbian life. People are generally not raised to be gay and are assumed to be heterosexual until they actively declare to themselves and others that they are lesbian, gay, bisexual, or transgender (LGBT). Prior to coming out, LGBT people may live a double life in which they either passively conceal their sexual identity because of shame or fear of retribution or actively lie about it, or both. While remaining in the closet may allow gays and lesbians to pass as straight in mainstream society, it typically comes with a price—accepting the shame associated with consistently misrepresenting one's own personality and opinions as well as hiding significant relationships and activities. Accordingly, coming out of the closet is often associated with a newfound pride, which can serve to transform shame into personal and political power in LGBT individuals as well as in the gay community. Coming out also serves to make LGBT people more visible in the general population, since greater numbers of straight people become aware that they have family, friends, and coworkers who are gay. This, in turn, is thought to foster greater acceptance and tolerance of alternative sexual identities. Therefore, it is argued, a formerly private sexual identity can become a potent political force simply through its public revelation.

Beginning in the late 1980s, however, some people began to force others out of the closet (a practice called "outing"). This transformed the act of coming out from a voluntary declaration of pride into a strategy for shaming those whose public positions were seen as being in conflict with their private lives. For example, some journalists thought they had a duty to reveal the gay identity of political figures who actively supported policies that disadvantaged LGBT populations, such as the Clinton administration's "Don't Ask, Don't Tell" policy that compelled gays serving in the military to remain closeted. During the 1990s, several celebrities came out as gay, some to increase awareness and others out of fear of being outed by the press. Recently, the increased visibility and growing acceptance of LGBT populations in public life has led some to argue that the coming out narrative is less central than it used to be. However, its importance as a personal and political practice is unlikely to recede completely as long as LGBT individuals fear that revealing their sexual identity may lead to rejection, discrimination, and even violence.

COMING OUT AND THE LGBT MOVEMENT

After the Stonewall Inn riots in June 1969, large numbers of people began to publicly identify as gay, lesbian, bisexual, or trangender. A powerful rejection of their previous isolation and shame, coming out also became linked to a larger political agenda that included equal rights and liberties for the LGBT population. A November 17, 1969, *Times* report titled "The Woman Homosexual: More Assertive, Less Willing to Hide" noted that the modern lesbian "to an increasing degree, is refusing to live with the limitations and restrictions imposed by society and is showing a sense of active resentment and rebellion at a condemnation she considers unwarranted and unjust." The piece stated that attendance at lesbian political and social groups such as the Daughters of Bilitis had increased 300 percent in recent years. In a lengthy *Times* piece on lesbians published in the Sunday

Magazine on March 28, 1971, Barbara Love (described as a "comely blonde") said, "People must speak up as lesbians. I am a lesbian. We've got to come out of the closet and fight, because we're not going to get anywhere if we don't." Similarly, the August 24, 1970, *Times* report "Homosexuals in Revolt" noted that gay men were increasingly "publicly identifying themselves as homosexuals, taking a measure of pride in that identity and seeking militantly to end what they see as society's persecution of them." This piece brought to the forefront two slogans that emerged in the wake of Stonewall: "Out of the closets and into the streets" and "Gay is good." In a *Times* essay that appeared in the Sunday Magazine on October 10, 1971, openly gay writer Merle Miller offered a relatively sober assessment, noting that while "many homosexuals still prefer the closet . . . I'm more optimistic that attitudes are changing."

One primary impediment to coming out that was identified early on was the potential negative impact on family relationships. A *Times* piece of September 1, 1972, noted that parental reactions ranged from outright rejection to limited acceptance within the home but not in public to active participation in the movement. While noting that it was becoming less difficult for gay people to come out to their parents, the report nonetheless detailed several cases of young adults being kicked out of the house, and one instance of a parent threatening suicide. To counter these negative responses, gay liberation groups emerged at colleges and universities across the country to offer support and encouragement to the local LGBT community. In 1973 the Gay Academic Union organized one of the first conferences designed to bring together gay professors and graduate students who could serve as positive role models for gay undergraduates at their institutions. The conference was held at John Jay College in New York City, and conference speakers encouraged participants to come out, especially tenured professors who could afford to push the limits of accepted behavior owing to their greater job security. Just a few years later, on June 19, 1975, *The Times* reported that new discos designed for teenage homosexuals were opening up in Los Angeles. Noting the fast pace of the recent changes, one of the owners of the disco said, "Gay kids today are coming out of the closet a lot earlier than past generations. And the day of the sleazy, back-alley gay bar is over. Some of these kids and their dates were dropped off by their parents."

Not everyone shared the view that coming out was unambiguously good. During the mid-1970s, *The Times'* conservative columnist William Safire commented critically in several opinion pieces on the relatively new phenomenon of gay people coming out. In an April 18, 1974, essay, he stated that "as homosexuals have gained the courage to come 'out of the closets and into the streets,' many have proceeded to overstate their case." Safire argued that rather than settling for the ability to "live and let live" in private, many gay people have also suggested that "criticism of homosexuality is bigoted and psychologically outdated," asserting that "their way of life is fulfilling and morally unassailable." Conceding that gays should have the freedom to live as they like in their private lives, Safire nevertheless concluded that "to be gay is to be abnormal" and "homosexuality should be discouraged."

In a later opinion piece of September 29, 1975, Safire contrasted the stories of Air Force sergeant Leonard Matlovich, who challenged the ban on gays in the military, and Oliver Sipple, a decorated Vietnam veteran outed as gay by the *San Francisco Chronicle* after foiling Sarah Jane Moore's attempted assassination of President Gerald Ford (see "Gays in the Military"). While the openly gay Matlovich welcomed the public attention, Sipple shrank from it. Predicting that most homosexuals would choose to remain closeted, and rightly so, Safire criticized Matlovich while applauding Sipple's desire to keep his sexuality private. "The essential point that perhaps Mr. Sipple catches and Sgt. Matlovich does not, is that homosexuality is an abnormality that will never really lose its stigma, because that stigma—and not the law—protects society and the family." The column does not mention that Sipple was estranged from his family for some time after he was outed. Following a lengthy and unsuccessful attempt to sue the *San Francisco Chronicle* for invasion of privacy, Sipple suffered from a variety of physical and mental illnesses prior to his death in 1989 at the age of 47.

Despite the objections of Safire and others, gay people continued to come out in larger numbers throughout the 1970s. By 1977 well-organized and openly gay communities had developed in various areas of New York City, including Greenwich Village and Chelsea, and Kenneth Sherrill had been elected leader of Manhattan's 69th Assembly district, becoming the first openly gay man to win public office in the state of New York. In addition, *The Times* reports of May 15, 1977, and August 24, 1980, indicated that homosexuals were also coming out in the suburbs, although much more slowly and selectively, frequently remaining closeted at work or in wider social circles. A spokesperson for the National Gay Task Force noted that "in the suburbs, you will find that many men and women discover their homosexuality after they are married. These people will usually stay married and have sexual relationships with their spouses, but also have homosexual relationships." A closeted clinical psychologist with a private practice in New Rochelle said that more suburban lesbians than gay men continue to conceal their sexual identity,

IN FOCUS

Boston's St. Patrick's Day Parade

Like gay pride festivities, St. Patrick's Day parades in Boston, New York City, and other communities were originally organized to demonstrate community strength and solidarity in the face of widespread prejudice. Well into the first decades of the twentieth century, Irish American immigrants routinely dealt with housing and employment discrimination. They were negatively stereotyped as drunkards, and some restaurants and bars reportedly posted signs in their windows reading "No Dogs or Irish."

Given this history, it is ironic that the organizers of St. Patrick's Day parades have vehemently fought against including Irish American LGBT groups in these events. Members of these groups viewed marching in their local St. Patrick's Day parade as a symbolic step toward full inclusion within the community. The organizers of the parade in Boston, the South Boston Allied War Veterans Council, originally rejected the Irish-American Gay, Lesbian, and Bisexual Group of Boston's request to march. The group took their case to court, and in 1994 the Supreme Judicial Court of Massachusetts ruled that the parade fit the definition of a "public accommodation" within the state's civil rights law and that exclusion of groups of sexual orientation was prohibited.

Following this decision the parade was cancelled in 1994, and the next year marchers carried black flags instead of green in protest against the court's decision. On June 19, 1995, the United States Supreme Court unanimously overruled the lower court's decision, arguing that the Constitution protects the right of the parade's private sponsors to exclude marchers whose message they reject. Arguing that the parade is a form of expression rather than a public accommodation, Justice David H. Souter said that "one important manifestation of the principle of free speech is that one who chooses to speak may also decide what not to say." He added that the government may not interfere with this right, even for the "enlightened" purpose of preventing discrimination. As of this writing, the Boston St. Patrick's Day Parade continues to bar LGBT groups from marching.

From *The New York Times*

Greenhouse, L. "The Supreme Court: The Boston March; High Court Lets Parade in Boston Bar Homosexuals." June 20, 1995.

noting that "many of them are afraid of losing income, jobs, children and husbands. But they are carrying on affairs with other women." In the wake of a major civil rights battle in Miami during which opponents characterized gay people as immoral child molesters (see the chapter "Gay Civil Rights Laws . . ."), the National Gay Task Force launched a series of open dialogues to correct such misconceptions and "to show the American people who we really are." Described in a *Times* report of June 19, 1977, the education campaign was titled "We are Your Children" and involved the orchestrated and public coming out of a wide variety of gays and lesbians in various cities across the country, with the aim of illustrating

that homosexuals are not "sinful, criminal, or sick" but rather "the people you deal with every day."

Although coming out was a major theme of gay activism in the 1970s, the issue has continued to have resonance for the LGBT community in recent years, as evidenced by the focus on coming out as "one of the people next door" at the 1993 March on Washington for Lesbian, Gay and Bi Equal Rights and Liberation, which was attended by "hundreds of thousands of homosexuals." As indicated by a *Times* report of April 26, 1993, "again and again, speakers hammered away at the theme of 'coming out.' However, although transgender people began establishing a network of organizations and communities after World War II (as noted in an article of September 7, 2006) and were involved in the gay civil rights movement since Stonewall (see the first chapter), this population's efforts to achieve public recognition, both within and outside the movement, have progressed more slowly. Historian Susan Stryker, a male-to-female transsexual, argues that most people are so invested in traditional gender roles that "if you fall outside that easy definition of what a man or a woman is, a lot of people see you as some kind of monster." For example, just as bisexuals were excluded from the title of the 1979 and 1987 marches on Washington for gay and lesbian rights, transgender people were similarly excluded as recently as 1993, even though issues specific to this group were included in the march's platform that year. To combat lingering exclusions and stereotypes, transgender people began to organize and come out more publicly in the mid-1990s, through organizations such as Transexual Menace, which had forty-six chapters in cities across the country by 1996, as well as the Gender Public Advocacy Coalition (GenderPAC), a lobbying group advocating for transgender civil rights and inclusion in hate crime legislation. In addition, out transgender people became more visible in popular culture beginning in the mid-1990s. Although significant progress has been made, more work is necessary to ensure transgender people even the limited level of public acceptance and protection currently afforded to many American gay men, lesbians, and bisexuals.

OUTING AND THE COMING OUT OF POLITICIANS

Because being gay was criminalized and stigmatized for many years, the press generally avoided publicizing the sexual orientation of gay and lesbian celebrities and other public figures even in the face of strong evidence of same-sex sexual behavior, unless this information had already been revealed by the individual in question. This reflected something of a double standard, since the media regularly published the names and occupations of ordinary people whom the police arrested in raids of gay bars. However, despite the increased coverage of gay and lesbian issues post-Stonewall, coming out remained largely at the individual's discretion until the late 1980s.

The onset of AIDS in the 1980s led to speculation that celebrities who contracted the infection (such as Rock Hudson) were hiding their sexual identity to protect their careers. Published in 1985, Hudson's obituary is believed to be the first to have mentioned AIDS as a cause of death.

(See In Focus, page 126.) Beginning in the late 1980s and continuing on through the 1990s, several journalists who worked at alternative newspapers began to purposefully "out" or reveal the allegedly gay identities of some public figures who had not previously revealed their sexual identity to the general public. Michaelangelo Signorile and Gabriel Rotello, both of whom worked at now defunct gay publication *Outweek,* were perhaps the most prominent of these journalists. As they outed significant public figures such as businessman Malcolm Forbes and Assistant Secretary of Defense Pete Williams, the ethics of outing became a subject of discussion in *The New York Times.* During the controversy, *The Times* refused to repeat the names of those outed, referring to Forbes only as "an unnamed businessman" and Williams as "a Pentagon official" in an interview with Signorile on April 25, 1993.

In a March 27, 1990, article, *The Times* described outing as a practice undertaken by "a faction among American gay people," employed to the end of "unmasking prominent people who [are said to be] secretly gay," noting that many viewed it as an invasion of privacy. Some journalists and civil libertarians criticized the tactic of outing, arguing that it could have severe negative consequences for those who were outed, similar to Sen. Joseph McCarthy's accusing many of his political enemies of being communists during the 1950s. Rotello and Signorile defended the practice, insisting that they were simply reporting the news in an unbiased manner, while lambasting the mainstream press for applying an inappropriate double standard that allowed for the coverage of straight but not gay sexual behavior. Rotello stated that "the media talks about the private lives of famous people in great detail. But when it comes to somebody being gay, there is a code of silence." Fueled by the lack of governmental response to the AIDS crisis, many activists specifically targeted public figures who were implementing policies disadvantageous to LGBT populations, such as bans on gay marriage, adoption, and military service. Robert Bray of the National Gay and Lesbian Task Force noted that the issue had been longstanding: "What do we do about homophobic homosexuals in positions of power? It's been a problem since Nazi Germany."

Coming out can be a particularly challenging decision for politicians. In 1987 *The Times* reported that Rep. Barney Frank declared himself gay in a front-page article in the *Boston Globe.* Despite fears that the news would alarm some of his constituents or cause them to see him as solely concerned with gay rights, Frank stated that he decided to come out because of the increasing public attention paid to the private lives of politicians. He noted that Rep. Stewart McKinney's recent death from AIDS involved "such an unseemly scuffle" in the press surrounding questions of McKinney's sexual identity, and Frank said he did not want news of his own eventual demise to focus on "Was he or wasn't he, did he or didn't he." He further expressed concern that a failure to come out would be inaccurately construed as shame about being gay. As a result, the four-term representative chose to take the initiative and reveal his sexual identity himself. Yet, despite this proactive strategy, Frank still felt forced out of the closet to some extent. "I had no choice" he is quoted as saying; "I don't remember making a lot of choices on this whole subject." Although gay politicians sometimes remain closeted for fear of retribution on the part of voters, Frank was reelected to his seat with over 90 percent of the vote in a subsequent election and later chaired the House's Financial Services Committee, a powerful position in the wake of the economic crash of 2008. The phenomenon of politicians coming out to avoid being outed is not confined to the United States, as evidenced by a November 12, 1998, *Times* piece reporting that British agricultural minister Nick Brown had recently declared he was gay after *The News of the World* threatened to publish an interview with one of his former lovers.

The outing of politicians continued as the debate about same-sex marriage began to emerge as a central issue in U.S. politics (see "Same-Sex Marriage and the Family"). When Congress voted on the Defense of Marriage Act (DOMA) in 1996, the three openly gay members of the House, Representatives Gerry Studds (D-MA), Barney Frank (D-MA), and Steve Gunderson (R-WI) all voted against it. However, Rep. Jim Kolbe (R-AZ), who voted in favor of the bill, found himself subject to an outing campaign, including a full-page ad publicizing his sexual identity in *The Washington Blade,* a gay newspaper published in the nation's capital. Kolbe eventually acknowledged that he was gay but defended his vote in favor of DOMA on the grounds that decisions about same-sex marriage should be decided at the state rather than the national level. In 2004, when President Bush formally endorsed a constitutional amendment prohibiting same-sex marriage, a similar outing campaign emerged that targeted gays who work for lawmakers supporting the amendment, as noted in a *Times* report of July 25, 2004.

In addition to celebrities and politicians, some religious leaders are particularly vulnerable to having their sexual identities revealed, since many mainstream religions do not allow LGBT people to serve in that capacity (see "The Intersection of Religion. . . "). As a *Times* report of March 19, 1995,

Rep. Jim Kolbe prepares to speak at an awards ceremony in 1997 for the National Log Cabin Republicans, a group of pro–gay rights Republicans. Kolbe was outed as gay in 1996 after voting for the Defense of Marriage Act.

Source: AP Images/Wilfredo Lee

noted, Bishop David Hope, the Church of England's third most senior cleric, was forced to come out when the group OutRage! "had threatened to go public with an allegation that he was gay unless he himself did so."

TEACHERS, TEENS, AND COMING OUT

While an admittedly stressful time for most gay, lesbian, bisexual, and transgender people, coming out poses unique difficulties for adolescents and those who work with them, especially teachers in primary and secondary schools. Lingering myths about gay recruitment and child molestation have made it difficult for many schoolteachers to acknowledge an alternative sexual identity, for fear of losing their jobs or being labeled mentally ill (see the second chapter, "Gay Civil Rights Laws"). Some teachers have chosen to come out in spite of the risks involved, arguing that such speech is political and thus protected by the First Amendment. An early example of this was reported in *The Times* on December 4, 1974, when Paramus, New Jersey, teacher John Gish refused his school board's order to undergo a psychiatric evaluation after announcing he was the new president of the Gay Activists Alliance (GAA) of New Jersey.

While barriers persisted into the 1990s and beyond, some teachers, such as high school English teacher Alta Kavanaugh in Alessandro, California, have come out as gay, only to find that most colleagues, parents, and students are supportive of the decision. In Kavanaugh's case, she was the subject of some defamatory graffiti but also unanimously chosen by that year's senior class to read their names at graduation. However, teachers of younger children often face stronger resistance. A *Times* report of June 11, 2000, noted that when first grade students in suburban Boston asked their teacher about his family during a lesson on biographies, some parents objected when David Gaita responded that "if he had a partner, 'someone you love the way your mom and dad love each other,' it would be a man." Although the Newton mayor and the school superintendent supported Gaita, a leader of a conservative parents' group complained that "a child's psychology isn't put together for any of this stuff." When students of a seventh grade teacher in the Bronx kept asking him if they were invited to his upcoming wedding, he found a venue that would accommodate a larger crowd and came out to his students as bisexual, inviting them and their parents to witness his commitment to another man. As noted in a *Times* piece of March 23, 2009, although most of the class attended the ceremony, two parents told the principal they didn't want Chance Nalley teaching their children. Noting that Nalley was the only math teacher in the school, the principal said the invitation was appropriate in a school that views itself as an extended family. Since Nalley's commitment ceremony, six students have come out to him as gay.

Gay teens often experience significant resistance regarding their sexuality from parents and other authority figures. Although many families become more accepting over time, the consequences of coming out can be devastating for some LGBT teens. In a *Times* report of May 17, 2007, teens described leaving home after being beaten for cross-dressing, threatened with a gun for hanging around with "tomboys," and raped by a family friend who wanted to "straighten out" a lesbian. Because so many of these teens are thrown out of their homes or decide to run away, studies suggest that up to half of homeless youth are gay, lesbian, or transgender. With limited skills and resources, these homeless teens often turn to sex work to support themselves, leading to high rates of drug use, HIV infection, and suicide. According to research, gay homeless youths are twice as likely to have attempted suicide as heterosexual homeless youths have. In addition, homeless shelters are often dangerous places for LGBT youth, as those unable to successfully pass as straight are frequently threatened and beaten by other residents and sometimes also mistreated by staff. As of 2007, more than twenty-five cities offer at least a few beds in emergency shelters for homeless gay youths, such as the Detroit area's Ruth's House, a ten-bed facility. One user said Ruth's House was "the only place I feel safe being me. Out there, I knew I wasn't safe. I knew I might be killed by someone realizing that I'm a girl looking like a boy." However, demand far exceeds the number of beds available at most of these shelters, leading to extensive waiting lists. Mika Major, director of a drop-in center in Cleveland, said, "The hardest part of the job is telling kids who show up with bruises or horrific stories that we don't have a safe place to send them."

Another challenge faced by some gay teens is reparative, or conversion, therapy. As minors, teens can be forced by their parents to enroll in programs such as Love In Action, an intensive fundamentalist Christian-based effort to help teens resist what are believed to be sinful homosexual urges. Although the teen version of Love in Action is a day-program, conversion therapy sometimes involves extended stays at a treatment facility. Similar to drug rehabilitation programs, these programs typically combine Bible study and talk therapy with behavioral modification techniques in an effort to control homosexual desire and encourage the adoption of heterosexual norms. The American Psychiatric Association has strongly criticized this practice, questioning both its methods and effectiveness, and even the supporters of conversion therapy acknowledge that their success rate is low. Fearful parents, however, continue to pay $1,000 a week or more in the hope of "curing" their LGBT children. When one teen known as "Zach, 16, from Tennessee," discussed on a Web page that his parents requested he enroll in such a program after he came out to them, friends posted additional comments on their own blogs. These were forwarded to other friends, creating a snowball effect that resulted in Love in Action receiving hundreds of e-mails, tens of thousands of Web site hits, a national protest coordinated by the Queer Action Coalition, and days of national media attention.

While many gays and lesbians are out to neighbors, friends, and coworkers in urban centers such as Manhattan, coming out is still often difficult for those living outside such areas, particularly in places where religious traditions or cultural attitudes about masculinity preclude greater tolerance. Many LGBT people in such situations continue to risk rejection, ridicule, or attack. While supportive institutions exist, such as gay bars in Brooklyn and a play group for children of gay parents at the Staten Island Children's Museum, they are sparse when compared with what is available in Manhattan and other urban centers in cities across the nation. A lengthy piece that appeared in *The Times'* Sunday Magazine on August 3, 2003, "Double Lives on the Down Low," suggests that many African American gay men remain closeted owing to an emphasis in mainstream black culture on the importance of masculinity and fatherhood and a widespread belief that homosexuality is a perversion that stems from white culture.

COMING OUT AND POPULAR CULTURE

An interesting feedback loop seems to exist between real life and popular culture. As LGBT people came out in the 1970s, gay characters began to show up in television and movies. As these fictional portrayals became increasingly sympathetic, they also seemed to play a role in normalizing gay identities and increasing popular acceptance, which, in turn, stimulated more people to come out. Homosexuality appeared on television for the first time in the 1960s as a topic of discussion on documentary news programs broadcast from locally based public stations in New York, San Francisco, and other major cities. The first of these, "The Rejected," was aired in 1961 on San Francisco's KQED-TV. New York followed suit, airing a British documentary in 1966. These programs typically featured interviews with gay men and lesbians from diverse backgrounds who discussed the difficulties associated with being homosexual in a predominantly heterosexual culture. Topics included relationships, gay bars, counseling services, police harassment, and job loss. While some used these programs as an opportunity to publicly declare their homosexuality, many took advantage of special camera placement and lighting techniques to hide their true identities. In 1967 Mike Wallace hosted the first major network program focusing on homosexuals, *CBS Reports: The Homosexual.* Because homosexuality was widely thought to be a psychological disorder at this time, programs typically also included sage advice from psychiatrists about how to correct or control the condition (see "Sexuality, Gender, and Science"). It was not until 1978 that a local New York affiliate aired a documentary report focused entirely on job discrimination and child custody issues faced by lesbians; "Lesbians: Women Without Rights?" was favorably reviewed in *The Times* on February 7, 1978.

Initially, some questioned whether pop culture would ever portray homosexuals as living normal, happy lives. In a *Times* piece of February 23, 1969 ("Why Can't 'We' Live Happily Ever After, Too?"), Donn Teal, a prominent gay activist writing under a pseudonym, noted that even though renowned film critic Judith Crist called 1968 "the year of the Third Sex," in most of the movies "writers and producers still feared to let the public see two homosexuals happily in love." A few months later Teal, writing under his own name, welcomed the success of *The Boys in the Band,* the first mainstream play focusing on homosexuality, but worried that the portrayal of the gay characters was largely negative and misleading. Arguing that it was "as if we arrived at our own Coming Out Party dressed in rags," Teal questioned whether audiences would recognize the guilt-ridden, self-loathing portrayals as caricatures. Even in a January 23, 1972, article titled "Why Do Homosexual Playwrights Hide Their Homosexuality?" the author of a play about a closeted homosexual playwright felt compelled to conceal his own identity, writing under a pseudonym and accompanied by a dramatic photograph in which the author's facial features were entirely obscured.

In 1971 the popular situation-comedy *All in the Family* addressed the issue of closeted homosexuality when its famously bigoted main character, Archie Bunker, discovered that his drinking buddy, an ex–pro football player, was gay, in an episode titled "Judging Books by Covers." Shortly thereafter, a lesser-known comedy, *The Corner Bar,* became the first to feature a recurring gay character, a designer by the name of Peter Panama. The quality of the television treatment of gay and lesbian characters varied greatly during this period. For example, the critically acclaimed *That Certain Summer* became the first made-for-television movie about homosexuality, focusing on a gay father who was compelled to come out to his 14-year-old son. A review published in *The Times* on November 3, 1972, contrasted its "intelligence and sensitivity [that are] essential for all television" with the sensational treatment of lesbians on a recently aired episode of the popular dramatic series *The Bold Ones,* which was said to simply inject "titillation into inane plots." Episodes of popular dramatic shows such as *Marcus Welby, M.D.* and *Police Woman* represented homosexuals as ill people, child molesters, and serial killers, while long-running situation comedies such as *Sanford and Son* found broad humor in the setting of a gay bar. Incidents like these led gay activists to protest the networks' representation as biased, including a protest involving an uninvited visit that disrupted the set of *The Today Show.* The broadcaster of the show, NBC, conceded in a *Times* report of October 27, 1973, that "the network had at times dealt unfairly with homosexuals in its programs" and promised to ask gay groups for advice when they covered topics relating to the LGBT community in the future.

In 1977, ABC aired *Soap,* a parody of daytime soap operas, featuring a gay character who was planning to have sex reassignment surgery so that he could be legally wedded to his closeted lover, an ex–pro football player. The network received protests orchestrated by conservative groups as well as by gay groups, including the International Union of Gay Athletes, which, in a *Times* report of August 8, 1977, called the character "a stereotype that would contribute to the ridicule of homosexuals." The National Gay and Lesbian Task Force objected to the fact that "the character is a joke because he's gay." He added that the networks "have stopped all that with blacks in television, and it is time they stopped it with us." It was not until 1982 that Hollywood released the film *Making Love,* which *The Times* called "the first sympathetic movie about gay lovers," in a report of April 26, 1992.

People with AIDS were typically not directly discussed on network television and at the movies in the early years of the crisis. One exception was the critically acclaimed made-for-television 1985 movie *An Early Frost,* which focused on a gay lawyer who is diagnosed with AIDS. *And the Band Played On,* a 1993 HBO drama based on a book by Randy Shilts, chronicled the failure of the government and the medical profession to take appropriate action to combat the AIDS crisis. In the same year the Hollywood film *Philadelphia* starred Tom Hanks as a lawyer who successfully sued his elite firm for firing him when its partners became aware that he had AIDS. The film, which eventually won two Oscars, took the unusual step of employing several people with HIV to play smaller roles. (See In Focus, page 130.) As late as 1991, half of PBS's affiliates refused to show Marlon Riggs's acclaimed documentary *Tongues Untied,* about black gay men and the struggle to deal with AIDS in the black community. As a *Times* report of May 19, 1991, noted, television offers "mixed signals" when it comes to gay images.

Other breakthroughs followed. In 1991 a bisexual lawyer kissed her girlfriend on the popular prime-time drama *L.A. Law,* the situation-comedy *Friends* celebrated a lesbian wedding in 1996, and finally, in 1997, the lead character of the prime-time television show *Ellen* came out of the closet in "The Puppy Episode," receiving enormous media attention as its star, Ellen DeGeneres, also came out as lesbian on the cover of *Time* magazine three weeks prior to the airing of the episode. In a piece titled "The 'Ellen' Striptease," *Times* columnist Frank Rich noted the enormous publicity gained by the pairing of the two events, pointing out that at least one cynical television executive saw it as a last-ditch attempt to boost the show's flagging ratings. Although *Ellen* was soon cancelled, *Will and Grace* debuted the following year in 1998, featuring the first main character on prime-time television

who was out from the start. In 2003 cable television network Bravo began to broadcast *Queer Eye for the Straight Guy,* in which out gay men not only starred but also offered advice to seemingly clueless straight men on how to dress, eat, decorate their apartments, groom themselves, and otherwise be hip. A *Times* piece of July 29, 2003, concluded that "several network and cable television executives said the Supreme Court's 6–3 decision in June, overruling a Texas sodomy law [see the next chapter, "The Right to Privacy"] and legalizing gay sexual conduct, underlined what they already knew: that the nation's attitudes toward gays and lesbians are radically changing."

Talking about the representation of transgender people in popular culture presents a unique challenge. Gender ambiguity has a long history as both a comedic device (as in Shakespeare's *As You Like It* as well as Hollywood classics such as *Some Like it Hot* and *Tootsie*) and as a sexually charged act of female transgression (such as Marlene Dietrich's provocative performance as the tuxedo-wearing nightclub singer in *The Blue Angel*). However, these were men or women self-consciously masquerading as the opposite sex with a wink and a nod toward the camera. Regardless of the characters' costumes or behavior, viewers were confident that Tony Curtis was still clearly a man and Marlene Dietrich was a woman. Movies and television shows did not start to depict transgender people until relatively recently. As with gays and lesbians, transgender characters first received prominent coverage through biographical movies (such as the *Christine Jorgensen Story* in 1970) and documentaries (including Jennie Livingston's 1990 film *Paris Is Burning,* profiling black and Latino transvestites and transsexuals who participate in elaborate New York City drag balls). Stepping outside these genres, *The Crying Game* became the most talked about movie of 1992, largely because of its dramatic revelation that the presumed female lead was actually a transgender character played by Jaye Davidson. Elaborate steps were taken to maintain the secret of Davidson's gender, including a lengthy profile in *The Times* on December 17, 1992, which cleverly offered seventeen paragraphs of description without once referring to its object of interest as either "he" or "she." In the mid-1990s, three successful comedies were released featuring transgender characters (although no transgender actors were cast in any of the lead roles): *The Adventures of Priscilla, Queen of the Desert* (1994), *To Wong Foo, Thanks for Everything, Julie Newmar* (1995), and *The Birdcage* (1996). Around this same time, RuPaul, a statuesque black drag queen, scored a dance hit with the song "Supermodel" and soon became a pop icon, guest starring on ABC's popular soap opera *All My Children,* scoring a major modeling contract with MAC cosmetics, and

IN FOCUS

Marketing to the LGBT Community

• •

As more LGBT people began to openly acknowledge their sexual orientation, American businesses became increasingly interested in marketing to this new (or at least newly visible) demographic. In the early 1990s, American Express, Philip Morris, Seagram, and Time Warner risked offending long-term customers by deliberately marketing to gay male consumers, a group perceived to be both affluent and brand-loyal. Although these advertisements generally appeared in publications targeting the gay community, the retail store Ikea broke new ground in 1994 by airing a television commercial featuring a gay male couple shopping for furniture.

In April 1994 the first National Gay and Lesbian Business Expo was held at the Meadowlands Convention Center in Secaucus, New Jersey. A total of 150 companies, including Columbia Records, AT&T, Continental Airlines, IDS Financial Corporation, and Waldenbooks, each paid $1,500 for a booth at the two-day event. Although gay- and lesbian-owned businesses made up the majority of the exhibitors, one-third of the participants had no connection to the LGBT community beyond a desire to sell vacation packages, real estate, bottled water, and a wide array of other consumer products and services.

In more recent years marketing to the LGBT community has expanded exponentially. Stores and Web sites are stocked with specialty items, including targeted travel guides and calendars, pornography and sex toys, compact discs and jewelry. Just about any product, including rainbow flag dog collars, pink triangle shower curtains, and T-shirts, may be emblazoned with pride slogans and symbols or other messages tailored to the LGBT community. An entire industry has developed to meet the needs of same-sex brides and grooms, including specialized invitations, planning services, venues, gifts, cards, and honeymoon destinations. Despite this explosion of products and services, however, it remains unusual to see images of LGBT people in advertisements aimed at a mainstream audience.

From *The New York Times*

Elliott, Stuart. "The Media Business; Advertising; This Weekend, A Business Export Will Show the Breadth of New Interest in Gay Consumers." April 14, 1994.

• •

hosting a talk show on VH1. Since this time, media portrayals of transgender issues have grown increasingly nuanced and diverse, including the PBS 1996 documentary *You Don't Know Dick: Courageous Hearts of Transsexual Men* and Hilary Swank's Oscar-winning performance in *Boys Don't Cry* (1999), the true story of Brandon Teena, a young transman raped and murdered when he was discovered to be biologically female. Felicity Huffman was also nominated for an Oscar for her portrayal of a male-to-female (MTF) transsexual in *Transamerica* (2005). As of 2009, RuPaul has hosted a reality television show, *RuPaul's Drag Race*.

Despite the changing attitudes, coming out as a LGBT actor remains a risky enterprise. While the number of out actors and gay roles has increased over the years, many in Hollywood choose to stay closeted for fear that they will no longer be cast in straight roles. Two popular television actors, Neil Patrick Harris and T. R. Knight, remained closeted until Harris was outed online and Knight's costar offered some virulently homophobic comments on the set of the popular drama *Grey's Anatomy*. While the impact on their careers of coming out is not yet certain, it is clear that filmmakers continue to consider these issues. The producer of the 2008 film *Milk*, a biopic about gay political leader Harvey Milk (see the chapter "Violence against LGBT People"), noted upon choosing straight actor Sean Penn to play the leading role, "We always have to ask that awful question: 'Who puts bodies in seats?" He concluded, "Sadly, there don't seem to be openly gay actors that could carry a movie, but I think that will change." Similarly, although the number of transgender characters is on the rise, few of these roles are filled by transgender actors. A notable exception was the character of Carmelita on ABC's *Dirty Sexy Money,* played by postoperative MTF actress Candis Cayne, who in 2007 became the first transgender performer to be cast in a reoccurring transgender role on a major television network.

Coming out as lesbian, gay, bisexual, or transgender is a process rather than an event. Although significant progress has been made over the past half century, additional steps will likely be taken in the years ahead to more fully integrate alternative sexual identities into family life and employment as well as public discourse and popular culture.

BIBLIOGRAPHY

Chauncey, George. *Gay New York: Gender, Urban Culture, and the Making of the Gay Male World, 1890–1940.* New York: Basic Books, 1994.

Signorile, Michaelangelo. *Queer in America: Sex, the Media, and the Closets of Power.* New York: Random House, 1993.

Tropiano, Stephen. *The Prime Time Closet: A History of Gays and Lesbians on TV.* Milwaukee, WI: Hal Leonard, 2002.

FROM *THE NEW YORK TIMES*

Barton, Lee. "Why Do Homosexual Playwrights Hide Their Homosexuality?" January 23, 1972.

Berke, Richard L. "Milestone for Gay Rights: March for Gay Rights; Washington Rally Puts Faces with Issues, but Probably Won't Create Change." April 26, 1993.

Brown, Les. "N.B.C. Acts after Complaints by Homosexual Organizations." October 27, 1973.

———. "Homosexuals Move to Protect Civil Rights on TV." August 8, 1977.

Clemetson, Lynette. "Proposed Marriage Ban Splits Washington's Gays." July 25, 2004.

Crosette, Barbara. "Homosexuality in the Suburbs." May 15, 1977.

Cunningham, Michael. "After AIDS, Gay Art Aims for a New Reality." April 26, 1992.

Darnton, John. "Gay Issue Roils the Church of England." March 19, 1995.

Denizet-Lewis, Benoit. "Double Lives on the Down Low." August 3, 2003.

Dominus, Susan. "Most of the Seventh Grade Will Be at the Commitment Ceremony." March 23, 2009.

Forsythe, Ronald. "Why Can't 'We' Live Happily Ever After, Too?" February 23, 1969.

Green, Penelope. "A Safe House for the Girl Within." September 7, 2006.

Johnson, Dirk. "Privacy vs. the Pursuit of Gay Rights." March 27, 1990.

Johnston, Laurie. "Homosexuals Plan Educational Drive." June 19, 1977.

Klemesrud, Judy. "The Disciples of Sappho, Updated." March 28, 1971.

———. "For Homosexuals, It's Getting Less Difficult to Tell Parents." September 1, 1972.

Lyall, Sarah. "London Journal; For Blair's Cabinet, These Outings Are Not Picnics." November 12, 1998.

Maslin, Janet. "Into the Limelight with: Jaye Davidson; A Star to Match a Mystery Role." December 17, 1992.

Miller, Merle. "What It Means to Be a Homosexual (Continued)." October 10, 1971.

Nemy, Enid. "The Woman Homosexual: More Assertive, Less Willing to Hide." November 17, 1969.

Nordheimer, Jon. "Coast Homosexuals Fight Repeal of Law." June 16, 1975.

O'Connor, John J. "TV: Homosexuality Is Subject of Two Programs." November 3, 1972.

———. "TV: WCBS 'Eye On' Focuses on Lesbian Couples." February 7, 1978.

———. "Gay Images: TV's Mixed Signals." May 19, 1991.

Pener, Degan. "Egos & Ids; Closets Are Out, but Outing Is Not." April 25, 1993.

Roberts, Steven V. "Homosexuals in Revolt." August 24, 1970.

Safire, William. "Don't Slam the Closet Door." April 18, 1974.

Unsigned. "Tests Ordered for Homosexual Teacher." December 4, 1974.

———. "Gay Teacher's Disclosure Spurs a Debate." June 11, 2000.

Urbina, Ian. "Gay Youths Find Place to Call Home in Specialty Shelters." May 17, 2007.

Weinraub, Bernhard, and Jim Rutenberg. "Gay-Themed TV Gaining a Wider Audience." July 29, 2003.

Williams, Lena. "Homosexual Men Discuss Life in the County." August 24, 1980.

Homosexual Scholars "Come Out" to Combat Discrimination

Rejecting the fear, isolation, and self-contempt common among homosexual academics, more than 200 professors and graduate students from across the country gathered in 1973 for a two-day conference organized by the Gay Academic Union. Held at the John Jay College of Justice in New York City, the gathering provided participants with the opportunity to "come out of the closet" as homosexuals and to begin serving as positive role models for young homosexual students. In addition, the scholars made plans to use their specific academic skills to combat the prevailing scientific view of homosexuality as an illness. Dr. Martin Duberman, a speaker at the conference and a professor of history at Lehman College, predicted that academics would soon begin studying homosexuality in a variety of scientific disciplines as well as including references to homosexuals in history books and in literature. Tenured and well-known, Duberman had publicly announced his own homosexuality more than a year before this *New York Times* article was written; however, he acknowledged that the risks of "coming out" were much higher for those without tenure. Despite these concerns, those in attendance urged closeted college professors to openly declare their homosexuality and join the fight to end homosexual discrimination on college campuses.

As the twentieth century went on and more and more persons of note revealed themselves as gay, Dr. Martin Duberman's prediction proved to be prescient. Today LGBT studies programs are an accepted curricular offering at many leading academic institutions.

NOVEMBER 24, 1973
200 START FIGHT ON HOMOSEXUAL 'MYTHS'
By BARBARA CAMPBELL

In a collective as well as an individual effort to publicly "come out of the closet," more than 200 homosexual faculty members and graduate students met yesterday to discuss methods of using their professional abilities to "combat the myths" of homosexuality.

The men and women, from colleges and universities in the city and across the country meeting at the John Jay College of Justice, urged other homosexual professors to declare their homosexuality and unite to end discrimination against homosexuals on campuses.

They were invited to the two day meeting by the Gay Academic Union, a 100-member organization of homosexual college professors formed here eight months ago.

"All week," said Dr. Martin Duberman, playwright, historian and professor of history at Lehman College, who addressed the group yesterday, "an opening phrase for this speech has been going through my mind. . . . 'Honored rabbi, dear parents and relatives' . . ."

Laughter filled the first-floor auditorium as he explained that the opening was from his speech at his bar mitzvah which marked his passage into manhood. "Today ours is also a rite of passage." Dr. Duberman said.

By meeting despite the traditional fear, secretiveness and conservatism of homosexual academics, Dr. Duberman said, the group had passed from isolation, self-contempt and fear into the open.

To meet publicly as homosexual scholars was not an easy decision, he said, because doing so presented risks for those teachers who were untenured. "It can mean losing your job, or for those graduate students, not getting a teaching job," he added, of being stereotyped and of having the avowal of homosexual treated as exhibitionism.

When he "came out" a year and half ago, after a lifetime of hiding his homosexuality, Dr. Duberman said, he did so from a "maximum-security position"—he was tenured and well-known and he included the fact of his homosexuality in a book of history called "Black Mountain College."

The situation of the homosexual scholars present is unique, he said, because they are organizing themselves around their skills as sociologists, biologists, historians, psychologists and scholars of all other disciplines to begin research into homosexuality. The aim is to present an authoritative alternate to the predominating heterosexual scientists' view of homosexuals as ill.

Scholars, he said, will begin study on the heterosexual reaction to homosexuality and include homosexuality in history books and in literature.

Before the conference began, Dr. Duberman said "no one likes to talk about his sex life, but this seems the only way to unite, no matter how uncomfortable it makes us."

He and Dr. Howard J. Brown, a New York University professor and a former member of Mayor Lindsay's cabinet, who made headlines several months ago when he announced that he was homosexual, maintained that their avowals set a "positive example for young homosexual students."

"There has been so much secrecy and silence that they don't know there are gay doctors and lawyers," Dr. Brown said. He was a member of a panel discussing "Scholarship and the Gay Experience."

A professor of health policy and administration at N.Y.U. and chairman of the National Gay Task Force, Dr. Brown said that since he had declared his homosexuality, homosexual students who "feel so alone" had sought him out to talk about their problems. "And surprisingly," he said, "parents who read about me for the first time began to talk to their sons about homosexuality."

The conference was interrupted for an hour after an anonymous caller phoned the policy emergency number, 911, to say there was a bomb on the third floor of the building, at 59th Street and Amsterdam Avenue. The police searched the building but found no bomb.

· ·

Safire Predicts Most Homosexuals Will Remain Closeted

In 1975 Air Force sergeant Leonard Matlovich challenged regulations banning homosexuals from service, insisting he "could be both a good airman and gay" (see "Gays in the Military"). Three days after a military panel disagreed and recommended his discharge, Oliver Sipple, a former marine, averted an assassination attempt against President Gerald Ford. As a result of media interest following this act of heroism, it soon became public knowledge that Sipple frequented homosexual bars in San Francisco. Under pressure from homosexuals to come out, and presumed pressure from his family to remain closeted, a visibly strained Oliver Sipple appeared at a press conference, stating, "My sexuality is a part of my private life and has no bearing on my response to the act of a person seeking to take the life of another."

In this opinion piece, William Safire contrasted the stories of Matlovich and Sipple to offer a "moralistic libertarian" position on the issue of gay rights. He argued that although homosexuality would always be viewed as abnormal and immoral, it should not be legally sanctioned. Laws regulating the private, consensual activity of adults should be repealed, including those limiting the military service of homosexuals, but Safire predicted that even when free from the risk of arrest or job loss, few homosexuals would ever choose to be open about their sexuality.

After 1975 many more prominent cases of homosexuals in the military would be brought to the attention of the American people. By the early 1990s many in the LGBT rights movement were clamoring for change in the armed forces policy that banned homosexual conduct. In 1992 Bill Clinton campaigned on a promise to repeal the ban; however, the majority of public opinion was against the idea, as was Congress. A compromise of sorts was reached in 1993 in a policy commonly known as Don't Ask, Don't Tell (DADT). Under DADT, gays and lesbians were allowed to serve as long as they remained closeted. Superiors were expected not to investigate the sexual orientations of their subordinates without cause. DADT came under fire immediately, as advocates of LGBT rights argued that the "Don't Ask" part of Don't Ask, Don't Tell was not being obeyed and that thousands of qualified gay military personnel, overwhelmingly female, were being dismissed unfairly as a consequence. In 2008, with the country involved in two wars, DADT came into question again. Barack Obama campaigned on a promise to end the military's ban on gays serving in the military. In 2010 the Pentagon began a formal review of the consequences of Don't Ask Don't Tell, which many believed would eventuate in the lifting of the ban. In November 2010 the Pentagon released the study, which indicated that most members of the service did not feel that including gays and lesbians in the military would negatively affect their work. In December of that year Congress voted to lift the ban on gays in the military.

SEPTEMBER 29, 1975
BIG WEEK FOR GAYS
By WILLIAM SAFIRE

Washington—How do you thank an alleged homosexual for saving the life of a President just after a military panel decides that homosexuals are unfit to protect the nation by serving in the armed forces?

"You acted quickly and without fear for your own safety," President Ford wrote to Oliver Sipple a few days ago, after the alert 32-year-old former Marine had spoiled the aim of a would-be assassin. "By doing so, you helped to avert danger to me and to others in the crowd. You have my heartfelt appreciation."

But by doing his duty as a citizen, Mr. Sipple stepped into the white circle of pitiless publicity that surrounds the President and his party. It was soon reported that he is supported by a disability award for the aftereffects of combat experience in Vietnam, and hangs around with the "gay community" in the homosexual bars of San Francisco.

"What's he trying to hide?" demanded one gay militant, sensing a propaganda coup if a genuine hero could be presented as a man proud to be a homosexual. Another leader, with more sympathy, said: "If in fact he is homosexual it would be beneficial to the community if he would come forth and state such, but I cannot condemn him for not doing so."

Under obvious strain, Mr. Sipple appeared at a press conference. Evidently the news not only of his bravery but of his reputed homosexual associations had reached his mother in Detroit, and he had suffered through a difficult family telephone call.

His prepared statement contained a sentence of considerable dignity: "My sexuality is a part of my private life and has no bearing on my response to the act of a person seeking to take the life of another."

Mr. Sipple is guilty of committing heroism in public, and is trying to hold on to the last shreds of the privacy that was stripped from him as a consequence of his selfless act. He is probably under family pressure to go one way, and under peer-group pressure to go the other, with publicity stakes fairly high. He will think twice before he does any good deed again.

The saving of the President by someone who might be a gay took place three days after the decision of a military panel in the case of T. Sgt. Leonard Matlovich. The bemedaled Air Force sergeant was testing the armed forces regulations against homosexuality, and argued that he could be both a good airman and a gay, He lost; the military judges recommended that he be given a general discharge, neither honorable nor dishonorable.

Most Americans would agree that the Air Force acted wisely, and a practical argument can be made that morale in the armed forces would suffer if homosexuality there were to be publicly tolerated. Moreover, such official toleration might lead to its unwelcome increase.

However, I think the decision is wrong. Homosexuality is a sin and not a crime. To practice it is to break all moral codes but no constitutional laws. The prattle of gay leaders that homosexuality is a beneficial "alternative lifestyle" strikes me as foolish, and the unsupported assertion of a psychologist that bisexual switch-hitting is the wave of the future is intellectually dishonest.

But the gay life is by no means the criminal life. All laws—Air Force regulations—that presume to tell consenting adults what to do in private ought to be struck down by the courts. Get out of the people's lives, Big Brother; when morality has to be legislated, morality loses its moral fervor.

The essential point that perhaps Mr. Sipple catches, and Sgt. Matlovich does not, is that homosexuality is an abnormality that will never really lose its stigma, because that stigma—and not the law—protects society and family life. Let the gays go their way; the straights do not have to be narrow.

As Mort Sahl used to say, is there anyone I haven't offended? This moralistic libertarian view of homosexuality infuriates the gays, who like to think they are merely different and by no means abnormal, and puzzles the straights, who do not want to encourage or legitimize the "queers."

But in time, homosexuals will gain their individual rights in law. Then the battle of sexuality will be fought fair and square, and the straight heterosexual line, traversing the shortest distance, will make its point.

For even when job discrimination against gays is a thing of the past, most homosexuals will choose to stay in the closet. And even when a gay's individual courage makes him an instant hero, his first thought is likely to be how to slip back into the cool shadow of personal privacy.

PROGRESS AND TENSION IN EMERGING HOMOSEXUAL COMMUNITIES

By the late 1970s significant progress had been made in the development of an organized and open gay community in New York City. An increasing number of professionals had come out, and homosexual neighborhoods formed in Greenwich Village, Chelsea, and other areas of the city. Residents of these new communities could now patronize homosexual-owned businesses, join a variety of homosexual organizations, and read homosexually oriented publications, such as *Gaysweek, Christopher Street,* and *Lesbian Tide.* In addition, Democratic mayoral candidates asked for the homosexual vote during interviews in the summer of 1977, and Kenneth Sherrill had been elected district leader of the 69th Assembly district, the first openly gay man to win a public office in New York state. H. Gerald Schiff, an accountant who recently returned to New York after a five-year absence, said "I came back to an entirely different city. It was very much more openly gay".

Despite this progress many homosexuals remained closeted because they feared that coming out would result in job loss, denial of child custody, or other negative consequences. According to Ginny Apuzzo of the National Gay Rights Lobby, fewer prominent women had come out because many still felt the risks outweighed the benefits. In addition, many lesbians felt that they continued to have a limited voice within the homosexual community and questioned the failure of gay men to support feminism.

OCTOBER 25, 1977
HOMOSEXUALS IN NEW YORK FIND NEW PRIDE
By GRACE LICHTENSTEIN

It was Yom Kippur at Congregation Beth Simchat Torah, Manhattan's four-year-old self-proclaimed "gay synagogue," and the temple facilities in Westbeth apartments in Greenwich Village were over flowing with more than 350 worshipers.

As the Kol Nidre services proceeded, the congregants, a majority of them in suits, prayer shawls and yarmulkes, joined the rabbi as he recited a special holiday "petition" for "gay liberation," which ended: "Fulfill your promise to lift the oppressed from degradation. Remove affliction and suffering from all gay people."

Four years ago, the synagogue consisted of a small band of homosexuals who gathered at irregular intervals for services. Now, it is a part of New York life, involved in United Jewish Appeal fund-raising efforts, tree-plantings in Israel and offering classes in Hebrew. It is one of many symbols of what some homosexual New Yorkers call "the new gay pride."

Gains Are Enormous

The city's homosexual population, which only a few years ago began to "come out of the closet" and into the street, has developed markedly in recent months into a cohesive, open and organized force.

Despite national setbacks, such as a recent unfavorable ruling by the United States Supreme Court on the dismissals of homosexual teachers, gains by homosexuals in New York and elsewhere have been enormous.

Many people still think of homosexual life in terms of interior decorators, Fire Island, and bars with a leather motif. This world does indeed exist and flourishes in some neighborhoods.

There have always been bars catering to homosexuals, where much socializing goes on and much information about homosexual concerns is exchanged.

But, increasingly, the homosexual community is very much one of lawyers, physicians, teachers, politicians, clergymen and other upper-class professional men and women. Aside from their sexual preference, many tend to live like their heterosexual counterparts.

One trustee of the synagogue for homosexuals, for instance, mentioned off-handedly, "My lover and I keep a kosher home now. We met at the synagogue. Everybody laughs because this is one of the traditional roles synagogues have always played."

Political Potential

Homosexuals are now showing a greater willingness to identify themselves. Homosexual neighborhoods, for example, are growing in parts of Greenwich Village, Chelsea, the Upper West Side and Brooklyn Heights. A variety of organizations, such as Parents of Gays and Salsa Soul Sisters, are proliferating, along with homosexual religious congregations.

No one claims to have accurate statistics on how many homosexuals there are in the city—10 percent of the population is the most-often cited figure—or how to identify them. But leaders of the community all contend their ranks are swelling and becoming visible.

"If the demographics are true," said Robert L. Livingston of the New York Political Action Council, "we ought to be able to make a Mayor."

H. Gerald Schiff, an accountant who helped found the Greater Gotham Business Council, returned to New York in 1975 after a five-year absence and found the change striking.

"I came back to an entirely different city," he said. "It was very much more openly gay, more willing to seek out gay professional people, gay clients, gay customers, more conducive to 'coming out.'"

Ronald Gold of the National Gay Task Force said: "I can get my windows washed by a gay person, get my television repaired, do anything and never see a straight person again."

The reason is that a network of homosexual-oriented services and enterprises has evolved over recent months, many of them listed in Greater Gotham's directory or the Gay Yellow Pages, a national and local publication, so that bars are no longer the sole source of information.

There is a Gay Switchboard and a Lesbian Switchboard, a Gay Men's Health Project; publications such as Gaysweek, Christopher Street and Lesbian Tide; the Gay Teachers Association; Dignity, a group of homosexual Roman Catholics; Integrity, a similar group of Episcopalians; a program "Gay Rap" on WBAI radio; travel agencies, as well as numerous clothing, accessory and book stores.

In addition to getting involved in these services and enterprises, the homosexual community has become active politically and the growing political consciousness, activists in the community say, will be a factor to be reckoned with.

Many homosexuals became involved politically when they battled for passage by the New York City Council of a measure that would have barred discrimination in housing and employment. Its passage has failed six times, most recently in September 1975.

But, as was the case nationally, with Anita Bryant's campaign in Florida, the defeats only strengthened the homosexuals' resolve to organize their forces better and to fight harder next time.

Candidates Evaluated

The Democratic mayoral candidates this summer acknowledged homosexuals' strength by appealing for their vote in interviews conducted by the New York Political Action Council. Edward I. Koch, the Democratic mayoral candidate and long a supporter of homosexual rights in Congress, got a "preferred" rating, as did Bella S. Abzug, Herman Badillo and Percy Sutton, Mario M. Cuomo, who is now the Liberal Party candidate, was rated "acceptable," Mayor Beame and Joel Harnett "unacceptable."

In the Democratic primary, Kenneth Sherrill, a candidate of the Gay Independent Democrats and other clubs, won the post of district leader in the 69th Assembly district on Manhattan's Upper West Side, becoming, he said, "the first openly gay man to be elected to any part or public office in New York State." . . .

Male Indifference Cited

The same kind of services and business have blossomed recently among lesbians as they have among homosexual men. (Many women prefer the term lesbian, arguing that the slang "gay" is usually thought of as meaning male.)

Thus there is a lesbian switchboard, newsletter, bookstores, restaurants and political groups, as well as a word-of-mouth list of doctors, lawyers, psychiatrists and stock brokers.

Nevertheless, some lesbian leaders admit they have a larger problem of "invisibility" to overcome than homosexual men have.

The network has "really escalated in the past three years," said Ginny Apuzzo of the National Gay Rights Lobby, a Washington-based group. Yet, "fewer prominent women have come out because they have more to lose and less to gain. They can gain as much by being just feminists."

Major groups such as the National Gay Task Force have made it a point to have equal male and female leaders. Nevertheless, while lesbians may support male homosexual groups and causes, they do not always agree.

All we have in common is same-sex preference," noted Andrienne Scott, a leader of the year-old Gay Rights National Lobby and a former editor of Blueboy, a slick magazine sometimes referred to as "Playboy for Gays."

"There are many gay men who can't relate to women and lesbians who can't relate to men," she said. There are lesbian separatist groups that will not join in "gay pride" demonstrations.

Some lesbians have also been distressed at male indifference to the women's movement.

"We come into the gay movement with an intellectual and emotional perspective that comes out of the feminist movement," said Ginny Apuzzo. "There's a real problem with many lesbian feminists when men choose to live and die with gay rights alone."

"It's an uphill struggle for the women to be heard" in the homosexual rights movement, she acknowledged.

Many Said to Stay Silent

Moreover, according to Betty Powell, a member of the New York State Advisory Committee to the United States Commission on Civil Rights, "lesbians still threaten many women in the feminist movement. That's still not resolved."

Indeed, there are serious divisions within the homosexual population in New York, not just between men and women, but between old and young, moderates and radicals, the wealthy and the poor.

Beyond this, there is what's thought to be the huge reservoir of "closet gays," men and women who still will not write out a check to an organization with "gay" in the title, who insist newspapers be sent in plain brown wrappers, or who simply feel that disclosing their sexual preference to the general public will endanger their jobs, home and family.

In addition, there are those, such as the priest from an Episcopal church, the trustee of Congregation Beth Simchat Torah, the homosexual father engaged in a custody battle over a child, who participate in "gay rights" activities but prefer not to have their names published. Too much exposure, they fear, would hurt their reputations because of still-existing biases in the "straight" world.

Often, in recent months, homosexuals who come out have been pleasantly surprised about the benign response. "Six months ago you wouldn't have caught me on television for anything," Mr. Schiff said.

He did appear, his neighbors in the small town in Connecticut where he has a weekend house saw him, "and the post-mistress thought it was simply interesting," he related, laughing.

However, Mr. Schiff's willingness to accept the new activism is not universal. "There's a whole generation in their 40's and 50's that has always played the role of trying to assimilate in the straight world," he noted. . . .

TRANSGENDER COMMUNITY FIGHTS STUBBORN TABOOS

More than forty years after the successful emergence of the gay rights movement, transgender people continue today to face public rejection, job discrimination, and the threat of violent attack. *Transgender* is an umbrella term that includes transsexuals, transvestites, intersex people, and others living on the border between male and female. According to historian Susan Stryker, an MTF transsexual, people are so invested in traditional gender roles that "if you fall outside that easy definition of what a man or woman is, a lot of people see you as some kind of monster." With the help of the Internet, a movement for transgender rights has been building over the past two decades. Transgender conferences currently draw hundreds of participants, and the protest group Transexual Menace had established forty-six chapters throughout North America by the end of the 1990s. A new advocacy group called GenderPAC is currently pursuing legal strategies to prohibit employment discrimination and to require the tracking of crimes against transgender people under the Hate Crimes Statistics Act. Advocates of traditional family values have been vocal in their criticism of the new movement, and even some gays and lesbians are uncomfortable allying with this group, fearing the inclusion of transgender people will undercut efforts to normalize homosexuality.

SEPTEMBER 8, 1996
SHUNNING 'HE' AND 'SHE,' THEY FIGHT FOR RESPECT
By CAREY GOLDBERG

In Boston, Nancy Nangeroni is helping arrange a courthouse vigil for a slain male-to-female transsexual. In Washington, Dana Priesing lobbies for laws that would ban discrimination against "transgendered" people. And in Southern California, Jacob Hale and the rest of the local Transgender Menace chapter occasionally pull on their black Menace T-shirts and go for a group walkabout, just to look people in the eye with collective pride in who they are.

All see themselves as part of a burgeoning movement whose members are only now, nearly two decades after gay liberation took off, gathering the courage to go public and struggle for the same sort of respect and legal protections.

The name that scholars and organizers prefer for this nascent movement is "transgender," an umbrella term for transsexuals, cross-dressers (the word now preferred over transvestites), intersexed people (also known as hermaphrodites), womanish men, mannish women and anyone whose sexual identity seems to cross the line of what, in 1990's America, is considered normal.

That line has certainly blurred. Dennis Rodman preens in his bridal gown, Ru Paul puckers for MAC cosmetics, and viewers flock to movies like "The Crying Game."

But members of the movement say they still cannot escape the feeling that in a society that has grown more responsive to other minorities, they are among the last pariahs. When they give up the old dream of simply "passing" as their desired sex, they face painful battles both in everyday life and in the political arena, where they are roundly condemned as deviants by religious conservatives and often spark controversy among more mainstream gay and lesbian groups.

Their very existence, they say, is such a challenge to universal gut-level ideas about a person's sex as an either-or category—as reflected in everything from binary bathrooms to "he" and "she" pronouns—that they are often subjected to scorn, job discrimination and violence.

"There's finally a voice saying, 'Enough,'" said Riki Anne Wilchins, a Wall Street computer consultant and organizer in the movement. "We pay taxes. We vote. We work. There's no reason we should be taking this. When you have people in isolation who are oppressed and victimized and abused, they think it's their own fault, but when you hit that critical mass that they see it happening to other people, they realize it's not about them. It's about a system, and the only way to contest a system is with an organized response."

No one knows exactly what that critical mass is. Experts say that in the more than 40 years since George Jorgensen emerged from the operating room as Christine, several thousand Americans have undergone sex-change surgery; they are believed to include nearly even numbers of men and women. Perhaps as many as 60,000 Americans consider themselves valid candidates for such surgery, based on what psychiatrists call "gender identity dysphoria," according to the Harry Benjamin Gender Dysphoria Association, the leading medical association of specialists—including sex-change surgeons—that sets guidelines for treating transsexuals. But that is only the tip of a far larger iceberg, organizers say, of cross-dressers—many of whom are heterosexual men—and people who live as the opposite sex but never undergo surgery.

The movement's growth, however, is easy to discern. Scores of participants rallied as part of a new advocacy group called Gender PAC for the first time in Washington last fall and plan to do the same in May, and transgender conventions now draw hundreds of people and number nearly 20 a year. Increasingly, a "T" can be found tacked onto the "G, L and B" of gay, lesbian and bisexual events and groups, from community centers to pride parades.

In San Francisco, which a survey has shown is home to about 6,000 of the movement's constituents, the San Francisco Human Rights Commission has formed a Transgender Community Task Force, and the protest group Transexual Menace now counts 46 chapters nationwide, some of which are called Transgender Menace. There is even a new national group, Transgender Officers Protect and Serve; members act as marshals at events when needed.

The movement's coalescence, which members say began over the last five years and accelerated in recent months, has gained particular momentum from the Internet, with its ability to connect far-flung people and afford them a sense of safety. On-line groups that began by swapping tips on using makeup and obtaining hormones now also spread word of the latest victims of violence and the next political protest.

But "the fundamental building block of the whole movement," said Dr. Barbara Warren of the Gender Identity Project at New York City's Lesbian and Gay Community Services Center, "is the willingness of transgender folk to put themselves out there and be visible." That takes more than the courage to face funny looks in the checkout line. The most painful of rallying points is the frequency with which they are attacked and even killed.

"I know so many people who've suffered from vilification in their daily lives just because people have heard they're transsexual, not because they look weird or act weird," said James Green, a female-to-male transsexual and head of FtM International, the biggest group for what many members call "transmen." "As soon as the fact is known, they're just targets, and people are still being murdered."

Since last year, Ms. Wilchins and Transexual Menace have taken to organizing vigils after the slayings of transsexuals. In May 1995 they protested outside the Lincoln, Neb., courthouse where the rapist and killer of Brandon Teena, a young woman living as a man, was coming to trial. Since then, they have marked the deaths of several transsexual women who were killed by men they dated. The next will come on Sept. 16 in Lawrence, Mass., where Deborah Forte, a transsexual, was killed.

"We're so invested in being men or women that if you fall outside that easy definition of what a man or woman is, a lot of people see you as some kind of monster," said Susan Stryker, a male-to-female transsexual with a doctorate in history whose book on changing sex is to be published by Oxford University Press next year.

Gender PAC, the advocacy group, is lobbying to have crimes against "transgendered people" included in the Hate Crimes Statistics Act, which lets the Justice Department track crimes based on race, religion, ethnicity and sexual orientation. (These crimes do not fall under the orientation category because "transgenderism" concerns sexual identity, not sexual practices, Gender PAC says; some male-to-female transsexuals are lesbians, for example.)

Gender PAC's other priority, said Dana Priesing, its main lobbyist—and a prominent Washington litigator until she began her sex change—is to get the group's constituency included in the Employment Nondiscrimination Act, a bill in the House of Representatives that would protect gay people from job discrimination.

Employees currently have no recourse if they are dismissed because they reveal their sexual identity or undergo "transition" except in a handful of cities—including

San Francisco, Seattle and Santa Cruz—and the state of Minnesota.

If Nancy Nangeroni is any judge, transsexuals still need help in the workplace. A 42-year-old, M.I.T.-educated computer designer, she found she could not get a job if she volunteered that she was a male-to-female transsexual, but had no problem if she kept silent. Ms. Nangeroni is not only open about her identity but also runs "Gender Talk," a radio talk show every Wednesday evening on WMBR-FM, a Boston-area station.

"There's a widespread discontent with gender roles," she said, "and transgenderism is trying to speak to that in a compassionate way, speaking only liberation and not doctrine. It's kind of like shooting fish in a barrel sometimes. People are very ripe for it."

Not everybody. Christian conservatives and advocates of traditional family values condemn the movement as decadent and unhealthy.

"This is yet another social pathology," said Robert H. Knight, cultural studies director for the Family Research Council, a think tank in Washington. "This is deviant behavior that seeks legitimization in the social, legal and political realms. It is part of a larger cultural movement to confuse the sexual roles and to usher in a relativistic mindset concerning sexuality itself."

The movement has also created some friction within the gay and lesbian groups that have generally accepted and aided it. Some gay and lesbian organizers have balked because its issues do not concern sexual orientation but rather identity. Others argued, usually sotto voce, that flamboyant "drag queens" and "stone butches" would further alienate straight America and belie their claims that gay people are really just like everybody else.

But "transgendered people" have long been at the heart of the gay rights movement, said Kerry Lobel, deputy director of the National Gay and Lesbian Task Force. Now, she said, "they're seeking and have found their own political power."

"All of a sudden a lot of people feel, 'Hey, I am proud,'" said Alison Laing, director of the International Foundation for Gender Education in Waltham, Mass. "It's like gay pride. People say, 'I didn't choose this, but I do choose my behavior and my attitude.'"

Alison Laing's life demonstrates the kind of freedom the movement espouses. A husband and father, "M. Laing" (to use the honorific proposed as an ungendered alternative to Mr. and Ms.) spends about 80 percent of the time dressed in women's clothes and 20 percent as Al, in men's clothing, showing that "we don't have to live in gender boxes."

· ·

REP. BARNEY FRANK COMES OUT

Massachusetts representative Barney Frank's homosexuality was publicly revealed in a front-page *Boston Globe* story in June 1987. According to Frank, his decision to come forward was motivated by several factors. Avoiding the issue was growing increasingly difficult as public attention to the private lives of politicians increased, and he wanted to avoid the sort of gossip that circulated following Rep. Stewart B. McKinney's death from AIDS in May 1987. In addition, although he believed his sexual orientation was irrelevant to his political decision making, Frank feared that if he continued to dodge the question, "the inference would be that I'm embarrassed or ashamed, when I'm not."

Although coming out is never easy, especially for a politician, Frank did so from a position of strength. The popular Democrat won his last election with 90 percent of the vote, most of his colleagues and some of his voters already knew he was gay, and a representative from an adjoining district, Rep. Gerry Studds, had already been reelected twice following House censure of his homosexual affair with a teenage page ten years previous to the revelation. In the wake of the revelatory newspaper article, both Republican and Democratic colleagues have expressed their support, and positive constituent mail is outweighing the negative by a ratio of 6 to 1. Still, Frank described himself as someone who had not sought excessive media coverage and said that he was uncomfortable with the increased attention. In addition, he was concerned that some voters would now assume he cares about gay issues only and that a few may even be afraid to shake his hand for fear of contracting AIDS. Representative Frank was chair of the powerful House Committee on Financial Services from 2007 to 2010.

JUNE 3, 1987
WASHINGTON TALK

Public Man, Private Life
Why a Congressman Told of his Homosexuality
By LINDA GREENHOUSE

On paper, Representative Barney Frank's decision to go public about his homosexuality ought to have been relatively painless.

Nearly all the Massachusetts Democrat's colleagues on Capitol Hill already knew. So did at least some voters in his diverse suburban Boston district, where he knew that his private life was a subject of rumor even as his House seat grew safer.

His constituents, evidently cherishing his blend of liberal politics, fast-talking irreverence and cerebral approach to issues, gave him 89 percent of the vote in the Democratic primary last year and re-elected him to a fourth term by 90 percent, his highest margin ever.

His Democratic colleague in an adjoining district, Representative Gerry E. Studds, has won re-election twice since being censured by the House in 1983 for having had a homosexual relationship with a teen-aged Congressional page 10 years earlier.

Periods of Introspection

So it is a measure of the extreme sensitivity of the issue of homosexuality in American public life that Mr. Frank's decision to come out of the closet was anything but painless. He made his disclosure last weekend in answer to a question from a reporter for The Boston Globe, a question that he knew would come someday from somewhere and that he had steeled himself for after long periods of introspection and discussions with friends and colleagues.

Mr. Frank discussed his decision and its consequences in an interview this morning in his office in the Longworth House Office Building. He received many interview requests in the wake of The Boston Globe's Page One

article last Saturday, and turned many down, including one from Playboy Magazine.

"I said I didn't want to be in Playboy and they said, 'Oh, but we also want your views on the issues.' I said, 'Why didn't you ask me for my views on the issues last week?'"

In the interview, Mr. Frank's fine-tuned sense of irony was as apparent as ever, but his customary brashness was not. As he drew on a cigar, his tone was subdued, almost somber, his rapid-fire delivery a few beats slower than usual.

More Public Scrutiny

Several factors contributed to his decision to bring an end to years of deflecting questions about his homosexuality, he said. One was the heightened public scrutiny to which the private lives of all politicians is now being subjected—most prominently in the case of Gary Hart, whose Presidential candidacy collapsed in the aftermath of reports that he had spent time with a Florida woman.

Questions were likely to increase, not diminish, Mr. Frank knew.

Another factor was the death from AIDS last month by a respected colleague, Representative Stewart B. McKinney, a Connecticut Republican. Mr. McKinney's physician asserted that his patient had contracted the disease from a blood transfusion, leaving it to newspapers to report that Mr. McKinney was known to colleagues to have been homosexual.

"There was such an unseemly scuffle after he died," Mr. Frank said. "I'm not criticizing the press; the problem was the way it was handled. I have no reason to expect anyone to be reading my obituary anytime soon, but I do fly home on weekends, and we can all be hit by a truck, and I don't want the focus to be: Was he or wasn't he, did he or didn't he. I just wanted to get rid of it."

Choice Was Made for Him

Mr. Frank said he decided that if he continued to avoid questions, "the inference would be that I'm embarrassed or ashamed, when I'm not." He said [he] continued to believe that his sexual preference was irrelevant to the way he did his job, "but being Jewish is also irrelevant, and I don't refuse to talk about being Jewish."

In the end, Mr. Frank said, "I had no choice." He added, in a nearly inaudible murmur: "I don't remember making a lot of choices on this whole subject."

The suggestion by some homosexual acquaintances that he was something of a hero for making the disclosure reminded him, he said, of John F. Kennedy's response to the question of how he became a war hero. "They sank my boat," was Mr. Kennedy's answer.

"You deal with the facts handed to you," Mr. Frank said. "Will I become a role model for thousands of young gay men who smoke cigars and talk too fast? I don't think so."

'I Had No Emotional Life'

Mr. Frank said he had decided not to expand upon his disclosure by talking about the details of his private life. But Mr. Frank, who is unmarried, did say that for much of his career—he served in the Massachusetts state legislature in the 1970's while also earning a degree from the Harvard Law School—he kept himself so busy with professional commitments as to close off the possibility of a private life.

"For 10 years I had no emotional life," he said. "When a public career has to carry the entire burden of an emotional life and a public life, it's too much, it's distorted."

That period ended when he came to Washington in 1981. "But by then I was 41 years old," he said with a slight smile. "Even if I had wanted to live life to the fullest, I was too tired to stay out that late." A severe weight loss regime did, however, give him a newly slender and fashionable image; a photograph of a rumpled, overweight figure, barely recognizable as Barney Frank, hangs as a reminder to the left of his desk.

Support From All Sides

Mr. Frank said he was relieved that the disclosure was behind him. His Capitol Hill colleagues have offered support across ideological boundaries. One of the first telephone calls was from Senator Alan K. Simpson of Wyoming, the acerbic and very conservative Republican whip, who told Mr. Frank he admired his courage and wished him well. Mail from constituents has been supportive at a ratio of about 6-to-1.

Yet Mr. Frank's relief is tempered by wariness, as though he were running in an election for which the returns are not yet in.

He said he was worried that his constituents would think "all I'm going to be now is a gay rights crusader." While he has in fact sponsored or co-sponsored homosexual rights legislation every year he has been in public office, he has spent most of his time on issues ranging from immigration to housing to textile imports.

"I've never tried excessively to get media attention," he said, referring to those issues. "Now I'm going to have to work harder to offset the suggestion that all I care about is gay rights."

The AIDS crisis made his decision more difficult, he said, because "it could make the political consequences worse."

'Strangers Are Looking'

He said: "The public perception is that all gays have AIDS and that AIDS is transmitted through casual contact. It is not helpful for people to be afraid to shake a politician's hand."

As for a politician's sexual orientation, Mr. Frank said, "My preference would be that no one cared. Maybe we'll get to that point someday."

In the meantime, Mr. Frank finds himself, after years in the public eye, trying to shake an acute self-consciousness. "I stand at the trolley stop, I go to the store, I take out the garbage, and you have a sense that strangers are looking at you, thinking about your private life."

But he said he expects to overcome his discomfort. He recalled that when he was a graduate student at Harvard, he moved into an apartment across the street from a firehouse. "Within two weeks, I was sleeping through the sirens," he said. "Human beings have an amazing capacity to adapt."

The "Outing" of Rep. Jim Kolbe

In 1996 a Hawaiian court was expected to rule that the state's refusal to grant marriage licenses to gay and lesbian couples amounted to sex discrimination. Anticipating this decision, Congress passed the Defense of Marriage Act (DOMA), denying federal recognition for same-sex marriages and allowing states to refuse recognition of gay marriages performed in other states. All three openly gay House members—Gerry E. Studds and Barney Frank, both Democrats from Massachusetts, and Steve Gunderson, a Republican from Wisconsin—voted against the bill. Rep. Jim Kolbe, a Republican from Arizona, voted for it. Divorced with no children, Kolbe was serving his sixth term and was best known for his support of the North American Free Trade Agreement. His "yes" vote on DOMA, however, angered gay activists, who orchestrated an "outing" campaign involving a flurry of e-mail messages and a full-page newspaper ad in a gay newspaper, the *Washington Blade.* The goal of this effort was to compel Kolbe to publicly acknowledge his homosexuality, and, under pressure, he finally did so. Kolbe insisted, "The fact that I am gay has never, nor will it ever, change my commitment to represent all the people of Arizona's Fifth District." He also defended his vote for DOMA, stating that states should be allowed to define marriage as they see fit and not be required to accept definitions adopted elsewhere. Openly gay Arizona state representative Ken Cheuvront predicted that Arizona voters would not be concerned by Kolbe's revelation but would be angry that he was forced out of the closet. "They think that outing is wrong," he said, "that what one does in the privacy of one's own home shouldn't be discussed in the papers."

Rep. Jim Kolbe continued to serve the people of Arizona's 5th district until his retirement in 2007. After revealing his homosexuality in 1996, Kolbe became one of the better-known members of the Log Cabin Republicans, a conservative group that advocates for LGBT rights.

AUGUST 3, 1996
A REPUBLICAN CONGRESSMAN DISCLOSES HE IS A HOMOSEXUAL
By DAVID W. DUNLAP

Three weeks ago, Representative Jim Kolbe, a Republican from Arizona, voted with the majority to deny Federal recognition to same-sex marriages and absolve states of the obligation to honor such marriages performed in other states.

In Washington, he is best known for having championed the North American Free Trade Agreement. But a number of gay-rights advocates said there was something else that should be known about Mr. Kolbe, who at 54 is serving his sixth term. Within days of the vote on the Defense of Marriage Act, they began a blistering campaign on the Internet to compel Mr. Kolbe to disclose that he himself was gay, a practice known as outing.

The campaign reached its peak last week with a full-page ad in The Washington Blade, a newspaper that reaches a nationwide gay audience, calling on "all closeted gay and lesbian members of Congress" to "end your silence and defend your community."

On Thursday night, Mr. Kolbe spoke.

"That I am a gay person has never affected the way that I legislate," he said in a statement. "The fact that I am gay has never, nor will it ever, change my commitment to represent all the people of Arizona's Fifth District," which includes Tucson and the southeastern corner of the state.

With his announcement, Mr. Kolbe became the fourth Congressman to identify himself publicly as gay. The other three are Gerry E. Studds and Barney Frank, both Massachusetts Democrats, and Steve Gunderson, Republican of Wisconsin.

All three voted against the Defense of Marriage Act, which was prompted by expectations that a Hawaii court would ultimately rule that the state cannot discriminate in issuing marriage licenses on the basis of sex. President Clinton has already said he will sign the bill.

Explaining his vote, Mr. Kolbe said: "If the citizens of Hawaii believe it to be in their public interest to permit same-sex marriages, they should be permitted to do so. By the same token, other states—as Arizona has done—should be allowed to define marriage differently and not be required to accept the definition adopted by others.

"There are some who have decided that their disagreement with this particular vote warrants their making public information about my private life."

Mr. Kolbe was elected to the Arizona State Senate in 1976 and to Congress in 1984. He won his most recent election with 68 percent and now serves on the Appropriations and Budget Committees. He is divorced and has no children.

The outing campaign took the form of E-mail messages that were widely distributed to journalists and others. Some messages called on Mr. Kolbe to reconcile his vote with his sexual orientation; others said his personal life was no one's business but his own.

Mr. Kolbe was too busy talking with constituents yesterday to grant interviews, said Ron Foreman, his press secretary. But he added that support from district residents had been effusive and that Mr. Kolbe had also received encouragement from Speaker Newt Gingrich and others in Congress.

Mr. Gunderson was one of them. "I don't believe in outing, yet I believe everybody ought to be out," he said. "The fact that Jim and I are both out continues to break down stereotypes and the Republican Party is going to have to deal with that."

From the other side of the aisle, Mr. Frank also welcomed Mr. Kolbe's announcement. "It's very helpful," he said. "That he is a respected, able, mainstream conservative has to diminish the prejudice somewhat."

Mr. Frank said Mr. Kolbe's vote on the marriage bill should not by itself make him anathema to lesbians and gay men. "In general, Kolbe has voted against bigotry and discrimination," he said, "so his overall record is intellectually honest on this issue."

State Representative Ken Cheuvront, Democrat of Phoenix, who was elected in 1994 as an openly gay candidate, said yesterday that Arizona residents "could care less" that Mr. Kolbe was gay but were "mad at the gay press."

"They think that outing is wrong," Mr. Cheuvront said, "that what one does in the privacy of one's own home shouldn't be discussed in the newspapers."

One of the architects of the campaign was Michael Petrelis, an advocate of gay rights who lives in San Francisco. "I think it's a terrific development that we now have an equal number of openly gay G.O.P. members of Congress," he said.

. . . .

Gay Teachers Still Face Barriers

Several events motivated Alta Kavanaugh, a 48-year-old teacher at Alessandro High School, to come out in 1994, including the harassment of a gay student who ultimately dropped out of school. Openly acknowledging homosexuality remains risky for teachers, owing to lingering myths about child molestation and recruitment. Although California teachers are largely shielded from employment discrimination based on sexual orientation, civil rights laws and union contracts vary widely from state to state. Kavanaugh informed her principal about her decision prior to coming out as a lesbian to her students during a lesson on prejudice. After she came out, a few parents complained, her name was featured in some homophobic graffiti, and some closeted teachers began to avoid her. Still, she insisted that the experience was less difficult than she had previously imagined. The majority of her colleagues were supportive, and the senior class unanimously chose Kavanaugh to read their names at graduation. Overall, she said that she was more comfortable being open about her sexuality: "I have more of a sense of humor and more tools to deal with it."

JULY 27, 1994
IN SCHOOL; A GAY TEACHER FINDS THAT COMING OUT WAS DIFFICULT, BUT NOT AS CATACLYSMIC AS SHE HAD FEARED

By JANE GROSS

"Alta's a dyke." Those words, scribbled in the margin of a textbook, sent a chill of fear up Alta Kavanaugh's spine three years ago. So she slammed the book shut and said nothing to her students or colleagues at Alessandro High School here.

The same words, a few months back, were scratched on a picnic table in the school's sun-baked courtyard.

But this time Ms. Kavanaugh, a 48-year-old English teacher, reacted far differently. She approached the offending students, took a pencil in hand and changed the graffito to read, "Alta's a lesbian."

"That's the word I prefer," Ms. Kavanaugh told them.

What has changed in the intervening years, Ms. Kavanaugh said, is her own sense of security since announcing that she is gay, a move fraught with risk for teachers across the United States—and nowhere more than in conservative communities like this one in rural Riverside County, set in the dusty embrace of the San Jacinto Mountains.

But even here in Hemet, with its fundamentalist churches, trailer parks for retirees and school board that favors an abstinence-only curriculum for sex education, Ms. Kavanaugh has found comfort in openness. "Now it doesn't create such a fear in me," she said. "I have more of a sense of humor and more tools to deal with it."

It was a gathering of events a few years back that persuaded Ms. Kavanaugh, a teacher for more than two decades, that it was time to reveal her secret at school, the setting where, the American Civil Liberties Union says, gay employees are most susceptible to dismissal or discrimination because of the abiding myths that homosexuals molest and recruit children.

First, Ms. Kavanaugh learned that one of her favorite students, Johnny Maiden, had dropped out of school after receiving death threats from classmates because he is gay. Ms. Kavanaugh blamed herself for not stepping forward to support him.

Then, at an AIDS fund-raising event in nearby Palm Springs, she bumped into the parents of a former student. The couple, Keith and Bonnie Froehlich, had recently formed a local chapter of an organization for the parents of homosexuals, an act of bravery in a place like Hemet. Ms. Kavanaugh had read of their activities, but she had not found the courage to acknowledge the couple's efforts until that day.

With those events fresh, Ms. Kavanaugh attended a professional conference in Los Angeles. At a workshop about suicide among gay teen-agers, she met the teacher who had introduced support groups for gay students in that city's high schools.

"How can you dare be out?" Ms. Kavanaugh asked her.

"Honey, it's your civil right," was Virginia Uribe's reply.

Armed with information from Ms. Uribe about the protections offered by union contracts and civil rights law, which vary from state to state but are quite strong in California, Ms. Kavanaugh got on the freeway for the long drive home.

"I cried all the way down the 405," she said. "I knew my sense of integrity demanded I do something, but I was so frightened." That night, she dreamed of yellow police tape across the door of her classroom.

Ms. Kavanaugh's colleagues at Alessandro High School had long known either explicitly or implicitly that she is gay. And before she told her students, she alerted the principal of her plans.

That day Ms. Kavanaugh was teaching a unit on prejudice, based on "Farewell to Manzanar," an account of a young girl's experience in a Federal internment camp for Japanese-Americans during World War II. She interrupted the regular lesson and wrote "homophobia" on the board, followed by a list of some ugly words common in the schoolyard.

Then, she took a deep breath. She told the students: "When you use those words, you hurt people deeply. And you hurt me. Because I'm a lesbian."

The students buffeted her with questions. When did she know? What about her ex-husband? Was she with somebody now? Could she be fired for telling them? A few hugged her. Two went to the principal and asked to be transferred, but he dissuaded them.

Ms. Kavanaugh said that in her classes since then, she has not harped on her sexual orientation.

She does make a point of mentioning gay writers, like Walt Whitman and Gertrude Stein. She hangs posters, with hot-line numbers, that say, "You Are Not Alone." And mounted on a rainbow flag is a quotation attributed to the German pastor Martin Niemoller, about his silence and thus implied assent when the Nazis persecuted Communists, Jews, trade unionists and Roman Catholics.

"Then they came for me," the quotation reads, "and by then there was nobody left to speak up."

In general, Ms. Kavanaugh said, her fears about coming out were worse than the reality.

A few parents have complained, but not many. The assistant superintendent tried to stand in her way when she took time off for related speaking engagements, she said. But she pressed her rights through the union and state labor commission; he has not bothered her since.

Fellow teachers at Alessandro have been supportive, and a gay counselor there has been more open about his homosexuality in the wake of Ms. Kavanaugh's announcement. But staff members at other schools, particularly closeted homosexuals, have given her a wide berth, perhaps, she said, from a "gut fear that I'll out them."

Student reaction, too, has been mixed. When Ms. Kavanaugh won an award and her picture was hung in the corridor, it was defaced with insults. But a group of students responded by circulating a petition of support. And the senior class voted unanimously to have her read their names at graduation.

Even the fundamentalist-dominated school board has minded its manners. "They are very polite," Ms. Kavanaugh said, adding that her mere presence keeps attention on issues that might otherwise be neglected.

And it was with great pleasure that she accepted a $150 prize recently from a local civic group. "One of the board members had to present it to me," she said.

· ·

COMING OUT LEADS TO HOMELESSNESS FOR MANY TEENS

As crowds gathered for the annual 2004 Pride Parade, New York's growing population of homeless gay youth continued their struggle to survive. Carl Siciliano, who manages a shelter for gay teens, estimated that they numbered in the thousands in New York alone and believed the numbers increased in part because gay rights activists and television shows such as *Will and Grace* encouraged teens to come out, not recognizing that many live in families completely unwilling to accept a gay child. As a result, many run away or are thrown out into the streets. Sex work is the only source of money for many of these youths, and the rates of drug use, HIV infection, and suicide are high. Although these teens are subject to abuse and violence in the general shelter system, only twenty-four beds are currently available for gay, lesbian, and transgender youth, leaving waiting lists of 100 or more on many nights. National studies suggested that as many as half of all homeless youth are gay or lesbian, said Omar-Xavior Ford, youth coordinator for Harlem's Gay Men of African Descent: "The streets of New York will eventually consume them. If it doesn't kill them, there's no way to reverse the damage it's caused."

JUNE 27, 2004
FOR YOUNG GAYS ON THE STREETS, SURVIVAL COMES BEFORE PRIDE
Few Beds for Growing Class of Homeless
By ANDREW JACOBS

David Antoine's coming out last year did not exactly fill his family with pride. A few months shy of his high school graduation, Mr. Antoine said, his mother told him to pack his bags, and he was suddenly out on the icy streets of Brooklyn, his life stuffed into a trash bag, his bed the hard back of a subway car rumbling from one end of the city to the other.

Brian Murray is still trying to find his place in what is known as the gay community. A good night is the soft bed of a stranger and $100 in the morning. A bad night is an empty stomach, a park bench and the rousing jolt of a nightstick on his bare feet as he is ordered to move on.

Like Mr. Antoine and Mr. Murray, his friends, Michael Leatherbury, 25, would consider cheering his gay brothers and sisters marching down Fifth Avenue this afternoon if he had a few coins in his pocket and a place to call his own. No sense flirting with strangers, he says, when home is a lumpy cot in a city shelter. "Being homeless is not exactly conducive to dating," he says with a shrug. "These days, I'm not feeling very prideful."

As hundreds of thousands of people flock to New York today for the annual celebration of the 1969 Stonewall uprising and the birth of the modern gay rights movement, few are likely to give a moment's thought to their homeless brethren, a growing legion of the disowned and the dispossessed, most of them black and Latino, an increasing number of them H.I.V. positive and still in the throes of adolescence.

With just two dozen beds available for gay, lesbian and transgender youth, they endure violence in the city's shelters, camp out in doorways in Harlem or pass the night at a 24-hour Internet cafe next to Disney's New Amsterdam Theater on 42nd Street. There, many of them trawl the Web for paying "dates" or try their luck on Christopher Street in the far West Village, where some quick work in a passing car might yield $30. "You've got to do what you've got to do to survive," says Mr. Murray, who is 22 and has been turning tricks in the Village since he was 15.

There is no official count of those who are homeless and gay in New York, but Carl Siciliano, who runs the city's largest shelter for gay young adults, puts their numbers in the thousands. Most national studies estimate that as many as half of all homeless youth are lesbian or gay, many of them tossed out by parents who scorn homosexuality for a variety of reasons.

As director of the Ali Fourney Center in Manhattan, Mr. Siciliano can shelter only 12 people at a time and wring his hands as the waiting list grows beyond 100. He seethes

with indignation when talking about the teenagers who are forced onto the streets, where they quickly become acquainted with drugs, hustling, violence and the virus that causes AIDS. For many, he says, suicide becomes the only way out.

The number of homeless teenagers is growing, Mr. Siciliano says, inadvertently fueled by the identity-affirming pitch of gay rights advocates and the feel-good wit of television shows like "Queer Eye for the Straight Guy" and "Will and Grace," which encourage adolescents to declare their sexuality to parents on the opposite side of a yawning generation gap.

"I think it's shameful that these kids are out there alone and in danger, in a city where gay men have so much money," he says.

Young black men like Mr. Antoine and Mr. Murray spend most of their time in Harlem, where they can melt into the bustle of 125th Street. Down in Greenwich Village or in Chelsea, Mr. Leatherbury says, "You feel like a foreigner, someone who doesn't belong."

When they are not looking for legitimate work, filling out applications in stores and restaurants, they cruise Marcus Garvey and Morningside Parks, or shop their wares along a gritty stretch of Third Avenue near the Willis Avenue Bridge. It is a perilous circuit, and in recent years, three gay homeless teenagers have been killed in Harlem, their deaths still unsolved.

During the day, as many as two dozen of them gather in the offices of Gay Men of African Descent in Harlem, commonly known as GMAD, where they play video games, grab cheese sandwiches and stuff condoms into AIDS-prevention handouts. Omar-Xavior Ford, the organization's overworked youth coordinator, serves as their surrogate father, offering job advice, wrangling beds in the better shelters and trying, with mixed success, to help them steer clear of the city's perils. "The streets of New York will eventually consume them," he says. "If it doesn't kill them, there's no way to reverse the damage it's caused." . . .

PROTESTS OF GAY TEEN "CONVERSION" PROGRAM SPARKED BY WEB POSTINGS

Referring to himself only as "Zach, 16, from Tennessee" a teen posted comments on his personal Web page in which he described coming out to his parents and, shortly after, his parents' request that he enroll in Refuge. This teen program is an offshoot of Love in Action International, a Christian organization in Memphis that claims to help gay men and lesbians change, or at least learn to control, their sexual orientation. Zach's friends posted comments and links to his site on their own blogs, and these were forwarded to others, ultimately causing a snowball effect that resulted in Love in Action receiving 100 e-mails a day and over 80,000 Website hits as well as calls from reporters and a multiday protest of their offices organized by the group Queer Action Coalition.

Reparative, or conversion, therapy emerged in the 1970s, when most counselors ceased to view, or treat, homosexuality as a form of mental illness. Rev. John J. Smid, executive director of Love in Action, has argued that programs such as Refuge are needed to help teens resist the harmful effects of society's increasing tolerance of homosexuality. Critics counter that these programs are rarely successful and merely increase the guilt and shame experienced by many gay teens.

JULY 17, 2005
GAY TEENAGER STIRS A STORM

By ALEX WILLIAMS

Memphis

It was the sort of confession that a decade ago might have been scribbled in a teenager's diary, then quietly tucked away in a drawer: "Somewhat recently," wrote a boy who identified himself only as Zach, 16, from Tennessee, on his personal Web page, "I told my parents I was gay." He noted, "This didn't go over very well," and "They tell me that there is something psychologically wrong with me, and they 'raised me wrong.'"

But what grabbed the attention of Zach's friends and subsequently of both gay activists and fundamentalist Christians around the world who came across the entry, made on May 29, was not the intimacy of the confession. Teenagers have been outing themselves online for years, and many of Zach's friends already knew he was gay. It was another sentence in the Web log: "Today, my mother, father and I had a very long 'talk' in my room, where they let me know I am to apply for a fundamentalist Christian program for gays."

"It's like boot camp," Zach added in a dispatch the next day. "If I do come out straight, I'll be so mentally unstable and depressed it won't matter."

The camp in question, Refuge, is a youth program of Love in Action International, a group in Memphis that runs a religion-based program intended to change the sexual orientation of gay men and women. Often called reparative or conversion therapy, such programs took hold in fundamentalist Christian circles in the 1970's, when mainstream psychiatric organizations overturned previous designations of homosexuality as a mental disorder, and gained

ground rapidly from the late 90's. Programs like Love in Action have always been controversial, but Zach's blog entries have brought wide attention to a less-known aspect of them, their application to teenagers.

Although Zach wrote only a handful of entries about the Refuge program, all posted before he arrived there in the Memphis suburbs on June 6, his words have been forwarded on the Internet over and over, inspiring online debates, news articles, sidewalk protests and an investigation into Love in Action by the Tennessee Department of Children's Services in response to a child abuse allegation. The investigation was dropped when the allegation proved unfounded, a spokeswoman for the agency said.

To some, Zach, whose family name is not disclosed on his blog and has not appeared in news accounts, is the embodiment of gay adolescent vulnerability, pulled away from friends who accepted him by adults who do not. To others he is a boy whose confused and formative sexual identity is being exploited by gay political activists.

In his last blog entry before beginning the program, at 2:33 A.M. on June 4, Zach wrote, "I pray this blows over," adding that if his parents caught him online he'd be in trouble. He described arguments he had been having with his parents, his mother in particular. "I can't take this," his post reads. "No one can. I'm not a suicidal person. I think it's stupid, really. But I can't help it—no I'm not going to commit suicide—all I can think about is killing my mother and myself. It's so horrible."

The Rev. John J. Smid, the executive director of Love in Action, declined to discuss the details of Zach's experience, citing the program's confidentiality rules. In an interview early this month at his headquarters, a weathered 1960's A-frame building, which was until recently a vacant Episcopal Church, Mr. Smid explained that teenage participants in Refuge are forbidden to speak with anyone the program does not approve of. Requests made through Mr. Smid to interview Zach's parents were declined.

Founded in California in 1973, Love in Action moved to Memphis 11 years ago. It is one of 120 programs nationwide listed by Exodus International, which bills itself as the largest information and referral network for what is known among fundamentalist Christians as the "ex-gay" movement. In 2003 Love in Action introduced the first structured program specifically for teenagers, 24 of whom have participated, Mr. Smid said. The initial two weeks costs $2,000, and many participants stay six weeks more, as Zach has.

The goal of the program, said Mr. Smid, who said he was once gay but now renounces homosexual behavior, is not necessarily to turn gays into practicing heterosexuals, but to "put guardrails" on their sexual impulses.

"In my life I've been out of homosexuality for over 20 years, and for me it's really a nonissue," Mr. Smid said.

"I may see a man and say, he's handsome, he's attractive, and it might touch a part of me that is different from someone else," he said. "But it's really not an issue. Gosh, I've been married for 16 years and faithful in my marriage in every respect. I mean I don't think I could white-knuckle this ride for that long."

Mr. Smid first learned that one of his teenage participants was a cause célèbre when protesters appeared outside his headquarters for several days in early June, carrying signs saying, "This is child abuse" and "Jesus is no excuse for hate."

He was bombarded by phone calls from reporters, he said, as well as by 100 e-mail messages a day from as far as Norway. Zach's writings, which appeared on his page on www.MySpace.com, were publicized by one of his online acquaintances, E. J. Friedman, a Memphis musician and writer, who read Zach's May 29 blog entry, "The World Coming to an Abrupt—Stop."

Mr. Friedman, 35, was disturbed by what he read and fired off an instant message. "I said: 'You should run away from home. There are people who will help you,'" Mr. Friedman recalled. "He said: 'I can't do that. I want to have my childhood. If this is what I have to go through to have it, then I will.'"

Mr. Friedman posted an angry message about Zach's impending stay at Refuge on his own blog. Mr. Friedman's friends picked up on the story and started spreading it on blogs of their own. Soon a local filmmaker, Morgan Jon Fox, who had met Zach through mutual acquaintances, joined with others to start a group called Queer Action Coalition, which organized the protests at Love in Action.

"We wanted to show support," said Mr. Fox, 26, who directed a fictional film about gay teenagers in 2003, shot at White Station High School in Memphis, where Zach is a student. "Then it kind of blew up."

Links to Zach's site bounced around the country. Mr. Friedman's Web page had so much traffic, "it blew my bandwidth," he said. Mr. Smid, too, was inundated with Internet traffic, much of it outraged at the attempts to change Zach's sexual orientation.

"All of a sudden, 80,000 Internet hits later on our Web site, the world has decided that he should be freed," Mr. Smid said. "Maybe he didn't ask for this. Maybe he doesn't really have the personality that really is going to be able to deal with this. And they talk about our 'abuse' of him." . . .

For Mr. Smid and his supporters, offering Love in Action to teenagers is vital to combat what they see as a growing tolerance of homosexuality among young people. "We just really believe that the resounding message for teenagers in our culture is, practice whatever you want, have sex however, whenever and with whoever you want," he said. "I very deeply believe that is harmful. I think exploring sexuality can lay a teenager up for numerous lifelong issues."

Critics of programs that seek to change sexual orientation say the programs themselves can open a person to lifelong problems, including guilt, shame and even suicidal impulses. The stakes are higher for adolescents, who are already wrestling with deep questions of identity and sexuality, mental-health experts say.

"Their identities are still in flux," said Dr. Jack Drescher, the chairman of the committee on gay, lesbian and bisexual issues of the American Psychiatric Association, which in 2000 formally rejected regimens like reparative or conversion therapy as scientifically unproven. "One serious risk for the parent to consider is that most of the people who undergo these treatments don't change. That means that most people who go through these experiences often come out feeling worse than when they went in." . . .

Zach is due to leave the program next week. His June 4 message expressed thanks for the more than 1,700 messages on his page, many voicing support. "Don't worry," he wrote. "I'll get through this. They've promised me things will get better, whether this program does anything or not. Let's hope they're not lying."

"Out"side Manhattan

Many gay men and lesbians live openly in Manhattan, holding hands on the street and freely acknowledging their sexual orientation with neighbors, friends, and coworkers. The situation is significantly different in the rest of the city. In Queens, Staten Island, Brooklyn, and the Bronx, differing religious traditions and cultural attitudes toward masculinity lead to decreased tolerance for homosexuals. However, gay and lesbian young adults from low-income families also have fewer options for leaving home. Many cannot afford college, and well-paid jobs are scarce. As a result, gay and lesbian New Yorkers outside Manhattan often remain closeted or semicloseted, perhaps telling their coworker but not family (or the reverse). Those who are openly gay risk being ostracized, ridiculed, or attacked. Although bars, organizations, and support services there are limited compared with what is available in Manhattan, some do exist. For example, a Brooklyn gay bar called The Starlight has been open since 1960, and the Staten Island Children's Museum recently started a play group for children of gay parents. Some gay men and lesbians say they would move to Manhattan if they could afford it, but Bronx native Elizabeth Marrero has decided to stay put. A 40-year-old Puerto Rican lesbian, she admits that her family did not accept her sexual orientation right away. But, she says: "I was raised with the courage to be what I wanted to be. If I was going to be gay, I was going to be gay in the place where I was born and bred."

JULY 18, 2004
LOVE ON THE QUIET
By SETH KUGEL

One breezy evening a few months ago, 19-year-old Joseph Briggs did something he had never before dared to do growing up gay in New York: he held hands with and kissed his boyfriend in his own neighborhood.

Being affectionate in public in a place like Greenwich Village was one thing. But the Fordham section of the Bronx was different. The children playing tag knew him, and the men and women sitting outside the weary apartment buildings were invariably eager for something to gossip about. And in fact, he and his boyfriend got some surprised looks. But no one said a word.

"At first, I was happy I was able to show people in my neighborhood," he said. "Then I had conflicting thoughts about safety and losing friends. But I was more overjoyed than negative." . . .

With more gay characters on prime-time television and the national spotlight focused on gay marriage—most recently last week, when the Senate blocked a proposed constitutional amendment to ban same-sex marriage—awareness of gay rights is increasing. But many gay New Yorkers predict that broader acceptance for gays outside Manhattan will not come quickly. For one thing, Manhattan is generally considered a safe space for gays; the same cannot be said for the other boroughs.

Or, as Mario de la Cruz, a gay man who helps run youth support groups at Bronx AIDS Services, put it: "You can smile at someone on Christopher Street and not be worried that they will misinterpret it. You can smile at someone just to be nice."

Less Money, More Taboos

A web of reasons helps explain why places like White Plains Road in the Bronx, Northern Boulevard in Queens and Atlantic Avenue in Brooklyn are still much closer to Main Street than Christopher Street.

Perhaps most important are cultural differences. While Manhattan is the perfect place to live anonymously among an often transient population, many communities in the other boroughs are tight knit, and the families who live there are often more traditional and consider homosexuality a taboo, if not an outright sin.

Economics also plays a role. Less money often translates into less independence for young gays living outside Manhattan. They often cannot afford to live on their own or go away to college. Many cannot find steady work. And they must often travel farther for social and medical services, including treatment for AIDS-related illnesses. "What is really clear is that the Bronx lesbian and gay community mirrors the Bronx community: people of color, low-income," said Mark Reyes, until recently the executive director of the Bronx Lesbian and Gay Health Resource Consortium. "The major issues are housing and employment."

Yet another issue involves the machismo common among Latin and West Indian cultures. Fausto Paez, the director of Latitud Cero (Zero Latitude), an Ecuadorean gay group whose members live mostly in Queens, discovered firsthand that homophobia from the home country can easily replicate itself here when he came out of the closet to relatives in Long Island City and found himself ostracized.

Nor is machismo limited to Latinos. Among black men, the desire to be seen as masculine means that some gay men have created a separate "down low" identity, having sex with men in secret and leading otherwise straight lives.

It is revealing that safe spaces and other institutions for gays are relatively uncommon outside Manhattan. In the latest edition of the Lesbian, Gay, Bisexual and Transgender Directory of Services and Resources, a guide to metropolitan-area gay resources released by the office of Comptroller William C. Thompson Jr., less than a quarter of the city organizations listed are outside Manhattan.

"How different it is in Chelsea, in the Village," Mr. Paez said. "There are bars, stores, bookstores, cafeterias, delis where people can gather easily, comfortably as can be, where there are no stereotypes. Queens? What it has are bars that are only open at night. In the day there is nothing. In the Bronx there is nothing."

Intolerance at the Doorstep

For Joseph Briggs, who finally dared to kiss his boyfriend on his own street, growing up gay was complicated by growing up poor in an often punishing environment. When he was a child, his family bounced between homeless shelters and housing projects in Brooklyn and Queens. He did a stint in foster care. By the time he was 14 and living in Bedford-Stuyvesant, Brooklyn, he was out of the closet, and paid a price; he often got jumped. After switching schools repeatedly, he finally dropped out.

"People didn't like it, because I'm very outspoken," he said. He even got kicked out of his church choir when it was discovered that he was dating his godbrother, also a church member.

In his teens, he became interested in women's clothing. He scavenged his mother's old outfits and made his own handbags. But the outfits he created were not for the neighborhood. Instead, he would cover them with baggy clothes, then climb aboard the J train to meet friends in the Village.

His transformation to Moniqua Alicia Jackson, his female alter ego, began at the last stop in Brooklyn before the Williamsburg Bridge. "When I got to Marcy Avenue," he said, "I opened up my bag. As the train pulled out of the station, I'd start putting on my lotion." By the time he crossed the bridge, his sweats were off, his hair was loose and his spandex was tight.

Although his mother, Priscilla Ford, now supports his sexuality, it was a slow road. "But it got to the point I wanted to meet his friends," she said recently. Now, she is even urging him to take her to see the gay scene in the Village.

Mr. Briggs's boyfriend, who spoke only on the condition of anonymity, is not so lucky. Although he was openly gay to his friends at Robert F. Wagner High School, an alternative school in Long Island City, Queens, he has not come out to his parents or neighbors. His mother is tolerant of gays, he said, but his father gets defensive around them, and is quick to dismiss them with epithets, as do some residents of the housing projects near his home in Astoria. . . .

Cautiously Comfortable

While some gays and lesbians who live outside Manhattan live openly and make no apologies for their lives, others follow a more muted and oblique path. Their families may know they are gay, but their work colleagues do not. Or vice versa. The neighbors might welcome them to block parties but would not care to see a same-sex couple holding hands.

Maria Romagnuolo, who lives with her partner, Wendy, and their 5-year-old twin sons in Dongan Hills, Staten Island, lives just such a nuanced life. One reflection of the complexity of being gay in Staten Island is the lack of gay bars; because many residents are ambivalent about gays, the occasional gay bar that does sprout on the island does not last long.

"People don't want to party in their backyard," Maria Romagnuolo explained. "If you're seen walking in, it's going to get back to Mommy." Yet in a small nod to the borough's gay families, the Staten Island Children's Museum began a playgroup last month for the children of gay parents.

The Romagnuolos, who have been together for 13 years, are cautiously, and complicatedly, comfortable in the borough generally considered the city's most conservative. So while they will not hold hands in public, Maria Romagnuolo is co-president of the PTA at her sons' school, Public School 52.

With more money or no children, she might move. "I'd go to Manhattan if it were up to me," she said. "You could hold hands and feel confident. You can be who you are. When I'm in Manhattan, I'm like, ahhhhhh." But Manhattan, along with gay-friendly places where the couple has traveled, like Provincetown, Mass., and Key West, Fla., are out of their economic reach.

"Whenever it's a gay community, you have to pay double," she said. "Where do we live? We live in a straight community that we can afford." Their story is common, especially among lesbian couples, who are more likely than gay male couples to live in suburban settings, largely because they are also more likely to have children, said Jason Ost, co-author of the Gay and Lesbian Atlas.

Very Gay, Very Proud

For all the obstacles to gay life in the boroughs, there are undeniable bright spots. Many gays outside Manhattan speak lovingly of the Starlite, a bar in Crown Heights, Brooklyn, that has been around since 1960 and claims to be the city's oldest bar under black gay ownership. . . .

And some gay residents of the boroughs beyond Manhattan, like Elizabeth Marrero, a 40-year-old Puerto Rican lesbian, have never been prouder of where they live.

Ms. Marrero, the house manager at the Bronx Academy of Arts and Dance in Hunts Point, grew up in what she describes as a "typical Latin household" in the Fordham section of the Bronx. Though she does not feel comfortable holding hands with her girlfriend in the neighborhood of her childhood, she insists she is not going anywhere.

"Being gay was definitely not something they were going to embrace quickly," she said of her family, "but I was raised with the courage to be what I wanted to be. If I was going to be gay, I was going to be gay in the place where I was born and bred."

Anonymous Homosexuals Receive Sympathetic Coverage

This *Times* review from 1966 applauded a British documentary on homosexuality as both thorough and tasteful, offering sincerely educational coverage without a hint of sensationalism. Part of an international exchange series, the hour-long program included excerpts from a series of interviews with homosexual men and lesbians who described their diverse backgrounds, relationship and loneliness, psychological troubles, police harassment, and frequent job losses then experienced by many homosexuals. Unusual camera angles and lighting techniques were used to maintain the anonymity of those who participated. Clubs for homosexuals in the Netherlands and a counseling service for London lesbians also were profiled. The program closed with information from Dr. Irving Bieber, a New York psychiatrist, about how parents may unintentionally contribute to the development of homosexual traits in childhood and how these symptoms can be corrected if caught at an early enough stage.

MAY 21, 1966
TV REVIEW

Channel 13 Presents a Homosexuality Study

By JACK GOULD

One of television's most mature and thoughtful examinations of homosexuality was presented on channel 13 on Thursday night. The program, which happened to conflict with Jack Paar's amusing hour of humor and politics, will be repeated at 10:35 P.M. on Monday. It is well worth seeing.

The study was produced by Associated Rediffusion, one of the major commercial program producers in London, as part of the international exchange series called "Intertel."

Bryan Magee, a British TV reporter, painstakingly explored the lives of a number of homosexuals and lesbians through a series of detailed interviews. In most cases the identities of the participants were protected either by having the cameras shoot over their heads or by leaving their faces in shadows.

The virtue of the hour was Mr. Magee's exceptionally skillful questioning, which combined thoroughness with taste. The personal experiences of men who found torment in relationship with women and relief in a liaison with members of their own sex was elicited with a quiet effectiveness that eschewed any suggestion of sensationalism and fulfilled an educational purpose.

The cross section of interviews pointed out that homosexuality was not confined to any particular social strata or income group. The viewer heard of one homosexual relationship that had lasted nearly 20 years and another that was dissolved after five when one of the men no longer felt a sense of dependence on his partner.

The British program expanded the television medium's usual consideration of homosexuality by also covering lesbianism. One of the interviews presented a former married woman who became dissatisfied with life with her husband and found several years of contentment with another woman, who, ironically, left her to get married.

The program, produced by Jeremy Isaacs, reported on clubs for homosexuals in the Netherlands and on a counseling service for lesbians in London. The loneliness of the homosexual in a heterosexual world, his psychological troubles and his frequent loss of employment, and the legal harassment homosexuals suffer in many countries were all discussed as part of the excellent social study.

Dr. Irving Bieber, New York psychiatrist, closed the hour on WNDT with helpful and specific analyses of how parents may unknowingly contribute to the development of homosexual traits in their children and how symptoms, if detected early enough, can often lead to corrective steps. All in all, the "Intertel" presentation was a superior example of the use of the home screen for stimulating a better understanding of a serious problem.

The importance of such dignified reportorial behavior needs to be stressed because there are some disquieting signs that the issue of homosexualism has become a plaything for odious wiseguys in broadcasting.

At least the National Broadcasting Company, which likes to boast of its sole control of the content of news broadcasts, recently allowed a gentleman name Joy Pyne to interview two homosexuals over its New York radio station, WNBC. He asked one of his guests whether a homosexual would make a good President of the United States and, upon receiving an affirmative answer asked the second guest whether he agreed with "his lover." Mr. Pyne also gratuitously injected the word "lavender" into his colloquy. Broadcasting can do without the likes of Mr. Pyne. . . .

MIXED REACTIONS TO HOMOSEXUALITY'S THEATRICAL "COMING OUT"

In this opinion piece, Donn Teal reflected on homosexuals' mixed reactions to the news that A&M Records reported strong sales for its 1969 recording of *The Boys in the Band*, Mart Crowley's successful off-Broadway tragicomedy. The play was set at a surprise birthday party attended by a small group of homosexual friends, a heterosexual man who is having marital troubles, and a homosexual prostitute. Although Teal praised the play as a "satanic gem" and applauded the quality of the recording, he had mixed reactions about the increased interest in homosexuality at the time shown by the general public. A question was posed: Is this a symptom of a new empathy for alternative forms of love or simply the desire for an original scapegoat or plot device? He also had mixed reactions to the play itself. Teal admitted that it was exciting to see aspects of homosexual life portrayed openly on stage—this was the first significant play about homosexuals—and he predicted many homosexuals would purchase the recording of it for this reason. Unfortunately, the portrayal of homosexuals in the play was neither flattering nor typical. Crowley's characters were immature, selfish, guilt-ridden, and self-loathing. Said Teal, it was "as if we arrived at our own Coming Out Party dressed in rags." Whereas New Yorkers attending the off-Broadway production might have had enough knowledge of homosexuals to recognize these portrayals as stereotypes, he worried that rural Americans exposed to the new recording would assume that it was an accurate reflection of homosexual life. Teal concluded with a hope that the play would perhaps lead to increased tolerance as well as a repeal of the laws criminalizing homosexuality.

JUNE 1, 1969
HOW ANGUISHED ARE HOMOSEXUALS?
By DONN TEAL

"Why?" is a question that will immediately come to mind. Why, when "Rosencrantz and Guidenstern Are Dead," "Plaza Suite" and other long-running Broadway hits past and present have not been recorded, has Mart Crowley's The Boys in the Band—an Off Broadway drama about the neurotic homosexual—joined the ranks of tragedies and comedies immortalized on disks?

Beyond doubt, "The Boys" is a deftly fabricated, sharp-angled monument of tragicomedy. Furthermore, it is having an unprecedentedly successful run for an Off Broadway production. By the reason "The Boys" achieved a recording derives simply from a circumstance for which it currently has no competitors, except nudity: the interest in homosexuality that has overtaken New York and other major cities. Thanks to A&M records' original-cast album (6001), this interest may soon spread to the smallest prairie town that has no local movie house where its populace might have seen "The Fox" or "The Sergeant."

Homosexuals greet this interest with mixed feelings, for we are not sure whether it stems from a broadminded Now Generation empathy with those who love, no matter whom they love (poet Rod McKuen's closing encouragement to his recent Carnegie Hall audience), or from the desire for a new stage and screen scapegoat, producers having exhausted plot variations based on hetero sex. We

homosexuals greeted "The Boys" with the same mixed emotions when it opened to raves on April 14, 1968, at Theater Four on West 55th Street: though it was our true dramatic debut in heterosexual society, it was a debasing one, as if we had arrived at our own Coming Out Party dressed in rags.

Yet Crowley's well- (if over-) wrought drama is a satanic gem, a veritable black diamond. It is set at an all-male, surprise birthday party given for Harold, a bitchy "32-year-old, ugly, pock-marked Jew fairy," in the apartment of Michael, his crony and equal in vindictiveness. Five friends arrive, plus a hustler—Emory's gift to Harold—and, unexpectedly, Alan, an old college friend of the host's who is in the depths after a rift with his wife. Alan's confrontation with the gay retinue, acid exchanges of camp humor, and a self-destroying "game" in which each guest must telephone the one person he has always loved best, soon transport the audience from a breezy first-act to a finale of absinthial tragedy.

In the recording, Michael's (Kenneth Nelson) caustic wit blazons forth as predatorily as onstage. Harold (Leonard Grey) fails only at times to sustain the bitchiness he displayed in the theater, and his convulsive, near-psychotic laughter and sword-crossing with Michael in Act Two come off magnificently. Emory (Cliff Gorman) is as fey—and endearingly human—as he was before the footlights. Technically, the recording is praiseworthy. Stereo effects are good, and even sighs and cigarette puffs are audible. Director Robert Moore and Gil Garfield, producer of the album, duplicated the stage setting in the recording studios, complete with furniture, props, and all sound effects. The cast seems quite at home.

A special problem, however, even for the listener who has viewed the play, is the seeming competition among the cast to hurl out their lines, evident notably at the beginning and, most disturbingly, in scenes where non-connected conversations are run together; the rapid-fire repartee frequently forces the auditor to guess what was said and who said it. The similarity of several male voices in the womanless cast contributes to the confusion. A text would have helped.

A&M Records already reports high sales for the album. It is to be hoped that an overwhelming majority of these are to homosexuals themselves, since the heterosexual buyer may not realize that "The Boys in the Band" presents a distorted picture of a subculture about which he may know merely a trifle. Crowley's characters in "The Boys" are, in the main, immature: Michael's line "What you see before you is a 30-year-old infant," is the truest in the play. The average among us are appalled that the heterosexual (and maladjusted homosexual) may believe our typical soirée founders on—or flourishes by—self-degrading confessions like "The Truth Game"; that we store up barbiturates as Harold does for "the long winter of his death"; that our parents have all been "killer whales"; and that we regularly address each other as "fairy" and "fag." "The Boys" exude selfishness, self-absorption, and self-indulgence. Worst of all, they not only bespeak, they *proclaim,* guilt feelings through every utterance Crowley has given them. Though we grant that the New York playgoer may

not be so blithely duped into accepting the stereotypes of this show, we wonder what will be the thoughts of, say, less up-to-date Kansas Citians when, turntables revolving, they hear Michael's second act wail: "If we could just learn not to *hate* ourselves so much!"

Self-hate and a feeling of guilt are not typical of today's homosexual, though it has been a labor to shake these leftovers of Judaeo-Christian Puritanism, and many of us are still wrestling with the inferiority complex which society has been only too glad to foist upon us. Then how to explain the fact that dozens—scores?—of homosexuals have returned to see "The Boys" twice, even three times, and will probably purchase the recording? Primarily because, although few of us can see ourselves therein— just as few heterosexuals could really picture themselves in "Who's Afraid of Virginia Woolf?"—many homosexuals can find *a bit* of their story and struggle in Michael, Harold, and Emory. And though we have overcome, we can nevertheless sympathize—as can every member of a "Boys" audience—with a defenseless, emasculated Michael, trembling and weeping in his friend's arms, in one of the most affecting conclusions in recent theater.

Realizing that the author's attempt was not to epitomize the normal American homosexual in "The Boys," any more than Albee's was to apotheosize the average (childless) American marriage in "Virginia Woolf," we are angry still that an ugly misrepresentation has been broadcast by an excellent play. If, however, audiences can gain a deeper understanding of the *minority* of homosexuals represented by Michael, Harold, and Emory and if, above all, legislators can be persuaded to take steps to legalize male/male and female/female adult sexual relationships in this country, then Crowley would deserve not only the accolades but even the adulation of the world he has so one-track-mindedly described.

SYNERGY: THE NEW LOVE THAT DARE NOT SPEAK ITS NAME

In this *Times* opinion piece Frank Rich marveled at Disney's ability to generate seven months of media attention over the decision to "out" the title character on the situation comedy *Ellen* (as well as Ellen DeGeneres, the actress who plays her). When the article was originally printed, the outing episode was still three weeks from being aired but, according to Rich, "feels like a rerun before it even arrives." The episode, its famous guest stars, and the plot had all been covered in numerous articles, and a public relations firm was hired to orchestrate interviews with DeGeneres. Two of these interviews had been hosted by *Prime Time Live* and *Oprah*, both of which were also Disney affiliates. Predictably, Rev. Jerry Falwell and other prominent conservatives were generating additional coverage by calling for an advertising boycott of the show.

Although some saw the groundbreaking show as a courageous effort to eliminate Hollywood's remaining barriers, at least one television executive read it as a last-ditch effort to boost the ratings of *Ellen*. The show would air for another season, ending its run in 1998.

APRIL 10, 1997
THE 'ELLEN' STRIPTEASE
By FRANK RICH

Only in America—Disney's America, at any rate—can the act of a TV sitcom heroine declaring her lesbianism be turned into a media epic that plays out over seven months, generating a striptease of publicity that in a simpler age would be beyond the imagination of even P. T. Barnum, if not Gypsy Rose Lee herself.

It's still three weeks until ABC unveils the all-star outing of "Ellen," featuring cameos by everyone from Demi Moore to Billy Bob Thornton. But like so many oversold events in American mass culture, it seems like a rerun well before it arrives. The episode's jokes, plot and emotions are all detailed in this week's news magazines—one of which, Time, runs a cover story (headline: "YEP, I'M GAY!") with the not-unexpected revelation that the show's eponymous star, the stand-up comic Ellen DeGeneres, is also gay.

More revealing is Newsweek's skinny that this announcement has been "carefully orchestrated" by a P.R. firm that "has been shopping interviews with DeGeneres, promising she'll talk about being a lesbian." Among those to whom she'll be talking are "Prime Time Live" and Oprah, both fellow Disney corporateers. These days synergy is the love that dare not speak its name.

The nation's opponents of all things homosexual, meanwhile, are following a script as predictable as that of Ms. DeGeneres's promoters, with Jerry Falwell, fresh from his joint "Larry King Live" appearance with Larry Flynt, getting plenty of airtime for his call for advertisers to abandon "Ellen." Some sponsors—Chrysler, J. C. Penney—are taking a pass, but ABC's own courage also has its limits. It has turned down one "Ellen" commercial—for a gay cruise-ship line—as too controversial. Am I the only parent who feels that the straight cruise-ship commercials starring Kathie Lee Gifford are more of a threat to my kids' view of heterosexuality than anything a gay sponsor could come up with?

A Hollywood executive I spoke to, and he's not alone, wonders if the network is taking a risk at all in outing "Ellen," given the show's flat quality and ratings. "There's no downside for Disney," he says. "If this works and people actually tune in, it's saved. If not, it was dead anyway." Yet there could be a downside for gay people. Though there are some two dozen gay characters on other network shows, "Ellen" is the first with a gay lead. If it fails, will the character's homosexuality, rather than the series' spotty quality, be held accountable? Even if "Ellen" is a hit, it remains to be seen how many doors it will open. Who in Hollywood will have the guts to hire Ms. DeGeneres, or any out gay actor, to play a straight lead in a TV series?

But at least one unusually expert observer regards "Ellen" as a serious breakthrough, tantamount to Bill Cosby's smashing of the color barrier for TV leads on "I Spy" in 1965: Sheila James Kuehl, a popular sitcom actress of the early 60's, fondly remembered as Zelda Gilroy, the smart but plain coed unrequitedly in love with the hero of "The Many Loves of Dobie Gillis." Speaking this week from California, where she is now Speaker Pro Tem of the State Assembly, Ms. Kuehl recalled how, as a closeted lesbian in her early 20's, she'd been up for her own spin-off series as "Dobie Gillis" concluded its run. "People were high on it," she said. "We thought it would really go. But all of a sudden there was a great silence, and it sank like a stone. A couple of weeks later, the director told me that the president of CBS thought I was a little butch.

"He didn't say I was gay, but I was completely panicked. I'd already been kicked out of my sorority at U.C.L.A. I thought of killing myself. I thought they'd tell my parents. . . . But nothing happened." Nothing, that is, except the rapid demise of her TV career—which would in turn lead her by a circuitous route to Harvard Law School and a career as the first openly gay legislator elected in the nation's largest state.

Not every story like this has so happy an ending, as Ms. Kuehl would be the first to acknowledge. Speaking of Ellen DeGeneres's coming out, she said, "Even in 1997, I think it is an act of courage." The extent to which that act makes a difference in the lives of today's young and frightened gay Americans will determine whether it is a landmark in the history of cultural civil rights or of show-business hype.

Coming Out Is Still a Risk for Actors

Although the number of lesbian and gay actors, television characters, and movie roles increased dramatically in the postmillennium era, Hollywood's homophobia had not entirely disappeared.

Some actors and actresses believed that they continued to be turned down for certain roles because of their sexuality, and others, while not exactly closeted, chose not to draw attention to their personal life for fear of its potential effect on their career. Even such prominent gay television actors as Neil Patrick Harris and T. R. Knight chose to remain closeted until online outing (in the case of Harris) or homophobic comments made by a costar (in Knight's case) brought the issue to light. Further, because both landed their high-profile roles prior to coming out, the ultimate impact of the revelation on their careers remained unclear. Although they were still able to find work, neither was likely to be offered the type of roles that would lead to superstardom. This was due to lingering concerns about gay actors' drawing power at the box office. As a result, the plum roles in heterosexual romances and action films continued to go to those who are either straight or at least believed to be so. Even the lead role in a 2008 movie about the assassination of Harvey Milk, an openly gay politician, was played by a straight actor, Sean Penn.

SEPTEMBER 28, 2008
OUT IN HOLLYWOOD
Starring Roles are Rare
By MIREYA NAVARRO
Los Angeles

There's a bisexual woman in "Bones" and a lesbian couple on "The Goode Family."

"Dirty Sexy Money" features a transsexual and "Brothers & Sisters" a gay marriage.

In "Mad Men," the Emmy-winning drama set in the early '60s, there's Salvatore Romano, a self-loathing homosexual who marries a woman but pines for a male co-worker.

Never before have gay story lines been so prominent. Nor have there ever been so many gay, lesbian, bisexual and transgender characters on television—83 by a recent count from the Gay and Lesbian Alliance Against Defamation, not counting reality shows, daytime dramas or gay-oriented cable networks.

Hollywood, with its depictions of cowboy lovers and lesbian neighbors, has done much to make gay men and women part of mainstream American life.

At the same time, gay actors like Neil Patrick Harris and T. R. Knight play heterosexual characters on TV and in film, while couples—Ellen DeGeneres and Portia de Rossi—are covered by celebrity magazines as if they were any old romance.

"We've gone from the revolution to the evolution," said Howard Bragman, a longtime Hollywood publicist who is gay and has advised actors like Amanda Bearse, of "Married . . . With Children" and Dick Sargent of "Bewitched" on how to handle their coming out.

Yet for most gay actors, Hollywood is not a warm and fuzzy episode of "Will & Grace." Today, it is certainly more acceptable to be openly gay. But these actors must still answer wrenching questions: Just how candid do you want to be? Would you be happy appearing only in comedies, or being pigeonholed as a character actor? And what does the line "You're just not right for the role" really mean?

Jasika Nicole, 28, an F.B.I. agent on "Fringe," a new Fox drama, said that as bigger parts became available, her manager, John Essay, sat her down and asked how public she wanted to be about being a lesbian. Some roles could be lost, he told her, as would some fans.

Mr. Essay, who is gay, said he encouraged openness but warned clients of the risks.

"If it becomes exaggerated," he said, "you just become the gay actress instead of a wonderful actress."

Perhaps, he suggested, she didn't want to be too vocal about it.

Ms. Nicole, who has a girlfriend, said she would just be herself. She has been open about her sexual orientation since she started dating women about 3 ½ years ago, while she was filming "Take the Lead" with Antonio Banderas in Toronto.

Now, as she becomes better known, "There's no way I can keep quiet," she said. "I want to be clear this is my partner. I don't want to make that shameful in any kind of way."

But most other actors calibrate just how out they want to be. Openly gay can still mean they would rather not talk about it. Most gay actors are mum in public or on the set, even if they don't hide their orientation in private, actors and others in the entertainment industry said. Although most may no longer participate in charades—the "girlfriend" on the red carpet, for instance—many adopt a don't ask, don't tell policy.

Why? For both men and women, being openly gay, at least for now, means giving up any hope of superstardom.

"The industry is persuaded that being known as gay will undermine your credibility both as romantic lead or an action star," said Larry Gross, director of the Annenberg School for Communication at the University of Southern California and author of a book on media portrayals of gays and lesbians.

"They don't test it," he said. "We're waiting for the Jackie Robinson moment when someone tests that assumption and discovers it's not true."

GAY actors don't just lose the potential of becoming the next Brad Pitt or Reese Witherspoon, they lose the opportunities for fame that ensure plum jobs, said Jason Stuart, an actor and comedian who chairs the lesbian, gay, bisexual and transgender committee of the Screen Actors Guild. It is no coincidence, he said, that even the title role in "Milk," based on the slain gay hero, Harvey Milk, went to Sean Penn, an Oscar-winning actor who is straight.

"There are not enough famous gay actors to play these roles," he said.

Dan Jinks, a producer of "Milk," agreed. The film's director, writer and two producers are openly gay and so are a number of actors who play gay and straight roles, including the Tony Award-winners Denis O'Hare and Stephen Spinella.

But for the lead, Mr. Jinks said, "Our first concern was to get the best actor that we could get who was enough of a movie star to get the movie made."

"When one is casting a film for a lead role we always have to ask that awful question: 'Who puts bodies in seats?'" Mr. Jinks said. "Who has carried movies previously? Sadly, there don't seem to be openly gay actors that could carry a movie, but I think that will change.'" . . .

One test of how far things have progressed, some industry analysts said, will be the kind of roles Mr. Harris and Mr. Knight are offered once they end their current hit shows. Although they are openly gay, they landed the parts before they came out. And tellingly, they made statements about their sexuality only after being outed by bloggers in the case of Mr. Harris, and by a homophobic incident with a co-star in the case of Mr. Knight. For now, more gay characters and better scripts are adding up to more fulfilling work. It wasn't too long ago that actors like Bryan Batt of "Mad Men" could find good parts only on the stage. Even in theater, he said, his agent was once told by a casting director, "I just can't see Bryan as a baseball player."

"I didn't know what to make of that," said Mr. Batt, 45, who came out publicly in the mid-90s when he landed the part of Darius in "Jeffrey," the off-Broadway play about sex and romance in the age of AIDS.

As an actor, Mr. Batt said, he doesn't want to be pigeonholed into playing only gay roles, but it's hard not to feel "proud and happy" with Salvatore. He begged Matthew Weiner, the show's creator, to let the character get married. "It's a realm of reality that television had not really explored," he said.

The character is addled by the kind of inner conflict—not able to be himself, forced to act like the sexist guys in the office—that "continues to happen," and not just in 1960s period dramas, Mr. Batt noted.

That such a meaty part went to an openly gay actor "speaks volumes about how far we've come," he said.

THE RIGHT TO PRIVACY AND THE DECRIMINALIZATION OF SODOMY

A *New York Times* report of April 13, 1969, asserted that "sex is illegal in so many ways in the United States that only the country's vast capacity to ignore its own laws has saved America from becoming a nation of jailbirds." Until recently, this has been particularly applicable to many gay men and lesbians, owing to antisodomy laws. While the specific content of these laws varied from state to state, generally such laws made it unlawful to engage in oral or anal sex, in some states only with persons of the same sex and in other states with persons of either sex. Because enforcement of these laws also varied, some gay men and lesbians were able to quietly cohabitate without undue fear of prosecution. However, regardless of the rates of enforcement, the existence of sodomy laws threatened to transform millions of otherwise law-abiding citizens into criminals, leaving them vulnerable to blackmail and police entrapment as well as loss of employment, housing, and child custody. Accordingly, the repeal of antisodomy laws was a critical component of the modern gay rights movement.

In 1953 a newspaper editorial titled "A Social Problem" stirred controversy throughout Great Britain regarding the increasing frequency of homosexual crimes (also referred to as "unnatural offenses" and "male perversions"). Records suggested that the number of court cases involving charges of homosexuality had increased by 400 percent since before World War II. As described in a *Times* story of December 11, 1953, David Maxwell Fyfe, the British home secretary, emphasized that this escalation represents a problem "because homosexuals in general are exhibitionists and proselytizers and a danger to others, especially the young." The perceived threat posed by male homosexuals was reflected in its punishment, with maximum sentences of life in prison for sodomy and up to ten years for "attempts to commit unnatural offenses." Interestingly, lesbianism was not punishable under British law at this time, perhaps because of the "greater public hostility to effeminacy in males than masculinity in women," according to a *Times* opinion piece of November 12, 1967.

The Moral Welfare Council of the Church of England requested that the British government set up an inquiry to investigate an appropriate state response. To tackle this sensitive issue as well as concerns regarding increased prostitution, a fifteen-person committee made up of prominent British citizens—including three women and two members of Parliament—was formed. After three years of study, the results of the committee's investigation were released in a publication that came to be known as the Wolfenden Report, after committee chair John Wolfenden.

The Wolfenden Report generated additional controversy when it recommended that the British government decriminalize private homosexuality when practiced by consenting adults above the age of 21. A *Times* article of September 22, 1957, noted that the report argued that moral and legal authority should be separated: "[T]here must remain a realm of private morality which is, in brief and crude terms, not the law's business." The Roman Catholic Social Guild appeared to agree, saying that decriminalizing homosexuality "is only acceptance of the fact that the community should not pry into the citizen's private deeds—even if they are misdeeds." Similarly, in a *Times* report of May 13, 1965, the archbishop of Canterbury, the leader of the Church of England, supported decriminalization but was careful to note that he did not condone homosexuality in doing so but felt that homosexual acts "should be placed in the realm of private moral responsibility."

Public resistance delayed the implementation of the Wolfenden Report's recommendations by nearly a decade. A 1957 Gallup Poll indicated that 47 percent of the British population opposed the decriminalization of homosexuality, 38 percent supported it, and 15 percent said they didn't know. In an unusual reversal, the traditionally socially liberal House of Commons at first rejected decriminalization, while the often socially conservative House of Lords embraced it. After debating the bill in several sessions over a ten-year period, the House of Commons eventually voted by a margin of 164–107 to decriminalize homosexuality in what a *Times* report of February 12, 1966, characterized as a "dramatic victory," repealing all criminal penalties against homosexual acts committed in private by consenting adults. Commenting on the vote, Home Secretary Roy Jenkins said that "the great majority of homosexuals are not exhibitionist freaks but ordinary citizens. Homosexuality is not a disease but is more in the nature of a grave disability for the individual, leading to a great deal of loneliness, unhappiness, guilt and shame." Conservative opponent Cyril Osborne said, "I am rather tired of democracy being made safe for the pimps, prostitutes, the spivs and the pansies, and now the queers." The Wolfenden Report also had significant influence in the United States, as evidenced when the Young Democrats of Wisconsin cited it as their inspiration for advocating for a party plank in the Democratic platform that would call for the decriminalization of sodomy. As reported in *The Times* on April 10, 1966, Wisconsin's Republican governor Warren Knowles derisively rejected the proposal, saying, "When the Young Democrats split into the 'homocrats' and the Democrats it is going too far."

Around the same time that the Wolfenden Committee was composed, similar efforts began in the United States. A group of law professors working with the American Law Institute (ALI) began to devise a model penal code that would recommend new legal definitions and penalties for a wide variety of crimes, including homosexuality. As reported in *The Times* on July 24, 1955, the group was chaired by one of the most eminent legal minds of the time, Professor Herbert Wechsler of the Harvard Law School. The new code sought to remove inconsistencies from the law, serving as a model that each state could look to as a guide while undertaking to reform its own criminal statutes. In a *Times* report of November 29, 1964, another member of the group, Judge Learned Hand, took note of the uneven enforcement of sodomy laws, concluding that "criminal law which is not enforced practically is much worse than if it was not on the books at all." He added, "I think it is a matter of morals, a matter largely of taste, and it is not a matter that people should be put in prison about." A year after Illinois became the first state to decriminalize homosexual sodomy, the committee completed the new penal code, in 1962, which included a recommendation to decriminalize all "sexual relations, normal or abnormal, between consenting adults in private."

In the 1965 case *Griswold v. Connecticut,* the U.S. Supreme Court struck down a Connecticut birth control law that prohibited married couples from using contraceptives in the privacy of their own homes. The decision in *Griswold* established a right to privacy that shielded married couples

from government intrusion into their intimate relations. The Supreme Court later extended the protection of the right to privacy to include unmarried individuals. As discussed in a July 12, 1970, *Times* report, this was a significant change because "America's traditional penchant for legislating morality has produced a mélange of laws against obscenity, adultery, fornication, homosexuality, sodomy and other activities, to the point that in some states virtually all sex is illegal except face-to-face relations between spouses." Still later, the right to privacy was extended to include other intimate matters, such as the controversial right to choose to have an abortion.

In 1969 a government-sponsored panel of doctors, lawyers, and social and behavioral scientists in the United States submitted a report to the National Institute of Mental Health (NIMH) that recommended the decriminalization of private homosexual relations between consenting adults. The panel was chaired by psychologist Dr. Evelyn Hooker of UCLA, who had conducted earlier studies that found homosexuals to be as psychologically well adjusted as heterosexuals (see In Focus, page 77). The panel also recommended that private employers review their employment policies regarding homosexuals. As noted in a *Times* report of October 21 of the same year, the group concluded that discrimination against homosexuals was the root of the problem that should be addressed, saying, "Homosexuality presents a major problem for our society because of the amount of injustice and suffering entailed in it, not only for the homosexual but also for those concerned about him." The report added that efforts to enforce laws criminalizing homosexual sodomy are uneven and often involve police entrapment.

Various states revised their penal codes in the wake of the ALI and NIMH reports, including Connecticut, which became the second state to decriminalize sodomy, in 1969. Several states, including New York, chose to accept the ALI's recommendation to modernize their penal codes while rejecting the specific recommendation to decriminalize sodomy. As noted in a June 4, 1965, *Times* report, New York adopted an amendment that retained laws criminalizing homosexuality by an overwhelming 115–16 margin. On February 3, 1975, however, *The Times* reported that a New York state judge ruled that homosexuals and unmarried people have a right to engage in consensual sodomy. Despite these developments, the U.S. Supreme Court affirmed without comment in 1976 a lower federal court ruling that upheld the constitutionality of a Virginia state law that made consensual sodomy punishable by up to five years in prison. Opponents of the ruling characterized it as a decision that would allow the government to "step into the American bedroom."

At this time thirty-seven states still had sodomy laws on the books, but throughout the late 1970s and early 1980s a number of states decriminalized homosexual sex. Given the importance of the issue and the conflicting understandings of the law that were emerging, some lawyers were surprised that the Supreme Court did not give the case a full hearing, while others anticipated that a more detailed consideration of the constitutionality of sodomy laws would be conducted in the near future. However, it would be nearly ten years before this predication would be fulfilled. While the European Court of Human Rights found that laws criminalizing sodomy were invalid under the European Convention on Human Rights in 1981, the drive to repeal state sodomy laws in the United States appeared to be waning. This may have been related to early connections drawn between homosexuality and the AIDS epidemic. Regardless, no state undertook to repeal its sodomy laws from 1984 to 1991, and it was in this context that the case of Bowers v. Hardwick was taken up by the U.S. Supreme Court.

THE SUPREME COURT UPHOLDS THE CRIMINALIZATION OF SODOMY IN THE *BOWERS* CASE

In Bowers v. Hardwick (1986), the U.S. Supreme Court granted a full hearing on the question of whether the Constitution protects consenting adults from being prosecuted for private, consensual sodomy, agreeing to hear a challenge to a Georgia law that criminalized anal or oral sex. A Times report of November 5, 1985, noted that the case would provide the Court with an opportunity to clarify the meaning of the right to privacy, which had been the basis for invalidating state restrictions on contraception, abortion, and interracial marriage.

The case began when police entered Michael Hardwick's bedroom and found him having sex with another man. Although the prosecution dropped the charges without going to trial, Hardwick challenged the constitutionality of the law, claiming that it put him at constant risk of arrest as a practicing homosexual. Under Georgia law, sodomy was a felony that was punishable with a prison term of up to twenty years.

A lower federal court subsequently found the Georgia sodomy law unconstitutional, so the state of Georgia appealed. The next highest court in the federal system, the U.S. Court of Appeals, said that homosexual relationships were "an intimate association protected against state interference," akin to marital intimacy, and as such protected by the Constitution. However, federal courts in other areas of the country had considered similar cases and found laws criminalizing sodomy to be constitutional. Bowers provided the U.S. Supreme Court with an opportunity to issue a ruling that would resolve this conflict among the lower courts.

By 1985 twenty-five states retained laws similar to Georgia's that criminalized homosexual relations, and nineteen of these, including Georgia, also outlawed heterosexual sodomy. Although unevenly enforced, these laws nevertheless had important consequences, as they were often used to justify differential treatment between gay and straight people, particularly in the areas of employment, child custody, and adoption.

As reported in The Times on April 1, 1986, Lawrence Tribe, a professor of law at Harvard University, made the case for Hardwick, arguing that the government should not be allowed to play the role of "Big Brother" by monitoring private sexual activity between consenting adults. Michael Hobbs, the assistant attorney general of Georgia, claimed that the law was designed to promote "a decent and moral society." In response, Tribe argued that the government should have a better reason to justify the law than simple "majority morality" because the case involved two important constitutional freedoms, the right to engage in private sexual relations and the right to be free from government intrusion in one's home.

In further defense of the law, Georgia's attorney general argued that if the Court found the sodomy law unconstitutional, it would also have to invalidate laws prohibiting polygamy, homosexual marriage, incest, adultery, prostitution, bigamy, and drug possession. Tribe countered that incest does not involve consent and that adultery laws were justified because of the state's recognized interest in protecting marital relationships. He also noted that moral condemnation of homosexuality had been receding in recent years, as evidenced by the decriminalization of homosexual sodomy in many states since 1961.

On July 1, 1986, the Supreme Court announced its decision to uphold the Georgia law. In a 5–4 vote, the Court said that the Constitution does not protect private, consensual sodomy practiced by homosexuals. Although the Georgia law also criminalized sodomy for heterosexuals, the Supreme Court decision focused on the constitutionality of prosecuting homosexual sodomy. Highlighting the landmark nature of the case, justices in both the majority and the minority read portions of their opinions from the bench, an atypical practice for the Supreme Court.

IN FOCUS

Justice Powell Changes His Mind

Supreme Court justice Lewis F. Powell Jr. played an important moderating role on the Court, drawing on his own experiences to make difficult decisions about laws related to abortion and affirmative action. According to his former law clerk and biographer, John C. Jefferies Jr., Powell's unwavering support for *Roe v. Wade* stemmed at least in part from the experience of an office worker at his Richmond law firm. According to Jefferies, Powell received a call from this young man in the middle of the night, asking for help because his girlfriend had bled to death as the two attempted to abort an unwanted pregnancy. As a result, Powell concluded that legal abortions were necessary, since driving the practice underground would increase the risk of injury or death, rather than decrease the demand for abortion.

However, Powell was 79 years old when *Bowers v. Hardwick* reached the Supreme Court, and he believed that he had little personal experience to draw on related to the issue of gay sex. At the time he told one of his clerks, "I don't believe I've ever met a homosexual." The clerk, who was himself gay, replied "Certainly you have, but you just don't know that they are." According to *Courting Justice,* a book on the Supreme Court's handling of gay rights issues, Powell had at least one gay law clerk in each of six consecutive terms in the 1980s. Powell was undecided as the Court considered *Bowers,* but he finally cast the deciding vote in the 5–4 decision, which allowed states to continue to criminalize sodomy, rather than finding that such laws abridged a constitutional right to privacy regarding intimate sexual matters.

Four years later, while speaking with a group of New York University law students, the retired justice surprised listeners by stating that he probably would vote differently if given the chance to reconsider the case. He said, "I think I probably made a mistake" and that, on reading the decision a few months after it was issued, "I thought that dissent had the better of the argument." According to Joyce Murdoch and Deb Price, authors of *Courting Justice,* "Doubts still gnaw at Powell's ex-clerks about whether they could or should have done more to educate him."

From *The New York Times*

Greenhouse, Linda. "Black Robes Don't Make the Justice, but the Rest of the Closet Just Might." December 4, 2002.

The majority of the Court dismissed the idea that the right to privacy would include homosexual relations, saying that it was "at best facetious" to imagine that the Constitution would protect homosexual rights. Emphasizing the "ancient roots" of criminal prohibitions on sodomy, they said it was up to the states to decide whether they wanted to retain such laws or repeal them. In dissent, the minority said that the Constitution's right to privacy allows individuals to conduct intimate relations as they see fit within their own homes.

In an additional *Times* report of July 1, 1986, supporters and opponents of the ruling agreed that the case signaled a very serious setback for the movement for gay and lesbian rights. The Reverend Jerry Falwell, head of the Moral Majority, applauded the Court for issuing a ruling that "recognized the right of a state to determine its own moral guidelines" and because it "issued a clear statement that perverted moral behavior is not accepted practice in this country." In yet another *Times* report issued that day, Atlanta lawyer Gil Robison, a member of the Atlanta Campaign for Human Rights, said that it was "ironic that the conservatives who are interested in getting government off people's backs would applaud this." Others predicted increased police harassment and difficulty obtaining professional licenses dependent on "a good moral character." Employment and child custody rulings involving gays and lesbians also were expected to be negatively impacted.

Protests of the ruling followed in various cities across the country. In the immediate aftermath more than 1,000 people marched through the streets of New York City, exclaiming their displeasure with the *Bowers* ruling and its implied designation of gays and lesbians as second-class citizens. Various speakers said the decision was destined to become the gay and lesbian version of the *Dred Scott* ruling, a now infamous case in which the Court ruled in 1857 that slavery was constitutional, exacerbating a crisis that led to the Civil War. Other speakers likened the *Bowers* case to *Plessy v. Ferguson,* the Court's 1896 decision upholding segregation.

A few months later several thousand gays and lesbians gathered in Washington, D.C., at the Supreme Court building in a nonviolent protest of the *Bowers* ruling. The protest was held as part of the 1987 March on Washington for Gay and Lesbian Rights, attended by an estimated 200,000–500,000 people in October of that year. Among the more than 600 people arrested was Michael Hardwick, the man whose case had led to the unsuccessful challenge of the Georgia law in *Bowers.* This demonstration marked the largest at the Court since a 1971 protest against the Vietnam War.

Although the *Bowers* ruling undoubtedly had enormously negative consequences for gay and lesbian rights, it did serve as a rallying point for the gay and lesbian movement, as evidenced by the large numbers attending the 1987 March on Washington for Gay and Lesbian Rights. In addition, the Lambda Legal Defense and Education Fund, perhaps the most prominent defender of gay and lesbian rights, doubled its budget in the year following the ruling. In a *Times* report of May 3, 1987, Lambda's executive director, Thomas Stoddard, said that the organization's "contributions shot up dramatically as a result of *Bowers v. Hardwick.*"

The Supreme Court eventually overturned the *Bowers* ruling in *Lawrence v. Texas* (2003). In the seventeen-year period between the two cases, several important events occurred on and off the Court. In 1996 the Court itself issued a landmark ruling, *Romer v. Evans,* that struck down an amendment to the Colorado constitution that denied civil rights protections to homosexuals (see the second chapter, "Gay Civil Rights Laws"). This was the first major Supreme Court ruling in favor of gay rights, and it served to give the community new hope that *Bowers* might be overturned in the not-too-distant future. A May 26, 1996, *Times* report on the *Romer* case quoted Urvashi Vaid, a former director of the National Gay and Lesbian

Task Force, who underscored the importance of the ruling, saying that "the gay movement had not had a big win in a while."

Despite the *Romer* ruling, *Bowers* continued to have a negative impact on gay and lesbian rights. In 1997 a high-profile case in Georgia highlighted the ongoing effect of *Bowers* in the area of employment discrimination. Michael Bowers, the attorney general of Georgia after whom the case was named, hired Robin Shahar to join his staff permanently after she had served as a temporary law clerk in his office during the summer. When he subsequently learned that she was a lesbian who had been married to another woman in a religious service, Bowers withdrew the appointment on the grounds that it would compromise the integrity of his office to hire a presumptive lawbreaker. Ironically, Bowers was later found to have had an adulterous affair for more than ten years, in violation of the Georgia law against adultery, as noted in a *Times* opinion piece by Anthony Lewis published on June 13, 1997.

By 1998 the Georgia Supreme Court had decided to overturn the sodomy law upheld in the *Bowers* case, stating that the constitution of the state of Georgia offers greater protection for the right of privacy than the U.S. Constitution. In doing so Georgia became the fifth state in recent years to overturn its sodomy law through the courts, while several others had accomplished the same goal through the legislature. Robin Shahar, the lawyer who had lost her job earlier because of the *Bowers* ruling, said that she was thrilled by the Georgia Supreme Court's action. Similarly, *The Times* issued an editorial applauding the decision. Several other states had recently decriminalized sodomy through legislative processes. However, nineteen states still had sodomy laws on the books at the time, and thirteen of those criminalized both heterosexual and homosexual sodomy conducted privately between consenting adults. The stage was set for the Court's dramatic ruling in *Lawrence v. Texas.*

THE SUPREME COURT DECRIMINALIZES SODOMY IN THE *LAWRENCE* CASE

The *Lawrence* case began in 1998, when police, responding to a report of an armed intruder, entered John Geddes Lawrence's apartment and found him having sex with Tyrone Garner. Lawrence and Garner pleaded no contest but challenged the constitutionality of the Texas law they were charged under, which criminalized homosexual sodomy. As noted in a *Times* report of November 21, 1998, Texas was one of nineteen states that still had sodomy laws on the books, and it was one of only five that punished only homosexual sodomy.

IN FOCUS

Historians Weigh in on Sodomy Case

Chief Justice Warren E. Burger defended the Supreme Court's 1986 decision in *Bowers v. Hardwick* by arguing that affirming a right to homosexual sodomy would "cast aside millennia of moral teaching." When the Supreme Court revisited the issue in 2003 in *Lawrence v. Texas,* nine prominent historians collaborated to correct the historical record. They argued that discrimination against gay people was "so pervasive and well-established" that the Court, along with the general public, had mistakenly assumed that such prejudices had always been a central feature of Western civilization. However, these historians suggested that such stigmatizing was a relatively new phenomenon, rather than a long-standing practice, as "it was only in the twentieth century that the government began to classify and discriminate against certain of its citizens on the basis of their homosexual status."

According to their research the term *sodomy* had been used throughout history in a variety of ways, at times referring to all forms of non-procreative sex, including masturbation, regardless of the sex or gender of the actors. Although engaging in gay or lesbian sex was typically considered a sin, those who engaged in this behavior with members of the same sex were not categorized as "gay" until the second half of the nineteenth century. Further, although sodomy was theoretically illegal and punishable by death, only twenty prosecutions and no more than five executions were documented during the entire colonial period in the United States.

It wasn't until the late nineteenth century that anti-vice crusaders began to fight for increased social control over gay and lesbian behavior, viewing homosexuality (along with drunkenness, prostitution, and contraception) as a threat to order and morality. In response, police instituted a policy of harassment that continued to escalate over the next several decades. By the 1950s employment restrictions and regulations related to liquor licenses were being used to systematically discriminate against gays and lesbians at work and in public accommodations, resulting in more than 1,000 arrests a year in many American cities.

Owing to the work of these historians, the Supreme Court Justices who heard *Lawrence v. Texas* in 2003 had access to a more nuanced understanding of the shifting American attitude toward gay sex, allowing Anthony M. Kennedy to argue, in his majority opinion that reversed *Bowers v. Hardwick* and overturned the country's remaining sodomy laws, "[T]here is no longstanding history in this country of laws directed at homosexual conduct in this manner."

From *The New York Times*

Edidin, Peter. "Word for Word/Educating the Court; In Changing the Law of the Land, Six Justices Turned to Its History." July 20, 2003.

Despite the constitutional challenge, the law was upheld by various courts in Texas and was eventually appealed to the U.S. Supreme Court.

By the time the case was heard by the Supreme Court, only thirteen state sodomy laws remained on the books, largely in the southern part of the country. According to a *Times* report of December 3, 2002, lawyers knowledgeable about gay rights said that the Court "would not have bothered to intervene in the case unless a majority of justices had concluded the time had come to revisit the issue," and *Bowers* supporters and opponents alike agreed that the Court's willingness to take the case seemed to indicate they were predisposed to finding the Texas law unconstitutional.

The coalition that supported overturning *Bowers* was somewhat unusual in that it included a significant portion of those conservatives known as libertarians because of their emphasis on securing individual liberty by limiting government regulation. In a *Times* report of March 19, 2003, Roger Pilon, vice president for legal affairs at the Cato Institute, argued that "government has no business in the bedroom or the boardroom." David Berliner of the Institute for Justice added, "If the government can regulate private sexual behavior, it's hard to imagine what the government couldn't regulate." Both organizations filed briefs with the Court indicating their support for decriminalizing sodomy. On the other hand, socially conservative organizations, such as Pat Robertson's American Center for Law and Justice as well as the Family Research Council and Focus on the Family, submitted briefs in favor of retaining Texas's sodomy law.

In anticipation of a landmark ruling, the Court was packed by 6:30 in the morning even though the arguments were not scheduled to begin until 11:00, as indicated by a *Times* report of March 27, 2003. The lawyers arguing the case "proved to be a mismatch of advocates to a degree rarely seen at the Court," with Paul Smith, a former Supreme Court clerk with significant experience in this setting, arguing the case for decriminalization against Charles Rosenthal, a local district attorney from Texas making his first appearance at the Court. Smith argued that a libertarian tradition of personal privacy was firmly rooted in the nation's founding and the right of individuals to define their own lives. He noted that when *Bowers* was decided in 1986, many people, including the justices on the Court, did not understand that established gay relationships and families existed, paralleling the straight relationships and families already protected by the right to privacy. Rosenthal countered that Texas had a right to set moral standards based on the beliefs of the majority. When asked by one justice what reason there was for excluding gays from privacy protection other than personal distaste or dislike of the group, Rosenthal was unable to answer.

On June 27, 2003, the Court issued what may be the most important gay rights decision in U.S. history, *Lawrence v. Texas.* By a 6–3 vote, the Court found sodomy laws unconstitutional, arguing that they demean homosexuals and threaten their ability to live as free and dignified people. In doing so the Court invalidated Texas's sodomy law as well as sodomy laws on the books in thirteen other states. While the decision to overturn such laws was expected, the decision's resounding support of gay rights came as a surprise to many. Gay and lesbian attorneys in the audience wept visibly as Justice Anthony Kennedy read portions of the majority's opinion from the bench, his voice breaking at times as he too appeared to be moved by the enormous importance of the landmark ruling. Kennedy said that the *Bowers* case had been decided incorrectly, arguing that the right to privacy covers homosexual as well as heterosexual expressions of intimacy, as part of the core freedoms available to all Americans. To reduce the meaning of this case merely to homosexual sex, he added, would be like saying that marriage is simply about heterosexual sex. Rather, he argued, the case centered on the freedom of individuals to live freely and to make autonomous decisions about the most important aspects of their lives. Notably, this was the first time that the Supreme Court invoked a decision of the European Court of Human Rights as precedent to support its own decision, as reported in *The Times* on July 1, 2003. In a concurring opinion, Justice Sandra Day O'Connor argued that moral disapproval of a group is an inadequate basis for state law that "runs contrary to the values of the Constitution."

Justice Antonin Scalia strongly dissented from the majority's ruling in *Lawrence,* arguing that the Constitution does not contain a right to homosexual sodomy and therefore the Court had no basis for making such a sweeping decision and overturning the Texas law and *Bowers.* He added that people who oppose sodomy laws should fight for their repeal at the state level, working to persuade democratically elected legislators rather than relying on undemocratic courts to produce the change they seek. Accusing the Court's majority of taking sides in a culture war and signing on to the "homosexual agenda," he predicted that the *Lawrence* decision would lead to the legalization of same-sex marriage, despite the majority's protestations to the contrary. Recognizing the enormity of the ruling, legal experts called the decision "historic and transformative."

In the wake of the decision, gays and lesbians celebrated in the streets of various cities across the country. Activists likened *Lawrence* to *Brown v. Board of Education,* saying it would further mobilize the lesbian, gay, bisexual, transgender (LGBT) movement, just as *Brown* had done for the civil rights movement. Some predicted that the decision would lead to gays and lesbians having rights equal to those of straight people in areas such as same-sex marriage, partner benefits, and parental rights. As noted in a *Times* piece of June 30, 2003, libertarian conservatives such as William Safire considered

John Lawrence and Tyron Garner celebrating at a 2003 victory rally after the landmark Supreme Court ruling in *Lawrence v. Texas,* a decision that decriminalized sodomy.

Source: AP Images/Michael Stravato

the decision "a victory in the war to defend everyone's privacy." Admitting that he "used to fret about same-sex marriage," Safire encouraged social conservatives to embrace the competition and "repair our own house" regarding marriage.

Opponents of the decision said that they did not believe it would compel states to recognize same-sex marriage. Just as the earlier decision in *Bowers* served as a wake-up call and rallying point for the LGBT movement, social conservatives came to view the pro–gay rights ruling of *Lawrence* as "an unexpected and welcome political opportunity" to further the conservative agenda, as noted in a *Times* piece of September 7, 2003. Noted conservative Rev. John Neuhaus said, "People really think that on this one they have a winner."

Be that as it may, the Massachusetts Supreme Judicial Court recognized same-sex marriage just two months later. Commenting on the development, Professor Suzanne Goldberg of Rutgers University said it was "impossible to overestimate how profoundly *Lawrence* changed the landscape for gay men and lesbians."

BIBLIOGRAPHY

Andersen, Ellen Ann. *Out of the Closets and Into the Courts.* Ann Arbor: University of Michigan Press, 2004.

Cain, Patricia. *Rainbow Rights: The Role of Lawyers and Courts in the Lesbian and Gay Civil Rights Movement.* Boulder, CO: Westview Press, 2000.

Richards, David A. J. *The Sodomy Cases:* Bowers v. Hardwick *and* Lawrence v. Texas. Lawrence: University Press of Kansas, 2009.

FROM *THE NEW YORK TIMES*

AP. "Study Group Urges U.S. to Ease Laws Concerning Homosexuals." October 20, 1969.

Emerson, Gloria. "Parliament to Study Reform of Penalties for Homosexuality." May 13, 1965.

Greenhouse, Linda. "Libertarians Join Liberals in Challenging Sodomy Law." March 19, 2003.

———. "Supreme Court Roundup; Justices to Reconsider Ruling against Sex between Gays." December 3, 2002.

———. "The Supreme Court: Texas Law; Court Appears Ready to Reverse a Sodomy Law." March 27, 2003.

———. "The Supreme Court: Overview; In a Momentous Term, Justices Remake the Law, and the Court." July 1, 2003.

Lewis, Anthony. "Morals Issue: Crime or Not?" November 29, 1964.

———. "Commons Endorses a Measure to Reform Homosexuality Law." February 12, 1966.

———. "Homage to Virtue." June 13, 1997.

Nagourney, Adam. "The Nation; Affirmed by the Supreme Court." May 26, 1996.

Rohter, Larry. "Friend and Foe See Homosexual Defeat." July 1, 1986.

Ronan, Thomas P. "Report on Sex Problems Stirs British Debate." September 22, 1957.

Rosen, Jeffrey. "How to Reignite the Culture Wars." September 7, 2003.

Safire, William. "The Bedroom Door." June 30, 2003.

Shipp, E. R. "Concern over AIDS Helps Rights Unit." May 3, 1987.

Silbey, John. "Assembly Passes a Total Revision of the Penal Law." June 4, 1965.

Taylor, Stuart, Jr. "Case on Rights for Homosexuals Will Be Heard by Supreme Court." November 5, 1985.

———. "Supreme Court Hears Case on Homosexual Rights." April 1, 1986.

Unsigned. "Homosexual Study Is Asked in Britain." December 11, 1953.

———. "A New Penal Code Is Being Drafted." July 24, 1955.

———. "In Lesbos." November 12, 1967.

———. "No Censorship in the Home." April 13, 1969.

———. "Broad Attack on Attempts to Regulate Sex Morals." July 12, 1970.

———. "National News Briefs; 2 Men Fined $125 Each For Sodomy in Private." November 21, 1998.

UPI. "Arrest in Man's Home Began Test of Georgia's Law." July 1, 1986.

Vescey, George. "Judge Supports 'Consensual Sodomy.'" February 3, 1975.

Wehrwein, Austin. "Freer Sex Plank Stirs Wisconsin." April 10, 1966.

BRITISH REPORT RECOMMENDS DECRIMINALIZATION OF HOMOSEXUALITY

In 1957, after three years of study, a committee appointed by the British government published a report advising Parliament to tighten prostitution laws and loosen those related to homosexuality. Called the Wolfenden Committee after its chair, John Wolfenden, this group of fifteen prominent British citizens found no evidence that homosexuality causes "demoralization and decay of civilizations" or that homosexuals are more of a security risk than those who drink, gamble, or engage in "compromising situations of a heterosexual kind." Therefore, despite protests from several members, the committee determined that as long as participants are consenting adults, homosexuality constitutes a private moral issue, rather than a public legal one. As a result, the Wolfenden Report recommended retaining the current maximum sentence of life imprisonment only for homosexual acts involving a person under the age of 16. Although this recommendation was expected to cause controversy among religious, feminist, and church reform groups, a spokesperson from the Roman Catholic Social Guild commented that decriminalizing homosexuality "is only acceptance of the fact that the community should not pry into the citizen's private deeds—even if they are misdeeds."

The Wolfenden Committee's report proved to be controversial. After the report was released in 1957, it would take the British Parliament ten years to implement the legal changes suggested, including the decriminalization of homosexual acts.

SEPTEMBER 5, 1957
VICE LAW REFORM URGED IN BRITAIN

Increased Fines and Prison for Streetwalkers Asked in Government Report

Other Changes Sought

Adult Homosexuality Viewed as Not a Criminal Offense—Controversy Likely

By WALTER H. WAGGONER

Special to the New York Times

LONDON, Sept. 4—A long-awaited report by a Government-appointed committee urged Parliament today to tighten British law against prostitution but to ease it with regard to homosexuality.

As to homosexuality, the report said that when practiced privately by persons 21 years of age or older it was a matter of morals and not of law and should no longer be regarded as a criminal offense.

The Report of the Committee on Homosexual Offenses and Prostitution was ordered by Parliament in August, 1954, and made public today.

It recommended that a heavier penalty than at present be imposed on the street walker, on the ground that her loitering or solicitation constituted an affront to public order and decency. London streets are notorious in this respect, the report observed.

Question of Law and Morals

The committee recommended many other changes in laws. It grappled also with the more abstract issue of the difference between public law and private morals. The report is expected to ignite a blazing controversy among church, feminist and prison reform groups.

The committee is known by the name of its chairman, Sir John Wolfenden, Vice Chancellor of Reading University. Among its fifteen members are some of Britain's most distinguished subjects, including three women and two Members of Parliament.

Several reservations by individual members were appended to the report. The most important protested against the conclusion that private homosexual acts by adults should not be considered criminal offenses.

The three women united in rejecting a conclusion by their colleagues that the maximum penalty of two years' imprisonment for the offense of "living on the earnings of prostitution" was adequate.

Prostitution in itself is not a criminal offense, but soliciting on the streets for prostitution is punishable by a fine of £2 ($5.60). The committee, observing that the present fine is 100 years old, asked for a maximum fine of £10 ($28) for a first offense, £25 ($28) for a second and three months' imprisonment for a third and subsequent offenses.

Numbers on Streets Deplored

These recommendations, the committee said, were based on evidence that "there is no doubt that the aspect of public prostitution which causes the greatest public concern at the present time is the presence, and the visible and obvious presence, of prostitutes in considerable numbers in the public streets of some parts of London and a few provincial towns."

"It has indeed been suggested to us in this respect some of the streets of London are without parallel in the capital cities of other civilized countries," the committee declared.

It explained that it was not trying to abolish prostitution or even to make it illegal.

The committee stated that forces responsible for the existence of prostitution would defeat any effort to abolish it by legislation. It stated, however, that the licensing of brothels was not the way either to control the problem or to clear the streets.

Peril to Civilization Doubted

Among the committee's conclusions relating to homosexuality were these:

There is no evidence supporting the view that homosexuality "is a cause of the demoralization and decay of civilizations."

Homosexuals are no worse "security risks" than drunkards, gamblers and those who become involved in compromising situations of a heterosexual kind.

The present penalties for acts of homosexuality range up to life imprisonment. The committee recommended that this penalty be applicable only in offenses involving persons under 16 years of age.

In a statement of support for the committee, Dr. Donald Soper, prominent British Methodist clergyman, said the report gave "a sense of hope and a promise of justice to a great many homosexual people in this country who are honestly trying to live straight and decent lives in conditions which have been almost intolerable."

A spokesman for the Roman Catholic Social Guild said that the committee's recommendations "seem to go as far as possible to diminish the public display and encouragement of sexual immorality."

"That the criminal charge is removed from the act of consenting by adult males," he continued, "is only acceptance of the fact that the community should not in general pry into the citizen's private deeds—even when they are misdeeds."

American Law Institute's Model Penal Code Recommends Decriminalization of Homosexuality

An independent association of America's most respected judges, law professors, and practicing lawyers gave final approval to a model penal code after ten years of discussion and revision. The American Law Institute undertook this project to make criminal laws and sentences "more civilized and organized." Before 1962 a felony conviction in New York could have resulted in a sentence ranging from two years to life imprisonment. In contrast, the new model code attempts to standardize sentencing practices by dividing all felonies into three degrees of severity. Two law professors, Herbert Wechsler of Columbia University and Louis B. Schwartz of the University of Pennsylvania, did the majority of the work on the new code. In addition, the late judge Learned Hand was influential in the decision to recommend decriminalization of all "sexual relations, normal or abnormal, between consenting adults in private." Some other key recommendations included a new definition of legal insanity, procedures for imposing the death sentence, and parameters for the use of force to defend life or property. Considered one of the most important legal developments at the time, the model penal code began to influence state and federal law even before its official approval.

MAY 25, 1962
MODEL PENAL CODE IS APPROVED BY THE AMERICAN LAW INSTITUTE
By ANTHONY LEWIS
Special to the New York Times

WASHINGTON, May 24—The American Law Institute gave final approval today to a model penal ode that has been under preparation for ten years.

The code is regarded by many authorities as one of the most important recent projects in legal scholarship. Even before its completion it had begun to influence the criminal law of the states and the Federal Government.

The code is intended to take a fresh look at all of criminal law—its philosophical underpinnings, its definitions of crimes, its provisions for sentencing and correction of offenders.

The principal work on the code was done by two law professors—Herbert Wechsler of Columbia University and Louis B. Schwartz of the University of Pennsylvania. They received a standing ovation from institute members after the final vote on the code.

The Law Institute is an association of the country's most distinguished judges, law professors and practitioners. It works to codify and modernize the law. It has completed such other projects as a uniform commercial code that has been adopted by many states, including New York.

Under the institute's procedure, sections of a work such as the model penal code are prepared by the principal draftsmen, then debated in various committees and before the full membership at the annual meeting here in Washington. Then further drafts are written and rewritten until the language is finally approved.

The late Judge Learned Hand was one of the many eminent figures who took part, under this procedure, in the shaping of the penal code.

One of his arguments was that the criminal law should not punish any kind of sexual relations, normal or abnormal, between consenting adults in private. The institute adopted his view, and it is reflected in the code approved today.

More important probably than any single provision of the new code is its over-all approach. It tries to bring a unified approach to criminal law, which has grown up in the United States by scattered and often inconsistent laws over the years.

Thus, for example, maximum sentences for various felonies in New York are two years, three, four, five, twenty-give, thirty, forty and life—with no particular logic in the distinctions. The model code substitutes three degrees of felony for sentencing purposes.

Before defining specific crimes the code devotes more than 100 pages to such general questions as when a former conviction should bar a new prosecution for the same offense, when it is permissible to use force in defense of person or property, and when a man is mentally responsible for commission of a crime.

The code's definition of what the layman calls legal insanity has won widespread approval. It says a person is not responsible for a crime if, as a result of mental disease or defect, he lacks substantial capacity to appreciate the criminality of his conduct or conform it to the law.

In addition to suggesting its own solutions to many controversial problems of criminal law, the code gives detailed reasons for its views and considers the advantages and disadvantages of other solutions.

Would Help States' Studies

The idea here—and one of the main purposes of the code—is to provide idea and material for the re-examination of criminal law now going on in many states. New York, for one, has a commission to revise the state's entire criminal law.

In undertaking the large project of the code ten years ago, the institute believed that most lawyers paid too little attention to criminal law, an important facet of a society. The code is an effort to meet the profession's responsibility.

The code's general thrust is to try to be more civilized and organized about invoking the state against the individual.

The definitions of particular crimes tend, therefore, to be more carefully drawn. Disorderly conduct, for example, which now can constitute almost anything the police dislike, is narrowly defined.

The code takes no position on the great question of capital punishment. But it does suggest a new procedure for imposing sentence in the states that retain the death penalty.

The jury, when there is one, would first bring in a verdict as to guilt and then, in a separate proceeding, decide whether there should be a death sentence. Unless the jury unanimously agreed that there should be, the judge could not impose the death penalty.

- -

British House of Commons Votes to Decriminalize Sodomy

In 1967 the House of Commons approved a long-debated bill that aimed to reform British law on homosexuality. Approval from the House of Lords followed, as the bill had been approved by the Lords twice in the past. Once approved, the new law decriminalized private consensual sex between adult homosexual men. Lesbians were not mentioned in the bill, since such practices were never criminalized "apparently because the Victorians who wrote the [initial] law did not believe such a thing existed." Some Conservative members of Parliament predicted catastrophe, warning that the reform would damage Britain's international reputation, provide enemies with further evidence of British degeneracy, and lead "decent people of Britain" to react violently.

The reform of the law stemmed from a report issued by the Wolfenden Committee in 1957, a group headed by John Wolfenden that recommended the liberalization of laws governing homosexual behavior. Debated for ten years, the bill was embraced early on by the typically more socially conservative House of Lords while being repeatedly rejected by the House of Commons. The government did not take a stand on the bill, leaving members of both parties free to vote their conscience on the matter. Opponents unsuccessfully attempted to kill the bill through filibuster as it became clear that proponents of reform had the votes necessary to win the debate. The bill became law following formal approval by the House of Lords.

JULY 5, 1967
COMMONS ADOPTS A BILL TO MODIFY PENALTY FOR ADULT HOMOSEXUALITY
By ANTHONY LEWIS
Special to the New York Times

LONDON, July 4—The House of Commons, after sitting through the night to overcome a threatened filibuster, voted today to approve the long-argued bill to reform British law on homosexual conduct.

The vote completed action in the Commons and should be decisive. Only approval by the House of Lords is needed to make the bill law, and the Lords have twice before voted in favor of reform.

The measure would repeal all criminal penalties for homosexual acts committed in private by consenting adults. It affects only men since the existing statute does not condemn Lesbian behavior, apparently because the Victorians who wrote the law did not believe such a thing existed.

As the bill passed early this morning, there were gloomy warnings from opponents that it would blacken Britain's reputation abroad. Rear Adm. Morgan Giles, a Conservative member, said the effect would be "catastrophic."

"In a world too ready to criticize us," he said, "this bill will be looked on as further evidence of Britain's degeneracy.

"I can imagine the headlines in foreign newspapers. It will only encourage our enemies and those who disparage us, and it can only dismay our friends."

Admiral Giles added that the decent people of Britain would react violently, and he voiced the hope that the newspapers would publish the names of those who had voted for the bill.

Sir Edward Boyle, a Conservative known for his liberal views on social questions, drew cheers when he responded that he would not mind having his name published as a supporter.

"The measure rightly humanizes the criminal law of this country," he said.

"I frankly am not concerned about what opinion overseas will think. I think we are right in this House to pursue what we think is right for this society."

The proposal for reform was originally made in 1957 by a committee headed by Sir John Wolfenden. Twice the House of Commons rejected it, but in recent years opinion has shifted.

The Church of England, the Roman Catholic Church and the Methodists all supported the Wolfenden proposal. The House of Lords, in its new guise as prime mover of social reform, gave it legislative impetus.

The Commons finally approved the bill in 1966, but it died when a new Parliament was elected in March of that year.

Opponents, seeing defeat near, decided this year to try to kill the bill procedurally. They hoped to use up the limited time available for debate, and the rare night session was called as an answer.

Traditionally the Government leaves this sort of bill to a free vote. As a private member's bill it is not subject to the strict time limitations applied to Government measures, so a filibuster is possible.

Actually the Labor Government, while remaining technically impartial, gave up much of its own time to advance the reform bill. The Home Secretary, Roy Jenkins, and other Cabinet members sat through last night to help out.

Most Members Absent

When the vote finally came, most members had slipped away. The bill passed, 99 to 14. Then, at 6:21 A.M., the House recessed.

The victory should improve the chances of another reform that has faced even more stubborn opposition—a bill to broaden the legal grounds for abortion, which was blocked last week by a filibuster that lasted through one night.

The Government must decide whether to allow it more time, and in light on the outcome on homosexuality, is likely to do so.

There was one angry moment in the House early this morning when an opponent of reform, Harold Gurden, a Conservative, intimated that some members supporting the bill were themselves homosexuals. He referred to surveys showing a substantial percentage of men with some homosexual experience.

"It would be a strange thing," Mr. Gurden said, "in a place of 600 members if there were not some M.P.'s in this house—and yet I haven't heard anyone declare an interest in respect of that."

Andrew Faulds, a bearded Labor Member known for his hot temper, shouted to Mr. Gurden: "We don't know about you, do we? It might be interesting!"

The Deputy Speaker, Sir Eric Fletcher, had to intervene before the House calmed down.

Future of U.S. Sodomy Laws Unclear in Wake of British Decriminalization

Should society punish individuals for private conduct that the majority of citizens find morally offensive? This difficult philosophical question received much attention in both Great Britain and the United States in the 1950s and 1960s, specifically regarding the legal status of homosexual behavior between consenting adults. In 1957 the Wolfenden Report advocated decriminalizing consensual sex between adult men in Britain, arguing that the state should not sanction private behavior that may deviate from the norm simply because most people found such behavior morally objectionable. Opponents of this view claimed that society had a right to maintain the social climate and moral values preferred by the majority of citizens.

The 1967 House of Commons vote in favor of decriminalizing homosexuality led to legal change throughout Britain. This sort of wide-sweeping change could not occur in the United States because each state is allowed to decide such matters as it sees fit, leading to the possibility of great variation across the country. Nonetheless, the prospects for liberalizing the law regarding homosexual behavior between consenting adults seemed promising in the wake of the British decision for several reasons.

Making the public more aware of the prevalence of homosexual behavior, the 1948 Kinsey Report led to a greater acceptance of homosexual behavior in the general public. In addition, laws in existence at the time designed to punish homosexual behavior were very old, biblically based, difficult to understand, and rarely enforced. The American Law Institute (ALI) recommended that states repeal existing sodomy laws, noting that such behavior should be punished only if it occurs in public or with minors. In 1961 Illinois became the first state to adopt the model code suggested by the ALI, while other states such as New York and Wisconsin declined to do so at the time, owing to powerful opposition from the Catholic Church and Republicans. Wisconsin's Republican governor derisively labeled Young Democrats advocating the decriminalization of sodomy, "homocrats," whereas North Carolina's Supreme Court asserted that imprisoning a homosexual was akin to "throwing brer rabbit into the briarpatch." When this *Times* article was written in 1967, there were fourteen states with a wide range of political cultures considering the adoption of the ALI's model code.

JULY 9, 1967
THE LAW: THE HOMOSEXUAL'S CASE
By FRED P. GRAHAM

WASHINGTON—One of the most difficult philosophical issues posed by the law is whether society should have the right to punish individuals for private conduct—even though not injurious to others—merely because it violates generally accepted moral precepts.

A decade ago in England, a royal commission under Sir John Wolfenden encountered this dilemma in a study of the country's harsh laws against homosexuality. Its conclusion:

There must remain a realm of private morality and immorality which is, in brief and crude terms, not the law's business.

In line with this principle, the commission recommended the abolition of laws against homosexual acts committed by consenting adults in private.

This touched off a national debate between backers of the Wolfenden report and those who argued that society must have the right to preserve the social climate and moral values that its members approve—even if it means punishing people for conduct that injures no one but themselves.

Last week, England seemed on the verge of resolving the controversy in favor of the Wolfenden view.

Enactment is Likely

The House of Commons voted, 99 to 14, to repeal criminal penalties for homosexual conduct by men over 21 (lesbianism has never been condemned by English law). Since the House of Lords has twice approved the change, prospects for enactment are considered very good.

Law reformers in the United States could never score a one-shot legislative victory of this magnitude, since morals legislation is a matter for each state to decide. But about a dozen legislatures are quietly moving toward consideration of Wolfenden-type repeal laws within the next couple of years, and the climate for change appears promising.

The shift in attitudes dates back to 1948, when the Kinsey Report showed that there are more homosexuals in the United States than most had thought.

Professor Kinsey found that at least 37 per cent of the men he interviewed had had at least one homosexual experience. This and other findings about the sexual misbehavior of American males led him to conclude that "if the existing laws were to be vigorously carried out, we would almost all of us be in jail, guarded presumably by females and eunuchs."

One reason why the laws are largely ignored is that they are archaic and difficult to understand. Many of the Victorian-minded legislators who passed them couldn't bring themselves to consider the subject closely, so they cribbed heavily from ecclesiastical law and even from the Bible.

The situation has prompted the American Law Institute to recommend, in its model penal code, that the states repeal their laws against homosexual behavior between consenting adults. Under the A.L.I. view, such conduct would be punishable only if it involved solicitation in public.

Illinois became the first state to adopt this model code provision in 1961, and although the idea has not spread to other states, it has been accepted calmly in Illinois.

Church Opposition

In the past two years, legislators in New York and Wisconsin have considered making the same change and have shied away. Determined opposition from the Roman Catholic Church did the trick in New York, and in Wisconsin the proposal became a political issue when the Young Democrats favored the idea and were labeled "homocrats" by the state's Republican Governor.

Yet officials of the A.L.I. believe that the recent adoption of the model code's liberal abortion law provisions by California, Colorado and North Carolina suggests that many legislatures—resuscitated by reapportionment—are ready to update other archaic laws involving sex.

At present the legislatures of 14 states are moving toward consideration of the model code: California, Connecticut, Colorado, Delaware, Hawaii, Iowa, Kansas, Maryland, Michigan, Montana, Ohio, Pennsylvania, South Carolina and Texas.

Many may decide that the action taken in the House of Commons is not for them. But others may decide that regulating such private conduct is not the province of the law, and that, as the North Carolina Supreme Court recently wrote in an opinion, putting a homosexual in prison is "a little like throwing brer rabbit into the briarpatch."

STATES BEGIN TO DECRIMINALIZE SODOMY

Following the recommendations of the ALI's Model Penal Code, the Connecticut House of Representatives approved a bill that would decriminalize sodomy between consenting adults. This made Connecticut the second state in the nation to do so after the bill passed the State Senate and the governor signed it. The most extensive revisions in the state's penal code came in the area of sexual freedoms. In addition to decriminalizing sodomy, revisions to the code also permitted fornication between unmarried consenting adults and downgraded adultery from a felony carrying a potential five-year sentence to a misdemeanor punishable by no more than one year in jail. The Supreme Court affirmed the constitutionality of Georgia's sodomy law in the 1986 case *Bowers v. Hardwick*, but it overturned the ruling in 2003 in *Lawrence v. Texas*, declaring such statutes unconstitutional.

JUNE 3, 1969
HARTFORD SUPPORTS HOMOSEXUALITY BILL
By JOHN DARNTON
Special to the New York Times

HARTFORD, June 2—A bill ending penalties for homosexual acts between consenting adults was approved today by the State House of Representatives.

The bill, part of a new penal code, would make Connecticut the second state in the nation to abandon penalties against adults practicing homosexuality in private. The only state with such a law is Illinois.

The new penal code, which would go into effect Oct. 1, 1971, also contains provisions retaining the death penalty but permitting a judge to overrule a jury's death verdict.

Passage of the homosexuality bill was by voice vote. It now goes to the Senate, where approval is expected before the mandatory adjournment date of June 4. Gov. John N. Dempsey is expected to sign the measure.

Criminal Law Codified

The bill represents the first codification of criminal law in Connecticut's history. It establishes categories and penalties for all crimes, and collects hitherto scattered criminal statutes into a single comprehensive system.

A number of statutes deemed obsolete, such as penalties for walking a cow along a roadside, have been dropped. Others have been revised.

The most extensive revision is in the area of sexual freedoms. The new code permits fornication between unmarried consulting adults, while several present statutes—although rarely enforced—make such persons liable to prosecution.

An amendment from the floor of the House retained a criminal statute for adultery, which had been dropped by the Judiciary Committee when it reported favorably on the bill.

In the code, however, adultery was dropped to the status of a misdemeanor, punishable by a year's imprisonment instead of the present five years.

Another amendment, to expand the code to allow abortion in certain cases, was ruled out of order as a reconsideration of a matter already voted down. The Judiciary Committee had knocked out a section of the code permitting abortion in instances of rape and incest.

Fruits of a 6-Year Study

The code is the product of a six-year study by a special commission that based it upon the Model Penal Code, advanced by the American Law Institute, and upon revisions in the New York State code. . . .

Supreme Court Upholds Sodomy Law without Comment

In 1976, upholding a lower court decision without comment, the United States Supreme Court affirmed the constitutionality of a Virginia law that made private homosexual sodomy between consenting adults punishable by up to five years in jail and a $1,000 fine. Characterizing the ruling as insensitive, shocking and highly destructive, opponents said the decision was a "government step into the American bedroom."

Bruce Voeller, the executive director of the National Gay Task Force, said that the Court's decision ran against the grain of the recent trend toward decriminalization at the state level, noting that laws against sodomy had been recently repealed in thirteen states prior to the 1976 decision. He argued that the decision was based in irrational fear of homosexuals rather than in the law, asserting that the Court failed to follow earlier cases that recognized a right to privacy in intimate associations. Aryeh Neier, the executive director of the American Civil Liberties Union, agreed, calling the Virginia law "obnoxious."

Opponents of the decision argued that the "government has no right to be in anyone's bedroom, and that the right of privacy that would apply there to an individual is a right equally possessed by homosexuals." While one New York lawyer expressed "utter shock" with the abbreviated process that the Court followed to render its decision, lawyers for the State of Virginia who defended the law applauded the Court's decision, emphasizing the amount of time that they had put in to defend it. In 2003 the Supreme Court struck down state sodomy laws in *Lawrence v. Texas*.

MARCH 30, 1976
HOMOSEXUALS AND A.C.L.U. DISMAYED BY COURT RULING
By ROBERT D. MCFADDEN

Spokesmen for homosexual and civil liberties groups voiced astonishment and dismay yesterday over the Supreme Court's affirmation of a state law against private homosexual acts, calling the decision [a] government step into the American bedroom.

"Insensitive," "shocking" and "highly destructive" were some of the terms used to characterize the Court's ruling, which upheld a Virginia law that makes sodomy by consenting adults in private punishable by up to five years in jail and a $1,000 fine.

Two anonymous homosexuals who had not been convicted or even accused had challenged the law, saying it violated their constitutional right to "seek and enjoy sexual gratification." A Federal Court disagreed, and the Supreme Court upheld that decision.

One of the plaintiffs, in a statement released through the National Gay Task Force here, said, "I am deeply disturbed and depressed by the Supreme Court's insensitivity to the right to privacy and all Americans."

Bruce Voeller, executive director of the group, which has a national membership of 3,000 and helped to pay some of the legal costs in the case called the ruling "an enormous disappointment."

Against a Trend

He said that the decision ran counter to a national trend in which laws against private and consensual sexual behavior have been repealed in at least 13 other states and eroded by a number of court decisions.

"This was a plain, simple example of homophobia—the irrational fear and loathing of homosexuals," Mr. Voeller said. "The court has abandoned the logic of the law and even of its own former rulings involving privacy."

Aryeh Neier, executive director of the American Civil Liberties Union, called the Virginia law obnoxious and the ruling shocking. He said, "The Supreme Court has demonstrated a great insensitivity to claims for individual privacy. This is typical of that trend."

Mr. Neier and Dr. Frank Kameny, a member of the District of Columbia Commission on Human Rights and a frequent spokesman for homosexual groups, both said that state sodomy laws were almost never enforced against private and consensual sexual activity. However, they noted that some cases had been brought against acts committed in movie theaters, cars and other public and quasi-public places.

But they asserted that the existence of such laws, even if never enforced, provided a pretext for discrimination against homosexuals in housing, employment, licensing, security clearances and other areas.

"The fact that there is a 'crime' of homosexuality allows them to say homosexuals are not of good moral character and to deny them their civil rights," Mr. Neier said. He reported that the A.C.L.U. currently was involved in more than 100 cases in defense of the rights of homosexuals.

Dr. Kameny, who gave a deposition in the challenge to the Virginia law, said such laws "create an aura of criminality" around homosexuals that he called "highly destructive."

John Grad, one of two cooperating attorneys for the A.C.L.U. who argued the Virginia case on behalf of the plaintiffs, expressed regret that the Supreme Court had not held "a full hearing on the merits" and had merely affirmed the lower court decision without arguments or explanations.

Opportunity Is Denied

He said the plaintiffs had been denied "an opportunity to present our argument that government has no right to be in anyone's bedroom, and that the right of privacy that would apply there to an individual is a right equally possessed by homosexuals."

E. Carrington Boggan, a New York lawyer who filed a friend-of-the-court brief in the case, said, "My reaction was utter shock that the Court could render such a decision on an issue which they know would have widespread impact without even permitting oral argument."

The Supreme Court had before it only abbreviated arguments that had been submitted for the purpose of appealing the lower court decision, he said. Fuller arguments would have been made in a hearing, he added.

Reno S. Harp, Virginia's Deputy Attorney General in charge of criminal cases, applauded the Court's decision.

"It's a case that we spent considerable amounts of time on," he said. "It's our responsibility to represent the commonwealth and to uphold state laws. Naturally, we are pleased the Court has upheld it."

Supreme Court Upholds State Sodomy Law in Landmark Case

In the 1986 *Bowers v. Hardwick* case, the United States Supreme Court ruled by a 5–4 margin that the Constitution does not protect private, consensual homosexual sexual relations from criminal prosecution, upholding a law passed by the state of Georgia that criminalizes the practice of oral and anal sex. At the time the ruling was expected to strengthen the case for discrimination against homosexuals in other areas, such as employment and adoption, or at least to slow recent advances in the drive for full rights of citizenship for homosexuals.

The decision was issued from a divided court in dramatic fashion. Justice Byron White took issue with the view that the right to privacy recognized in previous court decisions would protect all private sexual conduct between consenting adults, including homosexual sodomy. Although the *Bowers* case involved police entering the bedroom of Michael Hardwick while he was having oral sex with another man, Justice White emphasized that such arrests are rare. Subsequent to his arrest, Hardwick challenged the constitutionality of the Georgia law.

In a 1965 decision, *Griswold v. Connecticut,* the Court found unconstitutional a Connecticut law that barred married couples from using contraceptives in their own homes, establishing the right to privacy. This ruling was later extended to include single heterosexuals as well. Emphasizing the ancient roots of criminal prohibitions on sodomy, Justice White declined to extend the right to privacy to homosexual relations, saying that it was "at best, facetious" to say that the Constitution would protect homosexual rights. Suggesting that the Court should not create "a right to homosexual sodomy," White noted that all fifty states had outlawed homosexual sodomy until 1961, when Illinois decriminalized it. At the time of the ruling, twenty-six states had repealed their laws. Justice White said that this ruling would allow states to continue to repeal their laws through majoritarian processes, rather than through the courts. While Justice Powell agreed that states could continue to outlaw sodomy, he stated that Georgia's twenty-year penalty was "cruel and unusual" under the Eighth Amendment.

In his dissent, Justice Harry Blackmun said that the Constitution's right of privacy allows individuals to conduct intimate relations as they see fit within their own homes. Although the Georgia law appears to cover both heterosexual and homosexual sodomy, the Court declined to rule on the matter regarding heterosexuals. In his dissent, Justice John Paul Stevens said that previous cases had made it clear that such laws were unconstitutional when applied to heterosexuals. He also noted that the law should apply equally to the prohibited conduct, regardless of marital status or sexual orientation.

JULY 1, 1986
HIGH COURT, 5–4, SAYS STATES HAVE THE RIGHT TO OUTLAW PRIVATE HOMOSEXUAL ACTS;
Division is Bitter
By STUART TAYLOR JR.
Special to the New York Times

A bitterly divided Supreme Court ruled 5 to 4 today that the Constitution does not protect homosexual relations between consenting adults, even in the privacy of their own homes.

The Court held that a Georgia law that forbids all people to engage in oral or anal sex could be used to prosecute such conduct between homosexuals.

The majority said it would not rule on whether the Constitution protected married couples and other heterosexuals from prosecution under the same law. Associate Justice John Paul Stevens, however, said in a dissent that such laws were "concededly unconstitutional with respect to heterosexuals" under the reasoning of previous Supreme Court rulings.

Weakens Legal Position

The decision is unlikely to curb the growing visibility of homosexuality as a fact of daily life in America, but it weakens the legal arguments of homosexual activists against various forms of discrimination.

This does not necessarily mean it would allow discrimination against homosexuals in other contexts. However, both homosexual groups and their opponents agreed the ruling would slow the advancement of homosexual rights. [Page A19.] The announcement of the decision was unusually dramatic, with Associate Justices Byron R. White, author of the majority opinion, and Harry A. Blackmun, author of an impassioned dissent, both reading detailed passages from the bench.

Limits Effect of Past Rulings

The ruling limited past Supreme Court decisions by rejecting what Justice White called the view "that any kind of private sexual conduct between consenting adults is constitutionally insulated from state proscription."

While the Court has previously upheld a vague right of sexual privacy for heterosexuals, it has never specified, and did not say today, whether that right protects oral or anal sex between men and women.

Criminal prosecutions for private sexual conduct between consenting adults are rare in the case of homosexuals, the Court noted today, and almost unheard of in the case of heterosexuals.

The case ruled on today was a civil suit challenging the Georgia sodomy law brought by Michael Hardwick, a homosexual who had been arrested in his Atlanta bedroom while having sexual relations with another man.

The law defines sodomy as "any sex act involving the sex organs of one person and the mouth or anus of another."

A police officer had gone to his home to serve a warrant because Mr. Hardwick had not paid a fine for public drunkenness. The officer was given permission by someone who answered the door to enter the house and find Mr. Hardwick.

Was Not Prosecuted in Case

Mr. Hardwick was not prosecuted, but he challenged the law on the ground that it violated his constitutional right to privacy.

Justice White's opinion declined to extend to homosexuals a line of decisions involving heterosexuals—in particular a 1965 decision striking down a Connecticut law against contraception—in which the Court has recognized constitutional rights to sexual privacy. While the court did not specifically refer to homosexual acts between women, its reasoning would apparently apply to such acts.

Justice White stressed the "ancient roots" in English common law of statutes criminalizing homosexual relations, noting that all 50 states outlawed homosexual sodomy until 1961 and that 24 states and the District of Columbia still do.

"The Court is most vulnerable and comes nearest to illegitimacy when it deals with judge-made constitutional law having little or no cognizable roots in the language or design of the Constitution," Justice White said in explaining why it should not create a right to homosexual sodomy.

Justice Blackmun, in his dissent, said, "The right of an individual to conduct intimate relationships in the intimacy of his or her own home seems to me to be the heart of the Constitution's protection of privacy."

Justice Stevens, in a separate dissent, said the Court's rationale, like the Georgia statute and the English common law from which it was derived, "applies equally to the prohibited conduct regardless of whether the parties who engage in it are married or unmarried, or of the same or different sexes."

He said that the court's prior decisions indicated the Constitution barred governmental intrusion into private heterosexual relationships, and that the same protections should apply to homosexuals.

Severity of Punishment Cited

One member of the majority, Associate Justice Lewis F. Powell Jr., said in a separate concurrence that while states may criminalize homosexual sodomy, those who commit such acts may enjoy some protection from the Eighth Amendment's ban on "cruel and unusual punishments."

Noting that the Georgia law authorizes prison sentences of one to 20 years for a single homosexual act, he said, "In my view, a prison sentence for such conduct—certainly a sentence of long duration—would create a serious Eighth Amendment issue."

Others joining the majority opinion were Chief Justice Warren E. Burger and Associate Justices William H. Rehnquist and Sandra Day O'Connor.

Associate Justices William J. Brennan Jr., Thurgood Marshall and Stevens joined Justice Blackmun's dissent. The first two also joined Justice Stevens's dissent.

Twenty-six states have decriminalized sodomy, and five of the 24 that still make homosexual sodomy a crime have decriminalized heterosexual sodomy, at least in some contexts.

The New York Court of Appeals, in a 1980 decision apparently in conflict with today's Supreme Court decision, held the state's law barring sodomy unconstitutional. But a state official said the ruling would have no direct bearing on New York law.

"The New York State statute was struck down by our own state court of appeals, and that statute remains unconstitutional," said Timothy Gilles, a spokesman for State Attorney General Robert Abrams. Mr. Gilles said the Supreme Court had declined to rule on the New York case in 1981, letting stand the state court ruling.

New Jersey and Connecticut have decriminalized sodomy by legislation.

Noncommital on Desirability

Justice White stressed today that the case, Bowers v. Hardwick, No. 85–140, "does not require a judgment on whether laws against sodomy between consenting adults in general, or between homosexuals in particular, are wise or desirable," or about whether states should repeal such laws.

"The issue presented is whether the Federal Constitution confers a fundamental right upon homosexuals to engage in sodomy and hence invalidates the laws of the many states that still make such conduct illegal and have done so for a very long time," he said.

Justice White said that homosexual activity was not protected by previous decisions that have interpreted the 14th Amendment right not to be deprived of "liberty" without "due process of law" as including various "fundamental rights" not specified in the Constitution. He said these rights were limited to those "deeply rooted in this nation's history or tradition" or "implicit in the concept of ordered liberty."

In light of the law's longstanding condemnation of homosexual conduct, Justice White said, it would be "at best, facetious" to suggest that homosexual conduct qualified as a "fundamental right."

Privacy Argument Rejected

Justice White also rejected the argument that homosexual conduct should be protected at least where it occurs in the privacy of the home. "Otherwise illegal conduct is not always immunized whenever it occurs in the home," he said, citing laws against possession of narcotics and stolen goods as well as "adultery, incest and other sexual crimes."

In response to arguments that the Constitution bars majorities from imposing their view of morality on minorities, he said the law "is constantly based on notions of morality, and if all laws representing essentially moral choices are to be invalidated under the Due Process Clause, the courts will be very busy indeed."

A Federal appellate court in Atlanta had held that the Georgia law "infringes upon the fundamental constitutional rights of Michael Hardwick" to have private sexual relations, indicating it was likely to strike the law down after further proceedings. The state appealed to the Supreme Court.

Justice White noted that a husband and wife who had challenged the law along with Mr. Hardwick had been held by the lower courts not to have standing to sue because they had never been arrested.

He said: "The only claim properly before the Court, therefore, is Hardwick's challenge to the Georgia statute as applied to consensual homosexual sodomy. We express no opinion on the constitutionality of the Georgia statute as applied to other acts of sodomy."

MARCHERS PROTEST COURT'S DECISION ON HOMOSEXUAL SODOMY

On the Fourth of July 1986, more than 1,000 people marched in the streets of New York City to protest the Supreme Court's decision in *Bowers v. Hardwick* upholding state laws that criminalize homosexual sodomy. Organizers estimated the crowd at 3,000 to 6,000, while police said 1,200 had attended. One protester noted the irony of the timing of the ruling, stating, "I love this country and I love the principles on which this country is founded. Principles which state that we are all equal. We are not second-class citizens. We are entitled to all the rights and privileges enjoyed by all the people in this country."

Speakers at the rally likened the *Bowers* case to the infamous *Dred Scott* decision, in which the Court found slavery to be constitutional prior to the Civil War. Many vowed to work to get the decision overturned. After several speeches were given, protesters marched to the Federal Court House, blocking traffic at several points. Police prevented the demonstrators from moving toward Wall Street, and the march slowly dispersed.

The 1986 ruling of *Bowers v. Hardwick* was a major blow to the gay rights movement. Although the majority opinion ruled that the Constitution did not prevent states from making homosexual sodomy a criminal offense, after the case was decided, additional states repealed their sodomy laws. In 2003 *Bowers v. Hardwick* was overruled by the Supreme Court in the landmark case *Lawrence v. Texas*.

JULY 5, 1986
POLICE HALT RIGHTS MARCHERS AT WALL ST.

By ALAN FINDER

Hundreds of homosexual-rights activists, marching to protest a Supreme Court ruling on sodomy, confronted a police barricade yesterday in crowded lower Manhattan. After 15 tense minutes, in which some demonstrators urged a charge against the police lines, the march broke up without incident or arrests.

The faceoff, at Broadway and Wall Street, ended the march from a rally at Sheridan Square. The demonstration—estimated by the police to number 1,200 people and by the rally organizers at 3,000 to 6,000—followed one Tuesday night, when protesters blocked traffic on the Avenue of the Americas in Greenwich Village.

Many protesters yesterday remarked on the timing of the rally and the march, which coincided with the celebration of Independence Day.

"I love this country and I love the principles on which this country is founded," the vice president of the People With AIDS Coalition, Max Navarre, said. "Principles which state that we are all equal. We are not second-class citizens. We are entitled to all the rights and privileges enjoyed by all people in this country."

Dozens of Officers

The 90-minute rally, which started at noon, was organized so quickly that leaders were unable to obtain a police permit. The police, however, did nothing to stop it.

"Why have a confrontation?" asked Inspector Thomas Gallagher, who commanded the dozens of officers assigned to the event.

The crowd listening to speakers who denounced the court ruling filled Grove and West Fourth Streets and spilled onto Seventh Avenue South. Police officers directed traffic, which was light, around the gathering.

"Are you angry today?" shouted Andrew Humm, a member of the Coalition for Gay and Lesbian Rights and an organizer of the rally. "Yes," the crowd answered. Then the group chanted, "Not the church, not the state, we alone decide our fate."

'Bigotry of This Ruling'

"This week's decision is the Dred Scott decision for gay and lesbian Americans," Ronald Najman of the National Gay and Lesbian Task Force said. "No government is going to take my money and brand me a criminal at the same time. Not for long."

"The torch that is lit today had best cast some light on the dark, dank chambers of the Supreme Court," Raymond Jacobs of the Gay Men's Health Crisis said. "We will not allow America to accept the lies and bigotry of this ruling. And I truly believe America will not allow it either."

The Supreme Court decision that has angered homosexual-rights activists was issued Monday. It said the Constitution did not protect homosexual relations between consenting adults from prosecution.

After many speeches—including one from a lawyer about civil disobedience and what those arrested could expect to face from the police and the courts—the rally moved downtown. With a police escort, the line snaked down Seventh Avenue South, across Houston Street and down Lafayette Street, to the Federal Court House on Foley Square.

In front of the courthouse steps, the marchers raised their fists in unison and shouted, "Shame, shame, shame."

'You'll Get Lost'

The police had said earlier that they would not allow the demonstrators to march all the way into lower Manhattan. But when the crowd decided that it wanted to go to the Battery, the police initially obliged.

"Good luck," Inspector Gallagher told the crowd as it surged down Centre Street and passed City Hall. "Sooner or later, you'll get lost in all the people."

But at 3 o'clock, the police drew their line at Wall Street. Four rows of officers wearing helmets and holding clubs lined up behind the barricades blocking Broadway.

Various responses were urged by marchers. Finally, one demonstrator suggested that the marchers disperse in small groups and use side streets to reassemble in Battery Park. They slowly withdrew. A group of several hundred did re-form briefly in the park.

GAY AND LESBIAN PROTESTERS ARRESTED OUTSIDE SUPREME COURT

Several hundred gays and lesbians were arrested in 1987 at the Supreme Court building as they protested the Court's ruling in *Bowers v. Hardwick*. The nonviolent protest was the culminating event in the March on Washington for Gay and Lesbian Rights. The march crowd was estimated at 200,000 by police and at 500,000 by organizers. Police said roughly 600 people had been arrested at the Supreme Court building protest, making it the largest mass arrest since a 1971 protest against the Vietnam War. Among those arrested was Michael Hardwick, the man who had challenged the constitutionality of the Georgia law that criminalized homosexual sodomy.

Between 2,000 and 4,000 protesters watched as groups of 15–30 people breached police barricades, approached the Supreme Court building, and sat in the plaza, waiting to be arrested for attempting to enter the building for reasons other than official business. Organizers of the event explained that they wanted to approach the bench to state their disagreement with the Court's ruling in *Bowers*. At one point during the demonstration, several police officers donned white gloves, presumably as protection from AIDS infection.

OCTOBER 14, 1987
600 IN GAY DEMONSTRATION ARRESTED AT SUPREME COURT
By LENA WILLIAMS
Special to the New York Times

WASHINGTON, Oct. 13—Hundreds of gay men and women deliberately subjected themselves to arrest today by attempting to enter the Supreme Court building to protest a 1986 decision upholding a Georgia sodomy law's enforcement against homosexuals.

Quintin Peterson, a spokesman for the District of Columbia police, said about 600 people had been arrested, making this the largest mass arrest at the Court since May Day in 1971, when 7,000 antiwar protesters were detained.

Those seized today, many of whom had made public their intention to be arrested, were charged with attempting to enter the Court for reasons other than official business. That is an offense under a regulation that the Court's marshal, mindful of the planned demonstration, said last week that he intended to invoke.

Several of those arrested paid $100 fines and were released, but hundreds more were arraigned in Superior Court this afternoon, after they had refused to identify themselves or post bail.

Weeklong Events

The demonstration was the final act in a weeklong series of events in which homosexuals and their supporters from around the country held rallies and political forums, lobbied Congress and staged a dramatic march Sunday that drew what the police said were 200,000 participants and what organizers said were half a million.

Organizers of today's action said they had hoped to approach the bench and to air their grievances before the Justices.

Gay Americans lost a key legal case in June 1986, when the Supreme Court ruled, in Bowers v. Hardwick, that the constitutional right to privacy did not extend to homosexual relations. The Court held that a Georgia law forbidding all people to engage in oral or anal sex could be used to prosecute such conduct between homosexuals, even in the privacy of their homes, though it did not say the same law could be enforced against heterosexuals.

Among those arrested today was Michael Hardwick, the gay man whose arrest in his Atlanta bedroom, while having sexual relations with another man, led to the Supreme Court case.

Thousands Gather

The protest began about 8 o'clock this morning, when the demonstrators, estimated by the police at 2,000 and by the organizers at 4,000, congregated across the street from the Court's grounds. Starting about 9 A.M., the protesters, some carrying signs, began moving intermittently in groups of 15 to 30 past police barricades and toward the Court. These movements were peaceful and coordinated with the police, who pushed the barricades aside as each group moved forward.

The demonstrators would then sit in circles on the plaza of the grounds, where they were handcuffed by members of the Court's 65-member police force, who were joined by several officers from the District of Columbia police.

Many of the protesters walked quietly, escorted by policemen, to waiting city buses. Others were dragged across the plaza.

Although the demonstration was free of any major violent incidents, the police did wrestle to the ground five protesters who had attempted to cross a barricade at the rear of the building.

At one point, a group of demonstrators including some AIDS victims sat down on the steps of the building and began to chant, "We have AIDS, and we have rights." At another, as a group crossed the barricades to be arrested, some police officers at the top of the steps placed white gloves on their hands, ostensibly as a protection against AIDS, prompting the crowd to shout, "Shame, shame!" and "Your gloves don't match your shoes!" The arrests continued until 2 P.M. Under Section 13L of the United States Code, which deals with public space violation, the Court's marshal can declare the Court off-limits to the public. Under the regulation invoked last week by the marshal, Al Wong, and approved [by] Chief Justice William H. Rehnquist, access to the Court was limited today to those people wishing to view the public session in the courtroom or those having some official business. Violation of the regulation is punishable by a $100 fine and or 60 days in prison.

JUSTICE POWELL EXPRESSES REGRET OVER *BOWERS* DECISION

Justice Lewis Powell, who voted with the majority in the *Bowers* decision, stated publicly in 1990 that he probably would vote differently if hearing the case at the time of the statement. An admission of this sort is unusual and seems to suggest that personal values, rather than simply the law, can be influential in judicial decision making. In the case of *Bowers* such an admission is even more dramatic given that the case was decided on the basis of a 5–4 vote. Had Justice Powell changed his mind earlier, the landmark case would have been decided in favor of extending the right to privacy to include intimate homosexual relations. At this point of Powell's public revelation, his change of heart was no longer relevant, since he had retired the year following the *Bowers* case and was replaced by Justice Kennedy, who was thought to agree with the logic of the case. Since it was decided, the *Bowers* case proved to be a barrier in the further development of the right to privacy, as well as equal rights for homosexuals.

While several states repealed their antisodomy laws by way of legislative action or court ruling, *Bowers v. Hardwick* would not be overturned until 2003, in *Lawrence v. Texas*.

NOVEMBER 5, 1990
WASHINGTON TALK;
When Second Thoughts In Case Come too Late
By LINDA GREENHOUSE
Special to the New York Times

WASHINGTON, Nov. 4—The most interesting opinion to come from the Supreme Court since the new term began last month may well be the comments of a retired Justice, Lewis F. Powell Jr., on his second thoughts about a 1986 decision.

Talking with some New York University law students two weeks ago, Justice Powell said, "I think I probably made a mistake" in voting with the majority against applying the constitutional right of privacy to homosexual relations between consenting adults.

The vote in that case, Bowers v. Hardwick, was 5 to 4. Justice Powell acknowledged at the time that he had initially cast his vote in favor of extending the right to privacy. Before the decision was issued, however, he changed his mind. He cast the deciding vote in favor of Justice Byron R. White's opinion that the constitutional argument for defining homosexual conduct as a "fundamental right" was "at best, facetious."

Justice Powell's disclosure that he has now changed his mind again is a reminder, at once startling and sobering, of the human dimension at the heart of the judicial enterprise.

The case Bowers v. Hardwick—Michael J. Bowers is Georgia's Attorney General and Michael Hardwick a man arrested in his own Atlanta bedroom while having sex with another man—is not well-known to the public.

But among gay people the case is infamous. Gay rights advocates sometimes refer to Bowers v. Hardwick as the Plessy v. Ferguson of their cause, after the notorious 1896 Supreme Court decision that enshrined "separate but equal" as the rationale for racial segregation. As constitutional doctrine, Bowers v. Hardwick has proved a nearly impassable barrier in the path of development of the right to privacy.

According to a compilation by the Alliance for Justice, a liberal legal policy group here, the case has been cited in more than 100 state and Federal court decisions as authority for refusing to find a right to privacy in a variety of contexts. The decisions have included not only gay rights cases but also challenges to drug testing, seat belt requirements and state laws governing the naming of children, among other disputes about the exercise of government authority over individuals' lives.

In his conversation with the law students, Justice Powell did not explain his current view of Bowers v. Hardwick. According to an account of the session in The National Law Journal, the retired Justice, who is 83 years old, said that when he reread the decision a few months after it was issued, "I thought the dissent had the better of the arguments."

He said the majority opinion "was inconsistent in a general way" with Roe v. Wade, the 1973 decision that interpreted the right to privacy as giving women a constitutional right to obtain abortions. Justice Powell was in the majority in Roe v. Wade and supported the ruling throughout his remaining 14 years on the Court.

That so much could flow from the mutable instincts of one Supreme Court Justice is an obvious lesson but not the only one that can be drawn from this odd historical footnote. Charles Evans Hughes, Chief Justice in the 1930's, once observed that the Constitution is what judges say it is.

In modern times, conservatives have accused liberal judges of interpreting the Constitution through the prism of their own values instead of through a principled search for the "original intent" of the framers. But evidence for those origins is often so ambiguous that conservative judges are left having to make their own leaps of faith.

Beyond the personal dimension, this episode underscores the role of the historical moment in constitutional decision-making.

Despite its outcome, Bowers v. Hardwick, announced on June 30, 1986, may well be the high-water mark for the right to privacy.

A few months after the decision, Justice Antonin Scalia joined the Court. Justice Powell retired within a year, to be succeeded by Anthony M. Kennedy. There is little doubt that Justices Scalia and Kennedy would reject the privacy argument in a future Bowers v. Hardwick.

Justice Powell's moment of indecision in 1986 coincided with perhaps the last moment for a generation when the Supreme Court might have found a constitutional right to homosexual privacy. Intriguing as Justice Powell's second thoughts may be, the fact is that the moment passed.

• •

GEORGIA SUPREME COURT FINDS SODOMY LAW FROM *BOWERS* UNCONSTITUTIONAL

In 1998 by a 6–1 vote, the Georgia Supreme Court decided that the same sodomy law that was found valid under the federal Constitution in *Bowers v. Hardwick* was invalid under the Georgia state constitution. Supreme Courts in four other states had made similar rulings, all stating that the right to privacy in their state constitutions offered greater protection than the right to privacy in the federal Constitution. Eighteen states still had antisodomy laws as of the 1998 ruling, including thirteen that banned both homosexual and heterosexual sodomy and three that banned same-sex sodomy only. Although the Georgia challenge involved heterosexual sodomy, the entire law was struck down, making it legal for both homosexuals and heterosexuals to practice consensual sodomy in private.

In its decision, the court noted that moral condemnation of homosexuality does not constitute a compelling justification for state regulation of same-sex sodomy. Opponents of the decision argued that the ruling would undercut all regulation of private sexual behavior, including incest. Gay rights advocates applauded the decision, saying that it would remove some of the stigma associated with the *Bowers* ruling, which had been used to deny jobs, child custody, and visitation rights to gays and lesbians. For example, when Georgia attorney general Michael Bowers decided in 1991 to rescind a job offer to a lawyer after discovering she was a lesbian, Bowers defended his action by saying that it would compromise the integrity of his office to hire a presumptive lawbreaker. The dismissed lawyer, Robin Shahar, said she was thrilled by the Georgia Supreme Court's new ruling.

NOVEMBER 24, 1998
GEORGIA'S HIGH COURT VOIDS SODOMY LAW
By KEVIN SACK

WASHINGTON, Nov. 23—Twelve years after the United States Supreme Court upheld Georgia's anti-sodomy statute in a landmark decision, Georgia's own Supreme Court invalidated the law today by ruling that private consensual sodomy between adults is protected under privacy rights guaranteed by the State Constitution.

Although top courts in other states have struck down similar laws, the ruling today held special symbolic meaning for gay rights advocates because it was Georgia's anti-sodomy law that had prompted the United States Supreme Court to declare that "the Constitution does not confer a fundamental right upon homosexuals to engage in sodomy."

"This is especially sweet," said Stephen R. Scarborough, a lawyer with the Lambda Legal Defense and Education Fund, a gay rights organization that filed a friend-of-the-court brief challenging Georgia's law. "I think that it really sends the signal to other states who may be considering similar challenges that we are in a day and age where the government simply does not belong in bedrooms."

Georgia's became the fifth top state court to reject anti-sodomy laws since the United States Supreme Court, on a vote of 5 to 4, upheld the Georgia law in its 1986 decision, Bowers v. Hardwick, Lambda officials said. In each case, state courts ruled that their state constitutions afforded more extensive privacy rights than those guaranteed by the United States Constitution.

Georgia's Chief Justice, Robert Benham, noted in the decision today that "it is a well-recognized principle that while provisions of a state constitution may not be judicially construed as affording less protection to that state's citizens than a parallel provision in the Federal Constitution may provide, the state constitution may provide more protection than the U.S. Constitution."

The 6-to-1 ruling leaves 18 states with anti-sodomy laws of some kind. Thirteen prohibit both homosexual and heterosexual sodomy, while five ban only same-sex sodomy. Georgia's law, which dated from 1833, defined sodomy as "any sexual act involving the sex organs of one person and the mouth or anus of another."

Anti-sodomy statutes existed in every state as recently as the early 1960's. Twenty-five states, including New Jersey and Connecticut, have repealed their anti-sodomy laws, while top courts have struck down the laws in seven states, New York among them. Legal challenges are winding through the courts in several other states, including Texas, Arkansas and Louisiana.

Paradoxically, the successful challenge to Georgia's law came in a case involving heterosexual activity. In 1996, Anthony San Juan Powell was convicted of sodomizing his 17-year-old niece after both testified that he had had sexual intercourse with her and performed oral sex on her.

Mr. Powell was originally indicted on charges of rape and aggravated sodomy because his niece maintained that the sex had not been consensual, an accusation he denied. The jury acquitted him of those charges but convicted him of sodomy after the trial judge had made that option available. He was sentenced to five years in prison and served 14 months before being released on bond pending the outcome of his appeal, said his lawyer, Steven H. Sadow.

The United States Supreme Court's decision in 1986 focused on homosexual sodomy, with Warren E. Burger, who was then Chief Justice, writing that protecting homosexual sodomy as a fundamental right would "cast aside millennia of moral teaching." But the Georgia decision made clear that any sexual activity that is consensual, adult and private would be protected under privacy rights that, though not made explicit by the State Constitution, have been recognized by Georgia courts since 1905.

That recognition, Justice Benham wrote, does not mean that the court condones homosexuality. But he added, "While many believe that acts of sodomy, even those involving consenting adults, are morally reprehensible, this repugnance alone does not create a compelling justification for state regulation of the activity."

The lone dissenter, Justice George H. Carley, accused his colleagues of "acting as social engineers rather than as jurists." He said the decision would call into question any criminal statute proscribing a consensual act that does not harm anyone but the participants, including laws against consensual incest and drug use.

Lou Sheldon, the chairman of the conservative Traditional Values Coalition, echoed that concern.

"It seems that the Georgia Supreme Court is willing to allow incestual relationships and moral indecency to occur all in the name of 'privacy,'" he said in a statement. "Apparently laws can be discarded if they are broken privately."

Although prosecutions under Georgia's sodomy statute have been rare, gay rights advocates said the statute had been used to stigmatize homosexuals and to deny them jobs and child custody and visitation rights. Indeed, in 1991, Michael J. Bowers, then the Georgia Attorney General, rescinded a job offer to a lawyer, Robin J. Shahar, after learning that she is a lesbian. Among other reasons given for his decision, Mr. Bowers said his office's ability to enforce state laws would be compromised by hiring someone who, he assumed, was breaking the sodomy statute.

Today Ms. Shahar, a senior assistant city attorney in Atlanta, said she was thrilled by the ruling.

"Sodomy has really been used as a tool by people who want to discriminate against us, even when the statute doesn't apply," she said. "And the courts have been letting them get away with it."

THE TIMES APPLAUDS DECRIMINALIZATION OF SODOMY

A 1998 *Times* editorial applauded the Georgia Supreme Court for decriminalizing sodomy, characterizing antisodomy laws in other states as assaults on privacy. The Georgia law had initially been upheld by the United States Supreme Court, after Michael Hardwick protested his arrest in his own bedroom for consensual same-sex sodomy. His lawyer later took up this question, arguing that the central issue was not what Hardwick was doing in his bedroom, "but rather what the State of Georgia was doing there." In a case decided in November 1998, the Georgia court invalidated the law in question. Although nearly two-thirds of the fifty states had decriminalized sodomy, the state of Georgia's decriminalization was seen as an especially important victory by many gays and lesbians because of its historic role in the 1986 Supreme Court's *Bowers v. Hardwick* decision. The *Times* editors urged "the remaining holdouts" to "drop the last traces of this assault on privacy."

Unfortunately, Michael Hardwick would not live to see either the Georgia repeal or the Supreme Court's later decision in *Lawrence v. Texas;* he passed away in 1991 of an AIDS-related illness.

NOVEMBER 25, 1998
STRIKING DOWN THE SODOMY LAWS

When Michael Hardwick looked up from the privacy of his apartment in Atlanta one day 16 years ago, he was stunned to see a policeman standing in the door. "What are you doing in my bedroom?" he asked. It is a question that took on a special bitterness for gay men and lesbians after the United States Supreme Court in 1986 upheld the Georgia law against sodomy under which Mr. Hardwick was arrested that day. The law was 170 years old. It prohibited oral and anal sex by anyone, homosexual or heterosexual, and like all such laws in the United States it was modeled on old English law, which was shaped by religious teachings.

In his argument to the Supreme Court, the Georgia Attorney General, Michael Bowers, attacked homosexual sodomy as "anathema to the basic units of our society—marriage and the family." Five justices bought the argument, upholding the law in a decision that removed any claim homosexuals had to privacy or to protection from government intrusion in their bedrooms. To decide otherwise, Chief Justice Warren E. Burger said, would "cast aside millennia of moral teaching."

But the critical constitutional question, Mr. Hardwick's lawyer later wrote, "was not what Michael Hardwick was doing in his bedroom, but rather what the state of Georgia was doing there." On Monday, ruling in another case, the Georgia Supreme Court agreed and struck down the law. This case arose from heterosexual acts between a man and woman, but the Court made clear that Georgia's Constitution guarantees rights of privacy that make no distinction between homosexuals and heterosexuals. "We cannot think of any other activity that reasonable persons would rank as more private and more deserving of protection from governmental interference than consensual, private, adult sexual activity," it said.

The Georgia decision follows one by a city circuit judge in Baltimore last month who held that Maryland law could not discriminate by making sodomy illegal for homosexuals and not for heterosexuals. In Rhode Island, the legislature voted to repeal its anti-sodomy law earlier this year. One way or the other, in almost two-thirds of the states, outdated legal restrictions on private sex have fallen away. The remaining holdouts should drop the last traces of this assault on privacy.

- -

U.S. Has Opportunity to Demonstrate Human Rights Leadership through Gay Rights Case

In anticipation of the Supreme Court's reconsideration of sodomy law, this *Times* opinion piece pointed out that gay rights were by this time considered basic human rights by much of the world. Canada had recently ruled same-sex marriage constitutional on the grounds that heterosexuals and homosexuals should receive equal treatment under the law, thereby joining the Netherlands, Belgium, and seven other European countries that allowed some form of legal recognition for same-sex couples. In addition, the European Union requires equal treatment for gays and lesbians in the area of employment, a ruling that covers more than 380 million people. Further, gay rights were by then being protected in some South American and African countries, including Ecuador, Brazil, Namibia, and South Africa.

While a consensus in favor of gay rights seemed to be forming internationally, several states in the United States continued to criminalize sodomy and prohibit gay marriage or partner registry. This opinion piece argued that the Supreme Court should find a Texas law that banned private sodomy between consenting homosexuals unconstitutional and thereby overturn the Court's ruling in the 1986 case of *Bowers v. Hardwick.* By doing so, the Court would reaffirm the United States' long-standing reputation as a world leader in the protection of human rights and liberties.

Lawrence v. Texas effectively decriminalized homosexual sexual acts throughout the nation. American decriminalization trailed many decades behind Canada, which decriminalized homosexuality in 1969 and hundreds of years behind France, which did so in 1791.

JUNE 18, 2003
NOT LEADING THE WORLD BUT FOLLOWING IT
By LAWRENCE R. HELFER

Disparities in the legal treatment of lesbians and gay men in the United States and their treatment in the rest of the world are becoming more pronounced. As the United States Supreme Court considers an important gay rights case, expected to be decided this month, it should realize that much of the globe sees the issue as a matter of basic human rights.

Last week the Ontario Court of Appeal in Canada ordered the provincial government to grant marriage licenses to two same-sex couples, ruling that restricting marriage to heterosexual couples could not be squared with the fundamental right to equality in Canada's constitution. The Canadian court's decision is hardly an aberration. In the last decade, national and local lawmakers in dozens of countries have enacted laws to bar discrimination on the basis of sexual orientation in housing, employment, public accommodation and health benefits. Many of these countries are also beginning to recognize rights for lesbian and gay families.

Lesbian and gay couples now enjoy full marriage rights in the Netherlands and Belgium and may enter into registered partnerships in seven other European nations. In November 2000, the European Union adopted a new directive that mandates all member nations to provide equal treatment to lesbians and gay men in employment. At the time, this ruling covered 380 million people. With the union's expansion to 25 countries, it will soon cover millions more.

These legal protections are spreading to parts of the developing world, like Ecuador, Brazil and Namibia. South Africa's highest court has issued several rulings in favor of lesbians and gay men since that country became the first to outlaw discrimination on the basis of sexual orientation in its constitution.

The legal landscape in the United States is very different. Several states continue to impose a criminal ban on sex between consenting adults of the same gender, even in the privacy of their own homes. Others have enacted new laws restricting marriage to a union between one man and one woman. There are two states that recognize same-sex partnerships, and nearly a dozen states and many more municipalities have laws banning discrimination on the basis of sexual orientation in public accommodation and in employment. But the majority do not have such laws, and the prospects for enacting a federal antidiscrimination statute are bleak.

A ruling expected soon from the Supreme Court provides an opportunity to redress at least one of these issues. In the case of Lawrence v. Texas, the court is considering a constitutional challenge to the Texas sodomy law, which bans private, consensual sex between homosexual couples. When the court last reviewed a similar law in Georgia in a 1986 case, a 5–4 majority rejected the constitutional challenge.

Will the recent trend recognizing gay rights in other countries influence the court's decision this time around? The justices are sharply divided over whether it is appropriate to consider foreign and international law when interpreting the United States Constitution. But in a recent ruling banning executions of the mentally retarded, a majority of the court took into account that such executions had received condemnation from the world community.

The international consensus in favor of gay rights is still evolving. But the court can no longer state, as Chief

Justice Warren Burger did in that 1986 case, that a decision striking down a sodomy law would "cast aside millennia of moral teaching."

Recent events have created rifts between the United States and the rest of the world over important questions of law and policy. But respect for human rights should not be among them. When it comes to protecting the basic civil liberties of all people, including lesbians and gay men, the United States should lead the world, not lag behind it.

. . . .

U.S. SUPREME COURT DECRIMINALIZES SAME-SEX SODOMY, OVERTURNING *BOWERS V. HARDWICK*

In what may have been the most important gay rights decision in U.S. history, the Supreme Court overruled its previous decision of *Bowers v. Hardwick,* saying that antisodomy laws are a demeaning threat to the freedom and dignity of homosexuals. By a 6–3 vote in *Lawrence v. Texas,* the Court declared a Texas law criminalizing same-sex sodomy unconstitutional. While many believed that the Court would overturn the Texas law, most were surprised by the Court's resounding affirmation of gay rights.

Several gay and lesbian attorneys in the courtroom visibly wept as Justice Anthony Kennedy read aloud portions of the majority opinion from the bench. Kennedy argued that the *Bowers* case was incorrectly decided and inconsistent with the Court's previous rulings on privacy, as well as with rulings in other Western countries. Justice Sandra Day O'Connor concurred, while Justice Antonin Scalia issued a fiery dissent that accused the Court of taking sides in a culture war.

Ruth Harlow of the Lambda Legal Defense and Education Fund called the ruling "historic and transformative," while Suzanne Goldberg, a professor of law at Rutgers University, predicted the decision would impact various cases, saying, "*Bowers* took away the humanity of gay people, and this decision gives it back."

JUNE 27, 2003
THE SUPREME COURT:
Homosexual Rights;
Justices, 6–3, Legalize Gay Sexual Conduct in Sweeping Reversal of Court's '86 Ruling
By LINDA GREENHOUSE

WASHINGTON, June 26—The Supreme Court issued a sweeping declaration of constitutional liberty for gay men and lesbians today, overruling a Texas sodomy law in the broadest possible terms and effectively apologizing for a contrary 1986 decision that the majority said "demeans the lives of homosexual persons." The vote was 6 to 3.

Gays are "entitled to respect for their private lives," Justice Anthony M. Kennedy said for the court. "The state cannot demean their existence or control their destiny by making their private sexual conduct a crime."

Justice Kennedy said further that "adults may choose to enter upon this relationship in the confines of their homes and their own private lives and still retain their dignity as free persons." [Excerpts, Pages A18–19.]

While the result had been widely anticipated since the court agreed in December to hear an appeal brought by two Houston men who were prosecuted for having sex in their home, few people on either side of the case expected a decision of such scope from a court that only 17 years ago, in Bowers v. Hardwick, had dismissed the same constitutional argument as "facetious." The court overturned that precedent today.

In a scathing dissent, Justice Antonin Scalia accused the court of having "taken sides in the culture war" and having "largely signed on to the so-called homosexual agenda." He said that the decision "effectively decrees the end of all morals legislation" and made same-sex marriage, which the majority opinion did not discuss, a logical if not inevitable next step. Chief Justice William H. Rehnquist and Justice Clarence Thomas signed Justice Scalia's dissent.

While some gay rights lawyers said that there were still abundant legal obstacles to establishing a right either to gay marriage or to military service by gay soldiers, there was no doubt that the decision had profound legal and political implications. A conservative Supreme Court has now identified the gay rights cause as a basic civil rights issue.

Ruth Harlow, legal director of the Lambda Legal Defense and Education Fund and the lead counsel for the two men, John G. Lawrence and Tyron Garner, called the decision "historic and transformative." Suzanne Goldberg, a professor at Rutgers Law School who had represented the men in the Texas courts, said that the decision would affect "every kind of case" involving gay people, including employment, child custody and visitation, and adoption.

"It removes the reflexive assumption of gay people's inferiority," Professor Goldberg said. "Bowers took away the humanity of gay people, and this decision gives it back."

The vote to overturn Bowers v. Hardwick was 5 to 4, with Justice Kennedy joined by Justices John Paul Stevens, David H. Souter, Ruth Bader Ginsburg and Stephen G. Breyer.

"Bowers was not correct when it was decided, and it is not correct today," Justice Kennedy said. "Its continuance as precedent demeans the lives of homosexual persons."

Justice Sandra Day O'Connor, who was part of the 5-to-4 majority in Bowers v. Hardwick, did not join Justice Kennedy in overruling it. But she provided the sixth vote for overturning the Texas sodomy law in a forcefully written separate opinion that attacked the law on equal protection grounds because it made "deviate sexual intercourse"—oral or anal sex—a crime only between same-sex couples and not for heterosexuals.

"A law branding one class of persons as criminal solely based on the state's moral disapproval of that class and the conduct association with that class runs contrary to the values of the Constitution and the Equal Protection Clause," Justice O'Connor said.

Texas was one of only four states—Kansas, Oklahoma and Missouri are the others—to apply a criminal sodomy law exclusively to same-sex partners. An additional nine states—Alabama, Florida, Idaho, Louisiana, Mississippi, North Carolina, South Carolina, Utah and Virginia—have criminal sodomy laws on their books that in theory, if not in practice, apply to opposite-sex couples as well. As a result of the majority's broad declaration today that the government cannot make this kind of private sexual choice a crime, all those laws are now invalid.

Twenty-five states had such laws at the time the court decided Bowers v. Hardwick. The Georgia sodomy law the court upheld in that case was overturned by a state court ruling in 1998. Some of the other state laws have been repealed and others invalidated by state courts.

In the Texas case, Mr. Lawrence and Mr. Garner were discovered by the Houston police while having sex in Mr. Lawrence's apartment. The police entered through an unlocked door after receiving a report from a neighbor of a "weapons disturbance" in the apartment. The neighbor was later convicted of filing a false report.

The men were held in jail overnight. They later pleaded no contest, preserving their right to appeal, and were each fined $200. The Texas state courts rejected their constitutional challenge to the law.

Asked today for the Bush administration's reaction to the ruling, Ari Fleischer, the White House press secretary, noted that the administration had not filed a brief in the case. "And now this is a state matter," he said. In fact, the decision today, Lawrence v. Texas, No. 02–102, took what had been a state-by-state matter and pronounced a binding national constitutional principle.

The delicacy of the moment for the White House was apparent. Groups representing the socially conservative side of the Republican Party reacted to the decision with alarm and fury. On the other hand, important libertarian groups had supported the challenge to the Texas law. Justice Thomas, who is often in sympathy with libertarian arguments, wrote a brief separate dissenting opinion today with a nod in that direction.

He said he would vote to repeal the law if he were a member of the Texas Legislature. "Punishing someone for expressing his sexual preference through noncommercial consensual conduct with another adult does not appear to be a worthy way to expend valuable law enforcement resources," Justice Thomas said, but added that he could not overturn the law as a judge because he did not see a constitutional basis for doing so.

Charles Francis, co-chairman of the Republican Unity Coalition, a group of gay and heterosexual Republicans seeking to defuse the issue within the party, said today, "I hope the giant middle of our party can look at this decision not as a threat but as a breakthrough for human understanding." The group includes prominent Republicans like former President Gerald R. Ford, David Rockefeller and Alan K. Simpson, the former senator from Wyoming, who is its honorary chairman. No member of the Bush administration has joined the group, Mr. Francis said.

As the court concluded its term today, the absence of any sign of a retirement meant that the issue was not likely to surface in judicial politics anytime soon. There was a tense and ultimately humorous moment in the courtroom this morning when, after the announcements of decisions, Chief Justice Rehnquist brought the term to a close with his customary words of thanks to the court staff.

"The court today notes the retirement," he then said drily as those in the audience caught their breath, "of librarian Shelley Dowling." A collective sigh and audible chuckles followed as the marshal, Pamela Talkin, banged her gavel and the nine justices left the bench, all of them evidently planning to return when the court meets on Sept. 8 for arguments in the campaign finance case.

Earlier, as Justice Kennedy was reading excerpts from his decision, the mood in the courtroom went from enormous tension and then—on the part of the numerous gay and lesbian lawyers seated in the bar section—to visible relief. By the time he referred to the dignity and respect to which he said gays were entitled, several were weeping, silently but openly.

The majority opinion was notable in many respects: its critical dissection of a recent precedent; its use of a decision by the European Court of Human Rights, supporting gay rights, to show that the court under Bowers v. Hardwick was out of step with other Western countries; and its many citations to the court's privacy precedents, including the abortion rights cases.

The citations to Roe v. Wade and Planned Parenthood v. Casey appeared particularly to inflame Justice Scalia. If Bowers v. Hardwick merited overruling, he said, so too did Roe v. Wade. He also said that laws against bigamy, adultery, prostitution, bestiality and obscenity were now susceptible to challenges.

The majority opinion did not precisely respond to that prediction, noting instead that the right claimed by Mr. Lawrence and Mr. Garner did not involve prostitution, public behavior, coercion or minors.

The fundamental debate on the court was over the meaning of the Constitution's due process guarantee, which Justice Kennedy said was sufficiently expansive so that "persons in every generation can invoke its principles in their own search for greater freedom."

Thousands Welcome Landmark Decision Recognizing Gay Rights

Thousands of gay men and lesbians took to the streets to celebrate the U.S. Supreme Court's 2003 ruling in *Lawrence v. Texas,* which found a Texas antisodomy law to be unconstitutional, effectively voiding similar laws in thirteen other states. Many activists said that the *Lawrence* case would do for gay and lesbian rights what *Brown v. Board of Education* did for the African American civil rights movement. Kate Kendell of the National Center for Lesbian Rights stated that the "arsenal used against us, with sodomy laws being the foremost weapon, has been neutralized."

Opponents of the decision expressed dismay with the Court's rebuke to state power and emphasized that the ruling would not compel states to recognize same-sex marriages. However, Jane Dolkart, a professor of law at Southern Methodist University, said that the Court's decision was "following the nation, not leading it." The district attorney's office in the locality where the *Lawrence* case originated largely expressed disinterest saying, "I have a lot more serious criminal offenses in files on my desk than this."

JUNE 27, 2003
THE SUPREME COURT:

THE REACTION;

Gays Celebrate and Plan Campaign for Broader Rights

By DEAN E. MURPHY

SAN FRANCISCO, June 26—Gay men and lesbians poured into the streets today to celebrate a Supreme Court decision striking down or strictly limiting the country's last remaining sodomy laws in 13 states.

From Florida to Alaska, thousands of revelers vowed to push for more legal rights, including same-sex marriages.

Gay activists, many in tears, called the ruling the most significant legal victory in the gay rights movement, likening the decision to the seminal civil rights case, Brown v. the Board of Education of Topeka, Kan. They predicted it would embolden the movement and, as in the segregation era, encourage more people to step forward and demand an end to prejudice.

"I feel like I have been walking six inches off the ground," said Kate Kendell, executive director of the National Center for Lesbian Rights, one of many gay and lesbian groups based here in San Francisco, where revelers gathered in the Castro District. "The arsenal used against us, with sodomy laws being the foremost weapon, has been neutralized."

But the authorities in some states with sodomy laws warned against interpreting today's ruling too broadly. The Virginia attorney general, Jerry W. Kilgore, said the court had not created "any new rights for any particular group of people or the general population."

Mr. Kilgore, in a statement, also said the ruling did not prevent states "from recognizing that marriage is fundamentally between a man and a woman."

Even so, several legal scholars and gay and lesbian activists said the decision would probably have far-reaching implications for the popular discussion about gay rights.

Activists and scholars said that by essentially acknowledging gay relationships as legitimate, the Supreme Court justices gave the gay rights movement a new credibility in debates about marriage, partner benefits, adoption and parental rights.

"The court has put gay people in the mainstream of society for the first time," said Paula Ettelbrick, executive director of the International Gay and Lesbian Human Rights Commission. "The court understands gay sexuality is not just about sex, it is about intimacy and relationships. Now there is a real respect for our relationships, as us almost as families, that is not seedy or marginal but very much a part of society."

Some critics of the ruling said they feared it for the same reasons.

Henry McMaster, the South Carolina attorney general, described the possible ramifications as "complex and troubling." While acknowledging that the ruling rendered his state's sodomy law ineffective, Mr. McMaster, a Republican, insisted that the state had a fundamental right to bar behavior considered "inappropriate and detrimental."

In Virginia, Mr. Kilgore, a Republican, accused the court of undermining "Virginia's right to pass legislation that reflects the views and values of our citizens."

In Texas, whose sodomy law was the basis of the case—Lawrence and Garner v. Texas—decided today, celebrations took place in the streets of Austin, Dallas and Houston.

"The decision is a clear indication that our Texas politicians in 2003 are out of sync with the rest of America," said Randall K. Ellis, executive director of the Lesbian/Gay Rights Lobby of Texas. "Yesterday the relationship that I had with my boyfriend was illegal. Today it is legal, and this is one step in full equality for all Texans and for all Americans."

The authorities in Harris County, Tex., where John Lawrence and Tyron Garner were arrested in 1998 for having sex in Mr. Lawrence's apartment, said they had mixed feelings about the ruling.

"Obviously I am a little bit disappointed in the outcome because of the amount of work we put into it," said Bill Delmore, an assistant district attorney in Harris County, who was involved in the appeals of the case.

"But I have a lot more serious criminal offenses in files on my desk than this," Mr. Delmore said. "It is going to be something of a relief to leave the social implications and philosophy and all that behind, and just focus on putting the bad guys in prison."

Mr. Delmore, like the authorities in other states with sodomy laws, said today's ruling would have little impact on day-to-day law enforcement because the statutes had been rarely enforced.

In his 22 years with the Harris County district attorney's office, Mr. Delmore said, the only prosecution under the statute was that involving Mr. Lawrence and Mr. Garner.

More typically, he said, prosecutions of homosexual acts are brought under the state's public lewdness statute, which prohibits sexual acts—heterosexual as well as homosexual—in public places. Mr. Delmore said there was nothing in the today's decision that would prevent the [au] pursuit of those cases.

Similarly, in Idaho, an 1864 state law that forbids "crimes against nature" will still be applied to public sexual acts involving gays, said Michael Henderson, deputy attorney general. He added that the law would also still apply to acts with animals.

"The Supreme Court's decision applies to sodomy laws in certain cases," Mr. Henderson said. "We can't enforce our law of crimes against nature as it applies to private consenting adults now."

Speculation was already rife in several states about how today's decision might be leveraged by gay rights groups to attack other laws deemed antihomosexual.

In Texas, State Representative Warren Chisum said he expected a legal challenge to a law he wrote this year—called the Defense of Marriage Act—that bars Texas officials from recognizing same-sex unions performed in other states.

Mr. Chisum, a Pampa Republican, said today's ruling was nothing less than an assault on the ability of state legislators to uphold moral values. He said he had already assembled a group of lawyers to review how the marriage act might withstand a court challenge.

"It is kind of scary stuff," Mr. Chisum said. "I think the court really opened the Pandora's box here that legislatures are going to deal with for many years in the future if they are concerned about the moral values of this country."

Gay groups across the country said that Mr. Chisum's concern about new legal challenges was warranted. They said they intended to use today's victory to push for more legal rights and to ensure that the ruling on sodomy is not ignored.

"I am confident that never again will there be a serious claim made that a lesbian or gay person is a criminal based on the existence of a sodomy law and thereby fair game for being a victim of all sorts of other discriminatory state action," said Ms. Kendell of the National Center for Lesbian Rights.

Robin Tyler, a comic and producer in Los Angeles who helped organize some of the celebrations today, said many people were mindful of how difficult it had been for some civil rights decisions to become a reality in everyday life.

"This is just the beginning of the race for full equality," Ms. Tyler said. "There is going to be an enormous backlash from the radical right. It is not like everybody is going to suddenly say that now that we aren't criminals anymore, therefore we are entitled to housing, not getting beaten up and marriage."

Jane L. Dolkart, an associate professor of law at Southern Methodist University who specializes in sexuality and gender issues, said that today's decision did open a legal window for gay rights advocates, but that the court was in essence following the nation, not leading it.

Antihomosexual laws were already being removed from the books in most states, Professor Dolkart said, most notably in Georgia, the origin of the last major sodomy case to be heard by the Supreme Court, Bowers v. Hardwick in 1986. Today's ruling reverses that decision, which had upheld the Georgia statute.

"This ruling may have an effect that isn't strictly legal," Professor Dolkart said. "It may have an effect on the beliefs of people in this country."

Some gay groups, fearing the worst, had been preparing protests had the court ruled the other way. This morning they quickly printed up posters declaring "Terrific!" and "Victory!" and sent out e-mail messages with "talking points" for interviews with the news media.

As word of the ruling spread in San Francisco, a group gathered at the corner of Castro and Market Streets, where a rainbow flag—a symbol of the gay movement for the last 25 years—had regularly flown.

A small chorus of gay military veterans sang the national anthem as the rainbow flag was gently lowered, replaced with an American one.

Gay Rights Case Will Lead to Greater Freedom for All

Times editors described the U.S. Supreme Court's *Lawrence* decision, which struck down state antisodomy laws, as a landmark ruling and predicted that it would eventually lead to full citizenship rights for gays and lesbians. The decision found that criminalizing private sexual acts of homosexuals deprived gays and lesbians of freedom and privacy under the law. Recognizing the integrity of gay and lesbian relationships, Justice Kennedy said that the case was no more about sexual conduct than the right of heterosexuals to marry is simply about the right to have intercourse. By overruling *Bowers v. Hardwick,* the largely conservative Court reflected the general public's growing acceptance of gay and lesbian relationships. This opinion piece argued that the dissenters' opposition to the ruling was based on "the same old tired arguments that conservatives have long used to deny minority rights," likening their resistance to conservative justices of an earlier era who objected to the Court striking down state laws that banned interracial marriage. While the full impact of the decision is as yet unclear, it may well serve as a basis for upholding gay marriage in the future, a result that the *Times* editors applauded as a move toward greater freedom for all.

JUNE 27, 2003
A GAY RIGHTS LANDMARK

Gay Americans won a historic victory yesterday when the Supreme Court struck down Texas' sodomy law. The sweeping 6-to-3 decision made a point of overturning a 17-year-old precedent that was curtly dismissive of gay rights. Yesterday's ruling has implications that reach beyond sodomy, and is an important step toward winning gay men and women full equality under the law.

The challenge to Texas' "Homosexual Conduct" law was brought by two men who were convicted of engaging in "deviate sexual intercourse" in a private home. John Geddes Lawrence and Tyron Garner argued that the law denied them equal protection by criminalizing sexual acts of same-sex couples that were legal for different-sex couples. More broadly, they argued that criminalizing their private sexual acts deprived them of their liberty and privacy rights.

The Supreme Court could have ruled on relatively narrow equal protection grounds, and affected only states with laws singling out gays. But five justices went further, holding that any anti-sodomy law violates gay people's liberty rights. Justice Anthony Kennedy's majority

opinion noted that the case is really about gay people's ability to maintain personal relationships. It demeans gays, he wrote, to see it as a dispute about sexual conduct, "just as it would demean a married couple were it to be said marriage is simply about the right to have sexual intercourse."

The court took direct aim at Bowers v. Hardwick, the notorious 1986 ruling that rejected claims similar to the ones that prevailed yesterday. Declaring that Bowers "was not correct when it was decided, and is not correct today," the court overruled it. It is a testament to how much has changed that even today's conservative Supreme Court could see that Bowers belongs in history's dustbin.

The three dissenters accused the majority of advancing a "homosexual agenda." But their legal analysis relied on the same tired arguments conservatives have long used to deny minority rights. Justice Antonin Scalia, writing for the three, called the ruling "the invention of a brand-new 'constitutional right' by a Court that is impatient of democratic change." It is the same argument made in 1967 for upholding a Virginia law banning marriage between blacks and whites. The idea that minorities must wait for the majority to recognize their basic rights is as wrong today as it was then.

It is too early to say how profound an impact yesterday's decision will have. Gay-rights advocates will no doubt cite it in employment discrimination and gay adoption cases. And no less an authority than Justice Scalia, in his dissent, suggested it may provide a basis for upholding gay marriage. The majority opinion ended by noting the genius of our Constitution: that "persons in every generation can invoke its principles in their own search for greater freedom."

LAWRENCE Case Begins to Have Broad Effect

On the day following its ruling in *Lawrence v. Texas,* the U.S. Supreme Court vacated the sodomy conviction of a teenager who had been sentenced to seventeen years in prison under a Kansas law. The teen, who was 18 years old when he was convicted, had oral sex with another boy who was under 16, the legal threshold for statutory rape in Kansas. When both parties are teenagers, prosecutors are typically more lenient, and if the other teen had been a girl, the maximum sentence would have been fifteen months rather than seventeen years. Following *Lawrence,* the Court found that it was illegal to make the penalty for a crime dependent on the sexual orientation of the perpetrator. The teen's release was to occur immediately, since he had already served two years in prison, well beyond the fifteen-month maximum. Matthew Coles of the American Civil Liberties Union said that the case demonstrated the potential breadth of the ruling in *Lawrence,* stating that "when the Court finds that gay relationships are protected by the Constitution, it's answering the equality questions as well. It's an example of how much is now going to open up."

JUNE 28, 2003
SUPREME COURT ROUNDUP;
Justices Extend Decision on Gay Rights and Equality
By LINDA GREENHOUSE

WASHINGTON, June 27—In an immediate application of its new protective approach to gay rights, the Supreme Court today vacated the sodomy conviction of a Kansas teenager who received a 17-year sentence for having oral sex with a younger boy.

In a one-sentence order, the justices told the Kansas Court of Appeals to reconsider the conviction and sentence in light of the Supreme Court ruling on Thursday that overturned a Texas sodomy law.

Unlike the Texas law, which applied only to sexual relations between same-sex partners, the Kansas law at issue is a variety of a statutory rape law, making sodomy with any child under the age of 16 a crime.

Kansas, like other states with similar laws, treats the offense much more leniently, under a so-called Romeo and Juliet exception, if it involves a teenage couple, but only if the two teenagers are of opposite sex.

Matthew R. Limon had just turned 18 when he had consensual sex with a 14-year-old boy at the residential school for developmentally disabled youths where both were living. Had the younger child been a girl, the sentence would have been no longer than 15 months, instead of the 17 years for Mr. Limon.

Mr. Limon, represented by the American Civil Liberties Union's gay and lesbian rights project, challenged the

Kansas law unsuccessfully in state court as a violation of equal protection.

"Making the penalty for a crime depend on sexual orientation is antithetical to the basic promise of the Equal Protection Clause," his lawyers said in his Supreme Court appeal, Limon v. Kansas, No. 02–583.

Mr. Limon has now served more than two years in prison, longer than the sentence that he would have received had his challenge succeeded. A lawyer for Mr. Limon, Matthew A. Coles, said today that he expected to ask the Kansas court simply to order Mr. Limon's release.

Mr. Coles said the Supreme Court order today was a significant demonstration of the breadth of the decision on Thursday in Lawrence v. Texas. While Mr. Limon's challenge to the Kansas law was based on equal protection, and the majority opinion in the Texas case was based not on that constitutional ground but on due process, it was evidently sweeping enough to encompass equal protection cases as well, Mr. Coles said in an interview.

"It's an example of how much is now going to open up," he said, adding, "When the court finds that gay relationships are protected by the Constitution, it's answering the equality questions as well."

LAWRENCE MAY LEAD TO MARRIAGE LAW AFTER ALL

The U.S. Supreme Court's ruling decriminalizing sodomy specified that gay people were deserving of dignity and "respect for their private lives." Many believe that this determination influenced the decision by the Massachusetts Supreme Judicial Court to recognize same-sex marriage in that state. Although the U.S. Supreme Court insisted that its recognition of the integrity of gay relationships did not amount to a right to marry, several dissenting justices despairingly disagreed, saying that the decision paved the way for exactly that sort of recognition. Although many states have laws prohibiting same-sex marriage, the dissenters argued that such laws could be found unconstitutional following the human rights logic in Lawrence. Laurence Tribe, a professor of law at Harvard University, said that after Lawrence any law that gives "same-sex couples less than full respect is constitutionally suspect," meaning that states would have to provide compelling reasons for such differential treatment. The Massachusetts case applied this logic in its decision upholding the right of same-sex couples to marry there, stating that there were no rational reasons to exclude gay men and lesbians from the institution. While the Massachusetts Supreme Judicial Court asserted that its state constitution may well provide greater protection of individual rights and liberties than the federal Constitution, Professor Suzanne Goldberg said that it is "impossible to overestimate how profoundly Lawrence changed the landscape for gay men and lesbians."

Just two months after Lawrence v. Texas, Massachusetts became the first state to legalize same-sex marriage. The same-sex marriage debate became an important issue in the 2004 presidential campaign. During the election the ballots of eleven states contained propositions to prohibit same-sex marriage, and all of them passed. As of 2010, five states (Massachusetts, Vermont, Connecticut, Iowa, and New Hampshire) grant same sex marriages, as does the District of Columbia.

NOVEMBER 19, 2003
SAME-SEX MARRIAGE:

THE CONTEXT;

Supreme Court Paved Way for Marriage Ruling With Sodomy Law Decision

By LINDA GREENHOUSE

WASHINGTON, Nov. 18—In its gay rights decision five months ago striking down a Texas criminal sodomy law, the Supreme Court said gay people were entitled to freedom, dignity and "respect for their private lives." It pointedly did not say they were entitled to marry.

In fact, both Justice Anthony M. Kennedy, in his majority opinion for five justices, and Justice Sandra Day O'Connor, in her separate concurring opinion, took pains to demonstrate that overturning a law that sent consenting adults to jail for their private sexual behavior did not imply recognition of same-sex marriage, despite Justice Antonin Scalia's apocalyptic statements to the contrary in an angry dissent proclaiming that all was lost in the culture wars.

The Texas case "does not involve whether the government must give formal recognition to any relationship that homosexual persons seek to enter," Justice Kennedy wrote. And Justice O'Connor wrote: "Unlike the moral disapproval of same-sex relations—the asserted state interest in this case—other reasons exist to promote the institution of marriage beyond mere moral disapproval of an excluded group."

And yet, despite the majority's disclaimers, it is indisputable that the Supreme Court's decision in Lawrence v. Texas also struck much deeper chords. It was a strikingly inclusive decision that both apologized for the past and, looking to the future, anchored the gay-rights claim at issue in the case firmly in the tradition of human rights at the broadest level.

And it was this background music that suffused the decision Tuesday by the Massachusetts Supreme Judicial Court that same-sex couples have a state constitutional right to the "protections, benefits, and obligations of civil marriage." The second paragraph of Chief Justice Margaret Marshall's majority opinion included this quotation from the Lawrence decision: "Our obligation is to define the liberty of all, not to mandate our own moral code."

"You'd have to be tone deaf not to get the message from Lawrence that anything that invites people to give same-sex couples less than full respect is constitutionally suspect," Professor Laurence H. Tribe of Harvard Law School said in an interview. Professor Tribe said that had the Texas case been decided differently—or not at all—"the odds that this cautious, basically conservative state court would have decided the case this way would have been considerably less."

The Massachusetts decision was based on the state's Constitution, which Chief Justice Marshall described as "if anything, more protective of individual liberty and equality than the federal Constitution." She said the Massachusetts Constitution "may demand broader protection for fundamental rights; and it is less tolerant of government intrusion into the protected spheres of private life."

Clearly, the state ruling, Goodridge v. Department of Public Health, was not compelled by the Supreme Court's decision in Lawrence v. Texas and, given its basis in state law, cannot be appealed to the Supreme Court. Whether it will influence other state high courts remains to be seen. A similar case in the New Jersey state courts was dismissed this month at the trial level and is now on appeal.

Yet just as clearly, the Massachusetts decision and the Lawrence ruling were linked in spirit even if not as formal doctrine. The Goodridge decision "is absolutely consistent with and responsive to Lawrence," Suzanne Goldberg, a professor at Rutgers University Law School who represented the two men who challenged the Texas sodomy law in the initial stages of the Lawrence case, said in an interview. Ms. Goldberg added: "It's impossible to overestimate how profoundly Lawrence changed the landscape for gay men and lesbians."

Professor Goldberg said that sodomy laws, even if not often enforced, had the effect of labeling gays as "criminals who deserved unequal treatment." With that argument removed, discriminatory laws have little left to stand on, she said, adding that the Supreme Court "gave state courts not only cover but strength to respond to unequal treatment of lesbians and gay men."

The Massachusetts court considered and rejected the various rationales the state put forward to defend opposition to same-sex marriage. These included providing a "favorable setting for procreation" and child-rearing and defending the institution of marriage.

"It is the exclusive and permanent commitment of the marriage partners to one another, not the begetting of children, that is the sine qua non of civil marriage," Chief Justice Marshall said. Noting that the plaintiffs in this case "seek only to be married, not to undermine the institution of civil marriage," she said, "The marriage ban works a deep and scarring hardship on a very real segment of the community for no rational reason."

The decision will usher in a new round of litigation. The federal Defense of Marriage Act anticipated this development by providing that no state shall be required to give effect to another state's recognition of same-sex marriage.

On the books since 1996, the law has gone untested in the absence of any state's endorsement of same-sex marriage. With 37 states having adopted laws or constitutional provisions defining marriage as between a man and a woman, same-sex couples with Massachusetts marriage licenses may soon find themselves with the next Supreme Court case in the making.

GAYS IN THE MILITARY

In a historic policy shift that some likened to the end of racial segregation in the military, Congress voted in December 2010 to lift a longstanding ban on gays and lesbians serving openly in the military. This chapter traces the long struggle that led to this change in policy. Gay people have served in the United States military since its founding, at times tolerated and at other times disciplined. For example, during the Revolutionary War, Lt. Gotthold Ensilin was discharged for same-sex sodomy while Cpt. Friedrich von Steuben, according to Nathaniel Frank (*Unfriendly Fire,* 2009), was revered as a brilliant leader. Approximately 65,000 gay, lesbian, and bisexual people currently serve in the U.S. armed forces under similar circumstances, alternatively disciplined or accepted, depending on the situation at hand.

Consensual sodomy (anal or oral sex) practiced by either heterosexuals or homosexuals became a crime in the military during World War I. The first large-scale purge of suspected homosexuals occurred at Newport Naval Training Station in 1919. During World War II the military began to view homosexuality as a psychological dysfunction that could serve as grounds for exclusion or discharge. Purges continued, destroying the careers and reputations of many homosexual service members. At the same time, homosexuals continued to serve and were tolerated in many units, in part because of the continuing need for troops. In the documentary *Before Stonewall,* lesbian servicewoman Sgt. Johnnie Phelps recounts a story of Gen. Dwight D. Eisenhower ordering her to conduct a purge of lesbians serving in her Women's Army Corps (WAC) unit. She agrees to do it but tells him that the first name on the list of those to be discharged would have to be hers. Overhearing the discussion, another WAC within earshot of the conversation says that Sgt. Phelps's name might be the second name on the list, but that the first name would have to be her own, leading Sgt. Phelps to explain to Eisenhower that a purge would decimate their unit, given the large number of lesbians serving in that capacity. According to Sgt. Phelps, Eisenhower immediately decided to abandon the purge.

The military tolerated a variety of practices during World War II, such as drag shows and displays of same-sex intimacy. Some scholars argue that the modern gay and lesbian movement has its roots in this culture, since many gays and lesbians serving in the military became aware for the first time that they constituted a significant percentage of the general population. After the war many gay veterans relocated to port cities, establishing gay subcultures in cities such as New York and San Francisco that later became the source of gay and lesbian activism, such as the Stonewall Rebellion.

According to a *New York Times* article of July 21, 1950, the government began to purge homosexuals and other alleged subversives from public service after the war on the grounds that "sexual perversion" was a security risk linked to communism. As reported in *The Times* on July 3, 1953, the State Department discharged hundreds from service on morals charges in the early 1950s, in response to growing fears of communist infiltration raised by Sen. Joseph McCarthy (R-WI) and his allies in Congress. Forced to hide their sexuality or sacrifice their careers, many gay service members felt particularly vulnerable to blackmail, further increasing concerns about security. A *Times* report of May 17, 1967, discusses a nationwide blackmailing operation that extorted thousands of dollars from closeted gay men, including a high-ranking military officer who committed suicide the night before he was scheduled to testify on the matter.

While open resistance was very difficult during this period, a *Times* report of May 30, 1965, notes that members of the Mattachine Society, a homosexual advocacy group, marched outside the White House to protest discriminatory treatment of homosexuals in the military, including the government's practice of issuing less-than-honorable discharges to those removed from service. In 1966 several gay advocacy organizations across the country united to form the Committee to Fight Exclusion of Homosexuals from the Armed Forces, arguing that including homosexuals would increase the number of soldiers available for duty during the Vietnam War.

Mattachine members Barbara Gittings and Franklin Kameny also publicly defended individuals such as Bennett Wentworth, who challenged the government's right to rescind his security clearance on the basis of sexual orientation. On August 20, 1969, Gittings argued in *The Times* that "the only relevant question should be, 'Is this person capable of safeguarding classified material?'" This conclusion was supported in a piece published on June 27, 1972, celebrating Wentworth's victory over the government. In this article columnist Tom Wicker argued that while "brass hats don't have to believe that 'gay is good,' even in the security field they ought to restrict their inquisitions to the question of whether a person is capable of safeguarding classified material."

On July 19, 1971, *The Times* reported that the Institute for Sex Research, founded by Alfred Kinsey, had completed a study titled "Homosexuals and the Military" that characterized the military policy toward homosexuals as "unwise, unjust, and in essence unenforceable." The report noted that "the majority of homosexuals who serve do so with honor" and that "if an individual's sex life does not interfere with his service activities, it should be of no concern to military authorities."

While some gay and lesbian service members who were discharged during this period fought the ban with the support of the American Civil Liberties Union (ACLU) and other legal advocacy groups, none received as much attention as Sgt. Leonard Matlovich. A decorated, career U.S. Air Force member, Matlovich had served three tours of duty in Vietnam and had since served as a trainer in race relations. After declaring his homosexuality to his commanding officer in order to challenge the ban, the air force recommended that Matlovich receive a general (that is, less than honorable) discharge. He subsequently became the most well-known homosexual in the country, appearing on the cover of *Time* magazine and in numerous *Times* articles, including two lengthy feature stories published on May 26, 1975, and in the Sunday Magazine on November 9, 1975.

Raised as a strict Catholic and once a committed conservative supporter of the Republican Party, Matlovich argued that it was his patriotic duty to fight for the inclusion of gays in the military, a battle he viewed as parallel to the African American civil rights struggles. While an air force panel found him unfit for military service, as covered in a *Times* report of September 20, 1975, a subsequent piece on December 8, 1978, reported that a federal appeals court ruled his dismissal unlawful because the current policy gave the military too much discretion, making it impossible for the court to determine whether improper factors played a role. Matlovich welcomed the decision, saying, "In the past, the military

said, 'If you're gay goodbye.' Now they'll have to tell you why they want to discharge you and give you reasons for it."

Five years after initially declaring his homosexuality, Matlovich won a further victory when, following a series of court cases, *The Times* reported on September 10, 1980, that a court had ordered the air force to reinstate him with back pay. Characterized in a *Times* report of November 25, 1980, as "a rallying point for the national homosexual rights movement," Matlovich ultimately settled with the air force for $160,000 in exchange for an agreement that he would not try to enlist in any branch of the service. The air force stated that it had settled "because we continue to regard homosexuality as fundamentally inconsistent with military service and wanted to avoid returning Matlovich to active duty."

Despite Matlovich's triumph in court, the military continued to discharge gays and lesbians on a regular basis. As more homosexuals were discharged, lesbian, gay, bisexual, and transgender (LGBT) leaders pressured the federal government to lift the ban on gays in the military during meetings with an aide to President Jimmy Carter, as reported in *The Times* on March 27, 1977, and also as part of the first March on Washington for gay rights, as reported on October 15, 1979.

The military ban did not mention transsexuals, but at least one person was expelled for "homosexual tendencies" based on her marriage to a transsexual man who had been a WAC, as reported in *The Times* on July 21, 1977. In addition, although much of *The Times* coverage of this issue focused on gay men, women actually were discharged from service at a much higher rate. Particularly within the navy, which was beginning to send more women to sea, discharges of alleged lesbians increased. A *Times* editorial of September 4, 1980, questioned the wisdom of one such incident that resulted in the dismissal of several female crew members of the USS *Norton Sound*. Similarly, the ban on homosexuals in the military resulted in the discharge of nearly ten times more women than men within the U.S. Marines, including a 1988 extensive purge of women who were alleged to be lesbians at the Marine Corps Recruit Depot Parris Island.

Also in 1988 a federal appeals court issued a stunning ruling that found the military ban unconstitutional, prohibiting the U.S. Army from excluding people from service because of their sexual orientation. Likening discrimination against homosexuals to that of other minority groups such as blacks, Judge William Norris said that the military's arguments that homosexuals would harm morale and discipline

IN FOCUS

"In the Navy" Considered for a Military Recruitment Campaign

The Village People were created to appeal to disco's large gay male audience. Formed in 1977, the group chose a name suggestive of New York's Greenwich Village, an area famous for its high proportion of gay residents. Members wore flamboyant costumes reminiscent of stock characters out of gay fantasy, including a policeman, biker, cowboy, construction worker. They wore tight clothes, sported large mustaches, and danced provocatively to a string of hits that included "Macho Man," "Y.M.C.A.," and "In the Navy." Along with lesser-known tracks such as "Fire Island, Cruisin'" and "Hot Cop" these songs combine infectious melodies with tongue-in-cheek references to the gay male culture of the 1970s. Perhaps missing or ignoring this subtext, mainstream Americans bought millions of Village People albums, and they continue to use their arms to form the letters of *YMCA* at weddings and sporting events throughout the country.

Shortly after the release of "In the Navy," the group was contacted by U.S. Navy officials interested in using it in an upcoming recruitment campaign. In return for free rights to the song, the navy agreed to allow the group to film a video for "In the Navy" on the USS *Reasoner,* a naval ship docked in San Diego. However, after officials in Washington viewed the resulting tape, the navy decided against using the tune in future recruitment efforts. Officials stated that the decision was based on "budgetary and coordinating requirements" and had nothing to do with "the Village People's reputation as a group with a substantially homosexual following."

From *The New York Times*

Unsigned. "Navy Bars Recruiting to Beat of Disco Tune." April 1, 1979.

did not meet a heightened constitutional standard. While the core ruling finding the ban unconstitutional was ultimately overturned by the Ninth Circuit sitting en banc, openly gay Sgt. Perry Watkins, the subject of this case, was allowed to reenlist because the army had repeatedly allowed him to do so over his fourteen-year career with full knowledge that he was a homosexual.

Despite the government's continued resistance to lifting the ban, a Pentagon research center issued a report in 1989, again contending that exclusions of homosexuals were discriminatory. Noting that anyone with a secret is subject to blackmail, the report argued that homosexuals are no more susceptible than heterosexuals to such pressures, thus undermining the main argument that the government had been using to justify the exclusion of gays from the military. Although Defense Secretary Dick Cheney later agreed, characterizing the argument as "an old chestnut," Pentagon sources quickly disavowed the report as biased, while such advocates

of lifting the ban as Rep. Patricia Schroeder (D-CO) called it "an excellent academic survey." Two years later Congress's General Accounting Office found that enforcing the ban cost the government at least $27 million a year. Later the same summer, an August 20, 1992, *Times* story noted that both the *Army Times* and the *Air Force Times* newspapers had come out in favor of ending the ban.

During the 1992 presidential campaign, the discussion of gays in the military heated up as candidate Bill Clinton vowed to lift the ban, arguing that the country needed everyone willing and able to serve. In a piece published on June 24, 1992, *Times* columnist Anna Quindlen wrote about Col. Margarethe Cammermeyer, one of the highest-ranking officers to be discharged because of the ban. Calling her "one of thousands of Americans whose exemplary service has paled beside the military's determination to boot gay soldiers," Quindlen noted that arguments about military cohesiveness and order were once also used to keep African American soldiers in segregated units. Suggesting that "the military should reflect the simple notion of performance as the gauge of job fitness," she wryly concluded, "Maybe there are no homophobes in foxholes."

Alternatively, a *Times* article of August 26, 1992, reported that the chaplain of the Marine Corps, Capt. Larry Ellis, a Baptist minister, issued a position paper asserting that homosexuals are "a physical and psychological" threat to other troops, adding that homosexuals "would experience serious difficulty in controlling their behavior in cramped quarters." The commandant of the marines, Gen. Carl Mundy Jr., issued a memo to all senior marine officers, praising the paper as "extremely insightful" and "a sound basis for discussion of the issue." Rear Adm. Roberta Hazard, the highest-ranking woman in the navy, also endorsed the paper as a "highly reasoned and carefully nuanced approach."

Following the election in November 1992, President-elect Bill Clinton reaffirmed that he would fulfill his campaign pledge to lift the ban on gays in the military; however, there were many signs that the military would not readily accept this change in policy. That same year navy officials resisted when a federal judge ordered reinstatement of openly gay service member Petty Officer Keith Meinhold, who was discharged for stating on national television that he was a homosexual. In response to the navy's inaction, Judge Terry Hatter reissued the order, stating, "[T]his is not a military dictatorship. Here, the rule of law applies to the military." When the navy complied with this second order, Meinhold commented that his presence in the navy would effectively disprove the military's argument that gay service members undermine good order, morale, and discipline in the ranks.

Even more important, Gen. Colin Powell, chair of the Joint Chiefs of Staff, made it clear that he strenuously objected to the acceptance of homosexuals for military service, and suggested a "major confrontation is brewing" as noted in a *Times* report of November 14, 1992. In addition, several military leaders argued that lifting the ban could lead to mass resignations and recruiting difficulties. Some said that they resented such a major policy change coming from a president they considered to be a draft dodger. Although President Harry Truman issued an executive order to end racial segregation in the armed forces in 1948, Clinton instead opted to negotiate with Powell in an effort to end the ban on gays in the military. Several observers, including *Times* columnist Abe Rosenthal in an opinion piece of January 26, 1993, noted the irony that an African American general who had experienced segregation was resisting a policy that would end the exclusion of another minority group.

Another opinion piece published on February 1, 1993, said, "[S]ubstitute 'gays' for 'blacks' and you've pretty much got the situation facing President Clinton. The same chorus of protest, resistance to change, fear of the unknown."

A *Times* editorial of November 15, 1992, argued that while Powell and the Chiefs of Staff deserved a "respectful hearing," their views were "not a reason for inaction," as "the rationale for the ban has become increasingly dubious." Adding that lifting the ban would not undermine morale, order, and discipline, the editorial argued that "it is unreasonable to ban homosexuals based on the presumed reaction of straights." That same day, however, Clinton also received considerable public resistance from Sen. Sam Nunn (D-GA), chair of the Senate's Armed Services Committee and a senior member of Clinton's own party. Speaking on various Sunday morning news shows, Sen. Nunn openly opposed lifting the ban, stating that Congress should have a central role in forming any new policy the president might be considering.

Following his inauguration, Clinton announced that he would delay action until July 15, 1993, in order to give the Pentagon a chance to draft an executive order to lift the ban. In the interim the military was directed to stop discharging homosexuals and to stop asking recruits about their sexuality. A flurry of articles followed. On January 25, 1993, *The Times* reported that a confidential memo from Defense Secretary Les Aspin to President Clinton was leaked, indicating that not only top military leaders but also Congress would oppose lifting the ban, necessitating the inclusion of key senators such as Nunn in further negotiations. A January 29, 1993, *Times* editorial characterized Nunn's resistance as a sad "ceremony of his own ego." Nonetheless, by January 30, 1993, *The Times* had concluded that Nunn had seized control of the debate, promising to hold hearings on any plan that Clinton proposed and threatening to solidify the ban by making it statutory, thus preempting the possibility of an executive order to allow military service by gays and lesbians. Unnamed sources speculated that Nunn's open rebuke of the president was a result of Clinton bypassing Nunn for the position of secretary of state.

The Times offered extensive coverage of the ensuing debate, including numerous articles exploring various arguments on all sides of the issue. Issues regarding military morale, discipline, recruitment, and cohesiveness were explored in detail, as were assertions about a lack of privacy in shower rooms, concerns about homosexual promiscuity, and the spread of AIDS. Many of these claims were unsubstantiated. For example, a *Times* report of January 27, 1993, noted that navy spokesperson Cmdr. Craig Quigley offered "no evidence" to back his claim that "homosexuals are notoriously promiscuous." Thomas Stoddard, of the Lambda Legal Defense and Education Fund, argued that military leaders "can either give into the prejudice and coddle the bigots, or . . . address it and teach people the mistaken and unethical basis on which the prejudice rests."

Other *Times* pieces noted that both the general public and members of the military seemed split about the ban. According to a January 1993 *New York Times*/CBS News telephone survey of 1,179 adults, 42 percent favored "permitting homosexuals to serve in the military, 48 percent were opposed and 10 percent had no opinion on the issue." Similarly, an article that ran on January 28, 1993, noted that a small, informal survey of soldiers stationed at the Fort Benning army base found "a slim majority" opposed to allowing gays to openly serve in the military. One airman rejected the idea that the ban paralleled earlier patterns of discrimination against African Americans and women, saying that was "just prejudiced thinking. We're not that way at all. We just don't like homosexuals." Alternatively, an African American woman who had served in the army for eleven years saw the connection between the issues, saying, "[P]eople often use race and a lot of other things like this as a cop-out. I don't see a problem at all."

A *Times* piece published on January 31, 1993, revealed similar divisions. One sailor said that if a homosexual "comes on to me, I'll kick" him unconscious. Another argued that "people need to be judged on their ability to do a job, and as long as they can keep their sexual preference to themselves it shouldn't matter in the workplace." A third soldier added "I think the military is real adaptable, and will adapt to this. There's a lot of misconceptions about what could happen and will happen."

During this time, Allen Schindler was murdered and mutilated by two of his fellow sailors at a U.S. naval base in Japan shortly after coming out as gay to his commander. Some sailors noted that the killing was part of a pattern of harassment against gays at the base. A *Times* report of March 8, 1993, indicated that prior to his death, Schindler had described life on his ship as a "living hell" for homosexuals. Others speculated that it was connected to Clinton's proposal to lift the ban and was further indication that the military was not ready to deal with open homosexuality.

The Senate and the House both held various hearings on lifting the ban, including some that specifically addressed lesbians in the military. Randy Shilts's book on the subject, *Conduct Unbecoming,* estimated that 25 percent of the 200,000 women in the military were lesbians. Women are discharged for homosexuality about three times more often than men, and many are accused of being lesbians after reporting a higher-ranking male service member for sexual harassment. Col. Margarethe Cammermeyer, herself discharged by the army in 1992, said "[M]any men still don't think women belong in the military. The ban is a perfect mechanism to get us out."

During this time the Clinton administration considered several options, including the segregation of gay troops, an idea swiftly condemned by gay advocacy groups such as the newly formed Campaign for Military Service. These groups asked the president not to retreat from his promise to lift the ban, saying in a *Times* report of March 27, 1993, that an upcoming major March on Washington for Lesbian, Gay, and Bisexual Rights could turn into "either a celebration or a protest that we're not getting equal treatment." A *Times* report of April 26, 1993, noted that the military issue was raised repeatedly during the march. Noting the "thunderous applause, tears and screams" that emerged when gay military heroes appeared on stage, the report added that the crowd stilled when Dorothy Hajdys, the mother of Allen R. Schindler, a recently slain gay seaman, came to the stage and "expressed fear for every gay and lesbian service member." Prominent gay fund-raisers, many of whom had strongly supported Clinton during his campaign to become president, announced that they would stop collecting money for the party until he lifted the ban.

On July 20, 1993, President Clinton announced his plan to reform the ban on gays in the military. The new policy was quickly dubbed "Don't Ask, Don't Tell" (DADT) because it called for a reciprocal relationship in which commanders would not inquire about homosexuality if gay service members did not reveal it. In theory this allowed discrete gays and lesbians to serve and allowed investigation of only overt homosexual statements and behavior. When Clinton made the announcement, he was accompanied by the Joint Chiefs of Staff, but no gay rights advocates were in attendance. The same day, *The Times* issued an editorial that expressed disappointment in the modified ban, saying that Congress and the Joint Chiefs had left Clinton little choice but to offer gay soldiers "half a loaf."

The following day *The Times* reported that gay advocacy groups had denounced the new policy, characterizing it as "an overwhelming defeat." Miriam Ben-Shalom, a lesbian who had previously been discharged from the army, said the new policy was "nothing more than the old ban couched in doublespeak." Gay leaders promised to challenge the ban in court. On July 22, 1993, *The Times* reported that the military was pleased with the Clinton administration's new plan and characterized it as "purposefully ambiguous" and differing

IN FOCUS

Colonel Peck and His Gay Son, Scott

• •

Testifying before the Senate Armed Services Committee on President Clinton's proposal to end the ban on gay men and lesbians serving openly in the military, Col. Fred Peck made headline news when he announced, "My son Scott is a homosexual. I think he's a fine person. But he should not serve in the military."

Familiar to many Americans owing to his recent high-profile role as spokesperson for international relief operations in Somalia, the 44-year-old marine had learned that his son was gay only five days earlier. Scott had been aware of his sexual orientation since grammar school and had been slowly coming out while studying English at the University of Maryland, writing on gay topics for a school newspaper as well as telling friends and his stepmother. But he was hesitant to tell his father. Absent for the majority of Scott's childhood because of an early divorce, Col. Fred Peck invited his son to move in with him following the death of his mother when the boy was 15. Scott was unsure about how his father would take the news about his sexual orientation. "I had my own stereotypes about Marine Corps colonels, and I assumed because of the life style he chose, he would have certain political views."

However, shortly after he had published an article critical of radical gay activists, Scott learned that an acquaintance affiliated with the campus branch of Queer Nation was threatening to embarrass Col. Peck by publically "outing" Scott to the national media. As a result, Scott's stepmother told Col. Peck that Scott was gay, after which father and son had an emotional two-hour phone conversation. Scott said, "He told me he still loved me and accepted me." The two agreed that Col. Peck would disclose Scott's sexual orientation during his testimony. "I could not ask him not to appear at the hearing any more than he could ask me not to share my side of the issue," said Scott.

While denying that he was homophobic, Col. Peck testified that openly gay soldiers would damage morale and could face physical danger, even murder at the hands of many in the ranks who remain "fearful and distrustful" of homosexuals. His son disagreed during a subsequent telephone interview with *The Times*. "Once soldiers and marines discover that the men and women they've been serving with have been gay or lesbian all along," he said, "I think they'll see them as real people, not stereotypes." Despite their disagreement over this issue, Scott was pleased with his father's reaction to his sexual orientation. "After hearing his response, I wish I'd talked to him 10 years ago."

From *The New York Times*

Clines, Francis X. "Surprised by the Limelight, A Colonel's Gay Son Shines." May 17, 1993.
Schmitt, Eric. "Marine's Son Personalizes Gay Debate." May 13, 1993.

• •

"only slightly" from the previous policy. The policy was officially signed into law on November 30, 1993.

The ACLU and the Lambda Legal Defense and Education Fund made the first legal challenge to Don't Ask, Don't Tell (DADT) on behalf of six homosexual service members, as reported in *The Times* on March 8, 1994. The suit argued that the new policy violated the Constitution's guarantee of equality and free speech. Striking down the policy, a federal

judge characterized DADT as forging an "Orwellian" connection between sexual orientation and conduct as reported in *The Times* on March 31, 1995. He added, "Hitler taught the world what could happen when the government began to target people not for what they had done but because of their status." However, an April 6, 1996, *Times* article reported that a higher court ultimately upheld the policy on appeal, deferring to the power of Congress and the president to address issues pertaining to the military. In dissent one judge argued that the prohibition on "telling" in the policy penalized a gay soldier for "nothing more than an expression of his state of mind," punishing speech in a manner contrary to the First Amendment. The Supreme Court subsequently declined to hear the case.

Despite the promise of the new policy to reset the terms of gay participation in the military, the rate of gay discharges increased dramatically under the new policy. Military commanders continued to ask gay service members about their sexual identity and many continued to tell, prompting the Servicemembers Legal Defense Network to say that the new policy was "as bad, if not worse than, its predecessors." A Times report of April 7, 1998, noted that discharge rates had soared 67 percent since DADT had been adopted, affecting more than 1,000 service members a year by the end of 1998.

As The Times noted in pieces on March 15 and December 9, 1999, reports of antigay harassment were also on the rise in every branch of the service, including the murder of Pfc. Barry Winchell, who was beaten to death with a baseball bat by a member of his own unit as he slept. Michelle Benecke, a retired U.S. Army captain, said, "Private Winchell is only the latest example of the severe anti-gay harassment that service members face every day. Others called the slaying a classic hate crime and argued that Don't Ask, Don't Tell made life more difficult for gays in the military, "leaving many to suffer in silence or leave the service." In response the new policy underwent its first major revision. New limitations were placed on investigations, and antiharassment training was mandated for all service members. Spot-checks for gay harassment on bases also were ordered. A year later, as reported in The Times on March 26, 2000, a Pentagon report continued to find that harassment of gays and lesbians in the military was "widespread," stating that it was tolerated by superiors and peers "to some extent."

According to a Pentagon study reported in a Times article on February 15, 2006, ten years under the DADT policy cost approximately $364 million and resulted in rising reports of harassment as well as the discharge of roughly 10,000 service members. Following earlier patterns of increased tolerance during wartime, the rate of discharge of gays and lesbians dropped almost 50 percent in the first three years after the 9/11 attacks as the demand for troops rose owing to U.S. involvement in Iraq and Afghanistan, as reported in The Times on February 13, 2005. A December 10, 2003, Times report indicated that three high-ranking retired officers (two generals and an admiral) had come out as gay, noting that DADT had been ineffective and corrosive of core military values of truth, honor, dignity, respect, and integrity.

A Times report of August 15, 2006, noted that discharges began to rise again after 2005, particularly at Fort Campbell, Kentucky, where Private Winchell had been murdered, and Parris Island, South Carolina, where well-publicized purges of alleged lesbians had been conducted in the late 1980s. The policy continued to affect women disproportionately. In addition, by mid-2007 fifty-eight service members who spoke or had studied Arabic had been discharged under DADT, despite the military's pressing need for such translators, leading researcher Nathaniel Frank to argue that the ban on gays in the military was actually compromising national security.

President George W. Bush was not interested in altering the existing policy on homosexuals in the military. When he called for an overall increase in the size of the armed forces, retired general John Shalikashvili, chair of the Joint Chiefs of Staff from 1993 to 1997, wrote a Times opinion piece on January 2, 2007, indicating that conversations with military personnel had led him to his change of heart about lifting the ban. Noting that many nations now enlist homosexuals, he argued that "if gay men and lesbians served openly in the United States military, they would not undermine the efficacy of the armed forces." Echoing an argument made by President Clinton at the outset of the debate about lifting the ban, the general added, "Our military has been stretched thin by our deployments in the Middle East, and we must welcome the service of any American who is willing and able to do the job." The then-current chair of the Joint Chiefs, Gen. Peter Pace, expressed his support for the current policy, saying he believed that homosexuality was immoral and akin to adultery, as noted in a Times report of March 14, 2007.

Public opinion on this issue has slowly shifted over time. A Times report of June 8, 2007, indicated that, in 2006, 60 percent of Americans favored allowing gays and lesbians to serve openly, with only 32 percent opposed. According to Michael Dimock of the Pew Research Center, "[M]uch of the shift in attitudes is generational. Age is a huge factor."

In the 2008 presidential elections, several Democratic candidates indicated that they would be willing to reconsider the ban, but no Republicans expressed similar intentions. Like Bill Clinton before him, presidential candidate Barack Obama pledged to allow gays and lesbians to serve openly in the military. By the time Obama was elected president, 69 percent of those polled supported lifting the ban, including 58 percent of Republicans and 60 percent of those who describe themselves as weekly churchgoers. Yet, when an Ohio soldier sought to challenge Don't Ask, Don't Tell at the Supreme Court, the Obama administration successfully argued that the case should not be heard, in effect defending

Lt. Dan Choi (right) and his partner Matthew Kinsey at a rally in New York City in 2009. Lt. Choi, an Iraq veteran and Arabic linguist, became a national figure in the movement to repeal the "Don't Ask, Don't Tell" policy after he publicly announced that he was gay.

*Source: Michelle V. Agins/*The New York Times

the policy. James Pietrangelo II, the former army infantry-man who brought the case, said of Obama, "[T]his is a guy who spent more time picking out his dog, Bo, and playing with him on the White House lawn than he has working for gay people," as reported in a *Times* article of June 9, 2009. Noting that Obama had campaigned as a "fierce advocate" for equal rights for gays, many gay leaders continued to hope that he would soon act to lift the remaining restrictions on the service of gays and lesbians within the various branches of the United States military. In 2010 the Pentagon issued a report that suggested 70 percent of military personnel felt that allowing gays and lesbians to serve openly would not negatively affect their work. Based on this report, Congress repealed Don't Ask, Don't Tell on December 18, 2010, lifting the ban on gays serving openly in the military. A *Times* report of December 19, 2010, noted that President Obama embraced this change, saying that it was "time to close this chapter in our history." Another *Times* report of that day focused on implementation. While one army officer who supported lifting the ban argued that the first gay men to serve

in combat "are going to need very thick skins," another predicted that "if an individual is performing well on the battlefield, people won't care." A December 20, 2010, *Times* article titled "After Fall of 'Don't Ask,' Pushing for 'I Do'" predicted that this legislative victory would lead the LGBT movement to focus on legalizing same-sex marriage, shifting greater attention to state rather than federal policy.

BIBLIOGRAPHY

Bérubé, Allan. *Coming Out under Fire: The History of Gay Men and Women in World War Two.* New York: Free Press, 1990.

Frank, Nathaniel. *Unfriendly Fire: How the Gay Ban Undermines the Military and Weakens America.* New York: St. Martin's Press, 2009.

Rosenberg, Robert, John Scagliotti, and Greta Schiller (Producers) and Greta Schiller (Director). *Before Stonewall: The Making of a Gay and Lesbian Community.* First Run Features, 1999.

Shilts, Randy. *Conduct Unbecoming: Gays and Lesbians in the U.S. Military.* New York: St. Martin's Press, 1995.

From *The New York Times*

AP. "Judge Orders Air Force to Readmit Homosexual." September 10, 1980.

———. "U.S. to Pay $160,000 In Homosexual's Suit On Air Force Ousting." November 25, 1980.

Applebome, Peter. "Military People Split Over Ban on Homosexuals: Army; Ranks Are Split, As in Society." January 28, 1993.

Berke, Richard. "Gay Groups Warn President Not to Retreat on Lifting Ban." March 27, 1993.

Bumiller, Elisabeth. "Rare Source of Attack on 'Don't Ask, Don't Tell.'" October 1, 2009.

Clines, Francis X. "Killer's Trial Shows Gay Soldier's Anguish." December 9, 1999.

Cushman, John H., Jr. "The Transition: Gay Rights: Top Military Officers Object to Lifting Homosexual Ban." November 14, 1992.

Dao, James. "Backing 'Don't Ask' Repeal, with Reservations." December 19, 2010.

Duberman, Martin. "The Case of the Gay Sergeant." November 9, 1975.

Files, John. "Gay Ex-Officers Say 'Don't Ask' Doesn't Work." December 10, 2003.

———. "Number of Gays Discharged from Services Drops Again." February 13, 2005.

———. "Washington: $364 Million for Military Ousters." February 15, 2006.

———. "Military's Discharges for Being Gay Rose in '05." August 15, 2006.

Hunter, Charlayne. "Homosexual Seeks to Retain Security Clearance." August 20, 1969.

Johnson, Dirk. "Military People Split Over Ban on Homosexuals: Air Force; Are Homosexuals the New Enemy?" January 28, 1993.

King, Wayne. "Homosexual G.I.'s Ouster Is Recommended by Panel." September 20, 1975.

Lewis, Neil A. "Court Upholds Clinton Policy on Gay Troops." April 6, 1996.

Meyers, Steven Lee. "Gay Group's Study Finds Military Harassment Rising." March 15, 1999.

———. "March 19–25; Anti-Gay Bias in Military." March 26, 2000

Oelsner, Lesley. "Homosexual Is Fighting Military Ouster." May 26, 1975.

Quindlen, Anna. "Public & Private; With Extreme Prejudice." June 24, 1992.

Rohter, Larry. "The Gay Troop Issue; Off Base, Many Sailors Voice Anger toward Homosexuals." January 31, 1993.

Rosenthal, Abe. "On My Mind; General Powell and the Gays." January 26, 1993.

Roth, Jack. "Blackmail Paid By Congressman: Victim among Thousands of Homosexuals Preyed Upon by Ring of Extortionists." May 17, 1967.

Schmaltz, Jeffrey. "March for Gay Rights; Gay Marchers Throng Mall in Appeal for Rights." April 26, 1993.

Schmitt, Eric. "Military's Anti-Gay Rule Is Costly, a Report Says." June 20, 1992.

———. "Marine Corps Chaplain Says Homosexuals Threaten Military." August 26, 1992.

———. "The Inauguration; Clinton Set to End Ban on Gay Troops." January 21, 1993.

———. "Pentagon Chief Warns Clinton on Gay Policy." January 25, 1993.

———. "Military Cites Wide Range of Reasons for Its Gay Ban." January 27, 1993.

———. "Ego and Error on the Gay Issue. January 29, 1993.

———. "Military Praises Gay Policy for Ambiguity and Caution." July 22, 1993.

———. "Judge Overturns Pentagon Policy on Homosexuals." March 31, 1995.

Shalikashvili, John. "Second Thoughts on Gays in the Military." January 2, 2007.

Shanker, Thom. "Top General Explains Remarks on Gays." March 14, 2007.

Stolberg, Sheryl Gay. "After Fall of 'Don't Ask,' Pushing for 'I Do.'" December 20, 2010.

Thomas, Jo. "75,000 March in Capital in Drive to Support Homosexual Rights." October 15, 1979.

Thompson. Mark. "Dismay over Obama's 'Don't Ask, Don't Tell' Turnabout." June 9, 2009.

Toner, Robin. "For 'Don't Ask, Don't Tell,' Split on Party Lines." June 8, 2007.

Truscott, Lucian K, IV. "Truman's Legacy to Clinton." February 1, 1993.

Unsigned. "Senators Ask U.S. Dismiss 'Bad Risks.'" July 21, 1950.

———. "107 U.S. Aides Ousted on Morals, Security." July 3, 1953.

———. "Homosexuals Stage Protest in Capital." May 30, 1965.

———. "Army Clerk's Dismissal Upheld." July 21, 1977.

———. "Homosexuals in the Ranks." September 4, 1980.

———. "End Ban on Gay G.I's, 2 Service Papers Urge." August 20, 1992.

———. "Lift the Ban on Gay Soldiers." November 15, 1992.

———. "Gay Sailor Tells of a 'Living Hell.'" March 8, 1993.

———. "Gay Soldiers: Half a Loaf." July 20, 1993.

———. "'Don't Ask, Don't Tell' Is Challenged in Suit." March 8, 1994.

UPI. "Homosexual Leaders Meet at White House with Presidential Aide to Discuss Discrimination in Federal Law." March 27, 1977.

Van Gelder, Lawrence. "Armed Forces Assailed on Views of Homosexuals; Researchers Report Terms U.S. Policy 'Unwise' and 'Unjust' and States Authorities 'Pursue Group.'" July 19, 1971.

Verhovek, Sam Howe. "Gay Groups Denounce the Pentagon's New Policy." July 21, 1993.

Weiner, Tim. "Military Discharges of Homosexuals Soar." April 7, 1998.

Weinraub, Bernard. "Military, after Appellate Ruling, Starts Review on Homosexuality." December 8, 1978.

Wicker, Tom. "Is Gay a 'Security Risk?'" June 27, 1972.

MILITANTS SAY ENDING THE BAN ON HOMOSEXUALS IN THE MILITARY WOULD AID WAR EFFORT

The Committee to Fight Exclusion of Homosexuals from the Armed Forces launched a national campaign in 1966 designed to end the ban on gays in the military. Based in Los Angeles, the group argued that ending the ban would increase the number of soldiers available for the war in Vietnam. Characterized as an example of a new militancy in the homosexual movement, the group planned to raise public awareness on this issue by distributing leaflets, undertaking a letter-writing campaign to the president, and participating in public debates on local television and radio programs across the country. The effort culminated in parades and demonstrations in several major U.S. cities on May 21, 1966, in recognition of Armed Forces Day. This plan grew out of the two-day National Planning Conference of Homosexual Organizations, held in Kansas City in February, which drew more than forty homosexuals representing fifteen groups nationwide, including the Council on Religion and the Homosexual of San Francisco, the Mattachine Society of New York, and One, Inc. of Kansas City. These groups sought to challenge laws that discriminated against homosexuals and to set up a legal fund to defend those in trouble with the law.

APRIL 17, 1966
WAR ROLE SOUGHT FOR HOMOSEXUALS

Groups to Aid Deviates Ask End to Pentagon Ban
By PETER BART
Special to the New York Times

LOS ANGELES, CA, April 16—A national campaign to end the exclusion of homosexuals from the armed forces was set in motion here this week.

The campaign will culminate in a series of parades and demonstrations in major cities on Armed Forces Day, May 21.

The organization staging the campaign contends there are 17 million homosexuals in the nation, most of whom would be eager to fight for their country. The organization, called the Committee to Fight Exclusion of Homosexuals From the Armed Forces, argues that an end to the ban would ease the shortage of manpower available for service in Vietnam.

Donald Slater, a spokesman for the committee, which is based here, said the drive represented the first manifestation of a new militancy in "the homosexual movement." The campaign, he said, grew out of a convention of homosexual organizations held Feb. 19–20 in Kansas City.

The convention, which was formally called the National Planning Conference of Homosexual Organizations, is said to have represented the first major effort of homosexual groups throughout the nation to organize a unified self-improvement program.

About 40 homosexuals representing 15 groups attended the two-day meeting, among them members of the Council on Religion and the Homosexual of San Francisco; the Janus Society of America, Philadelphia; the Mattachine Society of New York, and One, Inc., of Kansas City.

The homosexuals also agreed to set up a national legal fund to defend homosexuals who are in legal difficulties and to fight against "restrictive" sexual laws.

Mr. Slater discussed the aims of his organization in the small, sparsely furnished offices of Tangents magazine, a homosexual literary periodical of which he is the editor. Tangents, an outgrowth of a defunct publication called One, has a circulation of 5,000, according to its editor, a small, slender man with graying hair. The walls of the office are lined with books dealing with homosexuality. A seminude male adorns a calendar on the wall.

Mr. Slater said he was encouraged to find an increased willingness of homosexuals across the nation to discuss their situation publicly.

He said he did not believe that the homosexual population was increasing relative to the total population but conceded that "it may seem that way because of the trend toward more open discussion."

The campaign on military policy, Mr. Slater said, will focus on distributing leaflets to the public and encouraging people to write to the President. To attract public attention, homosexual groups around the country will seek to go on radio and TV programs and to engage in public debates.

HOMOSEXUAL MARINE CHALLENGES DISCHARGE

A panel composed of three U.S. Marine Corps officers meeting in March of 1972 recommended an undesirable discharge for Lance Cpl. Jeffrey Arthur Dunbar, an avowed homosexual. Dunbar did not deny his homosexual identity but contended he had not engaged in homosexual activities with any marines or while on base. Other sexual activities, he argued, were his own private affair. The case arose when a letter to a man was found in Dunbar's wallet in November of 1971 after Dunbar was taken to the base hospital after attempting suicide. Following an investigation Dunbar's commander recommended an undesirable discharge, which was supported by the administrative panel.

An undesirable discharge falls below both an honorable and a general discharge but above bad conduct and dishonorable discharges. Dunbar hoped to work with the ACLU to form a class-action suit with other affected servicemen (including Ronald L. Stintson, who had received a general discharge from the navy in 1971) that would challenge the ban on homosexuals in the military.

More than thirty activists supporting Dunbar protested outside of the hearing. Franklin Kameny, the founder of the Mattachine Society, testified during the hearing that Dunbar should be given an honorable discharge, arguing that anything less would "permanently render a man unemployable or underemployable." David Addlestone of the ACLU agreed, saying that a less-than-honorable discharge "would only serve as a punishment for the rest of his life."

MARCH 22, 1972
MARINES URGE OUSTER OF A HOMOSEXUAL

Special to the New York Times

QUANTICO, Va., March 21—An administrative board at the Marine Corps base here recommended today that Lance Cpl. Jeffrey Arthur Dunbar, an avowed homosexual, be given an undesirable discharge.

The recommendation for an undesirable discharge, the lowest level of separation from the service that the three-officer panel could recommend, came in a case that attorneys for the American Civil Liberties Union plan to join with other similar suits in an eventual class-action challenge to the armed forces' policy on homosexuals.

Under the recommendation, which is expected to be approved within two months by Gen. Robert E. Cushman, the commandant of the Marine Corps, the 18-year-old marine would be separated from the service with a discharge that ranks below the two top grades of honorable and general, but above the bottom grades of bad conduct and dishonorable, which can only be imposed by a court-martial.

Activists at Hearing

The two-hour hearing today in the headquarters building of this 7,000-man base attracted more than 30 homosexual activists who support Corporal Dunbar.

Franklin Kameny, founder and president of the Mattachine Society, a homosexual organization, testified for nearly an hour and urged the panel to recommend that Corporal Dunbar be given an honorable discharge.

"Anything less than a full honorable discharge effectively means the man is thrown upon the human trash heap," Mr. Kamedy said. "Such a discharge permanently renders a man unemployable or underemployable."

David F. Addlestone, the attorney from the A.C.L.U.'s military law project, who represented Corporal Dunbar, said in his closing argument: "What has [Corporal Dunbar] done to hurt the Marine Corps? A less than honorable discharge would only serve as punishment for the rest of his life."

Class-Action Suit

Mr. Kameny said that homosexual groups and the A.C.L.U. planned to appeal the discharge given to Corporal Dunbar. He added that the case would eventually be joined with that of Ronald L. Stintson, a dental technician who received a general discharge from the Navy last fall for being a homosexual, in a class-action suit designed to bring about a revision of the armed forces' policy toward homosexuals.

Corporal Dunbar, a native of Falls Church, Va., who joined the Marines in August, 1970, after his junior year at George Mason High School in Falls Church, said in a written statement presented to the board: "I freely admit to being a homosexual and to having engaged in homosexual activities while a member of the United States Marine Corps."

Began in High School

Corporal Dunbar added, however, that he had not engaged in any homosexual activities with any marine nor on any Marine base, and contended that his sexual activities off base while he was off duty were his "private affair."

Speaking to reporters before the hearing, Corporal Dunbar said that he began his homosexual activities while in high school. He also said that he continued such activities during his 19 months in the Corps with homosexuals in the communities near the bases where he was stationed.

Corporal Dunbar said he had served as a cook and assisted in setting up physical fitness classes while serving in the Marines. He is expected to remain at this base while the panel's recommendation is being reviewed.

Corporal Dunbar's homosexual activities came to light after he attempted to commit suicide last November. When he was taken to the base hospital, a letter addressed to a man in Oklahoma was found in his wallet. After an investigation, his company commander urged that he be given the undesirable discharge that the administrative panel recommended today.

Seeking Equality for All, Matlovich Challenges Ban

While the U.S. Air Force sought to discharge Sgt. Leonard Matlovich, owing to homosexuality, in 1975, he continued to insist that he was still a patriot fighting to uphold constitutional ideals such as equal protection under the law. A twelve-year veteran and a decorated war hero, Matlovich served three tours of duty in Vietnam, receiving both a Bronze Star and a Purple Heart. In March 1974 Matlovich handed his superior officer a statement declaring his homosexuality. Shortly thereafter, he became one of the most widely known gay men in the country when his picture graced the cover of *Time* magazine along with the headline "I Am a Homosexual."

Matlovich believed that his challenge to the ban on gays in the military was akin to the challenge to racial segregation that occurred in the landmark case of *Brown v. Board of Education*. He maintained that his military oath required him to uphold the Constitution and thus to fight discrimination and other deprivations of equality.

Matlovich's challenge was particularly dramatic given his conservative political and religious background. His devoutly Roman Catholic parents both responded in a strong but ultimately accepting fashion. Matlovich himself, once a conservative Goldwater Republican, admitted that he had been biased against African Americans as a youth, although in the latter years of his service he had become a respected race relations counselor at his base, as testified to by several African American servicemen who spoke on his behalf at his separation hearing. He vowed to continue to fight even if the battle against his own discharge failed, saying that he would "go anywhere there's a soapbox to preach for equality and justice for all, not just gays."

SEPTEMBER 20, 1975
AIR FORCE SERGEANT FEELS HE IS A PATRIOT FIGHTING FOR FREEDOM
Special to the New York Times

HAMPTON, Va., September 19—T. Sgt. Leonard Philip Matlovich, a one-time Goldwater conservative who flew the flag each day from an 18-foot staff in front of his apartment, says that he is still a patriot. He served three tours in Vietnam, was severely wounded when he stepped on a land mine there and can, when he chooses, wear the Bronze Star and the Purple Heart on his Air Force blues.

But at home in his two-bedroom apartment across town from Langley Air Force Base, where he was a race relations counselor, the lanky, chestnut-haired sergeant favors bell bottom bluejeans and an open-collared shirt. On his walls are placards that say, "Legalize Freedom" and, in red, white and blue, "Trust God-She Provides."

The matches on his coffeetable carry the inscription: Say It Loud—Gay and Proud.

Sergeant Matlovich is 32 years old and has been in the Air Force for 12 years.

Proceedings Started

Until last March, when he handed his superior officer a statement declaring himself a homosexual and setting in motion the proceedings that will decide whether that condition is enough to bring about his discharge, Sergeant Matlovich was just another soldier, although one with a distinguished record of service.

Now, framed on his wall, is a recent Time magazine cover featuring a picture of the uniformed, beribboned sergeant with the pronouncement "I Am a Homosexual" emblazoned in bold black letters across his chest.

Why did he do it—"come out of the closet," as the expression goes?

Sitting cross-legged on the floor of his apartment, boyish and at ease, the sergeant recalled that when he had handed his "coming-out" statement to his superior, a black captain, the captain said, "What does this mean?"

"I said, 'It means Brown v. the Board of Education'—a test of sexual rights of landmark proportions equal to that of the 1954 Supreme Court decision outlawing school segregation.

"I told him to sit down before he read it. He didn't, but he sat down after he read it."

'Simply Another Cause'

For his parents, devout Roman Catholics living in Florida, the jolt was far more severe. When Sergeant Matlovich told his mother by phone, her stunned reply was, "God is punishing me for something I've done."

"Her next reaction," the sergeant recalled, "was that I hadn't prayed enough, that I hadn't seen enough psychiatrists."

Mrs. Matlovich told her son that she had known, or suspected, the truth since he was 19, but then settled on the conviction that her son was "simply trumpeting another cause," the sergeant said.

She refused to tell the sergeant's father, himself a former Air Force sergeant who now operates a refrigeration business. It was left for him to read about it in the newspapers.

"He cried for about two hours," Sergeant Matlovich said, "and then he told my mother, 'If he can take it, I can take it.'"

"They both say they still love me, and I talked to them by phone, but I haven't been home since then.

"I'm sure they're much different people now, hopefully, much better people."

Although Sergeant Matlovich said that he knew, or suspected, that he was homosexual as early as 12 ("I've never liked women, sexually, my whole life"), he did not act on that knowledge until two years ago when he was 30 and went into a "gay bar" in Pensacola, Fla., where he was stationed.

Exclusion Challenged

Frightened by his own feelings—"I'd read that all homosexuals were sadists or masochists"—and fearing to put himself into a den of homosexuals—"My God, I've heard of those 27 [homosexual] killings in Texas"—Sergeant Matlovich found that the bar was low-key and filled with people pretty much like himself, he said. Later, he became a practicing homosexual—his first sexual experience.

The experience, Sergeant Matlovich said, led him to challenge the exclusion of homosexuals from military service.

But why not go into a civilian profession more tolerant of homosexuals?

"First of all, I love the military," he said. "And the first time in the bar, I met a bank president who was petrified he'd be found out. I decided then and there I was not going to jump from job to job."

Also, Sergeant Matlovich contends that his military oath to uphold the Constitution requires him to fight what he believes is a deprivation of equal rights and protection under the law.

The acceptance of his homosexuality by his "straight" friends, who he avoided at first, has been heartening, the sergeant said.

"Last night, I got a call from my third-grade teacher wishing me luck," he said.

"A 46-year-old man from Massachusetts was calling me, but he's stopped. I'm afraid he's committed suicide. He was still celibate at 46, and he called and cried and cursed God. Then it stopped.

"I keep my phone listed because of things like that."

Increasingly liberal over the last few years, Sergeant Matlovich said that his days as a conservative were over.

Among his major supporters have been several blacks on the base who have testified to his abilities as a race-relations counselor.

"As each black witness got up there [at the Air Force hearing on his discharge], I felt a little shame, because a few years ago, I used the word nigger," he said. "When the blacks were seeking freedom in the sixties, I was against them; now they're defending me."

If his battle against discharge fails, the sergeant said, he will "go anywhere there's a soapbox to preach for equality and justice for all, not just gays." He went on:

"I'm going to hold up a Bicentennial 50-cent piece that says 200 years of freedom and say, 'Not yet—maybe someday, but not yet."

Court Rules in Favor of Homosexuals, Criticizing Policy Governing Ban

In December 1978 a federal court of appeals found that two homosexuals, Sgt. Leonard Matlovich of the air force and Ens. Vernon Berg of the navy, were wrongly dismissed from the armed forces, stating that the policy governing the discharge of homosexuals was insufficiently clear. The court noted that the military had retained some homosexuals, but that the policy in place at the time lacked a clear rule to guide such exceptions, making it impossible in the cases of Matlovich and Berg "to decide whether or not there has been an abuse of discretion in this instance or whether improper factors have played a material role."

DECEMBER 7, 1978
COURT SAYS 2 HOMOSEXUALS WERE WRONGLY DISMISSED FROM MILITARY

By A. O. SULZBERGER JR.

Special to the New York Times

WASHINGTON, Dec. 6—Two homosexuals were unfairly discharged from the military, the United States Court of Appeals for the District of Columbia ruled today.

The holding, which reverses two separate District Court decisions, means that former Tech. Sgt. Leonard P. Matlovich of the Air Force and former Ens. Vernon E. Berg 3d of the Navy must have further proceedings in their respective branches of the armed forces. The ruling leaves the way open for full trials.

The earlier Federal District Court decision was a summary judgment, which means that a full trial was not held.

In its ruling the court criticized the two branches for their failure to establish a clear policy on discharging homosexuals.

Told Office of Homosexuality

"The absence of articulated standards, policies, or considerations—plus the absence of any reasoned explanation in this case—makes it impossible to decide whether or not there has been an abuse of discretion in this instance or whether improper factors have played a material role," the court said.

"Mr. Matlovich, a decorated Vietnam veteran with 12 years of service, was given an honorable discharge from the Air Force in October 1975 after he told his commanding officer at Langley Air Force Base in Virginia, in a letter, that he was a homosexual.

In July 1976, Federal District Judge Gerhard A. Gesell upheld the right of the Air Force to discharge Mr. Matlovich.

But in today's ruling, the appeals court found that the Air Force had in the past retained on active duty personnel who had engaged in homosexual activity, making an exception to its usual practice of dismissal.

Remanded Case for Reconsideration

"But what disturbs us is that it is impossible to tell on what grounds the Service refused to make an exception or how it distinguished his case from the ones in which homosexuals had been retained," the court said.

For similar reasons, the appeals court remanded to the Secretary of the Navy the case of Mr. Berg, a former officer who acknowledged engaging in homosexual acts while in the service.

In May 1977, almost a year after his discharge with less than honorable conditions, later upgraded to honorable, Judge Gesell also dismissed Mr. Berg's suit seeking reinstatement and back pay.

"It is proper, therefore, to call upon the service for a fuller articulation and explanation of its policy on retention of homosexuals and the application of those standards to Berg's case," the appeals court said.

Women Discharged from Marines for Homosexuality at Higher Rates than Men

Defense Department statistics compiled between 1983 and 1988 showed that women were discharged for homosexual conduct nearly ten times more frequently than men were. During 1988, 18 of 120 women drill instructors were discharged or imprisoned for homosexual behavior as a result of an investigation into lesbian activities at Parris Island, South Carolina, a Marine Corps Recruit Depot. In response to charges by gay rights groups that such statistics may indicate selective prosecution, a Marine spokesperson for Parris Island denied any bias, saying that "the Marines treat men and women equally."

James Woodward of the San Diego Veterans Association argued that the military usually does not "go after gay men in the kind of coordinated, full-out way that they go after women." Comparing the Parris Island investigation to a McCarthy-like witch hunt, he argued that "it was precipitated not by any problems in the performance of duties, but from allegations of off-base, off-duty relationships." Noting that studies at the time estimated that 7 percent of men and 3 percent of women are homosexual, Thomas Stoddard of the Lambda Legal Defense and Education Fund said that "on the face of it, the only explanation why Parris Island would be discharging 10 times as many lesbians as gay men is selective prosecution."

DECEMBER 4, 1988
GAY GROUPS SUGGEST MARINES SELECTIVELY PROSECUTE WOMEN
By TAMAR LEWIN

Over the last year about 10 percent of the 120 women who were drill instructors at the Marine Corps Recruit Training Depot at Parris Island, S.C., have been discharged or imprisoned for homosexual behavior.

Since 1983, Defense Department statistics show, lesbians have been discharged for homosexual conduct at a rate almost 10 times that of homosexual military men.

Under the Uniform Code of Military Justice, homosexuality itself is not prohibited, but homosexual acts are. Gay rights groups say the marines may be guilty of selective prosecution, but the Corps denies that.

A Parris Island spokesman, Maj. Robert MacLean, said, "The Marines treat men and women equally."

Two drill instructors and a military policewoman from Parris Island are serving time in the brig at Quantico, Va., after being court-martialed and convicted of indecent acts or of sodomy. On Thursday the military policewoman, Cpl. Barbara J. Baum, was granted clemency and told she would be freed Dec. 15, rather than serving out the one-year sentence she began in June.

Granted Immunity for Testifying

"We're going to file an appeal anyway," said Corporal Baum's lawyer, Susan Masling, of Washington, D.C. "I think it's outrageous that she should have had to serve even a day in the brig for her sexual preferences."

Corporal Baum, 24 years old, of Mishawaka, Ind., was charged with sodomy, indecent acts and conspiring to obstruct justice after a former boyfriend of Lance Cpl. Diana Maldonado reported finding the two women in bed in a motel. After her conviction, Corporal Baum agreed to cooperate with investigators and was interrogated for 14 hours. Corporal Maldonado was granted immunity in return for testifying about lesbian activity at Parris Island.

Corporal Baum and the drill instructors may not speak to the press, but Ms. Masling and several gay rights groups say the Marine Corps may be guilty of selective prosecution in its yearlong investigation of lesbian activity at Parris Island.

Witch Hunts Are Evoked

"Very seldom does the military go after gay men in the kind of coordinated, full-out way that they go after the women," said James Woodward, public affairs officer for the San Diego Veterans Association of gay and lesbian veterans. "The Parris Island investigation has been the epitome of the old McCarthy witch hunts. It was precipitated not by any problems in the performance of duties, but from allegations of off-base, off-duty relationships. Throughout the investigation, the whole direction of the interrogations has been, 'If you give us names, we'll be easy on you.'"

Thomas Stoddard, executive director of the Lambda Legal Defense Fund, a New York-based gay rights group, said: "There are no good current statistics on homosexuality in the population, but back in the 1940's, the Kinsey Institute found that 7 percent of men and 3 percent of women are homosexual. So, on the face of it, the only explanation why Parris Island would be discharging 10 times as many lesbians as gay men is selective prosecution."

Martin Weinberg, a sociologist and sex researcher at Indiana University at Bloomington, has worked with the Kinsey Institute. He says that while the percentage of lesbians has probably increased since the early Kinsey studies, it has not increased enough to account for the differences in the discharge rates.

"It's possible that there are as many lesbians as gay men, but there certainly aren't 10 times as many," he said. "And while professional athletics and the armed services attract lesbians proportionately more than heterosexual women, we're still not talking about numbers big enough to account for that difference."

Ms. Masling, Corporal Baum's lawyer, said the military prosecutors were also selectively choosing to overlook heterosexual sodomy, though it is illegal under military law. "There's got to be sodomy occurring between heterosexuals and no one is going after that at all," she said. "The way the law is enforced is suspect and hypocritical since the statute, as it's written, is gender-neutral. The whole policy against homosexuality is wrong. These women are spending their careers trying to serve their country, and I think it's incredible that the U.S. Government should say they're not suitable to serve without evidence to back it up."

Treated Equally, Corps Says

Major MacLean, the spokesman for Parris Island, said the Marine Corps did not treat men and women differently. "When we run across infractions of the code of military justice, we take action aggressively in both cases," he said.

"I know some people would like to see us change our policy on homosexuality, but we don't formulate policy," Major MacLean said. "We have to enforce the rules Congress gives us and our policies are well known to everyone who enlists. They're asked on the enlistment form, in black and white, 'Are you homosexual or have you engaged in homosexual activities?'"

Parris Island, one of two Marine Corps boot camps and the only one where women are sent for basic training, has about 80 female drill instructors at a given time, or about 120 over the course of a year.

As a result of an investigation into lesbian activities at the boot camp, 11 women among drill instructors, along with 7 other women, have been administratively discharged for homosexual behavior, or court-martialed and charged with sodomy and indecent acts.

- - -

PENTAGON RESEARCH CENTER ASKS MILITARY TO RECONSIDER BAN ON HOMOSEXUALS

The Pentagon's Personnel Security Research and Education Center issued a draft report in 1989 that called for the ban on gays in the military to be rethought, contending that the practice of exclusion was discriminatory and without merit. The report recommended that the Pentagon develop programs "to test the hypothesis that men and women of atypical sexual orientation can function appropriately in military units" similar to the manner in which African Americans were integrated into the military in the late 1940s.

The Pentagon quickly rejected the report as "biased, flawed, offensive and wasteful of Government resources," arguing that the center had exceeded its mandate by considering homosexuals' suitability for military service rather than simply the potential threat they posed to security. Stating that this was "a distinction without a difference," Rep. Patricia Schroeder (D-CO), a member of the House Armed Services Committee, said that the report was based on "an excellent academic survey of the available literature." She added that "the problem is that the Defense Department doesn't want to deal with it."

The report found no evidence that homosexuals posed a greater security risk than heterosexuals. Dr. Theodore Sarbin, a research psychologist who authored the report, said that anyone with a secret could be blackmailed "whether homosexual or heterosexual. It can be anything— adultery, bankruptcy, unprosecuted felonies." In addition, there was no correlation between homosexuality and standard indicators of suitability for service. The report considered those with "nonconforming sexual orientation as a minority group," a categorization "more in tune with current behavioral science theory than earlier constructions: sin, crime and sickness."

Noting that upcoming court challenges and congressional initiatives were likely to compel the military to rethink the ban, the report stated that the military's workforce needs could be better met if the ban were lifted. Current military policy bars those who engage in homosexual conduct from serving in the military on the grounds that they would undermine discipline, good order, and morale. A 1981 update of the policy further excluded those who demonstrated not only homosexual conduct but also a propensity to engage in homosexual activity.

OCTOBER 22, 1989
REPORT URGING END OF HOMOSEXUAL BAN REJECTED BY MILITARY

By ELAINE SCIOLINO
Special to the New York Times

WASHINGTON, Oct. 21—A draft report by a Pentagon research center concludes that the American military should consider ending discriminatory practices against homosexuals and allowing them in the services.

But the Pentagon has rejected the report as exceeding its mandate. Calling it biased, flawed, offensive and wasteful of Government resources, a senior official said in internal Pentagon correspondence that the report went far beyond its task of determining security risks posed by homosexuals in the military when it examined the broader question of their suitability for military duty.

Representatives Release Report

The unclassified report and the Pentagon correspondence were made available by members of Congress who believe that homosexuals should be permitted to serve in the military.

The report, "Nonconforming Sexual Orientations and Military Suitability," was completed 10 months ago by the Defense Department's Personnel Security Research and Education Center in Monterey, Calif.

The Pentagon created the center in 1987 after a spy network was discovered operating in the Navy. The center's purpose is to study behavioral aspects of personnel security and analyze what kind of people make good custodians of classified information. The small research unit has no authority to make policy recommendations.

The report says the Pentagon should rethink its policy of barring homosexuals from service. The Pentagon has long held that those who engage in homosexual conduct in the military undermine "discipline, good order and morale." In 1982, that policy was broadened to include men and women who demonstrate a "propensity" to engage in homosexual activity.

Legal Change Is Seen

The report said the Government would probably be forced by court rulings to undertake such a re-examination.

The Pentagon's policy has faced several legal challenges in recent years and a number of court cases are pending.

The report dealt only briefly with the security issue, concluding that there was no evidence that homosexuals were any greater security risk than heterosexuals and no more likely to be liable to blackmail.

The Pentagon said in a written statement Friday after being asked about the study: "The report was merely a draft recommendation, which was not accepted by the Department of Defense because it was not responsive to the original research request. We cannot comment on matters that remain unresolved before the court."

Center Defends Report

Defending its approach, the research center, in a memorandum to the Pentagon last January, implied that the Pentagon would have found the report "instrumental" if its findings had supported current Pentagon policy. The memo said the findings "should not be invalidated because the results turned out to be problematic from a policy perspective."

Pentagon officials have asked a co-author of the report, Dr. Theodore R. Sarbin, to prepare a new report focusing solely on the security question. Dr. Sarbin, a research psychologist and a part-time consultant at the research center, stood by the validity of his report and said he expected the new report to draw the same conclusion as the original.

Dr. Sarbin, a professor emeritus in psychology and criminology at the University of California at Santa Cruz, said of the report's conclusions in a telephone interview from his home in Carmel, Calif.: "I don't think anything there can be challenged. All the information is contained in documents already in the public domain."

Dr. Sarbin wrote the report with Capt. Kenneth E. Karols, a psychiatrist and surgeon, who is still in the Navy but no longer with the research center.

Manpower Needs Cited

The center's official position on the draft report is not known. The current acting director, Dr. Roger Denk, who took over after the report was completed, did not return a reporter's telephone call seeking comment.

The report examined data relating to why people were found unsuitable for the military and concluded that there was no correlation between homosexuality and other indicators of suitability. Citing continuing manpower needs in

the armed forces and social pressures to remove barriers to homosexuals, the report concluded that the Pentagon should begin to think about accepting homosexuals into the services.

"Our analysis directs us to regard people with non-conforming sexual orientation as a minority group," the report says, adding that such categorization "is more in tune with current behavioral science theory than the earlier constructions: sin, crime and sickness."

It said that if the military's current policy survives, either the courts or Congress will force it to be re-examined.

The report's primary recommendation was that the Pentagon develop research programs "to test the hypothesis that men and women of atypical sexual orientation can function appropriately in military units" in the same way that blacks were integrated into the military 40 years ago.

Primary Personnel Problem

But the presence of homosexuals in the military is legally the most sensitive personnel problem facing the American military today, and the unclassified report has caused a firestorm of protest at the Pentagon.

In a letter last January to the director of the research center, Craig Alderman Jr., Deputy Under Secretary of Defense for Policy, said the organization had no authority to conduct research on whether homosexuals were suitable for military service.

He added that the Pentagon found the report "to be technically flawed, to contain subject matter (Judeo-Christian precepts) which has no place in a Department of Defense publication, to reflect significant omissions with respect to relevant court decisions concerning personnel security and to suggest a bias"—a bias, he said, that did justice to neither the research center nor the Defense Department.

In an internal Defense Department memorandum in February, Mr. Alderman predicted that the study "will probably cause us in Washington to expend even more time and effort satisfying concerns in this whole issue area both in Congress and the media, and within the department itself."

'Excellent Academic Survey'

A number of lawmakers who have read the report have asked the Pentagon to make it public.

"The report was an excellent academic survey of the available literature," said Representative Patricia Schroeder, a Colorado Democrat who is a member of the House Armed Services Committee. "The problem is that the Defense Department doesn't want to deal with it."

In a meeting to discuss the report last Wednesday, Ms. Schroeder said she was told by Maynard Anderson, Assistant Deputy Under Secretary of Defense for counterintelligence and security policy, that the research center was nearing completion of a new report focusing on whether homosexuals in the military are susceptible to blackmail.

"We asked for an explanation of why the Defense Department killed the report," she said. "We were told the report's mandate was to look at the reliability of homosexuals for security reasons, not the suitability of homosexuals for military service. I found that a distinction without a difference."

Mr. Alderman and Mr. Anderson said through a Pentagon spokesman that they had no comment on the report.

Same Conclusion Drawn

Dr. Sarbin acknowledged that he did not draw a sharp distinction between the "suitability" of a homosexual for military service and the person's "reliability" for access to classified information, a subtle but important distinction within the military bureaucracy.

Dr. Sarbin said his new report focusing on security issues would contain the same basic conclusions as the original, particularly that homosexuals are no greater security risks than heterosexuals.

Only a small portion of the original report dealt with security, concluding that the number of cases of blackmail as a result of past investigations of homosexuals is negligible.

"Anybody who has a secret is a potential for blackmail, whether homosexual or heterosexual," said Dr. Sarbin. "It can be anything—adultery, bankruptcy, unprosecuted felonies, adultery and sexual orientation. That conclusion will be borne out in the new report."

COURT FINDS MILITARY BAN ON GAYS UNCONSTITUTIONAL

In 1988, for the first time in U.S. history, a federal appeals court prohibited a branch of the military from excluding people from service on the grounds of sexual orientation. Finding that homosexuals had been discriminated against in a manner that "is plainly no less pernicious or intense than the discrimination faced by other groups," the U.S. Court of Appeals in San Francisco called the U.S. Army's ban unconstitutional, saying that the Fifth Amendment entitles homosexuals to equal protection under the law in a manner similar to racial minority groups. Writing for the court, Judge William Norris said that the ban on homosexuals was as legally suspect as laws that prohibited interracial marriage, which were struck down by the Supreme Court in 1967. He added that the nation's historical experience of discrimination makes laws based on race and sexual orientation constitutionally suspect absent a strongly persuasive argument offered by the government. Norris said that the army's argument that the presence of homosexuals would harm military morale and discipline did not pass constitutional muster.

The ruling arose from the case of Sgt. Perry Watkins, who had acknowledged his homosexuality repeatedly over his long career in the army, beginning with a medical form he filled out prior to enlisting in the army in 1967. At that time soldiers could be discharged only for homosexual acts. In 1981 the policy was amended to allow service members to be discharged as well for claiming to be a homosexual. Although Watkins was never said to have committed specific homosexual acts, he was discharged in 1984 for being a homosexual, four years short of retirement with a pension. Like many of the approximately 1,400 service members who were annually discharged for homosexuality at that time, Watkins's ability to perform his job was never in question.

Thomas Stoddard, of the Lambda Legal Defense and Education Fund, called the ruling "the most important judicial opinion issued in the history of the gay rights movement," stating that it could have broad implications, possibly extending to custody, immigration, and other cases involving homosexuals. Some experts questioned whether the ruling would stand given the precedent of *Bowers v. Hardwick,* a 1986 case that allowed states to pass laws criminalizing sodomy (see the previous chapter). Judge Norris argued that *Bowers* was not pertinent because antisodomy laws are based on actual conduct, unlike the military ban, which is based simply on a declared sexual orientation. However, Judge Stephen Reinhardt, the sole dissenter in the case, said that *Bowers's* precedent made it impossible for him to vote to overturn the ban.

FEBRUARY 11, 1988
HOMOSEXUAL BAN IN ARMY REJECTED BY APPEALS COURT
By TAMAR LEWIN

A Federal appeals court in San Francisco struck down the Army's ban on homosexuals yesterday, ruling that homosexuals are entitled to as much protection against discrimination as members of racial minority groups.

The United States Court of Appeals for the Ninth Circuit ruled 2 to 1 that the discrimination that homosexuals face "is plainly no less pernicious or intense than the discrimination faced by other groups."

The ruling was the first by a Federal appeals court prohibiting a branch of the armed services from excluding people on the basis of sexual orientation. The Army had argued that homosexuals would impede recruitment and create problems of morale and discipline.

Legal Experts See an Appeal

The Defense Department had no immediate comment on the ruling. The decision was hailed by a representative of the gay rights movement, who said it could have implications far beyond the military if it is upheld.

Richard K. Willard, head of the Justice Department's civil division, said he could not say whether there would be an appeal until he saw the decision.

Legal experts said an appeal was almost certain.

Whether the ruling would stand on appeal is unclear, however. In recent years, the United States Supreme Court has not been receptive to homosexual rights cases. In 1986, in Bowers vs. Hardwick, the Court upheld a Georgia anti-sodomy law allowing criminal prosecution for private homosexual acts.

Judge Kennedy Could Be Key

And Anthony M. Kennedy, who is to join the Supreme Court next week, upheld the Navy's right to exclude people for homosexual conduct in a case he decided in 1980 when he was a judge on the same court that issued yesterday's decision.

However, several legal experts said Judge Kennedy's reasoning in that case was so nuanced that it was impossible to be sure how he would rule in the current case. This case is different from the earlier one in that it does not involve charges of specific sexual conduct but a soldier's statement that he is homosexual.

Judge William A. Norris, in the 60-page decision, which was joined by Judge William Canby, drew a distinction between the Georgia sodomy case and the military ban on homosexuality, holding that the High Court's 1986 ruling did not necessarily apply to the case at hand, since the sodomy laws were based on actual conduct, while the military ban was based simply on "sexual orientation."

Judge Norris said the Army ban would apply even to those who desired homosexual contact but committed no sexual act, while heterosexuals who engaged in homosexual acts while intoxicated might not come under the ban.

"If a straight soldier and a gay soldier of the same sex engage in homosexual acts because they are drunk, immature or curious, the straight soldier may remain in the Army while the gay soldier is automatically terminated," the decision said. "In short, the regulations do not penalize soldiers for engaging in homosexual acts; they penalize soldiers who have engaged in homosexual acts only when the Army decides that those soldiers are actually gay."

The majority said the military rules therefore violate the Fifth Amendment, which bars discrimination by the Government without compelling justification.

Judge Norris wrote that the ban on homosexuals in the military was just as offensive, legally, as the old laws against miscegenation.

"Laws that limit the acceptable focus of one's sexual desires to members of the opposite sex, like laws that limit one's choice of spouse (or sexual partner) to members of the same race, cannot withstand constitutional scrutiny absent a compelling governmental justification," he said.

'Most Important Opinion'

Thomas Stoddard, executive director of the Lambda Legal Defense and Education Fund, said: "This is the most important judicial opinion issued in the history of the gay rights movement. I'm sure that it will be appealed to the Supreme Court, but if it stands, it will have an impact far beyond the military. The court's broad endorsement of gay people's constitutional rights would affect custody and immigration cases involving homosexuals, and make it easier for gay people to work in the F.B.I or the C.I.A."

In a dissenting opinion, Judge Stephen Reinhardt said that while he felt the military ban was unconstitutional, the High Court's decision in the sodomy case left him no choice but to uphold the ban.

Dissent Cites High Court

"Like the majority, I believe that homosexuals have been unfairly treated both historically and in the United States today," he said in his opinion. "Were I free to apply my own view of the meaning of the Constitution and in that light to pass upon the validity of the Army's regulations, I too would conclude that the Army may not refuse to enlist homosexuals."

Judge Reinhardt said that although he was certain that Bowers v. Hardwick "will be overruled by a wiser and more enlightened Court," the decision as it stands appeared to him to uphold the legality of the military ban.

"Homosexuals are defined by their conduct—or, at the least, by their desire to engage in certain conduct," Judge Reinhardt said. "With other groups, such as blacks or women, there is no connection between particular conduct and the definition of the group. When conduct that plays a central role in defining a group may be prohibited by the state, it cannot be asserted with any legitimacy that the group is specially protected by the Constitution."

Judge Reinhardt said that because of the Bowers v. Hardwick decision, he could not agree with the majority opinion that homosexuals must be treated as a class entitled to special protection under the Constitution.

Case Sent Back to Trial Court

Exactly how widely yesterday's ruling will apply was unclear. In its ruling, the appeals court sent the case back to the trial court, with instructions to declare the Army regulations constitutionally void. Technically, the ruling applies only to the states in the Ninth Judicial Circuit: California, Oregon, Washington, Idaho, Arizona, Nevada, Montana, Alaska and Hawaii.

But lawyers specializing in constitutional litigation said that as a practical matter, the Army would probably stop enforcing the regulations nationwide, as would other branches of the military, which apply the same policies on homosexuality.

In Bowers v. Hardwick, the High Court ruled 5 to 4 that neither the 14th Amendment guarantee of liberty nor the constitutional right to privacy created a right to engage in homosexual sodomy.

The fifth vote for the majority came from Lewis F. Powell Jr., the Justice whose place Judge Kennedy will take.

Yesterday's ruling came in the case of Perry Watkins, a career soldier who repeatedly acknowledged his homosexuality, starting with a statement on a preinduction medical form he filled out when enlisting in 1967.

At the time, the Army's policy was to discharge soldiers for sodomy, but not simply for being homosexuals.

Sergeant Watkins was not found to have committed any specific sexual acts and the Army never contended that his job performance was impaired, but the Army regulations were changed in 1981 to require that all homosexual be discharged. Sergeant Watkins was discharged in 1984, four years short of the 20 years required for a pension.

The decision ordered the Army to reconsider Mr. Watkins's application for re-enlistment.

1,400 Homosexuals Discharged

About 1,400 men and women a year are discharged from the military on the grounds of homosexuality.

The Watkins case, brought by the American Civil Liberties Union of Seattle, has been in the courts for several years. In fact, the same appeals court that issued yesterday's opinion upheld the military's right to discharge homosexuals in a 1983 ruling in Mr. Watkins's case. That decision was not based on the constitutional arguments, but was limited to arguments that the Army was barred from discharging him on the grounds of homosexuality since he had disclosed his homosexuality at the time he joined the military.

Judge Norris dissented in the court's 1983 decision.

In the decision yesterday, Judge Norris said that the Army's argument that homosexuals in the military would hurt morale and discipline was no more acceptable legally than the similar concerns military officials used to offer to justify racial segregation in the ranks.

Mr. Stoddard of Lambda Legal Defense Fund said the military adopted an explicit policy against homosexuals in the late 1940's.

"It was very closely tied to the McCarthy business and the fear of communism, the notion that homosexuals are unstable and dangerous because of their terrible secret," he said. "I say that with irony."

Openly Gay Service Member Reinstated in the Navy

In 1992 a federal judge ordered an openly gay service member to be reinstated to his post in the U.S. Navy. The case arose when Keith Meinhold, a twelve-year military veteran, stated that he was a homosexual on national television in May 1992. Appearing on ABC's *World News Tonight,* Meinhold asserted that the navy had been conducting a witch hunt for homosexuals. He was honorably discharged in August, and he sued to be reinstated, arguing that the ban on gays in the military violates the Constitution's equal protection clause.

The navy initially refused to reinstate him despite a court order. Upon arriving at his base, Meinhold was told in writing that he would not be reinstated. In response, Judge Terry Hatter said, "This is not a military dictatorship. It is not the former Soviet Socialist Republic. Here, the rule of law applies to the military." Pentagon spokesperson Pete Williams said that Meinhold would be sworn back into the navy following the Veterans Day holiday.

Meinhold's attorney argued that the visible presence of a known gay man would undermine the military's argument that homosexuals undermine good order, morale, and discipline in the ranks. Although some gay rights advocates worried that the ruling could be overturned by a higher court, thus creating a potential obstacle to President-elect Clinton's vow to reverse the ban on gays in the military, Meinhold's lawyer said, "[B]etween then and now I think we should fight the policy with all the ammunition at our disposal."

NOVEMBER 11, 1992
NAVY WILL OBEY ORDER TO RESTORE GAY SOLDIER'S JOB
By SETH MYDANS

LOS ANGELES, Nov. 10—The Navy said today that it would comply with a Federal judge's order to reinstate temporarily a sailor who had been discharged after declaring on national television that he was homosexual.

The judge, Terry J. Hatter Jr. of the United States District Court, declared, "This is not a military dictatorship," in reaffirming his order to the Navy to reinstate the sailor, Keith Meinhold, by Thursday.

"It is not the former Soviet Socialist Republic," the judge went on. "Here, the rule of law applies to the military."

He said he would hear arguments next Monday on a motion by the Navy to overturn his original order, a temporary injunction issued on Friday while the merits of the case are considered.

The Navy refused to comply with that order on Monday and barred the sailor from his base. At the hearing today the sailor's lawyers asked to have the Navy declared in contempt for its action on Monday, but Judge Hatter reaffirmed his order, giving the Navy a second opportunity to comply with it.

The Navy issued a one-sentence statement that it would comply with today's order. A Justice Department spokesman in Washington, Joe Krovisky, said the department was "studying the judge's order and considering our options."

Soon after the court hearing, a Pentagon spokesman, Pete Williams, said the Navy would swear Mr. Meinhold back into the Navy on Thursday. Wednesday is a holiday, Veterans' Day. "The sailor is supposed to show up on Thursday, the oath of office will be administered and he will be immediately reinstated," Mr. Williams said. "He will pick up in his old job where he left off."

'Broad Ramifications'

At his home in Palo Alto, where a gay-pride rainbow flag flies alongside an American flag, the 30-year-old Mr. Meinhold said: "I'm elated. Hopefully I'll be in a nice shipshape Navy uniform by Thursday morning."

His lawyer, John McGuire, said: "Come Thursday morning it will be the first time any openly gay service member will be reinstated in the military. I think it will have broad ramifications on policy because the Navy has alleged up till now that the presence of gays is disruptive of good order, morale and discipline."

Gay-rights advocates praised the ruling but said that it could paradoxically be a setback for their cause.

President-elect Bill Clinton has declared his readiness to sign an executive order that would overturn the current ban on homosexuals in the military. But the gay-rights advocates said that if the case reached the United States Supreme Court before Mr. Clinton's inauguration, it could be overturned in a ruling that could impede the gay-rights movement.

Tom Stoddard, a leading gay-rights lawyer, praised Judge Hatter, but he added, "I'm worried about the ultimate disposition of this case by a hostile Supreme Court."

On Friday, Judge Hatter had ordered the Navy to reinstate Mr. Meinhold to his job as a sonar crew instructor at the Moffett Field Naval Air Station in Sunnyvale, Calif., near San Jose. But 15 minutes after Mr. Meinhold reported for work on Monday, he walked out with a letter from the station's legal adviser, Lieut. Janice Monk. "I must advise you that local Navy authorities at Naval Air Station Moffett Field are not authorized to reinstate you," it said.

Temporary Reinstatement

That led to Judge Hatter's reaffirmation of his reinstatement order today. The judge, who was appointed by President Jimmy Carter, said his ruling was not on the merits of Mr. Meinhold's suit and added that the reinstatement order was effective only until the newly scheduled hearing next Monday.

The Navy's lawyers argued today before Judge Hatter that his order for reinstatement "flies in the face of present military policy, rules and regulations designed to promote military order and discipline, morale and combat effectiveness."

Mr. Meinhold, a 12-year veteran, made his homosexuality public on the ABC News program "World News Tonight" in May. At the time he said he was gay and accused the Navy of conducting a witch hunt for homosexuals.

The Navy gave him an honorable discharge in August. He sued to be reinstated, arguing that the military's ban on homosexuals violated the Constitution's equal protection clause and provisions that prohibit punishment of a particular class of people. Since August, Mr. Meinhold has been working as a computer salesman in Palo Alto.

Finding Encouragement

His lawyer, Mr. McGuire, said he was encouraged by the strong words from Judge Hatter. "He said that his decision was not based on some technicality," the lawyer went on, "but on his finding that once the case comes to trial that it was likely that Michael would be able to prove that the Navy's regulation is unconstitutional."

Asked about the assertion that this case could be a setback for gay rights if it moved quickly to the Supreme Court, he replied: "I trust President-elect Clinton. I believe he's going to reverse the ban. In the amount of time we have between now and then I think we should fight the policy with all the ammunition at our disposal."

He added that it was his job to work to advance his client's own interests, and that Mr. Meinhold is eager to return to his post.

Wearing a red plaid shirt and blue jeans, the thin, blond sailor seemed elated after the judge's ruling today. But he cautioned other gay sailors, saying, "I wouldn't come flying out of the closet now until the policy has changed, but it looks like there is light at the end of the tunnel."

CLINTON RENEWS PROMISE TO OVERTURN BAN

In 1992 President-elect Clinton vowed to fulfill his campaign pledge to lift the ban on gays in the military, while Gen. Colin Powell, chair of the Joint Chiefs of Staff, said that reversing the ban would disrupt good order and discipline in the military. Although Clinton could unilaterally lift the ban by issuing an executive order, much the same as President Truman did in 1948 when he ended racial segregation in the armed forces, many experts anticipated that he would negotiate the manner and timing of the change with Gen. Powell. Public opinion polls indicated at the time that most Americans favored lifting the ban.

A Pentagon study released prior to 1992 undermined the longstanding argument that homosexuals were more susceptible to blackmail, showing that homosexuals were no more a security threat than heterosexuals. Despite his ongoing support for the ban, Defense Secretary Dick Cheney characterized the claim that homosexuals present an increased security risk as "an old chestnut."

While many military leaders acknowledged at the time that homosexuals served in secret, they worried that open homosexuality would seriously disrupt unit morale and management, perhaps leading to mass resignations and recruiting difficulties. An unnamed official said that Clinton was sensitive to the enormity of this change for military culture and wanted to move forward with the input of military leaders.

NOVEMBER 12, 1992
THE TRANSITION:
News Analysis—
Challenging the Military;
In Promising to End Ban on Homosexuals, Clinton Is Confronting a Wall of Tradition
By ERIC SCHMITT

WASHINGTON, Nov. 11—In saying today that he would honor his campaign pledge to lift the military's ban on homosexuals, President-elect Bill Clinton is challenging one of the military's most entrenched traditions.

Gen. Colin L. Powell, the Chairman of the Joint Chiefs of Staff, has said that removing the ban "would be prejudicial to good order and discipline." The military has dismissed more than 15,000 homosexuals in the last decade to enforce the policy.

As Commander in Chief, Mr. Clinton can impose his order on the armed forces, just as President Harry S. Truman did in 1948 did when he ordered the integration of the Army, and Mr. Clinton's aides say he will do that shortly after he becomes President on Jan. 20. But his remarks today seemed to acknowledge a need to negotiate the method and pace of the change with General Powell and his colleagues to gain their support. Mr. Clinton addressed the issue a day after the Navy said it would comply with a judge's order to reinstate a gay sailor, Keith Meinhold.

Worries About Discipline

Senior military commanders acknowledge that tens of thousands of homosexuals already serve in the 1.8-million-member military but keep their sexual orientation secret. Many officers say that the problem is not that homosexuals are there but that if the ban is lifted they will openly display their homosexuality, possibly undermining the morale and discipline of fighting units.

Field commanders insist that sharing barracks, showers, latrines—especially at sea or in extreme combat conditions—would create serious management problems.

"It is difficult in a military setting where there is no privacy, where you don't get choice of association, where you don't get choice of where you live, to introduce a group of individuals who are proud, brave, loyal, good Americans but who favor a homosexual life style," General Powell said in testimony before the House Budget Committee earlier this year.

Clinton campaign advisers are poring over various proposals of how to rescind the ban against homosexuals in the military. Some Clinton advisers say that senior members of the transition team in Little Rock, Ark., and in Washington are in the early stages of formulating a new policy.

'Huge Culture Shock'

"This is a huge culture shock to the military, and he's sensitive to that culture," said one official familiar with Mr. Clinton's transition team. "You can't expect people to change attitudes overnight. It's one of the most tricky issues that could be raised."

In remarks to reporters following a Veterans Day address at the Capitol in Little Rock, Mr. Clinton said: "How to do it, the mechanics of doing it, I want to consult with military leaders about that. There will be time to do that. My position is we need everybody in America that's got a contribution to make that's willing to obey the law and work hard and play by the rules."

Mr. Clinton is walking a fine line between keeping his promises to gay people who backed him in the Presidential campaign and avoiding a rash of resignations that has been threatened in the tradition-bound military, as well as recruiting problems.

"There's a huge amount of superstition, hostility and ignorance about what gay people are," one senior Pentagon official said today. "Certainly it's wrong-headed, but it's real and exists. So the question becomes: How do you do this in a way that says to the country, 'I'm committed to change but I don't want to degrade the ability of the military'?"

Variety of Proposals

Some proposals that Clinton advisers are reviewing would halt the discharge of homosexuals, most of whom are given an honorable but involuntary discharge when their sexual orientation is discovered. After the discharges are halted, the proposals anticipate moving gradually to study broader steps. But it is more likely that the ban will be lifted immediately, allowing homosexuals to enlist in the services and enabling existing service members to stop hiding their sexual orientation. Some proposals go as far as reinstating discharged service members with back pay, a financial burden that Mr. Clinton is unlikely to accept.

"I don't think there will be any kind of fine lines drawn or lengthy executive order," said David Mixner, an influential fund-raiser and adviser to the Clinton campaign on gay issues. "The only commitment he made was that there'd be no discrimination against gays in the military in the future."

Public opinion polls show that most Americans favor lifting the ban, though it is unclear how deep that support runs.

One traditional reason for keeping homosexuals out of the military has been discarded. A study done for the Pentagon a few years ago found that homosexuals were no more of a security risk, in this case, being susceptible to the threat of blackmail, than other soldiers. Defense Secretary Dick Cheney himself called that reasoning an "old chestnut" last year, but still said he supported the ban.

The General Accounting Office, an investigative arm of Congress, released a report in June that found that the ban on homosexuals cost the Pentagon at least $27 million a year in investigations and perpetuated a policy that was unsupported by science and sociology.

Former service members discharged from the military for homosexuality say that General Powell and other commanders who oppose rescinding the ban vastly overstate the potential for disruption.

"If you are a gay man or lesbian and join the military, you want to fit in, you want to conform," said John McGuire, a lawyer who served as an Army captain for four years.

"People I worked with in the Army knew I was gay, but I didn't hold up a huge sign. My commanders never asked me about it. In a lot of cases, I'm sure it never crossed their minds."

Mr. Clinton's promise to rescind the ban is likely to render moot a growing number of court challenges to the policy, including the one by Mr. Meinhold which led the Navy to agree on Tuesday to reinstate him.

· ·

SENATOR NUNN TAKES CONTROL OF DEBATE ON GAYS IN THE MILITARY

Sen. Sam Nunn (D-GA) seized control of the national debate regarding the role of gays in the military in 1993 as President Clinton continued to work out the specifics of his proposal to lift the ban. Arguing that the decision should not be made unilaterally, Nunn openly challenged Clinton on national television, emphasizing the complexity of the issue and promising to hold hearings on any proposed plan. The move came as a shock to many, since both Nunn and Clinton were Democrats. Noting that Nunn had embarrassed Clinton, an unnamed senator said, "I think there are still fingerprints on the president's face from being slapped around."

At the time Nunn's record on homosexuals and military service was split. While he had said that the ban was too inflexible and that it compelled homosexuals to begin their careers in the service by lying, he had also said that rights of privacy and free expression enjoyed by civilians are not appropriate for military life. In the 1980s, Nunn asked two aides to resign from the Armed Services Committee upon learning that they were homosexuals, arguing that they posed a security risk.

JANUARY 30, 1993
THE GAY TROOP ISSUE;
This Time, Nunn Tests a Democrat
By MICHAEL WINES

WASHINGTON, Jan. 29—For a man whose military experience is limited to a year in the Coast Guard, Sam Nunn displays an uncanny knack for single-handedly surrounding the White Houses and taking its occupant political prisoner.

When the victims were Ronald Reagan and George Bush, Mr. Nunn's fellow Democrats rallied round and cheered. This time, Democratic opinion is a bit more divided.

Just as President Clinton was struggling to define his policy on admitting avowed homosexuals to the military, Mr. Nunn, the chairman of the Senate Armed Services Committee, stepped onto the national stage again this week and seized control of the debate. When Mr. Clinton announced a tentative ruling on the matter today, it was only after Mr. Nunn had twice lectured him, by way of network television, on the complexities of the issue, voiced his disagreement and made it clear that he would oversee hearings on any final plan.

Claiming a Role for Congress

"This is certainly an appropriate issue for the President in terms of his powers," Mr. Nunn, a Georgia Democrat, said Wednesday in a speech on the Senate floor. "But it's not in a unilateral sense. The Constitution makes it very clear that Congress also has a responsibility."

Admirers call this classic Nunn: a fine blend of reverence for procedure, social conservatism and command of military policy that has worn exceedingly well in Georgia for 20 years now.

But not until this week's debate have those traits converged on the national political scene. There, they are viewed as the clearest challenge yet to Mr. Clinton's authority by a member of his ostensibly unified party. And the Democratic establishment is abuzz over his motives.

One school of thought has Mr. Nunn engaging in a fit of pique, taking measured revenge on Mr. Clinton for, in Mr. Nunn's view, not consulting with him adequately on military matters and, more important, for failing to name him Secretary of State, a job Democratic colleagues say he longed for.

Mr. Nunn's denials of any grievance with the President fall on deaf ears.

"Nunn was not given the deferential treatment he expected during the transition," said one Democratic Senator, expressing a view held by many of his colleagues. That Senator, like many others interviewed, refused to be identified.

Slapping Clinton?

"What Nunn did on the Senate floor was embarrass Clinton," said one former Democratic Senate aide who had dealt directly with Mr. Nunn on military issues. "I think there are still fingerprints on the President's face from being slapped around."

A second, less critical school holds that Mr. Nunn is simply being a senator, and a good one—relentlessly protective of his turf, cautious about basic changes in military policy, more concerned about principle than party loyalty.

"This is completely consistent with his modus operandi," said Sean O'Keefe, the Bush Administration's Navy Secretary and the Pentagon's former comptroller. "He fully explores issues as opposed to reaching quick judgments. He protects his legislative prerogatives. It's not so much turf as making damn sure Congress has a role to play." . . .

Mr. Nunn's stance on Government service and homosexuals has received attention before.

As was reported last year, in 1981 and 1982 Mr. Nunn separately advised two aides on the Armed Services Committee to resign after he discovered that they were homosexuals.

The Senator has suggested that he had no choice, because the men's jobs required access to military secrets that intelligence agencies do not grant to homosexuals. He has since said that he has employed people "who did a tremendous job and who have stayed on my staff who are homosexual" but who do not require security clearances.

Faced this week with similar questions, Mr. Nunn has split the difference. He has implied that the military ban is overly inflexible and only encourages homosexuals to begin their service with a lie. But he has also disputed Mr. Clinton's position, saying the rights to privacy and free expression so prized by civilians are fundamentally at odds with the strictures of military life.

· ·

Openly Gay Sailor Killed, Questions Arise about Ending the Ban

In 1993 an openly gay sailor was killed at an American naval base in Japan shortly after coming out to his commander as gay. Allen Schindler was found beaten to death against a public toilet, his head crushed, ribs smashed, and penis cut. Owing to the extent of his injuries, his mother was forced to rely on his tattoos when identifying the body. Witnesses saw two sailors running from the crime scene, both of whom were arrested the following morning. Charles Vins was subsequently court-martialed after admitting his role in the killing and promising to testify for the prosecution, in exchange for which he received a four-month sentence and a bad conduct discharge. Terry Helvey also was court-martialed and received a sentence of life in prison.

The killing shocked many at the base, leading some to speculate about its connection to President Clinton's proposal to end the ban on gays in the military. Various sailors characterized the killing as a gay bashing, noting that it had been one of several instances of harassment at the base. Many said that while the murder was unjustifiable, it was also an indication that the military was unprepared to deal with open homosexuality in its ranks. A gay group called Queer Nation said that it intended "to make Schindler the gay Rodney King."

JANUARY 31, 1993
THE GAY TROOP ISSUE;

Death of a Gay Sailor:
A Lethal Beating Overseas Brings Questions and Fear
By JAMES STERNGOLD

SASEBO, Japan, Jan. 28—Six days before the U.S.S. Belleau Wood arrived at this sleepy American naval base last Sept. 30, Allen R. Schindler, a 22-year-old radioman, ended months of inner turmoil and told his commander that he was homosexual. As expected, he was informed that he would be discharged, but he wrote in his diary of his relief at finally showing his "true self."

After being confined to ship for a month, Mr. Schindler was allowed to go ashore in late October, and he quickly made his way to the knot of pubs known here as Sailor Town. There, he met several American entertainers, some gay, who were singers and dancers at a nearby theme park. He spoke of his homosexuality and the harassment he was enduring from other sailors as word of his sexual orientation spread.

A couple of days later, a month after his confession, the sailor went to a nearby park and was battered to death against the fixtures of a public toilet. Two other seamen from the Belleau Wood, a large amphibious assault ship, were arrested the next day. One has been sentenced as part of a plea agreement and the other is awaiting trial.

Victim Becomes a Symbol

The killing of Mr. Schindler has shocked many at this modest-sized base. Although the incident occurred months ago, reports about it have begun circulating only recently as the United States debates whether homosexuals should be allowed in the military. As a result, Mr. Schindler has been transformed into a symbol of the powerful anxieties that have been unleashed by President Clinton's proposal to end a ban on homosexuals in the military. Both sides have seized on the case as evidence for their arguments.

But here, in the far southwest corner of Japan, there is an edge of fear to the discussions because of the horrific nature of the crime. The attack left Mr. Schindler so badly disfigured, his mother said, that she could identify his body only by the tattoos on his arms.

Navy officials declined requests for interviews and did not acknowledge Mr. Schindler might have been killed because he was gay until the American entertainers he met here wrote a letter last November to Pacific Stars and Stripes, the military newspaper, which published an article on the case on Dec. 13.

But more than a dozen sailors here were willing to talk about what they generally described as a clear case of gay-bashing. They also said it was one of four previously undisclosed cases of harassment of homosexuals at a normally quiet base that experienced a spasm of violence after the Belleau Wood arrived last fall.

'It Just Can't Work'

One point agreed upon by several of the seamen, whether they supported or opposed allowing homosexuals in the military, was that this killing exposed how generally unprepared the military is to deal with either the substantial number of homosexuals already in its ranks— last year they were discharged at the pace of about two a day—or the prospect of permitting them to enlist openly.

"I don't know anybody who thinks you can have them on ships," said one sailor who, like the others, spoke on condition of anonymity. "I don't think there's a place for them in the Navy. It just can't work. But no matter how you feel, he didn't deserve what happened to him. There are crazy people in the Navy who are going to do this kind of thing, though. You can't control them."

The Navy insists that it is investigating the Schindler case fully. But the group of entertainers Mr. Schindler met here and his mother say they fear that the Navy has been seeking to cover up a hate crime.

"We wrote the letter because we knew this wasn't getting out and we were outraged," said Eric Underwood, a member of the group who now lives in New York. Michael Petrelis, an official in the gay-rights group Queer Nation, said he intended "to make Schindler the gay Rodney King."

Dorothy Hajdys, Mr. Schindler's mother, said she was groping to understand. She said she still doubted that her son was gay, even though he told her so in 1991 and wrote of a homosexual encounter in Hawaii in a journal he kept, which was recently given to her by the Navy. But most of all, she said, she wanted to get to the bottom of the case.

"I just can't believe that anyone could be so angry that they could do what they did to my son," she said.

Dreaming of the Midway

Mr. Schindler left high school in Chicago Heights, Ill., when he was 18 and joined the Navy. In his journal he wrote that his ultimate desire was to serve on the aircraft carrier Midway, which he did starting in 1991. "Some dreams do come true," he wrote.

But he came back down to earth when he was assigned to a new ship at the end of 1991, the Belleau Wood. The ship, which carries a crew of 930, had a reputation for roughness that Mr. Schindler quickly found was justified. He noted his growing unhappiness in his journal and to some friends.

Jim Jennings, who said he had been Mr. Schindler's lover in San Diego, recalled him complaining of being called "faggot" and "queer" by shipmates even before the sailor's announcement to his commander. . . .

It is not clear whether Mr. Schindler went to the park with his assailants or met them there. A little after 11 P.M. on Oct. 27 several witnesses saw him being battered relentlessly against the fixtures of a public restroom in the park. His head was crushed, his ribs smashed and his penis, according to the Navy, was cut. Trails of blood suggested that Mr. Schindler may have escaped the restroom briefly, and then been dragged back in.

Two sailors were seen running from the scene. The next morning, the military police arrested Airman Charles E. Vins and Airman Apprentice Terry M. Helvey, both 20 years old. . . .

Mr. Vins was court-martialed in November after admitting his involvement in Mr. Schindler's murder and agreeing to testify for the prosecution. He received what was effectively a four-month sentence as well as a bad-conduct discharge for failing to report a serious crime and resisting arrest. Mr. Schindler's mother and gay activists have voiced outrage over the sentence.

Mr. Helvey is expected to face formal charges soon and a court-martial. A recommendation on the precise charges was sent Friday to Capt. Douglas Bradt, commander of the Belleau Wood.

· ·

The Strange Career of Gays in the Military

The role of gays in the military has always been complicated. Concerned about the psychological state of homosexuals, the military devised new ways to identify and discharge them beginning in 1942. These discharges have typically been most frequent during peacetime, such as the McCarthy era in the 1950s, and less common during times of conflict, such as World War II and the Vietnam War. Women are particularly vulnerable to being discharged on charges of homosexuality, and some have argued that these charges have often been used as retribution against female soldiers who have rejected and/or reported the sexual advances of male service members.

Many scholars argue that the military was pivotal in the development of the modern gay rights movement. Although discharges still occurred, many relatively open homosexuals were allowed to serve during World War II. At this time significant pockets of acceptance existed, as evidenced by drag shows, lectures on alternative sexuality, and tolerance for intense emotional intimacy between members of the same sex. After World War II many gay veterans relocated to port cities and were influential in the development of majority-gay communities in New York City and San Francisco.

There were hopes of ending the sporadic tradition of barring homosexuals from openly serving in the military with the election of Bill Clinton, who campaigned to lift the ban. In 1993 public opinion was split on the wisdom of this decision. Some regarded it as a civil rights issue, while others argued that the inclusion of gays would undermine combat effectiveness. Ironically, opinions varied regarding the exact nature of the threat homosexuals posed. While some worried that gays would aggressively prey on unsuspecting straight males in showers and elsewhere, others took the opposite view, arguing that effeminate homosexuals would feminize the military, creating a passive presence that would weaken it as a fighting force. Still others expressed concern that a wave of violence could break out against gays if they were allowed to serve openly. Adm. William Crowe, former chair of the Joint Chiefs of Staff, rejected this last suggestion, noting that the discipline of the services is uniquely suited to control such violence.

APRIL 18, 1993
THE ODD PLACE OF HOMOSEXUALITY IN THE MILITARY
By CATHERINE S. MANEGOLD

Until 1942, no specific proviso barred homosexuals from serving in the military. That year, military psychiatrists, new to the ranks, warned of the "psychopathic personality disorders" that would make homosexuals unfit to fight. Then they devised supposedly foolproof guides to ferret them out: an effeminate flip of hand or a certain nervousness when standing naked before an officer.

It never really worked. Homosexuals served throughout World War II and after. In the repressive atmosphere of the 1950's, discharges for homosexuality soared; at the height of the Vietnam War, when recruitment drives were at their peak, enforcement was lax.

That military tradition of keeping out homosexuals could end on July 15, when President Clinton has said he will lift the ban. Pentagon officials, who had been notably recalcitrant in cooperating with the plan, said last week that they are rushing through several studies to address key matters like housing.

As things have stood, homosexuals could serve so long as they could hide. In the 1940's, if something untoward occurred, it was ascribed to "emergency" or "deprivation" homosexuality, according to John Costello in "Virtue Under Fire," a 1985 study of changing sexual mores brought about by World War II. Homosexual interludes were discounted as sparked by frustration. The armed forces thus maintained the facade of sexual purity (read: heterosexuality).

With President Clinton's announcement in January that the ban on homosexuals in the military would be lifted, a military tradition became harder to keep. Gay advocacy groups like the Campaign for Military Service saw the issue rapidly expand into a national debate on the worthiness of homosexuals. They have spent millions of dollars on a neatly packaged, well-advertised battle, underscored by a march on Washington next Sunday, to win inclusion in the ranks as blacks and women did before them.

Polls show that the nation remains divided, working its way through a subject as fiery as abortion yet imbued with more primal fears and deep social and religious constraints. The result has often been the rhetorical equivalent to the fog of battle, a fog in which women have been peculiarly absent, the ghosts of the debate.

Sex and Puritanical Roots

The argument has many voices. Some say it's a question of civil rights. Others say combat effectiveness. Or fear. Or homophobia and a surge in gay bashing that would devastate unit cohesiveness. Perhaps it is really about control and what would happen to one of the last bastions of American traditionalism if its defining social order were tampered with.

The argument is also, inevitably, about sex. That may be why keeping the subject hidden has always had a certain intrinsic appeal in a country with puritanical roots.

Military leaders who reject the civil rights analogy say the controversy is not about sex or even equal rights, but the agenda of a special interest group. They fear that complying with President Clinton's orders would set a precedent, inviting demands for inclusion by everyone from the mentally handicapped to other sexual minorities like transsexuals. They also argue that it is a privilege to serve in the fighting forces, not a right. "It's a nightmare as far as the military is concerned," said Bernard E. Trainor, a retired Marine lieutenant general. "It threatens the strong, conservative, moralistic tradition of the troops."

Not everyone in the military agrees. Adm. William J. Crowe Jr., a former Chairman of the Joint Chiefs of Staff, told The Washington Post recently that the argument was fueled "more by emotion than by reason." He said that the armed forces' culture of strict discipline is, in fact, uniquely suited to control the behavior of both homosexuals and the heterosexuals who might bash them—more so than civilian society.

Randy Shilts, the author of "Conduct Unbecoming," a new history of homosexuality in the military, points to the armed forces' policies on AIDS to illustrate how well the four services can cope with thorny problems when they must. "The armed forces has some of the most enlightened policies on H.I.V. in the country," he said. Discounting fears that wounded AIDS-infected soldiers might bleed on their buddies, he cited as an example the fact that regulations already prevent those soldiers from going into combat.

But even if the military can manage the transition, that does not necessarily mean the controversy will fade. There is a deeper source of discontent: "They want us to move faster than the country," said a former general who did not wish to be identified. Sodomy laws based on religious proscriptions against sex for sex's sake are still on the books in 24 states. The District of Columbia recently moved to drop its sodomy law, but Congress, which has final say, blocked a similar attempt in 1981.

The Supreme Court, too, was disinclined to undo a taboo that it says dates to biblical times. In its 1986 decision Bowers v. Hardwick, the Court upheld Georgia's sodomy law.

So for months now, Americans have been watching ominous shower shots on the nightly news and wrestling with their fears. Women soldiers have voiced support for the policy change and do not express the fear of being attacked by same-sex predators that preoccupies some men. Many of their male comrades, some of whom still believe that women are ancillary to the fighting troops, have made macho threats about just what they would do if they found a gay man in their midst.

Another widespread objection is that it would feminize a male club. Enduring images of homosexual men depict them as effeminate, therefore weak, therefore a drain upon a mighty fighting force. Yet that ignores the role of a dominant participant in homosexual sex, a partner who takes the aggressive "male" role. The argument also raises the question whether anything could have feminized the force more than women. And women are already there.

Yet some soldiers are so perturbed by the prospect of including gay men in the ranks that they are willing to break the rules by assaulting fellow soldiers. Their explanation is that they fear attack or unwanted sexual advances—sexual harassment—as if they really don't believe that no means no. It is likely, too, that some fear their own reactions and the prospect that they might respond sexually. "Hatred of gay men," Ken Corbett, a psychologist, wrote in an Op-Ed article for The New York Times in February, "is based on fear of the self, not of an alien other." For decades, psychologists have said that at the core of homophobia is repressed fear and latent homosexuality.

Psychologists point to a rich history of songs, drag shows and jokes in the military that serve to neutralize powerful feelings. As early as 1941, the psychiatrist William Menninger described the typical soldier's wartime relationship as one of "disguised and sublimated homosexuality," a theme given voice in the popular war song, "My Buddy": "I miss your voice and the touch of your hand, my buddy."

That intense companionships were both so common and so acceptable in pop culture must have alleviated some soldiers' fears about unexpected longings. With those fears neutralized and the relationships the cause of celebration, the military became a safe place for the emotional intimacy so compelling to men and women facing the chaos and terror of war.

Seen from a distance, the logic of the military's denial of homosexuality in the ranks was simple: as long as no homosexuals were enlisted, soldiers could play at being lovers (and even consummate the roles) without ever having to acknowledge those feelings. Whatever happened, happened. There was a war on.

The implied double standard was made official in 1982. The Department of Defense regulations adopted that year allow a heterosexual to have homosexual sex and to be exonerated—so long as he or she states that the incident was a lapse. Gay and lesbian soldiers, by contrast, are discharged just for identifying themselves as such.

Women More Vulnerable

Col. Margarethe Cammermeyer, a much-decorated nurse in the Army National Guard who was discharged last May for her sexual orientation, says the ban has left women particularly vulnerable. "There is a tremendous amount of lesbian-baiting in the service," she said. "Any straight man who propositions a woman and she's not interested, well, it can't be because he's not attractive. So it must be because she's a lesbian. It's used as a threat all the time."

Because homosexuals now have to hide, anyone in the armed forces, she says, can sabotage the career of another by making allegations about their sexuality. If homosexuals were allowed to be open, that disruption would disappear. Though men are equally susceptible to such accusations, they are less likely than women to be dismissed because of their orientation. Lesbians are discharged at a rate from two to six times higher than gay men, depending on the branch of the service.

Several books, but most notably Allan Berube's "Coming Out Under Fire," trace the start of a gay rights movement in America to the military itself. They argue that the relative openness of gay and lesbian relationships in the military in World War II eventually led to those veterans settling in port cities like San Francisco and New York where, for the first time, they established identifiable subcultures.

Depending on its own convenience, the military operated with a double standard: while there were purges and discharges during that war, scores of written accounts show an easy acceptance among the Allied forces (German S.S. officers, in contrast, faced death by firing squad). Women in particular were likely to escape punishment. The Women's Army Corps actually dealt with lesbianism as a normal part of life. "A lecture to WAC officer candidates on homosexuality, prepared by the Surgeon General's Office and revised by WAC officials," wrote Mr. Berube, included the observation that "every person is born with a bisexual nature." In that corps, discharge was used only as a last resort in cases that disrupted a unit.

Men, too, often seemed to accept their gay comrades. Ben Small, a gay Army Air Corpsman stationed near New Guinea, once wrote away for a pile of dresses for a drag show. When the dresses arrived, he recounted in Mr. Berube's study, "Well, here's everybody in the office from the lieutenant on down trying on dresses! Everybody suddenly becomes a drag queen!"

Such tolerance would not last through the cold war. By the 1950's, Senator Joseph McCarthy was well into a civilian witch hunt that would quickly bleach the military's ranks as well. At the time, Senator McCarthy's righthand man, Roy Cohn, and J. Edgar Hoover of the Federal Bureau of Investigation, both closeted themselves, presented the argument that homosexuals were the agents of communism. "One homosexual can pollute a Government office," concluded a report authorized by the Senate in 1950. Military discharges based on sexual orientation doubled in the 1950's and then increased by half again in the 1960's.

When recruitment demands were high during the Vietnam War, the situation loosened. Cal Anderson, an Army court reporter who would later join the Washington State Assembly, recalled in "My Country, My Right to Serve," that he was once caught in the act. The commander's reprimand was short and mild: "Now, I don't care what people do in their own time," he told the terrified young soldier. "But the Army doesn't feel that way, so in the future, be more discreet."

Klinger in Drag

By 1972, the popular television show "M*A*S*H" featured a soldier who almost always appeared in drag: Corporal Klinger, played by Jamie Farr. Though the show stopped short of explicitly dealing with his sexuality—always leaving open the question that he was merely trying to get a discharge—the character became one of the most beloved in the series.

Today, many senior officers see the issue in a long historical perspective. Steeped in military lore that traces homosexuality to pre-Christian history, they point to tales of homosexuality on the front lines from the Sacred Band of Thebes in 338 B.C. (where each soldier was said to be a lover of another) to such military giants as Alexander the Great, Richard the Lion-Hearted and T. E. Lawrence (popularly known as Lawrence of Arabia). Seen in that context, said a retired general, the issue becomes more a matter of management than revolution.

In an open letter to his soldiers printed in the Marine magazine "Leatherneck" last month, Gen. Carl

E. Mundy Jr., the Marine Corps Commandant, advised: "We are made up not of individuals who seek self-identity, but of selfless men and women who place country and corps ahead of self . . . whatever their privately held preferences or belief may be." He urged tolerance: "We treat all marines with firmness, fairness and dignity."

Those comments were supportive, but typically oblique. General Trainor, who now directs the national security program at Harvard's Kennedy School of Government, may have encapsulated the military's gut reaction best. Given half a choice, he said, the military would have looked long and hard at the matter and then decided: "Listen, I'd rather not deal with it."

Congress to Debate the Ban on Lesbians in the Military

Although gay women are more likely to have served in the military than straight women, they have played only a small role in the debate about gays in the military. A 1993 book on gays in the military estimated that 25 percent of the 200,000 women in the military at the time were gay, and Pentagon statistics show that women have been discharged for homosexuality roughly three times more often than men. Congress held a round of hearings addressing how the ban has affected these soldiers.

Gay women may be more attracted to the military because it offers an alternative to traditional femininity. Yet because they must keep their sexual identity hidden, they often find themselves in a bind, compelled to behave as traditional women in a masculine culture. "Many men still don't think women belong in the military. The ban is a perfect mechanism to get us out," said Col. Margarethe Cammermeyer, who was discharged by the army under the current ban. In addition, many servicewomen say that if they accuse someone of sexual harassment, they are often charged with being a lesbian.

MAY 4, 1993
LESBIANS, LONG OVERLOOKED, ARE CENTRAL TO DEBATE ON MILITARY BAN

WASHINGTON, May 3—When Congress begins a new round of hearings on homosexuals in the military this week, it will take its first long look at the group that is believed to be most affected by the current ban on such soldiers: women.

So far, the debate has been cast largely in terms of gay men: Would they hurt combat morale? Would they spread sexually transmitted diseases? What about communal showers?

But to the extent that facts can be obtained in the elusive world that gay soldiers inhabit, many experts, from historians to advocates for homosexual rights, say a disproportionate number of homosexuals in the military are women.

A Surprising Estimate

The evidence is mostly anecdotal, because it is impossible to quantify the presence of homosexuals in an institution that officially excludes them.

But the documentation is often startling. Randy Shilts, author of a new book about homosexuals in the military, said in a recent interview that most of the several hundred lesbians he interviewed for his book, "Conduct Unbecoming" (St. Martin's Press), estimated that 25 percent of the 200,000 or so women in the armed forces are gay.

Similarly, a 1984 study in the Journal of Homosexuality found that gay women were "significantly more likely to have served" in the military than heterosexual women, while homosexual and heterosexual men were "equally likely" to have served.

Because of this, gay-rights advocates and some military analysts say allowing homosexuals in the military would have a more immediate effect on women than men.

To explain why lesbians may be more attracted to the military than gay men, many gay women have said that the military offers them the opportunity to escape traditional female roles.

But gay women in the military say they are doubly vulnerable, as homosexuals who must keep their sexual identity secret and as women in what is still a masculine culture.

And many heterosexual women say that an accusation of homosexuality has become a weapon in the arsenal of sexual harassment.

"If you're a woman in the military, you can't make sexual-harassment charges, because you're going to face the countercharge that you're a lesbian," said Representative Patricia Schroeder, Democrat of Colorado. "As a result, you're going to have a culture that tolerates sexism more."

Ms. Schroeder said that at hearings starting on Tuesday before the House Armed Services Committee she would focus on Pentagon statistics showing that females have been discharged for homosexuality at roughly three times the rate of men over the last decade.

Pentagon spokesmen say the statistics do not prove the military is discriminating against lesbians because the numbers of men and women dismissed for being gay are so small.

Other military authorities say this discrepancy is attributable to the apparent overrepresentation of lesbians. Still other service members have suggested that because women are so greatly outnumbered by men, they are easier to single out.

But Ms. Schroeder and other advocates contend that the military investigates suspected gay females more aggressively than males, partly out of hostility toward women in the military.

"Many men still don't think women belong in the military," said Margarethe Cammermeyer, a former colonel and chief nurse of Washington Veteran's Hospital who was discharged by the Army. "The ban is the perfect mechanism to get us out."

A 1990 memorandum issued by the commander of the Navy's surface Atlantic fleet, for example, has become legend among lesbians in the military. In it, Vice Adm. Joseph S. Donnell instructed his officers to step up their efforts to root out lesbian sailors even though they were "among the command's top performers."

Mass investigations and discharges are far more common for women than men, Mr. Shilts said. A 1988 inquiry at Parris Island, S.C., the only boot camp for female Marines, for example, grew to involve 70 suspected lesbians.

Lawyers who represent lesbians in the military say that investigations of their clients often begin with their rejection of a male officer's advances, a contention that finds some support outside the ranks of gay-rights advocates.

"I think a lot of the initial inquiries about women are a result of their spurning men's sexual advances," said Lawrence J. Korb, an Assistant Secretary of Defense under President Ronald Reagan.

Even heterosexual women say sexual-harassment charges can set off a homosexuality investigation.

After serving as an operations officer during the gulf war, Capt. Victoria Hudson of the Army charged that a superior asked about her sexual orientation after she refused to write him an erotic letter.

* *

CLINTON ANNOUNCES COMPROMISE ON MILITARY BAN

With the support of the Joint Chiefs of Staff, President Clinton announced his plan to ease the ban on homosexuals in the military in 1993. The recommended compromise was known informally as Don't Ask, Don't Tell because commanders would not ask about sexual identity and gay service members would not offer such information. Homosexuals would be allowed to serve, if discreetly, while military officers would refrain from investigation in cases that lacked overt expression of homosexual orientation or conduct.

Although the support of senior military officials was in doubt as recently as six months before this, Colin Powell, the chair of the Joint Chiefs, called the new policy "an honorable compromise." Conversely, gay congressperson Barney Frank (D-MA) said that it "falls short of where I thought we would be." Sen. Sam Nunn, chair of the Armed Services Committee, reserved final judgment but indicated that he felt generally positive about the new policy. President Clinton acknowledged that the compromise was not perfect, but he argued that it offered "a sensible balance between the rights of the individual and the needs of the military." Gay rights advocates said they would rely on the courts to eradicate the ban in its entirety. In the Clinton years, such efforts had limited success.

JULY 20, 1993
GAY RIGHTS IN THE MILITARY:
Chiefs Back Clinton on Gay-Troop Plan;
President Admits Revised Policy Isn't Perfect
By THOMAS L. FRIEDMAN

WASHINGTON, July 19—Flanked by the Joint Chiefs of Staff, President Clinton today presented his plan for easing the ban on homosexuals in the military and appealed to his generals and admirals to find in their hearts "the will and the desire" to carry it out.

Immediately after the President laid out his policy, which was announced in a speech to a friendly audience of military officers at the National Defense University at Fort McNair in Washington, the top commanders of the Army, Navy, Air Force, Marines and Coast Guard as well as Gen. Colin L. Powell, Chairman of the Joint Chiefs of Staff, met with reporters.

The chiefs, who were in a nearly open revolt six months ago over Mr. Clinton's plan to lift the ban on homosexuals unconditionally, took turns expressing their support for the new policy's limited opening to homosexuals.

Requiring Silence

Mr. Clinton's plan will permit homosexuals to serve in the military if they do not engage in homosexual behavior on or off base and remain quiet about their sexual identity. But it also makes it difficult for commanders to initiate investigations without clear evidence of homosexual behavior, thereby implicitly creating a zone of privacy for gay soldiers and sailors. [Text of policy guidelines, page A12.]

Calling this "an honorable compromise" after "difficult" debates, General Powell said the military chiefs "fully, fully support" it.

But Representative Barney Frank, the openly gay Massachusetts Democrat who tried to work with Mr. Clinton to get the ban fully lifted, said the plan "falls short of where I thought we would be."

"This does not meet the minimum," he added.

'Not a Perfect Solution'

Mr. Clinton acknowledged that the compromise formula "is not a perfect solution" or "identical with some of my own goals." During the Presidential campaign, he called for lifting the ban on homosexuals unconditionally.

"It certainly will not please everyone—perhaps not anyone—and clearly not those who hold the most adamant opinions on either side of this issue," he added.

The President's very choice of his audience to announce his plan demonstrated the balance of power that in the end shaped the new policy. It was an audience made up of military officers, with not a single gay or lesbian representative present.

The issue of whether to lift the Pentagon's 50-year-old ban began with a casual campaign pledge but was transformed into one of the thorniest issues of the Clinton Presidency. It involved six months of difficult negotiations with Congress and the military brass and called into question the President's willingness to stand by his principles.

At first, conservatives were infuriated by the effort to help homosexuals; then liberals became enraged by the President's retreat. In the end, only homosexuals in the military—whose lives will be affected, if only to a limited degree—seemed pleased, and their joy was savored quietly.

The message of the Clinton plan is twofold: To homosexuals in the military, it says that they can serve if they are extremely discreet about their sexual identity and behavior. To military officers, it says that they must tolerate the right of homosexuals to serve discreetly, but it gives them license to initiate investigations of anyone involved in ostentatious expressions of homosexual orientation or conduct.

But the rules leave ample gray areas for subjective interpretation, and the difficulty will come when some homosexuals try to assert their identities in ways they believe are legitimate, but are in fact proscribed, and when some overzealous commanders try to implement the policy more strictly than its drafters intended.

Declaring that his plan was a "a substantial advance" over the half-century ban on homosexuals in the military that he inherited, Mr. Clinton said it struck a "sensible balance between the rights of the individual and the needs of the military."

Mr. Clinton's presentation and the military chiefs' display of support seemed to calm ripples of discontent still visible on Capitol Hill.

'Don't Pursue'

The policy, which Secretary of Defense Les Aspin issued today in the form of a directive to the civilian service secretaries and to General Powell, takes effect Oct. 1, the start of the new Federal fiscal year and the date of General Powell's retirement. It has been characterized by the Administration as: "don't ask, don't tell, don't pursue."

The "don't ask, don't tell" elements of the policy are clear. The order states that "applicants for military service will no longer be asked or required to reveal" their sexual orientation. At the same time, the policy formally prohibits homosexual members of the military from disclosing their status, saying the military continues to reserve the right to discharge members who engage in homosexual conduct on- or off-base. It defines homosexual conduct "as a homosexual act, a statement that the member is homosexual or bisexual, or a marriage or attempted marriage to someone of the same gender."

The key to the new policy is the strict guidelines for pursuit of homosexuals. Those guidelines are designed to be strict enough to force homosexuals to remain discreet but loose enough to allow a discreet homosexual to live his or her life without harassment, including being able to visit gay bars, attend gay marches and quietly identify oneself to a friend as homosexual, provided no sexual relations are involved.

The pursuit order states that "no investigations or inquiries will be conducted solely to determine a service member's sexual orientation."

In addition, it says, the mere "statement by a service member that he or she is homosexual" is not grounds for dismissal by itself. Such a statement, however, does create "a rebuttable presumption that the service member is engaging in homosexual acts or has a propensity or intent to do so."

People who identify themselves as homosexual would be taking a chance that they might be challenged as to whether they are engaging in homosexual activities; if they deny that they are, which may require lying on their part, they will not be dismissed.

The policy states that sexual orientation alone, "absent credible information that a crime has been committed, will not be the subject of a criminal investigation." Also, "an allegation or statement by another that a service member is a homosexual, alone, is not grounds for either a criminal investigation or a commander's inquiry."

In part, the policy notes, this is designed to avoid "victimization of homosexuals through blackmail."

Permissible Behavior

The policy also explicitly states that activities like associating with "known homosexuals, presence at a gay bar, possessing or reading homosexual publications, or marching in a gay rights rally in civilian clothes will not, in and of themselves, constitute credible information that would provide a basis for initiating an investigation or serve as the basis for an administrative discharge." The same is true for listing someone of the same sex as an emergency contact or beneficiary of a will.

To avoid frivolous or arbitrary investigations, the order says, commanders are urged to "exercise sound discretion regarding when credible information exists to launch an investigation." Only an officer of the rank of major or above can order such an inquiry.

Officers, the policy says, "will investigate allegations of violations of the Uniform Code of Military Justice in an evenhanded manner without regard to whether the conduct alleged is heterosexual or homosexual or whether it occurs on base or off base."

Senator Sam Nunn, the Georgia Democrat who heads the Armed Services Committee, said he felt "positive" toward the President's proposal but would reserve final judgment. The committee is to take testimony from the Joint Chiefs on Tuesday.

White House officials had been casting anxious glances toward Mr. Nunn since Friday, when he announced his intention to write a new policy on homosexuals in the military into this year's defense authorization bill. At one point he seemed to be threatening to trump Mr. Clinton's executive order with a more restrictive law, but that prospect seemed to recede today.

Homosexual rights advocates said they would look to the courts to erase the ban entirely.

* *

GAYS DISCHARGED FROM MILITARY AT INCREASED RATE DESPITE NEW POLICY

In the years following 1993's Don't Ask, Don't Tell (DADT) policy, evidence came to light to suggest that military commanders were still asking and gay service members were continuing to tell about sexual identity, just years after the initial announcement of the Clinton administration's DADT policy, which was designed to reset the terms of gay participation in the military. Seventeen percent more gay service members were discharged in 1995, compared with the previous year, prompting the Servicemembers Legal Defense Network to comment that the new policy was "as bad [as], if not worse than, its predecessors."

MARCH 3, 1996
WORD FOR WORD: MILITARY GAY POLICY;
When 'Don't Ask, Don't Tell' Means Do Ask and Do Tell All
By PHILIP SHENON

WASHINGTON—When the Clinton Administration announced a policy of "don't ask, don't tell" for homosexuals in the military, the rules seemed clear enough: Gay soldiers could serve so long as they kept quiet about their sexuality. Commanders would no longer be allowed to ask about a soldier's sexual orientation.

But on the policy's second anniversary, the evidence suggests that some military commanders continue to ask. And under duress, some soldiers continue to tell.

While the "don't ask, don't tell" policy was meant to make it easier for gays to serve in the military, the number of soldiers, sailors and marines discharged last year for homosexuality jumped 17 percent over the year before.

A study released last week by the Servicemembers Legal Defense Network, a Washington-based lawyers' group, found that the new policy in practice was "as bad, if not worse than, its predecessors," and that witch hunts for gays were still common. . . .

* *

DON'T ASK, DON'T TELL POLICY REVISED TO ADDRESS GROWING HARASSMENT

On August 14, 1999, the Clinton administration's DADT policy regarding gays in the military underwent its first major revision, placing new limitations on investigations of homosexuality and instituting mandatory antiharassment training at all levels of the military. The new requirements responded to concerns about the intrusive nature of such investigations as well as the increased number of discharges and reports of gay harassment under the new policy. Gay rights advocates were unconvinced that the new rules would adequately address problems with the policy, arguing that the guidelines needed to be more specific to prevent harassment and physical violence, such as the murder of Pvt. Barry Winchell by a member of his own unit at Fort Campbell, Kentucky.

AUGUST 14, 1999
REVISED MILITARY GUIDELINES FAIL TO QUELL GAY CONCERNS
By PHILIP SHENON

WASHINGTON, Aug. 13—The Pentagon today announced its first major revision of guidelines for its "don't ask, don't tell" policy on homosexuals in the military, including a new requirement that commanders seek approval from senior civilian officials at the Pentagon before opening certain types of investigations of troops who acknowledge that they are gay.

The revised guidelines failed to satisfy gay rights advocates, who say that the new directives do not go far enough and that pervasive hostility toward homosexuals in uniform continues to result in violent harassment. They pointed to the murder last month of an Army private in Kentucky as evidence of the entrenched hostility.

Under the guidelines, the Pentagon ordered that commanders institute anti-harassment training at all levels of the military, beginning with basic training, and that low-level military lawyers consult with senior lawyers before opening an investigation of anyone suspected of being gay.

The new directives also require commanders to seek approval from the military secretary that they serve—the Army Secretary, in the case of an Army commander—before opening an investigation in the dozen or so cases a year when "a service member made a statement regarding his or her homosexuality for the purpose of seeking separation" from the service.

The requirement appears to have been designed to answer criticism from gay rights advocates that the military has conducted intrusive investigations into the sex lives of troops who admit their homosexuality and are preparing to leave the service.

The investigations, the advocates charge, are an effort to find damaging information that can be used to force troops to pay back military scholarships and other benefits.

"I've made it clear there is no room for harassment or threats in the military," Defense Secretary William S. Cohen said in issuing the directives, which the Pentagon described as an effort to spell out the policy more clearly to avoid abuses.

"I've instructed the military services to make sure that the policy is clearly understood and fairly enforced," Mr. Cohen said. "The department is determined to implement the homosexual conduct policy with fairness to all concerned."

While the five-year-old "don't ask, don't tell" policy was designed by the Clinton Administration to make it easier for homosexuals to serve in uniform, gay rights advocates contend that the instances of anti-gay harassment in the military have increased.

And the numbers of gay and lesbian soldiers facing discharge from the service has grown dramatically under the policy. Last year, 1,145 people were discharged from the armed services for homosexuality, compared with 997 in 1997 and 617 in 1994, the year the policy took effect.

The military continues to bar openly gay people from serving in uniform. Under the policy, homosexuals can serve in the armed forces as long as they do not discuss their sexual orientation, and commanders are barred from asking troops whether they are gay.

The new guidelines also remind commanders that they cannot begin investigations of the sexual orientation of troops without credible information, that they must promptly investigate when troops complain that they are being taunted because of the perception or accusation that they are gay, and that those troops cannot be the subject of retaliation for filing complaints.

They also for the first time give a specific order to internal investigators in each of the branches of the military—the inspectors general—to review whether commanders and military lawyers are properly carrying out the "don't ask, don't tell" policy. . . .

Michelle M. Benecke, a retired Army captain who is co-director of the Defense Network, said that while the group was pleased with the wording of Mr. Cohen's statement and with some elements of the directives, the new guidelines would leave many members of the military vulnerable to harassment and violence. "This is not a new day," Ms. Benecke said.

She said the guidelines, which have been delayed for months, did not provide the detailed direction to commanders that might prevent the kinds of abuse that appear to have led to the death last month of a soldier at Fort Campbell, Ky.

The soldier, Pfc. Barry Winchell, was allegedly beaten with a baseball bat by a member of his unit after his homosexuality became known on the base, one of the nation's largest.

"Pfc. Winchell is only the latest example of the severe anti-gay harassment that service members face every day," Ms. Benecke said.

"We've pressed Secretary Cohen for two years now to tell commanders the investigative limits and how to properly implement these policies, and there's nothing in the package today that does that," she said. "What's here is inadequate to address the magnitude of the problem." . . .

* *

RESEARCHER ARGUES BAN DECREASES NATIONAL SECURITY

Owing to the increasing demand for troops in the Iraq war, this opinion piece suggests that Don't Ask, Don't Tell may well be weakening military readiness instead of strengthening it. Rather than promoting unit cohesion, it compels service members to hide their identity, preventing them from forming personal relationships with others in their unit. In addition, more than 10,000 service members have been discharged under the policy, including 9 highly competent Arabic translators at a time when such intelligence is drastically needed. Further, recent polls indicate that 64 percent of Americans are in favor of allowing gays to serve openly in the military, while the number of officers who are uncomfortable with gays has dropped significantly. Finally, twenty-four allied countries, including Britain, Canada, Australia, and Israel, have lifted their bans without damaging unit cohesion and readiness. Rather than posing the issue as a tension between civil rights and military readiness, it would be better to think about how repealing the ban could serve to increase national security and lessen prejudice.

NOVEMBER 28, 2003
WHY WE NEED GAYS IN THE MILITARY
By NATHANIEL FRANK

Ten years ago Sunday, President Bill Clinton signed into law the "don't ask, don't tell" policy on gays in the military. The law, which has resulted in nearly 10,000 discharges to date, bans openly gay people from serving in the armed forces, requires those who do serve to conceal their sexual orientation and avoid homosexual conduct, and prohibits military personnel from being asked about their sexual orientation. With American soldiers, gay and straight, fighting for their country in Iraq, the wisdom of this policy is increasingly suspect.

The last time Americans seriously debated gays in the military, after Mr. Clinton's broken campaign promise to lift the ban outright, political and military leaders framed the discussion as a choice between the civil rights of gays and the requirements of national security. Few argued that national security might require letting gays serve. Many believed that homosexuality was incompatible with military service. In the language of the law, letting gays serve openly in the military would threaten the "high morale, good order and discipline, and unit cohesion" of the American forces.

In the decade since the policy was put into place, however, and particularly since 9/11, it has become clear that it is not the presence of gay soldiers that undermines security. It is the ban itself which does so. Indeed, the policy may be weakening what it was intended to protect: military readiness.

The ban was supposed to safeguard unit cohesion, the watchword of military analysts who oppose letting gays serve. The law states that the presence of openly gay people in the services would create an "unacceptable risk" to unit cohesion, which is generally defined as the bonds of trust among service members that make the combat effectiveness of a unit greater than the sum of its parts.

Yet soldiers I have interviewed about their experience serving in the Middle East say the policy has had the opposite effect. One soldier told me that when he was in a unit where he couldn't tell people that he was gay, it was more difficult for him to form close personal relationships within his unit. Serving under the gay ban, he said, erodes the mutual trust that is essential not only to effective bonding but also to effective fighting.

The gay ban was also said to protect military readiness. Most Americans agree, especially after 9/11, that national security should be paramount in any debate over who can serve. That's why the nation was dismayed to learn, last fall, that the Army fired nine gay Arabic-language translators at a time when national security experts were worrying about a dire shortage of intelligence personnel capable of translating Arabic.

Just last month, the Pentagon acknowledged that the military has hired many translators since 9/11 without full background checks. The result? At least three translators now face espionage charges, and the military faces yet another intelligence imbroglio. In short, the government is drastically lowering its standards for critical intelligence agents while throwing out highly competent ones just because they are gay.

The growing understanding that the gay ban is bad for national security may explain why even those who once supported the ban now support letting gays serve. The former judge advocate general for the Navy, Rear Adm. John D. Hutson, who was involved in the development and enforcement of the policy, recently said that the ban is a failed policy whose elimination would strengthen the military. A Fox News poll conducted in August shows that 64 percent of Americans now favor allowing gays to serve openly in the military, up from 56 percent in a similar poll taken in 2001.

Even within the military, anti-gay sentiment has declined over the past decade. One study conducted at the Naval Postgraduate School in California found that between 1994 and 1999, the percentage of Navy officers who feel uncomfortable in the presence of gay people decreased to 36 percent from 58 percent.

The debate over gays in the military was never really about balancing civil rights with national security. Britain, Israel, Canada and Australia are among 24 militaries that lifted bans on gay soldiers without undermining unit cohesion or combat readiness. These experiences show that the choice is not between gay rights and military readiness. It is between prejudice that compromises national security and equality that enhances it. And that's no choice at all.

GAY LEADERS STILL WAITING FOR OBAMA TO FULFILL PROMISE TO LIFT BAN

Following up on a promise made in his campaign, in 2009 President Barack Obama reaffirmed his vow to allow gays to serve openly in the military. Speaking in front of the Human Rights Campaign, a leading gay advocacy group, he nevertheless failed to provide a specific timetable for effecting this change in policy. Although Obama campaigned as a "fierce advocate" of equal rights for gays, he has made limited progress in many areas, such as hate crime legislation and partner benefits, leaving many movement leaders disappointed. "An opportunity

Sen. Joe Lieberman (left) shakes hands with Maj. Mike Almy, who served in the Air Force for thirteen years until being discharged under "Don't Ask Don't Tell." Lieberman had just introduced a 2010 bill that would end DADT, and introduce specific protections for gays and lesbians in the military.

*Source: Stephen Crowley/*The New York Times

was missed tonight," said Aubrey Sarvis, the executive director of the Servicemembers Legal Defense Network. Since then, Congress and the Obama administration have agreed to lift the ban, pending the outcome of a Pentagon study that will explore whether allowing gays and lesbians to serve openly will negatively impact military effectiveness.

OCTOBER 11, 2009
OBAMA PLEDGES AGAIN TO END 'DON'T ASK, DON'T TELL'
By SHERYL GAY STOLBERG

WASHINGTON—President Obama on Saturday renewed his vow to allow gay men and lesbians to serve openly in the military, but failed to offer a timetable for doing so—an omission likely to inflame critics who say he is not fighting aggressively enough for gay rights.

"I will end 'don't ask, don't tell,'" Mr. Obama told an audience of nearly 3,000 people at a fund-raising dinner for the Human Rights Campaign, the nation's largest gay advocacy group. "That is my commitment to you."

The president's emphatic declaration, on the eve of a major gay rights rally here, brought a huge roar from the crowd at the star-studded black-tie dinner, where tickets cost as much as $1,000 and entertainment was provided by the singer Lady Gaga and the cast of the new Fox comedy

"Glee." But outside the room, the president's words met with a chillier reception.

Bil Browning, a blogger for Bilerico Project, a Web site aimed at a gay audience, said moments after the speech ended that the site was flooded with critical comments by people who said they had heard nothing new. "I could have watched one of his old campaign speeches and heard the same thing," one wrote.

Even inside the room, reaction was mixed. Terry Penrod, a real estate agent from Columbus, Ohio, said some gay rights advocates were being impatient with the president, while Raj Malthotra, 29, a management consultant from Washington, said he thought the speech was a rehash of Mr. Obama's past promises.

"For him, it's buy more time until he needs our votes again," Mr. Malthotra said.

Mr. Obama campaigned as a "fierce advocate" of equal rights for gays, he said, and he used Saturday's speech to lay out his vision of the day when, as he said, "we as a nation finally recognize relationships between two men or two women are just as real and admirable as relationships between a man and a woman," and when "no one has to be afraid to be gay in America."

Yet the president's relationship with the gay community has been a conflicted one. He does not support gay marriage—as a matter of Christian principle, he has said— and he got off to a bad start with the gay community when he invited the Rev. Rick Warren, who opposes same-sex unions, to deliver the invocation at his inauguration.

In the nine months since, Mr. Obama has made only limited progress on the issues that are important to gays. He has pushed for hate crime legislation, and a bill, approved in the House on Thursday, now appears headed for passage. He has put forth a package of domestic partnership benefits for federal workers, but faced criticism that the effort did not include health benefits. He has said he would push to repeal the Defense of Marriage Act, which allows states to refuse to recognize same-sex marriages in other states, but it remains on the books.

But of all the issues Mr. Obama has vowed to address, the Clinton-era "don't ask, don't tell" policy is perhaps the one that stirs the most emotion. Mr. Obama said Saturday night that he was working with the Pentagon and with House and Senate leaders to repeal the policy, but many gay rights supporters have accused him of dragging his feet.

In the days before the speech, many advocates for gay rights said they hoped he would lay out a timetable for overturning the policy or otherwise offer specifics on how he will achieve his goal.

"An opportunity was missed tonight," Aubrey Sarvis, executive director of Servicemembers Legal Defense Network, which represents gay and lesbian soldiers, said in a statement afterward.

Mr. Obama spoke for about 20 minutes inside the packed Washington Convention Center; outside, a small band of protesters on the sidewalk carried banners urging the president to live up to his promises. Among them was Mark Katzenberger, a software trainer from San Francisco, who said that despite his disillusionment with Mr. Obama, he would probably vote for him again.

Capturing the feeling of many in the gay community, Mr. Katzenberger said, "Even our friends sometimes need a kick in the butt."

Congress Allows Gays to Serve Openly in the Military

In December 2010 the LGBT movement obtained a major victory in its struggle for equal rights when Congress voted to repeal Don't Ask, Don't Tell, lifting the longstanding ban on gays and lesbians in the military. The historic measure passed with bipartisan support in both the House of Representatives and the Senate. Sen. Joseph I. Lieberman (I-CT) said that Congress had "righted a wrong" and "done justice." While President Obama welcomed Congress's action, arguing that it would strengthen the armed forces, recent Republican presidential candidate Sen. John McCain (R-AZ) argued that the legislation would do "great damage," repeating concerns about unit cohesion and battle effectiveness. Sen. Carl Levin (D-MI), chair of the Senate Armed Services Committee, countered McCain's concern, noting the long history of gay and lesbian service in the armed forces: "Men and women wearing the uniform of the United States who are gay and lesbian have died for this country. . . . [G]ay and lesbian men and women wearing the uniform of this country have their lives on the line right now."

DECEMBER 18, 2010
SENATE REPEALS BAN AGAINST OPENLY GAY MILITARY PERSONNEL
By CARL HULSE

WASHINGTON—The Senate on Saturday struck down the ban on gay men and lesbians serving openly in the military, bringing to a close a 17-year struggle over a policy that forced thousands of Americans from the ranks and caused others to keep secret their sexual orientation.

By a vote of 65 to 31, with eight Republicans joining Democrats, the Senate approved and sent to President Obama a repeal of the Clinton-era law, known as "don't ask, don't tell," a policy critics said amounted to government-sanctioned discrimination that treated gay and lesbian troops as second-class citizens.

Mr. Obama hailed the action, which fulfills his pledge to reverse the ban. "As commander in chief, I am also absolutely convinced that making this change will only underscore the professionalism of our troops as the best led and best trained fighting force the world has ever known," Mr. Obama said in a statement after the Senate, on a 63–33 vote, beat back Republican efforts to block a final vote on the repeal bill.

The vote marked a historic moment that some equated with the end of racial segregation in the military.

It followed a comprehensive review by the Pentagon that found a low risk to military effectiveness despite greater concerns among some combat units and the Marine Corps. The review also found that Pentagon officials supported Congressional repeal as a better alternative than a court-ordered end.

Supporters of the repeal said it was long past time to end what they saw as an ill-advised practice that cost valuable personnel and forced troops to lie to serve their country.

"We righted a wrong," said Senator Joseph I. Lieberman, the independent from Connecticut who led the effort to end the ban. "Today we've done justice."

Before voting on the repeal, the Senate blocked a bill that would have created a path to citizenship for certain illegal immigrants who came to the United States at a young age, completed two years of college or military service and met other requirements including passing a criminal background check.

The 55–41 vote in favor of the citizenship bill was five votes short of the number needed to clear the way for final passage of what is known as the Dream Act. The outcome effectively kills it for this year, and its fate beyond that is

uncertain since Republicans who will assume control of the House in January oppose the measure and are unlikely to bring it to a vote.

The Senate then moved on to the military legislation, engaging in an emotional back and forth over the merits of the measure as advocates for repeal watched from galleries crowded with people interested in the fate of both the military and immigration measures. "I don't care who you love," Senator Ron Wyden, Democrat of Oregon, said as the debate opened. "If you love this country enough to risk your life for it, you shouldn't have to hide who you are."

Mr. Wyden showed up for the Senate vote despite saying earlier that he would be unable to do so because he would be undergoing final tests before his scheduled surgery for prostate cancer on Monday.

The vote came in the final days of the 111th Congress as Democrats sought to force through a final few priorities before they turn over control of the House of Representatives to the Republicans in January and see their clout in the Senate diminished.

It represented a significant victory for the White House, Congressional advocates of lifting the ban and activists who have pushed for years to end the Pentagon policy created in 1993 under the Clinton administration as a compromise effort to end the practice of banning gay men and lesbians entirely from military service. Saying it represented an emotional moment for members of the gay community nationwide, activists who supported repeal of "don't ask, don't tell" exchanged hugs outside the Senate chamber after the vote.

"Today's vote means gay and lesbian service members posted all around the world can stand taller knowing that 'don't ask, don't tell' will soon be coming to an end," said Aubrey Sarvis, an Army veteran and executive director for Servicemembers Legal Defense Network.

The executive director of the Log Cabin Republicans, a gay group that challenged the policy in federal court, thanked Republican senators for participating in a historic vote. The director, R. Clarke Cooper, who is a member of the Army Reserve, said repeal will "finally end a policy which has burdened our armed services for far too long, depriving our nation of the talent, training and hard won battle experience of thousands of patriotic Americans."

A federal judge had ruled the policy unconstitutional in response to the Log Cabin suit, but that decision had been stayed pending appeal.

Aaron Belkin, director of the Palm Center in California, a research institute at the University of California in Santa Barbara that studies issues surrounding gays and lesbians in the military, said that the vote "ushers in a new era in which the largest employer in the United States treats gays and lesbians like human beings."

In a statement on the group's website, Mr. Belkin said: "It has long been clear that there is no evidence that lifting the ban will undermine the military, and no reason to fear the transition to inclusive policy. Research shows that moving quickly is one of the keys to a successful transition. If the President and military leadership quickly certify the end of 'don't ask, don't tell,' they will ensure an orderly transition with minimal disruption."

Organizations that opposed repeal of the ban assailed the Republican senators who defied their party majority.

The Center for Military Readiness, a group that specializes in social issues in the military and has opposed repeal, said the new legislation "will impose heavy, unnecessary burdens on the backs of military men and women." It said the Senate majority voted with "needless haste" by not waiting for hearings into a recent Department of Defense study of the "don't ask, don't tell" policy. Elaine Donnelly, president of the group, said that the Pentagon's survey indicated that 32 percent of Marines and 21.4 percent of Army combat troops would leave the military sooner than planned if "don't ask, don't tell" were repealed.

Kris Mineau, president of the Massachusetts Family Institute, said senators like Scott Brown, a Republican from Massachusetts, "broke trust with the people" by voting on repeal before the federal budget was resolved and "have put the troops at risk during wartime."

During the debate, Senator John McCain, Republican of Arizona and his party's presidential candidate in 2008, led the opposition to the repeal and said the vote was a sad day in history. "I hope that when we pass this legislation that we will understand that we are doing great damage," Mr. McCain said. "And we could possibly and probably, as the commandant of the Marine Corps said, and as I have been told by literally thousands of members of the military, harm the battle effectiveness vital to the survival of our young men and women in the military."

He and other opponents of lifting the ban said the change could harm the unit cohesion that is essential to effective military operations, particularly in combat, and deter some Americans from enlisting or pursuing a career in the military. They noted that despite support for repealing the ban from Defense Secretary Robert M. Gates and Adm. Mike Mullen, chairman of the Joint Chiefs of Staff, other military commanders have warned that changing the practice would prove disruptive.

"This isn't broke," Senator James M. Inhofe, Republican of Oklahoma, said about the policy. "It is working very well."

Other Republicans said that while the policy might need to be changed at some point, Congress should not do so when American troops are fighting overseas.

"In the middle of a military conflict is not the time to do it," said Senator Saxby Chambliss, Republican of Georgia.

Only a week ago, the effort to repeal the "don't ask, don't tell" policy seemed to be dead and in danger of fading for at least two years with Republicans about to take control of the House. The provision eliminating the ban was initially included in a broader Pentagon policy bill, and Republican backers of repeal had refused to join in cutting off a filibuster against the underlying bill because of objections over the ability to debate the measure.

In a last-ditch effort, Mr. Lieberman and Senator Susan Collins of Maine, a key Republican opponent of the ban, encouraged Democratic Congressional leaders to instead pursue a vote on simply repealing it. The House passed the measure earlier in the week.

The repeal will not take effect for at least 60 days while some other procedural steps are taken. In addition, the bill requires the defense secretary to determine that policies are in place to carry out the repeal "consistent with military standards for readiness, effectiveness, unit cohesion, and recruiting and retention."

Because of the uncertainty, Mr. Sarvis appealed to Mr. Gates to suspend any investigations into military personnel or discharge proceedings under the policy to be overturned in the coming months.

Mr. Lieberman said the ban undermined the integrity of the military by forcing troops to lie. He said 14,000 members of the armed forces had been forced to leave the ranks under the policy.

"What a waste," he said.

The fight erupted in the early days of President Bill Clinton's administration and has been a roiling political issue ever since. Mr. Obama endorsed repeal in his own campaign and advocates saw the current Congress as their best opportunity for ending the ban. Dozens of advocates of ending the ban—including one wounded in combat before being forced from the military—watched from the Senate gallery as the debate took place.

Senator Carl Levin, the Michigan Democrat who is chairman of the Armed Services Committee, dismissed Republican complaints that Democrats were trying to race through the repeal to satisfy their political supporters.

"I'm not here for partisan reasons," Mr. Levin said. "I'm here because men and women wearing the uniform of the United States who are gay and lesbian have died for this country, because gay and lesbian men and women wearing the uniform of this country have their lives on the line right now."

YOUTH AND EDUCATION

Opportunities and Challenges for Today's LGBT Youth

Lesbian, gay, bisexual, and transgender (LGBT) youth now have access to information and support unimaginable to past generations. In a March 3, 1996, interview, Dan Woog described what it was like to be a gay teen in the early 1970s: "I knew I was different from about the age of 3 or 4, but not like I was able to put any kind of definition on it. It was not talked about, could not be talked about." Today, most LGBT teens grow up with an awareness of homosexuality, and many have relatives or friends who are openly gay or lesbian. In addition, more schools are including value-neutral discussions of LGBT issues in their sex education curriculum as well as sponsoring Gay-Straight Alliances. "Coming out of the closet" is likely to still be somewhat difficult and usually requires a period of adjustment, but more parents and peers are tolerant and accepting than ever before. Even LGBT youth growing up in unsupportive communities and families now have access to numerous Internet sites specifically geared toward teens, including Planned Parenthood's Teen Talk site and Rutgers University's Sexetc.org site.

Despite the progress that has been made, childhood and adolescence are still challenging times for most LGBT individuals. First, as Dr. Amy Kohn says in a November 5, 1995, *New York Times* article, gay teens are raised in the same homophobic society as everyone else, and "they have these feelings, and they think 'It's gross, it's disgusting.'" She adds, "At the same time, they ask, 'Why does it feel so natural?' It's a terrible struggle." In addition, although society as a whole is becoming more accepting, many individuals, religions, and regions of the country have not altered their position on these issues. As a result, a significant number of LGBT youth continue to feel unsafe in their homes, schools, and communities. While many carefully guard the secret of their sexual or gender orientation in an attempt to protect themselves from emotional and physical harm, such secrecy can also lead to increased feelings of shame and isolation. Others will choose to come out or be "outed" involuntarily by others. For this latter group, the teasing and bullying can be intense. According to a survey by the Gay, Lesbian and Straight Education Network, four out of five LGBT students report being verbally harassed at school because of their sexual or gender orientation; two out of five report physical harassment, such as being shoved or pushed; and one out of five report physical assaults by classmates within the past year. Transgender students report the highest rates of all types of harassment.

In some instances school violence can turn deadly for LGBT youth, as in the case of Lawrence King. A fifteen-year-old junior high school student, King had recently come out as gay to his classmates and sometimes wore high-heeled boots and makeup to school. As described in a *Times* article on February 23, 2008, he and twenty-four other students were working in a computer lab when fourteen-year-old Brandon McInerney drew out a gun and shot Lawrence in the head. The youth was rushed to the hospital, where he died two days later. Some news outlets reported that King asked McInerney to be his valentine a few days prior to the shooting. At the time of this writing, McInerney is awaiting trial as an adult for murder and related offenses and faces a maximum sentence of fifty-four years. Said Masen Davis, executive director of the Transgender Law Center, Brandon "is just as much a victim as Lawrence. He's a victim of homophobia and hate."

LGBT youth differ from most other minorities because they are often outsiders even within their own families. Many continue to experience denial, rejection, shaming, and prohibition at the hands of homophobic relatives. In some cases, these teens may even be beaten, raped, institutionalized, or forced to leave home by family members unable or unwilling to come to terms with their sexual or gender orientation. Ryan Kim's story is told in a December 8, 2004, *Times* article. When Kim came out as gay in his senior year of high school, his parents withdrew their financial support for his college education and, instead of taking freshman classes at New York University, as had been planned, he found himself living in a room at the Salvation Army and working two jobs to pay his bills. Kim eventually enrolled at Princeton, thanks in part to financial support and mentors provided by the Point Foundation, which was founded to provide scholarships and other assistance to successful students marginalized as a result of their gender or sexual orientation. For many LGBT youth, however, being forced to leave home leads to a downward spiral that may include homelessness, sex work, drug use, sexually transmitted diseases, violence, and even death.

The advent of the Internet offers new threats as well as opportunities to isolated LGBT youth. Although it can provide useful information and supportive contacts for isolated LGBT youth, it can also expose teens to hard-core pornography, sexually explicit chat rooms, and virtual sexual experiences that they may not be emotionally mature enough to handle. A lengthy December 10, 2000, *Times* article describes both the benefits and pitfalls, including the story of a thirteen-year-old midwestern boy who spends several hours a day online, visiting gay porn sites, engaging in online sex with multiple partners, and occasionally being "pestered" by adults for an in-person meeting. While sexual predators pose a real threat, much of the Internet's danger for teens stems from its unique ability to foster relationships that combine both anonymity and intimacy. Although they may never have been on a date or even been kissed, gay teens can create alternate, idealized versions of themselves online and then interact with others who may also be misrepresenting themselves, sometimes developing deep emotional commitments to people whom they have never met and who may suddenly disappear without a word of explanation. When rejected by a long-term online boyfriend after the two swapped photos, one teenager described his confusion at the intensity of his emotional reaction, saying, "It's like, Oh, my God, I'm crying over someone I've never seen, I've never touched. It's kind of scary."

Given the challenges they face, it is perhaps not surprising that LGBT teens continue to be more likely to suffer from poor self-esteem and depression than their heterosexual counterparts. They are also more likely to abuse drugs or alcohol, drop out of school, and consider or attempt suicide. It is estimated that 30 percent of the homeless teens in the United States are gay, lesbian, bisexual, or transgender. As Allan Van Capelle, executive director of the Empire State Pride Agenda, stated in an August 8, 2008, article, "In a 'Queer Eye for the Straight Guy,' 'Will and Grace' world, kids are coming out at a much younger age. As a community, we have done a woefully inadequate job of protecting them." However, it is also true that millions of LGBT Americans have successfully navigated their teen years to become happy, healthy adults with productive careers, satisfying romantic relationships, and extended networks of supportive family, friends, organizations, and communities.

GAY CURRICULUM AND CLUBS IN THE PUBLIC SCHOOLS

To help LGBT youth make the difficult transition to adulthood, some public schools have tried to offer various forms of support in recent decades. However, as illustrated by Anita Bryant's successful antigay rights campaign (see the second chapter), associating the issue of homosexuality with children often results in an emotional and political uproar. This is illustrated by a December 5, 1974, *Times* story of two Baptist ministers who threatened legal and divine retribution over a plan to require all sixth graders to take home economics because "by having a young boy cook or sew, wearing aprons, we're pushing a boy into homosexuality." Although this is perhaps an extreme reaction, it is by no means unique. In the 1980s, changing public attitudes as well as high rates of AIDS infection among gay men provided new impetus for discussing the issue of homosexuality as part of a comprehensive sexual education curriculum within the public schools. However, when the Stafford County Prenatal and Family Planning Clinic in Dover, New Hampshire, created a curriculum for teens that suggested homosexuality was both normal and healthy, a political firestorm ensued. The curriculum was distributed to public schools only on request and was primarily focused on helping teens engage in discussions about pregnancy, contraception, and rape. Nonetheless, its stance on homosexuality was deemed so controversial that Gov. John Sununu asked the state attorney general to investigate blocking its further distribution, Sen. Gordon Humphrey requested an investigation into the use of taxpayer money to produce the manual, and the Stafford County commissioners threatened to cut off the clinic's financial support.

New York City's battle over the "Children of the Rainbow" curriculum in the early 1990s provides another example of the intense interaction of emotion and ideology that tends to swirl around this issue. As argued in a December 3, 1992, *Times* article, the controversy over the curriculum may have been primarily a fight over local versus centralized control of the city schools, further aggravated by animosity toward New York City schools chancellor Joseph A. Fernandez.

Nonetheless, the topic of homosexuality in the classroom is what finally ignited the long-smoldering tension.

Dr. Fernandez was a nationally known school reformer when he was unanimously selected to be the chancellor by the New York City Board of Education in 1989. He was an appealing candidate, a native of New York City who had dropped out of high school, earned a GED, and eventually gone on to successfully manage Miami's public school system. However, he and the relatively conservative New York City Board of Education soon clashed over educational priorities, including Dr. Fernandez's efforts to encourage comprehensive AIDS-prevention education and condom distribution within the schools. The relationship did not improve, and Dr. Fernandez took the unusual and perhaps politically unwise step of publishing a tell-all memoir titled *Tales Out of School: Joseph Fernandez's Crusade to Rescue American Education.* Further conflict seemed inevitable.

At this time a new first-grade diversity curriculum was to be introduced into the New York City schools that primarily focused on songs and activities from various cultures, including the Mexican hat dance, a recipe for Greek New Year's Day bread, and a Japanese version of rock, paper, scissors. The 443-page instructor's guide also included a few sections addressing the issue of homosexuality, such as a passage that urged teachers to "include references to lesbians and gays in all curricular areas" and a bibliography listing *Heather has Two Mommies* and other children's books with homosexual themes. Members of many of New York City's thirty-two local school boards were uncomfortable with discussing homosexuality with elementary school children, particularly in the first grade, and several local boards voted to not implement this portion of the new curriculum.

School District 24 took the issue one step further. Covering a primarily working-class, ethnically diverse region of western Queens, this district's school board refused to adopt the "Children of the Rainbow Curriculum" and, when pressed by Dr. Fernandez, refused to provide an equivalent replacement or even to meet to discuss the issue. The controversy quickly escalated, with Dr. Fernandez suspending all members of the dissenting school board, only to have the NYC Board of Education immediately reinstate them. Public meetings scheduled to discuss the new curriculum brought out hundreds of people on both sides of the issue. One meeting had to be ended early when the participants became uncontrollable, shouted, and shoved one another. After being vilified by many in the press and receiving at least two death threats, Fernandez was ousted from his position on a 4–3

Lexie Levitt, Danica West, and Sam Verde walk to class at Hunter High School in West Valley City, Utah. The three students belong to the school's Gay-Straight Alliance. A similar club started by Kelli Peterson in 1996 at her Salt Lake City, Utah, high school generated a firestorm of controversy leading to a ban on school clubs and a walk-out by students.
*Source: Jeffrey D. Allred/*The New York Times

vote by the Board of Education, following a six-hour meeting punctuated by shouting board members as well as more than 200 spectators. When asked what advice he'd give to his successor, a February 14, 1993, *Times* article reported that Dr. Fernandez said, "Don't come."

In middle and high schools, controversy has frequently developed over the formation of Gay-Straight Alliances and other clubs designed to provide support for LGBT teens. Although the first such club was organized in Massachusetts in 1988, the issue received national attention in 1996 when Kelli Peterson and two classmates attempted to organize a Gay-Straight Alliance at East High School in Salt Lake City, Utah. The seventeen-year-old senior was hoping to ensure that future LGBT students did not suffer the same sense of isolation and rejection that she felt after coming out as a lesbian during her sophomore year. However, approximately half of Salt Lake City's residents are members of the Mormon Church; in 1991 church leaders issued a statement condemning homosexuality and stating, "[S]uch thoughts and feelings, regardless of their causes, can and should be overcome and sinful behavior should be eliminated." Despite the community's generally conservative position on this issue, the federal Equal Access Act of 1984 effectively prevented the local board of education from banning Peterson's club.

Ironically, this law, which requires public schools to treat all proposed clubs the same regardless of content, was sponsored by Sen. Orrin Hatch (R-Utah) and was originally intended to ensure that Christian groups could not be barred

IN FOCUS

Same Sex Proms and Homecoming "Royals"

In 1979 seventeen-year-old Paul Guilbert made headlines when he requested permission to bring a male date to the junior prom being held at his Cumberland, Rhode Island, high school. Guilbert was refused permission by his principal and also denied a hearing before the Cumberland School Committee. Although the Rhode Island branch of the American Civil Liberties Union considered fighting the decision, the group reluctantly decided not to pursue the case, largely because Guilbert's parents had expressed disapproval of their son's prom plans and the proposed legal action. The local ACLU executive director attributed the decision to a concern that "the issue of homosexual rights would be overshadowed by the parents' rights."

By the early 2000s, however, communities throughout the country were beginning to host "gay proms," although not without controversy. Some parents were excited that their LGBT teens would be among the first to proudly engage in this traditional rite of American adolescence. Others were strongly opposed, seeing these events as condoning deviant sexual relationships in a manner that might give impressionable teens the idea that homosexuality is an acceptable alternative to heterosexuality. Commenting on same-sex proms held on Long Island in 2001, Rev. John F. Harvey, a local Catholic priest, said, "This just shows how sick we are as a civilization." However, one bisexual teen planning to attend said, "This gives us a chance to go with who we really want to go with and imagine what it would be like if it was our real school prom and we were accepted."

Changes have also begun at some high school and college homecoming celebrations. Throughout the country, men have been elected homecoming queens and women have been crowned homecoming kings. Many of those running are LGBT students, motivated by desires to question the sexist and heterosexist assumptions behind the tradition or to play with the campy drag possibilities of fancy dress, tiaras, and ribbon sashes. However, straight students also have been the recipients of gender-bending crowns, including a young woman who successfully ran for homecoming king at her San Francisco high school simply because she didn't want to compete with her best friend for the queen title. Further, some schools have chosen to eliminate gender distinctions from these competitions altogether, electing a set number of "royals," which may include two women and no men, as was the case at University of Washington's homecoming in 2004. Because the honors came with a $1,000 scholarship, the student body decided that the decision-making process should be gender neutral. Newly crowned royal Glorya Cho, a nineteen-year-old heterosexual woman majoring in international studies, commented, "I think that the gender-specific titles are becoming obsolete."

From *The New York Times*

Baker, Al. "With Pride and Corsages, Gay Proms Reach Suburbs." April 23, 2001.

Kershaw, Sarah. "Gay Students Force New Look at Homecoming Traditions." November 27, 2004.

Unsigned. "Homosexual Denied Male Escort Plans to Picket Providence Prom." April 22, 1970.

———. "Boy, 17, Seeks to Take Male Date to the Prom." April 11, 1979.

IN FOCUS

LGBT Youth Fight School Dress Codes

In 2004 the ACLU filed suit against a Missouri high school for prohibiting sixteen-year-old Brad Mathewson from wearing a T-shirt that read, "I'm gay and I'm proud." Similarly, in 2009 several schools have been threatened with legal action for attempting to force students to conform to gender norms. These conflicts have often involved male students wearing wigs, makeup, or women's clothing. However, one school in Mississippi stirred controversy by refusing to publish the yearbook photo of a tuxedo-clad lesbian. Although it is difficult to estimate how frequently these incidents occur, they appear to be on the rise. "This generation is really challenging the gender norms we grew up with," said psychologist and gender expert Diane Ehrensaft. "A lot of youths say they won't be bound by boys having to wear this or girls wearing that. For them, gender is a creative playing field."

On the one hand, some administrators argue that schools are communal environments and, just like in the workplace, certain elements of personal expression must be toned down to promote concentration and productivity. For example, when a Florida school sent home a boy wearing high-heeled boots and a padded bra on the grounds that such clothing abridged a requirement that students dress "in keeping with their gender," a district spokesperson commented, "He was cross-dressing, and it caused a disruption in the normal instructional day. That's the whole point behind the dress code." However, others point to the shooting of Lawrence King (see the introduction) as evidence that schools are unable to adequately protect LGBT students from the often violent, and occasionally lethal, reactions of their classmates.

Although schools regularly impose dress codes limiting sexually provocative outfits or gang-related clothing choices, placing limits on students' desire to wear clothing that reflects their sexual orientation or gender identity is more complicated. Advocates for LGBT teens suggest that the line between protecting these students and further adding to their harassment is unclear. In addition, many argue that restricting boys from wearing clothing, makeup, or accessories that would be deemed acceptable for girls is gender discrimination.

The law related to this issue remains unclear, but some school administrators are now attempting to enforce gender-neutral dress codes. Dr. Alan Storm, former assistant superintendent of a school district in Tucson, reports that principals would regularly call his office for clarification regarding transgender students. "They'd say, 'Johnny just showed up in a cutoff top! Should I suspend the kid or make him change his clothes?' And I'd say, 'Is there a bare midriff?' 'No.' 'Then it doesn't violate your dress code. You have no right to make the kid change his clothes. But it is your absolute policy to keep the kid safe.'"

From *The New York Times*

Hoffman, J. "Can a Boy Wear a Skirt to School?" November 8, 2009.

Lewin, T. "Battle on Gay Pride Shirts Leads to Suit against School." November 24, 2004.

from meeting in school facilities. Rather than allow the creation of a Gay-Straight Alliance at East High School, the Salt Lake School Board voted to ban all student clubs at high schools throughout the school district. In response, hundreds of angry students walked out of school and marched on the state capital in protest. Although the East High School club received support from a national gay group to form as an independent community group and eventually rented meeting space at the high school, a *Times* article on December 7, 1998, reported that student morale was badly damaged and many seniors were worried about the effect their lack of extracurricular activities would have on college admissions boards. According to one East High School teacher, "It has been a disaster." High-profile disputes over the establishment of Gay-Straight Alliances have also occurred in many other states, including Kentucky, Texas, California, and Georgia.

To date, the discussion of homosexuality in the public schools and the rights of LGBT students continue to be controversial topics. Throughout the country conservative and progressive community members are still fighting over whether homosexuality has a place in sexual education or diversity curriculums and, if it does, at what age it should be introduced, and what the content of the message should be. A September 14, 2007, *Times* article describes a school district almost evenly divided—50.4 percent for and 49.5 percent opposed—regarding an educational video aimed at third graders called "That's a Family!" Along with interracial and adopted children, the film offers short profiles of children raised by two gay dads. In an August 15, 2007, *Times* article, conservative groups in Montgomery County, Maryland, promised to appeal a court decision allowing lessons on homosexuality and condom use for eighth and tenth graders.

Similarly, although there are now more than 4,000 active Gay-Straight Alliance groups in high schools and middle schools across the country, Utah passed a seventeen-page law in 2007 that, along with detailed requirements regarding club formation, content, membership, and discipline, mandates that students obtain written parental permission prior to joining any school club. A *New York Times* article on March 17 of that year quotes Utah state senator Scott D. McCoy as saying, "This is all about gay-straight alliance clubs, and anybody who tells you different is lying." In 2009 the American Civil Liberties Union filed suit on behalf of two Florida students prohibited from forming a club promoting gay tolerance at Yulee High School. On a related issue, a December 2007 *Times* article describes efforts by the Advocates of Faith and Freedom and other conservative organizations to

block a California bill that would protect students in public schools from discrimination on the basis of sexual orientation and gender identity. Although the general trend is toward increased LGBT education and tolerance within the public schools, this issue continues to be a contentious one for many communities.

SEXUAL AND GENDER ORIENTATION ON COLLEGE CAMPUSES

Because of college's *en loco parentis* role, homosexuality has been an issue of controversy on campuses for decades. This Latin phrase literally means "in the place of a parent" and refers to a long-standing tradition by which college administrators took responsibility for safeguarding and disciplining students in the way that a parent might if these students were still living at home. As a result, universities used to enforce curfews (sometimes as early as 10 P.M. for female students), bar visitors of the opposite sex from entering dorm rooms, and otherwise attempt to regulate students' social and sexual behavior.

Homosexual students were typically viewed as a threat to the morality of others rather than as individuals in need of protection themselves. As a result LGBT students needed to carefully conceal their sexual orientation and relationships or risk being expelled. A November 30, 2002, *Times* article describes papers found in Harvard's archives that vividly document a 1920 investigation resulting in the dismissal of eight students and one professor on grounds of homosexuality. After a sophomore at Harvard committed suicide, his brother discovered letters in his room that provided information about the existence of a gay subculture on campus. The college president appointed a group of administrators to investigate, and this "court" (as they referred to themselves) proceeded to interrogate students as well as local men not enrolled at Harvard about their sex lives. Most students were found guilty and asked to leave both the college and the city of Cambridge. Two later committed suicide. According to George Chauncey, author of a book on New York's gay culture between 1890 and 1940, Harvard's reaction was typical for colleges at that time.

The dismantling of en loco parentis traditions began in 1961 with a landmark case, *Dixon v. Alabama,* in which a federal appeals court found that a public university could not expel students without due process. Although this case dealt with black students dismissed from Alabama State College for participating in civil rights demonstrations, the precedent it set had wider implications. Combined with a loosening of sexual mores and a general liberalization of American culture in the 1960s, this led to swift and dramatic changes for many gay, lesbian, and bisexual college students.

In 1965 the Group for the Advancement of Psychiatry released the 129-page study "Sex and the College Student." In addition to offering college administrators advice on issues related to birth control, sexually transmitted diseases, and abortion, the report recommended a then-radical change in policy toward gay and lesbian students. Based on the results of their study, the authors discouraged automatically expelling the "active homosexual individual," instead advocating a policy similar to that extended to other sexually active students. If conducted in a sensitive and discrete manner, the report suggested, both homosexual and heterosexual behavior should be ignored, with college administrators stepping in only when "a student's failure to insure the privacy of his sexual life places it outside the private domain and in the realm of public concern." Although this appears to be a recommendation for equal treatment, it is important to remember that the definitions of appropriate public behavior remained vastly different for heterosexual and homosexual couples at this time. As a result, even on progressive campuses that adopted the new recommendations, gay couples were not free to behave like ordinary straight couples (for example, openly discussing their relationship, dancing together in public, and holding hands while walking to class).

Faced with this double standard and emboldened by the black civil rights movement, some students began to question why lesbians, gays, and bisexuals did not have the same rights as their heterosexual peers. (The struggle for transgender rights did not gain momentum until much later. See Introduction.) In 1967 students at Columbia University organized the Student Homophile League, the first officially recognized campus group dedicated to seeking equal rights for homosexuals. Although the group's declaration of principles asserted, "The homosexual has a fundamental human right to live and work with his fellow man as an equal," the membership list of the Student Homophile League was initially kept confidential and the group's president employed a pseudonym when interviewed by *The Times*. According to a May 11, 1967, *Times* article, critical comments by both the director of Columbia's counseling service and the college dean were printed in the school newspaper, describing the group's efforts as "angry exhibitionism" and suggesting that its presence might hinder college fund-raising efforts.

Despite this rocky beginning, homosexual organizations were soon springing up on campuses throughout the country. According to a December 15, 1971, *Times* article, their activities had expanded to include the coordination of socializing opportunities such as parties, dances, and dedicated campus lounges as well as the publication of newsletters and the staffing of emergency hotlines, counseling programs, offices, and speaker bureaus, all dedicated to improving campus acceptance and quality of life for gay, lesbian, and bisexual students. At that time it was estimated that groups had formed on more than 150 campuses, receiving little resistance from college administrators and, in some cases, even being awarded student activity fee funding.

Throughout the 1970s, campus groups for lesbian, gay, and bisexual students continued to grow in number, size, and militancy, but many students remained fully or partially closeted, fearful of negative reactions from family, fellow students, professors, and future employers. As quoted in an extensive March 12, 1978, *Times* article titled "Homosexuality on Campus," Dave (no last name given), the leader of the Gay People's Union at Stanford, commented, "Coming out is a very liberating experience, but you have to be awfully sure of yourself to handle negative attitudes."

In the 1980s the election of Ronald Reagan heralded a conservative shift within American culture, including decreased support for taxes, regulation, and social welfare programs coupled with increased concern for national defense and traditional family values. This new mood became a force to be reckoned with on many college campuses, often with the help of independently owned newspapers such as the *Dartmouth Review*. Founded in 1980, the *Dartmouth Review* was written and edited by students but received significant outside funding from conservative foundations as well as the support of such well-known Republican politicians and conservative powerbrokers as Patrick Buchanan and William F. Buckley Jr. The weekly paper swiftly gained national attention for its provocative approach. During its first year the *Dartmouth Review* claimed the college gave preferential treatment to minority students, suggested that a women's studies class should be renamed "lesbian studies," and hosted a free dinner with champagne and lobster during a campuswide fast designed to raise awareness about world hunger. The following year, after the Gay Student Alliance reported files had disappeared from its office, the *Dartmouth Review* printed a list of members' names and excerpts from private correspondence.

Following the success of the *Dartmouth Review*, similar papers were started at colleges throughout the country, and as the culture wars heated up, these publications contributed to the polarization of a variety of campus issues, including homosexuality. The University of Iowa's *Campus Review* ignited controversy by printing, displaying, and selling T-shirts that read "Stop AIDS" and depicted two men engaged in a sexual act within a slashed red circle. Campus protests resulted after Harvard's *Peninsula* magazine published an entire issue on homosexuality in November 1991, characterizing same-sex relationships as "bad" for both individuals and society. And across the country, right-wing students organized Conservative Awareness Weeks and Straight Pride Rallies to protest what some perceived to be a pervasive liberal and prohomosexual bias on many college campuses.

Despite this conservative backlash, in recent years most campuses have generally become more accepting places for gay, lesbian, bisexual, and even transgender students. An increasing number of schools are offering courses, certificates, and, in a few cases, entire majors devoted to the academic study of LGBT issues related to literature, philosophy, history, and other traditional areas of study. In addition to social and support groups, some colleges now have policies prohibiting discrimination based on sexual orientation and offer special scholarships and housing options targeted to LGBT students.

As described in a March 16, 2008, *Times* article, transgender students have been fighting for recognition on campuses for several years, and these efforts are beginning to pay off. More than 140 schools now include gender identity in their nondiscrimination policies, and some are starting to provide single-stall lockable public bathrooms, a critical amenity for individuals who feel uncomfortable or unsafe entering traditional multistall, gender-segregated facilities. In addition, a few schools allow transgender students to choose the gender of their roommate, and some professors now inquire about preferred names and pronouns, allowing transgender students to opt for neutral options such as "ze" and "hir."

JAMES DALE AND THE BOY SCOUT BAN

No discussion of youth and sexual orientation would be complete without a consideration of the Boy Scouts' long-standing ban on openly gay members and troop leaders. Ironically, this group was founded in 1908 by Lord Baden-Powell, who may himself have been a practicing homosexual according to a biography by Tim Jeal that was reviewed in *The Times* on April 1, 1990. The group quickly spread from Britain to the United States, and by 1928 more than a million American boys were gathering to build fires, tie knots, and learn other skills needed by "healthy pioneers, good citizens, and energetic patriots." Boy Scout administrators have long struggled with the issue of attracting appropriate male role models to serve as volunteer troop leaders while effectively weeding out sexual predators.

In a June 9, 1935, *Times* article, Chief Scout Executive Dr. James E. West described a system developed to minimize this risk. An alphabetical card catalog was kept of all men who had been dismissed from Boy Scout service, and against which all new applicants names were checked prior to acceptance as a volunteer. Of the 2,919 cards in the file, Dr. West said that about 30 percent were "morally unfit," and he went on to explain, "We still have those who seek to enter Scouting and contact boys who are unbalanced morally . . . and sometimes give way to temptation and develop practices which make them degenerate." A few high-profile cases demonstrated the validity of these concerns, including one described in an April 12, 1977, *Times* article that involved seventeen New Orleans men investigated regarding "the use of a Boy Scout troop to supply boys for homosexual acts."

Controversy arose as cultural attitudes began to shift on the issue of homosexuality. First, as more gay men began to come out of the closet, the Boy Scouts took steps to formally ban their participation in the program, stating, "We believe that homosexual conduct is inconsistent with the Scout oath that a Scout be morally straight and in the Scout law that a Scout be clean in word and deed." Although most Americans continued to strongly support the need to protect children from sexual predators, many also came to understand that the vast majority of gay men are no more sexually interested in children than their heterosexual peers. As a result, the Boy Scouts' ban on all homosexual Scouts and Scout leaders ceased to seem like a prudent safety policy and began to feel more like discrimination to an increasing number of people.

James Dale became the public face of this issue in 1992, when he sued the Boy Scouts of America for revoking his membership. A long-standing member of the Scouts, Dale had been an Eagle Scout, the highest possible rank, and earned more than thirty merit badges. He remained active in the Scouts while attending Rutgers University by serving as an assistant Scoutmaster for his childhood troop. However, when a local newspaper printed an article in which Dale acknowledged being gay, the Monmouth Council of the Boy Scouts of America revoked his membership, stating that as a private club they had a right to set standards that prohibited membership to known homosexuals. Although the New

In 2000 the U.S. Supreme Court upheld the right of the Boy Scouts of America to exclude gay scout leaders. Viewing the organization's policies as discriminatory, the Philadelphia City Council voted in 2007 to end the lease on the municipally owned land on which the Boy Scouts' council headquarters, pictured here, were situated.

*Source: Jessica Kourkounis/*The New York Times

Jersey Superior Court originally supported the Boy Scouts' position in 1995, a New Jersey appeals court reversed this decision in 1998. According to a *Times* article on March 3 of that year, the judges ruled 2–1 that the Boy Scouts' support by public schools and civic groups had essentially transformed the group from a private club into more of a public accommodation, such as a hotel or restaurant, making the Boy Scouts subject to a New Jersey law prohibiting discrimination on the basis of sexual orientation in public places. Accordingly, they ordered the Scouts to reinstate Dale as a member in good standing.

The Boy Scouts appealed the decision to the New Jersey Supreme Court, which again found in favor of James Dale, stating in a unanimous 7–0 decision that the revocation of his membership was "based on little more than prejudice" and that "a lesbian or gay person, merely because he or she is a homosexual, is no more or less likely to be moral than a person who is heterosexual." On hearing the decision, James Dale said, "This is what Scouting taught me: Goodness will

prevail." However, the Boy Scouts again appealed the decision, and in 2000 the United States Supreme Court ruled 5–4 in favor of the Boy Scouts. Chief Justice William H. Rehnquist wrote the decision, which hinges on the assertion that forcing the Boy Scouts to include homosexuals would limit the Boy Scouts' ability to advocate for the viewpoint that homosexuality is incompatible with their oath, "particularly with the values represented by the terms 'morally straight' and 'clean.'" Writing in dissent, Justice John Paul Stevens said that neither morally straight nor clean "says the slightest thing about homosexuality." Quoting Justice Brandeis, he added that "we must be ever on our guard, lest we erect our prejudices into legal principles."

Despite winning in Court, the Boy Scouts lost significant public and financial support in the wake of the Supreme Court decision. Some parents pulled their sons from participating in the program, local troops have circulated petitions protesting the national policy, and "Scouting for All," a group initially formed by a fifteen-year-old scout, has organized protests in several cities. In addition, Chase Manhattan Bank, Textron, Inc., and other companies have ceased to provide financial support, while some cities and school districts have placed new restrictions on the Boy Scouts' use of parks, classrooms, and other facilities. As described in a December 6, 2007, *Times* article, local Boy Scout councils continue to struggle to find common ground amid the competing demands of various supporters.

Although homosexuality is often a controversial topic in America, this is particularly true when dealing with issues related to children, teens, and young adults. Whether discussing sexual education in the public schools, support programs for LGBT teens, or United Way funding for the Boy Scouts, these debates continue to be heated and are unlikely to be fully resolved anytime soon.

BIBLIOGRAPHY

Gray, Mary L. *Out in the Country: Youth, Media and Queer Visibility in Rural America.* New York: NYU Press, 2009.

Sears, James T. *Gay, Lesbian and Transgender Issues in Education: Programs, Policies, and Practice.* New York: Routledge, 2005.

Shephard, Tom (Producer and Director). *Scout's Honor* [Documentary]. United States: Independent Television, 2001.

FROM *THE NEW YORK TIMES*

Barbanel, Josh. "Under 'Rainbow,' a War: When Politics, Morals and Learning Mix." December 27, 1992.

———. "FEB. 7-13: A Reformer is Fired; Can Anyone Survive the System to Rebuild New York Schools?" February 14, 1993.

Berger, Joseph. "A Mix of Earlier Skirmishes Converges in the Rainbow Curriculum Battle." December 3, 1992.

Cathcart, Rebecca. "Effort to Block California Anti-Bias Bill." December 30, 2007.

———. "Boy's Killing, Labeled a Hate Crime, Stuns a Town." February 23, 2008.

Celis, William III. "Schools Across U.S. Cautiously Adding Lessons on Gay Life." January 6, 1993.

Clendinen, Dudley. "Conservative Paper Stirs Dartmouth." October 13, 1981.

Colapinto, John. "Armies of the Right; The Young Hipublicans." May 25, 2003.

Egan, Jennifer. "Lonely Gay Teen Seeking Same." December 10, 2000.

Freedman, Samuel G. "A Refuge for Gay Students When Families Turn Away." December 8, 2004.

Hanley, Robert. "Appeals Court Finds in Favor of Gay Scout." March 3, 1998.

———. "New Jersey Court Overturns Ouster of Gay Boy Scout." August 5, 1999.

Hechinger, Grace, and Fred M. Hechinger. "Homosexuality on Campus." March 12, 1978.

Johnson, Kirk. "Utah Sets Rigorous Rules for School Clubs, and Gay Ones May Be Target." March 17, 2007.

Jones, Richard G. "Film with Same-Sex Parents Splits School District." September 14, 2007.

Knowlton, Brian. "American Topics." December 7, 1988.

Lombardi, Kate Stone. "Facing the Agony of Being Different." November 5, 1995.

———. "Long Days, Long Hallways." January 27, 2002.

Medina, Jennifer. "New York State Senate Gets Bill Banning Bullying Acts in the Schools." August 8, 2008.

Quart, Alissa. "When Girls Will Be Boys." March 16, 2008.

Reinhold, Robert. "Campus Homosexuals Organize to Win Community Acceptance." December 15, 1971.

Schumach, Murray. "Criticism by Two Officials at Columbia Angers Leaders of Student Homophile League." May 11, 1967.

Steiner, Zara. "There Is a Brotherhood of Boys." April 1, 1990.

Unsigned. "Boy Scouts Head Explains 'Red' List." June 9, 1935.

———. "Around the Nation: 17 Men Accused of Abusing Boys in Scout Troop." April 12, 1977.

———. "Excerpts from the Supreme Court's Ruling on Gays and the Boy Scouts." June 29, 2000.

———. "In Harvard Papers, a Dark Corner of the College's Past." November 30, 2002.

Urbina, Ian. "Boy Scouts Lose Philadelphia Lease in Gay-Rights Fight. December 6, 2007.

Weizel, Richard. "Connecticut Q&A: Dan Woog; Taking Gay Issues into the Schools." March 3, 1996.

Whitaker, Barbara. "To Outlaw Gay Group, District May Ban Clubs." February, 10, 2000.

GAY TEENS STILL STRUGGLE TO FIND ACCEPTANCE

Adolescence is a challenging time for most people, but for many lesbian, gay, bisexual, and transgender teens, it can be a particularly difficult transition. In addition to the issues dealt with by all teens, members of this group often struggle to accept a sexual identity that they may initially find somewhat unappealing, often without a supportive parent, peer group, or school system to turn to for help. Attitudes toward homosexuality are changing slowly, and more LGBT teens now receive support from understanding family members and Gay-Straight Alliance programs in high school. But many are still subject to harassment and bullying at school as well as frequent and sometimes violent conflicts at home. Says one social worker with experience in this area, "For some kids, sometimes staying in the closet is an adaptive response" that can protect them until they are old enough to graduate and leave home. Whether out or closeted, LGBT youth continue to suffer from higher rates of depression, drug and alcohol abuse, suicide, and homelessness. These teens are also more likely than their straight peers to drop out of school or become the victims of violent crime.

In an effort to support these vulnerable youth, Westchester Jewish Community Services founded Center Lane in 1995. This community center for gay, lesbian, and bisexual teenagers is located in White Plains, New York, a suburban community just north of New York City. Serving 130 teens from throughout Westchester County, the center offers educational and recreational activities, counseling, advocacy services, support groups, and a drop-in center where teens can meet others like themselves in an informal, safe environment. Since this article was written, Center Lane has expanded its services to include transgender youth and has opened a branch office in Yonkers, New York.

AUGUST 29, 1999
A CENTER OFFERS A SAFE HAVEN FOR GAY TEEN-AGERS
By MERRI ROSENBERG

With a mixture of lassitude and restlessness, a dozen 15- to 20-year-olds sprawled across battered couches, played computer games, drank sodas, ate snack foods and demonstrated the fine art of hanging out.

There was nothing out of the ordinary in the activity, paralleled across the county in many suburban family rooms and basements on a warm summer afternoon. What was different was the fact that the young people here were relaxing in Center Lane, Westchester's only community center for gay, lesbian and bisexual teen-agers.

At a time when national attention is increasingly focused on what happens to teen-agers who feel alienated, places like Center Lane, which offer a haven for teen-agers who are different from the majority of their peers, take on added importance.

"What happens to a lot of gay kids in school is that when they come out, they become 'the gay kid,'" said Jill Schreibman, a certified social worker and the coordinator of the Center Lane program. "Instead of being the captain of a team or debate club president, they are the 'gay team captain' or 'gay club president.' It becomes their primary identity, and a label, and it can be a difficult label to carry around." Adolescence in general is often marked by a difficult quest for identity and figuring out where to belong, and that quest for gay, lesbian and bisexual teen-agers can be particularly perilous, experts say.

"Gay and lesbian teen-agers face all of the same challenges, struggles and difficulties in their journey toward identity," said Dr. Amy Kohn, associate executive director of Westchester Jewish Community Services, the nonprofit agency that runs Center Lane. "But the gay and lesbian teen-ager often does so in isolation. The whole life experience they go through is so much more profound."

For many teen-age homosexuals, depression, drug and alcohol abuse—even suicide attempts—are a response to their situation, which can be exacerbated by rejection from their parents, hostility from their peers and teachers and other problems that are easily magnified by adolescent self-analysis, Dr. Kohn said. According to a study by the United States Department of Health and Human Services, homosexual teen-agers are two to three times more likely than their heterosexual counterparts to attempt suicide. They are also at increased risk of dropping out of school, becoming homeless or victims of violence.

"The stresses of trying to deal with this in middle and high school are so great," Dr. Paul Bloom, a pediatrician who helps lead some of the groups at Center Lane said, referring to the quest for identity. "Being different when you're in middle school is depressing. There are many kids in Westchester who have serious emotional problems and have been depressed and hospitalized, from being harassed."

Finding a safe place can be difficult. "Some kids get kicked out of their home by their parents," said Jill Schreibman, a clinical social worker and the coordinator of the Center Lane program. "It's difficult for any gay kid in any school. A lot of it is homophobic. For some kids, sometimes staying in the closet is an adaptive response."

The stories that the teen-agers here told reflected the range of their experiences.

The parents of a 19-year-old from Yonkers who attended a Catholic high school reacted to the news that she was a lesbian by committing her to a mental hospital. Her parents never visited her there.

A 16-year-old boy from White Plains said: "My mother doesn't know I'm here. When I told her I was gay, she ripped the phone off the wall." She also took away his connection to America on Line and cable television and told him he could no longer talk to his sister.

And Kevin Slavin Jr., 20, said: "I was banned from coming here by my parents. When I told them about this place, they thought that if I hung around gay people, I'd stay gay. When they found out about me, I was banned from using the phone for a week. And I was verbally harassed in high school by the students, even though the faculty and staff were supportive."

Some high schools are more accepting of homosexual students, which makes the school day less difficult. Schools like Horace Greeley in Chappaqua, Mamaroneck

High School, Scarsdale High School and White Plains High School, which have active after-school gay and straight alliance organizations, "create an environment of tolerance," Ms. Schreibman said.

A 15-year-old boy from White Plains said: "The teachers are really supportive and don't care about your life style. It's more acceptable than it was 10 years ago. Even if the majority of parents think this is wrong, most people our age are more tolerant."

Not every coming-out experience is painful or tense. An 18-year-old woman from Hastings-on-Hudson said: "My parents are great about it. My father has been awesome, and my mom has been cool."

And a 15-year-old girl from Hawthorne added: "My parents are gung-ho. It's impossible to hide your life style for a long amount of time. I didn't tell them until the beginning of last year, but I always was a guy. In my high school, I know everyone and everyone knows me, so that kind of overrides the gay thing. I think it's where racism was a generation ago. Our generation is more accepting of gay people."

For some of the young adults, moving on to college can provide a respite from the narrow-mindedness found in some high schools.

"I'm at Westchester Community College now, and people are very tolerant," James Andrade, 20, said.

Teen-agers and young adults at Center Lane say they get security from being with others like themselves. For the 15-year-old from Hawthorne, Center Lane offers hours upon hours "of the best conversation I have anywhere."

"It's a place where I understand everyone's point of view."

Center Lane is housed in a bright and cheerful basement downstairs from the Loft, a gay and lesbian community support service for adults on the commercial stretch of North Broadway in White Plains. It was begun by Westchester Jewish Community Services in July 1995, and today it offers a supervised after-school drop-in center, movie nights, counseling, support groups for teen-agers and their parents, a peer leadership program, community educational outreach training and recreational activities, including a gay prom in the spring.

Center Lane initially drew about 65 teen-agers and now serves 130. "The center itself has changed things," Dr. Kohn said. "It's a place that validates their existence and offers a place for adults to refer kids."

Some of the mental health programs involve recreational activities and groups for teen-agers with like-minded and supportive peers. "We run groups and trips, multicultural events, even a Passover seder," Ms. Schreibman, the program's coordinator, said. "It's all youth driven." Participants, many of whom use the county's public bus system to reach White Plains, come from communities throughout the county, including Ardsley, Hastings, Hawthorne, New Rochelle, Tuckahoe and White Plains. The center relies on about a dozen volunteers.

Center Lane, which has a yearly budget of $85,000, received a Distinguished Service Award from the White Plains Commission on Human Rights in 1997 and a $57,000 State Department of Health grant last year. Funds are also provided by United Way, Westchester County and private donors. The number to call for information is 948–1042.

Parents and Experts Unclear on Best Approach to Raising Transgender Child

As one parent of a transgender child describes it, life is an ongoing series of difficult judgment calls, with "every day feeling like a balance between your kid's self-esteem and protecting him from the hostile outside world." In the past children who intensely identified with the opposite gender were either referred for therapy or simply forced to conform, often resulting in childhoods blighted by misery, shame, and high rates of depression, suicide, and self-mutilation. To prevent these negative outcomes, gender-identity rights advocates are encouraging families and schools to take a new approach, allowing these children to be "who they are" from kindergarten onward. However, as was the case in 2006, only a few states have laws protecting the rights of transgender children, and even in the most progressive schools and families, a child who persistently challenges traditional gender norms may raise numerous difficult issues, including conflict over dress codes, bathroom usage, and pronoun choice. Parents and teachers are also likely to struggle with how to respond to questions from other children and adults, how to protect the child from bullying and physical violence, and, most controversially, whether it is appropriate to use pharmaceuticals to block the onset of puberty as the child reaches adolescence.

Confused parents and school administrators face conflicting recommendations from experts about how to negotiate these difficult issues. Although few professionals would advocate the harsh treatment routinely recommended for these children in the past, the field is currently divided on whether it is more helpful to wholeheartedly support or gently discourage alternative gender expression in young children. The issue is further clouded by research that suggests that the majority of these children do not grow up to be transgender adults. As one father says, "As a parent you're in this complete terra incognita."

DECEMBER 2, 2006
SUPPORTING BOYS OR GIRLS WHEN THE LINE ISN'T CLEAR
By PATRICIA LEIGH BROWN

OAKLAND, Calif., Dec. 1—Until recently, many children who did not conform to gender norms in their clothing or behavior and identified intensely with the opposite sex were steered to psychoanalysis or behavior modification.

But as advocates gain ground for what they call gender-identity rights, evidenced most recently by New York City's decision to let people alter the sex listed on their birth certificates, a major change is taking place among schools and families. Children as young as 5 who display predispositions to dress like the opposite sex are being supported by a growing number of young parents, educators and mental health professionals.

Doctors, some of them from the top pediatric hospitals, have begun to advise families to let these children be "who they are" to foster a sense of security and self-esteem. They are motivated, in part, by the high incidence of depression, suicidal feelings and self-mutilation that has been common in past generations of transgender children. Legal trends suggest that schools are now required to respect parents' decisions.

"First we became sensitive to two mommies and two daddies," said Reynaldo Almeida, the director of the Aurora School, a progressive private school in Oakland. "Now it's kids who come to school who aren't gender typical."

The supportive attitudes are far easier to find in traditionally tolerant areas of the country like San Francisco than in other parts, but even in those places there is fierce debate over how best to handle the children.

Cassandra Reese, a first-grade teacher outside Boston, recalled that fellow teachers were unnerved when a young boy showed up in a skirt. "They said, 'This is not normal,' and, 'It's the parents' fault,'" Ms. Reese said. "They didn't see children as sophisticated enough to verbalize their feelings."

As their children head into adolescence, some parents are choosing to block puberty medically to buy time for them to figure out who they are—raising a host of ethical questions.

While these children are still relatively rare, doctors say the number of referrals is rising across the nation. Massachusetts, Minnesota, California, New Jersey and the District of Columbia have laws protecting the rights of transgender students, and some schools are engaged in a steep learning curve to dismantle gender stereotypes.

At the Park Day School in Oakland, teachers are taught a gender-neutral vocabulary and are urged to line up students by sneaker color rather than by gender. "We are careful not to create a situation where students are being boxed in," said Tom Little, the school's director. "We allow them to move back and forth until something feels right."

For families, it can be a long, emotional adjustment. Shortly after her son's third birthday, Pam B. and her husband, Joel, began a parental journey for which there was no map. It started when their son, J., began wearing oversized T-shirts and wrapping a towel around his head to emulate long, flowing hair. Then came his mother's silky undershirts. Half a year into preschool, J. started becoming agitated when asked to wear boys' clothing.

En route to a mall with her son, Ms. B. had an epiphany: "It just clicked in me. I said, 'You really want to wear a dress, don't you?'"

Thus began what the B.'s, who asked their full names not be used to protect their son's privacy, call "the reluctant path," a behind-closed-doors struggle to come to terms with a gender-variant child—a spirited 5-year-old boy who, at least for now, strongly identifies as a girl, requests to be called "she" and asks to wear pigtails and pink jumpers to school.

Ms. B., 41, a lawyer, accepted the way her son defined himself after she and her husband consulted with a psychologist and observed his newfound comfort with his choice. But she feels the precarious nature of the day-to-day reality. "It's hard to convey the relentlessness of it," she said, "every social encounter, every time you go out to eat, every day feeling like a balance between your kid's self-esteem and protecting him from the hostile outside world."

The prospect of cross-dressing kindergartners has sparked a deep philosophical divide among professionals over how best to counsel families. Is it healthier for families to follow the child's lead, or to spare children potential humiliation and isolation by steering them toward accepting their biological gender until they are older?

Both sides in the debate underscore their concern for the profound vulnerability of such youngsters, symbolized by occurrences like the murder in 2002 of Gwen Araujo, a transgender teenager born as Eddie, southeast of Oakland.

"Parents now are looking for advice on how to make life reasonable for their kids—whether to allow cross-dressing in public, and how to protect them from the savagery of other children," said Dr. Herbert Schreier, a psychiatrist with Children's Hospital and Research Center in Oakland.

Dr. Schreier is one of a growing number of professionals who have begun to think of gender variance as a naturally occurring phenomenon rather than a disorder. "These kids are becoming more aware of how it is to be themselves," he said.

In past generations, so-called sissy boys and tomboy girls were made to conform, based on the belief that their behaviors were largely products of dysfunctional homes.

Among the revisionists is Dr. Edgardo Menvielle, a child-adolescent psychiatrist at the Children's National

Medical Center in Washington who started a national outreach group for parents of gender-variant children in 1998 that now has more than 200 participants. "We know that sexually marginalized children have a higher rate of depression and suicide attempts," Dr. Menvielle said. "The goal is for the child to be well adjusted, healthy and have good self-esteem. What's not important is molding their gender."

The literature on adults who are transgender was hardly consoling to one parent, a 42-year-old software consultant in Massachusetts and the father of a gender-variant third grader. "You're trudging through this tragic, horrible stuff and realizing not a single person was accepted and understood as a child," he said. "You read it and think, O.K., best to avoid that. But as a parent you're in this complete terra incognita."

The biological underpinnings of gender identity, much like sexual orientation, remain something of a mystery, though many researchers suspect it is linked with hormone exposure in the developing fetus.

Studies suggest that most boys with gender variance early in childhood grow up to be gay, and about a quarter heterosexual, Dr. Menvielle said. Only a small fraction grow up to identify as transgender.

Girls with gender-variant behavior, who have been studied less, voice extreme unhappiness about being a girl and talk about wanting to have male anatomy. But research has thus far suggested that most wind up as heterosexual women.

Although many children role-play involving gender, Dr. Menvielle said, "the key question is how intense and persistent the behavior is," especially if they show extreme distress.

Dr. Robin Dea, the director of regional mental health for Kaiser Permanente in Northern California, said: "Our gender identity is something we feel in our soul. But it is also a continuum, and it evolves."

Dr. Dea works with four or five children under the age of 15 who are essentially living as the opposite sex. "They are much happier, and their grades are up," she said. "I'm waiting for the study that says supporting these children is negative."

But Dr. Kenneth Zucker, a psychologist and head of the gender-identity service at the Center for Addiction and Mental Health in Toronto, disagrees with the "free to be"

approach with young children and cross-dressing in public. Over the past 30 years, Dr. Zucker has treated about 500 preadolescent gender-variant children. In his studies, 80 percent grow out of the behavior, but 15 percent to 20 percent continue to be distressed about their gender and may ultimately change their sex.

Dr. Zucker tries to "help these kids be more content in their biological gender" until they are older and can determine their sexual identity—accomplished, he said, by encouraging same-sex friendships and activities like board games that move beyond strict gender roles.

Though she has not encountered such a situation, Jennifer Schwartz, assistant principal of Chatham Elementary School outside Springfield, Ill., said that allowing a child to express gender differences "would be very difficult to pull off" there.

Ms. Schwartz added: "I'm not sure it's worth the damage it could cause the child, with all the prejudices and parents possibly protesting. I'm not sure a child that age is ready to make that kind of decision."

The B.'s thought long and hard about what they had observed in their son. They have carefully choreographed his life, monitoring new playmates, selecting a compatible school, finding sympathetic parents in a babysitting co-op. Nevertheless, Ms. B. said, "there is still the stomach-clenching fear for your kid."

It is indeed heartbreaking to hear a child say, as J. did recently, "It feels like a nightmare I'm a boy."

The adjustment has been gradual for Mr. B., a 43-year-old public school administrator who is trying to stop calling J. "our little man." He thinks of his son as a positive, resilient person, and his love and admiration show. "The truth is, is any parent going to choose this for their kid?" he said. "It's who your kid is."

Families are caught in the undertow of conflicting approaches. One suburban Chicago mother, who did not want to be identified, said in a telephone interview that she was drawing the line on dress and trying to provide "boy opportunities" for her 6-year-old son. "But we can't make everything a power struggle," she said. "It gets exhausting."

She worries about him becoming a social outcast. "Why does your brother like girl things?" friends of her 10-year-old ask. The answer is always, "I don't know." . . .

MINISTERS CLAIM HOME ECONOMICS LEADS TO HOMOSEXUALITY

When in 1974 the New Milford, Connecticut, school board decided to allow all seventh- and eighth-grade students to choose between home economics and industrial arts, it seemed reasonable to require all sixth graders to take one semester of each. "That way, they can know what they're choosing for the next two years," the local superintendent of schools explained. However, this decision resulted in ministers from the local Faith Baptist Temple threatening lawsuits and divine retribution. Although the school board voted to continue the new policy despite these protests, Rev. Clemmons's son was excused from taking home economics for religious reasons.

DECEMBER 5, 1974
TWO MINISTERS THREATEN SUIT OVER BOYS' COOKING CLASSES
By MICHAEL KNIGHT

The New Milford, Conn., school board scoffed yesterday at complaints that its policy of requiring sixth-grade boys to study home economics is leading to "homosexuality" and "moral decay."

J. Thomas Eagen, the president of the school board, said the policy would continue despite threats by two Baptist ministers to begin court action and bring the wrath of God upon the Candlewood Lake community.

The Rev. James Clemmons and the Rev. Lynn Mays, who preach together at the Faith Baptist Temple in a trailer off U.S. Route 7, have promised to sue the school board for its decision this year to make shop and home economics classes mandatory for both boys and girls.

"By having a young boy cook or sew, wearing aprons, we're pushing a boy into homosexuality," the Rev. Mays insisted. "It's contrary to what the home and the Bible have stood for. When God set up the human race, there was a division of sexes."

"A woman's place is in the home," he said, adding "that's where God put them, barring unusual circumstances."

Daniel Center, the superintendent of schools, said that prior to this fall the boys in the town's middle

school took only industrial arts courses and the girls took only home economics courses as a matter of official policy.

This fall, he said, because of new civil rights legislation, the classes are integrated and children in grades seven and eight are free to choose which of the two courses to take. But the 330 sixth-grade students are required to take both one semester of home economics and one semester of industrial arts.

"That way, they can know what they're choosing for the next two years," Mr. Center explained. "It's only for 16 hours of a whole semester, so I don't know what the fuss is all about. I think we are right in this and we are going to continue it."

The Rev. Clemmons, however, said he felt the requirement erodes his constitutional and religious right as a father to determine the pattern of his children's lives.

"My son doesn't want the course and I don't want him to be a sissy," he said.

Mr. Center said Reverend Clemmons' son, James, had been excused from the home economics courses for "religious reasons."

"We try to make adjustments for people's religion," he explained.

Teacher's Guide Claims "Homosexuality Normal"

A political uproar arose in New Hampshire in 1988 over the publication of the sixty-page manual "Mutual Sharing, Mutual Caring: A Sexuality Education Unit for Adolescents." Developed by a New Hampshire prenatal and family-planning clinic with support from a federal grant, the manual was distributed to school districts only upon request and was designed to facilitate conversations between teachers and teens on critical issues such as pregnancy, rape, and contraception. Homosexuality was not recommended as a discussion topic, but the guide included information in the introduction to help teachers support homosexual teens and to discourage homophobic behavior in the classroom. Controversy arose over specific statements in this introduction, including "Gay and lesbian adolescents are perfectly normal and their sexual attraction to members of the same sex is healthy." Following criticism from many quarters, including Gov. John H. Sununu and Sen. Gordon J. Humphrey, county officials threatened to cut off funding for the clinic and the federal Department of Health and Human Services attempted to block further distribution of the manual. The clinic's executive director defended the contents of the curriculum, stating that it reflected mainstream professional opinion and was simply an attempt to protect homosexual teens from prejudice and violence.

APRIL 24, 1988
SEX EDUCATION MANUAL PROMPTS MORAL OUTRAGE
By ROD PAUL
Special to the New York Times

CONCORD, N.H., April 22—A federally financed manual outlining a curriculum of sex education for teen-agers has touched off a political firestorm in this conservative state because it describes homosexuality as normal.

Since January more than 200 copies of the 60-page manual, which also discusses such issues as pregnancy, rape, contraception and sexual abuse, have been distributed to medical, family planning and government agencies around the state, and school districts have requested copies of it.

The manual has been criticized by county, state and Federal officials, including Gov. John H. Sununu. The Federal Government has begun action to try to block its distribution.

Program 'Should Be Expelled'

Senator Gordon J. Humphrey, a Republican, has asked Federal officials to investigate how the manual came to be produced with taxpayers' money, saying: "The program deserves an F. It should be expelled from New Hampshire."

The manual, "Mutual Sharing, Mutual Caring: a Sexuality Education Unit for Adolescents," was prepared for the Strafford County Prenatal and Family Planning Clinic in Dover with a $161,000 Federal grant. Cooper Thompson, an educator who is a member of the Campaign to End Homophobia, based in Cambridge, Mass., spent more than three years developing it, working with community groups, schools and youth organizations to test the curriculum.

The manual is intended for discussions about sex issues by groups of about a dozen teen-agers and a teacher.

According to the manual, "Gay and lesbian adolescents are perfectly normal and their sexual attraction to members of the same sex is healthy."

'Homophobia Is the Problem'

Chuck Rhoades, the Dover clinic's executive director, defended the manual, saying: "It recognizes that there are some young people who are homosexual and that these young people are often the targets of hatred, prejudice and violence. Those are the types of attitudes labeled homophobia. The manual, in part, seeks to address homophobia. Our position is consistent with every mainstream medical, psychological, educational and legal group in the country. We say that homophobia is the problem."

He said critics should be aware that the manual did not call for specific discussion sessions on homosexuality or homophobia. "What exists in the manual are comments in the introduction which are intended to help teachers give support to homosexual teen-agers in the classroom," he said. "Also, there are ways the teacher might respond firmly to disparaging remarks against homosexual teen-agers."

The reaction to the manual has been unrelenting since its distribution became publicly known two weeks ago. Now, the Federal Department of Health and Human Services has moved to block the clinic from distributing the manual.

Nabers Cabanis, a Deputy Assistant Secretary, has asked public health officials to "take whatever action is necessary to suspend dissemination" of the curriculum, "pending a review."

Clinic Funds in Jeopardy

Ms. Cabanis questioned whether the curriculum complied with Federal regulations on family planning grants like the one that paid for the manual.

Governor Sununu said: "It is not the kind of document that I would like governing any kind of programs that my kids are exposed to." He asked the State Attorney General to see if distribution of the manual could be blocked.

Stafford County commissioners voted to cut off financial support to the clinic but later backed off, offering to reinstate the financing if the clinic agreed to stop distributing the manual. The county provides $39,000 of the clinic's $580,000 annual budget. State lawmakers from the county have scheduled an April 29 meeting to discuss the matter.

"I'm not against sex education, but when teachers start telling kids if you are lesbian or homosexual then you are all right, normal and healthy," said Roland Roberge, a Commissioner. "That's not O.K."

Cutoff 'Will Hurt a Lot'

The New Hampshire chapter of the National Organization for Woman has threatened a lawsuit unless county officials keep financing the clinic.

Mr. Rhoades says a cutoff of funds by the county could jeopardize the family planning services the clinic provides to as many as 300 pregnant women, mothers and infants each year.

"It will hurt a lot, especially the low-income women and girls," he said. "But as far as I am concerned I stand by what was written in the curriculum."

· ·

Diversity Curriculum Encourages Respect for Gay People—Chaos Ensues

In 1992 in an effort to combat prejudice and intolerance, Chancellor Joseph A. Fernandez recommended the "Children of the Rainbow" diversity curriculum for use in all first-grade classrooms in New York City Public Schools. The primary focus was on songs and activities from various cultures, including the Mexican hat dance, a recipe for Greek New Year's Day bread, and a Japanese version of rock, paper, scissors. However, there are a few references to homosexuality in the 443-page instructor's guide, including a passage that urges teachers to "include references to lesbians and gays in all curricular areas" and a bibliography that contains children's books with homosexual themes—*Daddy's Roommate, Heather has Two Mommies,* and *Gloria Goes to Gay Pride.*

Many of New York City's thirty-two local school boards adopted the curriculum but did not plan to introduce classroom discussions of homosexuality until fifth or sixth grade. One district, however, chose to draw a line in the sand on this issue. Covering a primarily working-class, ethnically diverse region of western Queens, District 24's school board refused to adopt the guide, provide a suitable replacement or even meet with the schools' chancellor, Joseph A. Fernandez, to discuss the issue. When Chancellor Fernandez moved to suspend the dissenting board, the central Board of Education failed to back him up, reinstating the dismissed members and encouraging the chancellor to be more conciliatory. However, feelings on this issue continued to run high as evidenced by a meeting of the Board of Education on this topic. As a long line of individuals took turns providing testimony for or against the new curriculum, representatives from opposing factions eventually began shouting at and shoving each other. After several fruitless attempts to restore order, the board president called in security to end the meeting early and clear the room despite a backlog of sixty people still waiting to speak.

DECEMBER 17, 1992
FRACAS LEADS BOARD TO END A MEETING
By JOSEPH BERGER

Tensions over the "Children of the Rainbow" curriculum caused an uproar at a New York City Board of Education meeting last night, as ideological antagonists shouted and at times pushed one another, forcing an abrupt adjournment of the heated session.

When H. Carl McCall, the board's president, directed security guards to clear the room, more than 60 people were still waiting to speak, mostly on the disputed curriculum, which includes passages teaching respect for gay people.

The boards hold public meetings every two weeks at which virtually anyone can speak on any school-related topic, and recent meetings have been dominated by three-minute speeches from supporters and opponents of the curriculum. While the meetings are always heated, they had not produced a dispute as violent as the one that erupted last night.

James S. Vlasto, a spokesman for the board, said the conflict began when a woman charged that the curriculum was being foisted on the school system by "white gay men."

When the woman, whom Mr. Vlasto said he could not identify, returned to her seat, she was surrounded by supporters of the curriculum, several of them from Act Up, an organization that protests for and advocates rights for people with AIDS.

The two factions engaged in a shouting match, and soon shouting and some shoving erupted throughout the meeting room.

Mr. McCall banged his gavel futilely and called repeatedly for order. He finally adjourned the meeting.

Security guards had to force some spectators out of the hall, at which point the arguments continued in front of television cameras.

"It was a bedlam," said Robert H. Terte, another board spokesman.

Schools Chancellor Joseph A. Fernandez has been trying to get the city's 32 local schools boards to adopt a 443-page teaching guide intended to combat discrimination based on race, religion, sex or sexual orientation. But the guide's few references to gay men and lesbians, urging that they be treated the same as other people, has roused fierce opposition.

Many of the 32 boards have changed the guide, postponing lessons about homosexuals to the fifth and sixth grades, and one district, District 24, in a working-class section of Queens, has rejected the guide entirely and refused to meet with Mr. Fernandez to work out possible changes.

After Mr. Fernandez suspended that board two weeks ago, the central Board of Education rebuffed him by reinstating the Queens board and asking him to try a more conciliatory approach.

Conciliation Breaks Down

That approach appears to be breaking down this week. Mr. Fernandez is on the verge of sending in three trustees to take over the curricular functions of the board . . .

SALT LAKE CITY BANS ALL SCHOOL CLUBS TO THWART GAY-STRAIGHT ALLIANCE

In 1996 the Salt Lake City Board of Education chose to ban all clubs from city high schools rather than allow the formation of a Gay-Straight Alliance Club at East High School. The group was proposed by three students, including senior Kelli Peterson, who said that when she came out as a lesbian her sophomore year, she "immediately lost all [her] friends." Despite protests from local and national conservative groups, the Board of Education was not able to simply ban the club because of the federal Equal Access Act of 1984, which states that public schools must treat all student groups the same. Ironically, this legislation was sponsored by Sen. Orrin Hatch of Utah and was originally intended to ensure Christian groups would not be barred from meeting in school facilities.

Although some students at Kelli Patterson's high school supported her efforts, many believed homosexuality was a sin and were angry that unrelated clubs had been affected. Hundreds of students marched on the state capital in protest, and several at East High requested permission to form an "Anti-Homosexual League."

FEBRUARY 28, 1996
WILL BANNING OF CLUBS TO BLOCK GAY GROUPS EXTEND ACROSS THE COUNTRY?
To Be Young, Gay and Going to High School in Utah
By JAMES BROOKE

LAKE CITY, Feb. 27—For Kelli Peterson, a 17-year-old senior at East High School here, the Aztec and U.F.O. clubs held no appeal; her primary concern was intensely personal—easing the loneliness she felt as a gay student. "I thought I was the only lesbian student in East High," she said outside school here today. "As a sophomore I was really pressured by my friends to date. I came out that year, and immediately lost all my friends. I watched the same cycle of denial, trying to hide, acceptance, then your friends abandoning you."

So last fall, she and two other gay students formed an extracurricular club called the Gay/Straight Alliance. With that, the three set off a furor that now involves national conservative leaders, the State Legislature and the local school board.

Anti-gay leaders believe that a strong stand in Utah will help turn the national tide against gay clubs in high schools, which have sprung up in the last decade from Boston and New York to San Francisco and Los Angeles. They point to Utah's precedent-setting legislation last year that formally banned same-sex marriages. Although Utah is politically more conservative than most states, this year, 15 other state legislatures are debating similar bans.

"We are going to win this battle—and Utah will again be in the forefront," said Gayle Ruzicka, president of the Utah Eagle Forum, an affiliate of Phyllis Schlafly's national organization. "Homosexuals can't reproduce, so they recruit. And they are not going to use Utah high school and junior high school campuses to recruit."

Ms. Peterson scoffs at the idea: "Nobody led me to become a lesbian. My parents are heterosexual. I was taught to be heterosexual. I was taught to get married and to have children."

Paradoxically, 12-year-old conservative-sponsored Federal legislation would have forced the district to allow Ms. Peterson's club to meet in the school. The law, the Federal Equal Access Act of 1984, was intended to allow Bible clubs to meet in schools. Sponsored by Senator Orrin G. Hatch of Utah, the law says local school boards cannot pick among campus clubs. Last week, Mr. Hatch, a Republican, fumed. "The act was never intended to promulgate immoral speech or activity," he said.

Fearing lawsuits—and loss of Federal aid—Salt Lake City's Board of Education chose last week to ban all clubs from city high schools, from the Polynesian Club to Students Against Drunk Driving.

In response, hundreds of students poured out of city high schools last Friday, marching on the State Capitol. In the protest, one 14-year-old girl was run over by a car and critically injured.

Last month, as anti-gay feelings started to crystallize, Utah's Senate violated the state's public meetings law and met in secret to watch an anti-gay video. Senators later said they were so shocked that they would vote to ban gay clubs in schools, even if it meant risking $100 million a year in Federal aid to Utah schools.

Last week, the Senate easily approved a bill forbidding teachers from "encouraging, condoning or supporting illegal conduct." An amendment to preach "tolerance" was defeated. With sodomy a misdemeanor in Utah, the bill's sponsor said the measure was aimed at keeping avowed homosexuals out of public schools.

"Young people reach their teen-age years, and their sexuality starts developing," said State Senator Craig Taylor, the sponsor. "And I believe they can be led down that road to homosexuality."

Earlier this month, a political group, Gay Lesbian Utah Democrats, pressured Democratic legislators to try to legalize sodomy. In response, the state's party leadership demanded that the group drop "Democrats" from its name.

With battle lines drawn sharply, both sides believe that a struggle of national importance is being fought in this desert state of two million people. Defenders of gay high school clubs say that Utah's opponents are fighting a doomed battle. Nationwide, the number of high school gay clubs have mushroomed from a handful in 1992 to hundreds today, according to the Gay Lesbian Straight Teachers Network, a group based in New York. . . .

At East High, a neo-Gothic structure that disgorged student protesters last Friday, the divisions of Utah's larger society are mirrored among the 1,400 students.

Last week, several students asked the principal for permission to form a club called "the Anti-Homosexual League." Then, at last Friday's walkout, some boys threw snowballs at their protesting classmates.

"I'd rather do away with all the clubs, than have that club," Joseph Emerson, a high school senior, said Monday in the warmth of his pickup truck in the school parking lot.

"It's against our religion," the senior, a Mormon, said as two friends nodded assent. "Ban homosexuality, not clubs—we should have a demonstration like that."

Students like Ms. Peterson say that it was precisely these sentiments that led them to form the Gay/Straight Alliance last fall. Erin Wiser, a 17-year-old lesbian, said, "When my girlfriends would talk about marriage or boys, I would feel isolated."

A 16-year-old bisexual girl who asked not to be identified said that the alliance had sought a low profile, meeting quietly in classrooms, coffee houses or family living rooms.

"All we asked for is classroom time," said the girl, a junior. "We never used the intercom at student announcement time. We didn't ask for a picture in the yearbook."

Denying accusations that they were forming a "sex club," Ms. Peterson said the alliance is not about "technique," but about "identity."

Kelli's mother, Dee Peterson, recalled Kelli's hospitalization for depression last year after realizing her orientation. "Being gay you don't have a choice," Mrs. Peterson said. "You either are or you aren't."

While state officials may succeed in keeping homosexuality out of the state sphere, gay high school students vow to keep meeting, either on campus in school hallways or off-campus in coffeehouses. . . .

CONSERVATIVES TARGET HOMOSEXUALITY IN PUBLIC SCHOOLS

In the 1990s homosexuality in public schools became an increasingly important issue for many on the political right, and individuals on both sides of the debate reported that "they have never seen passions about public school activities run so high." Specific areas of contention included whether it was appropriate for public schools to sponsor clubs that focus on the issue of homosexuality or introduce the topic in the classroom, particularly in the earlier grades. Conservative groups across the nation successfully organized to block value-neutral discussions of homosexuality in sex education classes, as well as the formation of Gay-Straight Alliances, both of which had become increasingly popular. In addition, bills were introduced in at least two states to limit minors' access to books with homosexual themes. According to Mathew D. Staver, president of the conservative Liberty Counsel, many Americans are "concerned about the effort to capture youth through indoctrination into the homosexual lifestyle. Students are a captive audience, and they are being targeted."

JUNE 9, 2005
GAY RIGHTS BATTLEFIELDS SPREAD TO PUBLIC SCHOOLS
By MICHAEL JANOFSKY

Emboldened by the political right's growing influence on public policy, opponents of school activities aimed at educating students about homosexuality or promoting acceptance of gay people are mounting challenges to such programs, at individual schools, at statehouses and in Congress.

Chief among the targets are sex education programs that include discussions of homosexuality, and after-school clubs that bring gay and straight students together, two initiatives that gained assent in numerous schools over the last decade.

In many cases, the opponents have been successful. In Montgomery County, Md., for example, parents went to court to block a health education course that offered a discussion of homosexuality, while in Cleveland, Ga., gay and lesbian students were barred from forming a high school club of gay and straight youths.

Leading figures on both sides of the fight say they have never seen passions about public school activities run so high. They agree that much of the reason is conservative groups' eagerness to meet their adversaries with a forcefulness more common to modern-day election campaigns.

"The intensity of the culture wars has heated up over the last few years," said J. Michael Johnson, a lawyer with the Alliance Defense Fund, a conservative group that specializes in issues involving religion. "People are becoming more aware that they have rights, and they're feeling more emboldened to defend them. Across the country, people are saying enough is enough."

Mathew D. Staver, president and general counsel of another conservative group, Liberty Counsel, said: "We're concerned about the effort to capture youth through indoctrination into the homosexual lifestyle. Students are

a captive audience, and they are being targeted by groups with that as an agenda."

The growing conflicts are centering on three issues: whether classrooms are an appropriate venue to explore issues of homosexuality, whether schools should lend sanction to extracurricular activities in which gay culture is a focus and whether textbooks that acknowledge homosexual relationships are suitable for younger children.

This spring, in one instance of the conservative response, the Alliance Defense Fund organized its first national Day of Truth for high school students uncomfortable with the National Day of Silence, an event sponsored for nine years by the Gay, Lesbian and Straight Education Network to protest discrimination in schools.

"We needed to present a counter or Christian perspective," said Mr. Johnson, whose event attracted participation by 340 schools. Kevin Jennings, founder and executive director of the gay education network, said more than 3,700 junior and senior high schools took part in his group's event.

Mr. Jennings and other gay rights leaders say the growing opposition to their efforts is in keeping with a predictable trend set off by disputes over issues like same-sex marriage that are playing out on the national stage.

"These are a bunch of people who very much want to remove from public discourse any mention of homosexuality," said James Esseks, litigation director of the Lesbian and Gay Rights Project of the American Civil Liberties Union. "They don't want any mention of the fact that gay people exist."

The struggles have broken out everywhere.

Last month in Montgomery County, Md., a parents' group, alarmed because revisions to a health education course for 8th and 10th grades included a discussion of homosexuality and a video that demonstrated how to use a condom, went into federal court and gained a restraining order to halt them. The county school board then voted 7 to 1 to eliminate the amended program, six months after unanimously approving it.

Conservative groups applauded the board's vote as a victory for religious conviction, and described the litigation strategy as a model for school districts across the country.

"This was huge," said Robert H. Knight, director of the Culture and Family Institute, which seeks to apply biblical principles to public policy.

Another battle involved student journalists at East Bakersfield High School in California. They wrote a series of articles for the school newspaper this spring that explored gay issues through student experiences. But the principal, John Gibson, citing concern for the safety of students who had been interviewed and photographed, would approve publication only if their identities were withheld.

The journalists refused and, with the help of the American Civil Liberties Union, sued the school district on May 19, seeking an emergency order that would have allowed the articles to be published in the final issue of the year, six days later. A county judge declined to overrule Mr. Gibson, saying the issues were too important for an instant ruling.

Christine Sun, a lawyer for the A.C.L.U., said that if Mr. Gibson had been motivated only by concern for student safety, "his actions are completely illogical."

"These kids were already 'out' on campus," Ms. Sun said of the articles' subjects. "To the extent there is any threat against them, neither they nor their parents were notified by the principal or anyone from law enforcement."

Mr. Gibson did not respond to a call seeking comment.

The war is being waged at the state level as well. Alabama lawmakers are considering a bill that would bar state spending on books or other materials that "promote homosexual lifestyle." Oklahoma passed a resolution last month calling on public libraries to restrict children's access to books with a gay theme. Louisiana is considering a similar measure.

Charles C. Haynes, a senior scholar at the Freedom Forum, a nonpartisan free-speech advocacy group, said

gay rights issues involving public schools had become a litmus test to many religious conservatives.

"They feel the public schools are getting ahead of the country," Mr. Haynes said. "They believe the schools are imposing a view of homosexuality that offends their faith and is not consistent with where we are as a country."

Two members of the Southern Baptist Convention have prepared a "resolution on homosexuality in public schools," to be introduced at the denomination's annual gathering this month. The resolution implores Baptist churches to determine whether schools in their area have "homosexual clubs or curricula or programs" and, if so, to encourage parents to remove their children from the schools.

"Churches and parents need to be aware of what's going on," said Bruce N. Shortt, a Houston lawyer who is a co-author of the resolution.

After-school clubs known as Gay-Straight Alliances, which draw together students to share common experiences and concerns, have become a particular source of conflict. The issue has roiled a number of communities, including Ashland, Ky.; Klein, Tex.; Hanford, Calif.; and Cleveland, Ga., where a small group of gay and lesbian students were denied permission this year to form an alliance at White County High School.

Federal law often frowns on administrators' barring some clubs while allowing others, but Cleveland school officials told the students that they would abolish all after-school organizations before allowing a gay-straight alliance.

"They're just scared of change," said Kerry Pacer, 17, who is leading the students' effort. "We live in the Bible Belt. Anything that threatens change, people here don't want that."

Complaints over the students' endeavor led State Senator Nancy Schaefer to introduce a bill that would have required a parent's written permission before a student could join any after-school club. The legislature later deferred to the Georgia Department of Education, which is now considering a modified approach allowing each local school board to develop its own policy.

Ms. Schaefer dismisses the compromise as too weak.

"I just don't feel like homosexual clubs have anything to do with readin,' writin' and 'rithmetic," she said.

Five-Year Legal Battle over Three-Hour Homosexuality Curriculum

Montgomery County, Maryland, a well-educated and politically liberal area just north of Washington, D.C., instituted a new curriculum on homosexuality for all eighth- and tenth-grade health education classes in 2007. Two forty-five-minute modules were developed for each grade, and these were to be delivered in combination with a video on how to correctly use a condom. School officials said that the classes did not promote a political agenda and were simply an attempt to provide students with basic cultural literacy about the diversity of sexual identity. Specific messages to students regarding tolerance as well as respect for themselves and others were in keeping with the county's overall sex education and diversity programming. Despite these assurances, Citizens for a Responsible Curriculum and other conservative groups fought implementation of the new curriculum in the courts for the five years prior to the 2007 approval and vowed to challenge a legal defeat that recently paved the way for the program's long-delayed implementation.

AUGUST 15, 2007
LESSONS ON HOMOSEXUALITY MOVE INTO THE CLASSROOM
By DIANA JEAN SCHEMO
ROCKVILLE, Md.

After five years, one legal defeat and a challenge on the way, Montgomery County, Md., is at the frontier of sex education in the United States. This fall, barring last-minute court action, the county will offer lessons on homosexuality in its 8th- and 10th-grade health education courses.

To school officials, the lessons are a natural outgrowth of sex education and of teachings on tolerance and diversity. They consist of two heavily scripted, 45-minute lessons for each grade and a video demonstrating how to put on a condom. The lessons' central message is respect and acceptance of the many permutations of sexual identity, both in others and in one's self.

School officials said they were not seeking to promote a political agenda, beyond tolerance and a kind of cultural literacy. "Our charge starts with educating students," said Betsy Brown, who supervised the curriculum's development in consultation with the American Academy of Pediatrics. "This is part of education."

But critics, who have filed lawsuits seeking to stop the lessons, contended that the Montgomery County schools, just north of Washington, have gone too far.

John Garza, president of the Citizens for a Responsible Curriculum, a group leading the opposition, said parents can block television shows they deem morally questionable, "but then we have the schoolteacher affirming unhealthy behavior."

Montgomery is a mostly well-educated, politically liberal enclave. But opponents of the new curriculum, portrayed as a vocal minority by school officials, may be more in sync with the mood of parents nationally.

According to a 2004 national poll by the Kaiser Family Foundation, Harvard University's Kennedy School of Government and National Public Radio, roughly three out of four parents say it is appropriate for high schools to teach about homosexuality, but about half say it is appropriate in middle school.

When asked about the issue in greater detail, more than 50 percent of high school and middle school parents supported teaching what homosexuality is about "without discussing whether it is wrong or acceptable." Only 8 percent of high school parents and 4 percent of middle school parents said schools should teach "that homosexuality is acceptable." The survey had a margin of error of 6 percentage points.

Montgomery County may be ahead of the country on sex education, but it may also just be out there, stranded on its own.

The controversy illustrates how fraught the road can be for educators who venture beyond academics to influence students about sensitive social issues, risking not just lawsuits, but also losing step with parents and voters. In New York City, the controversy 14 years ago over the "rainbow curriculum," which included the book "Heather Has Two Mommies" as a first-grade text, cost Chancellor Joseph A. Fernandez his job.

"It's a myth that our schools don't teach values about lots of things," said Debra W. Haffner, director of the Religious Institute on Sexual Morality, Justice and Healing, which promotes discussions about sexuality. "We don't put communism, socialism and capitalism on an equal footing in our classes on government."

But for a raft of reasons, many of them unconscious, teaching about sexuality is different, said Susan K. Freeman, a historian at Minnesota State University, Mankato.

For many parents, boy-girl dating may not mean that their child is sexually active, she said. By coming out as gay, though, "they're announcing their sexuality." Parents make a tacit assumption of sexual activity, and "that presents a problem for a lot of people," she said.

The Montgomery County lessons begin by defining terms like "prejudice," "homosexual" and "transgender," and warn students not to assume that because they are not yet attracted to the opposite sex, they must be gay. The eighth-grade curriculum tells gay students that "concerns about how family and friends will accept the situation are reasonable, and fears about being teased or even attacked are not unfounded."

In the 10th grade, the lessons, which presume that sexual identity is innate, again discuss the stresses of coming out, but add, "Many people who are gay, lesbian, bisexual or transgender celebrate their self-discovery."

Kevin Jennings, the executive director of the New York-based Gay, Lesbian and Straight Education Network, said the curriculum could reduce bullying over sexual identity.

"I don't know how denying information to young people about sexuality or sexual orientation does anything to promote their health and well being," he said.

Mr. Garza objected to schools teaching that homosexuality is not subject to change and failing to mention higher rates of some venereal diseases among gay men. "When you get into these hotly contested areas of moral judgment, that's where the school needs to get out of it, or at least teach all sides," he said.

THREE HUNDRED MIDDLE AND HIGH SCHOOL STUDENTS ATTEND GAY-STRAIGHT CONFERENCE

Approximately 200 adults and 300 middle and high school students converged on the Westchester County (New York) Center for the 2007 PrideWorks conference, a daylong event held for members of gay-straight clubs from forty area schools. The conference was organized by the Hudson Valley chapter of the Gay, Lesbian and Straight Education Network and received sponsorship support from numerous sources, including a state senator, a nearby Merrill Lynch office, the local branches of the PTA and School Boards Association, and many other community groups. Although short workshops were offered on topics ranging from coming out to homophobia in hip-hop music, the best part of the day for many participants was the rare opportunity to meet and talk with other teens like themselves. Anna Trejo said that the event gave her fifteen-year-old gay son the opportunity "to see that there's all this out there, a positive life where he never has to be ashamed or put his head down."

DECEMBER 16, 2007
FOR GAY TEENAGERS, HOPE IN NUMBERS
By MICHAEL WINERIP
WHITE PLAINS

Michael Moreno, a 15-year-old 10th grader from Brewster, could not believe what he was seeing as he walked into the big hall at the Westchester County Center, and he grew quiet. There, for as far as the eye could see, were hundreds of boys and girls who belonged to gay-straight clubs at area middle schools and high schools.

"This is a great moment for him," said his stepfather, Hector Ramos. "He's always felt so isolated."

Michael had so been looking forward to the daylong PrideWorks conference that he'd jumped out of bed that morning at 5:30. He was so happy and nervous, he kept forgetting basic pieces of information. "Dad, what's my cellphone number?" he asked at one point.

The boy has felt different forever, long before he had a name for it, at least since age 5, he said. He told his mom when he was in the eighth grade, and she wasn't surprised. "She figured how I was," said Michael.

"He'd hang out with the girls, not the boys," said Anna Trejo, his mother, a court worker.

"He had female tendencies and a sensitive part," said Mr. Ramos, a flooring contractor.

For these differences, Michael suffered. He was treated for depression. Knowing no one like himself, he spent long hours on the computer. Several months ago he told his parents he'd met a nice boy from Australia online and wanted to bring him here for a visit. "He wanted us to pay for it," said Mr. Ramos. "He was upset when we wouldn't."

How does a parent make friends for a child? "I had this weight on my shoulders," said Ms. Trejo. "I didn't know where to go and what to do. As his mother, I can help him only so much." Which is why the family had put a good deal of hope in the conference here. As Michael said: "I was feeling kind of lonely and stuff. I wanted to meet people."

This was the ninth year of the PrideWorks gathering, which is put on by the Hudson Valley chapter of the Gay Lesbian and Straight Education Network. The conference is sponsored by numerous community groups, including a local Merrill Lynch office, the Westchester-Putnam School Boards Association, the Westchester-East Putnam Region PTA and a state senator, Suzi Oppenheimer, a Democrat from Mamaroneck.

In the beginning, in 1999, there were no students, just 125 adults, mostly educators who worked with gay children. This year, there were about 200 adults along with 300 boys and girls. Some, like Michael, attended with their parents. More arrived in school buses with their Gay Straight Alliance clubs.

At the outset, each of the 40 school delegations was announced, and the hall filled with cheers and woo-woos. There were 20 students from Eastchester High, 21 from Tuckahoe High, 22 from Putnam Valley High, 24 from Rye Middle School. In the spirit of gay-straight clubs, while many were gay, some were straight and supportive.

Michael Campion, 17, who is president of the Lakeland High club and straight, persuaded his dad, Norman, the police chief of Briarcliff Manor, to run a seminar that discussed legal protections for gays and police prejudices.

Much of the day was filled with hourlong seminars: Coming Out—How, When, Where?; Gay Straight Alliance in Middle School; Hip-Hop and Homophobia; What Is Transgender?; Healthy Relationships for Lesbian-Gay-Bisexual-Transgender Youth.

But the heart of things for these teenagers was just being with and talking to and seeing so many others like themselves. "When I first walked in, I felt like crying," said Brian Lindley, 14. "So many people were meeting so many people for the first time."

Brian came out in seventh grade. "I'd be walking in the hallway, and kids would yell 'fag!'" he said. In eighth grade, he said, a group of boys in gym told him he had to wait for them to leave the locker room before changing into his gym uniform. "I didn't want to make a big deal, so I just waited," he said. Then the gym teacher asked why he wasn't getting dressed with the others. "I said because I'm gay and they don't feel it's appropriate. He said, 'I can't say I disagree with them.'"

It got so bad that Brian's family discussed moving to another school district. "We didn't want Brian to be known as the gay kid his whole high school career," said Andrea Werner, who lives with Brian's divorced dad and is helping raise the boy. At the end of eighth grade she took Brian for a daylong visit to John Jay High in Katonah, which, unlike the high school in the district where Brian had been living, has a gay-straight club. "I loved it there," Brian said. "I didn't say much about it to anybody, but I felt secure there." Last summer, they moved to Katonah, and Brian is now a freshman at John Jay. "It's just nice to be able to walk down the hallway without people screaming at you," he said.

Linda Barat's son, Robert, 17, a junior at New Rochelle High, came out to her last spring when she was driving him to Hebrew school. At the time, she didn't have a clue. "He just said, 'Mom?' 'Uh-huh.' 'I'm gay.' I'm driving along. What do I say? I said, 'O.K., I love you.'"

Robert was not happy when his mom pulled him away from lunch at the conference to talk to a reporter; he'd been busy meeting kids.

Was he surprised, he was asked, to find so many gay teenagers in one place? "Surprised?" he said. "Not really . . . well . . . yeah." When told he could go back to lunch, he looked like he'd just hit the Powerball lottery. "Nice meeting you," he called, racing out of the room.

"I'm sorry about that," his mom said, "but it's wonderful there are so many people here for him."

While a few students had brightly dyed hair and exotic piercings and dressed Goth, most wore the standard teenage uniform, a hooded sweatshirt and jeans, which pleased Mr. Ramos. "I was telling Michael on the way here, I don't want him to be overly flamboyant in his sexuality," he said. "Same as straight people, we're not going to throw it in their faces and they're not in our faces."

Michael didn't talk much during the four seminars he attended that day. "I talked a little bit," he said. "I was still getting warmed up. I'm so new to it, I'm still getting used to it."

His parents, however, could tell what the day meant. "Every time I looked at Michael," said his mom, "all I could see was a big, cheesy smile." He told her he was thinking about going to an empowerment retreat next month. "For him to see that there's all this out there," she said, "a positive life where he never has to be ashamed or put his head down. . . ."

That night, when Ms. Barat and her son, Robert, got home, they went over the day in great detail. At one point, the mother asked Robert if he was sure he felt comfortable being quoted in the newspaper.

"Definitely," said Robert. "I'm tired of people assuming I'm straight."

- -

COLLEGES ENCOURAGED TO TOLERATE DISCRETE HOMOSEXUALS

In 1965 the Group for the Advancement of Psychiatry released a 129-page study titled "Sex and the College Student" and offered recommendations to college administrators on appropriate campus policies regarding student sexuality. With what was described as "open-mindedness toward homosexuality," the authors argued that many heterosexuals show signs of overt homosexuality at some point in their youth, making it "difficult to define the boundary between serious psychopathology, transient aberrations and normal adolescent development." Finding no evidence that the presence of an "actively homosexual individual" would lead to an overall increase in homosexual behavior, the report suggested that college administrators should not "automatically dismiss known homosexuals from the campus." Instead, the report said, there should be little difference between policies for heterosexual and homosexual college students. Accordingly, sexual activity conducted in a private, discrete, and sensitive manner should largely be ignored, but "a student's failure to insure the privacy of his sexual life places it outside the private domain and in the realm of public concern." The study also recommended that colleges develop specific guidelines for educating and advising students on birth control, venereal disease, and abortion. The report was edited by Dr. Harris P. Eddy, former psychiatric consultant at Vassar College, and was based on the professional experience of Group members as well as interviews with college deans and counselors and an examination of the relevant policies at thirty-seven schools.

DECEMBER 12, 1965
PSYCHIATRISTS OFFER COLLEGES SEX ADVICE

By ERIC PACE

A group of 260 psychiatrists declared yesterday that the private heterosexual and homosexual behavior of students need not become the direct concern of college administrators.

This opinion was made in a 129-page study, entitled "Sex and the College Student," prepared by a committee of members of the Group for the Advancement of Psychiatry. The study also recommended that the college draft explicit rules governing some areas of sexual behavior, provide information about birth control and venereal disease and give counsel on aspects of abortion to girl students who are considering termination of pregnancy.

"Private homosexual, like heterosexual, behavior need not become the direct concern of the administration," the study said.

"The student's privacy requires respect," it said, and a college administration should not act on "sexual activity privately practiced with appropriate attention to the sensitivities of other people."

As to heterosexual behavior alone, the study concluded, "a certain amount of freedom in the area of student social and sexual interaction with the opposite sex is now taken for granted within limits of personal integrity and public decency."

"At the same time," it said, "we believe that changing sexual mores and new social realities require the college to be explicit about its view toward sexual conduct on the campus."

The authors put a premium on discretion in all sexual behavior.

"Sexual activity that is not private is likely to be disturbing to others, and a student's failure to insure the privacy of his sexual life places it outside the private domain and in the realm of public concern."

The authors took the view that homosexuality among students may be only a passing phase.

"Manifestations of homosexual feelings during the period of young adulthood vary widely," they said. "[T]he ultimately successful heterosexual adaptation of many students who reveal overt homosexual manifestations at some point in their adolescence or early adulthood makes it difficult to define the boundary between serious psychopathology, transient aberrations and normal adolescent development."

The report also says that "instances of homosexuality occur among women students probably as frequently as they do among men, particularly in residential colleges."

Nevertheless, the study finds "there is no evidence that the presence per se of an actively homosexual individual on campus will necessarily increase the incidence of homosexuality."

Accordingly, the authors said it was doubtful whether college administrators should automatically dismiss known homosexuals from the campus.

The committee's open-mindedness toward homosexuality reflects changing and often conflicting attitudes on the subject in recent years. The British Parliament has debated legislation on homosexuality. In New York homosexual relations have been suggested as a ground for divorce.

A former psychiatric consultant at Vassar College, Dr. Harris P. Eddy, edited the report. Other committee members included Dr. Robert Arnstein of the Yale University health department, and Dr. Tom Stauffer, psychiatric consultant at Sarah Lawrence College. John T. Rule, a former dean of students at Massachusetts Institute of Technology, was a consultant.

Dr. Esther Raushenbush, president of Sarah Lawrence College, praised the report yesterday. She called it "a book by people with wisdom, wide professional knowledge of college students, understanding and compassion.

"I'm glad this vexed subject is discussed by such people," she said in a statement. "They write more circumspectly about some matters, as perhaps befits psychiatrists, than I would. But they will help everyone think more intelligently about a subject administrators must think about."

At the press conference, Dr. Eddy said: "We're trying to put into everyday language things that have been discussed in this field for half a century."

He said the committee's thinking had been influenced by the views of Dr. Anna Freud, a psychoanalyst and daughter of Sigmund Freud. Miss Freud takes a tolerant view of what the report calls "the healthy turmoil of adolescence."

As to contraception, the study favors providing students with information, but not medical materials. Information about "the public health aspects of venereal disease" is suggested on the same basis.

The report said a college health service should also be ready to help the unmarried girl student "in making the diagnosis of pregnancy as early as possible in order to give [her] and her partner as much time as possible to consider alternative plans."

If she is considering abortion, counseling may "pave the way toward a more satisfactory resolution," the study said.

In preparing the study, committee members interviewed various college deans and counselors, studied the rules of 37 schools, and drew on their own professional experience.

College rules, the report said, should be made flexible, so that "the student who finds rules useful as a protection or a limit will have some acceptable backing, and the student who feels less need for rules will have avenues open to establish greater independence."

But it also urged college administrators to spell out their policies on campus sex.

The report was compiled by the organization's Committee on the College Student. The organization itself is known as GAP. Copies of the report can be obtained from the group's office at 104 East 25th Street for $1.50.

Columbia Is Home to First Student Group for Homosexuals

Columbia University was the first college in the country to recognize a student group seeking equal rights for homosexuals. Called the Student Homophile League, the group reportedly had twelve members as of its founding in 1967, including one female student from Barnard. There was some delay in obtaining a charter for the group because school policy required submission of the names of all officers as well as five additional group members. League members wished to keep their identities concealed and were unwilling to comply with this requirement until assurances were provided that the list would remain confidential. Campus reaction to the group was mixed. Some students initially dismissed it as an April Fools' joke, and the school newspaper has printed letters both for and against the group's formation. Funding was provided by Columbia alumni who reportedly became aware of the group through advertisements in homosexual magazines. There were plans to start additional groups at colleges throughout the country. After obtaining recognition, the group at Columbia struggled to build membership while still maintaining existing members' anonymity. The chairman of the League, using the pseudonym Stephen Donaldson, said during a phone interview that the group would need to figure out some way to confidentially prescreen people who express an interest in joining.

MAY 3, 1967
COLUMBIA CHARTERS HOMOSEXUAL GROUP
By MURRAY SCHUMACH

Columbia University has issued a charter to a student group that seeks equal rights for homosexuals.

The organization, called the Student Homophile League, is reported to have about a dozen members, and it says it has both homosexual and heterosexual members. A girl from Barnard is reported to be a member.

According to the chairman of the Student Homophile League, this is the first such group ever chartered by a college in this country. He says that charters will be sought at other colleges including Stamford, the University of Chicago, the University of California at Berkeley, the University of Connecticut, Trinity, Bucknell and the University of Maryland.

The chairman, who used the pseudonym Stephen Donaldson, said in a telephone interview last night that the organization had been formed because "we wanted to get the academic community to support equal rights for homosexuals."

Before the university issued the charter, there were delays because the league refused to give the names of its officers and of five members. The charter was granted on April 19, after the names were supplied with the understanding they would be kept confidential.

The charter was issued by the Committee on Student Organizations, which is made up of student and faculty officials. The chairman of the committee, Dr. Harold E. Lowe, assistant to the vice president of Columbia, refused the petition until the names were supplied.

Dr. Lowe said last night that before the charter was granted the eight names submitted by the league were checked and found to be students.

"It is a bona fide student organization," he said, "and we saw no reason why we should turn down the request for a charter."

The head of the Student Homophile League said last night, in reply to a question, that before he first began campaigning for a charter his roommates had asked him to move from their quarters after they learned that he was homosexual.

"But I should say," he added, "that they asked me with great apologies and said they realized they shouldn't feel that way, but that they felt uncomfortable and uneasy."

The chairman of the league, who said he is bisexual, moved. He said that this incident was not the reason he decided to try to charter the Student Homophile League.

"It was just the general situation that prompted this," he said.

In their effort to get the charter, the league members conferred frequently with the Rev. John D. Cannon, chaplain of the university.

The Episcopalian said in an interview yesterday that he pointed out to them that as members of such an organization they might subject themselves, eventually, to dangers of discrimination. They look upon this as a civil libertarian organization," he said. "To my knowledge there has been no adverse reaction among the faculty."

However, there has been a mixed reaction among the students, as indicated by letters that followed appearance of the story in [the] school's paper, the Columbia Spectator, on April 27.

"At first," said Charles L. Skoro, who wrote the story in The Spectator, "the students seemed to think it was some sort of April Fool hoax, but now they realize it is for real."

An editorial in the college daily has praised the action, which has been defended and attacked in letters from students.

In its declaration of principles, the league lists 13 points including the following:

"The homosexual has a fundamental human right to live and to work with his fellow man as an equal in their common quest for the betterment of human society."

"The homosexual has a fundamental human right to develop and achieve his full potential and dignity as a human being and member of human society."

The declaration then says that "the homosexual is being unjustly, inhumanly and savagely discriminated against by large segments of American society."

The first discussions among the students that led to the charter began about a year ago. For several months, according to the chairman, it operated as a complete "underground group."

Funds Donated by Alumni

Last October, the students got in touch with school officials and a closed meeting was held with administrators and counselors of Columbia and Barnard on Oct. 28. Three days later, the group began the first of a series of talks with the Committee on Student Organizations. The hitch developed on submission of the names of the three officers and five other members.

Funds were said to have been supplied for the organization by some Columbia alumni who were reported to have learned about it from advertisements in magazines for homosexuals. The chairman of the league says it is not controlled by any other group but "maintains liaison" with homosexual groups.

With permission of the chaplain, the league has been using his office for meetings when he is not working there. In the sessions since obtaining a charter, the league has considered the possibility of how to go about opening a drive for members. This is admittedly difficult since the members now in the league are trying to conceal their identities.

"But somehow," said the chairman of the league, "we have to work out some way of interviewing persons who say they want to become members."

Conservative Campus Paper Markets Homophobic T-Shirt

Controversy erupted at the University of Iowa over a display case decorated by the school's privately owned conservative newspaper, *The Campus Review*. In addition to copies of the paper, the display featured a T-shirt showing two men engaged in a sexual act within a red slashed circle, with the caption "Stop AIDS" in large black print. The back of the T-shirt included the name of the newspaper and the tagline "The Right Side of the Story." *The Campus Review* sold the T-shirt for $10 as a fund-raiser for the paper.

In response, university students as well as the Women's Resource and Action Center and the Gay People's Union circulated fliers and petitions in protest. In addition, the Women's Resource and Action Center set up its own display next to the case containing the T-shirt, urging students to protest the administration for allowing this violation of the school's policy against discrimination on the basis of sexual orientation. At least one student felt the administration demonstrated its own homophobia by allowing the offensive T-shirt to be displayed, while the director of the Women's Resource and Action Center said it encouraged harassment of gay students. Jeffrey Renander, editor in chief of *The Campus Review,* defended the display, saying, "The bottom line is it's a free country. People should lighten up."

AUGUST 13, 1989
CAMPUS LIFE: IOWA;
T-Shirt Included in AIDS Display Leads to Protests

IOWA CITY – A display case put up by a conservative newspaper at the University of Iowa that contained a T-shirt depicting a homosexual act has drawn protests from homosexual and feminist groups on campus.

The case was placed in the Iowa Memorial Union last month by The Campus Review, a privately owned monthly newspaper published in Iowa City, employing university students and distributed to students. The display consisted of several copies of the newspaper and a T-shirt that depicts two men within a slashed red circle. Underneath the circle are the words "Stop AIDS" in large black print. The back of the shirt, which was made especially for the newspaper and is sold by it for $10, has the newspaper's name and the words "The Right Side of the Story."

"It points out the obvious: to stop AIDS you have to stop homosexual intercourse," said Jeffrey Renander, editor in chief of The Campus Review.

Some groups on campus did not see it that way. University students, along with the University of Iowa Women's Resource and Action Center and the Gay People's Union, protested the display by circulating fliers and petitions in the union. The Women's Resource and Action Center set up a counter-display next to The Review's.

'Encourages Harassment'

The counter-display described The Review's handiwork as "discrimination," and urged students to protest to the university's administration for allowing it. The counter-display also contained several brochures about AIDS placed under the title, "Stop AIDS," in large black type.

Susan Buckley, director of the Women's Resource and Action Center and a staff member of the university's Office of Student Services, said The Review's display was in violation of the university's human rights policy and should not have been allowed. "The policy explicitly states that protection from discrimination is extended to gays and lesbians," Ms. Buckley said. "In my mind, that display encourages harassment."

To put a display in the union, a group must file a request with its board of directors. If the group is a recognized student group—which The Campus Review is because it employs university students—it can use a display case any way it wants for two weeks, said Phillip

Jones, dean of student services. Both displays were removed after two-week periods.

'A Forum for Ideas'

"There are procedural rules, but none for content," Mr. Jones said. "The Campus Review has the right to express its political and social point of view in a forum for ideas."

But Virgil Hare, a senior in liberal arts who is president of the Gay People's Union on campus, said the administration was displaying a "homophobic" attitude in allowing the display to be put up.

Mr. Renander, who graduated last year from the university's College of Law, said that he did not feel the display was discriminatory and that protesting groups were taking it too seriously.

"The bottom line is, it's a free country," Mr. Renander said. "People should lighten up. This was meant to be humorous, to be a kind of fund-raiser and I wish people would see it that way."

Protestors Greatly Outnumber Participants at UMASS "Straight Pride" Rally

One of the scheduled events at the University of Massachusetts at Amherst's 1991 Conservative Awareness Week was a "straight pride" rally. At the appointed time 50 people gathered outside the student union wearing buttons with blue squares, an apparent parody of the pink triangle buttons sometimes worn as a symbol for gay pride. During his speech, the rally's founder, Theodore G. Maravelias, said of homosexuals, "They don't want rights; they want to force a sexuality on me. Keep it in the closet!" However, his remarks were difficult to hear owing to the crowd of 500 protesters dancing, kissing, and shouting "Shame!" as well as "Hey, hey, ho, ho, homophobia has got to go."

Conservative Awareness Week was organized by a variety of campus groups, including the Republican Club and the monthly newspaper, *The Minuteman*. Regarding the straight pride rally, Republican Club president Glen Caroline said it was not about gay bashing but simply providing an opportunity for heterosexual students to "proudly declare their sexuality." However, Laura Silver said that campus discrimination and harassment led her to organize a local chapter of the militant homosexual rights group Queer Nation. According to Ms. Silver, two seats allocated for gay representatives on a student governing body were recently eliminated, and after she and another student protested, they began to receive threatening phone calls. In response to the threats, the UMass Lesbian, Bisexual and Gay Alliance planned to present a list of demands to university administrators, including a request for increased campus protection for gay students.

MARCH 10, 1991
CAMPUS LIFE: MASSACHUSETTS;
Angry Gay Groups Drown Out Rally by Conservatives

AMHERST, Mass. – Conservative Awareness Week at the University of Massachusetts at Amherst backfired on student organizers last week when gay rights proponents outnumbered conservatives at their own events.

Organizers of the week, including the Republican Club, Young Americans for Freedom, the New Americans and The Minuteman, a monthly newspaper, met with particularly harsh criticism from gay-rights supporters for voicing anti-gay opinions at scheduled events.

On Thursday, about 50 conservatives, wearing the white pins emblazoned with blue squares emblematic of "straight pride," gathered at noon outside the student union for the second annual "straight pride" rally.

But a crowd of about 500 protesters, including some from nearby colleges like Amherst, shouted "Shame" and "Hey, hey, ho, ho, homophobia has got to go" to drown out the hourlong event, saying it was homophobic and intended to hurt homosexuals. Many waved posters of pink triangles—symbols of gay pride. Triangles were also painted on the red brick student union building.

'Declare Their Sexuality'

The president of the Republican Club, Glen Caroline, a senior political science major from Canton, Mass., said conservative students on campus had organized the rally to "proudly declare their sexuality."

"This will not consist of an hour of gay-bashing" but rather of heterosexuals proclaiming pride in their sexual orientation.

The counterprotest was marked by dancing, kissing and continuous shouting to drown out the speakers. The two groups were separated by wooden barricades and by the campus police.

"We'll do anything we need to be able to live our lives free of harassment and with dignity," said Laura Silver, a junior history major from Storrs, Conn. Ms. Silver is a member of Queer Nation, a militant gay rights organization founded last December.

Seats on Board Eliminated

Ms. Silver said she helped organize a Queer Nation chapter after conservative members of the Board of Governors, a student group in charge of allocating office space in the campus center and student union,

removed two seats on the board itself for gay student representatives.

She and another student, Jason MacDonald, a freshman liberal arts major from Boston, said they had received harassing telephone calls including death threats since they staged a "kiss in" at the Republican Club a few days after the removal of the seats.

The founder of the "straight pride" rally, Theodore G. Maravelias, spoke briefly at the rally, saying the gay rights law enacted last year in Massachusetts and other gay rights actions were distracting attention from more important issues, like the decline of the traditional family.

"They don't want rights, they want to force a sexuality on me," said Mr. Maravelias, a senior in political science from Danvers, Mass.

"Keep it in the closet!"

After the rally, students from Queer Nation and the UMass Lesbian, Bisexual and Gay Alliance entered the Republican Club's office and applied to join, Ms. Silver said.

A spokesman for the UMass Lesbian, Bisexual and Gay Alliance, Sean Sullivan, said the group planned to formulate a list of demands, including more protection for gay students on campus, and present them to the administration. "No way are we going to be marginalized or pressed, especially in the Pioneer Valley, which is supposedly one of the most liberalized places in the United States," said Mr. Sullivan, a freshman from West New York, N.J.

The turnout of protesters grew significantly from last year's "straight pride" rally in April, which the campus police said drew about 150 people.

The rally ended a week of smaller protests. More than 300 students turned out for a talk show on Tuesday night that focused mostly on gay rights. The police said about 150 protesters attended the conservatives' anti-abortion rally on Wednesday.

COLLEGE GUIDE TARGETS LGBT STUDENTS

Alyson Books began targeting a growing college demographic in 2006 with its publication "The Advocate College Guide for LGBT Students." The 400-page book profiled 100 schools, taking into consideration a range of issues, including whether the school has a nondiscrimination policy, gay-friendly housing options, active student groups, and courses geared to the specific interests of LGBT students. Although the colleges were not ranked, each received a "Gay Point Average" of up to twenty points. This resource has become increasingly necessary, according to Bruce Steele, the guide's editor-in-chief, because more teens are coming out in high school, so "unlike in the past, the experience they will have on a campus is something they can think about before they go to college." In addition, Mr. Steele hopes that publicizing cutting-edge programs and policies will accelerate change by encouraging additional colleges and universities to adopt them over time.

SEPTEMBER 14, 2006
IS THIS CAMPUS GAY-FRIENDLY?
By STEPHANIE ROSENBLOOM

This fall, stacked amid the hefty new college admissions books like "The Best 361 Colleges" and "Financial Aid for the Utterly Confused" is a guide about an entirely different sort of college acceptance.

"The Advocate College Guide for LGBT Students" (Alyson Books) profiles 100 of the country's "best campuses" for lesbian, gay, bisexual and transgender students, and it arrives at a time when gay students are more vocal and visible.

"It's looking more like half or most gay and lesbian Americans are coming out before they get to college," said Bruce Steele, the guide's editor in chief. "Unlike in the past, the experience they will have on a campus is something they can think about before they go to college."

Among the top 20 colleges in the guide are the University of Pennsylvania and the University of Southern California.

Lance Sun, 17, of Flushing, Queens, said he had purchased the glossy yellow guide as a supplementary resource to help him gauge how well he might fit in at various campuses.

"I remember a few months ago I was looking for a Web site or guide," he said. "I tried really hard and I couldn't find one."

But a few weeks ago he received an e-mail message from the Gay, Lesbian and Straight Education Network, a national education organization, about the new guide.

"I was really excited," Lance said. "It was perfect timing."

There is ample evidence that in recent years gay students have become more outspoken about their identity. Most Gay-Straight Alliances registered with the Gay, Lesbian and Straight Education Network are in high schools, and today there are more than 3,000 of them, up from 750 in September 2001.

Grant Hoover, a 21-year-old senior at the University of Southern California who was the executive director of the university's Gay, Lesbian, Bisexual and Transgender Assembly last year, said the Advocate guide is "definitely a step in the right direction."

"I think it reflects growing visibility on a national level," he said. "And a growing need."

For decades college guides have offered advice on subjects as varied as tuition, dorms and even where students can buy the best marijuana. Yet books devoted entirely to gay students' experiences have been scarce. New York University Press published "The Gay, Lesbian and Bisexual Students' Guide to Colleges, Universities and Graduate Schools," but that was in 1994.

Kevin Jennings, the executive director of the Gay, Lesbian and Straight Education Network and a former high school teacher, said the Advocate guide is the first book that really takes on the questions of non-straight students comprehensively.

The Advocate guide, about 400 pages, does not rank the schools but has a Gay Point Average Official Campus Checklist, which scores campuses (up to 20 points) on their policies, programs and practices affecting lesbians, gays, bisexuals and transgender people. That includes whether a school has nondiscrimination statements, if there are housing options or themes, if there is a student group devoted to the population, and if there is a variety of related courses.

Each profile also has a "Fun Queer Stuff to Know" box that includes information like "best LGBT-cool athletic sport" and "best LGBT-accepting religious/spiritual organization."

For many non-straight students the guide is a sign of how progressive many American campuses have become and proves that the students do not necessarily have to go to a big city college to feel comfortable. It can help parents find schools where their children will not only be safe, but welcomed. And, Mr. Steele said, it may make colleges and universities more aware of one another's practices and foster more change.

Yet several students said they were surprised their schools were in the guide because they still have a long way to go to stem homophobia.

Jeremy Marshall, a 20-year-old junior at Duke University and the president of Duke Allies, a student organization for those who support lesbian, gay, bisexual and transgender people, said he was surprised Duke was listed among the top 20 friendliest schools.

Boy Scouts Sued for Revoking Membership of Gay Eagle Scout

As a Boy Scout, James Dale achieved the coveted rank of Eagle Scout and continued to serve as an assistant Scoutmaster of Troop 73 while attending Rutgers University. However, when in 1990 a local newspaper printed an article in which Dale acknowledged being gay, the Monmouth Council of the Boy Scouts of America revoked his membership, stating that as a private club it had the right to set membership standards that prohibit known homosexuals from participating. In 1991 New Jersey passed a law that prohibited discrimination on the basis of sexual orientation, and it is under this law that Dale filed suit against the Boy Scouts of America, requesting a reinstatement of his membership as well as compensatory damages. Said Dale, "Being proud about who I am is something the Boy Scouts taught me. They taught me to stand up for what I believe in."

JULY 30, 1992
EX-EAGLE SCOUT SUES OVER BAN ON HOMOSEXUALS

TRENTON, N.J., July 29—James Dale says the Boy Scouts taught him to take pride in who he is. Today he sued the organization, saying his membership was revoked two years ago after the Scouts found out he was gay.

"I owe it to the organization to point out to them how bad and wrong this policy is," said Mr. Dale, a 21-year-old Rutgers student and former Eagle Scout. "Being proud about who I am is something the Boy Scouts taught me. They taught me to stand up for what I believe in."

The Monmouth Council of the Boy Scouts of America said Mr. Dale did not meet the standards of leadership set by the national organization, which prohibits homosexuals.

Blake Louis, spokesman of the Boy Scouts of America, based in Dallas, said: "We don't think a homosexual presents a role model that's consistent with the expectations of mainstream American families."

And James Kay, the executive director of the Monmouth Council, said: "The issue is purely and simply one that says we have a right to set standards for membership."

30 Merit Badges

Mr. Dale, of Port Monmouth, was an Eagle Scout, the highest rank in scouting, with Troop 73 in Matawan and held 30 merit badges. He received a letter in August 1990 saying his membership was terminated, said his lawyer, Evan Wolfson. When asked why, the Monmouth Council told Mr. Dale it was because he was gay, the lawyer said.

The Boy Scouts learned of Mr. Dale's sexual orientation after a newspaper article appeared about a seminar on gay and lesbian youth at which he was a speaker.

The lawsuit in Monmouth County Superior Court, against the Monmouth Council and the Boy Scouts of America, was filed under a state law that took effect this year prohibiting discrimination on the basis of sexual orientation. The suit asks the court to reinstate Mr. Dale's membership and award him compensatory damages.

A similar case against the Boy Scouts is pending in California, said Mr. Louis, the Scout spokesman.

* *

SUPREME COURT UPHOLDS BOY SCOUTS' RIGHT TO EXCLUDE HOMOSEXUALS

After a court battle that lasted from 1992 to 2000, the Supreme Court ruled that New Jersey may not require the Boy Scout troop to reinstate an openly gay troop leader. This *New York Times* opinion piece argues that gays and lesbians may legitimately argue against discrimination in employment, housing, and many other areas but that they do not have a civil right to "assist in raising other people's children." According to the author, although choosing to exclude some people may seem intolerant, it is central to the First Amendment's free association clause, which guarantees the right of people to join with others to share and promote common interests. Using antidiscrimination laws to force private clubs to admit everyone would fundamentally undermine this right. The Supreme Court agreed, stating in a 5–4 ruling that forcing a group to accept certain individuals could impair the group's ability to "express those views, and only those views, that it intends to express."

JUNE 30, 2000
A CASE THE SCOUTS HAD TO WIN
By STEFFEN N. JOHNSON

CHICAGO – To the dismay of gay rights groups and some civil libertarians, the Supreme Court ruled on Wednesday that it is unconstitutional for the state to require a Boy Scout troop to admit a gay scoutmaster. The court's decision, however, goes to the heart of the First Amendment's guarantee of free association. It may be a civil right to have access to employment, or to transportation, or to hotels and restaurants. But it is not a civil right to assist in raising other people's children.

In the past, the court had understandably ruled that society's interest in ensuring access to certain opportunities like jobs, school and other basic necessities must sometimes override the right to associate with whomever one pleases. Everyone needs to make a living. Everyone needs an education. Thus, the court ruled that businesses or commercial gatherings like the Rotary Club cannot exclude women from their ranks.

But serving as a role model for young children whose parents share common values is not the same sort of privilege as a job or an education. It is a service, and one entrusted to few people.

To extend the reach of anti-discrimination laws to private groups whose purpose is not to make a profit, but to bring together people with similar values, would destroy the nation's diverse tradition of voluntary collaboration for common causes. And a world in which the government could declare which causes and which moral positions benefit society, and which do not, could only be described as Orwellian.

The case arose when the Scouts informed James Dale that he could not serve as a leader of a troop in Monmouth

County, N.J. Mr. Dale sued, claiming that the Scouts had unlawfully discriminated against him because he was gay, and the New Jersey courts agreed. But the Supreme Court, in a 5–4 ruling, said that forcing a group to accept certain members may impair its ability to "express those views, and only those views, that it intends to express."

Exercising the right to exclude others may seem intolerant, but such a right is indispensable to private groups seeking to define themselves, to chart their own moral course, and to work together for common ends. If the Boy Scouts were required to admit leaders who advocated a position contrary to its own, then men could assert the right to lead the Girl Scouts, gentiles could assert the right to head Jewish groups and heterosexuals could assert the right to lead gay groups.

Mr. Dale's supporters said that the case was about status-based discrimination and that enforcing anti-discrimination laws against voluntary groups like the Scouts was valid because anti-gay beliefs are not what brought the Scouts together. But a group should not need to have an anti-gay agenda to hold the view that homosexual behavior is wrong. Many churches, for example, teach that homosexual activity is immoral while affirming that gay people should be treated with equal dignity and respect. That does not mean that they have given up their right not to appoint homosexuals to leadership.

Like many Americans, the Boy Scouts attempt to walk the line between tolerance of everyone and disapproval of certain types of conduct. That they wish to express their view by example or by quiet persuasion, rather than an outspoken campaign, does not diminish their right to take a position on moral issues.

As the court's majority understood, people's rights to hold moral positions, to associate with others who share the same views, and to instill those views in their children without threat of outside interference are liberties that belong as much to gay men and lesbians as to the Boy Scouts, as much to those who advocate alternative lifestyles as to those who advocate traditional morality.

Continued Ban on Homosexuals Leads to Loss of Support for Boy Scouts

Citing discomfort with the group's exclusion of homosexuals at the turn of the twenty-first century, many individuals, organizations, and communities began to rethink their role in supporting the Boy Scouts. Since the Supreme Court upheld the constitutionality of the ban in June 2000, the group lost significant financial and in-kind support from a wide variety of sources. The Boy Scouts sued the State of Connecticut over its decision to not allow state employees to choose to support the group with their contributions to a state-run charity. In addition, Chase Manhattan Bank, Textron, Inc., and other companies ceased to provide financial support, while some cities and school districts placed new restrictions on the Boy Scouts' use of parks, classrooms, and other facilities. Some parents chose to remove their children from local troops, and Scouting for All, a group organized by a fifteen-year-old Scout to protest the ban, held protests in several cities in August 2000.

For many, the decision required a painful choice between ethical/legal issues related to antidiscrimination and the high-quality recreational opportunities provided by the Boy Scouts, sometimes in neighborhoods where positive activities and options for boys are severely limited. Although some local troops and councils did not agree with the ban on homosexual members and would be willing to sign nondiscrimination policies, Boy Scouts of America insists that local groups are not allowed to establish policies contrary to those of the national organization and that to do so would result in loss of affiliation.

AUGUST 29, 2000
SCOUTS' SUCCESSFUL BAN ON GAYS IS FOLLOWED BY LOSS IN SUPPORT

By KATE ZERNIKE

Correction Appended

In the two months since the United States Supreme Court ruled that the Boy Scouts of America have a constitutional right to exclude gays, corporate and governmental support for the organization has slipped markedly.

Chicago, San Francisco and San Jose, Calif., have told local Scout troops that they can no longer use parks, schools and other municipal sites. Companies like Chase Manhattan Bank and Textron Inc., have withdrawn hundreds of thousands of dollars in support to local and national scouting groups nationwide. Dozens of United Ways from Massachusetts to San Francisco have cut off money amounting to millions of dollars each year.

And Connecticut, in what may become a test case, has banned contributions to the Scouts by state employees through a state-run charity. The state is also considering whether to block the Scouts from using public campgrounds or buildings.

"It's a watershed issue," said C. Joan Parker, assistant counsel to the Connecticut Commission on Human Rights and Opportunities, which must issue a ruling by Nov. 8 on whether the Scouts violate state antidiscrimination laws.

If the commission rules that the group does violate those laws, the Boy Scouts would be prevented from using any public facilities.

"We have to decide, are we aiding and abetting someone that discriminates?" Ms. Parker said. "Clearly, any public entity needs to have clean hands."

Gregg Shields, a national spokesman for the Scouts, said the organization respected the right of private companies to donate only to groups of their choice. But the organization is suing the State of Connecticut to restore state employees' ability to donate to the Scouts, and Mr. Shields said his group would fight to maintain access to public schools and public places in other states as well.

"The Boy Scouts of America since 1910 have taught traditional family values," Mr. Shields said. "We feel that an avowed homosexual isn't a role model for those values."

For public and private officials around the country, the problem is a complex and painful one. On the one hand, they do not want to cut off valuable opportunities for the young or run afoul of First Amendment principles. On the other hand, by allowing a group that bans gays to use public facilities and supporting it, they violate their antidiscrimination statutes.

The trim uniform of the Boy Scouts has become almost a cherished national symbol. But at a time when same-sex benefits, diversity training and nondiscrimination policies have become routine, some companies and organizations say the Scouts' refusal to admit gays has come to seem almost un-American.

"Their position is, on the face of it, in conflict with our commitment and our values on diversity," said Jim Finn, a spokesman for Chase, which had contributed about $200,000 annually to the Boy Scouts until stopping it last month.

The Supreme Court ruled in June by a 5-to-4 vote that the organization had a constitutional right to exclude gays because opposition to homosexuality is part of the organization's "expressive message."

The decision overturned a ruling last year by the New Jersey Supreme Court that applied the state's law against discrimination in public accommodations to require a New Jersey Scout troop to readmit a longtime member and assistant scoutmaster, James Dale, whom it had dismissed after learning he is gay. But the ruling did not address the merits of the ban on gays, only whether the Boy Scouts is a private group, and so has the right to set its own membership rules.

The Scouts, whose membership has grown to 6.2 million, said that the group's charter since 1910 had promoted "family values," and that its oath pledged a "morally straight" life. A homosexual, the organization said, is not the proper role model for those values.

While the decisions to withhold support will not seriously dent the $125 million raised annually by the Scouts national organization, the growing effort to block local chapters from meeting in places like public schools and state campgrounds raises practical problems for the Scouts. Since the ruling, many public bodies, charities and companies, including Merrill Lynch, are beginning the discussion that has taken place in Hartford. The options, they say, are equally unpleasant: hurting children who are benefiting from scouting, or supporting a position they find ethically untenable.

"Do we just cut off funding, and so hundreds of kids in Hartford aren't getting a program they so desperately need?" asked Susan Dunn, senior vice president of the United Way of the Capital Area. "Our mission is to serve our community, especially children. But it's also in our mission that we don't discriminate. That's where it becomes difficult."

The American Civil Liberties Union filed a lawsuit against the city of San Diego on Monday asking a federal court to revoke a 50-year-old agreement that lets the Scouts lease 18 acres of parkland for $1 a year. The lease is set to expire in 2007.

In Fall River, Mass., the executive director of the local United Way, Bob Horne, said he was stunned at how swiftly and strongly his board had acted to cut support to any Scout troops that did not sign a form saying they would not endorse the Scouts' ban on gays.

"I thought that some people would try to skirt the issue," Mr. Horne said. "But attendance was unbelievable, the best attendance we've had all year. It could not have been a more unanimous, enthusiastic vote. Obviously, there was concern for the kids, but it all came down to we really have an obligation to do the right thing."

More than half the population of Fall River, an old mill city, has Portuguese immigrants in its background, and an influx of Cambodians has arrived in the past few years.

"With those growing groups," Mr. Horne said, "people are being more aware of diversity and doing things right and being fair and not setting up separate views, the idea that people are people. "People felt very strongly that we should take this step." Those who are eliminating or reconsidering their support are trying to respect, as the Supreme Court affirmed, the Scouts' right to set its own mission.

And cutting off money or access to one private group raises more questions, officials say. Do those same charities then cut off financing to groups chartered to serve, say, Latinos? Do states stop allowing Roman Catholic youth groups to use public campgrounds or school meeting rooms because the church does not ordain gays?

Among those debating whether to end support, some are reluctant to do so because they believe the local Scout chapters do not agree with the ban on gays, which was put into effect by the national organization.

"Everyone knows their work with kids is good, and it's a policy that's not commonly enforced," said Marty Milkovic, executive director of the United Way of Northern Fairfield County, in Connecticut.

Like chapters in many other cities, the Southeastern New England United Way in Providence, R.I., has said it will require any Scout council to sign a form saying it will not discriminate. But the Boy Scouts' Narragansett Council, which receives $200,000 from the United Way, has said it must abide by the national policy. And Mr. Shields, the spokesman for the national group, said local councils were not allowed to disavow any part of the national charter, so the councils are not allowed to sign any nondiscrimination policy that would require them to admit gays. Troops that disobey the national charter could face eviction.

Within the local councils, though, there is increasing dissent from the policy. Scouting for All, a group started by a 15-year-old scout in California, that advocates opening up the organization to gays, held a national protest day outside Boy Scout headquarters in several cities last week. In Montclair, N.J., parents in a local Cub Scout troop are signing a petition saying they do not endorse the national policy.

In New Milford, Conn., Gale Alexander said he and his wife were torn about whether to allow their 9-year-old son to remain in the Boy Scouts. They like the skills and self-confidence the program has taught but, Mr. Alexander said, "I couldn't look at my friends if I couldn't stand up and say this is not right."

So as a compromise, the Alexanders are letting their son continue scouting, but they have decided to become vocal in their opposition to the policy. In conversations, they have discovered that other parents do not agree with it, either.

"The idea that all the rank and file is just fine with this is just a bunch of malarkey," Mr. Alexander said. "It's time now for parents to speak up and say, I don't agree with it. It's time for people to start fighting from within."

Correction: September 6, 2000, Wednesday. A front-page article on Aug. 29 and an editorial on Sunday about a falloff in support for the Boy Scouts because of their exclusion of gays misstated two cities' reactions to the ban. Chicago no longer lets the Boy Scouts use parks, city buildings and schools without charge. The public schools of San Francisco no longer sponsor Scout recruitment drives or other programs during school hours. The Scouts are not barred from using parks, schools and other sites. The article also misstated the timing of those restrictions. They began before the Supreme Court upheld the ban in June, not afterward. The article also cited one city erroneously among those that bar the Scouts from their facilities. Although one San Jose elementary school district, Alum Rock Union, does not permit recruiting or other Scout programs during school hours, the ban is attributed to demands on instructional time, not to the Scouts' policy. The article also misstated the number of United Way organizations that have stopped raising funds for the Scouts. It is about a dozen, not dozens. In addition, the article misstated the Roman Catholic Church's stance on the ordination of gays. Ordination requires a promise to live a celibate life. While the church condemns homosexual activity, it does not have a policy against ordaining gay men.

VIOLENCE AGAINST LGBT PEOPLE

HOMOPHOBIA AND THE ROOTS OF VIOLENCE

According to David Wertheimer (then of the New York City Gay and Lesbian Anti-Violence Project, currently working for the Bill and Melinda Gates Foundation), *The New York Times* is the first mainstream publication to seriously address the issue of violence against lesbian, gay, bisexual, and transgender (LGBT) people, beginning with a William Greer article published in November 1986. While stories about individual instances of vandalism, harassment, arson, assault, and murder had explicitly referenced homosexuals as targets since the early 1970s, Greer's article took the additional step of acknowledging violence against gays and lesbians as a unique category of crime that was on the rise and worthy of public concern. For the LGBT population, this certainly did not constitute breaking news. Since the early 1980s, a grass roots antiviolence movement had sprung up in many U.S. cities with large gay and lesbian populations. Disturbed by what appeared to be an increase in both the frequency and severity of attacks, groups were formed to document violent incidents, provide support to victims, and demand increased protection from law enforcement.

Violence against LGBT people is a by-product of homophobia, the hatred of those who do not conform to mainstream society's norms about sexuality or gender. One theory suggests that individuals use homophobia to manage fears about their own sexuality. Even for those who consider themselves heterosexual, it is not unusual to experience a sexual response or engage in sexual activity with someone of the same sex, particularly during adolescence. Because of this, some people become fearful or insecure about their own sexual or gender identity. For men in particular, this doubt may feel so uncomfortable or unacceptable that they develop a hatred of those perceived to be effeminate or gay as a strategy for reassuring themselves of their own masculinity and heterosexuality. This may help to explain why lesbians are less likely to be the victims of antigay violence than gay men or transgender people. It may also shed light on statistics that suggest that the typical aggressor in antigay attacks is a young man under the age of twenty-one, often acting as part of a group. "If you feel insecure about your own sexuality, as so many adolescents do, you can reassure yourself by attacking gays," explains Dr. Gregory Herek, a psychologist at the University of California at Davis.

Another frequently cited cause of homophobia is society's repeated reinforcement of the idea that LGBT people are inherently bad or inadequate. Homosexuality remains illegal in nearly eighty countries, and two-thirds of United Nations' members—including the United States, Russia, and China—recently refused to support a nonbinding declaration acknowledging the basic human rights of gay and lesbian people. Although the U.S. Supreme Court deemed sodomy laws unconstitutional in 2003, antigay bias is still institutionalized through limitations in areas such as marriage and adoption (see the chapter that follows). In addition, although much is made of increased American tolerance toward LGBT people, a 2007 survey of LGBT middle and high school students found that 86 percent had been verbally harassed (and 44 percent physically harassed) in school within the past year because of their sexual orientation (see "Youth and Education," page 294). Unlike racial stereotypes, it is still widely considered acceptable to use gay stereotypes as a source of humor, and as described in an October 28, 2005, *Times* article, gay slurs continue to be used unselfconsciously in the context of professional sports. In preparing for his 2009 inauguration, President Obama made the calculation that it was still politically safe for him to choose Rev. Rick Warren, a megachurch minister who has publicly compared gay relationships to incest and child molestation, to give the invocation, as reported in a December 28, 2008, *Times* opinion piece. These incidents combine with many others to create a context that appears to condone homophobia.

Paradoxically, efforts to increase the visibility of LGBT people may simultaneously foster acceptance and reinforce homophobia. On the one hand, because more people have "come out," more Americans are aware of having an LGBT family member, friend, or colleague, and these relationships help to undermine the myths and stereotypes on which homophobia is built. Combined with the increased

IN FOCUS

The Assassination of Harvey Milk

• •

When Harvey Milk (1930–1978) was elected to serve on San Francisco's board of supervisors in 1977, he became the first openly gay man to be elected to public office in the United States. He was nicknamed "The Mayor of Castro Street," the center of a gay neighborhood in the city of San Francisco.

By the time of his election, Milk had been receiving death threats for several years and predicted his own assassination in a tape-recorded message found after his death, which included the directive, "If a bullet should enter my brain, let that bullet destroy every closet door."

On November 27, 1978, Dan White assassinated Milk and San Francisco mayor George Moscone. White had resigned from the board of supervisors a few weeks earlier but had since changed his mind, asking Moscone to reappoint him. While Moscone initially considered doing so, he ultimately decided against it. White killed Moscone in his city hall office first, then killed Milk as well. Both were shot in the head at close range. In his confession White said that he shot Milk when he "started smirking because he knew that I wasn't going to be reappointed." As word of the shootings became public, a group of at least 25,000 people came together on Castro Street and marched to city hall by candlelight, where thousands of others had already gathered.

White offered an insanity defense at his trial, claiming that he had cracked under pressure and that his diet of junk food had caused "biochemical change" in his brain, which many papers dubbed the "Twinkie defense." Although eligible for the death penalty, White was found guilty of involuntary manslaughter and sentenced to a maximum of five years in prison. Thousands in San Francisco protested the leniency of the jury's verdict, leading to the "White Night" riot. More than 3,000 people took to the streets shouting "He got away with murder," setting fire to police cars, and smashing the glass doors of city hall, while a version of "Danny Boy" was broadcast on the police shortwave radio and officers wreaked havoc on a gay bar and its patrons in response to the uprising. More than 150 police officers and civilians were hospitalized and over $1 million in damages accrued.

Less than two years after his release from prison in 1984, White killed himself. Milk has since been called a martyr for the gay rights movement. In 2008 the feature-length film *Milk* was received with critical and popular acclaim, introducing a new generation to Milk's story. In 2009 he was posthumously awarded the Presidential Medal of Freedom and California designated an annual Harvey Milk Day, inducting him into the state's Hall of Fame.

From *The New York Times*

Carlsen, William. "Ex-Aide Held in Moscone Killing Ran as Crusader Against Crime." November 29, 1978.
Ledbetter, Les. "2 Deaths Mourned by San Franciscans." November 29, 1978.
Turner, Wallace. "Jury to Get Case of San Francisco Mayor's Murder." May 16, 1979.
———. "Ex-Official Guilty of Manslaughter in Slayings on Coast; 3,000 Protest." May 22, 1979.

• •

representation of LGBT people in the media, this has led to an overall reduction in antigay bias, particularly among younger people. As reported in a *Times* article on June 28, 2009, 32 percent of surveyed Americans opposed gay people serving openly in the military, compared with 45 percent in 1994. The same article cites a *New York Times*/CBS News poll that found 57 percent of people under 40 support same-sex marriage, compared with 31 percent of those over 40.

As these numbers indicate, however, a significant proportion of Americans continue to oppose expanding LGBT rights. Research suggests that this resistance is most often grounded in a deeply held religious conviction that homosexuality is a sin. As LGBT people become more visible and accepted in mainstream society, individuals operating out of religiously based homophobia are unlikely to alter their beliefs and may instead feel that cherished values and institutions are being undermined. This viewpoint is repeatedly reflected in a July 7, 1998, *Times* article on resistance to the gay rights movement in South Carolina. In this piece, Governor Beasley defended the state's ban on same-sex marriage by stating, "America is in a moral meltdown today because its leaders, under pressure from special-interest groups, want to always appear tolerant." Similarly, a local minister is quoted as saying, "We really believe this is the last bastion of moral decency left in America." Summing up these positions, political science professor Charles W. Dunn says, "People here perceive themselves on the defensive, defending their culture, their religion, their communities against outside forces." Feeling attacked and fearful, those with religiously based homophobia may become even more intensely angry as a direct result of increasing social acceptance of LGBT people, which may help to explain the apparent increase in violent incidents over the past three decades.

Hate Crimes

The National Coalition of Anti-Violence Projects (NCAVP) includes thirty-five organizations in twenty-five states that are currently working to address and eliminate violence against LGBT people. As part of this effort, NCAVP regularly publishes reports on the nature and frequency of violent attacks within the areas covered by its member organizations. Based on reports from thirteen organizations in eleven states, 2,424 individuals reported being the victim of antigay violence in 2008, including 29 murders, 138 sexual assaults, and 216 attacks that resulted in serious physical injury. Twelve percent of these incidents involved antitransgender bias, and only 28 percent were reported to the police.

One of the most disturbing aspects of attacks on LGBT people is the excessive level of violence that is often involved. In 1994 a study on bias-related killings of homosexuals uncovered 151 murders in twenty-nine states and the District of Columbia that occurred over a span of just under two years. Nearly 60 percent of these deaths included evidence of "overkill." As the name implies, overkill refers to assaults in which the violence used exceeds what is necessary to kill and typically involves victims who are shot or stabbed more than three times, who are severely beaten, or on whom more than one killing method has been used. When victims were analyzed by race and ethnicity, Latino and black victims were found to have suffered even higher rates of brutality, with overkill rates of 71 percent and 63 percent, respectively. One person involved in the study was quoted as saying, "The level of violence in these homicides is really gruesome."

Another aspect of this type of bias-motivated crime is its ability to affect the lives of all who belong to the targeted group, not just the specific victim. As David Leavitt wrote in a powerful *Times* opinion piece following the murder of Matthew Shepard in 1998, "Gay killings are not everyday occurrences, any more than lynchings were ever a daily event in the South, but the fear colors everything." Like acts that are more typically labeled "terrorism," the brutal murder of a person because of his or her sexual orientation or gender identity is meant to instill terror in all LGBT people in order to intimidate and disempower them regardless of whether they themselves are victims of physical violence.

The long history of distrust and poor communication between the LGBT community and law enforcement makes combating this type of violence particularly challenging. In addition to pre-Stonewall harassment, entrapments, and arrests, the legal system has frequently failed to take antigay crimes seriously, looking the other way, failing to conduct thorough investigations, and, in the rare instances when a case came to trial, avoiding convictions altogether or imposing unusually light sentences. One such case that received extensive coverage in *The New York Times* was that of Michael Maye's alleged assault on Morty Manford. On April 15, 1972, a professional association for reporters was hosting a dinner for members and local politicians in the grand ballroom of the New York Hilton. In an effort to protest the way that homosexuals were being portrayed in the media, twenty-one-year-old Manford and several other members of the Gay Activists Alliance entered the ballroom and attempted to distribute brochures. They were soon asked to leave, and as they did so, several dinner guests followed them out, including Michael

IN FOCUS

The Film *Cruising*

● ●

Released in theaters across the country in 1980, the film *Cruising* was based on a murder mystery written by *New York Times* reporter Gerald Walker that focused on a serial killer who targeted gay men in New York City. In the movie the killer picks up his victims at gay bars, takes them to seedy motels, ties them up, and stabs them to death. By the end of the movie, the officer assigned to investigate the killings (played by Al Pacino) himself becomes homosexual and a copycat killer. While some viewers claimed that the film accurately depicted aspects of the libertine cruising culture of gay male bars in the city before the rise of AIDS, many in the gay community argued that it offered a bigoted view of homosexuality. As reported in *The Times* on July 26, 1979, the National Gay Task Force called the movie "a gross distortion of the lives of gay men by portraying them as violent and sex-obsessed." Some activists feared that the film would encourage hate crimes against gay men.

While *Cruising* was being filmed in New York City, hundreds of demonstrators tried to disrupt the making of the movie by blowing whistles, ringing bells, blasting air horns, playing loud music, and shining mirrors at the sets, hoping to call attention to the biased representation of gay men. The National Gay Task Force initially asked the city of New York to rescind permission to film on location in the city; however, it withdrew the request after the producer, Jerry Weintraub, met with gay leaders and encouraged them to continue to air their views. Perhaps in recognition of the controversy, the original film included a disclaimer that read, "This film is not intended as an indictment of the homosexual world. It is set in one small segment of that world, which is not meant to be representative of the whole." Nonetheless, gay activists across the country picketed theaters showing the film, which was widely panned by the critics.

From *The New York Times*

Ferretti, Fred. "Filming of 'Cruising' Goes More Calmly." August 7, 1979.
Unsigned. "Protesters Call the Film 'Cruising' Antihomosexual." July 26, 1979.

● ●

Maye, a former national Golden Gloves champion and the president of the Uniformed Firefighters Association.

What happened next is the subject of controversy, but within a few days members of the gay rights group filed assault charges against Maye and six unknown assailants. As described in a May 2, 1972, *Times* article, four city officials who were attending the dinner testified that they had seen Maye punch Manford and then repeatedly kick him in the stomach and groin as he lay, semiconscious, on the steps of an escalator. Despite this evidence, Maye was not charged with a crime for over a month. In the intervening time, one of the witnesses, Ethan Geto, an assistant to the Bronx borough president, stated during a press conference that he was prepared to testify to "police inaction" in the case, and members of the Gay Activist Alliance staged at least one protest outside the home of District Attorney Frank Hogan (see the related *Times* article on May 5, 1972). When Maye was finally charged on May 23, 1972, the grand jury panel considered a charge of assault, a crime punishable by up to five years in prison, but instead chose to indict the accused attacker for harassment, a noncriminal violation similar to a speeding ticket and carrying a maximum penalty of fifteen days in jail. At his trial, Maye claimed that he became involved in the conflict only in an effort to rescue his friend from "a band of angry homosexuals" and denied kicking or stomp-ing Manford. Although he admitted to throwing one punch, Maye insisted it was only because one of the protesters grabbed at his groin and tore his pants. Despite the graphic descriptions several city officials provided of the assault on Manford, a July 7, 1972, Times article reports that the trial of Michael Maye concluded with the harassment charge against him being dismissed.

Cases like this one served to escalate existing tensions between the LGBT community and local law enforcement, often resulting in anger, accusations, and misinformation on both sides. This is reflected in The New York Times coverage of a series of killings in January 1973. Three men known to frequent Greenwich Village leather bars were found dead from multiple stab wounds within a few weeks of one another. Gossip quickly spread throughout the gay community that additional bodies had been found and that some had been decapitated. Police efforts to quash these rumors had little impact. The Gay Activists Alliance issued a statement accus-ing the police of intentionally withholding information and showing only "half-hearted interest" in investigating the mur-ders. In turn, a homicide detective speculated that the lack of forced entry suggested that the killer may have been someone the victims "had met in a bar and taken home." The detective went on to imply that the gay community was overreacting to and perhaps somewhat to blame for these deaths because "when they pick up a stranger on the street they're taking a chance." Some gay men appeared to accept the suggestion that the deaths were sex crimes perpetrated by someone from within their own community. However, others with knowledge of the local leather scene argued that this explanation just didn't ring true because those into sadomasochism were "more into costumes than violence" and knew how to keep bondage, domination, and other potentially dangerous ele-ments of their sexual activity "within carefully prescribed limits." Although as many as four other local murders were tentatively linked to these three, no one was arrested and the crimes remained unsolved.

With reports of gay-bashing incidents steadily increas-ing in the late 1970s and early 1980s, the National Gay Task Force began organizing around the issue of violence against gays and lesbians in 1982. Headed by Kevin Berrill, the group surveyed more than 2,000 gay men and lesbians in six cities in 1984 and found that 44 percent had been threatened with physical violence and 19 percent had been physically assaulted at least once owing to their sexual ori-entation. Twenty percent reported being victimized by the police. Responding to pressure from the National Gay Task

Force and other groups, Rep. John Conyers (D-MI) sponsored congressional hearings in 1986 on bias crimes against gays and lesbians, which included testimony from Dr. Gregory Herek, Kevin Berrill, and other experts, as well as several victims of antigay assaults. In 1988 Representative Conyers introduced the Hate Crimes Statistics bill, mandating that the Justice Department collect and publish annual statistics on bias crimes related to sexual orientation as well as race, religion, and ethnic origin. This bill received strong support in both the House and the Senate and was signed into law by President George H. W. Bush on April 23, 1990.

The Hate Crimes Statistics Act's ultimate impact was limited because local law enforcement's collection and submission of data was not mandated and, as reported in a January 6, 1993, Times article, less than 20 percent com-plied during the first year, resulting in an official national count of 421 hate crimes motivated by sexual orientation in a year when the National Gay and Lesbian Task Force docu-mented more than 1,000 in only five cities. Nonetheless, by acknowledging the connection between antigay violence and other bias-related crimes, this law strengthened the relationship between LGBT groups and other constituen-cies active in antiviolence efforts. In addition to groups that represented traditional targets of bias crime, such as the National Association for the Advancement of Colored People (NAACP) and the American Jewish Congress, this coalition included those motivated to oppose all violence—owing to their religious beliefs—as well as some conservatives com-mitted to being tough on crime. Moving forward, this broad base of support would make it significantly more difficult for politicians to dismiss antigay violence as an issue outside the realm of mainstream concerns.

The prosecution of Julio Rivera's killers illustrates both progress and continued problems in efforts to appropriately punish antigay crimes in the 1990s. On July 2, 1990, Daniel Doyle and Erik Brown, both twenty-one years old, left a party with Esat Bici, nineteen. As Doyle later testified, the three men wanted to find and beat up "a drug dealer or a drug addict or a homo out cruising." They came upon Julio Rivera, a twenty-nine-year-old gay bartender, in an area of Jackson Heights, Queens, often frequented by drug dealers and gay men seeking sexual partners. Erik Brown lured Rivera into a nearby schoolyard by offering him drugs and sex. Once there, the other two men approached, and Bici repeatedly struck Rivera in the head and back with a hammer. Doyle then struck the fatal blow by driving a knife into Rivera's back.

Initially, police classified the murder as drug related because of the area where it occurred and the victim's history of cocaine use; however, after angry demonstrations by gay and lesbian groups, the death was eventually reclassified as a bias crime. Once the three suspects were apprehended, Doyle was allowed to plead guilty to manslaughter in return for his testimony against the other two, both of whom were eventually found guilty of second-degree murder for "acting in concert" with Doyle in the killing of Julio Rivera. Daniel Doyle received the maximum sentence for first-degree manslaughter: eight and one-third to twenty-five years in prison. Both Erik Brown and Esat Bici received sentences of twenty-five years to life. Commenting on the verdicts in a November 21, 1991, *Times* story, a friend of Rivera's said, "We've accomplished something: justice. We have rights." Similarly, national groups anticipated that the Rivera case would have a lasting impact on LGBT people's relationship with the legal system. "There are so many victims out there who refuse to come forward because they do not believe their crimes will be treated seriously, who believe that they will be victimized a second time, not by the thug but by the system," said Gregory J. King of the Human Rights Campaign Fund, a national gay rights group. He added: "A jury verdict such as this gives them a sense of hope."

This sense of hope soon began to dim. In 1995 Brown and Bici's murder convictions were overturned on appeal. Brown pleaded guilty to the lesser charge of manslaughter and agreed to testify against Bici in return for a sentence of five to fifteen years. Out on bail, Bici skipped town and was never apprehended, eventually dying in what appeared to be a drug-related shooting in Tijuana, Mexico, as reported in a *Times* article on October 13, 2002. Shortly after Bici failed to appear for his court hearing, a staff member of the Hispanic AIDS Forum commented on the demoralizing effect these setbacks were having on the gay community. "You can be angry the first time, and angry the second time, and angry the third time" he said. "But then you see that there is no point."

Police sensitivity to issues of both sexual orientation and race drew national attention following the 1991 arrest of Jeffrey Dahmer on suspicion of murdering at least seventeen men and boys in Milwaukee. Two months earlier, a woman had called the police to report that a naked, bleeding, and disoriented Laotian boy, later identified as fourteen-year-old Konerak Sinthasomphone, was staggering in the street. Dahmer invited the responding police officers into his apartment and convinced them that the incident was nothing more than a domestic dispute between lovers. A recording from that evening captures the officers laughing as they inform their dispatcher that "an intoxicated Asian, naked male was returned to his sober boyfriend." Dahmer later told authorities

that he was concealing a dead body in his bedroom that night and killed Sinthasomphone shortly after the police left. The young man's dismembered remains were later recovered from Dahmer's apartment. The officers involved in this incident were suspended, but local LGBT activists claimed the problem was not the poor judgment of a few individuals but, rather, a pervasive police attitude that systematically undervalued the lives of homosexuals and people of color.

These events, combined with changing attitudes toward homosexuality and steadily increasing reports of antigay violence in the early 1990s, led some police departments to begin working to improve their relationship with the LGBT community. An August 9, 1991, *Times* article describes how Houston police worked with the local gay community to develop a sting operation in which undercover officers walked, either alone or posing as a gay couple, in a neighborhood known for its gay bars. Both gay activists and the police department were surprised by the dramatic response. After only one week, three of the undercover officers had been attacked, and thirteen people had been arrested.

As described in an April 7, 1992, *Times* article, the LGBT community in some cities organized unarmed groups of volunteers to patrol gay neighborhoods. Beginning as early as the late 1970s with the "Butterfly Brigades" in San Francisco, groups such as the Pink Panthers (New York City) and the Pink Angels (Chicago) worked closely with local law enforcement, reporting the license plate numbers of those engaged in verbal harassment, interrupting potentially violent encounters, and, when necessary, calling in the police for help. Other police departments provided officers with new forms of sensitivity and diversity training. The police department in Jackson Heights, Queens, the same neighborhood where Julio Rivera was murdered three years previously, piloted a training program that involved local gay and lesbian residents as instructors. Specifically designed to overcome years of misunderstanding and mistrust, the course included four sessions and covered topics such as how to respond to a complaint of same-sex domestic abuse, how to investigate a bias crime related to sexual orientation, and how to sensitively question someone who is "closeted."

On October 6, 1998, twenty-one-year-old Matthew Shepard, an openly gay college student, struck up a conversation with Russell Henderson, twenty-one, and Aaron McKinney, twenty-two, at the Fireside Bar in Laramie, Wyoming. The three ended up leaving together in McKinney's pickup truck, and Henderson and McKinney began beating Shepard as they drove to an isolated area just outside of town. The two assailants tied their five-foot two-inch victim to a fence and hit him repeatedly with a .357 magnum handgun as he "begged for his life." Eighteen hours later a passing bicyclist found Matthew Shepard, still tied to the fence and nearly lifeless. He died five days later without ever regaining consciousness.

The two killers were swiftly apprehended. Henderson pleaded guilty to murder and testified against McKinney in order to avoid the death penalty. McKinney stood trial for the murder, and, in a victory for LGBT activists, the judge refused to allow his lawyer to introduce a "gay panic" defense. As described in a November 2, 1999, *Times* article, this was a legal strategy devised to combat a growing tendency among juries to break with tradition and view the beating or murder of a homosexual as a crime worthy of serious jail time. In this case the proposed defense was that McKinney should be charged with manslaughter because he was temporarily unable to control his rage owing to his having been the victim of sexual abuse at the hands of a man during childhood. Judge Barton R. Voigt rejected this as an attempt to argue diminished capacity, which cannot be used to reduce sentences under Wyoming law. Although eligible for the death penalty, both killers ultimately received two consecutive life sentences each. In an emotional statement following McKinney's sentencing, Matthew Shepard's father spoke to the defendant about the family's decision not to push for a sentence of death, saying, "May you live long, and may you thank Matthew every day for it."

Given the number of hate crimes that are reported, it is difficult to say why this particular incident had such a powerful impact on the national imagination. Perhaps it was because of Shepard's clean-cut, boyish charm or that the position in which his body was tied was so suggestive of a

Russell Henderson, Aaron McKinney, and Chastity Pasley as they wait to be arraigned in the murder of Matthew Shepard. Sheppard, an openly gay college student at the University of Wyoming, was beaten, burned, and left to die on a fence.

Source: AP Images/Ed Andrieski

crucifixion. It may have been the waiting—the eighteen hours that he had to wait to be found and the days the nation waited to see if he would recover. Whatever the cause, candlelight vigils were held in communities throughout the country and, as described in an October 21, 1998, *Times* article, a protest march in New York City unexpectedly drew more than 4,000 people, interfering with traffic and ending in 120 arrests. To the initial dismay of his family, Matthew Shepard had become the face of antigay violence overnight, and as with the Julio Rivera murder verdicts, LGBT activists had high hopes that national indignation over his death would swiftly lead to advances in hate crimes legislation at the state and federal levels.

Although the 1969 Federal Hate Crimes Law allowed for stronger penalties to be applied to bias-motivated crimes, it covered only those victimized as a result of their race, color, religion, or national origin and was valid only for crimes committed when individuals were engaged in certain federally protected activities, such as voting, enrolling in school, or traveling on an interstate highway. At the time that Shepard was killed, forty states had similar legislation, but only nineteen included protection for those victimized because of their sexual orientation. Ten states, including Wyoming, had not yet passed hate crime legislation. In the months following the murder in Laramie, President Clinton again urged Congress to expand the federal categories of those protected by federal hate crimes legislation to include sexual orientation, sex, and disability. During this same time period, nine states also considered adopting hate crimes legislation or adding protections for gays and lesbians to their existing hate crimes laws, or both of these options. However, despite the horror of Matthew Shepard's murder, the federal bill failed, and of the nine states considering hate crimes legislation, only Hawaii, in 2001, obtained coverage for those victimized for their sexual orientation. The other eight (Colorado, Idaho, Montana, New Mexico, Oklahoma, Utah, Virginia, and Wyoming) all defeated similar efforts in the short run, and only two (Colorado and New Mexico) include this coverage in their state hate crimes legislation at the time of this writing.

A 2001 case, however, suggests that attitudes were changing toward LGBT violence, even in traditionally conservative areas of the country. A twenty-five-year-old immigrant from Jordan, Muna Hawatmeh, said her Roman Catholic family "never accepted" that she was a lesbian, even when she was living with her girlfriend, Leticia Rivera, in Provo, Utah. On a 2001 visit to her family, Hawatmeh reported that her parents and brothers imprisoned her in the family home and demanded that she end her relationship, while hitting,

kicking, verbally abusing, and threatening her with death over a span of approximately four hours. Overcome by pain and humiliation, she agreed to return to Jordan and become "a different person." However, Leticia Rivera reported the situation to the police after being physically threatened when she attempted to approach the family on their way to the airport. The police took swift action, contacting the family and insisting that Hawatmeh be brought to the Sandy police station to verify that she was leaving the country voluntarily. After the young woman told her story to the officers on duty, her father, mother, and two brothers were charged with aggravated kidnapping and assault. Although the case never came to trial, it is significant that police in suburban Utah were prepared to respond to concerns raised by a lesbian about her girlfriend's safety while in the company of immediate family members. This case also illustrates the complications that arise at the intersection of various types of identity, for local LGBT activists refused to label the incident a hate crime, owing to its "particular cultural circumstances."

Although it continues to be difficult to live as an openly gay, lesbian, or bisexual person in many communities, acceptance of alternative sexual orientations has proceeded at a much swifter pace than has acceptance of alternative or ambiguous gender expression. According to Susan Stryker, a male-to-female transsexual and transgender historian quoted in a September 8, 1996, *Times* article, people are "so invested in being men or women that if you fall outside that easy definition of what a man or woman is, a lot of people see you as some kind of monster." This reaction places transgender people in a difficult bind. If they are open about their alternative gender identity, they face a daily struggle against public mockery and hostility, as well as the very real possibility of job discrimination, family rejection, and violent attack. However, the cases of Brandon Teena and Angie Zapata provide stark examples of the risks taken by transsexuals who conceal their biological gender and attempt to "pass" as someone of the opposite sex.

Brandon Teena has become a household name as a result of the 1998 documentary *The Brandon Teena Story* and Hillary Swank's Oscar-winning performance in the 1999 movie *Boys Don't Cry*. Born biologically female, twenty-one-year-old Teena was living as a man in a small Nebraska town, befriending other young men and dating local girls. When he was arrested for passing bad checks in December 1993, the police discovered his biological sex and publicized this information. After learning of the gender deception, two male friends raped Teena on Christmas Day and then murdered him and two companions the following week. In 2008 eighteen-year-old Angie Zapata had been living as a woman for several years when she met Allen Andrade on a social-networking site. After learning that Zapata had male genitalia, Andrade used his fists and a fire extinguisher to beat Zapata to death in her Greeley, Colorado, apartment.

The Teena and Zapata murders occurred only fourteen years apart, and the public response to these two crimes shows changes in societal attitudes toward transgender people. The initial *New York Times* report of Brandon Teena's death used the female pronoun when referring to the victim and described the young transgender person as "a woman posing as a man, implying a fraudulent identity." Teena's mother subsequently sued the Richardson County sheriff for failing to arrest the two men for rape and thereby contributing to her child's murder. As described in an April 21, 2001, *Times* article, the judge in this case initially found that Teena was partially responsible for his own death, because of his "lifestyle," although this ruling was subsequently overturned by the Nebraska Supreme Court.

In contrast, *The New York Times* coverage of the 2008 murder refers to the victim as a "transgender woman" and uses the pronouns "she" and "her" in accordance with Angie Zapata's chosen gender, not her biological one. Rather than blaming the victim, legal authorities in this later case made national news by declaring Zapata's death a hate crime, making it the first death of a transgender person in which this designation was used. At trial, Andrade requested leniency based on a "trans-panic" defense. His lawyer attempted to argue that the shock of discovering that he had engaged in a sexual act with a man should be grounds for finding Andrade less than fully responsible for his violent actions. This defense failed, and he was found guilty of first-degree murder and committing a hate crime, in addition to other charges.

Despite these signs of progress regarding societal acceptance of alternative gender identities, the rate of transgender violence remains alarmingly high. Following the brutal 1998 stabbing death of transgender woman Rita Hester in Allston, Massachusetts, San Francisco activists organized a "Remembering Our Dead" vigil on November 20, 1999. Since then, this day has become known as the Transgender Day of Remembrance and is recognized with ceremonies, workshops, and candlelit marches throughout the country. In addition to memorializing those who have died as a result of transgender violence, these events are also designed to raise awareness and encourage an end to all forms of discrimination against transgender people.

At the time of this writing, thirty-two states currently have hate crimes legislation that protects those victimized because of their sexual orientation, and eleven states also specify protections for those targeted for their gender identity. The state where Matthew Shepard died—Wyoming—remains one of five lacking any state-level hate crimes law. Regarding federal legislation, bills were repeatedly submitted between 2001 and 2007 to expand the categories and crimes covered. Each was defeated, typically getting stuck in committee in either the House or Senate. Congress eventually passed such a bill, and on October 28, 2009, President Obama signed the Matthew Shepard and James Byrd Jr. Hate Crimes Prevention Act into law. Included as a rider to a military spending bill, this legislation expands the categories of those federally protected to include individuals victimized because of their gender, gender identity, or sexual orientation. The law also provides additional funding for hate crimes investigations, removes the limitation that victims must be engaged in a federally protected activity (such as voting) when attacked, and allows federal authorities to investigate hate crimes not pursued by local authorities. Finally, the law mandates that the FBI begin tracking hate crimes against transgender people. Following the signing of this law, thirty organizations issued a joint statement, "History in the Making," which read, in part, "It took too long . . . and came at too high a price . . . but this week, the president put pen to paper and . . . made an imperative statement to the country and the world: Our nation will no longer tolerate hate-motivated violence against lesbian, gay, bisexual and transgender (LGBT) people."

Bibliography

Human Rights Campaign. "Transgender Day of Remembrance." 2009. www.hrc.org.

Kenny, Jo, et al. "History in the Making." (Press release). National Gay and Lesbian Task Force, 2009. www.thetaskforce.org.

Kosciw, Joseph G., Elizabeth M. Diaz, and Emily A. Greytak. *National School Climate Survey: The Experiences of Lesbian, Gay, Bisexual and Transgender Youth in Our Nation's Schools.* Gay, Lesbian and Straight Education Network, 2007. www.glsen.org.

Mucciaroni, Gary. *Same Sex, Different Politics: Success and Failure in the Struggles over Gay Rights.* Chicago: University of Chicago Press, 2008.

Skolnik, Avy A., et al. *Hate Violence against Lesbian, Gay, Bisexual, and Transgender People in the United States 2008.* National Coalition of Anti-Violence Programs, 2009. www.ncavp.org.

Wertheimer, David M. "The Emergence of a Gay and Lesbian Anti-Violence Movement." In *Creating Change: Sexuality, Public Policy and Civil Rights,* edited by John d'Emilio, William B.Turner, and Urvashi Vaid. New York: St. Martin's Press, 2000.

From *The New York Times*

Fosburgh, Lacey. "Maye Is Held as Harasser in Gay Alliance Outbreak." May 23, 1972.

Fried, Joseph P. "'Gay Bashing' Death Convictions Voided." February 2, 1995.

Frosch, Dan. "Murder and Hate Verdict in Transgender Case." April 23, 2009.

Goldberg, Carey. "Shunning 'He' and 'She,' They Fight for Respect." September 8, 1996.

Janofsky, Michael. "Judge Rejects 'Gay Panic' as Defense in Murder Case. November 2, 1999.

Johnston, Laurie. "Bronx Official Backs 'Gay' Complaint." May 2, 1972.

Labaton, Stephen. "Poor Cooperation Deflates F.B.I. Report on Hate Crime." January 6, 1993.

Myers, Steven Lee. "For Gay Citizens, Unexpected Justice." November 21, 1991.

Nagourney, Adam. "Political Shifts on Gay Rights Lag behind Culture." June 28, 2009.

Rich, Frank. "You're Likable Enough, Gay People." December 28, 2008.

Roberts, Selena. "Homophobia Is Alive in Men's Locker Rooms." October 28, 2005.

Sack, Kevin. "Gay Rights Movement Meets Big Resistance in S. Carolina." July 7, 1998.

Seelye, Katharine Q. "Citing 'Primitive' Hatreds, Clinton Asks Congress to Expand Hate-Crime Law. April 7, 1999.

Terry, Don. "'Pink Angels' Battle Anti-Gay Crime." April 7, 1992.

Unsigned. "Hogan's Home Is Picketed by Homosexual Protesters." May 5, 1972.

———. "Gay Activist Member Charges 2nd Fireman with Beating Him." July 7, 1972.

———. "Houston Police Set Trap to Quell Tide of Violence Against Homosexuals." August 9, 1991.

———. "No Way to Handle a Protest." October 21, 1998.

———. "Court Increases Award to Kin in Hate Crime." April 21, 2001.

Worth, Robert F. "A Fugitive in the Murder of a Gay Man Is Found Slain." October 13, 2002.

Gay Activists Testify to "Epidemic of Violence"

In a 1986 hearing before the House Judiciary Subcommittee on Criminal Justice, stories and statistics were shared suggesting that the rate of violent crime against homosexuals had increased significantly over the previous three years. In addition, these attacks seemed to be more violent than in the past, and an increasing number of assailants were reported to have made derogatory remarks about AIDS at some point during the assault. Some had speculated that this escalation of violence was the result of increased visibility of gays and lesbians, the association of homosexuals with AIDS, and institutionalized homophobia.

Although surveys had been done that suggested this population was at higher risk than the general population for violent attack, this trend was difficult to verify because law enforcement agencies had not tracked these incidents as a specific category of crime. In addition, it was estimated that up to 90 percent of these attacks were never reported to the police. While local authorities had a history of providing inadequate response to this type of crime, New York City and Washington, D.C., police departments had begun treating these incidents as bias crimes, and other cities were considering taking similar action.

Testimony at the hearing was provided by David M. Wertheimer, executive director of the New York City Gay and Lesbian Anti-Violence Project, as well as representatives from similar organizations throughout the country. These groups had formed in the mid-1980s to raise awareness, fight for increased protection, and provide support to victims of violent attack. Testimony was also provided by individuals assaulted because of their sexual orientation and by Dr. Gregory M. Herek, an assistant professor of social psychology at City University of New York Graduate Center who studied homophobia and violence against homosexuals.

As a result of these hearings, Rep. John Conyers Jr. (D-MI), chair of the Criminal Justice Subcommittee, planned to ask the Justice Department to begin compiling statistics on violence against homosexuals and to recommend increased federal protection for gays and lesbians victimized for their sexual orientation.

NOVEMBER 23, 1986
VIOLENCE AGAINST HOMOSEXUALS RISING, GROUPS SEEKING WIDER PROTECTION SAY
By WILLIAM R. GREER

Attacks on homosexuals appear to have increased sharply around the nation in the last three years as homosexuals have become more vocal in their pursuit of civil rights and more visible because of publicity surrounding the spread of AIDS.

Law-enforcement agencies do not record crimes against homosexuals as a specific category. In several cities, however, homosexuals have formed organizations to document what they say is growing violence against them, to lobby for more protection and to counsel the victims.

At a hearing last month before the House Judiciary Subcommittee on Criminal Justice, these groups presented surveys they had conducted at the local, state and national levels that seemed to document a rise in such violence and suggest some of the underlying causes.

"It seems clear from the testimony," said Julian Epstein, a spokesman for Representative John Conyers Jr., the Michigan Democrat who heads the subcommittee, "that there have been dramatic increases in violence directed against gay men and lesbians, and the violence seems to be connected with the AIDS problem and a general hostility directed against the gay and lesbian population."

New York Cases Said to Double

David M. Wertheimer, executive director of the New York City Gay and Lesbian Anti-Violence Project, formed in 1980 after a series of gang attacks on homosexuals in Manhattan's Chelsea section, testified that the project had counted 351 incidents, from homicides to verbal attacks, aimed at homosexuals in the first nine months of 1986, as against 167 incidents in that time last year.

So far this year the group has counted 17 homicides where the victim appeared to have been selected because he was a homosexual, Mr. Wertheimer said.

The homosexual rights groups say that homosexuals have always been victims of violence but that the attacks have become more brutal and more frequent and that the assailants have increasingly referred specifically to acquired immune deficiency syndrome, which cripples the body's immune system.

In the United States most AIDS victims have been male homosexuals or intravenous drug users and their sexual partners. AIDS is spread through sexual intercourse or exchanges of blood.

Taunts Accompany Attacks

In 28 percent of all New York incidents reported in 1985, Mr. Wertheimer said, assailants taunted their victims with comments about AIDS. He estimated that the percentage of such cases was roughly the same this year.

"We're in the middle of an epidemic of violence against gay men and lesbians," Mr. Wertheimer said.

A San Francisco group, Community United Against Violence, said at the hearing that through September, 150 homosexuals reported being physically assaulted by attackers who shouted insults related to homosexuality, a 23 percent increase over the 116 such assaults in the same period last year.

The surveys presented at the hearing indicate that homosexuals are more often the victims of violent crimes than the general public. Surveys in cities from Richmond to Minneapolis to Des Moines, and in states from Maine to Alaska, found that 15 to 20 percent of homosexuals interviewed said they had been beaten in incidents related to their sexual orientation.

A survey of 2,074 homosexuals in eight cities by the National Gay and Lesbian Task Force found that 1 in 5 homosexual men and 1 in 10 homosexual women reported having been physically assaulted in their lifetimes because of their homosexuality.

A Matter of Perception

Some of these victims said they were perceived to be homosexuals because they were walking arm in arm with a partner or leaving a bar frequented by homosexuals, but others could not explain why they were selected. The survey also found that some heterosexuals, including a married couple walking together in Queens, had been attacked by assailants shouting epithets about homosexuality.

As Matthew Holloway, a homosexual who works for a major financial institution in San Francisco, waited for his roommate outside a supermarket last December, a teenage man and woman began to shout at him.

"We should kill you first, because you're gonna give us AIDS," Mr. Holloway said they shouted. He said that a few minutes later, as he and his roommate drove from the parking lot, they were attacked by the couple and a dozen other young people. His roommate, David Johnson, was dragged from the car and beaten with chains and skateboards. He suffered three broken ribs, a broken jaw and bruises. Mr. Holloway fought to stay in the car and was unharmed. The attackers fled before the police arrived; no suspects were arrested.

Police Don't Separate Data

Because the police do not systematically collect statistics on crime against homosexuals specifically, as the police and the homosexual rights groups acknowledge, a rise in such violence cannot be officially documented.

Moreover, such incidents are often not reported—some surveys say 90 percent go unreported—and the way the police classify crimes that result from bias differs from the way the groups classify them.

Mr. Epstein, the aide to Representative Conyers, said that as a result of the hearing, the Congressman planned to ask the Justice Department to compile statistics on such crimes. He said Mr. Conyers would also include protection for homosexuals in the civil rights provisions of the Federal criminal code, like provisions for blacks and other minority groups.

Federal Protection Sought

Such a change would allow the Federal Bureau of Investigation, United States Attorneys and other Federal agencies to intervene in cases as investigators and prosecutors, Mr. Epstein said. "The response on the part of local law enforcement has not been adequate," he said. "Most other groups that have been particularly targeted for violence because of who they are and what they believe enjoy Federal protection. Gays and lesbians don't."

The New York City and Washington police departments have assigned special units to investigate crimes against homosexuals in the way they investigate crimes against blacks or Jews. The Boston Police Department is considering similar measures. Robert M. Morgenthau, the Manhattan District Attorney, has appointed a prosecutor and a liaison officer for homosexual groups to handle cases of violence.

Since last July, when the Bias Unit of the New York City Police Department expanded its responsibility for crimes resulting from ethnic or religious bias to include bias based on sexual orientation, it has classified only 13 cases as such, according to its commanding officer, Capt. Donald J. Bromberg.

He said some incidents reported to the homosexual rights groups would not be classified by the police as crimes resulting from bias. "Our statistics do not show any type of increase for the most part," he said. "We also are aware that there are many cases out there that aren't reported to the police."

Brooklyn Man Recalls Beating

A homosexual man said in an interview that he walked around the corner from his Brooklyn apartment at 8 A.M. one Saturday last summer and three young men grabbed him. As his assailants shoved him back and forth, punching him in the chest and midsection, he said, they shouted: "Faggot! You faggots give us AIDS."

No one came to help, recalled the man, who works in the Mayor's office and asked that his name not be used to protect his privacy. He later reported the case to the police.

Since then, he said, he has been taunted twice by other groups and once was struck by a thrown bottle.

"What I find frightening is these groups don't seem to have any fear of verbally or physically assaulting people in the middle of the day, in a shopping center, in front of businesses, with hundreds of people around," he said. "Somehow they've gotten the message that their action will be condoned or at least ignored."

Social psychologists and psychiatrists who counsel victims of violence against homosexuals say AIDS has led to an increase in such violence by providing people a justification for their existing hostility to homosexuals. News about the disease has also forced some people to confront a population that they had ignored.

Dr. Gregory M. Herek, an assistant professor of social psychology at the City University of New York Graduate Center, said, "Homophobia also occurs at the institutional level when churches, the popular media, the schools and government pretty much teach people that there is something wrong with homosexuality and in fact it is appropriate to do bad things to them." Dr. Herek is chairman-elect of the American Psychological Association's Committee on Lesbian and Gay Concerns.

Vatican Letter Angers Groups

Homosexual rights groups say a statement by the Vatican last month in a letter on homosexuality to Roman Catholic bishops, for example, as well as speeches by

religious fundamentalists have led some people to rationalize aggression against homosexuals.

The Vatican letter deplored crimes against homosexuals but said that "when civil legislation is introduced to protect behavior to which no one has any conceivable right," people should not be surprised when "irrational and violent reactions increase."

Dr. Herek said the violence toward homosexuals was similar in some respects to the increase in violence against blacks in the 1960's at the peak of the civil rights movement.

But, he said, violence against homosexuals differs significantly from violence against other groups. Most attackers of homosexuals, he said, are adolescents seeking both to gain acceptance among their peers and to alleviate anxieties they may have about their own sexuality.

FEAR AND SELF-RIGHTEOUSNESS CITED AS CAUSE OF INCREASING VIOLENCE AGAINST GAYS

According to the National Gay and Lesbian Task Force, reported incidents of antigay violence and harassment steadily increased throughout the 1980s. In 1989 more than 7,000 incidents were reported throughout the United States, including 62 bias-motivated murders. Further, because many gay victims do not report being harassed or attacked, the actual number was likely much higher. When surveyed, as many as one in four gays and lesbians reported having been the victim of a physical attack.

Although AIDS had been cited as a possible cause for increased antigay violence, research indicated that people with a long-standing hatred of gays and lesbians may simply have been using the epidemic to justify their acts of aggression. Evidence suggested that homophobia often stems from the belief that homosexuality is inherently evil and therefore a threat to morality and society. This belief was further strengthened by legal and religious codes that institutionalized bias against gays and lesbians (such as the barring of homosexuals from serving in the military or as members of the clergy) as well as by the persistence of negative myths and stereotypes (for example, that gay men are effeminate or child molesters). Because of this, research suggested that antigay violence continued to be seen as acceptable in a way that violence against other minority groups is not.

Men under the age of twenty-one were the most frequent perpetrators of attacks on gays and lesbians, and they often attacked in groups. The most frequent victims were an individual man or two men walking together. According to Dr. Gregory Herek, a psychologist at the University of California at Davis, "In gangs of teen-age boys who go out looking for gays to attack, the gay symbolizes an outsider." The attack served to simultaneously reaffirm the boys' heterosexuality, group membership, and shared values.

Antigay bias is resistant to change, particularly when motivated by religious conviction. Nonetheless, "coming out" may be the best long-term strategy for combating homophobic violence and harassment. Although increased visibility may also lead to more attacks, the hope is that spending time with gays and lesbians who are out will eventually generate a greater level of understanding and acceptance.

JULY 10, 1990
HOMOPHOBIA: SCIENTISTS FIND CLUES TO ITS ROOTS
By DANIEL GOLEMAN

A Rise in hostile actions against homosexuals can be traced primarily to hatred based on fear and self-righteousness rather than to the AIDS epidemic, researchers are finding. Although polls show more Americans are beginning to accept homosexual men and women and support their rights, there has been a great increase in reports of anti-gay bias since the beginning of the epidemic. But rather than creating the new hostility, researchers have found, the disease has given bigots an excuse to act out their hatred.

In studying the virulence and tenacity of anti-gay feelings, psychologists are finding clues to the deeper sources of homophobia. The new findings confirm the theory that some men use hostility and violence to homosexuals to reassure themselves about their own sexuality. But the greatest portion of anti-homosexual bias, psychologists now say, arises from a combination of fear and self-righteousness in which homosexuals are perceived as contemptible threats to the moral universe.

Such attitudes are supported, researchers say, by the fact that unlike any other minority, homosexuals still find themselves the target of institutionalized bias. They are barred from the armed services, and in many states sodomy laws make their sexual activities illegal. Until 1980, the official psychiatric diagnostic manual listed homosexuality as a mental disorder.

"It's as though our very existence is somehow a threat," said Naomi Lichtenstein, a social worker at the New York City Gay and Lesbian Anti-Violence Project who counsels victims of attacks.

One of the most troubling findings for those trying to combat anti-gay bias is data showing the hostility is far more accepted among large numbers of Americans than is bias against other groups. In surveys, about three-quarters of homosexuals say they have been harassed by people calling them names, and as many as one in four say they have been physically assaulted.

"Anti-gay violence is still acceptable because while leaders decry racial and religious bigotry, they ignore violence against gays and lesbians," said Matt Foreman, executive director of the New York City Gay and Lesbian Anti-Violence Project.

A 1988 study by the State of New York for the Governor's Task Force on Bias-Related Violence concluded that of all groups, "the most severe hostilities are directed at lesbians and gay men."

In "one of the most alarming findings" the report found that while teen-agers surveyed were reluctant to advocate open bias against racial and ethnic groups, they were emphatic about disliking homosexual men and women. They are perceived "as legitimate targets which can be openly attacked," the report said.

In a survey of 2,823 students from 8th to 12th grade, three-quarters of the boys and half the girls said it would be bad to have a homosexual neighbor. The feelings were as strong among 12-year-olds as among 17-year-olds. Many students added gratuitous vicious comments about homosexuals; that was not the case with other groups.

Scientists who study attitudes toward homosexuals say the largest group among people who are biased are those for whom homosexuals "stand as a proxy for all that is evil," said Dr. Gregory Herek, a psychologist at the University of California at Davis.

"Such people see hating gay men and lesbians as a litmus test for being a moral person," said Dr. Herek, who has done extensive research on attitudes toward homosexuals. Often they act out of adherence to religious orthodoxy in faiths that hold homosexuality to be a sin.

Dr. Herek does not see AIDS as having increased anti-gay feelings as much as offering "a convenient hook on which they can hang their pre-existing prejudices."

The affirmation of one's own values through anti-gay sentiment, his research has found, is the most common motive. For instance, in a study of attitudes toward homosexuals in 248 college students, Dr. Herek found this was the source of hostility in just over half those who held an anti-gay bias.

Bob Altemeyer, a psychologist at the University of Manitoba who has developed a scale measuring attitudes toward homosexuals, has found that those with the most intense hostility have an extreme fear that the world is an unsafe place and that society is at risk, and a self-righteousness that leads them to judge those who hold different values as morally inferior.

"They see homosexuality as a sign that society is disintegrating and as a threat to their sense of morality," said Dr. Altemeyer. "Their self-righteousness makes them feel they are acting morally when they attack homosexuals. It overcomes the normal inhibitions against aggression."

Religion Makes Change Difficult

Dr. Altemeyer tells his students that he is gay. "For most, over the course of the year it makes their attitudes toward gays more positive," he said. "But if their hostility toward gays is based on religion, their views are hardest to change."

Once a person has an anti-gay bias, it is difficult to change, Dr. Herek said, "even when reality contradicts it." Thus the stereotypes of gay men as feminine and lesbians as masculine persist in people's minds even though most gay men and lesbians do not, in fact, conform to those images.

In an article to be published later this year in "Homosexuality: Social, Psychological and Biological Issues" (Sage Publishers), Dr. Herek reviewed a case in point: the tenacity of the belief that homosexuals should not be teachers because they might sexually molest children.

Persistence of Stereotypes

Citing studies showing that child molesters are overwhelmingly heterosexual or simply fixated on children, not homosexual, Dr. Herek notes that despite the facts, many people continue to believe that gay men are child molesters.

"Once parents perceive a threat to their children," Dr. Herek said, "their emotionality makes them prone to simplistic thinking. It is such emotionality that makes anti-gay stereotypes so hard to change."

In a classic study of stereotyping, Mark Snyder, a psychologist at the University of Minnesota, gave people a description of the life history of a woman named "Betty K." After reading the history, some were told that Betty later had a lesbian relationship and lived with her female lover. Others were told that Betty married a man.

"It made a dramatic difference in how people remembered and interpreted her life," said Dr. Snyder. While there was nothing negative in what people remembered, Dr. Snyder found that people selected facts that supported stereotypes about lesbians and ignored those that might contradict them. That normal tendency, he said, can build into a bias.

Negative Attitudes Snowball

"If your attitude is negative, it snowballs, and you only notice and remember facts that are negative, until it becomes a full-blown prejudice," said Dr. Snyder. "And you tend to assume everyone feels as you do. As you become more convinced, you are more likely to take the next step and put your beliefs into actions like outright discrimination or violence, whether it's against blacks or gays."

Defensiveness about their own sexuality is another common source of people's hostility toward homosexuals. In Dr. Herek's research, for instance, this was the second most common motive, accounting for about 40 percent of those hostile to homosexuals.

This explanation for homophobia is the oldest, dating back at least to a 1914 essay by Sandor Ferenczi, one of Freud's original followers who proposed that feelings of disgust toward gay men by heterosexual men are defensive, a reaction against their own similar attraction to other men. That view stems from Freud's theory that all people are originally bisexual in early childhood, and repress their attraction to the same sex as they grow.

"Homophobia has much to do with the stereotypic perception of gays as feminine: the more feminine a gay man appears, the more hostility he evokes in other men," said Dr. Richard Isay, a psychiatrist at Cornell Medical College and author of "Being Homosexual."

Dr. Peggy Hanley-Hackenbruck, a psychiatrist at Oregon Health Services University and president of the Association of Gay and Lesbian Psychiatrists, said, "In insecure heterosexual women, a lesbian can arouse fears of their own latent homosexual feelings, and so provoke hostility."

But Dr. Isay said, "Seeing a feminine man evokes a tremendous amount of anxiety in many men; it triggers an awareness of their own feminine qualities, such as passivity or sensitivity, which they see as being a sign of weakness. Women, of course, don't fear their femininity. That's partly why men are more homophobic than women, and why those biases are so strong in groups where men are selected for their masculine qualities, such as the army or sports."

Other psychoanalysts see the expression of anti-gay bias by men as being a way to reassure themselves that they are not homosexual.

"By hating gays, they can reassure themselves they are not gay," especially if they harbor doubts about their sexual orientation, said Dr. Jennifer Jones, a psychologist at the Sexuality Research Program at the State University of New York at Albany.

Both factors can be at play. "In gangs of teen-age boys who go out looking for gays to attack, the gay symbolizes an outsider," said Dr. Herek. "The attack solidifies the attackers' membership in their group, and affirms their shared values. But it's also crucial that it is their sexuality that defines homosexuals as outsiders. If you feel insecure about your own sexuality, as so many adolescents do, you can reassure yourself by attacking gays."

A Steady Rise in Violence

An exact accounting of such violence against gays is difficult, since many victims are reluctant to contact the police. But there were three times more attacks against gays reported to the New York Police Department Bias Crime Unit in the first half of 1990 as against the same period the year before.

In 1989 just over 7,000 incidents of violence and harassment were reported against gay men and lesbians in the United States, including 62 bias-motivated murders, according to a report released last month by the National Gay and Lesbian Task Force. The figures through the 1980's show a steady rise, peaking in 1988 and remaining at about the same level in 1989.

While most racial attacks are matters of turf in which people are attacked when they enter into another group's neighborhood, that is not so with homosexuals. Those who attack gays more often travel to a gay neighborhood to attack, Ms. Lichtenstein said. The most frequent pattern of attack, according to Ms. Lichtenstein, is against a lone man or two men walking together.

As with other bias crimes, the most frequent attackers are young men 21 or under who act in groups, according to a study of 331 incidents, to be published in an article by Kevin T. Berrill, director of the anti-violence project of the National Gay and Lesbian Task Force, in the September issue of The Journal of Interpersonal Violence.

"The attacks are intended to drive us back to the invisibility and isolation of the closet," Mr. Berrill said.

"Coming out" is one of the most powerful strategies for attacking anti-gay prejudice, Dr. Herek said. This approach is particularly effective on those whose anti-gay attitudes are based on a negative stereotype that has never been challenged by socializing with someone who is gay. Paradoxically, that approach may also lead to a rise in anti-gay incidents, gay rights leaders say.

"Although the data might suggest that intolerance is gaining ground, I believe the opposite is true," Mr. Berrill said. "In the years to come, I think that lesbian and gay people will experience both increased acceptance and increased violence."

U.S. Fails to Support U.N. Declaration of Homosexual Human Rights

In 2008 the United States refused to support a nonbinding United Nations declaration calling for increased global protection for homosexuals. The official reason given was that a phrase in the document—"without distinction of any kind"—could be seen as an effort to impinge on states' rights related to gay marriage and similar issues. At least one human rights activist suggested that the real issue was the Bush administration's close ties with the religious right.

Sponsored by France, the declaration was the first related to gay rights ever to be read before the UN General Assembly. It states that homophobic human rights violations are in conflict with the Universal Declaration of Human Rights. Adopted by the United Nations in 1948, the Universal Declaration of Human Rights was developed to provide a common worldwide foundation for the just treatment of people. Although it does not directly speak to the issue of homosexuality, it contains statements about privacy, family, equality, and due process that could be interpreted to support the rights of LGBT persons.

A total of sixty-six countries supported the declaration. Russia and China were among those that did not; nor did the Roman Catholic Church. In addition, the Organization of the Islamic Conference read an opposing statement that was supported by nearly sixty countries. It claimed that decriminalization of homosexuality would serve to legitimize pedophilia and other "deplorable acts." Nearly eighty countries, primarily in the Middle East, Africa, and Asia, currently ban homosexuality, and at least six allow the death penalty to be imposed for those convicted.

DECEMBER 19, 2008
IN A FIRST, GAY RIGHTS ARE PRESSED AT THE U.N.
By NEIL MACFARQUHAR

UNITED NATIONS – An unprecedented declaration seeking to decriminalize homosexuality won the support of 66 countries in the United Nations General Assembly on Thursday, but opponents criticized it as an attempt to legitimize pedophilia and other "deplorable acts."

The United States refused to support the nonbinding measure, as did Russia, China, the Roman Catholic Church and members of the Organization of the Islamic Conference. The Holy See's observer mission issued a statement saying that the declaration "challenges existing human rights norms."

The declaration, sponsored by France with broad support in Europe and Latin America, condemned human rights violations based on homophobia, saying such measures run counter to the universal declaration of human rights.

"How can we tolerate the fact that people are stoned, hanged, decapitated and tortured only because of their sexual orientation?" said Rama Yade, the French state secretary for human rights, noting that homosexuality is banned in nearly 80 countries and subject to the death penalty in at least six.

France decided to use the format of a declaration because it did not have the support for an official resolution. Read out by Ambassador Jorge Argüello of Argentina, the declaration was the first on gay rights read in the 192-member General Assembly itself.

Although laws against homosexuality are concentrated in the Middle East, Asia and Africa, more than one speaker addressing a separate conference on the declaration noted that the laws stemmed as much from the British colonial past as from religion or tradition.

Navanethem Pillay, the United Nations high commissioner for human rights, speaking by video telephone, said that just like apartheid laws that criminalized sexual relations between different races, laws against homosexuality "are increasingly becoming recognized as anachronistic and as inconsistent both with international law and with traditional values of dignity, inclusion and respect for all."

The opposing statement read in the General Assembly, supported by nearly 60 nations, rejected the idea that sexual orientation was a matter of genetic coding. The statement, led by the Organization of the Islamic Conference, said the effort threatened to undermine the international framework of human rights by trying to normalize pedophilia, among other acts.

The Organization of the Islamic Conference also failed in a last-minute attempt to alter a formal resolution that Sweden sponsored condemning summary executions. It sought to have the words "sexual orientation" deleted as one of the central reasons for such killings.

Ms. Yade and the Dutch foreign minister, Maxime Verhagen, said at a news conference that they were "disappointed" that the United States failed to support the declaration. Human rights activists went further. "The Bush administration is trying to come up with Christmas presents for the religious right so it will be remembered," said Scott Long, a director at Human Rights Watch.

The official American position was based on highly technical legal grounds. The text, by using terminology like "without distinction of any kind," was too broad because it might be interpreted as an attempt by the federal government to override states' rights on issues like gay marriage, American diplomats and legal experts said.

"We are opposed to any discrimination, legally or politically, but the nature of our federal system prevents us from undertaking commitments and engagements where federal authorities don't have jurisdiction," said Alejandro D. Wolff, the deputy permanent representative.

Gay-rights advocates brought to the conference from around the world by France said just having the taboo broken on discussing the topic at the United Nations would aid their battles at home. "People in Africa can have hope that someone is speaking for them," said the Rev. Jide Macaulay of Nigeria.

- -

MURDERERS OF GAYS MORE LIKELY TO "OVERKILL" AND LESS LIKELY TO BE CAUGHT

According to a 1994 study of 151 bias-related homicides of homosexuals, 60 percent showed evidence of "overkill," with the victims being beaten, shot, or stabbed more than three times or assaulted with more than one type of weapon. The rate of overkill was even higher for black and Hispanic victims. Although the national homicide arrest average was 66 percent, only 51 percent of these deaths resulted in an arrest. The deaths occurred over a two-year time period in twenty-nine states and the District of Columbia. A 1993 FBI study found that 12 percent of hate crimes were motivated by prejudice regarding the victim's sexual orientation.

In one case, sixteen-year-old Marvin McClendon was convicted of shooting Joseph Shoemaker and Robert Walters in Laurel, Mississippi. McClendon was sentenced to two consecutive life terms in jail. McClendon's lawyer unsuccessfully argued that McClendon's actions were partially justified owing to his fear that the two were HIV positive. Despite the guilty verdict, gay rights advocates were dismayed that the jury was apprised of the fact that Walters was HIV positive, saying that allowing the victim's HIV status to be used as evidence at trial was "prejudicial."

DECEMBER 21, 1994
SURVEY DETAILS GAY SLAYING AROUND U.S.
By DAVID W. DUNLAP

Bias-related slayings of homosexuals are often gratuitously violent and many go unsolved, according to a report released yesterday by 23 victims services and anti-violence groups nationwide.

The report, described by its compilers as the first national study of its kind, listed 151 such homicides in 29 states and the District of Columbia from January 1992 until early this month. All but eight victims were men.

The report does not claim to record the actual number of bias-related slayings. Rather, it is intended to examine the nature of such crimes and how they are handled.

Almost 60 percent of the homicides in the survey, released yesterday at a news conference in Manhattan, involved what the report called "overkill": victims had four or more gunshot or stab wounds or were beaten, or assailants used more than one killing method.

"The level of violence in these homicides is really grue-some," said Bea A. Hanson, director of client services for the New York City Gay and Lesbian Anti-Violence Project, which oversaw the survey.

The violence described in the report is in line with findings by crime experts that bias murders of all types tend to be extremely bloody. In the survey yesterday, the degree of violence was even more striking when broken down along racial and ethnic lines: 71 percent of Hispanic victims and 63 percent of the black victims were "overkilled," the report said, in contrast to 52 percent of white victims.

Of the victims whose ethnic background was known, 67 were white, 32 black and 14 Hispanic.

Arrests have been reported in only 51 percent of the cases studied. In contrast, 66 percent of homicides nationally were cleared by arrest in 1993, according to the Federal Bureau of Investigation's uniform crime reports.

"We have to ask the local police and the F.B.I. to take this much more seriously than they have been taking it," said Representative Jerrold Nadler, Democrat of New York City, who attended the news conference, held outside police headquarters in Manhattan. . . .

At the news conference in New York yesterday, Assemblywoman Deborah J. Glick, a Manhattan Democrat, said of the survey findings: "We can't look at this in a vacuum. We've seen a rise in the hostile rhetoric that justifies—to the ignorant, uneducated or fearful—a reason why it's O.K. to physically assault lesbians and gay men."

Wayne R. Koka, who coordinates the compilation of hate-crime statistics for the F.B.I., said yesterday that he could not comment on the report but said generally that bias-motivated crimes of all kinds were "more prone toward violence." . . .

· ·

MAYE DENIES ATTACK DESPITE TESTIMONY OF MULTIPLE WITNESSES

On April 15, 1972, protesters from the Gay Activist Alliance interrupted an Inner Circle dinner for politicians, political reporters, and their spouses being held at the New York Hilton Hotel. One of the guests attending the dinner, Michael Maye, was charged with harassment for kicking and shoving twenty-one-year-old Gay Activist Alliance member Morty Manford and repeatedly grinding his shoe into Mr. Manford's groin as he lay on the steps of a descending elevator. President of the Uniformed Firefighters Association and a former national Golden Gloves champion, Maye claimed that he ejected the protesters from the event because they were shouting obscenities in front of his wife and other female dinner guests. Despite the testimony of several prosecution witnesses to the contrary, Maye denied losing his temper, shouting profanities at the protestors, kicking Manford, or grinding a foot into his crotch. Maye claimed to have thrown only one punch during the entire incident and then only because a "golden-haired" man "grabbed" Maye's groin as he was attempting to rescue a fellow firefighter from a "band of angry homosexuals" that was waiting at the bottom of the escalator.

JUNE 28, 1972
ATTACK CHARGES DENIED BY MAYE
Never Kicked Homosexual, He Testifies in Defense
By LACEY FOSBURGH

Far from kicking or stomping anyone during disturbances at the New York Hilton Hotel three months ago, Michael Maye, president of the Uniformed Fire Fighters Association, testified yesterday, he never touched anyone except one unidentified "golden-haired" homosexual who "grabbed" his groin and tore his pants.

"I threw a punch at him," he admitted. Mr. Maye, in his first public explanation of what occurred at the hotel April 15 when the Gay Activist Alliance held a demonstration there, was a witness for two hours yesterday at his trial on harassment charges in Manhattan Criminal Court.

He told the court that he hit a "tall young blonde man" who allegedly was one of the group of intruders who demonstrated during an intermission at a banquet and show at the hotel.

Mr. Maye said he ejected the intruder from the ballroom after obscenities were shouted in front of his wife and other women.

The key charge against Mr. Maye is that he kicked and shoved 21-year-old Morty Manford, a member of the homosexual group who was lying prone on an escalator that was moving down, and then ground his shoe into his groin area a number of times.

'Professional Soldier'

When the assistant district attorney, Roger Hayes, asked Mr. Maye yesterday if he had done that with his foot, he answered:

No, I did not. Mr. Hayes, he'd be dead. I'm a professional combat soldier and you could kill a man that way."

In fact, Mr. Maye testified, far from having time on the escalator to do any such thing to Mr. Manford, he was trying to save another fireman, also lying on the escalator, from being hurt by the demonstrators.

His friend, David McCormack, an official of the Uniformed Fire Officer's Association, was caught on the escalator "in a jumble" with two demonstrators—he did not know if one was Mr. Manford, he said—and a band of angry homosexuals were waiting for him at the bottom of the moving steps.

He did go bounding down the escalator he testified to save him. He said he reached his arm into the group of three bodies and lifted his friend out by the shoulders without doing anything to the two demonstrators.

A series of prosecution witnesses who attended the 50th annual dinner of the Inner Circle, an organization of present and former newsmen at City Hall, testified that at this point Mr. Maye assaulted Mr. Manford with his hands and feet.

Throughout his testimony, Mr. Maye pictured himself as a man who was temperamentally incapable of committing any such violence.

First of all, he said, he never loses his temper because to remain "cool," as he puts it is the essence of a firefighter's skills. Furthermore, he testified, he could never had uttered the profanities that the prosecution witnesses said they heard him deliver to demonstrators because he never uses such language.

In addition, he said, he makes it a habit never to get into fights with people because, as a former national Golden Gloves champion, he is too powerful to risk hurting someone.

Three Gay Leather Men Found Stabbed to Death in Lower Manhattan

Three gay residents of lower Manhattan were savagely murdered within a few days of each other. Ronald Cabo, Donald MacNiven, and John Beardsley were each stabbed repeatedly and left in apartments that were then set on fire. All three victims frequented "leather" bars and may have been involved in New York's gay sadomasochist or "S and M" scene. Because the apartments did not show signs of forced entry, the police believe the men may have been killed by someone they picked up in a bar and voluntarily brought home. However, some have argued that the gay S and M scene is more about appearance than behavior and that those involved keep their sexual violence "within carefully prescribed limits."

In the wake of these murders, rumors spread throughout the gay community, alleging that additional deaths have occurred and that some of the bodies have been decapitated. Although police insisted that there are only three victims and that none of the bodies had been mutilated, some homosexual activists pointed out that city officials did not have a good track record of communicating openly with gay residents about this crime or other homosexual problems. Writer and activist Arthur Bell described the mood of the community as "very worried," while a local bar tender attempted to downplay the concern, saying that people are no more afraid than "a woman might be afraid after hearing about a rapist." After the Gay Activists Alliance issued a statement criticizing the police for failing to aggressively investigate the deaths, Capt. William J. Kelly met with gay community representatives to offer assurances the police were working on finding the killer.

JANUARY 18, 1973
HOMOSEXUALS IN 'VILLAGE' FEARFUL AFTER SERIES OF SIMILAR KILLINGS
By GRACE LICHTENSTEIN

Three similarly violent murders in three weeks in lower Manhattan involving men the police said were part of the "leather bar" scene have sent waves of rumors and fear through the area's homosexual community.

All three men were stabbed numerous times and found in apartments apparently deliberately set on fire, according to the police.

The first victim was Ronald Cabo, 29 years old of 234 Thomson Street who was found early Jan. 4, dead on a burning couch.

The other two were Donald MacNiven, 40 and John P. W. Beardsley, 53 who occupied separate apartments at 11 Varick Street. They were found Jan. 8, stabbed to death and lying in the living-room floor of Mr. MacNiven's apartment.

Mr. Beardsley, a 1942 graduate of Harvard College is listed in both the New York and Philadelphia Social Registers.

Meanwhile a new rumor began circulating yesterday that a body in a leather jacket had been found on the Morton Street pier in Greenwich Village.

But the police said that the partly decomposed body of a 23-year-old Queen's College student had been found floating in the Hudson off the pier yesterday afternoon. But they said the student, identified as Robben Borrero of 990 East 165th Street, the Bronx, was wearing dungarees and a turtleneck sweater. They said that he had been missing for five weeks and that his death was apparently unrelated to the three murders.

According to police, as well as those active in the homosexual community, rumors have been flying for a week in homosexual bars and bookstores that there have been additional murders, including decapitations and near-killings in the trucking area southwest of Greenwich Village frequented by some homosexuals.

One group, the Gay Activists Alliance, issued a statement yesterday accusing the police of "half-hearted interest" in the three murders. They said the police had imposed a blackout on information until the press picked up the story.

Yesterday morning officials of the alliance and another homosexual organization, the Mattachine Society, met with Capt. William J. Kelley at the West 10th Street Precinct station.

Afterward, Lieut. Richard Jason of that precinct said that the rumors were "grossly exaggerated." He said Captain Kelley had sought to assure the homosexual community leaders that the police were working on the killings.

Ronald Gold, public-relations officer for the Gay Activists Alliance, said later that the police had "more or less apologized for not giving us the straight dope in the first place." He said the Alliance hoped to have its own telephone line to receive information on the murders in operation by 9 A.M. this morning. The number is 966–6963.

Lieut. James J. Skennion of the First Detective District Homicide-Assault Squad, which is investigating the three murders, said that "there is no doubt" they could have been the work of one perhaps demented person.

He said the police had no suspects as yet, but believed that the men might have been killed by someone they had met in a bar and taken home, since there were no signs of forced entry at either location.

Lieutenant Skennion said that the police had been warning patrons of homosexual bars "to be careful of whom they pick up."

"We're trying to tell them that when they pick up a stranger on the street they're taking a chance, but sometimes they overreact to our warnings," he said.

Both he and Lieutenant Jason said they had received dozens of calls from persons who had heard talk of "bodies chopped up" and "heads cut off." The police said they had no evidence of either kind of mutilation.

The rumors were still very much alive yesterday, although Bruce Voeller, president of the Gay Activists Alliance, and others expressed concern that the murders might be over sensationalized by the press.

"Heterosexual murders are just as violent," said one patron of the Roadhouse, a bar at Hudson and 11th streets.

Arthur Bell, a writer and movement activist, said that "all up and down the Village on Sunday, people were stopping me and telling me stories of what they'd heard." The feeling was, he said, that there was a single killer who hated homosexuals.

The 'S and M' Scene

Mr. Bell and Lieutenant Skennion confirmed that the dead men had been known as patrons of "leather" bars, which cater to homosexuals who dress in leather jackets and dungarees. They are said by some homosexuals to be synonymous with the "S and M"–sado-masochist—scene.

"Normal S and M types, who are usually bravura types, are very worried," Mr. Bell said.

In Ty's, a bar at 114 Christopher Street said to be frequented by homosexual who are "into leather," the owner, who gave his name only as Ty, acknowledged that his patrons were "concerned, naturally," but added: "People are no more afraid of this than women might be afraid after hearing about a rapist."

At the Roadhouse, known as both a "neighborhood" and a "leather" bar, the bartender, who gave his name only as Rex, said that last Sunday night another bartender had broadcast a warning about the murders over the bar's loudspeaker system.

"He just said, 'The stories of violence that you've heard are not just stories, they're fact so watch out," Rex said.

One of the bars that reputedly had been favored by the dead men, as well as the "heavy leather" crowd—the Eagle's nest at 21st Street and 11th avenue—was not open yesterday afternoon.

Elsewhere, bar patrons and homosexual activists disagreed about the significance of the possible "S and M" connotations of the killings.

Mr. Gold, who asserted that the activist's alliance had tried unsuccessfully for five months to arrange a meeting on homosexual problems with Mayor Lindsay, said "People who are S-M do not stab people to death."

Others declared that homosexuals involved in sado-masochism were "more into costumes than violence" and kept the violence of their sexual activity within carefully prescribed limits.

But some patrons at the Roadhouse said any homosexual knew the risks of taking a stranger home with him. "We've been living with this all our lives," one of them said.

- -

Antigay Violence Included in Federal Study of Hate Crimes

In April 1990 homosexual rights activists were invited to participate in an official White House ceremony for the first time. The occasion was the signing of the national Hate Crimes Statistics Act. This bill, which directed the Justice Department to conduct a five-year study of crimes motivated by racial, ethnic, or sexual prejudice, received overwhelming support in both the House and Senate. The goal of the law was to determine the extent of the problem and evaluate whether additional legislation or enforcement efforts were warranted. In signing this law, George W. Bush became the first American president to finalize legislation that includes gays and lesbians with racial, ethnic, and religious minority groups. As the administration anticipated, the public event resulted in rare praise for the president from gay rights groups, the American Civil Liberties Union, and the NAACP. Representatives of gay rights organizations were invited on condition that they would not use the opportunity to agitate for increased federal spending on AIDS research or treatment.

APRIL 24, 1990
PRESIDENT SIGNS LAW FOR STUDY OF HATE CRIMES

By ANDREW ROSENTHAL
Special to The New York Times

WASHINGTON, April 23—Appearing before an audience that included liberal Democrats, conservative Republicans and the first homosexual rights advocates invited to a White House ceremony, President Bush today signed a law ordering a detailed study of crimes motivated by racial, ethnic or sexual prejudice.

"The faster we can find out about these hideous crimes, the faster we can track down the bigots who commit them," Mr. Bush said as he signed the law, which requires the Justice Department to conduct a five-year statistical study on crimes of hate.

"Enacting this law today," he said, "helps us move toward our dream, a society blind to prejudice, a society open to all."

Mr. Bush spoke at a ceremony in the Old Executive Office Building next to the White House, where he drew unusual praise from gay and lesbian organizations, the American Civil Liberties Union, the National Association for the Advancement of Colored People and other groups that have criticized his record on civil rights.

Agreement Against Protests

The expectation of such praise and the public relations benefit that could come from it were part of the Administration's calculation when it decided to hold a public ceremony for the signing of the bill, officials said.

It was the first time a President has signed legislation that includes homosexuals with members of more traditional groups like racial and religious minorities. It was also the first time that supporters of gay and lesbian rights had been invited to a White House event.

Administration officials and representatives of the homosexual organizations who took part said the White House had invited the advocates to the ceremony only after obtaining an agreement that they would not turn it into a protest seeking more Federal money for AIDS research and treatment than Mr. Bush has sought.

"Both sides agreed that this was a different issue," said Perry Jude Radecic, the legislative director for the National Gay and Lesbian Task Force, at the ceremony today.

"This was the President inviting us to his house," she added. "But we also assured the White House that we would continue to speak out on the AIDS issue."

Overwhelming Support for Bill

The National Hate Crimes Statistics Act, which was strongly backed by the Administration, was passed overwhelmingly by the House this month and by the Senate in February.

The law requires the Justice Department to spend five years gathering data on crimes motivated by prejudice about race, religion, ethnic background or sexual orientation. The Department has established a toll-free number—1–800–347-HATE—that will be available for the public to report such crimes starting next Monday.

Administration officials have said the study will help Federal and local policy makers and law-enforcement officials decide whether they need to change laws or enforcement methods to deal with hate crimes.

Diann Y. Rust-Tierney, the legislative director for the A.C.L.U.'s Washington office, called the new law a sign of a "national consensus that the issue of hate crimes is important."

Particular praise for Mr. Bush came from the gay rights advocates, who had occasionally worked quietly on legislation at the White House in the Administration of President Jimmy Carter but had never been included in a public event.

Senator Orrin Hatch, the Utah Republican who sponsored the bill in the Senate with Paul Simon, the Illinois Democrat, said the advocates who worked to have the words "sexual orientation" added to the measure "certainly deserved to be there" today.

Mr. Hatch said he was startled when he arrived at the ceremony and heard applause from groups with which he has had political battles.

"I turned around to see who might have come in behind me," he said, "but to my amazement, it was me they were applauding."

"I Killed Him Because He Was Gay"

In 1991 Erik Brown, age twenty-one, and Esat Bici, nineteen, were found guilty of murder for "acting in concert" with twenty-one-year-old Daniel Doyle in the savage killing of a gay man from Jackson Heights, Queens. This verdict was seen as a triumph by gay activists because the legal system has a history of minimizing the seriousness of antigay attacks. Activists hoped that the murder verdicts obtained in this case would encourage more victims to report gay-bashing incidents to the police. "There are so many victims out there who refuse to come forward because they do not believe their crimes will be treated seriously, who believe that they will be victimized a second time, not by the thug but by the system" said Gregory King, a spokesperson for the Human Rights Campaign Fund.

On the night of July 2, 1990, Brown, Bici, and Doyle went out looking for "a drug dealer or a drug addict or a homo" to beat up and ended up at a Queens schoolyard known to be a gay male cruising area. The men lured Julio Rivera, a twenty-nine-year-old bartender, into the yard and repeatedly struck him in the head with a hammer. During the trial Doyle admitted that it was he who actually killed Rivera by plunging a knife into his back, stating "I killed him because he was gay." In return for providing testimony against Brown and Bici, Doyle was allowed to plead guilty to the lesser charge of manslaughter.

NOVEMBER 24, 1991
IDEAS & TRENDS

A Murder Verdict Becomes a Rallying Cry
By JOSEPH P. FRIED

In the early morning darkness of July 2, 1990, a 29-year-old man named Julio Rivera approached a Queens schoolyard known as a gay cruising spot. Three younger men also approached it. Minutes later, Mr. Rivera was the victim of a savage and deadly attack. Murder verdicts were delivered in a New York courtroom last week, and gay-rights groups said the circumstances and the outcome of the case would have national reverberations.

One of the three men lured Mr. Rivera, who was gay, into the Jackson Heights schoolyard, according to testimony at the trial, which ended Wednesday. Another repeatedly smashed him in the head with a hammer. The third stuck a knife in his back, inflicting the fatal wound.

Originally charged with murder, the third attacker was allowed to plead guilty to a lesser charge of manslaughter in return for becoming the main prosecution witness against the two others, who were found guilty of murder for "acting in concert" with him.

The verdict surprised and galvanized gay-rights advocates following the trial. They now plan to use the verdict as a weapon in their fight to stop violent crimes against homosexuals, a trend they say is steadily rising.

During the trial, the man who admitted the stabbing, 21-year-old Daniel Doyle, told the jury, "I killed him because he was gay." He said he and his two friends, Erik Brown, also 21, and 19-year-old Esat Bici, had been looking for "a drug dealer or a drug addict or a homo out cruising" to beat up.

Gay rights advocates say the verdict was surprising because often in the past if a case of anti-homosexual violence made it to the courts, it was brushed off. "This is one of the first times a crime against a gay or lesbian person has been taken this seriously in any judicial system," said Robert Bray, spokesman for the National Gay and Lesbian Task Force.

"We'll use this case as an example of why it's so important for gay and lesbian victims to participate in the legal justice system," said Gregory J. King, communications director of the Human Rights Campaign Fund, a gay-advocacy group that claims 35,000 members.

"There are so many victims out there who refuse to come forward because they do not believe their crimes will be treated seriously, who believe that they will be victimized a second time, not by the thug but by the system," Mr. King said. "A jury verdict such as this gives them a sense of hope." The Human Rights Campaign Fund, he said, would publicize the case to "make sure every activist in the country knows there has been a major victory here." . . .

No Justice for Julio

Gay activists were discouraged in 1995 when an appeals court overturned the second-degree murder convictions of Erik Brown and Esat Bici. In what was then seen as a triumph of justice over homophobia, the two men were found guilty in the beating and stabbing death of Julio Rivera, a twenty-nine-year-old gay bartender. Brown has since pleaded guilty to the lesser charge of manslaughter in return for testifying against Bici. Bici, who was out on bail, failed to appear for a court hearing regarding the next phase of his case, and both his lawyer and his family said that they had not heard from him. "The system is not taking this matter as seriously as they should," said one local resident.

As some gay activists made plans to protest this latest development in the Rivera case, others seemed to have given up. "You can be angry the first time, the second time" said Daniel Castellano of the Hispanic AIDS Forum, "but then you see there is no point."

MAY 19, 1996
NEIGHBORHOOD REPORT

Jackson Heights
Still Waiting for Justice in Gay-Bias Killing
By DAVID W. DUNLAP

"Justice for Julio" was the refrain in Jackson Heights six years ago after Julio Rivera, a 29-year-old bartender, was lured into a gay cruising area on 37th Avenue by assailants who beat him and stabbed him to death. For months, gay organizers prodded the authorities to handle the case with a greater sense of urgency.

When Erik Brown and Esat Bici were convicted in 1991 of second-degree murder, homosexuals thought justice had been done. A third man, Daniel Doyle, had already admitted to stabbing Mr. Rivera.

Their feelings of vindication began to erode last year, however, when the convictions were overturned by an appeals court. Now, any sense of justice has vanished.

Mr. Bici, who was free on $350,000 bail, failed to appear for a court hearing Tuesday, a day after Mr. Brown pleaded guilty to a lesser charge of manslaughter and agreed to testify against him. Judge Thomas A. Demakos revoked Mr. Bici's bail and ordered his arrest. His lawyer, Barry Gene Rhodes, said that neither he nor the Bici family had heard from the young man.

Douglas Sullavan, 75, a Jackson Heights resident, sounded angry but not surprised that the defendant disappeared. "The law, the system is not taking this matter as seriously as they should," Mr. Sullavan said.

The latest development in the Rivera case will almost surely dampen the fourth annual gay pride march on June 2 along 37th Avenue, between 75th and 89th Streets. For the last few years, when the lead contingent reaches the yard of Public School 69, where Mr. Rivera was killed, the marchers have paused for a moment of silence.

Daniel Dromm, co-chairman of the Queens Lesbian and Gay Pride Committee, said he and others were considering a protest. But several residents said indignation might be giving way to resignation.

"People are so drawn out that we get deadened," said Howard Cruse, 52, an author. "In some ways, it's analogous to dealing with the epidemic. If everything had happened in the space of a week, you'd have people pouring into Sheridan Square."

Daniel Castellanos, 32, who works at the Hispanic AIDS Forum, also noted an erosion of outrage. "You can be angry the first time, and angry the second time, and angry the third time," he said. "But then you see that there is no point."

DAHMER CASE RAISES CONCERNS ABOUT POLICE RACISM AND HOMOPHOBIA

In 1991 prominent minority and gay activists complained that the way Milwaukee police handled a 911 call illustrated the department's culture of racism and homophobia. Two months prior to the arrest of serial killer Jeffrey Dahmer, police were called to his apartment building by a neighbor who had seen a Laotian boy (later identified as four-teen-year-old Konerak Sinthasomphone) staggering in the street, naked and bleeding. After questioning Dahmer, police left the boy in his care and joked with the dispatcher that "an intoxicated Asian, naked male was returned to his sober boyfriend." Sintha-somphone was one of seventeen men and boys Dahmer later admitted to killing and dismembering.

Sgt. Leonard Wells, a black officer and veteran of the department said, "If you're poor, black, Hispanic, gay or lesbian, then in the eyes of many on the Milwaukee Police Department you are engaging in deviant behavior." Local gay organizers said they had requested improved police training on homosexual issues for years because the department was slow to respond to reports of gay bashing and had shown a persistent lack of sensitivity regarding same-sex domestic abuse complaints.

AUGUST 2, 1991
SERIAL MURDER CASE EXPOSES DEEP MILWAUKEE TENSIONS
By DON TERRY

MILWAUKEE, Aug. 1—Almost day and night for a week, there have been angry news conferences, marches and rallies against the police in this wounded city.

Bitter charges of racism and homophobia in the police department have been provoked by the handling of the Jeffrey L. Dahmer serial murder case and the belief that some of the killings could have been prevented.

Tension heightened today as the chief of police announced that unspecified departmental charges had been filed against the three officers at the center of the public's anger.

The announcement by Chief Philip Arreola followed the department's release of recorded conserva-tions between a woman, 911 emergency operators and police officers on May 27, two months before Mr. Dahmer was arrested and the horrors inside his apartment were discovered.

The woman reported seeing a bleeding boy, stagger-ing along the street. But when officers arrived, Mr. Dahmer was able to convince them that the boy was his drunken friend and they left.

At one point on the tape an officer tells the dispatcher that "an intoxicated Asian, naked male was returned to his sober boyfriend." Then there is laughter.

Before announcing the charges, Chief Arreola said "the Police Department should be commended" for its efforts since Mr. Dahmer's arrest. He said the language used by the officers on the tape recordings was "not common, it's not tolerated."

Also today, the Milwaukee Journal reported that the three officers actually entered Mr. Dahmer's apartment. There were . . . photos of previous victims strewn on the floor, the newspaper said, and Dahmer has since told investigators that a body was in an adjoining room.

But The Associated Press reported that a spokeswoman for the police union said the officers saw no evidence to suggest anything was wrong.

'Treated Differently'

The case has badly shaken the 2,000-officer department, pitting the police union against the chief, at a time when officers are struggling to adapt to an increasingly diverse and complicated city.

"It's a great city by a great lake, but it depends on what color you are," said the Rev. LeHarve Buck, a neighborhood organizer and housing advocate. "If you're not an Anglo-Saxon white male, you're treated differently by the police in this city. The police have a picture of what a good citizen looks like. If you don't fit that description, you're not a good citizen and you're not worth serving." . . .

To be sure, there is tension in other cities between the police, minority populations and others who say they are neither served nor protected by the police. In Los Angeles, the shock waves are still reverberating five months after officers were videotaped beating a black motorist. But Mr. Dahmer and his confessions of murder and dismemberment has exposed what many here say is a long pattern of police indifference to minority citizens and homosexuals.

"Milwaukee is a sick town and it's been swept under the carpet for years," said the Rev. Gene Champion, a black Baptist minister. "But this has lifted up the carpet and the whole world can see the dirt."

But change is in the wind. The department, which is still 80 percent white, was taken [over] just less than two years ago by Chief Arreola, who has a Hispanic background and has begun steps to adapt the department to the city's changing makeup.

A Victim Nearly Rescued

The division between police and community was never more evident or tragic than on the May night two months and four killings before Mr. Dahmer's arrest last week.

That night, the police went to Mr. Dahmer's apartment building on North 25th Street but apparently dismissed what they saw: a teen-age Laotian boy whom neighbors say was bleeding and naked and being pursued by Mr. Dahmer. The officers considered it a routine domestic dispute between homosexuals. Two months later, the 14-year-old boy was identified as one of 17 men and boys that the 31-year-old former chocolate factory worker says he killed here and in Ohio. . . .

"If you're poor, black, Hispanic, gay or lesbian, then in the eyes of many on the Milwaukee Police Department you are engaging in deviant behavior," said Sgt. Leonard Wells, an 18-year veteran of the department and the president of the League of Martin, an organization of black officers named for the Rev. Dr. Martin Luther King Jr.

Organizers of Milwaukee's homosexuals say they have been asking for years for a police liaison to their population and for improved training about homosexuals.

"We want the police department to listen to the community," said Scott Gunkel of the Lambda Rights Network, a homosexual educational and political group. "We want them to wake up that this is no longer just a white city. It is a diverse city, with diverse needs."

But frustration and anger with the police is growing among homosexuals.

Some here say the police did not arrest Mr. Dahmer in May because the officers regarded a dispute between homosexuals as hardly worth the time to write a police report about.

"Instead of protecting the gay community," said Kitty Barber, "in many, many incidents, the Milwaukee Police Department has a history of harassing us."

Terry Boughner, the editor of a gay-oriented newspaper here, said reports of assaults on homosexuals are in every issue. "And somebody will call the cops for help and they don't come for 30, 45 minutes," he said. "A couple of weeks ago, two cops watched while five men beat up two gay people. They did absolutely nothing." . . .

Support for Police

There are also voices of support for the police.

"To fault the police for all this is wrong," said Jason Bridgemen, a 41-year-old building superintendent, as he walked past Mr. Dahmer's apartment building last week.

"This is a tough neighborhood to be a cop in," he said. "I spent 16 months in Vietnam but I felt safer there than here."

A few blocks away, Officer Jim Sobek, 38, was walking his beat on Wells Street. "A lot of people are jumping to conclusions about this case and what happened," he said. "That's what's causing the problems in the city. Everybody needs to calm down." . . .

GAY RESIDENTS DEVELOP TRAINING WITH JACKSON HEIGHTS POLICE

In the years after Julio Rivera's 1990 murder in a nearby schoolyard, gay and lesbian residents of Jackson Heights, Queens, have been meeting regularly with local police. The initial purpose was simply to decrease tensions and increase mutual understanding between the two groups. There had been complaints of Jackson Heights' police verbally abusing and unfairly detaining homosexual residents as well as being insensitive and lax in their response to problems within the gay community. As a result, a hostile climate developed and many gay and lesbian residents did not feel safe going to the police for help.

The two groups developed a series of trainings to teach police officers what they need to know to work more effectively with gay and lesbian residents. Topics covered include how to investigate a bias crime, discreetly question closeted homosexuals, and appropriately respond to a gay domestic abuse complaint. In addition to disseminating much-needed information, workshop attendance results in police officers and homosexual instructors spending several hours together, talking about a variety of issues. It was hoped that as the two groups got to know each other better, long-standing barriers would begin to break down; however, some participating police officers voiced concerns about the topics covered and the intimate nature of some of the information being shared. Others worried that additional neighborhood groups would also want the opportunity to engage in a similar level of dialogue.

APRIL 19, 1993
HEALING WOUNDS AND SEEKING UNDERSTANDING
Police and Gay Residents of the 115th Precinct Work Together to Find Common Ground
By RAYMOND HERNANDEZ

In an experiment being closely watched at Police Headquarters, efforts are under way to ease long-standing tensions between homosexuals and the police in Jackson Heights, Queens, the neighborhood with the largest number of gay and lesbian residents outside Manhattan.

It has been almost three years since the killing of a gay man in the neighborhood, a crime that brought gay groups together in anger after the police initially refused to classify it as a bias crime.

For more than a year now, officers and many gay and lesbian residents of the neighborhood have gathered at the 115th Precinct station house, discussing topics like AIDS and gay households, performing skits, and swapping intimate stories about themselves in an effort to reconcile two distinctly different cultures.

"We've had to learn the ways and life style of the gay community," Officer Bill Facciola said. "It was almost like dealing with a whole new set of foreigners with their own ways."

The most concrete result of the meetings has been to outline a series of training sessions that many regard as the most comprehensive way so far of teaching about gay and lesbian life styles to officers in a department long reviled in the gay community for its 1969 raid on a Greenwich Village homosexual bar, the Stonewall Inn. The raid helped ignite the gay rights movement.

It is too early to assess the classes' success, but the Police Department—which itself is coming to terms with a growing number of gay and lesbian officers in its ranks—plans to expand the sessions to other precincts where there are a large number of gay residents. These include the 78th in the Park Slope section of Brooklyn, and the 120th in St. George, Staten Island. The program may also be introduced into some Manhattan neighborhoods if the precincts and gay residents there feel it is needed.

"It seems to be our best hope for imparting this sort of information," said Deputy Inspector Louis Pietroluongo, who commands the department's quality control section. Part of the reason the program is so promising, he and others said, is that it brings gay instructors and officers together in an intimate setting over many hours.

"It takes a while to break down the barriers," Deputy Inspector Pietroluongo said.

Backdrop of Suspicion

At one session, for instance, one gay resident of Jackson Heights, Ed Sedarbaum, handed out 11 photographs of friends who had died of AIDS. Some officers remained expressionless and passed the photographs along, while others studied them closely. One took Mr. Sedarbaum aside afterward and confided that he, too, had known a gay man who died of AIDS.

"My guess is that he wanted me to know that he knew what I was talking about," said Mr. Sedarbaum, co-chairman of Queens Gays and Lesbians United. "It was a gesture of camaraderie."

Both groups have worked against a backdrop of misunderstanding and suspicion at a time when lesbians and gay men are asserting their political voice throughout the borough. In Ridgewood, about 400 gay marchers on Saturday protested the local school board's campaign against a curriculum teaching tolerance of homosexuals. In Jackson Heights, homosexuals complain that police officers had at times verbally abused or unfairly detained gay residents of the neighborhood.

And, they say, the police were particularly callous and inattentive to disputes and other problems involving lesbians and gay men like the bias attack and killing of Julio Rivera in July 1990, creating a hostile climate in which many lesbians and gay men were wary of turning to the police.

New View of Problems

Now among a number of practical lessons for officers at the 115th, the classes include instruction on how to handle a bias-crime investigation and discreetly question homosexual victims at a time when many gay men and lesbians are wary of professing their sexual orientation.

"The class definitely has opened my eyes to the problems that group has," said Officer Michael Monteverde, who recently got a taste of the problems that arise in places like Jackson Heights and other neighborhoods with openly gay communities.

While on patrol near Junction Boulevard, he came across a gay man with fresh bruises from an attack by about 10 teen-agers who hurled insults and a bottle at him. Prodding gently so as not to put the man on the defensive, Officer Monteverde listened as the man explained that the group had frequently harassed him in the past because he was gay.

Then, the two set off on foot through the neighborhood's bustling streets before the man led Officer Monteverde to one of the attackers. "It wasn't right that he had to go through that for all that time," the officer said. "But I think he was probably afraid to come forward to the police."

Questions and Responses

At times, though, the tensions in Jackson Heights have arisen not from hostility but rather from misunderstanding.

When Susan Caust and her lover called the police to their apartment after spotting a man with a gun outside their window, both women became uneasy as one of the officers who responded snooped around before asking them how many bedrooms there were in the apartment.

"As lesbians, our antennas went up, and we wondered why this guy wanted to know how many bedrooms we had," Ms. Caust recalled, acknowledging "paranoia" on her part. "We became very resistant to their questions after that."

It turns out, she later learned at one of the sessions at the 115th, that the officer was simply following police procedure by staking out the apartment for his own protection.

'Spilling Their Guts to Us'

For more than two decades, large numbers of gay men and lesbians have sought a more suburban life style in Jackson Heights, a middle- and working-class neighborhood of elegant garden apartments and squat row houses far removed from the bustle of Greenwich Village, where gay men and lesbians years ago established a community.

But relations with the police were largely tense, many people say, until Deputy Inspector Henry C. Roge, the 115th's new commander, invited the neighborhood's gay men and lesbians to discuss their concerns in the wake of widespread protests over Mr. Rivera's killing.

"We were on one end of the spectrum and they were on another," he said.

Bridging those worlds, though, has not come easily.

One officer, for instance, recalled an early meeting during which he and other officers became increasingly uneasy as several gay visitors recounted intimate details about their lives.

"I felt like I was at an A.A. meeting," the officer, Gene Jackson, said, noting that some officers protested the topic. "They were spilling their guts to us."

Special Treatment?

While Officer Jackson said he benefited from the meetings, not everyone has been convinced of the merits of the gatherings.

"My feeling is that we're giving one group special treatment by meeting like this," said one officer who spoke on the condition of anonymity. "If they can get us to sit down with them for a few hours, why can't other groups ask us to do the same?"

The other night, about eight officers, mostly rookies, sat across from four gay and lesbian instructors for the third of four classes they would have.

The topic, violence in gay and lesbian households, aroused discussion about how guarded homosexuals feel around the police, [elicited?] declarations from officers insisting that a person's sexual orientation was of no concern to them and led both sides to act out a situation in which officers responded to a domestic dispute between two male lovers.

"It's ironic the two groups would get together like this based on our experience in the past," Officer Facciola remarked after attending the two-hour session. "It's been pretty enlightening."

THE BEATING OF MATTHEW SHEPARD

On the night of October 6–7, 1998, Matthew Shepard, a twenty-one-year-old University of Wyoming student was drinking in the Fireside Bar in Laramie, Wyoming, when he was approached by Russell Henderson, twenty-one, and Aaron McKinney, twenty-two. Shepard was very open about his sexual orientation and had just attended a meeting of the university's Lesbian, Gay, Bisexual, Transgender Association. He reportedly told Henderson and McKinney that he was gay, and they said they were also. Shortly after midnight, the three left the bar together and departed in McKinney's pickup truck. The two men began beating Shepard in the truck. They then drove to an isolated area, tied the 5-foot 2-inch gay man to a fence, and hit him repeatedly with a .357 magnum handgun as he "begged for his life." After reportedly burning Shepard and nearly beating him to death, Henderson and McKinney stole his wallet and shoes and then left. Matthew Shepard was found by a passing bicyclist eighteen hours later, still tied to the fence and nearly lifeless. Shepard never regained consciousness and died on October 12.

In 1999 Henderson and McKinney were found guilty of the kidnapping and murder of Matthew Shepard and each given two consecutive life sentences. Two female friends also faced charges as accessories after the fact for helping them dispose of their bloody clothes. One pleaded guilty and was given a prison sentence of fifteen months to two years, while the other was put on probation.

OCTOBER 10, 1998
GAY MAN BEATEN AND LEFT FOR DEAD
2 Are Charged
By JAMES BROOKE

LARAMIE, Wyo., Oct. 9—At first, the passing bicyclist thought the crumpled form lashed to a ranch fence was a scarecrow. But when he stopped, he found the burned, battered and nearly lifeless body of Matthew Shepard, an openly gay college student who had been tied to the fence 18 hours earlier.

Today, Mr. Shepard, a 22-year-old University of Wyoming student, was in a coma in critical condition. At the Albany County courthouse here, Russell A. Henderson, 21, and Aaron J. McKinney, 22, were arraigned on charges of kidnapping, aggravated robbery and attempted first-degree murder. Two women described as friends of the men, Kristen Leann Price, 18, and Chastity Vera Pasley, 20, have been charged as accessories after the fact to attempted first-degree murder.

Mr. Shepard's friends said he did not know his alleged tormentors. The Laramie police say the primary motive was robbery, although court papers filed today indicate that Mr. Shepard's homosexuality may have been a factor. Mr. Shepard's friends call the attack a hate crime.

"He was very open about his sexuality," Tina LaBrie, an anthropology student here, said of her friend. "I admired him for that because it is very courageous to be yourself even when others disagree."

A few hours before he was beaten, Mr. Shepard, who is 5 feet 2 inches tall, had attended a meeting of the Lesbian, Gay, Bisexual, Transgendered Association, said Walter T. Boulden, a friend of Mr. Shepard.

"He was sitting at the bar, having a beer, when two men came up and talked to him," Mr. Boulden, a 46-year-old university lecturer of social work here, said today between tears. "He indicated he was gay, and they said they were gay, too."

"Now, he is in a coma," continued Mr. Boulden, who visited his friend at a hospital in Fort Collins, Colo., on Thursday. "I don't think anybody expects him to pull through." . . .

Although Wyoming often bills itself as the "equality state," the state Legislature has repeatedly voted down hate crime legislation on the ground that it would give homosexuals special rights.

"Wyoming is not really gay friendly," Marv Johnson, executive director of the Wyoming chapter of the American Civil Liberties Union, said from Cheyenne. "The best way to characterize that is by a comment a legislator made a few years back, when he likened homosexuals to gay bulls as worthless and should be sent to the packing plant." . . .

Calvin Rerucha, the County Attorney, charged in court documents today that Mr. McKinney and Mr. Henderson posed as homosexuals and lured Mr. Shepard out to Mr. McKinney's pickup truck just after midnight early Wednesday.

Beating him inside the truck, the pair drove him one mile southeast to an isolated part of a new rural subdivision, the County Attorney's report said. There, it said, the men tied their captive to a fence and pistol-whipped him with a .357 magnum handgun "while he begged for his life."

Relatives said that Mr. Shepard also suffered burns on his body.

After nearly beating the young man to death, said the Laramie Police Commander, David O'Malley, the assailants stole his wallet and shoes and left him tied to the fence.

Commander O'Malley said that when his officers arrested the two men on Thursday, they found in Mr. McKinney's pickup truck a .357 magnum pistol covered with blood and Mr. Shepard's shoes and credit card. He said they found Mr. Shepard's wallet at Mr. McKinney's home.

The police commander said that the two women helped the two men dump their bloody clothing, and that they reported hearing the men make anti-gay remarks. Ms. Pasley, a freshman art student at the university, lived with Mr. Henderson. Ms. Price lived with Mr. McKinney. The police did not say what the other three did for a living.

Today, friends and Laramie residents struggled to understand the incident.

Mr. Shepard, some said, may have felt a false sense of confidence because the local Gay Association completed plans on Tuesday night for Gay Awareness Week 1998. The weeklong series of events starts here Sunday with a local observance of National Coming Out Day and a lecture on Monday by Leslea Newman, the author of "Heather Has Two Mommies," a book about lesbian families.

"If I were a homosexual in Laramie, I would hang low, very low," said Carla Brown, manager of the Fireside. "Openly gay behavior is not only discouraged, it's dangerous."

. . . .

AN EVER-PRESENT FEAR

In this opinion piece, David Leavitt describes how all gay men were affected by the hatred and violence that led to the beating death of Matthew Shepard several days prior to its publication. Murders motivated by homophobia are rare, but the terror that they instill in the gay community is often substantial. Even the author, who has lived with his long-term partner for years and feels fully accepted by family, friends, and neighbors, does not feel safe holding hands with his boyfriend while walking down a city street. And if violence comes, it may come in the guise of love or friendship, as it did for Matthew Shepard. Loneliness may lure the unsuspecting into a dangerous situation that ends in robbery, taunts, and physical attack. If the victim survives, he probably will not report the incident to the police, and if he doesn't, the concern generated by his death will do little to undermine the systematic persecution of gay men.

OCTOBER 18, 1998
THE HATE EPIDEMIC
By DAVID LEAVITT

When I read the account of Matthew Shepard's murder, the words that I could not forget were those reportedly used by one of his killers after he and a companion had lured Mr. Shepard out of a Laramie, Wyo., tavern and into the pickup truck in which they would drive him to his place of execution: "Guess what? I'm not gay—and you just got jacked."

These words—odors from the abyss, as Forster might have put it—recalled others spoken by the narrator of Eudora Welty's 1963 story "Where Is the Voice Coming From?" which she wrote in a white heat after the assassination of the civil rights leader Medgar Evers. "Now I'm alive and you ain't," Evers's killer tells his dead victim in the story. "We ain't never now, never going to be equals, and you know why? One of us is dead."

Certain commonplaces cannot be restated enough: hatred of gay men in this country is an epidemic as pernicious as AIDS, and as unfathomable. Nor is any gay man untouched by this epidemic.

It haunts not only the drag queen who takes her life in her hands every time she steps onto the street, not only the middle-aged man who invites a stranger home with whom he has spoken on a phone sex line, not only the isolated college student in Wyoming longing for friendship and trusting in the overtures of moles from the Stasi of hate, but also the forward-thinking, well-adjusted, worldly homosexual man who imagines that in his urban corner of sanity and tolerance, in Greenwich Village or Los Angeles or London, he is somehow immune.

He is not immune—either from hatred or from the fear of hatred, which is in many ways even more destructive. Thus even though Mark Mitchell and I have lived together for almost seven years, even though when we stay at the homes of our enlightened parents we are treated by them no differently than, say, my brother and his wife, even though we share a house, a bed, a car and a bank account, when we walk together in any city we never hold hands—and not because we flinch at "public displays of affection" (as might my brother and his wife, for whom such decisions carry little weight) but because we are afraid of being killed.

No, gay killings are not everyday occurrences, any more than lynchings were ever a daily event in the South, but the fear colors everything—especially in a year when reported bias crimes against gay people in New York City have increased 81 percent.

Certain commonplaces cannot be restated enough. In the brutal con game to which Matthew Shepard fell prey, what was exploited was nothing less than a young man's

trust and hope and eager longing, if not for love, then at least for friendship, for camaraderie.

In this game, kindness can be held out as bait; sex can be used as a lure. The payoff may be death, as it was for Matthew Shepard, or it may be robbery or gay-bashing or merely unkind, ignorant words. But few of us walk away unscarred, if we are lucky enough to walk away at all.

For years AIDS conveniently helped the hate-mongers do their job, by wiping out gay men in appalling numbers. But now, for the first time in more than a decade, AIDS deaths are down, and it seems as if ignorance is stepping in and pick[ing] up the slack.

· ·

WITH GAY PANIC DEFENSE DISALLOWED, CONVICTED KILLER RECEIVES TWO CONSECUTIVE LIFE SENTENCES

The lawyers for Aaron McKinney, one of two men charged in the beating death of Matthew Shepard, had hoped to offer a "gay-panic" defense. Their plan was to show that because the defendant was sexually abused by a man in childhood, he was unable to control his revulsion when Shepard allegedly made a pass at him and was therefore not fully responsible for his actions on the night of the murder. However, Judge Barton R. Voigt ruled that Wyoming law does not allow for this sort of diminished capacity defense to be used to seek a lesser sentence, and McKinney was subsequently found guilty of second-degree murder, robbery, and kidnapping, a verdict that made him eligible for the death penalty.

The jury was about to begin discussions regarding McKinney's punishment when a surprise sentencing agreement was announced. After consulting with the victim's family, the prosecutors agreed that the convicted man would receive two consecutive life sentences in return for waiving his right to appeal. Gay and lesbian rights groups applauded both Judge Voigt's decision and the agreed-upon sentence for sending a strong message that hate crimes will no longer be tolerated and that those who commit them can anticipate severe consequences.

Although the prosecutor did not favor making the sentencing deal, Judy Shepard, Matthew's mother, insisted. She did not speak in court, but Matthew's father, Dennis, offered some insight into the family's decision making during his statements. He said that he would never forgive McKinney for robbing him of his son, that his family did not necessarily oppose the death penalty, and that "he would like nothing better" than to see the convicted man die. However, he also suggested that in order to begin healing, it was necessary to be merciful with McKinney even though the killer had failed to show mercy to his son.

Russell Henderson, the other man charged with beating and abandoning Matthew Shepard, pleaded guilty and received approximately the same sentence earlier that spring. Judy Shepard spent the months since her son's death working to pass hate crime legislation that would include protection for those victimized as a result of their sexual orientation. By 2010 thirty-one states had hate crimes laws in effect that address sexual orientation–based crimes. As of 2010, Wyoming did not have any laws specifically dealing with hate crimes. In October 2009 President Obama signed into law expanded federal hate crimes legislation.

NOVEMBER 5, 1999
PARENTS OF GAY OBTAIN MERCY FOR HIS KILLER
By MICHAEL JANOFSKY

DENVER, Nov. 4—With a call for mercy from the parents of the gay student he beat and left for dead on a prairie fence, Aaron J. McKinney was spared the death penalty today in a courtroom in Laramie, Wyo.

"I would like nothing better than to see you die, Mr. McKinney," the dead man's father, Dennis Shepard, said in a long and impassioned statement in which he called his son, Matthew, "my hero" for his courage in enduring slights and discrimination. "However, this is the time to begin the healing process, to show mercy to someone who refused to show any mercy."

Responding to a request from the court-appointed lawyers for Mr. McKinney, prosecutors consulted with the Shepard family and agreed to accept two consecutive life sentences rather than to push for the death penalty. In exchange, Mr. McKinney relinquished his right to appeal.

After the sentencing, Mr. Shepard told the defendant: "Mr. McKinney, I am going to grant you life, as hard as it is for me to do so, because of Matthew. Every time you celebrate Christmas, a birthday or the Fourth of July, remember that Matthew isn't. Every time you wake up in that prison cell, remember that you had the opportunity and the ability to stop your actions that night." He concluded, with obvious emotion: "You robbed me of something very precious, and I will never forgive you for that. May you live a long life and may you thank Matthew every day for it."

His wife, Judy, did not address the court.

The jury of seven men and five women in Wyoming District Court convicted Mr. McKinney on Wednesday of second-degree murder, robbery and kidnapping, a combination of charges that made him eligible for execution, which is by lethal injection in Wyoming. Today he told the court, "I really don't know what to say other than I'm truly sorry to the entire Shepard family."

The sentencing agreement came as something of a surprise on the first day the jury was expected to consider punishment for Mr. McKinney, a 22-year-old former roofer, who, with a friend, had lured Mr. Shepard out of a bar on Oct. 6, 1998, robbed him of $20, beat him with a pistol butt and left him for dead, tied to a wooden fence at the edge of Laramie.

Mr. Shepard, 21, was found unconscious the next morning and taken to a hospital in Fort Collins, Colo., where he died five days later.

The friend, Russell A. Henderson, 22, pleaded guilty and accepted virtually the same deal last spring that Mr. McKinney received.

While the case was widely perceived as a hate crime, Wyoming is one of eight states that have no such official designation.

Gay and lesbian rights groups praised the sentencing agreement as fair and benevolent. "Gay and lesbian Americans can now have renewed faith in our justice system," said David M. Smith, a spokesman for the Human Rights Campaign, the nation's largest gay rights group. "We can only hope a strong message was sent, that in America hate crimes will not be tolerated and that there are severe consequences for violent, hateful actions."

That sentiment was echoed by President Clinton, who said in a statement, "We cannot surrender to those on the fringe of our society who lash out at those who are different."

Cal Rerucha, the Albany County prosecutor, said he had not been in favor of offering Mr. McKinney a deal. But Mr. Smith said it largely came about at the insistence of Mrs. Shepard, who has spent months since the killing campaigning for more states and the federal government to pass laws that include a victim's sexual orientation as a basis for designating the crime as a hate crime. So far, only 21 states have such provisions; a federal proposal died in conference this year.

In his statement to the court, Mr. Shepard conceded that to some people, his son had become "a symbol, some say a martyr, putting a boy-next-door face on hate crimes."

He said that he and his family opposed an earlier deal for Mr. McKinney because they believed that Mr. McKinney was their son's principal antagonist, which Mr. McKinney's confession to the police confirmed, and they wanted a full public airing of what happened. "A trial was necessary," Mr. Shepard said, "to show that this was a hate crime and not just a robbery gone bad."

But that did not mean he, his wife or their son philosophically opposed capital punishment, Mr. Shepard told the court. He recalled a conversation with his son in which they agreed that some killers, like those convicted of murdering James Byrd Jr. of Jasper, Tex., by dragging him to his death, deserved to be executed.

"Little did we know," he said, "that the same response would come about involving Matt."

In a critical evidentiary ruling, Judge Barton R. Voigt said that Mr. McKinney's lawyers could not engage in a so-called gay-panic defense.

They had planned to present evidence showing that Mr. McKinney had suffered from homosexual abuse as a child and that in attacking Mr. Shepard, their client had acted out of sheer revulsion from a sexual advance they claimed Mr. Shepard had made toward him.

But Judge Voigt ruled that Wyoming law did not provide for such a defense as a basis for seeking conviction on a lesser charge, and the decision was hailed by gay rights groups as a victory against future attackers seeking to escape more severe punishment.

As a result, Mr. McKinney's lawyers tried to convince the jury that drugs and alcohol had played a role in Mr. McKinney's violent actions.

In his remarks to the court, Mr. Shepard thanked Judge Voigt for the ruling.

"By doing so," he said, "you have emphasized that Matthew was a human being with all the rights and responsibilities and protections of any citizen of Wyoming."

Despite Shepard Murder, Wyoming and Other States Balk at Extending Hate Crimes Protection

According to a 1999 report, 1,102 crimes motivated by sexual orientation were logged by the FBI's voluntary reporting system in 1997. However, neither this grim statistic nor the 1998 murder of Matthew Shepard in Wyoming seems to have made much of an impact on Rocky Mountain lawmakers. Colorado, Idaho, Montana, and Utah all rejected bills in the late 1990s that would have added crimes motivated by sexual orientation to those covered by existing hate crimes legislation. Further, if lawmakers in New Mexico had succeeded in passing a similar bill through its Democrat-controlled legislature, Republican governor Gary E. Johnson vowed to veto it. Nevertheless, hate crimes legislation with specific protections for LGBT people did get passed in New Mexico in 2003. Wyoming still has not passed hate-crimes legislation that is inclusive of sexual orientation and gender identity.

Typically, hate crimes laws result in higher fines or longer jail sentences for crimes motivated by hatred of a particular minority group. When this *Times* article was written, nineteen states had added sexual orientation as a protected category within this legislation, and Hawaii, Oklahoma, and Virginia were considering the adoption of hate crimes laws that include protection for gays and lesbians. By 2010 thirteen states had added sexual orientation into the language of their hate crime laws.

Those opposed to hate crimes legislation argue that all citizens should be protected "not just a few groups who claim victim status." One local resident suggested during a legislative hearing that Wyoming was the true victim of bias crime because of the way it was portrayed by national media during coverage of Matthew Shepard's murder.

FEBRUARY 5, 1999
ROCKY MOUNTAIN STATES RESISTING MOVE TO BROADEN HATE-CRIME LAWS
By JAMES BROOKE

DENVER, Feb. 4—Last fall, national revulsion over the killing of Matthew Shepard, a gay college student in Wyoming, seemed strong enough to push legislatures in the Rockies to expand hate-crime laws to include sexual orientation.

But this winter lawmakers in Colorado, Idaho, Montana and Utah have defeated bills that would add sexual orientation to categories of people protected by existing hate-crime laws. In Wyoming legislators have defeated all efforts to pass that state's first hate-crime law.

In New Mexico, which has the region's lone Democratic-controlled legislature, lawmakers are expected to pass a hate-crime bill that includes sexual orientation. But Gov. Gary E. Johnson, a Republican, has vowed a veto, saying, "All crimes are hate crimes."

Kerry Lobel, executive director of the National Gay and Lesbian Task Force, a Washington group that pushes for hate-crime legislation, said: "We are incredibly disappointed. We looked to the Wyoming Legislature for leadership and legislation, not lip service."

The votes came as the Federal Bureau of Investigation on Jan. 21 released its latest tally of hate crimes. In 1997, sexual orientation was the motivation for 14 percent of reported hate crimes, or 1,102 crimes out of 8,049, the bureau said. Under the bureau's voluntary reporting system, police departments covering about 80 percent of the country's population report their hate crimes.

Forty states have some kind of hate-crime legislation, generally laws that increase fines and add jail time for crimes motivated by hatred of a specific group. Of those states, 19 have laws that specify sexual orientation as a category for protection. Ten states, largely in the South and Southwest, do not have any hate-crime legislation.

Outside the Rockies, legislatures in Hawaii, Oklahoma, and Virginia are considering hate-crime bills that include sexual orientation.

Antipathy toward hate-crime legislation seems to stem from several factors, including a belief that the laws would confer special rights on the groups named and a backlash against publicity resulting from the Shepard killing.

Sally Vaughan, a resident of Remington, Wyo., complained two weeks ago at a legislative hearing in Cheyenne about what she called "the vicious smear campaign" by the national press in its coverage of [the] Shepard killing. Wyoming became the true victim of bias crime, Ms. Vaughan said.

Doug Thompson, who recently formed a Wyoming group called Citizens for Equal Protection, urged lawmakers in Cheyenne to protect all citizens "and not just a few groups who claim victim status."

Gov. Jim Geringer, a Republican, gave general support to a hate-crime bill but also warned legislators about yielding to "external pressure."

In the end, a hate-crime bill that six weeks ago seemed destined for passage died yesterday in the Senate Judiciary Committee.

"The part of the bill that made people the most uncomfortable was the provision for sexual orientation," State Senator John C. Schiffer, a Republican who is the committee chairman, said today, adding, "My feeling right now is that the committee is tired of discussing bias crimes." . . .

· ·

JORDANIAN FAMILY CHARGED WITH ASSAULTING AND KIDNAPPING LESBIAN DAUGHTER

Muna Hawatmeh, a twenty-five-year-old lesbian who immigrated to the United States with her family in the late 1980s, was living with her girlfriend, Leticia Rivera, in Provo, Utah, when she began to receive threatening phone calls from her two brothers. Unable to accept her sexual relationship with another woman, the brothers repeatedly demanded that she break up with Rivera and move back into their parents' home. When Hawatmeh finally agreed to meet with her family to discuss the situation, she was repeatedly kicked, hit, and told "You are going to die tonight; we are going to kill you." Humiliated, covered in bruises, and fearing for her life, the young woman agreed to change her sexual orientation and return to Jordan with her family. Rivera met up with the family as they headed to the airport and notified the police after one of Hawatmeh's brothers threatened her life and tried to grab her. The police then attempted to verify that Hawatmeh was leaving the country voluntarily, and she told them about the emotional and physical abuse she had endured from her family over the previous twelve hours. As a result, Utah officials charged the young woman's parents and brothers with assault and aggravated kidnapping, an offense punishable by up to life in prison. Local gay activists expressed concern for Hawatmeh's safety but were hesitant about calling the incident a hate crime, owing to the "particular cultural circumstances." During the court proceedings, Hawatmeh was barred from speaking with her family, and the prosecutor reports that this estrangement had been hard, saying, "Muna really misses contact with her parents, especially her mother. They used to be very close."

APRIL 21, 2001
FAMILY, CULTURE AND LAW MEET IN A UTAH COURT CASE
By MICHAEL JANOFSKY

SALT LAKE CITY, April 20—She was much like any other young immigrant from a faraway country, eager to absorb American culture and make a new life for herself.

But over several hours one night 18 months ago, Muna Hawatmeh said she found that her closest relatives were not so willing to abandon the ways of old. In a case now under review by the Utah Supreme Court, Ms. Hawatmeh claims that her two brothers, Iehab and Shaher, and her parents, Jamil and Wedad, felt that her lesbian relationship so shamed the family that they beat her and tried to take her back to their native Jordan.

The four family members were charged with aggravated kidnapping, a felony punishable by up to life in prison, and assault, a misdemeanor. After a preliminary hearing, a trial judge reduced the more serious charge to simple kidnapping, which carries a maximum penalty of 15 years. But two weeks ago, the Utah attorney general asked the higher court to reinstate the original charges.

All four have pleaded not guilty.

The accusations surprised many in the city. Despite the overwhelming presence of the Mormon Church, which frowns on same-sex relations, Salt Lake City in recent years has become more diverse. Local gay rights leaders said they did not see the case as a hate crime because of the particular cultural circumstances.

"I certainly think everyone in our community was aware of the situation and had concern for the safety of this woman," said Darin Hobbs, assistant executive director of the Gay and Lesbian Community Center of Utah. But, he continued, "it's hard to make a connection to the gay and lesbian community at large."

Mahnaz Afkami, an expert in Middle Eastern culture and president of the Women's Learning Partnership, an international human rights organization, said a woman having a sexual relationship outside marriage, especially one with another woman, was considered shameful in Middle Eastern cultures, regardless of their religion.

The Hawatmehs are Roman Catholic.

In her court testimony, Ms. Hawatmeh, 25, described her brothers' reaction to her relationship with Leticia Rivera, a graphic artist. Ms. Hawatmeh, who was still learning English at the time, told the court: "They never accepted it. They were hurt about it and they were, like, cannot believe, you know, a lesbian, and they never accept it." . . .

Ms. Hawatmeh told the court that for weeks, her brothers tried an assortment of tactics—she called them threats—to persuade her to break off the relationship with Ms. Rivera, with whom she was living in Provo, Utah. The brothers, who own thriving computer parts businesses, wanted her to return to their parents' home in Sandy, a Salt

Lake suburb, she said. Several times, she told the court, someone left messages on her answering machine, saying, "'Lesbians must die." She identified the voice as that of Shaher, now 35.

After weeks of explaining to them that she did not want to leave Ms. Rivera, Ms. Hawatmeh said she agreed to meet the family.

She returned to her parents' house on Oct. 13, 1999, and found, as she told the court, that they were still "very mad" at her and had no intention of allowing her to return to Ms. Rivera.

Over the next four hours, she testified, the family members hit her, kicked her and verbally abused her until she kissed her father's feet and promised to change her sexual orientation.

"'I was just in shock," she told the court. "I cannot believe it. I was, I was just—I didn't know how to react. I did not. It was like, you know, my family, my own family were doing this to me. I was just in shock."

At one point, she said, Shaher held a large knife toward her: "And he said, 'You going to die tonight.'"

She said Iehab repeated the threat, "saying you are going to die tonight; we going to kill you."

Ms. Hawatmeh said she was overcome with pain and humiliation, and begged them not to kill her. She said she agreed to return to Jordan the next day, saying, "I'll be a different person." She said her body ached and was covered with bruises. (The brothers came to the United States from Jordan about 15 years ago, followed by their parents and sister.)

The next morning, Ms. Hawatmeh testified, as the brothers were about to drive her to the Salt Lake airport, they encountered Ms. Rivera driving toward the family house. She said Iehab threatened Ms. Rivera's life and tried to grab her before she sped off. The brothers then took Ms. Hawatmeh to the airport, she said.

But before they checked in, she told the court, a police officer, alerted by Ms. Rivera, called on Iehab's cell phone, insisting that the brothers take their sister to the police station in Sandy to prove she was leaving on her own accord.

At the police station, she told officers everything she said she had endured over the previous 12 hours. That led to the charges against the four family members.

As part of the court proceedings, Ms. Hawatmeh is not allowed contact with her family. Ms. Barton, the prosecutor, said the estrangement had been hard for Ms. Hawatmeh.

"This was once a very loving family," Ms. Barton said. "This has devastated her. Muna really misses the contact with her parents, especially her mother. They used to be very close."

· ·

The Murder of Brandon Teena

Twenty-one-year-old Brandon Teena was living as a man just outside the small southeastern Nebraska town of Humboldt. After being arrested for alcohol and forgery charges, Brandon was discovered to be a woman whose legal name was actually Teena Brandon. Friends reported that Brandon claimed to be a hermaphrodite in the process of undergoing a surgical change of sex.

After Brandon's biological gender became known, police charged that John Lotter, twenty-two, and Marvin Nissen, twenty-one, kidnapped and sexually assaulted their former friend on December 25. Brandon was found shot to death with roommate Lisa Lambert, twenty-three, and a friend, Phillip DeVine, twenty-two, both of whom were also shot and killed in the incident. Lambert's infant son was also present but not injured. Lotter and Nissen were arrested for the murder and were held in the county jail. Police refused to speculate on the motive for the killings at the time.

JANUARY 4, 1994
WOMAN WHO POSED AS A MAN IS FOUND SLAIN WITH 2 OTHERS

HUMBOLDT, Neb., Jan. 3—A woman who had posed as a man and dated women was found shot to death on Friday, two weeks after residents of this rural area learned her true identity, the authorities said today.

The body of Teena Brandon was found along with the bodies of Lisa Lambert, 23, and Phillip DeVine, 22, both of whom had also been shot, in a farmhouse about three miles south of Humboldt, a southeastern Nebraska town of 1,000 residents.

Ms. Brandon shared the rented house with Ms. Lambert and Ms. Lambert's infant son, who was not harmed. Mr. DeVine was from Fairfield, Iowa, and his stepfather said in a telephone interview that Mr. DeVine had left home to visit friends in Nebraska.

John Lotter, 22, and Marvin Nissen, 21, both of Falls City, were arrested for investigation of murder and held in the county jail. They were also charged with kidnapping and sexually assaulting Ms. Brandon on Dec. 25, said the Richardson County Attorney, Douglas Merz.

The authorities refused to say if they believed the slayings were connected to the earlier assault complaint, to Ms. Brandon's double life or to some other incident.

Stories of Sex Change Surgery

Friends said Ms. Brandon, 21, had posed for two months as a man, using the name Brandon Teena, and had told stories of an incomplete sex-change operation or of being a hermaphrodite.

"She said she felt like a man inside, but she was a female outside," said Michelle Lotter, a friend of Ms. Brandon and a sister of Mr. Lotter.

Ms. Brandon had lived with Ms. Lambert for about three months, but their relationship was unclear, Mr. Merz said. Her friends said she moved to the area from Lincoln about three months ago and went by the name Brandon Teena.

One woman she dated was Lana Tisdel, 19, of Falls City, who said she met Ms. Brandon at a party in November.

The two dated for about a week, and Ms. Tisdel said she had believed that Ms. Brandon was male until Ms. Brandon was arrested about two weeks ago on alcohol and forgery charges.

After the authorities referred to Ms. Brandon as a woman, Ms. Tisdel said, she confronted her. "She told me that she had a sex change and it's not all done," Ms. Tisdel said.

* *

MAN CHARGED WITH HATE CRIME FOR MURDERING HIS TRANSGENDER DATE

Angie Zapata, eighteen, was found beaten to death in her Greeley, Colorado, apartment on July 17, 2008. Born biologically male, Zapata was described as a glamorous person who turned heads everywhere she went and who had dreams of becoming a cosmetologist or a professional drag queen. According to her sister, however, she was also lonely and wanted to date someone who would be proud to be with her.

Zapata had been living as a woman for several years when she met Allen R. Andrade, thirty-one, through an online dating service. The two went out on a date, and Zapata performed oral sex on Andrade. The following evening, Andrade confronted Zapata about her gender and, upon discovering that she had male genitalia, proceeded to beat her with his fists and a fire extinguisher. Andrade was arrested and, according to the official affidavit, told the police he thought he had "killed it." In addition to murder, the Weld County district attorney charged Andrade with committing a hate crime. In May 2009 Andrade was convicted of a bias-motivated crime. The sentence along with the murder conviction and habitual offender conviction led to a sentence of life in prison without parole, as well as an additional sixty years.

AUGUST 2, 2008
DEATH OF A TRANSGENDER WOMAN IS CALLED A HATE CRIME
By DAN FROSCH

GREELEY, Colo. – Angie Zapata began living as a woman six years ago even though she was born male and named Justin.

While Ms. Zapata, 18, was accepted by her many friends and five siblings, she was bullied in school and at times was lonely and troubled, an older sister, Monica, said. Eventually, Ms. Zapata dropped out of school and got her own apartment here in Greeley.

It was in that apartment that Ms. Zapata's badly beaten body was found on July 17.

On Wednesday, the police arrested Allen R. Andrade, 31, and charged him with murder. According to the authorities, Mr. Andrade had gone out on a date with Ms. Zapata, and upon discovering she had male genitalia, beat her to death—starting with his fists and then with a fire extinguisher.

Mr. Andrade told investigators that he thought he had "killed it," according to an affidavit filed by the police. Mr. Andrade, who is in custody, has said nothing publicly about the killing, and his arraignment has not yet been scheduled.

On Thursday, the Weld County district attorney announced that he would prosecute the killing as a hate crime, which carries an additional 18-month sentence if Mr. Andrade is convicted.

"We applied the law to the facts, and we thought the law was appropriate," said the district attorney, Kenneth R. Buck.

The killing has both shaken and rallied this rural, conservative town about 60 miles north of Denver, where there has long been a sense that minorities face discrimination, a feeling that became especially inflamed among Hispanics after a federal immigration raid on a meatpacking plant here in 2006.

"We've heard from so many people expressing not only just outrage but also shock as to how this could happen," said Chris Fiene, a board member for the Lambda Community Center in nearby Fort Collins, which provides services for the gay, lesbian, bisexual and transgender community.

At a recent memorial service, nearly 200 people filled the church Ms. Zapata had attended. A vigil is being planned for this month. With her long hair, baby-smooth face and distinctive looks, Ms. Zapata cut a glamorous figure, friends and family members said.

"We loved to take her out, because she got so much attention," her sister Monica, 32, said. "I couldn't even take her to Wal-Mart because people would turn around. Everybody knew Angie."

According to the Colorado Anti-Violence Program, there were 121 incidents of violence committed against gay, lesbian, bisexual or transgender people in Colorado last year, numbers that have held relatively steady over the past few years.

In 2007, however, there was a 24 percent increase nationally in the number of victims reporting such violence, said Avy Skolnik, coordinator of statewide and national programs for the National Anti-Violence Project in New York City. Ms. Zapata's death is emblematic of a surge in the violence over the past month, Mr. Skolnik said.

Ms. Zapata had dreamed of moving to Denver, becoming a professional drag queen and working as a cosmetologist. But she started hanging out with a rough crowd and dated too many men, some of them dangerous, her sister said.

"One time she came home crying saying, 'Why, Monica, why won't people accept me?'" Monica Zapata said. "All my sister wanted was somebody who would take her down the street and be proud of who she was."

Monica Zapata said her sister had drifted into drugs and at one point talked about prostitution to make extra money.

"I worried about her every time she left my house," she said. "I couldn't fix her loneliness."

According to an arrest affidavit, Ms. Zapata met Mr. Andrade on an Internet dating site. They spent time together at Ms. Zapata's apartment on July 15, and she performed oral sex on him. But Mr. Andrade told the police that Ms. Zapata would not let him touch her, and that they slept in separate rooms that night.

The next evening, after viewing photographs in her apartment, Mr. Andrade confronted Ms. Zapata over her sexual identity just before killing her, the affidavit said. "I am all woman," Ms. Zapata told him, according to the affidavit.

• •

LGBT AMERICANS ONE STEP AWAY FROM PROTECTION UNDER FEDERAL HATE CRIMES LEGISLATION

In the more than ten years since Matthew Shepard was murdered, federal hate crimes protection for LGBT Americans was within sight. Previous legislation covered those victimized because of their race, color, religion, or national origin. The law debated in Congress in 2009 extended this coverage to those who are targeted for attack because of their gender, gender identity, or sexual orientation. It also allocated additional money to local jurisdictions to help defray the costs of investigating hate crimes and empower federal agencies to assist with local investigations and prosecutions upon request.

The measure was sponsored by Sen. Patrick J. Leahy, a Democrat from Vermont, who introduced it as an amendment to an essential military-spending bill. Although opponents acknowledged the horrifying nature of bias crimes, they argued that these offenses were already punishable under existing laws and that the new legislation constituted an "Orwellian" move designed to punish "thought crime." Despite these objections, the motion passed the Senate with a 68–29 vote, two weeks after the House approved it, 281 to 146. The legislation then went to President Obama, who signed it into law on October 28, 2009.

OCTOBER 23, 2009
SENATE APPROVES BROADENED HATE-CRIME MEASURE
By DAVID STOUT

WASHINGTON – The Senate voted Thursday to extend new federal protections to people who are victims of violent crime because of their sex or sexual orientation, bringing the measure close to reality after years of fierce debate.

The 68-to-29 vote sends the legislation to President Obama, who has said he supports it.

The measure, attached to an essential military-spending bill, broadens the definition of federal hate crimes to include those committed because of a victim's gender or gender identity, or sexual orientation. It gives victims the same federal safeguards already afforded to people who are victims of violent crimes because of their race, color, religion or national origin.

"Hate crimes instill fear in those who have no connection to the victim other than a shared characteristic such as race or sexual orientation," Senator Patrick J. Leahy, Democrat of Vermont and chairman of the Senate Judiciary Committee, said afterward. "For nearly 150 years, we have responded as a nation to deter and to punish violent denials of civil rights by enacting federal laws to protect the civil rights of all of our citizens."

Mr. Leahy sponsored the hate-crimes amendment to the military bill and called its passage a worthy tribute to the late Senator Edward M. Kennedy of Massachusetts, who first introduced hate-crimes legislation in the Senate more than a decade ago.

Opponents argued to no avail that the new measure was unnecessary in view of existing laws and might interfere with local law enforcement agencies. Senator Jim DeMint, Republican of South Carolina, said he agreed that hate crimes were terrible. "That's why they are already illegal," Mr. DeMint said, asserting that the new law was a dangerous, even "Orwellian" step toward "thought crime."

Ten Republicans voted for the hate-crimes measure. The only Democrat to oppose it was Senator Russ Feingold of Wisconsin, who said he could not vote for the current bill "because it does nothing to bring our open-ended and disproportionate military commitment in Afghanistan to an end and/or to ensure that our troops are safely and expeditiously redeployed from Iraq." The Senate action came two weeks after the House approved the measure, 281 to 146, and would give the federal government the authority to prosecute violent, antigay crimes when local authorities failed to.

The measure would also allocate $5 million a year to the Justice Department to assist local communities in investigating hate crimes, and it would allow the agency to assist in investigations and prosecutions if local agencies requested help.

Federal protections for people who are victims of violent crime because of their sexual orientation have been sought for more than a decade, at least since the 1998 murder of Matthew Shepard, a gay Wyoming college student.

SAME-SEX MARRIAGE AND THE FAMILY

INTRODUCTION

The drive for same-sex marriage has been part of a more general challenge to laws that discriminate against homosexuals (see discussion in the first two chapters). Same-sex couples began to apply for marriage licenses in the 1970s in order to obtain legal recognition of their families as well as rights and privileges equal to those awarded to heterosexual marriages, such as hospital visitation rights, coadoption privileges, joint property ownership and inheritance rights, workers' compensation benefits, family leave, and immunity from being compelled to testify, as well as various other legal, insurance, and tax advantages. Although alternative strategies to marriage have been developed to access many of these benefits, such as domestic partner benefits, civil unions, and living wills, American citizens have traditionally received them through marriage. Every alternative strategy short of marriage leaves significant gaps in coverage. Hence, the drive for equality in this area has largely focused on marriage, heightening conflict between advocates of gay marriage on the one hand and, on the other, many social conservatives and evangelical religious people who wish to maintain the tradition of reserving marriage to opposite-sex couples.

Another wave of challenges to marriage laws began in the early 1990s, when many assumed that Hawaii was about to become the first state to recognize same-sex marriage. Although states typically accept marriages performed in other states as valid, several states responded to developments in Hawaii by passing laws that explicitly deny recognition out-of-state same-sex marriages. During this period the federal government also adopted a law, known as the Defense of Marriage Act (DOMA), that stated that the federal government would not recognize such marriages.

A subsequent wave of challenges began when the state of Vermont became the first state to legalize same-sex civil unions and the state of Massachusetts became the first to recognize same-sex marriages in 2000 and 2004, respectively. In the wake of these developments, several states adopted laws that legalized same-sex unions and marriages, while many more states passed laws and constitutional amendments that prohibited the recognition of same-sex couples, suggesting that conflict over the issue would persist for some time into the future. Recent developments in California, Iowa, and Maine make the ultimate outcome of this debate uncertain as of this writing.

EARLY CHALLENGES

The New York Times coverage of the issue began on January 10, 1971, when *The Times* published a single paragraph story simply titled "Court Won't Let Men Wed." This piece noted that two gay men, Jack Baker and James McConnell, had challenged the constitutionality of a law that made it illegal for the state of Minnesota to grant them a marriage license. Despite the fact that they had been married by a duly ordained Methodist minister in 1970, the state's highest court turned down Baker and McConnell's request for a license. That ruling was upheld by the United States Supreme Court when it refused to review the case "for want of a substantial Federal question." Later the state of Minnesota allowed McConnell to adopt Baker, making the two gay men a family in the eyes of the law. As reported in a *Times* piece on August 26, 1971, establishing this relationship allowed the two gay men to inherit each other's property without fear of a legal challenge to their wills, a very real possibility at that time, according to McConnell. The couple subsequently attempted to file joint federal tax returns, despite the fact that such a filing would have led to a smaller refund, but a *Times* article of January 5, 1975, noted that the return was rejected by the Internal Revenue Service.

When two men succeeded in obtaining a marriage license in Boulder, Colorado, on March 26, 1975, it was the first time that a same-sex couple had been legally married in the United States without being immediately challenged. Several other same-sex couples quickly followed suit. Because most states, including Colorado, did not explicitly prohibit same-sex marriage at that time, the Boulder county clerk saw no reason to exclude such couples, stating that it was not her business "why people get married," and that "no minority should be discriminated against." Although the state's attorney general said that he did not believe the marriages were legal, he also said he saw no reason to challenge

Tori and Kate Kuykendall were married in June 2008 in West Hollywood, California, shortly after the California Supreme Court legalized gay marriage in the state. The passage of Proposition 8 in November of that year halted same-sex marriages.
*Source: Monica Almeida/*The New York Times

licenses that had already been issued. One couple said that the marriage would allow him and his Australian partner to live together in the United States, while others reported that state recognition of their marriages had "psychological benefits."

The issuance of same-sex marriages also became more visible during the highly charged debate over the ratification of a proposed amendment to the U.S. Constitution that was designed to protect equal rights regardless of sex. Popularly known as the Equal Rights Amendment (ERA), it aimed to grant women rights equal to those of men. Despite the focus on women's equality, opponents regularly suggested that the ratification of the ERA would compel states to recognize same-sex marriages, as noted in pieces published in *The Times* on September 18, November 2, and November 6, 1975. When the ERA failed to pass, supporters bitterly asserted that such arguments had "intentionally distorted" the meaning of the amendment, directly contributing to its defeat. The ERA was not the only seemingly unrelated

issue that raised the specter of same-sex marriage in the 1970s. When Dade County (Miami), Florida, was considering whether to repeal a law that protected the civil rights of homosexuals, the state legislature responded by approving bills that outlawed same-sex marriage and prohibited homosexuals from adopting children, as noted in a *Times* story of May 31, 1977.

The legal status of gay couples arose not only in the context of marriage, but also in the context of divorce and alimony. As part of their divorce settlements, many men had signed orders promising to support their ex-wives until the latter remarried or died. As a growing number of divorced women formed long-term lesbian relationships in the 1970s, some judges began to rule that long-term lesbian relationships were also grounds for termination of alimony, granting a measure of legal recognition to those relationships. A *Times* report of February 27, 1979, on a case of this sort decided in Minnesota prompted Jean O'Leary of the National Gay Task Force to assert that the lesbian relationship involved "certainly is the equivalent of a marriage situation." She added that "we could solve all these problems just by legalizing homosexual marriages, and we wouldn't have to go through this."

The city of San Francisco has long been thought of as a center of gay culture, with gay residents composing an estimated 15 percent of the city's population. On November 28, 1982, *The Times* reported that San Francisco was seeking to become the first major city in the country to allow "domestic partners" of city employees to be put on their health coverage, including both long-term homosexual and heterosexual couples. Although the bill passed by an 8–3 margin, Mayor Dianne Feinstein subsequently vetoed it. A *Times* report of December 10, 1982, noted that Feinstein was praised by the Roman Catholic archbishop, who called the veto "a courageous act." Seven years later, in a unanimous vote, San Francisco became the first major city to provide a domestic partnership registry for unmarried homosexual and heterosexual couples. Designed to parallel marriage licenses given to heterosexual couples, the measure provided a basis for requesting hospital visitation rights equal to those regularly given to married couples. Across the country, in New York, another city with a very visible gay community, Mayor Ed Koch extended the city's bereavement policy to include unmarried employees, giving them the same right to paid leave after the death of a partner. As noted in a *Times* report of July 10, 1989, this action followed an important court decision that allowed a gay man to inherit his deceased partner's rent-controlled apartment.

Legal recognition of unmarried domestic partners became an issue of public concern partially because of health issues that arose during the AIDS crisis, as well as in response to the high-profile struggle of Karen Thompson to gain the right to see her long-term lesbian partner Sharon Kowalski, who had been severely disabled in a 1983 automobile accident. After the accident, Kowalski's father won legal guardianship over Sharon, denying Thompson any visitation or access to her. While a married partner would have immediately been recognized as the rightful guardian of a disabled spouse, Thompson was initially not allowed to care for Kowalski, even though both women consistently said that they wished to remain together as a family.

The Kowalski case highlighted the precarious status of same-sex relationships and became a centerpiece of the drive for legal recognition of gay and lesbian partnerships. *The Times* published numerous articles documenting Thompson's protracted court battle, including a February 8, 1989, piece noting that marches and vigils had been organized in twenty-one cities on August 7

to mark "National Free Sharon Kowalski Day." A *Times* report of December 18, 1991, noted the entire saga when a judge finally concluded that Thompson was Kowalski's rightful legal guardian. William Rubenstein, director of the Gay Rights Project at the American Civil Liberties Union (ACLU), commented that the Kowalski ordeal "exemplifies the difficulties lesbians and gay men have in safeguarding our relationships," adding that it, "underscored why we need legal protection, and created a terrific incentive to fight for these kinds of marital rights and recognition of domestic partnership."

Hawaii and Its Aftermath

As gay and lesbian partnerships were slowly coming to be recognized in instances such as the Kowalski case, some began to speculate that Hawaii might become the first state to legalize same-sex marriage. In May 1993 that state's supreme court announced in the case of *Baehr v. Lewin* that the current ban on gay and lesbian marriage could be interpreted as a violation of the state constitution's prohibition of sex discrimination. The court relied on a 1967 U.S. Supreme Court decision, *Loving v. Virginia,* which held that it was unconstitutional to prohibit mixed-race marriages, even though both black and white people were prohibited from marrying across race, much the way that both women and men have traditionally been prevented from marrying within their own sex.

Noting that marriage is a basic civil right, the Hawaii Supreme Court asked the state to defend its decision to exclude same-sex couples from marriage in a subsequent trial. Before the trial began, other states responded to the possibility that same-sex marriages might be legalized in Hawaii. By longstanding custom, U.S. states have recognized marriages performed in other parts of the country, even when the requirements for such marriages—such as those related to the age of consent—differed from the recognizing state. In March 1995, however, the state of Utah became the first state to pass a law explicitly denying recognition of out-of-state same- sex marriages not conforming to Utah law. Similar bills were considered in South Dakota and Alaska. Supporters of same-sex marriage argued that such laws violated the Full Faith and Credit Clause of the U.S. Constitution, which guarantees that each state will recognize the laws and public acts of other states. Similar arguments were made about anti-miscegenation laws before the U.S. Supreme Court ruled that prohibiting mixed-race marriage was unconstitutional.

Responding to this controversy, Congress passed the Defense of Marriage Act by overwhelming margins of 85–14 in the Senate and 342–67 in the House. President Bill Clinton signed the bill into law on September 21, 1996. DOMA defined marriage as a union between one man and one woman. In apparent conflict with the Constitution's Full Faith and Credit Clause, DOMA also said that states were not required to recognize public acts (such as marriage) of other states. While supporters of the bill said that it was necessary to defend traditional marriage owing to challenges in Hawaii, opponents called it a divisive, vote-getting ploy. Ralph Reed, the executive director of the Christian Coalition, described this law's passage as "a huge victory for the pro-family movement." However, Rep. Bob Barr (R-GA), the author of DOMA, has since said that it should be repealed, and former president Bill Clinton has since stated that people should be free to enter into whatever relationships they see fit and that the matter should be decided at the state rather than the national level. Some have speculated that his initial support was motivated by his desire for reelection in 1996. Others argue that, like that of many other Americans, Clinton's understanding of the issue evolved over time.

Back in Hawaii, the state was unable to provide evidence to support its claim that same-sex marriages should not be recognized because heterosexual marriages were in the best interest of children. Nevertheless, the ruling was "stayed" (prevented from being put into effect) pending an appeal to the Hawaii Supreme Court. In the meantime, voters were slated to decide on an amendment to Hawaii's state constitution that proposed to make same-sex marriage unconstitutional. A few months later Hawaii passed a law that offered many of the benefits of marriage to gay couples, siblings, and roommates, as a way of heading off the drive for same-sex marriage in the state. As reported by The Times on July 9, 1997, the law provided inheritance rights, the right to own property jointly, and the right to sue for wrongful death.

By a margin of 2 to 1, Hawaii voters subsequently approved an amendment to the state constitution that prohibited same-sex marriage, and the Hawaii Supreme Court allowed the ban to stand, effectively ending the drive for recognition of gay and lesbian marriages in the state. As noted in a Times report on December 10, 1999, thirty states and Congress had passed laws banning gay marriage by this time. In an editorial on December 20, 1999, The Times characterized this development as "an ugly backlash." Despite this, the editors argued, events in Hawaii had also had "a positive cultural impact," by convincing "fair-minded Americans" that same-sex marriage was not a threat. Concluding that "important civil rights battles are rarely won in the first round," the editorial anticipated the next stage in the conflict.

CIVIL UNIONS IN VERMONT AND SAME-SEX MARRIAGE IN MASSACHUSETTS

Vermont became the next battleground in the debate about whether same-sex couples should be legally recognized. In a Times report of November 19, 1988, Nina Beck and Stacy Jolles explained that they were one of three gay couples fighting for legal recognition because Jolles had been prohibited from seeing Beck during a medical emergency related to labor complications that resulted in Beck being sent to the hospital. Rather than being admitted, as any heterosexual spouse would have been, staff asked Jolles, "Who are you? Do you have legal papers to be there?" Noting that state courts overturned laws prohibiting mixed-race marriages long before the U.S. Supreme Court did so in 1967, Beck and Jolles's lawyer argued that it was time for Vermont to lead the way in a similar fashion with regard to same-sex marriage.

Subsequently, the Vermont Supreme Court ruled unanimously that the state had to provide the same benefits and protections to gay and lesbian couples that it does for heterosexual couples who are married, including health insurance, tax breaks, inheritance rights, and hospital visitation rights. Grounding the ruling in "recognition of our common humanity," the court said that the legislature should pass a law allowing for either same-sex marriage or a form of domestic partnership that would entitle gay and lesbian couples to state recognition and benefits. A Times editorial of December 22, 1999, said the ruling was characterized by "eloquence and passion." While opponents branded the decision "judicial tyranny," supporters of the ruling noted that it was "the courts that ended race discrimination in civil marriage, not the people and not the legislatures first," according to a subsequent Times report of December 26, 1999.

In anticipation of the legislature's decision, traditional New England–style town meetings were held across Vermont, in addition to two mass public hearings at the State House that drew over 1,000 people each. As a Times report of February 3, 2000, explained, that number constituted an astonishing one-half of 1 percent of Vermont's total population of 600,000. To put the size of that number in perspective, the report explained that one-half of 1 percent of a state as large as New York would amount to a gathering of roughly 90,000 residents.

Advocates from both sides of the debate received extensive coverage, as noted in a *Times* report of February 6, 2000, which documented opponents arguing that such recognition would contradict the Bible and thousands of years of tradition. Supporters of same-sex marriage, some of whom were themselves church members, responded that the Bible and tradition had also condoned slavery and other practices that would never be seen as acceptable in contemporary society. In a subsequent report of March 8, 2000, opponents pointed to nature, arguing that only opposite-sex deer mated, while others expressed a kind of passive support for the new legislation, saying that it would not make a difference to them or to their children if same-sex partnerships were legally recognized by the state.

In response to the controversy, the Vermont legislature opted for a compromise, recognizing "civil unions" that would give gays and lesbians virtually all the benefits of marriage at the state level. The Vermont House voted 76–69 and the Senate 19–11 in favor of the measure. A *Times* report of March 17, 2000, noted that opponents called the civil unions marriage in all but name, registering their disapproval by distributing plastic ducks to lawmakers, recalling the old saying, "If it looks like a duck and walks like a duck, then it is a duck." The Roman Catholic bishop of Burlington called it "a very sad day for the majority of Vermonters," and a *Times* report of April 20, 2000, stated that several representatives were in tears. Although this display of emotion on the part of lawmakers may have reflected the momentous nature of the decision, it may also have been motivated by fears regarding their political futures, since opponents of the measure had repeatedly warned of retribution at the ballot box for those who voted in favor of the new law. Many representatives who had supported civil unions reported that their cars had been vandalized and that they had been the recipient of obscene gestures and harassment in person as well as through the mail. Several said that such responses had steeled their resolve for civil unions, explaining that such abusive behavior made them wonder if gays have had to deal with this sort of inappropriate behavior throughout their entire lives.

Although many were ecstatic with Vermont's decision, as indicated by the March 18, 2000, *Times* report "Gay Couples Are Welcoming Vermont Measure on Civil Union," some gay rights advocates were disappointed that the final decision fell short of actual marriage. Many noted that the bill represented progress but expressed concerns that civil unions were "separate but equal," paralleling the notorious practice of racial segregation through Jim Crow laws in the South, when African Americans were relegated to facilities separate from whites that were said to be equal but that were in fact often substandard. Similarly, a *Times* editorial of March 18, 2000, hailed civil unions as "a crucial step forward" if an "imperfect" one. Gov. Howard Dean said that the bill was a logical extension of Vermont's tradition of treating people equally, harking back at least as far as the eighteenth century, when the state constitution banned slavery well in advance of the nation's resolution of that issue in the Civil War. In a *Times* report of April 26, 2000, Dean called for the end of division and the beginning of a "healing process." A subsequent *Times* report of April 16, 2001, noted that Who Would Have Thought, Inc., a group opposed to civil unions, was invoking the traditional myth connecting same-sex relationships with child molestation by implying that Governor Dean supported pedophilia. Despite such opposition Dean was reelected handily. Nevertheless, seven Senate and twenty-nine House members who voted in favor of civil unions either retired or were defeated in the fall 2000 election cycle. Vermont eventually approved same-sex marriage nine years later.

As was the case with Hawaii, the recognition of civil unions in Vermont engendered strong reactions in other states. Nebraskans voted to amend their constitution to ban not only gay marriage but also civil unions and domestic partnerships. Some said that the language of the Nebraska amendment was so broad that it could invalidate binding contracts in place between same-sex couples such as powers of attorney, wills, and medical directives. Supporters of the ban argued that it was not about bigotry but simply a matter of drawing the line before "a man and a dog can get married."

The issue of gay and lesbian marriage was also becoming an issue of public concern throughout the world. In 2000 the Netherlands decided to recognize same-sex marriage, joining Belgium, which was the first country to offer legal recognition to such unions. Canada followed suit in 2003. A *Times* report of December 20, 2000, noted that Dutch law would not foster "marriage tourism," which occurs when people who are not residents of the country travel there to wed, because it stipulated that those married must be legal residents. However, Canada's marriage laws did not include a residency requirement. Because of its geographical proximity and close cultural and political ties to the United States, the decision in Canada reverberated strongly in the States. Marriages conducted in Canada have always been recognized in the United States. As a *Times* report of June 19, 2003, noted, the practice of comity between nations has typically meant that the United States recognizes marriages performed in foreign countries and can expect its own marriages to be recognized abroad.

IN FOCUS

Times Reports Gay Commitment Ceremonies

• •

On August 17, 2002, *The Times* announced that it would begin to include reports of gay commitment ceremonies in its Sunday Styles section alongside its longstanding coverage of heterosexual marriages, joining about seventy other newspapers across the country. Changing the name of the pages from "Weddings" to "Weddings/Celebrations," the new coverage includes same-sex commitment ceremonies as well as formal registrations of gay and lesbian partnerships. Stating that the change was prompted by the "newsworthiness of gay and lesbian commitment celebrations," Howell Raines, the executive editor of *The Times,* noted that coverage of the gay marriage issue would remain impartial in the rest of the paper. Letters to the editor that followed on August 20, 2002, expressed both pleasure and regret in the fact that *The Times'* decision to include gay commitment announcements would undoubtedly set an example for newspapers across the country to follow.

The first announcement appeared on September 1, 2002, when *The Times* noted that Daniel Gross and Steven Goldstein were affirming their partnership that day in a civil union ceremony in Vermont. The announcement followed the *Times'* general practice of including a story of how the couple met, in this case through a personal ad that Gross had placed and Goldstein answered, which read: "Nice Jewish boy, 5 feet 8 inches, 22, funny, well-read, dilettantish, self-deprecating, Ivy League, the kind of boy Mom fantasized about." Shortly after the couple began dating, Gross went home to visit his parents for Thanksgiving and his mother said that he seemed as if he was in love. "I am," he responded. "His name is Steven." "Oy," his mother responded and went silent. All of the parents now support the relationship, which was ten years old at the time of the ceremony. When asked why they had chosen to affirm the relationship after all those years, Goldstein said, "September 11 accelerated the process. We all began to think of our own mortality."

One year after the first announcement, more than fifty gay and lesbian couples had been featured in *The Times* and about 150 newspapers nationwide had begun to include gay commitment ceremonies alongside heterosexual marriage announcements.

From *The New York Times*

Letters to the Editor. "Gay Couples Unions." August 20, 2002.
Unsigned. "Times Will Begin Reporting Gay Couples' Ceremonies." August 18, 2002.
———. "Weddings/Celebrations; Daniel Gross, Steven Goldstein." September 1, 2002.

• •

By 2003 the number of states that had adopted laws prohibiting the recognition of same-sex marriages had risen to thirty-seven; however, a *Times* report of July 6, 2003, also noted that states such as Connecticut and Rhode Island had begun to consider permitting same-sex marriage. In addition, California adopted a domestic partnership law in 2003 that gave same-sex couples nearly all the rights and responsibilities of married couples at the state level, such as health coverage, child support, and alimony, as noted in a *Times* report of September 20, 2003.

In one of the biggest developments in this debate to date, on November 18, 2003, the supreme court of Massachusetts declared that same-sex couples have the right to marry on the grounds that the state constitution "forbids the creation of second-class citizens." The ruling, deemed a "political earthquake" by some experts, made Massachusetts the first state in the nation to grant legal recognition to same-sex marriages. Gov. Mitt Romney pledged to pursue an amendment to the state constitution that would overturn the ruling; however, an amendment of this sort could not take effect for at least three years, since it would have to be approved by two successive sessions of the legislature as well as by voters in a statewide referendum. As reported in *The Times* on May 17, 2004, same-sex marriages began to be performed in Massachusetts and efforts to amend the constitution subsequently failed.

Reaction to the decision at the national level was also strong. A *Times* report of November 19, 2003, noted that House majority leader Rep. Tom DeLay (R-TX) denounced the decision, calling the court "a runaway judiciary." Conservative leaders pledged to seek an amendment to the U.S. Constitution that would prohibit same-sex marriage. Such an amendment would require passage by at least a margin of two-thirds in the House and Senate as well as by three-fourths of the states. Many political observers predicted that the issue would significantly affect the 2004 presidential election. A February 8, 2004, *Times* report titled "Conservatives Using Issue of Gay Unions as a Rallying Tool" noted that conservative Christians felt that this issue was even more effective at mobilizing grassroots support than *Roe v. Wade* (the 1973 decision recognizing a woman's right to choose abortion). Some Republicans, however, argued that President George W. Bush would have to tread carefully to avoid scaring off moderate voters.

Although a *Times* report of November 20, 2003, noted that President Bush very clearly stated his opposition to the Massachusetts ruling, he had not yet declared support for an amendment to the U.S. Constitution barring same-sex marriage. In an editorial published on the same day, *The Times* declared that "the Constitution has never been amended to take away minority rights, and now would be a poor time to start." As stated in a *Times* opinion piece of November 20, 2003, "Toward a More Perfect Union," the adoption of domestic partnership laws in Hawaii and California, civil unions in Vermont, and same-sex marriage in Massachusetts meant that about 42 million residents, or about 15 percent of the population of the United States, lived in states offering some form of legal recognition to gay and lesbian couples. It was further estimated that nearly one in five same-sex couples lived in these states. Based on this reality, the piece went on to argue that "there is no evidence" that same-sex unions have any harmful impact on marriage, children, or society and that the recognition of same-sex couples in jurisdictions across the country has already shown that the

"doomsday claims" and distortions of opponents "have not come to pass."

SAME-SEX MARRIAGE IN CALIFORNIA

In response to President Bush's opposition to same-sex marriage in his 2004 State of the Union address, San Francisco mayor Gavin Newsom, who had attended the speech, took the unusual step of allowing same-sex marriages to be performed in the city of San Francisco, in apparent contradiction with a California state law that prohibited it. He argued that the state law was unconstitutional and that the U.S. Constitution required him to provide equal treatment to all his constituents. The first couple to be married was Del Martin, eighty-three and Phyllis Lyon, seventy-nine, two leaders in the gay and lesbian movement who had been living together for more than fifty years. While opponents said the marriages were worthless and that the mayor was acting above the law, supporters argued that Newsom was acting responsibly by taking a courageous stand against unjust legislation. In a February 19, 2004, *Times* piece, Newsom explained his position: "He [Bush] is the president of the United States, and I am just a guy who does stop signs and tries to revitalize parks. But I also know that I've got an obligation that I took seriously to defend the Constitution. There is simply no provision that allows me to discriminate."

In the twenty-eight days that followed, more than 4,000 same-sex couples were married while opponents argued that the new policy amounted to "municipal anarchy," as reported in a *Times* piece of February 14, 2004. At a news conference Newsom responded by saying, "I am here to tell you how encouraged we all are, how proud we are to stand up and fight for civil rights, stand up for individual rights, and stand up against discrimination and advance this cause." He said that his main objective was to put a "human face" on the gay marriage debate. Indeed, long lines of exultant couples waited outside city hall while listening to the San Francisco Gay Men's Choir singing "Going to the Chapel" and other jubilant songs. As noted in a February 17, 2004, *Times* report, many couples said that they viewed their participation as an act of civil disobedience. Not knowing how long the opportunity would remain, thousands of gay and lesbian couples from locations across the country came to San Francisco to be married. When a court initially refused requests from opponents to halt the marriages, *The Times* reported on February 18, 2004, that Jeff Adachi, the San Francisco public defender, responded by asking, "What better place for this to happen than in San Francisco?" an apparent reference to the city's large and visible gay and lesbian culture.

Two weeks after San Francisco began to recognize same-sex marriages, President Bush announced that he supported an amendment to the U.S. Constitution that would ban gay marriage. After noting that thirty-eight states and Congress had already passed defense of marriage laws, Bush argued that the decisions of activist judges in Massachusetts and the city officials in San Francisco to recognize same-sex marriages necessitated a new constitutional amendment. Arguing that marriage is "the most fundamental institution of civilization," he called for a constitutional prohibition on same-sex marriage while conceding that states should be free to recognize gay unions short of marriage. *The Times* responded with an editorial on February 25, 2004, asserting that such a constitutional amendment "would inject mean spiritedness and exclusion into the document embodying our highest principles and aspirations." A *Times* report of February 26, 2004, noted that the Democrats characterized the proposal for an amendment as an attempt to "drive a political wedge" into the presidential race. The amendment has yet to be approved by Congress. As a *Times* piece of July 14, 2004, noted, Republicans had difficulty gaining a simple majority to support it in the Senate as well as the House, let alone the two-thirds supermajority required for constitutional amendments.

Events in San Francisco apparently inspired other localities to recognize same-sex marriage, however briefly. In New Mexico a county near Albuquerque briefly issued licenses to same-sex couples, as did the town of New Paltz, New York, where, according to a *Times* report of February 27, 2004, Mayor Jason West said he was "willing to go to jail to uphold these marriages. This is a stand any decent American should take." West was eventually fined and charged with a misdemeanor for issuing nineteen illegal licenses. Marriage licenses were also issued for a time in Multnomah County, Oregon, which includes the city of Portland, and Asbury Park, New Jersey. As reported in *The Times* on March 27, 2004, Willamette County, Oregon, took the unusual step of refusing to issue any marriage licenses—to either gay or straight couples—in order to ensure equal treatment under the law.

The Times reported on March 13, 2004, that the supreme court of California had put an end to the dramatic period in which same-sex marriages had been recognized in San Francisco. Conservative groups rejoiced in the decision, while many gay couples were seen openly weeping in front of city hall. Predicting that such measures would help motivate traditionalist voters to go to the polls, experts anticipated that the issue of same-sex marriage would be central in swing states in the 2004 presidential election, including Oregon, Michigan, and Ohio, where there were anti–same sex marriage measures on the ballot. A Bush strategist said,

"It could well be what swings the election." Democratic strategists agreed that this could be the case, particularly in Ohio. On Election Day voters in Ohio backed the amendment by a large margin, leading many to attribute President Bush's razor-thin margin of victory in that state, as well as in the national election, to the anti–same sex marriage amendment. Eight other states also voted in favor of additional restrictions on same-sex marriage during the 2004 presidential election.

The debate did not subside after the election. In April 2005 voters in Kansas adopted a constitutional amendment banning same-sex marriage, making it the eighteenth state with a constitutional prohibition, while thirteen others were slated to consider similar amendments that year. Also in 2005, Connecticut joined Vermont in offering civil unions, while the predominantly Catholic country of Spain legalized gay marriage, with a *Times* report of July 1, 2005, noting that 55 to 65 percent of Spaniards supported same-sex marriage. In December 2006 New Jersey became the third state to adopt civil unions for gay couples. In a *Times* report of December 16, 2006 a seventy-seven-year-old woman who had been with her lesbian partner for thirty-six years lauded the development, saying, "I was in New York when the cops used to raid bars. You had to show papers. They'd say, 'Does your mother know who you are?'"

In a blockbuster ruling that rivaled the earlier Massachusetts decision in impact, the supreme court of California legalized same-sex marriage in May 2008, saying, "In view of the substance and significance of the fundamental constitutional right to form a family, the California Constitution must be properly interpreted to guarantee this right to all Californians, whether gay or heterosexual, and to same-sex couples, as well as opposite-sex couples." The decision was made by a split court, with a 4–3 vote on the ruling. While supporters of gay rights welcomed the decision, arguing that same-sex marriage harmed no one, opponents pledged to fight the ruling, saying that "the court brushed aside the entire history and meaning of marriage in our tradition."

More than 17,000 same-sex couples had been married in the state by the time a referendum on the issue appeared on the California ballot during the 2008 presidential election. The referendum, known as Proposition 8, passed with 52 percent of the vote, halting same-sex marriage in California for the second time. A *Times* report of November 6, 2008, noted that exit polls (surveys that asked voters to indicate how they had voted as they exited polling places) indicated that the large black and Hispanic turnout to support Barack Obama's candidacy for president had also supported Proposition 8.

California's Proposition 8 was a successful 2008 ballot initiative to amend California's constitution to allow marriage only between a man and a woman. Here, both supporters and opponents of the measure gather in Los Angeles in the days leading up to the election.

*Source: J. Emilio Flores/*The New York Times

Although he pledged during the campaign to be a champion for gay rights, Obama also opposed same-sex marriage. Financial backing of over $5 million from the Mormon Church in the final days of the campaign for Proposition 8 also was said to be a significant factor in its success, leading thousands to protest outside the headquarters of the Mormon Church in Salt Lake City, Utah. A *Times* report of November 9, 2008, noted that gay rights supporters carried signs with slogans such as "Mormons: Once persecuted, now persecutors."

Proposition 8 also led to a new wave of activism in the gay community, dubbed "Stonewall 2.0," referencing the beginning of the gay movement at the Stonewall Inn in June 1969, as well as the activists' use of new social networking tools available on the Internet to organize large numbers of protesters. Activists successfully encouraged gay rights supporters to join in a series of large-scale protests after Proposition 8 passed. When thousands turned out at demonstrations in

cities across the country, many gay rights activists called it a watershed moment on a par with Stonewall and protests held during the height of the AIDS crisis in the 1980s; they called it "the greatest civil rights battle of our generation," suggesting that the influence of this grassroots movement on the debate might well be significant. In addition, the constitutionality of Proposition 8 is currently being challenged in federal court. Despite these developments, activists on both sides of the debate acknowledged that the momentum had at least temporarily swung in favor of those who oppose same-sex marriage.

IOWA AND MAINE AND THE FUTURE OF THE SAME-SEX MARRIAGE DEBATE

In April 2009 the Iowa Supreme Court overturned a law that limited marriage to a man and a woman, becoming the first state outside of the Northeast or the West Coast to recognize same-sex partnerships. As noted in the April 26, 2009, *Times* report "Same-Sex Ruling Belies the Staid Image of Iowa," the state had refused to recognize slaves as property well before the Civil War and was the first to allow women to practice law, in addition to desegregating its schools nearly a century before the U.S. Supreme Court ruled in 1954 that the country must do so.

David Twombley, a sixty-seven-year-old gay man and member of one of the six couples that had challenged the Iowa law, said "There's been a perception that it couldn't happen here. But yes, it happened, right here in Iowa. There's something about that, about it happening in the heartland, that has got to accelerate this process for the whole country." One opponent of the ruling said, "I'm almost ready to up and leave Iowa and move back to Minnesota." A *Times* editorial of April 5, 2009, approvingly noted that Republican appointee Justice Mark Cady's decision argued that the law should be overturned because it "excluded a historically disfavored class of persons from a supremely

IN FOCUS

Gay Adoption

• •

The legality of gay adoption varies from state to state. As of this writing, ten states (California, Connecticut, Illinois, Indiana, Maine, Massachusetts, New Jersey, New York, Oregon, and Vermont) and the District of Columbia allow same-sex couples to jointly adopt children. Nine states (California, Colorado, Connecticut, Illinois, Massachusetts, New Jersey, New York, Pennsylvania, and Vermont) and the District of Columbia also permit second-parent adoptions, meaning that a gay person is allowed to adopt the child of his or her partner. In addition, certain jurisdictions in several other states allow joint and second-parent adoptions.

The rules governing gay adoptions include outright prohibition in some states. For example, Florida prohibits all adoptions by single or coupled homosexuals, while Mississippi bans adoption by couples of the same gender. Court rulings have been issued in Kentucky, Nebraska, Ohio, and Wisconsin that prohibit same-sex couples from undertaking second-parent adoptions in those states. Arkansas and Utah prohibit adoptions by any individual who lives with an unmarried sexual partner, whether opposite or same-sex.

Despite continuing restrictions in some states, it is clear that gay adoption has become much more widely accepted as the gay rights movement has gained strength over the past forty years. Perhaps one sign of this acceptance is the 2010 opening of an Off Broadway play focused on gay adoption, *The Kid.* Based on a memoir by nationally syndicated sex columnist Dan Savage, the play chronicles the trials and tribulations of Savage and his partner, Terry, as they adopt a baby of a sixteen-year-old unmarried girl living on the streets of Portland, Oregon. A *Times* reviewer noted that the play "keeps telling its audience, 'Gays, they're just like us,'" as the audience comes to "realize how genuinely conventional Dan and Terry are." The lyricist for the play, Jack Lechner, commented, "A musical needs a great big protagonist with a great big want. . . . The dream of having a family is about as big a hope as you can get."

From *The New York Times*

Brantley, Ben. "Just Like Other Dads (Well, Almost)." May 11, 2010.
Healy, Patrick. "A Gay Adoption Becomes a Musical." May 7, 2010.

• •

important civil institution without a constitutionally sufficient justification."

As a *Times* report of April 5, 2009, stated, the Iowa
decision appeared to turn the momentum back toward
those favoring same-sex marriage. Activists in New England
initiated a campaign called "Six by Twelve," identifying
the goal of having all six states in New England (Vermont,
Massachusetts, Connecticut, Maine, New Hampshire, and
Rhode Island) recognize same-sex marriage by 2012. After
Maine and New Hampshire legalized same-sex marriage in
May 2009, attaining this goal seemed inevitable to many,
with only Rhode Island remaining. However, in the November
2009 election, the people of Maine rejected same-sex marriage in a statewide vote, reversing the momentum in the
debate once again and becoming the thirty-first state to block
gay marriage through a public referendum.

As of this writing, same-sex marriage is legal in five
states and Washington, D.C. In addition, nine states offer a
form of civil union or similar benefits to gay couples. Forty-
one states ban same-sex marriage, while nineteen prohibit
recognition of gay civil unions. A *Times* news analysis of
December 3, 2009, argued that while public support of
gay rights was surely increasing, the push for gay marriage
may have come too fast for some. Noting that young people
are most supportive of change on this issue, the analysis
anticipated greater acceptance of same-sex marriage in
the future. Others, such as Republican strategist Matthew
Dowd, counseled the lesbian, gay, bisexual, and transgender
(LGBT) movement to campaign for civil unions, rather than
marriage, on a state-by-state basis, saying, "It would allow
the public to see that crazy things aren't going to happen.
And over time, they'll say, 'What's the difference between
civil unions and marriage?'" While Dowd may or may not be
correct, forty years of *Times* coverage of this debate suggests
that the momentum is likely to swing back in favor of supporters of same-sex marriage before long. It is too soon to
tell whether advocates of same-sex marriage will retain the
advantage in the next round of this debate in some more permanent fashion or whether the momentum will again swing
back to their opponents.

BIBLIOGRAPHY

Badgett, M. V. Lee. *When Gay People Get Married: What
    Happens When Societies Legalize Same-Sex Marriage.*
    New York: New York University Press, 2009.
Mello, Michael. *Legalizing Gay Marriage.* Philadelphia:
    Temple University Press, 2004.
Pinello, Daniel R. *America's Struggle for Same-Sex
    Marriage.* Cambridge, MA: Cambridge University
    Press, 2006.
Snyder-Hall, Claire. *Gay Marriage and Democracy: Equality
    for All.* Lanham, MD: Rowman and Littlefield, 2006.

FROM *THE NEW YORK TIMES*

Associated Press. "Court Won't Let Men Wed." January 10,
    1971.
———. "Mormon Church Draws Protest over Marriage
    Act." November 9, 2008.
Barringer, Felicity. "Media; National Spotlight for Vermont
    Paper." April 16, 2001.
Belluck, Pam. "Same-Sex Marriage: The Overview;
    Hundreds of Same-Sex Couples Wed in
    Massachusetts." May 17, 2004.
Bohlen, Celestine. "Koch Widens City's Policy on Family."
    July 10, 1989.
Brozan, Nadine. "Woman's Hospital Visit Marks Gay Rights
    Fight." February 8, 1989.
Davey, Monica. "Same-Sex Ruling Belies the Staid Image of
    Iowa." April 26, 2009.
Fahim, Kareem. "In New Jersey, Gay Couples Ponder
    Nuances of Measure to Allow Civil Unions."
    December 16, 2006.
Goldberg, Carey. "Vermont Supreme Court Takes Up Gay
    Marriage." November 19, 1998.
———. "The Nation; Redefining a Marriage Made New in
    Vermont." December 26, 1999.
———. "Forced into Action on Gay Marriage, Vermont
    Finds Itself Deeply Split." February 3, 2000.
———. "State House Journal; A Kaleidoscopic Look at
    Attitudes on Gay Marriage." February 6, 2000.
———. "Vermont Town Meeting Turns into Same-Sex
    Union Forum." March 8, 2000.
———. "Vermont's House Backs Wide Rights for Gay
    Couples." March 17, 2000.
———. "Gay Couples Are Welcoming Vermont Measure on
    Civil Union." March 18, 2000.
———. "Vermont Senate Votes for Gay Civil Unions." April
    20, 2000.
———. "Vermont Gives Final Approval to Same-Sex
    Unions." April 26, 2000.
Goodnough, Arby. "A Push Is On for Same-Sex Marriage
    Rights across New England." April 5, 2009.
Hulse, Carl. "Gay-Marriage Ban Faces Loss in Early Vote."
    July 14, 2004.

Kershaw, Sarah. "Adversaries on Gay Rights Vow State-by-State Fight." July 6, 2003.

Kirkpatrick, David D. "Conservatives Using Issue of Gay Unions as Rallying Tool." February 8, 2004.

Marquis, Christopher. "U.S. Gays Who Marry in Canada Face Hurdles." June 19, 2003.

Marshall, Carolyn. "Rushing to Say 'I Do' Before City Is Told 'You Can't.'" February 17, 2004.

McKinley, Jesse, and Laurie Goodstein. "Bans in 3 States on Gay Marriage." November 6, 2008.

McLean, Renwick. "Spain Legalizes Gay Marriage: Law Is Among the Most Liberal." July 1, 2005.

Murphy, Dean E. "Bid to Stop San Francisco from Letting Gays Marry." February 14, 2004.

———. "Bay Area Judges Stop Short of Banning Gay Weddings." February 18, 2004.

———. "San Francisco Mayor Exults in Move on Gay Marriage." February 19, 2004.

———. "San Francisco Sees Tide Shift in the Battle Over Marriage." March 13, 2004.

Nagourney, Adam. "Same-Sex Marriage: News Analysis; A Thorny Issue for 2004 Race." November 19, 2003.

Rubenstein, William B., and R. Bradley Sears. "Toward a More Perfect Union." November 20, 2003.

Seelye, Katherine Q. "Conservatives Mobilize against Ruling on Gay Marriage." November 20, 2003.

Tavernise, Sabrina, and Thomas Crampton. "Gay Couples to Be Wed Today in New Paltz, Mayor Declares." February 27, 2004.

Toner, Robin. "Democrats Join Fray on Marriage." February 26, 2004.

Turner, Wallace. "Couple Law Asked for San Francisco." November 28, 1982.

———. "Partnership Law Vetoed on Coast." December 10, 1982.

Unsigned. "Student Adopted by His Roommate." August 26, 1971.

———. "Homosexual Couple Contest I.R.S. Ban on a Joint Return." January 5, 1975.

———. "As New York Vote on Equal Rights Nears, Two Sides Speak Out." September 18, 1975.

———. "Polls Show Voters in Doubt on E.R.A." November 2, 1975.

———. "Defeat of Equal Rights Bills Traced to Women's Votes." November 6, 1975.

———. "Florida House Votes Homosexual Controls." May 31, 1977.

———. "Hawaii Gives Gay Couples Marital Benefits." July 10, 1997.

———. "Hawaii Court Lets Gay Marriage Ban Stand." December 10, 1999.

———. "Hawaii's Ban on Gay Marriage." December 20, 1999.

———. "Vermont's Momentous Ruling." December 22, 1999.

———. "Legal Unions for Gays in Vermont." March 18, 2000.

———. "Same-Sex Dutch Couples Gain Marriage and Adoption Rights." December 20, 2000.

———. "National Briefing/West: California: New Domestic Partner Rights. September 20, 2003.

———. "A Victory for Gay Marriage." November 20, 2003.

———. "Putting Bias into the Constitution." February 25, 2004.

———. "Iowa Decency." April 5, 2009.

Van Gelder, Lawrence. "Termination of Alimony to Lesbian Adds to Legal Debate." February 27, 1979.

Zernike, Kate. "Gay? No Marriage Licenses Here. Straight? Ditto." March 27, 2004.

———. "News Analysis; Amid Small Victories, Advocates Lose the Marquee Battles." December 3, 2009.

SAME-SEX COUPLES LEGALLY MARRY IN COLORADO

On March 26, 1975, two men obtained marriage licenses and were subsequently married in Boulder, Colorado, marking the first time that same-sex couples were married in the United States without meeting an immediate challenge. Several other same-sex marriages followed across Boulder County. These marriages were part of a national movement designed to challenge laws that discriminated against homosexuals. While some legal experts expected a higher court to strike down the Boulder marriages, others claimed that they were defensible under the U.S. Constitution's guarantee of equal protection under the law. The Colorado attorney general said that he believed the marriages were not valid because legally marriage can only be between a man and a woman; however, he added that he would not challenge licenses that had already been granted.

When same-sex couples in other localities such as Phoenix tried to obtain marriage licenses, they were immediately charged with filing false documents. The earliest reported challenge occurred in Minnesota in 1971, when the marriage attempt of two men was denied by the state supreme court. While most states at the time did not specifically prohibit same-sex marriage, such unions remained controversial because the language of the law concerning marriage typically refers to male-female couples.

Same-sex couples married in Boulder County touted the psychological benefits of state recognition of their marriages. One gay man said that marriage to his Australian partner would allow them to stay together in the United States. Their minister called the development in Boulder "a breakthrough," adding, "I feel like I imagine Moses felt when he split the Red Sea."

The licenses in Boulder County were issued by County Clerk Clela Rorex, who said that while she knew very little about homosexuality, "it's not my business why people get married." She added, "No minority should be discriminated against." In the wake of her actions, Rorex received nearly 100 obscene phone calls, many of which included biblical references. William Wise, the county's assistant district attorney, commented, "Who is it going to hurt?"

APRIL 27, 1975
HOMOSEXUAL WEDDINGS STIR CONTROVERSY IN COLORADO
By GRACE LICHTENSTEIN
Special to the New York Times

BOULDER, Colo., April 25—A few weeks ago, two persons from Colorado Springs obtained, without fanfare, a marriage license at the County Clerk's office here. Then they were married. The wedding would have passed unnoticed, except that the partners were homosexual men.

Their action has touched off a string of successful applications by couples of the same sex for marriage licenses, a well-publicized homosexual marriage in a Denver church, a series of obscene telephone calls to the Boulder County Clerk, and a legal brouhaha that could extend far beyond the courts of this somewhat liberal university town—perhaps eventually, as far as the United States Supreme Court.

Moreover, the move toward legally sanctioned marriages between persons of the same sex is considered by homosexual rights groups to be an important part of their national drive to overcome what they regard as discriminatory laws.

Legal Precedents

Those familiar with the situation say this appears to be the first time a series of couples of the same sex have obtained marriage licenses in the United States without being immediately challenged. However, most of the legal precedents in other states are against such licenses.

One expert in family law says higher courts would probably strike down the Boulder licenses. But a homosexual rights legal counsel argues that such licenses are defensible under the 14th amendment which guarantees equal protection under the law.

J.D. MacFarlane, the Colorado Attorney General, said today that, in his opinion, the Boulder licenses were not valid, because, in his interpretation of the state law, a legal marriage can only be that between a man and a woman. However, he is not planning a court challenge to the license already issued.

'Phenomenal Benefits'

Meanwhile, Colorado has become a mini-Nevada for homosexual couples. Six couples—two women and four men—obtained licenses from Boulder County Clerk Clela Rorex as of Tuesday.

Anthony Sullivan, a 33-year-old Australian, clasped the hand of his spouse, Richard F. Adams, 28, of Los Angeles, after their wedding at the First Unitarian Church of Denver last Monday and said that the psychological benefits of their union were "absolutely phenomenal."

He also said that he married Mr. Adams to test the immigration laws that permit a foreigner to remain in this country if he marries a citizen. Mr. Adams added that they "wanted to have the full benefits of other married couples—income tax returns, inheritance, wills, and so on."

'A Breakthrough'

Their ceremony was a simple one derived from the Book of Common Prayer, performed in a chapel almost empty except television crews and a handful of well-wishers. The Rev. Robert Sirico of the Metropolitan Community Church of Los Angeles, part of a national organization of predominantly homosexual churches, officiated with the help of a woman minister, Freda Smith. They changed the words "husbands" and "wives" to "spouses" with Mr. Sirico inserting the phrase "as long as there is love" before "til death do us part."

Afterward, the two men smiled, kissed, held hands, and spoke to reporters. They were dressed nearly identically in dungarees, and white shirts decorated with a sprig of flowers.

The minister, a native of Brooklyn, called the licenses and the marriage "a breakthrough," remarking with a grin, "I feel like I imagine Moses felt when he split the Red Sea."

Mr. Sirico and other same-sex spokesmen note that thousands of homosexual couples have been united in religious ceremonies in recent years without benefit of a government document. Others have received licenses by having one partner pose as a member of the opposite sex.

Rejected by Courts

Boulder was not the first county to issue a license to a couple of the same sex. In January, two men in Phoenix were granted a license, but the Maricopa County Attorney charged one man with filing false documents, since he had filled out the woman's section. Last month a local court voided the marriage.

According to Henry H. Foster, professor of law at New York University and a vice-president of the family law section of the American Bar Association, most states do not specifically prohibit marriage between persons of the same sex because the language of the law is so clear in referring to male-female couples.

Test cases have all gone against couples of the same sex. The most important occurred in Minnesota in 1971, when two men attempting to get a marriage license were turned down by the state's highest court. The United States Supreme Court then refused to review their case. The two men are still trying to file a joint income tax return.

In New York, spokesmen for both the City Corporation Counsel and the Manhattan City Clerk said they interpreted the state law's definition of marriage as a union of a man and a woman, making marriages between persons of the same sex illegal.

Clela Rorex, the Boulder County Clerk, took the opposite position March 26 when she issued the first same-sex license in Colorado after getting a favorable opinion from William C. Wise, the county's assistant district attorney.

"I don't profess to be knowledgeable about homosexuality or even understand it," she said. "But it's not my business why people get married. No minority should be discriminated against."

Obscene Phone Calls

By last Tuesday, she had issued marriage licenses to six homosexual couples. She had also received nearly 100 phone calls, many of them obscene. "Most of the nasty calls centered around renditions from the Bible," she said, adding that others have told her, "I hope you suffer because God doesn't like this."

Callers have telephoned Mr. Wise in the middle of the night with proposals of marriage and proposals of something else, he said.

Although Boulder has a reputation as a liberal bastion, there is already talk of taking a vote to recall Miss Rorex from office. Last year, the city recalled a councilman and nearly recalled its mayor over their advocacy of an equal rights law for homosexuals.

To demonstrate his disgust of the situation, one local cowboy marched to the County Clerk's office last week with a request to marry his favorite horse. The request was denied on the grounds that the horse, an 8-year-old mare, was underage.

Subject to Harassment

The homosexual couples themselves have been subject to harassment and ridicule. A homosexual man from Wyoming who received a license from Boulder to marry was dismissed from his job. And Mr. Sullivan, the Australian homosexual who was married last Monday, has been disowned and denounced by his mother.

The legal issue, according to Professor Foster, boils down to the classic definition of marriage, written in the eighteen-sixties by Lord Penzance of Britain: "A voluntary union for life of one man to one woman to the exclusion of all others."

Miss Rorex, like members of homosexual rights groups, thinks that could be resolved by eliminating the gender words. For same-sex couples, she has crossed off "male" and "female" on the Boulder applications, substituting "person."

"Who is it going to hurt?" asked Mr. Wise.

SAN FRANCISCO BECOMES FIRST MAJOR CITY TO ADOPT REGISTRY FOR UNMARRIED DOMESTIC PARTNERS

In 1989 the city of San Francisco became the first major city to allow homosexuals and unmarried heterosexual couples to register formally as domestic partners, paralleling the process of obtaining a marriage license. The law provided hospital visitation rights to all unmarried partners who are registered with the city. Registered city employees were granted the same bereavement leave as other, married city workers. The registry was expected to have a significant impact, owing to the size of San Francisco's gay community and the incidence of AIDS within it.

Couples who registered with the city had to live together in a committed relationship, share household expenses, and pay a $35 registry fee. Other cities such as Boston and New York were expected to follow suit. In 1982 San Francisco had voted to extend health care benefits to domestic partners, but the move was vetoed by Mayor Dianne Feinstein. The Catholic Archbishop of San Francisco called both the health care proposal and the new registry an attack on marriage and family life.

Smaller California cities such as Berkeley, Santa Cruz, and West Hollywood also recognized domestic partnerships at the time, some of which include health benefits for their city workers, while Los Angeles allowed unmarried city workers to use sick and bereavement leave to attend to the illness or death of a domestic partner. San Francisco mayor Gavin Newsom created headlines in 2004 when he called for the city to grant marriage licenses to same-sex couples. Thousands of people came to the city to get married, although the licenses were later invalidated.

MAY 31, 1989
SAN FRANCISCO GRANTS RECOGNITION TO COUPLES WHO AREN'T MARRIED
By KATHERINE BISHOP
Special to the New York Times

SAN FRANCISCO, May 30—The city's Board of Supervisors today passed an ordinance giving legal recognition to the "domestic partnership" of homosexuals and unmarried heterosexual couples.

By a vote of 9 to 0, with two board members absent, San Francisco became the first major city to provide for the public registration of these relationships in the same way that other couples file marriage licenses.

The immediate impact of the measure will be to extend to domestic partnerships the same hospital visitation rights accorded to married couples. In addition, city employees in a domestic partnership will now have the same bereavement leave policy as married city workers. Both of these benefits are crucial issues to San Francisco's gay community, which has been hit hard by the AIDS epidemic.

The ordinance also mandates that the city and county, in instituting new policies or practices, cannot treat marital status differently from domestic partnership.

Mayor Art Agnos is expected to sign the ordinance within 10 days, a spokesman said.

Rules for Recognition

The ordinance defines domestic partnerships as "two people who have chosen to share one another's lives in an intimate and committed relationship." The two must live together and be jointly responsible for basic living expenses; neither may be married to anyone else. The couple must file a declaration of domestic partnership with the county clerk and pay a $35 fee. The partners must also file a notice of termination if their relationship ends.

Harry G. Britt, the president of the Board of Supervisors and a leader in the gay community here who sponsored the ordinance, predicted that other cities would now follow San Francisco's example. "There was a nervousness about this issue that needed to be overcome," he said.

Gay rights groups in Boston and New York are already organizing efforts to have such measures adopted.

Arthur Leonard, a professor at New York Law School, said a group called the Family Diversity Coalition is meeting with members of the New York City Council to find a sponsor for the measure. He also said candidates for Mayor would be questioned on the issue at a forum tonight sponsored by the Stonewall Democratic Club, a predominantly gay political group.

Veto of 1982 Measure

In 1982 the San Francisco board, by a vote of 8 to 3, passed a measure that extended health insurance coverage to domestic partners, but it was vetoed by Mayor Dianne Feinstein. Two years later she also rejected the recommendation of her Task Force on Equal Benefits to extend health benefits to the partners of city employees.

In both 1982 and this year the Roman Catholic Archdiocese of San Francisco strongly objected to the ordinances. In a statement issued May 23, Archbishop John Quinn called the current measure an attack on marriage and family life.

The current measure gives a committee 90 days to create a plan under which the domestic partners of city workers may be included in health insurance coverage. The plan would have to be adopted by the Health Services System, which administers health benefits offered to city employees.

The workers themselves would bear the cost of adding domestic partners to the plan because San Francisco does not pay for health insurance for the spouses or dependants of most city employees.

Three smaller California cities, Berkeley, Santa Cruz and West Hollywood, have already passed ordinances that to some degree recognize domestic partnerships. In 1985, for example, Berkeley extended health benefits to the unmarried partners of city workers.

Last year Los Angeles allowed unmarried city employees to use sick leave and bereavement leave upon the illness or death of a domestic partner if the couple has privately registered with the city after living together at least a year.

- -

STATE APPEALS COURT RECOGNIZES PARTNER RIGHTS SIMILAR TO SPOUSAL RIGHTS

A Minnesota appeals court gave Karen Thompson guardianship of her lesbian partner, Sharon Kowalski, who had been physically and mentally disabled as a result of a car accident caused by a drunk driver. Because guardianship rights of this sort would typically be taken for granted by married couples, the case was hailed by supporters as granting to a gay partner rights "tantamount to those of a spouse."

Kowalski required extensive care since an automobile accident left her quadriplegic and brain damaged. In 1985 her father won guardianship rights and denied Thompson any visitation. Thompson challenged the decision, causing her plight to become a high-profile issue in the national gay rights movement. The appeals court noted that "Thompson's suitability for guardianship was overwhelmingly clear from the testimony of Sharon's doctors and caretakers."

Noting that the victory was seven years in the making, William Rubenstein, director of the ACLU's Gay Rights Project, said, "This case exemplifies the difficulties lesbians and gay men have in safeguarding our relationships." He added, "It's underscored why we need legal protection, and created a terrific incentive to fight for these kinds of marital rights and recognition of domestic partnership."

The decision was handed down on the twelfth anniversary of Kowalski and Thompson's commitment ceremony. Kowalski's parents indicated that they would not visit their daughter while she was living with Thompson.

DECEMBER 18, 1991
DISABLED WOMAN'S CARE GIVEN TO LESBIAN PARTNER
By TAMAR LEWIN

After a seven-year legal battle that became a rallying cause for gay rights groups, a Minnesota appeals court yesterday granted guardianship of Sharon Kowalski, a 35-year-old woman left brain-damaged and quadriplegic in a 1983 car accident, to her lesbian lover.

"This seems to be the first guardianship case in the nation in which an appeals court recognized a homosexual partner's rights as tantamount to those of a spouse," said M. Sue Wilson, the lawyer for Ms. Kowalski's lover, Karen Thompson.

Ms. Thompson had fought since 1984 to be named guardian, over the objections of Donald and Della Kowalski, who said their daughter had never told them she was a lesbian and who barred Ms. Thompson from visiting their daughter's nursing home for several years after the accident.

A Cause Taken Up

Ms. Thompson's fight to be reunited with her lover became a cause celebre among groups advocating gay rights and rights for the disabled. These groups organized

vigils and processions in 21 cities on Aug. 7, 1988, which was called "National Free Sharon Kowalski Day."

"This case exemplifies the difficulties lesbians and gay men have in safeguarding our relationships," said William Rubenstein, director of the American Civil Liberties Union's Lesbian and Gay Rights Project. "The remarkable thing about this case is not that Karen Thompson finally won guardianship, but that it took her seven years to do so, when guardianship rights for a heterosexual married couple would be taken for granted."

Mr. Rubenstein said the Thompson case had struck a responsive chord among homosexuals, coming just as many gay men whose partners had died of AIDS were finding that they had no legal rights to stay in their apartments, share in the estates or decide where their partners would be buried.

"This case, and AIDS, have been the defining events of the 1980's in this area," Mr. Rubenstein said. "It's underscored why we need legal protection, and created a terrific incentive to fight for these kinds of marital rights and recognition of domestic partnership."

The Minnesota Court of Appeals said the St. Louis County District Court in Duluth had abused its discretion in denying Ms. Thompson's petition to become Ms. Kowalski's caretaker and instead appointing a third party, who was a close friend of Ms. Kowalski's parents.

"Thompson's suitability for guardianship was overwhelmingly clear form the testimony of Sharon's doctors and caretakers," the appeals court said.

A Battle's History

Ms. Kowalski, a former high school gym teacher, has required around-the-clock care since the automobile accident left her nearly paralyzed, with severe short-term memory loss and impaired ability to speak.

Her father, a retired mining foreman, won sole guardianship in July 1985, moved his daughter to a nursing home in Hibbing, Minn., and barred any visits by Ms. Thompson, a 44-year-old physical education professor at St. Cloud State University.

Over the next three years, Ms. Thompson filed appeals in local, state and Federal courts, seeking to change the guardianship decision and charging that Ms. Kowalski was being denied access to the therapy she needed.

In September 1988, Judge Robert Campbell of the St. Louis County District Court ordered a comprehensive evaluation of Ms. Kowalski, and she was moved to a Duluth nursing home, where Ms. Thompson was allowed to resume visits to the woman with whom she had exchanged wedding bands.

Last year, Mr. Kowalski resigned his guardianship, citing heart problems and weariness with the extended court proceedings. In April, Judge Campbell awarded guardianship to a third party, Karen Tomberlin, Ms. Kowalski's high school track and volleyball coach.

Judge Campbell likened Ms. Kowalski to a child over whom divorcing parents were battling and concluded that she could not express a reliable preference for guardianship. But in reversing that decision, the appeals court disagreed.

Deciding Kowalski's Choice

"All the medical testimony established that Sharon has the capacity reliably to express a preference in this case, and she has clearly chosen to return home with Thompson if possible," the court said. "This choice is further supported by the fact that Thompson and Sharon are a family of affinity, which ought to be accorded respect."

The appeals court also noted that Ms. Thompson was the only person willing or able to care for Ms. Kowalski outside an institution and that she had built a house fully accessible by wheelchair.

The court also rejected Judge Campbell's finding that Ms. Thompson had acted contrary to Ms. Kowalski's best interests by making public their lesbian relationship.

Ms. Tomberlin, reached yesterday at Greenway High School in Coleraine, Minn., said she had not seen the opinion or decided whether she would appeal.

"The worst thing about the decision is that Karen apparently wants to bring Sharon home to St. Cloud, but because of the years of hurt and pain, Sharon's parents have said they will never go see her again if she lives there," she said. "The void is too deep."

Ms. Tomberlin said she had not been able to reach the Kowalskis to discuss the opinion, and a call to their home was answered by a machine. Ms. Thompson's lawyer said yesterday that her client did plan to bring Ms. Kowalski to St. Cloud, about 60 miles northwest of Minneapolis, where they had lived together before the crash.

"This decision came out on the 12th anniversary of the commitment ceremony where they exchanged rings and promised to love each other their whole lives," said Ms. Wilson, the lawyer. "Karen and Sharon talked today about what they were going to do to celebrate. Sharon doesn't have the short-term memory to remember what happened an hour ago, but she does remember Karen and the past, and that she is a lesbian."

HAWAII MAY BECOME FIRST STATE TO RECOGNIZE SAME-SEX MARRIAGE

In 1993 the supreme court of Hawaii issued a ruling indicating that a ban on same-sex marriage may violate the state constitution's prohibition against sex discrimination. The Hawaii Supreme Court has a reputation of recognizing broader rights in a variety of areas under its own state constitution as compared with the federal Constitution. Noting that "marriage is a basic civil right," the Hawaiian high court sent the case back down to the trial level, where the state was asked to defend its decision to exclude same-sex couples. The court said that the strictest standard of review should be applied to evaluate the state's reasoning.

Relying on a 1967 U.S. Supreme Court ruling that found state bans on mixed-race marriages unconstitutional, the Hawaii Supreme Court rejected an argument that same-sex marriage bans do not entail discrimination because both men and women are not allowed to marry members of the same sex under current law. In the 1967 case opponents of mixed-race marriage made a similar argument asserting that laws prohibiting such marriages were constitutional because both whites and blacks were prohibited from marrying members of the opposite race. That argument was rejected by the U.S. Supreme Court on the grounds that it was grounded in bias that favored white people. The Hawaii Supreme Court extended the logic of that case to cases involving same-sex marriage.

The move fueled speculation that Hawaii might become the first state in the country to recognize same-sex marriages, entitling couples to tax breaks as well as health and survivor benefits. Many believed that recognition of same-sex marriage by one state could have implications for the entire country, since states typically recognize marriages that have been performed in other states even when they don't meet the legal requirements of the recognizing state. The ACLU's Gay Rights project director, William Rubenstein, called the decision a "major breakthrough," while Hawaii attorney general Robert Marks said that he was "not ready to conclude that this is lost." In 1998 voters in Hawaii passed a constitutional amendment that permitted the state legislature to define marriage as being between a man and a woman. In 2010 Hawaii governor Linda Lingle vetoed legislation that would have legalized same-sex unions (but not marriage).

MAY 7, 1993
IN HAWAII, STEP TOWARD LEGALIZING MARRIAGE
By JEFFREY SCHMALZ

Hawaii's highest court has taken a long step toward making the state the first in the country to recognize marriages between couples of the same sex, ruling that a ban on such marriages may well violate the State Constitution's prohibition against sex discrimination.

In a 3-to-1 ruling on Wednesday in a case brought by three homosexual couples, the State Supreme Court stopped short of striking down the ban, instead sending the case back to a trial court for review.

But in the majority opinion, Justice Steven H. Levinson wrote that "marriage is a basic civil right" and that "on its face and as applied," the Hawaii law "denies same-sex couples access to the marital status and its concomitant rights and benefits."

Legal experts said the case would not wind up in the United States Supreme Court because it was based solely on state law. But if Hawaii were to recognize gay marriages, the decision would have implications nationwide.

Crossing State Lines

No state currently allows such marriages. But each state recognizes marriages performed in another state. Thus, unless other states acted to change current practices, gay couples married in Hawaii would have to be recognized as married couples in other states, thereby entitling them to the tax breaks, health benefits and survivor benefits that accrue to married partners.

Robert Marks, Hawaii's Attorney General, said his office was still reviewing the ruling.

"I'm not ready to conclude that this is lost," he said, adding: "I'm no homophobe, but I think the issue should be left to the Legislature. I think it will come as a surprise to the Legislature that when they put in the Equal Rights Amendment, this is how it would be interpreted."

But gay advocates were ecstatic. "This is a major breakthrough," said William Rubenstein, director of the American Civil Liberties Union's national homosexual rights project. "This is the first court decision to give serious consideration to gay marriage."

The ruling follows a pattern in Hawaii over the last few years, since appointments to the court by Gov. John Waihee 3d, a Democrat. In recent rulings, the court has tended to use the State Constitution to impose broader rights than those interpreted under the Federal Constitution by the United States Supreme Court. In October, for example, the state court ruled that protections against unreasonable search and seizure barred some types of airport searches that are permitted by the Supreme Court.

This week's ruling came in a suit filed in 1991 by a gay male couple and two lesbian couples, who asserted that the ban on same-sex marriage violated their rights of privacy and equal protection. In October 1991, the lower court, the First Circuit Court, granted the state's motion to dismiss the suit, holding that the ban on same-sex marriage was well within the state's regulatory powers.

The Supreme Court criticized the lack of a thorough review by the lower court and applied the strictest standard for it to meet in rehearing the case.

'Compelling State Interest'

In finding that the ban probably violates the state constitutional prohibition against sex discrimination, the court required the Government to provide a "compelling state interest" that justifies the ban. If the court had not invoked sex discrimination, the lowered standard would have been "any reasonable justification."

In a dissent, Justice Walter M. Heen rejected the finding of sex bias in the law, saying the intent was not bias but a recognition that heterosexual couples further the propagation of the species. He said there was no bias because men and women were affected equally by the ban on gay marriages.

The majority opinion dismissed that argument and relied heavily on a 1967 Supreme Court ruling that overturned bans on mixed-race marriages. Supporters of that ban had argued that it was not discriminatory because it equally affected blacks and whites. The Supreme Court rejected that argument, as Hawaii's State Supreme Court pointed out Wednesday, extending the logic of the racial decision to one involving same-sex marriages.

"We reject this exercise in tortured and conclusory sophistry," the state court's opinion concluded.

The case was not the first time sex discrimination had been argued by gay-rights advocates. It has been raised for a quarter of a century without success.

But some advocates said yesterday that the ruling was consistent with a trend that has been building in family law: the growing recognition that gay couples constitute families.

In 1989, New York State's highest court recognized gay couples as a family for purposes of rent-control protection. In Minnesota, in 1991, Karen Thompson was appointed legal guardian of her lesbian lover, Sharon Kowalski, who had been paralyzed in a car accident. In the last 10 years, about 30 municipalities, including New York City and San Francisco, have adopted policies recognizing gay couples as "domestic partners" and granting them limited benefits.

- -

States Respond to Same-Sex Marriage Possibility in Hawaii

In 1995 Utah became the first state to pass a law that denied recognition to marriages performed in other states that do not conform to its own marriage laws. The move by the Utah legislature was widely understood to be a response to the possibility that Hawaii might soon recognize same-sex marriages. Similar bills were introduced in other states, including South Dakota and Alaska.

Gay rights advocates denounced these developments, arguing that "radical-right legislators will attempt to block recognition of marriages once we win them in the future." Opponents of same-sex marriage argued, "Same-sex couples do not qualify. It might be called a partnership, but if it's called marriage, it's a counterfeit version." While opponents argued that same-sex marriage undermines family life, advocates noted with irony that gays are often "labeled promiscuous, but when we ask for recognition of our long-term relationships, we're denied."

States have long recognized marriages performed in other states, even when the terms of such marriages are different from their own. The Utah law was thought by some to have abridged the Full Faith and Credit Clause of the U.S. Constitution, which says that each state will recognize, or give full faith and credit, to public acts, records, and judicial proceedings of other states. Some legislators argued that states may declare exceptions under the clause. The director of the South Dakota Gay, Lesbian and Bisexual Foundation noted that similar arguments were made in an earlier era when some states relied on antimiscegenation laws that made mixed-race marriages illegal in their states, in order to avoid recognizing mixed-race marriages that had been performed in other states.

MARCH 15, 1995
SOME STATES TRYING TO STOP GAY MARRIAGES BEFORE THEY START
By DAVID W. DUNLAP

A battle over the very definition of marriage, which began two years ago in Hawaii, is spreading through Western states as lawmakers hasten to foreclose any possible legalization of homosexual matrimony.

Homosexual marriages are not now legally recognized anywhere in the nation, but commitment ceremonies have become an increasingly common feature of gay life.

Anticipating that Hawaii may one day sanction gay weddings, Utah legislators voted overwhelmingly this month to deny recognition to marriages performed elsewhere that do not conform to Utah law. This would include same-sex unions.

On the same day, March 1, a bill rendering any same-sex marriage "null and void" failed by one vote to get on the calendar of the South Dakota Senate. It had already been approved by the state's House of Representatives.

Two days later, a bill was introduced in the Alaska House by Representative Norman Rokeberg, a Republican, to make it explicit that "marriage is a civil contract entered into by one man and one woman."

This legislative trend has alarmed gay and lesbian organizations.

"Radical-right legislators will attempt to block recognition of marriages once we win them in the future," said Evan Wolfson, senior staff attorney of the Lambda Legal Defense and Education Fund, "and will prevent the American people from having a serious discussion about the denial of marriage rights."

For opponents of same-sex marriages, however, there is nothing to discuss and nothing radical about the proposition that the family has a man and a woman at its nucleus. This traditional structure cannot be expanded to embrace gay couples, they say.

"Marriage is the basis of family life, and families are central to civilization," said Robert H. Knight, director of cultural studies for the Family Research Council in Washington.

"The law doesn't discriminate against homosexuals," Mr. Knight said. "It merely says that each sex must be represented in marriage. Same-sex couples do not qualify. It might be called a partnership, but if it's called marriage, it's a counterfeit version. And counterfeit versions drive out the real thing."

What Mr. Knight sees as counterfeit, many gay and lesbian organizers see as a legitimate expansion of what family means. "We're labeled as promiscuous," said Robert Bray, of the National Gay and Lesbian Task Force, "but when we ask for recognition of our long-term relationships, we're denied."

Chris Ryan, president of the Utah Log Cabin Club, a group of gay Republicans, said, "All we want are the legal rights that go along with marriage." He mentioned visiting a partner in the hospital, inheriting property, providing insurance coverage, filing a joint tax return and distributing assets in a divorce.

In 1993, the Hawaii Supreme Court ruled that a refusal to grant marriage licenses to three same-sex couples presumptively violated the State Constitution. It sent the case back to a lower court.

That case is pending and, depending on the outcome, could pave the way to legalized gay marriage.

Such a development would set off not only a social debate but also a constitutional one, over the applicability of Article 4, which says in part: "Full faith and credit shall be given in each state to the public acts, records and judicial proceedings of every other state."

Unless a state explicitly declares an exception, State Representative Roger Hunt of South Dakota said, "it may be obligated to give full faith and credit to a marriage entered into by two people of the same gender in another state."

"I believe, by and large, that would be counter to what, in this state, has been the sanctity of families for the last 100 years," said Mr. Hunt, a Brandon Republican who was the legislation's main sponsor.

But Barry Wick, executive director of the South Dakota Gay, Lesbian and Bisexual Federation, called the bill "patently offensive to anyone who remembers the miscegenation laws of the South that banned interracial marriage" as late as 1967.

Lynn D. Wardle, a law professor at Brigham Young University, said the new Utah law was designed to close a loophole that might have compelled local authorities to recognize marriages of gay or lesbian couples—including Utah residents—who traveled to Hawaii to be wed.

The law would also ban recognition of marriages performed in other states or countries if they involved incest, bigamy or minors under the age of 14.

"No one is going to lose any rights they didn't already have," said State Representative Norm L. Nielsen, the Orem Republican who introduced the bill. "All it did was make our laws consistent."

A spokeswoman for Gov. Michael O. Leavitt of Utah, a Republican, said Mr. Leavitt was likely to sign the bill when it reached his desk.

CONGRESS PASSES DEFENSE OF MARRIAGE ACT, RESPONDS TO POSSIBILITY OF SAME-SEX MARRIAGE AT STATE LEVEL

In 1996, by an 85–14 margin, the U.S. Senate voted overwhelmingly to pass a bill that banned federal recognition of same-sex marriages performed at the state level. Called the Defense of Marriage Act (DOMA), the measure had already passed the House by a vote of 342 to 67, and President Clinton had promised to sign the bill into law.

Sen. James Jeffords (R-VT) explained the seemingly contradictory outcome for gay rights by arguing that while "people don't want to go too far on changing marriage and traditional relationships. . . . the feeling is when someone wants to work someplace, they ought to be able to get a job." DOMA supporters said the bill was necessary because at the time Hawaii was expected to soon allow same-sex marriage and thus would have become the first state in the country to do so. While states such as Hawaii would be allowed to legalize same-sex marriages under DOMA, the couples would not receive federal benefits, since neither the federal government nor other states would be compelled to recognize such unions.

While supporters of the bill such as Sen. Trent Lott (R-MS) insisted that DOMA was "not mean- spirited or exclusionary," opponents such as Sen. Edward Kennedy (D-MA) argued that it was "designed to divide Americans, to drive a wedge between one group of citizens and the rest of the country solely for partisan advantage," a reference to the upcoming election cycle.

SEPTEMBER 11, 1996
SENATORS REJECT BOTH JOB-BIAS BAN AND GAY MARRIAGE

By ERIC SCHMITT

WASHINGTON, Sept. 10—The Senate voted overwhelmingly today to deny Federal benefits to married people of the same sex and to permit states to ignore such marriages sanctioned in other states. The bill now goes to the White House for President Clinton's promised signature.

But in a surprisingly narrow outcome on another measure involving gay rights, the Senate defeated by a single vote a separate bill that for the first time would have banned discrimination against homosexuals in the workplace.

The message sent by the lopsided vote against recognizing same-sex marriages, 85 to 14, and the much closer margin, 50 to 49, on the anti-discrimination bill, cast in relief the point at which the United States Senate draws a line on gay rights. No Republican voted against the marriage bill, while eight Republicans voted for the anti-discrimination bill. Among Democrats, 27 voted both to bar Federal benefits in same-sex marriages and to protect homosexuals in the workplace.

"People don't want to go too far on changing marriage and traditional relationships," said Senator James M. Jeffords, a Vermont Republican who supported the marriage bill and the anti-discrimination measure. "But the feeling is when someone wants to work someplace, they ought to be able to get a job."

The bill barring Federal recognition of same-sex marriages, the Defense of Marriage Act, is identical to legislation the House approved in July, 342 to 67. The President promised weeks ago to sign the bill, blunting an election-year issue the Republicans had hoped to use against him.

Today's vote on the anti-discrimination bill ends its chances in this Congress. A Democrat who would probably have voted in favor of the bill, Senator David Pryor of Arkansas, was absent because of his son's cancer surgery in Little Rock. Vice President Al Gore, who was campaigning in the Northeast, was prepared to fly back to Washington had his vote been necessary to break a tie, Democrats said. But even had the Senate approved the bill, the measure faced stiff opposition in the House, which had not taken it up.

Nonetheless, the bill's supporters were elated by today's razor-thin loss, claiming a symbolic triumph that gives their cause momentum for another vote next year.

"We came within a breath of victory today," said Elizabeth Birch, executive director of the Human Rights Campaign, a gay-rights advocacy group. "We'll hit the ground running in the 105th Congress."

The only suspense surrounding the same-sex marriage bill was how lopsided the final vote would be. Ultimately, 32 Democrats joined all 53 Republicans in supporting the bill.

The bill's sponsors, mainly conservative Republicans, said the measure was necessary because of expectations that a Hawaii court would rule that the state must recognize same-sex marriages.

Hawaii would be the first state to grant such recognition, but the bill's supporters foresee far wider consequences: Article IV of the United States Constitution requires that "full faith and credit shall be given in each state to the public acts, records and judicial proceedings of every other state."

The bill does not ban marriages between partners of the same sex but is intended to inoculate states against having to recognize homosexual marriages, although critics of the measure say states already have the authority under the Constitution to ignore laws of other states.

"It is not mean-spirited or exclusionary," said Senator Trent Lott, the Mississippi Republican who is majority leader. "It is a pre-emptive measure to make sure that a handful of judges, in a single state, cannot impose a radical social agenda upon the entire nation."

The bill's sponsors said the institution of marriage was under assault.

"The drive for same-sex marriage," said Senator Robert C. Byrd, Democrat of West Virginia, "is, in effect, an effort to make a sneak attack on society by encoding this aberrant behavior in legal form before society itself has decided it should be legal.

"Let us defend the oldest institution, the institution of marriage between male and female as set forth in the Holy Bible."

Senator Daniel R. Coats, Republican of Indiana, sounded a similar theme, saying, "Our urgent responsibility is to nurture and strengthen that institution, not undermine it with trendy moral relativism."

Opponents said the bill was unnecessary, unconstitutional and driven by election-year politics.

"This bill," said Senator Edward M. Kennedy, Democrat of Massachusetts, "is designed to divide Americans, to drive a wedge between one group of citizens and the rest of the country solely for partisan advantage."

Senator Carol Moseley-Braun, Democrat of Illinois, said, "This bill expands government intrusiveness into our everyday lives and represents just the opposite of smaller government."

Critics argued that many things threatened traditional marriages today but that loving gay or lesbian couples were not among them.

"If this were truly a Defense of Marriage Act," said Senator John Kerry, Democrat of Massachusetts, "it would expand learning experiences for future husbands and wives, treatment on demand for alcohol or substance abuse, guarantee day care and expand protection against abused children."

Of the 100 senators, at least 20 have been divorced.

The bill's provisions barring Federal recognition of same-sex marriages would preclude spousal benefits that are distributed by Government programs like Social Security and veterans services.

"This is a huge series of victories for the pro-family movement," Ralph Reed, executive director of the Christian Coalition, said in a telephone interview.

Supporters of the anti-discrimination measure originally tried to attach it to the same-sex marriage bill. But after Senator Lott and Senator Kennedy exchanged procedural threats, the Republicans agreed to allow a vote on a free-standing anti-discrimination bill.

VERMONT SUPREME COURT CALLS FOR EQUAL RIGHTS FOR GAY COUPLES

In a unanimous ruling, the Vermont Supreme Court in 1999 said that same-sex couples are entitled to the same benefits and protections as opposite-sex couples under its state constitution as "a recognition of our common humanity." Such benefits include health insurance, tax breaks, inheritance rights, and hospital visitation rights. Although California and Hawaii both recognize domestic partnerships, Vermont's coverage became the broadest in the nation at this time. The court deferred to the legislature as to whether equal protection was to entail gay marriage or domestic partnership recognition. In 2000 the Vermont legislature became the first state to legalize same-sex civil unions.

While Peter Shumlin, the president pro tempore of the Vermont Senate, said that Vermonters wanted to respond positively to "a class of people whose civil rights are being trampled upon," Gov. Howard Dean said that same-sex marriage "makes me uncomfortable, the same as anybody else." At the time he expected that the legislature would pass a domestic partnership law in response to the court's ruling. However, Beth Robinson, a lawyer for the plaintiffs argued that partnership would not entail federal benefits, whereas marriage would. With thirty states having already passed legislation banning gay marriage, the possibility that Vermont could legalize same-sex marriage potentially raised thorny legal issues on a national scale.

Jay Sekulow of the American Center for Law and Justice, a conservative group, said that the decision was "a slap in the face for marriage between a man and a woman." Holly Puterbaugh and Lois Farnham, one of three couples who brought the challenge to the court, were ecstatic. Having been together for twenty-seven years, they said that they were "look[ing] forward to the time when they can finally make it official." Matt Coles, director of the Gay and Lesbian Rights Project at the American Civil Liberties Union said that the term *domestic partnership* was invented only nineteen years prior to the Vermont Supreme Court's 1999 decision. He said, "If you think about the way that law and society move, to go from San Francisco considering domestic partnerships too far out there in 1981, to all five justices of the Vermont Supreme Court taking equal treatment for granted in 1999—it's astonishing, it really is."

DECEMBER 21, 1999
VERMONT HIGH COURT BACKS RIGHTS OF SAME-SEX COUPLES
By CAREY GOLDBERG

BOSTON, Dec. 20—The Vermont Supreme Court unanimously ruled today that the state must guarantee the very same protections and benefits to gay and lesbian couples that it does to heterosexual spouses. The court left it to the Legislature to either legalize gay marriage, which no state has yet done, or adopt a domestic partnership law, which would be the most sweeping in the country.

To extend equal rights to homosexual couples "who seek nothing more, nor less, than legal protection and security for their avowed commitment to an intimate and lasting relationship is simply, when all is said and done," the ruling said, "a recognition of our common humanity."

The court found that it was unconstitutionally discriminatory in Vermont to deny marriage licenses to homosexual couples, depriving them of the myriad benefits, from inheritance rights to health insurance to tax breaks, that accrue to heterosexual married couples. It is up to the Legislature to decide whether to establish a system recognizing gay couples as domestic partners, with the benefits like those of spouses, or to simply include homosexual partners in the state's marriage laws. It gave lawmakers an unspecified "reasonable period of time" to consider.

Peter Shumlin, the president pro tempore of the Vermont Senate, said today that the state's predominantly Democratic lawmakers might decide in the coming session how to respond. Mr. Shumlin said he expected it would be much easier to get votes for a domestic partnership law than one creating full-fledged gay marriages, but "both are strong possibilities," he said.

"When the court says, 'You have a class of people whose civil rights are being trampled upon,' Vermonters want to remedy that," he said.

Some state officials say they support gay marriage. But Gov. Howard Dean, a Democrat, said he thought the Legislature would pass a domestic partnership law. Same-sex marriage, he said, "makes me uncomfortable, the same as anybody else," The Associated Press reported.

William Sorrell, the Vermont attorney general, said of domestic partnership: "It would likely be a civilly sanctioned relationship that would, for all intents and purposes, have the benefits and protections a traditionally married couple would have but wouldn't be called a marital relationship. They wouldn't be called spouses, they'd be called domestic partners, and for a number of people, that makes an enormous difference."

But Beth Robinson, a lead lawyer for the plaintiffs, said that unlike marriage, domestic partnership would not entitle couples to benefits from the federal government and all private employers.

Piecemeal systems of protections and benefits for gay and lesbian couples have been enacted in recent years around the country, but advocates for gay rights said today that because the Vermont ruling would cover all possible benefits, it would put the state far ahead of all others. California and Hawaii have statewide domestic partnership systems, they said, but they pale next to what is coming in Vermont.

If Vermont chooses full-fledged gay marriage and homosexual couples begin flocking to the state to wed, their legal status in their home states would prove a very tangled issue, experts said today.

The campaign to legalize gay marriage has inspired a vigorous opposition. Since the prospect arose in a Hawaii case in 1991, nearly 30 states have passed laws against gay marriage. But gay rights advocates say it is not clear whether those laws would stand against challenges. Most likely, legal experts say, there would be state-by-state battles over recognizing same-sex marriages performed in Vermont.

Today's decision, written by Chief Justice Jeffrey L. Amestoy, exhilarated the three couples who brought the case against the state, as well as their lawyers and the many gay and civil rights groups supporting them.

"We celebrated our 27th anniversary together in October," one of the couples, Holly Puterbaugh and Lois Farnham, said in a joint statement. "We look forward to the time when we can finally make it official."

But the ruling brought expressions of dismay from religious and conservative groups and others who oppose gay marriage.

"The decision is not only troubling but it is tremendously disappointing," said Jay Sekulow, chief counsel of the American Center for Law and Justice, a national conservative group, in a statement. "While this legal decision is designed to elevate the status of same-sex couples, it really represents a slap in the face for marriage between a man and a woman."

In Vermont, Craig Bensen, an evangelical pastor and vice president of Take It to the People, a coalition that opposes gay marriage, said the group was considering a strategy like those used in Hawaii and Alaska, where opponents of gay marriage put the idea to a referendum and got enough votes to block it. The Hawaii Supreme Court dismissed as moot the gay-marriage case there on Dec. 10, because a 1998 ballot measure had authorized lawmakers to restrict the definition of marriage to man-woman unions.

"We suspect there will be momentum for a constitutional amendment to clarify the nature of marriage," Mr. Bensen said. "The difficulty is, we've got the toughest Constitution to amend in the country."

Though the ruling went against them, Mr. Bensen and those sharing his beliefs said they were happy to see the issue go to the Legislature.

Attorney General Sorrell said, "It's an important public policy question, and where important public policy should be debated and decided is in the Legislature, not the courts."

Mr. Sorrell noted that because the decision was based on the state Constitution rather than the federal one, the ruling cannot be appealed to the United States Supreme Court.

The provision of the Vermont Constitution referred to by the court was the common benefits clause, which says that the government ought to be "instituted for the common benefit, protection and security of the people, nation or community, and not for the particular emolument or advantage of any single person, family or set of persons who are a part only of that community."

Although the court's ruling focused on benefits rather than marriage itself, lawyers for the same-sex couples said today that they believed that the Legislature would ultimately choose full-fledged marriage for same-sex couples. A domestic partnership system would not go far enough to secure gay couples the exact privileges accorded heterosexual ones, like access to benefits from the federal government and private employers, they said.

"This legal status of marriage carries with it a lot of baggage," said Ms. Robinson, the lawyer for the couples. "The Legislature will come to understand that as a practical matter, you can't call it something different and have it be truly equal."

Matt Coles, director of the Lesbian and Gay Rights Project of the American Civil Liberties Union, noted that the phrase "domestic partnership" was invented only 19 years ago, when there was virtually no recognition of gay and lesbian relationships and the whole idea was so radical that when the San Francisco City Council passed a domestic partnership law, Mayor Dianne Feinstein, now a United States senator, vetoed it.

"If you think about the way law and society move," Mr. Coles said, "to go from San Francisco considering domestic partnerships too far out there in 1981, to all five justices of the Vermont Supreme Court taking equal treatment for granted in 1999—it's astonishing, it really is."

While the justices, who are appointed by the governor and can be removed by the Legislature, concurred that gay couples should be protected from discrimination, one, Denise R. Johnson, wrote that the court should order the state to let them marry. To do otherwise, she wrote, would consign them to "an uncertain fate in the political cauldron" of a moral debate in the Legislature.

The case began in 1997 when the three couples— Ms. Puterbaugh and Ms. Farnham, Stan Baker and Peter Harrigan, and Nina Beck and Stacy Jolles—filed suit after their local town clerks denied them marriage licenses. A Superior Court judge turned them down, but they appealed to the State Supreme Court, which heard their arguments last year.

The ruling, Ms. Puterbaugh told reporters today, will make this a special Christmas.

"I think there's going to be a little extra feeling of family now," she said.

Nebraska to Consider Strict Antigay Marriage and Union Law in Upcoming Election

In response to Vermont's decision to allow same-sex civil unions, voters in Nebraska were given the chance to decide whether to pass the most stringent antigay marriage law in the country during the 2000 election cycle. While thirty-three states had approved similar laws in order to ban gay marriage, the proposed constitutional amendment in Nebraska would also declare same-sex civil unions and domestic partnerships invalid. In the lead-up to the vote, the amendment was expected to pass.

Supporters of the amendment included a coalition of national Roman Catholic, Mormon, and evangelical groups. Nearly 95 percent of the funds raised to support the amendment came from out of state. Nevertheless, the leader of the coalition, Kay Orr, declined to be interviewed, saying, "I don't feel it advances our cause to be a part of any other newspaper article outside of Nebraska."

Opponents of the measure, such as the interim chancellor of the University of Nebraska, Harvey Perlman, argued that the amendment could impede new businesses and employees from being recruited to the state, noting that many applicants for jobs had expressed concern about the proposal. Others said that it might threaten gay couples' hospital visitation rights, adoption rights, powers of attorney, wills, and medical directives.

Despite the fact that retiring senator Bob Kerry opposed the amendment, both candidates in a close race for his seat strongly supported it. When asked why a same-sex relationship could not be as strong as an opposite-sex one, Don Stenberg, the Republican candidate, replied, "Or a man and a dog can get married? Where are you going to draw the line? A son and a mother? A father and a daughter?" Democratic candidate Ben Nelson argued for tolerance but added that the amendment "makes a statement for traditional marriage," adding that he was taught that a homosexual union "was not a moral relationship." When Nebraska voters went to the polls in November, they passed the ballot measure by a wide majority.

OCTOBER 21, 2000
NEBRASKANS TO VOTE ON MOST SWEEPING BAN ON GAY UNIONS
By PAM BELLUCK

OMAHA – Nebraskans will vote this Election Day on the country's most sweeping effort to bar gay unions, a proposed amendment to the state Constitution that not only bans gay marriages but also declares same-sex civil unions and domestic partnerships invalid.

Polls show that the measure has a good chance of passing.

Supporters of the proposed amendment have been helped by a coalition of national Roman Catholic, Mormon and evangelical groups and out-of-state contributors. Less than 6 percent of the more than $500,000 donated to support the amendment has come from Nebraska residents.

Opponents have raised about $100,000, most of it from Nebraskans.

Still, the battle is heating up. In recent days, the state's major newspapers have editorialized against the amendment. Leaders of some churches and synagogues have voiced opposition. And the interim chancellor of the University of Nebraska spoke against the amendment, saying it could discourage employees and businesses from moving to the state.

Opponents say they fear that the amendment would dissuade employers and insurers from offering health benefits for same-sex partners. And they are concerned that government agencies, hospitals and other institutions would interpret it to mean, for instance, that gays could be prevented from making decisions about their hospitalized partners or from adopting their partners' children.

"It shoves lesbians and gay Nebraskans out of every family protection in Nebraska, large or small," said Evan Wolfson, director of the marriage project for the Lambda Legal Defense Fund. "And it is intended to cast a cloud over private sector measures to assist gay and lesbian families as well."

Both sides expect a court challenge if the measure passes.

The proposal, Initiative 416, reads: "Only marriage between a man and a woman shall be valid or recognized in Nebraska. The uniting of two persons of the same sex in a civil union, domestic partnership or other similar same-sex relationship shall not be valid or recognized in Nebraska."

Proponents call the measure a response to a court decision last year in Vermont that stopped short of legalizing gay marriage but held that gay couples were entitled to the same benefits as heterosexual ones. This spring, to comply with the ruling, the Vermont Legislature passed a law recognizing "civil unions" for homosexuals.

Backers of Initiative 416 say they fear that gay couples might enter into civil unions in Vermont or another state that adopts a similar law and seek to have Nebraska recognize the unions.

"Because of the action in Vermont, we really feel we've been forced to adopt this language to close this loophole," said Dan Parsons, a spokesman for the Nebraska Coalition for the Protection of Marriage, the group leading the campaign for the amendment.

Mr. Parsons said the movement by gay advocates to persuade other states to copy Vermont "will place our definition of marriage at risk."

Thirty-three states have passed what they call "defense of marriage acts," which generally specify that only marriage between a man and a woman is valid.

Lesbian and gay activists say some states have used the laws to deny gay couples access to benefits enjoyed by heterosexual ones. In Idaho, a judge invoked the state's marriage law in refusing to allow a lesbian to adopt her partner's child.

But with the Nebraska amendment, opponents say, the language is so broad that it is unclear how it would be applied.

"My binding contracts, my power of attorney, wills and medical directives will be viewed as contracts or partnerships between two people of the same sex and no longer be recognized or valid in the state of Nebraska," said M. J. McBride, a campaign coordinator with Nebraskans Against 416.

Tension over the issue of same-sex unions has simmered for several years in Nebraska. Since 1996, bills to ban gay marriage have been introduced in the Legislature, sponsored by more than half the senators, only to be blocked.

But Initiative 416 seems to have greater momentum. In an Omaha World-Herald poll in mid-September, 59 percent of voters surveyed said they would support the measure; 34 percent said they would oppose it.

The undecided are being lobbied by a glossy television commercial that features a panorama of wedding portraits arranged on a mantle. And they are being courted by a coalition led by a former Republican governor, Kay A. Orr. Though Mrs. Orr is the most prominent voice for the amendment, she declined to be interviewed.

"I don't feel it advances our cause to be a part of any other newspaper article outside of Nebraska," Mrs. Orr said.

Both candidates in a tightly contested race for an open seat in the United States Senate—Don Stenberg, the Republican, who is the state's attorney general, and Ben Nelson, the Democrat, who is a former governor—also support the amendment.

At a recent news conference, Mr. Stenberg was asked why a relationship between two men could not be as strong as a heterosexual union.

"Or a man and a dog can get married?" Mr. Stenberg replied. "Where are you going to draw the line? A son and a mother? A father and a daughter?"

Mr. Nelson supports the amendment, even though the leaders of his party and Bob Kerrey, the retiring Democratic senator, believe it discriminates against gays.

Mr. Nelson said in an interview that while he believed "we should be tolerant of people, even if we disagree with them," he backed Initiative 416 because "it makes a statement for traditional marriage" and because he was taught that a homosexual union "was not a moral relationship."

Mr. Parsons, the spokesman for the group behind the amendment, said proponents were "not trying—even if we wanted to—to dictate relationships."

"This is not about bigotry," he said.

But opponents say the measure is already having negative effects.

Harvey Perlman, interim chancellor of the University of Nebraska, said applicants for faculty and administrative posts had expressed concern about Initiative 416. Mr. Perlman said he believed the measure "would hurt employers generally in Nebraska trying to recruit a skilled work force."

Several companies in Nebraska said they would continue to offer domestic-partner benefits. But even some businesses that do not offer such benefits said the amendment might discourage some employees from moving there.

"It's hard to recruit to the Midwest anyway, and this won't make it any easier," said Mark Ebes, director of employment for First Data Resources in Omaha, which does not offer domestic-partner benefits.

Because under other Nebraska laws, the phrase "domestic partnership" also refers to business partnerships formed within the state, opponents of Initiative 416 claim it could be interpreted to end businesses like a father-son farming operation. The measure's proponents say it is clear that those relationships are not what the amendment is addressing.

- -

Canada to Adopt Gay Marriage

Canada appeared poised to become the third country to allow same-sex unions as the cabinet approved a new national policy in 2003 that would allow gay couples to marry, joining the Netherlands and Belgium. The House of Commons drafted supporting legislation within a few months of the Canadian cabinet's approval in June 2003. The decision was presumed to have an impact on the continuing controversy over same-sex marriage across the border, because Canada has no residency requirement for marriage and Canadian marriage licenses have always been recognized in the United States.

Then–prime minister Jean Chrétien, said, "You have to look at history as an evolution of society. According to the interpretation of the courts, these unions should be legal in Canada." Little opposition was mounted as Canadian polls indicated that a majority of the public supported the change. John Fisher, director of advocacy for the gay rights group Égale Canada, hailed the development, saying, "Every movement has its human rights milestones. Just as the day women acquired the right to vote, when racial segregation was ruled unconstitutional, so too, same-sex couples have finally acquired the right to marry." Religious institutions were allowed to opt out of conducting same-sex marriages.

JUNE 18, 2003
CANADIAN LEADERS AGREE TO PROPOSE GAY MARRIAGE LAW
By CLIFFORD KRAUSS

TORONTO, June 17—The Canadian cabinet approved a new national policy today to open marriage to gay couples, paving the way for Canada to become the third country to allow same-sex unions.

"You have to look at history as an evolution of society," Prime Minister Jean Chrétien told reporters after a meeting of his cabinet. "According to the interpretation of the courts these unions should be legal in Canada. We will

ensure that our legislation includes and legally recognizes the union of same-sex couples."

The decision to redefine marriage in Canada to include unions between men and between women will immediately take effect in Ontario, Canada's most populous province. Last week, the province's highest court ruled that current federal marriage laws are discriminatory and therefore unconstitutional.

Once aides to Mr. Chrétien draft the necessary legislation, the House of Commons is expected to pass it into law in the next few months. Although leaders of the two conservative parties and some Liberals have expressed reservations, there is little organized opposition to such legislation, and public opinion polls show a solid majority in favor of the change.

The policy opens the way for same-sex couples from the United States and around the world to travel here to marry, since Canada has no marriage residency requirements. In addition, gay-rights advocates in the United States are already declaring that Canada will serve as a vivid example to Americans that same-sex marriage is workable and offers no challenge to traditional heterosexual family life.

No American state allows same-sex marriage, but Vermont has enacted a law providing for civil unions, which allow gay couples many of the benefits of marriage.

Canadian marriage licenses have always been accepted in the United States, but now that the definition of marriage in the two countries appears likely to diverge, legal challenges to same-sex couples claiming rights and privileges deriving from their Canadian marriages seem certain to arise in at least some states.

Issues including adoption rights, inheritance, insurance benefits and matters as mundane as sharing health club memberships are likely to arise in courts and state legislatures.

Canada's new marriage policy comes at a time when the government is also pushing for legislation that would decriminalize the possession of small amounts of marijuana, another policy that diverges sharply from American federal practices.

Polling experts and social scientists note that conservative religious views are much less influential here than in the United States, with regular church attendance far lower and with fundamentalist Protestant groups attracting far less support.

Mr. Chrétien said the government would also ask the Supreme Court for advice to make the new legislation invulnerable to appeals by provincial governments seeking to invalidate it in their jurisdictions.

However, the conservative premier of Alberta, Ralph Klein, has threatened a legal fight to exclude his province from the new rules.

Gay-rights advocates celebrated the decision as a civil-rights milestone.

"June 17 of 2003 is going to be a day gay and lesbian people remember for a long, long time to come," said Svend Robinson, a gay member of the House of Commons from the left-of-center New Democratic Party, in a television interview immediately after the announcement.

Canada's action follows in the steps of the Netherlands and Belgium, but it is likely to have a much larger impact on the United States. Only a few American same-sex couples have taken advantage of expanded marriage laws in the Netherlands because of its long residency requirement, and Belgium will only allow marriages of foreign couples from countries that already allow such unions. But Canada is nearby and has no such restrictions.

"What this presents for American couples is an opportunity to easily enter into a legal marriage and come back to the United States with a powerful tool to break down the remaining discrimination here," said Lavi Soloway, a Canadian-born lawyer and founder of the Lesbian and Gay Immigration Rights Task Force in New York.

Mr. Soloway said Canada's marriage reform would go a long way to changing public perceptions and attitudes in the United States, although he added that the march to full acceptance would be slow.

"What we are in for is a long gradual struggle to win full equal recognition of these marriages," he said.

Since the Ontario appeals court ruled last Tuesday in favor of same-sex unions, only a few minor hurdles stand in the way of legalizing them throughout Canada. Since the court decision last week, Ontario has already issued 131 marriage licenses to same-sex couples, including four from the United States.

The most important remaining step is a vote in the House of Commons sometime in the next few months, one in which Mr. Chrétien said he will allow Liberal members to vote their consciences.

Leaders of the Bloc Québécois and the New Democratic Party have said their members are solidly behind the change, and with a majority of Liberals they should be able to enact the legislation easily despite opposition from two conservative parties.

The Supreme Court, which has ruled repeatedly in favor of extending gay rights, appears to support the efforts of the government to extend marital rights.

"Every movement has its human rights milestones," said John Fisher, director of advocacy for Égale Canada, a group that has been working for same-sex marriage in the courts. "Just as the day women acquired the right to vote, when racial segregation was ruled as unconstitutional, so too, same-sex couples have finally acquired the right to marry."

To protect religious freedom, the cabinet decided that the planned federal legislation would allow religious institutions to refuse to conduct same-sex marriages.

A three-member panel of the Ontario Court of Appeal declared unanimously last week that the definition of marriage as currently set by federal government—as a union between a man and a woman—was invalid and must be changed immediately to include same-sex couples.

It ruled that under the Charter of Rights and Freedoms, roughly the Canadian equivalent of the Bill of Rights, "the existing common-law definition of marriage violates the couple's equality rights on the basis of sexual orientation."

It added, "In doing so, it offends the dignity of persons in same-sex relationships."

The ruling was similar in argument but more immediate in impact to two previous decisions by provincial courts in Quebec and British Columbia.

Last year, the Quebec Superior Court ruled that the prohibition of same-sex marriage was unconstitutional, and the British Columbia Court of Appeal did likewise last month. They gave the federal government until mid-2004 to change its marriage rules. Since then legislative panels have been studying ways to put the rulings into effect.

Members of the Liberal federal cabinet overwhelmingly supported granting same-sex couples marriage rights, but members were divided over whether to legislate an immediate change or first to request guidance from the federal Supreme Court. After hours of debate, the cabinet decided to do both, hoping for the imprimatur of both government bodies to assure maximum popular acceptance of the new law.

"I think on balance people recognize that the decisions of the courts are really pointing in a direction from which it would be difficult—if we wanted to—to turn back," said Deputy Prime Minister John Manley, who is also a candidate to replace Prime Minister Chrétien as Liberal Party leader later this year.

MASSACHUSETTS BECOMES FIRST STATE TO GUARANTEE SAME-SEX MARRIAGE

In 2004 the Massachusetts Supreme Judicial Court ruled that gay couples have the right to marry, making it the first state in the nation to recognize same-sex marriage. The state legislature was given 180 days to pass a bill conforming to the ruling. The court said that the Massachusetts constitution would not allow the state to deny to same-sex couples the benefits conferred by marriage. While affirming "the dignity and equality of all individuals," the court added that the Massachusetts constitution "forbids the creation of second-class citizens." The court rejected Massachusetts' attempt to defend the exclusion on the grounds that the purpose of marriage is procreation and child rearing, noting that not being allowed to marry "works a deep and scarring hardship" on homosexual families, many of which include children.

The decision was a 4–3 ruling, with three of the four justices in the majority having been appointed by Republican governors. The ruling produced strong reaction from both supporters and opponents. "This comes pretty close to an earthquake politically," said political science professor Alan Wolfe of Boston College, who expected a backlash against the decision. The executive director of Parents, Families, and Friends of Lesbians and Gays, David Tseng, called it "a tremendous victory for fairness and for families." The president of the conservative Family Research Council, Tony Perkins, said, "We must amend the Constitution if we are to stop a tyrannical judiciary from redefining marriage to the point of extinction."

Experts predicted that the ruling was likely to make same-sex marriage central to the 2004 presidential election. President Bush opposed same-sex marriage but had yet to call for a constitutional amendment prohibiting it. Calling marriage a "sacred institution between a man and a woman," he said that the Massachusetts decision "violates this important principle." He pledged to work with Congress to defend "the sanctity of marriage." Polls taken as of the 2004 Massachusetts decisions showed that the majority of Americans did not support same-sex marriage. Thirty-seven states at the time had laws that defined marriage as between only a man and a woman.

Gov. Mitt Romney said that he would support an amendment to the Massachusetts constitution to ban gay marriage, stating, "Of course we must provide basic civil rights and appropriate benefits to nontraditional couples, but marriage is a special institution that should be reserved for a man and a woman."

Several of the seven couples who challenged the law had been together for many years, and many of them said that they had been denied access to their partners when they were hospitalized. "We never have to worry about going to the hospital and negotiating our way through hospital teams because now we have the opportunity to protect ourselves through marriage," said one of the partners.

NOVEMBER 19, 2003
LEGISLATURE TOLD TO CLEAR WAY—COURT CITES STATE CONSTITUTION
SAME-SEX MARRIAGE: THE OVERVIEW;
MARRIAGE BY GAYS GAINS BIG VICTORY IN MASSACHUSETTS
By PAM BELLUCK

BOSTON, Nov. 18—Massachusetts' highest court ruled on Tuesday that gay couples have the right to marry under the state's Constitution, and it gave the state legislature 180 days to make same-sex marriages possible.

The 4-to-3 decision was the first in which a state high court had ruled homosexual couples are constitutionally entitled to marry, and legal experts predicted it would have ramifications across the country.

"The question before us is whether, consistent with the Massachusetts Constitution, the commonwealth may deny the protections, benefits and obligations conferred by civil marriage to two individuals of the same sex who wish to marry," wrote Chief Justice Margaret H. Marshall of the state's Supreme Judicial Court. "We conclude that it may not. The Massachusetts Constitution affirms the dignity and equality of all individuals. It forbids the creation of second-class citizens." [Excerpts, Page A24.]

The decision, which did not explicitly tell the state legislature how to carry out the ruling, sent lawmakers and legal experts scrambling to determine what options exist short of legitimizing gay marriage. Other experts said that the court appeared determined to extend full marriage rights to gay men and lesbians.

The decision ignited a storm of reaction throughout the nation, with gay groups and some liberals heralding the ruling, and conservatives and some religious groups denouncing it.

"We're thrilled and delighted the highest court in the state of Massachusetts confirms that our community has the right to enter into civil marriage the same as other couples," said David Tseng, the executive director of Parents, Families and Friends of Lesbians and Gays, who noted that three of the four justices in the majority were appointed by Republican governors. "This is a tremendous victory for fairness and for families."

Tony Perkins, president of the Family Research Council, a conservative group, said, "it is inexcusable for this court to force the state legislature to 'fix' its state constitution to make it comport with the pro-homosexual agenda of four court justices."

Mr. Perkins and other conservatives said the decision underscored the need for a federal constitutional amendment banning gay marriage.

"We must amend the Constitution if we are to stop a tyrannical judiciary from redefining marriage to the point of extinction," he said.

It also seemed likely that the court ruling would catapult same-sex marriage into a major issue in the presidential campaign. Virtually every Democratic presidential candidate issued a statement on Tuesday that tried to find a middle ground on an issue that is nothing if not polarizing. Most did not express support for gay marriage or a constitutional amendment banning it, but said they supported giving gay couples the benefits heterosexual couples receive.

President Bush, who has opposed same-sex marriage but not embraced the idea of a constitutional amendment, said in a statement: "Marriage is a sacred institution between a man and a woman. Today's decision of the Massachusetts Supreme Judicial Court violates this important principle. I will work with Congressional leaders and others to do what is legally necessary to defend the sanctity of marriage."

In defending the current practice of restricting marriages to heterosexual couples, Massachusetts officials had argued that the main purpose of marriage was procreation, that heterosexual marriage was best for child-rearing, and that gay marriage would impose a financial burden on the state. But Justice Marshall dismissed those arguments, saying that the state "has failed to identify any constitutionally adequate reason for denying civil marriage to same-sex couples."

Some legal experts said they thought the ruling might allow room for Massachusetts to embrace a parallel system like the civil unions allowed by Vermont. Other experts said the 34-page ruling left little doubt that the court intended that full-fledged marriage be extended to gays and lesbians. Robert E. Travaglini, president of the State Senate, who has said he supports civil unions but not same-sex marriage, said on Tuesday that "the strength of the language and the depth of the decision" makes it clear that marriage, and not civil unions, "is the wish of the court."

Because it is based in state law, the ruling cannot be appealed to the United States Supreme Court. And it cannot be overturned by the legislature. But the legislature could try to amend the state Constitution to ban gay marriage, an option that Gov. Mitt Romney said on Tuesday that he favored. Such a process, though, would take at least three years.

Polls show that many Americans, while more tolerant of homosexual relationships, still do not support homosexual marriage. And some experts predicted that the court decision would increase support for laws banning gay marriage in states and at a national level. Already, 37 states have passed measures defining marriage as between men and women.

"This comes pretty close to an earthquake politically," said Alan Wolfe, a professor of political science at Boston College. "I think it's exactly the right kind of material for a backlash."

The decision was a personal victory for at least 14 people: the gay and lesbian partners who were plaintiffs in the court case. The seven couples from across the state, most of whom had lived together for years and some of whom are raising children, all sought marriage licenses in 2001 from their town or city offices.

A lower-court judge dismissed the case in May 2002 before it went to trial, ruling that because same-sex couples cannot have children, the state does not give them the right to marry.

"Without a doubt this is the happiest day of our lives," said one plaintiff, Gloria Bailey, 62, of Cape Cod, as she stood, teary-eyed, at a news conference with her partner of 32 years, Linda Davies, 67. "We've been wanting to get married practically since the day we met. We didn't know if it would happen in our lifetime. We're planning a spring wedding."

Several of the couples told stories of being denied access to their partners when they were hospitalized.

Hillary Goodridge, 46, of Boston, had to say she was the sister of her partner, Julie Goodridge, 45, to see Julie when she was rushed to the neonatal intensive care unit after giving birth to their daughter, Annie.

David Wilson, 58, was not able to say he was the brother of his partner, Robert Compton, 53, because Mr. Wilson is black and Mr. Compton, who has been hospitalized five times in the last five years, is white.

"We never have to worry about going to the hospital and negotiating our way through hospital teams because now we have the opportunity to protect ourselves through marriage," said Mr. Wilson, smiling at Mr. Compton.

Being legally married in Massachusetts would entitle same-sex couples to numerous other rights and benefits, including those related to property ownership, insurance, tax consequences and child custody. The marriage would not automatically be considered valid by the federal government or other states, which would probably have to decide on their own whether to recognize a Massachusetts gay marriage.

In the ruling, Justice Marshall wrote about the benefits of marriage for children and said that not being allowed to marry "works a deep and scarring hardship" on homosexual families.

"It cannot be rational under our laws, and indeed it is not permitted, to penalize children by depriving them of state benefits because the state disapproves of their parents' sexual orientation," she wrote.

In the dissent, Justice Robert Cordy wrote that the marriage law was intended to apply to a man and a woman, and "it furthers the legitimate state purpose of ensuring, promoting and supporting an optimal social structure for the bearing and raising of children."

As it considers how to respond to the ruling in the next 180 days, the legislature will most likely consider several options. Already, in recent months, three different efforts have begun in the legislature: a drive to amend the state Constitution to ban gay marriage, a bill to establish civil unions and a bill that would allow for same-sex marriage.

Kate Zezima contributed reporting for this article.

The politics of Massachusetts make the issue especially tricky. The legislature is majority Democratic, but also largely Catholic, and the Roman Catholic Church is strenuously opposed to gay marriage. On the other hand, the Democrats are rarely aligned with Governor Romney, a Republican, who indicated on Tuesday that he would support some effort to extend benefits and rights to gay couples, though he would not support marriage.

"Marriage is an institution between a man and a woman," he said. "I will support an amendment to the Massachusetts Constitution that makes that expressly clear. Of course, we must provide basic civil rights and appropriate benefits to nontraditional couples, but marriage is a special institution that should be reserved for a man and a woman."

Arthur Miller, a Harvard law professor, said he thought that given the closeness of the court decision, there might be room for the legislature "to create a relationship that might not necessarily be called marriage but allows for the recognition of property passage and joint ownership and insurance and even child custody."

But Elizabeth Bartholet, a family law expert at Harvard Law School, said the extensive discussion of marriage in the decision made it unlikely the court would allow civil unions.

If the legislature did nothing or failed to comply, Professor Bartholet said, "I would assume after 180 days the Supreme Judicial Court would say this is law and the state would have to issue marriage licenses."

SAN FRANCISCO OFFERS SAME-SEX MARRIAGE, CHALLENGING CALIFORNIA LAW

In 2004 the city of San Francisco began to perform same-sex marriages in apparent conflict with California law, which held that "only marriage between a man and a woman is valid or recognized in California." Mayor Gavin Newsom said that he allowed the marriages to take place because the state constitution prohibits discrimination. Kate Kendell of the National Center for Lesbian Rights conceded that California law recognizes only opposite-sex marriages, but she argued that such a requirement was unconstitutional. She maintained, "It is in the highest order of civil responsibility when you see a law that does not treat your citizens equally to make a stand."

The first couple married under the city directive was Phyllis Lyon and Del Martin, long-standing leaders in the movement for gay rights. Lyon and Martin had been living together for more than fifty years. At least fifty other same-sex couples were married after Lyon and Martin, with more in the following days.

Lyon said that her work in the women's movement had led her to oppose marriage for both straight and gay couples until marriage had become such an important political issue in the fight for equal rights for gays and lesbians. She said, "We are fairly well united behind this because it's being fought so hard by the other side. If we let them beat us down on this one, it will be a long time before we make other advances."

Matthew Staver, president of the conservative Liberty Counsel, said that the mayor was inappropriately acting above the law and that the marriages "were not worth the paper they are written on." In August 2004 the California Supreme Court put an end to the issuing of same-sex marriage licenses in San Francisco. In 2008 that court said it was unconstitutional to prevent same-sex couples from marrying. Later in 2008 this ruling was overturned by popular referendum, which in turn was found unconstitutional by a federal district court in 2010. The latter ruling is expected to be appealed all the way to the U.S. Supreme Court.

FEBRUARY 13, 2004
DOZENS OF GAY COUPLES MARRY IN SAN FRANCISCO CEREMONIES
By CAROLYN MARSHALL

SAN FRANCISCO, Feb. 12—Two lesbians who have been living together for more than 50 years were the first to marry at city hall Thursday under a new city directive, leading the way for a host of other same-sex marriages and setting the stage for a heated debate over the legality of the ceremony.

California family law states that "only marriage between a man and a woman is valid or recognized in California." Nonetheless, the San Francisco county clerk issued the women, Phyllis Lyon, 79, and Del Martin, 83, an official marriage certificate and said the act was legal. They were married by the county assessor.

By late Thursday afternoon, at least 50 other gay couples had been married and others, some dressed in wedding gowns and dark suits, were waiting their turn.

"The marriages will be recognized in San Francisco, but I can't say how they will be viewed anywhere else," said the county clerk, Nancy Alfaro.

Mayor Gavin Newsom had urged the county clerk's office this week to begin issuing the marriage certificates, asserting that the state Constitution prohibits discrimination in such matters.

The clerk had not been expected to act on the request until next week, but the schedule was moved forward when the Campaign for California Families, a group that opposes gay marriage, announced it would file a lawsuit against the city and county on Friday.

Ms. Lyon said "it was exciting" to get married, even though the couple had no rings, had not written vows and just found out Wednesday night that the ceremony could take place.

Although Ms. Lyon, who met Ms. Martin in 1953, said she opposed marriage for straight and gay couples during the women's movement, she said it had become an increasingly important political issue for gay men and lesbians in the last two years.

"It's of crucial importance for the movement," Ms. Lyon said. "We are fairly well united behind this because it's being fought against so hard by the other side. If we let them beat us down on this one, it will be a long time before we make other advances."

Mathew D. Staver, president and general counsel of Liberty Counsel, the lawyers for the group that plans to sue, said the marriage certificates issued Thursday were "not worth the paper they are written on."

He added that Mr. Newsom was "giving the impression that mayors are above the law."

Hallye Jordan, a spokeswoman for the California attorney general, Bill Lockyer, said Mr. Lockyer had not been asked to render an opinion on the matter, but that he was investigating the constitutional issues surrounding gay marriage.

Asked if the marriage certificates issued in San Francisco were legal, Ms. Jordan said, "We don't know."

Kate Kendell, executive director of the National Center for Lesbian Rights, served as a witness to the Lyon-Martin marriage.

Ms. Kendell acknowledged that under California law marriage must be between people of opposite sex, but she said the requirement was unconstitutional.

"It is in the highest order of civic responsibility when you see a law that does not treat your citizens equally," Ms. Kendell said, "to make a stand."

· ·

BUSH SUPPORTS CONSTITUTIONAL AMENDMENT BANNING SAME-SEX MARRIAGE

President Bush announced his support for an amendment to the U.S. Constitution that would ban gay marriage, arguing that allowing such unions is a threat to society. In a brief statement made in 2004 at the White House, Bush said that "activist judges" were trying to redefine marriage, which he called, "the most fundamental institution of civilization." He argued that the amendment would protect marriage and allow states to make alternative legal arrangements for same-sex couples other than marriage.

While Bush acknowledged that the issue concerned private practices, noting that "America's a free society," he added that "freedom, however, does not require the redefinition of one of our most basic social institutions." White House officials later struggled to provide examples that showed how gay marriage would undermine American society, stating that "ages of experience have taught humanity that the commitment of a husband and wife to love and to serve one another promotes the welfare of children and the stability of society."

Conservative supporters had been calling on Bush to support the amendment prior to the upcoming presidential election, particularly in the wake of the recent recognition of same-sex marriages in Massachusetts and San Francisco. Although the Democratic frontrunner for president, Sen. John Kerry (D-MA) opposed same-sex marriage, he was one of only 14 senators to vote against the Defense of Marriage Act in 1996. Kerry favors civil unions as an alternative to gay marriage.

Rev. Richard Land, of the Ethics and Religious Liberty Commission of the Southern Baptist Convention, said that he was delighted and pleased, but not surprised by Bush's announcement, stating that "The president's been signaling this for quite a while that he would support this if we reached the last resort." He added: "Our forefathers gave us this procedure in times of crisis when the people's will is being disregarded." Calling the president's move a "declaration of war on gay America," Matt Foreman, of the National Gay and Lesbian Task Force, said it was "a transparent attempt to use our lives and our families to drive a wedge into the electorate purely for political gain."

In order to pass, the amendment would need two-thirds approval in both the House and the Senate, as well as passage in three-fourths of state legislatures within a seven-year period. Although many versions of an amendment have been circulating in Congress, only one has been introduced formally, by Rep. Marilyn Musgrave (R-CO). While 64 percent of the American public opposes legalizing gay marriage, only 41 percent favor an amendment that would prohibit states from recognizing gay marriage. Patrick Guerriero of the Log Cabin Republicans, a group of gay conservatives, vowed that his group would attend the Republican Convention in "record numbers," to defend "part of the American family."

FEBRUARY 25, 2004
SAME SEX MARRIAGE: THE PRESIDENT;
BUSH BACKS BAN IN CONSTITUITON ON GAY MARRIAGE
By ELISABETH BUMILLER

WASHINGTON, Feb. 24—President Bush on Tuesday declared his support for an amendment to the Constitution that would ban gay marriage, saying the union of a man and a woman is "the most fundamental institution of civilization" and that it cannot be separated from its "cultural, religious and natural roots" without weakening society.

In a five-minute announcement in the Roosevelt Room of the White House, Mr. Bush said that he was acting because "activist judges" had made aggressive efforts to redefine marriage and that preserving the institution was now a matter of national importance.

Mr. Bush said states should be permitted to have gay civil unions, even though White House officials said he would not have endorsed such unions as governor of Texas.

"The amendment should fully protect marriage while leaving the state legislatures free to make their own choices in defining legal arrangements other than marriage," said Mr. Bush, who took no questions from reporters and left the room after completing his remarks. [Transcript, Page A18.]

Mr. Bush was acting under enormous pressure from conservative supporters, who insisted that he speak out in an election year on a matter of critical importance to many of his Christian backers.

The pressure has increased in the wake of recent events in Massachusetts and San Francisco. Massachusetts is under court order to begin issuing same-sex marriage licenses on May 17 and San Francisco's City Hall has been transformed into a marriage parlor for thousands of gay and lesbian couples. Mayor Gavin Newsom of San Francisco,

who authorized the issuance of marriage licenses to same-sex couples, responded defiantly on Tuesday to Mr. Bush's remarks. [Page A19.]

Republicans said Mr. Bush was also seeking to draw a sharp distinction between himself and the Democratic front-runner in the primaries, Senator John Kerry of Massachusetts. In 1996, Mr. Kerry was one of 14 senators to vote against the Defense of Marriage Act, which defined marriage as a union between one man and one woman. Mr. Kerry opposes gay marriages but supports civil unions.

Mr. Bush's announcement, even though widely expected, immediately ignited a furious debate between conservatives who applauded it and gays who denounced it.

"It's a declaration of war on gay America," said Matt Foreman, executive director of the National Gay and Lesbian Task Force. "This is such a transparent attempt to use our lives and our families to drive a wedge into the electorate purely for political gain. I knew this was coming for a long time, but to actually read it in print, and to see him say it, left me shaking in both hurt and anger."

The Rev. Richard D. Land, the president of the Ethics and Religious Liberty Commission of the Southern Baptist Convention, embraced the decision, saying: "I'm delighted and I'm pleased, but I'm not surprised. The president's been signaling this for quite a while that he would support this if we reached the last resort. And we've now reached the last resort. Our forefathers gave us this procedure in times of crisis when the people's will is being disregarded."

Mr. Bush urged the Congress to move quickly on an amendment, which needs approval from two-thirds of the

House and the Senate and then passage in at least three-fourths of the state legislatures, or 38, over a period of up to seven years.

On Capitol Hill, Senate Republican leaders said an amendment could reach the floor before November, with hearings as early as next week. But Representative Tom DeLay of Texas, the House majority leader, was more cautious about the timing.

"This is so important we are not going to take a knee-jerk reaction to this," Mr. DeLay said. "We are going to look at our options and be deliberate about what solutions we may suggest."

Republicans said Mr. DeLay, who commended Mr. Bush for his leadership on the issue, was strategically reluctant rather than ideologically to move quickly on the amendment. Mr. DeLay said on Tuesday that it would be "very difficult" to get such a measure through Congress and that some Republicans were strongly resistant to changing the Constitution.

No House or Senate advocates of an amendment have come to any agreement on its wording, though various proposals are circulating. White House officials said Mr. Bush liked the language in the only amendment introduced so far, by Representative Marilyn Musgrave, Republican of Colorado.

That proposal states: "Marriage in the United States shall consist only of the union of a man and a woman. Neither this constitution or the constitution of any state, nor state or federal law, shall be construed to require that marital status or the legal incidents thereof be conferred upon unmarried couples or groups."

Senator Kerry's chief rival for the Democratic presidential nomination, Senator John Edwards of North Carolina, does not support gay marriages either, saying instead that the government could take other steps for gay couples, like provide partnership rights and adoption rights.

Recent opinion polls have consistently found that the majority of Americans oppose gay marriage. A CNN/USA Today/Gallup poll conducted Feb. 16–17, for example, found that 64 percent thought that gay marriage should not be recognized by the law as valid.

But there is less support in opinion polls for amending the Constitution to prohibit gay marriage. In a New York Times/CBS poll in mid-December, 55 percent said they favored an amendment banning gay marriage; in the National Annenberg Election Survey in mid-February, 41 percent said they supported a constitutional amendment to prohibit states from enacting same-sex marriage.

In his remarks, Mr. Bush said he was reacting to the ruling by the Massachusetts Supreme Judicial Court, which essentially ordered the state to begin granting marriage licenses to gay couples on May 17, and to city officials in San Francisco who have issued thousands of licenses.

Those actions, he said, could have "serious consequences throughout the country." There was no assurance, he added, that the Defense of Marriage Act would not itself be struck down by "activist courts."

The only recourse, he said, was to amend the Constitution on an issue that he acknowledged reached into Americans' most private activities.

"America's a free society, which limits the role of government in the lives of our citizens," he said. "This commitment of freedom, however, does not require the redefinition of one of our most basic social institutions."

At the end of his remarks, Mr. Bush spoke of the need for tolerance, saying there was "no contradiction" between a government that respected every person but also protected the institution of marriage.

Neither Mr. Bush nor White House officials defined what they viewed as the difference between gay marriages and civil unions, which would extend legal rights to gay partners. But in supporting the rights of states to offer civil unions, Mr. Bush opened himself up to criticism from some of his most conservative supporters.

"We are concerned that he left the door open for the states to create gay marriage by another name, namely civil unions or domestic partnerships," said Robert Knight, the director of the Culture and Family Institute. "He started out great, but at the end he basically gave a green light to cities and states to create gay marriage by another name."

Gay supporters of Mr. Bush were also unhappy, some saying he was pandering to extreme conservatives.

"This is reminiscent of Pat Buchanan's culture-war speech at the 1992 Republican convention that helped lose the election for the first President Bush," said Patrick Guerriero, the executive director of the Log Cabin Republicans, a group of gay conservatives.

Mr. Guerriero said his group would attend the Republican convention in "record numbers" to defend "part of the American family" if the party chose to marginalize it.

Mary Cheney, a Bush campaign official and the openly gay daughter of Vice President Dick Cheney, had no comment on the announcement. Neither did Mr. Cheney.

Last month, in interviews with The Rocky Mountain News and Denver Post, Mr. Cheney said he would support the president on the issue.

"At this stage, obviously, the president is going to have to make a decision in terms of what administration policy is on this particular provision," he said, "and I will support whatever decision he makes."

Carl Hulse contributed reporting for this article.

White House officials struggled to cite examples of how allowing gay marriage would undermine the social fabric of the United States, as Mr. Bush suggested in his remarks.

Scott McClellan, the White House press secretary, said Mr. Bush addressed that question when he said that "ages of experience have taught humanity that the commitment of a husband and wife to love and to serve one another promotes the welfare of children and the stability of society."

- -

CALIFORNIA SUPREME COURT HALTS GAY MARRIAGE IN SAN FRANCISCO

In a unanimous ruling, the California Supreme Court said that Mayor Gavin Newsom exceeded his authority by allowing same-sex marriages to be performed in San Francisco between February 12 and March 11, 2004. In a 5–2 vote the court also ruled that same-sex marriage licenses issued during that time should be removed from the public record. The decision did not address the constitutionality of state law limiting marriage to opposite-sex couples, leading two justices to argue that the discarding of those licenses was premature. However, the majority's nullification of same-sex marriages that had been performed made it the most definitive reversal of gay unions to date. Newsom responded to the court's action, saying, "I think what we did was right and appropriate and history will judge that." Jordan Lorence, a lawyer with the conservative Alliance Defense Fund, said the decision sent a "huge message" to gay rights advocates.

Although city officials informed couples that the legal standing of the marriages was uncertain at the time they were performed, some couples had obtained benefits previously denied to them as a result. Molly McKay said that she and her lesbian spouse had received an auto insurance discount that they were unable to obtain when they were registered only as domestic partners.

In its decision, the court argued that actions such as Newsom's were based on an individual interpretation of the law and could lead to "confusion and chaos." The court emphasized that it is the judiciary's duty, not the mayor's, to interpret the law. Newsom said that he would respect the ruling but disagreed with it.

AUGUST 13, 2004
CALIFORNIA COURT RULES GAY UNIONS HAVE NO STANDING
By DEAN MURPHY

SAN FRANCISCO, Aug. 12—The California Supreme Court ruled Thursday that a blitz of same-sex weddings here in February and March had no standing under state law and declared the marriages "void and of no legal effect from their inception."

In a unanimous ruling, the justices said that Mayor Gavin Newsom of San Francisco had exceeded his authority in allowing the marriages. By a 5-to-2 vote, the court also rendered the licenses, more than 4,000 in all, nothing more than a collector's item, ordering city officials to remove any record of them from the books and to offer the couples refunds of license fees.

The decision was narrow legally, applying only to the issue of executive authority and not to the constitutionality of state law limiting marriage to unions between a man and a woman.

Yet in practical terms, though previous rulings here and elsewhere in the country have placed thousands of same-sex marriages in limbo, the decision on Thursday was the biggest and most definitive reversal of gay weddings anywhere because of the nullification of the marriages.

"Withholding or delaying a ruling on the current validity of the existing same-sex marriages might lead numerous persons to make fundamental changes in their lives or otherwise proceed on the basis of erroneous expectations, creating potentially irreparable harm," Chief Justice Ronald George wrote for the majority.

In a dissenting opinion, Justice Joyce L. Kennard said it was too early to throw out the licenses because of a separate constitutional challenge now in San Francisco Superior Court to the prohibition on gay marriage in California state law.

"It is premature and unwise to assert, as the majority essentially does, that the thousands of same-sex weddings performed in San Francisco were empty and meaningless ceremonies in the eyes of the law," Justice Kennard wrote.

In issuing the licenses between Feb. 12 and March 11, when the Supreme Court ordered a halt to them, city officials warned the same-sex couples that the marriages had uncertain legal standing. But in the general euphoria of the time, few of the couples cared much about the caveat. In the early days before an appointment system was put in place, thousands of people lined up at City Hall in the hope of getting married.

Some of the same-sex married couples said they later used the licenses to obtain benefits previously denied them, like discounts on insurance.

Dennis Herrera, the San Francisco city attorney, said Thursday that he could offer no guidance to couples who had received such benefits, suggesting only that they consult a lawyer. Molly McKay, a lawyer who is associate executive director of Marriage Equality California, a gay rights group, said her own auto insurance discount of $316 might now be in jeopardy.

"Every year we called them to determine whether we qualify for the marital discount as domestic partners," Ms. McKay said of her insurance company, "and every year they said no." But after Ms. McKay and her partner of seven years got married, she said, "We called our agent and said: Guess what? We're married. Do we get the discount? And they said sure."

Ms. McKay, who showed up outside the courthouse on Thursday and wore her wedding dress, and the leaders of other gay and lesbian groups said the ruling had unleashed a torrent of questions from scores of suddenly unmarried same-sex couples. The National Center for Lesbian Rights posted a series of "Frequently Asked Questions" on its Web site to help address some of the concerns.

"The interesting question is, what happens next?" Ms. McKay said. "Do we file a joint tax return for the six months of our marriage and then file another return for the rest of the year separately as single?"

Yet even with the many pragmatic concerns, the most prevalent reactions to the ruling among gay-marriage advocates were anger and sadness. Several gay couples gathered on the steps outside the Supreme Court here to wait for the ruling and wept as excerpts from the court's 114-page decision were read aloud.

"I feel more pain than I expected to," said Kate Kendell, a lawyer who is the executive director of the National Center for Lesbian Rights and who acted as a witness at the first gay wedding on Feb. 12. "My lawyer brain is being seeped into by my human brain."

The decision was hailed by conservative groups opposed to same-sex marriage as an important repudiation of San Francisco's bid to skirt a state law, approved by voters in 2000, that defines marriage as "a personal relation arising out of a civil contract between a man and a woman."

Jordan Lorence, a lawyer for the Alliance Defense Fund, a Christian advocacy group that sued the city over the same-sex marriages, said the decision amounted to a "huge message" to Mr. Newsom and other gay-marriage advocates that they cannot break the law.

In issuing their ruling, the Supreme Court justices said Mr. Newsom, who had argued the state law on marriage was unconstitutional, had invited chaos by overstepping his bounds as mayor.

"This conclusion is consistent with the classic understanding of the separation of powers doctrine—that the legislative power is the power to enact statues, the executive power is the power to execute or enforce statutes, and the judicial power is the power to interpret statutes and to determine their constitutionality," Chief Justice George wrote.

"There are thousands of elected and appointed public officials in California's 58 counties charged with the ministerial duty of enforcing thousands of state statutes," he wrote later. "If each official were empowered to decide whether or not to carry out each ministerial act based upon the official's own personal judgment of the constitutionality of an underlying statute, the enforcement of statutes would become haphazard, leading to confusion and chaos."

Hailing the ruling, Mr. Lorence said, "Change comes by respecting regular procedures, not by defying state law."

He and others who had challenged the marriages gathered across the street from the Supreme Court building.

Another lawyer for the group, Joshua Carden, said the court had rendered the San Francisco marriages meaningless.

"It's like counterfeit money," Mr. Carden said of the licenses, "you can't spend it and you can't cash it."

Mr. Newsom, speaking at a news conference at City Hall, said he would respect the ruling, though he said he disagreed with it. He offered no apologies for his actions, except to say that his bid to bring same-sex marriage to California would take longer than he had hoped.

"I think what we did was right and appropriate and history will judge that," Mr. Newsom said.

As satisfying as the ruling was for the opponents of gay marriage, many agreed that the biggest fight was yet to come. In issuing its ruling, the Supreme Court expressly sidestepped the fundamental question of whether the state's ban on same-sex marriage was constitutional. That question is the subject of a separate lawsuit that could take several years before reaching the State Supreme Court.

With that fight in mind, gay-marriage advocates organized a protest march late on Thursday, beginning in the heavily gay Castro district and ending at Civic Center Plaza near the Supreme Court.

Mr. Newsom said he was convinced that gay-marriage proponents would achieve victory in his lifetime and in the lifetimes of the first couple to be married at City Hall, Del Martin, 83, and Phyllis Lyon, 79.

Mr. Lorence, the lawyer for the Alliance Defense Fund, disagreed. "People will step in," he said. "Previous political actions in various states have shown that the voters will step in when the states get it wrong."

Carolyn Marshall contributed reporting for this article.

* *

SAME-SEX MARRIAGE ISSUE TO PLAY A ROLE IN PRESIDENTIAL ELECTION

Experts on both sides of the debate agreed that it was inevitable that the issue of same-sex marriage would become entwined with the 2004 presidential election, particularly on the heels of the court decision that nullified unions performed earlier in the year in San Francisco. Conservative organizations succeeded in placing anti–same-sex marriage constitutional amendments on the ballot in several states, including such key swing states in the upcoming presidential election as Michigan, Ohio, and Oregon.

Conservative strategists believed that the proposed constitutional amendments would motivate traditionalists, a significant portion of the Republican base, to turn out to vote come Election Day. Republican strategist Grover Norquist said, "it could well be what swings the election." Phil Burress, a conservative leader in Ohio, further explained the somewhat ironic relationship between conservative organizing and judicial rulings that favor same-sex marriage: "What would really have fired us up is if it had been a decision that would have been more judicial tyranny. When we win one, it doesn't fire us up."

Cheryl Jacques of the Human Rights Campaign, a gay advocacy group based in Washington, D.C., predicted that the strategy would backfire, saying, "most people don't wake up in the morning thinking about gay and lesbian marriage or any gay issue. They wake up in the morning thinking about jobs and health care and the war in Iraq." Celinda Lake, a pollster associated with the Democratic Party, agreed, arguing that the Republicans were "using this to distract and deflect from their failures on Iraq and the economy." However, Lake conceded that having a constitutional amendment against same-sex marriage might make a difference in Ohio because a small increase in voters from one Party could influence the outcome due to the closeness of the race. A spokesperson for Democratic presidential candidate John Kerry said that Kerry opposes same-sex marriage, but that he "doesn't think that the Constitution should be used as a way to divide the country."

Tony Perkins of the conservative Family Research Council emphasized the importance of the polls, saying that opponents of same-sex marriage planned to encourage greater numbers of church members to vote in November through national telecasts as well as local influences. Gay groups, on the other hand, anticipated continuing to fight the battle in the courts, having obtained a favorable ruling recently in Washington State. Additional judicial rulings were pending at the time in New Jersey, Oregon, Florida, and California.

AUGUST 14, 2004
GAY MARRIAGE BECOMES A SWING ISSUE WITH PULL
By DAVID D. KIRKPATRICK

Supporters and opponents of same-sex marriage called this week's California Supreme Court decision nullifying San Francisco's marriage licenses a minor prelude to bigger battles at the ballot box. Both social conservatives and gay rights groups say their debate is becoming increasingly intertwined with the presidential election.

Social conservatives have argued for months that voters, not judges, should ultimately settle the issue of legal recognition for gay couples. They have organized to put constitutional amendments blocking same-sex marriages on the ballots in a dozen states this fall, including the pivotal swing states of Oregon, Michigan and Ohio.

And after the strong turnout in support of a similar measure in Missouri on Aug. 3, some conservative strategists said that the referendums could help President Bush by motivating traditionalists to vote. "It could well be what swings the election," said Grover Norquist, a strategist close to the Bush campaign.

Phil Burress, a veteran organizer who is working to amend the Ohio Constitution, said a California ruling in favor of same-sex marriage might actually have helped his efforts even more. "What really would have fired us up is if it had been a decision that would have been more judicial tyranny," Mr. Burress said. "When we win one, it doesn't fire us up. It surprises us that the judges got it right. We

high-fived for a couple of minutes around the office and then we went back to work."

But in a shift from their previous strategy, some gay rights groups fighting the amendments banning same-sex marriage said yesterday that they, too, would use advertisements aimed at making the debate an issue in the presidential election.

Cheryl Jacques, executive director of the Human Rights Campaign, one of the main groups fighting for gay marriage, said the group plans to argue in advertising campaigns in Ohio and other swing states that the Bush campaign and its allies are orchestrating the marriage amendment efforts in order to distract voters from other issues.

"There is a single puppet master behind these efforts, and that is George W. Bush and his allies," Ms. Jacques said in an interview. "They will try to make this an issue, and are going to remind people what they already know, that most people don't wake up in the morning thinking about gay and lesbian marriage or any gay issue. They wake up in the morning thinking about jobs and health care and the war in Iraq."

To suggest that Mr. Bush's campaign is behind the state initiatives, advocates of same-sex marriage have pointed to a letter that Ken Blackwell, a Republican who is secretary of state of Ohio, wrote to his supporters saying that the Bush campaign had asked him to support the state's amendment. Representatives of Mr. Blackwell and Mr. Bush did not dispute the letter.

But Mr. Burress said Republican leaders in Ohio had initially resisted his efforts to put the amendment on the ballot.

Some conservatives contended that accusing Mr. Bush of fighting same-sex marriage would help him and hurt Mr. Kerry, the Democratic candidate. In the Missouri election, gay rights groups spent $450,000 and their opponents only $19,000. The turnout was twice as high as in a typical state primary and the amendment to ban gay marriage passed with 71 percent support.

"I would think the Kerry campaign would want to talk to the Human Rights Campaign," said Gary Bauer, a candidate for the Republican presidential nomination in 2000 and founder of the organization American Values. "If I am for marriage between a man and a woman, then I should vote for George Bush. I think that is the last message Senator John Kerry wants to be connected with in the minds of voters."

Steve Schmidt, a spokesman for the Bush campaign, said: "The president has made his position clear, that he believes the institution of marriage should be preserved. This issue was forced on the country by a group of activist judges, and states across the country have measures on the ballot for the fall election which will preserve the institution of marriage, and voters will let their voices be heard."

Some Democrats argued that the ballot measures might not damage Mr. Kerry. Phil Singer, a spokesman for Mr. Kerry, said Mr. Kerry also opposed same-sex marriage, although he opposed amending the federal Constitution to ban same-sex unions. "John Kerry believes a marriage is between a man and a woman but doesn't think that the Constitution should be used as a way to divide the country," Mr. Singer said.

Celinda Lake, a Democratic pollster who has worked for the Human Rights Campaign, argued that the Bush campaign's support for the amendments could backfire. "Voters will say this is not the priority right now," she said. "The issue here is Iraq and the economy, not gay marriage. They are using this to distract and deflect from their failures on Iraq and the economy. Which are you more worried about?"

Of the three swing states where same-sex marriage amendments are likely to appear on the ballot, Ms. Lake argued, Ohio was the only one where it might make a difference. She argued that the amendment was not very popular in Oregon and that Mr. Kerry could carry Michigan by turning out voters among traditionally Democratic groups like union members and African-Americans.

"Ohio is a different story," Ms. Lake said. "It is very close and it could have an impact there."

Both sides of the marriage battle say they plan to step up their efforts as the election nears. Tony Perkins, president of the conservative Family Research Council, said opponents of same-sex marriage were relying on like-minded churches to turn out their members, just as they did in Missouri. On Sept. 19, he and other well-known conservative Christians will hold their third national telecast to churches around the country this year to discuss the issue.

They will speak from the First Baptist Church of Springdale, Ark. The organization Americans United for Separation of Church and State has argued that the church violated the requirements of its tax-exempt status by engaging in politics.

Gay groups, meanwhile, are continuing to press their case in courts. Last week, a court in Washington State ruled in favor of a same-sex couple's right to marry, setting the stage for an appeals battle there. Other cases are pending in state courts in New Jersey and Oregon, and a Constitutional challenge is under way in federal court in Florida.

Another case is pending in California, too. The court's ruling this week addressed only the procedural matter of whether the mayor of San Francisco could issue marriage licenses. Another case working its way through the court system will settle the underlying issue of same-sex marriage rights under the state Constitution, but that case could take years to resolve.

Still, Jordan Lorence, a lawyer with the Alliance Defense Fund, a socially conservative legal group that has filed briefs in many of the cases, argued that court victories for same-sex marriage were unlikely to settle much. Even in Massachusetts, he said, opponents were still trying to change the state Constitution. "The final decision is going to be made by the voters," he said.

THOUSANDS RALLY IN SUPPORT OF GAY MARRIAGE IN CITIES ACROSS THE NATION

Tens of thousands of people showed their support for same-sex marriage by gathering in cities across the country such as San Francisco, Los Angeles, Washington, New York, Las Vegas, Little Rock, Boston, and Minneapolis. The rallies were organized to show support for gay rights despite the fact that California voters had recently handed the movement a significant defeat by approving Proposition 8, a referendum that would overturn a 2008 judicial decision supporting same-sex marriage in California. Although polls had long indicated that voters would fail to approve Proposition 8, the gap closed in the months before the election and the measure passed with 52 percent of the vote.

Several participants in the rallies likened the response to the passage of Proposition 8 to that of earlier watersheds moments in the gay rights movement, such as the Stonewall riots of 1969 and sustained public outcry of the gay community during the AIDS crisis in the 1980s. Because the Proposition 8 protests were organized using social networking and other newer Internet technologies, some referred to it as Stonewall 2.0. Rallies included a mix of gay and straight people, many of whom held signs with messages such as "Straights Against Hate."

More than 4,000 people gathered in protest at city hall in New York, where many called same-sex marriage "the greatest civil rights battle of our generation." Despite the emergence of wildfires outside of the city, a crowd estimated at 9,000 gathered in Los Angeles, where Mayor Antonio Villaraigosa said, "I have come here from the fires because I feel the wind at my back as well. It's the wind of change that has swept the nation. It is the wind of optimism and hope."

Comedian Wanda Sykes publicly announced to a crowd of more than 1,000 in Las Vegas that she was gay and had wed her partner in California earlier, adding that the success of Proposition 8 made her feel "like I was being attacked, personally attacked—our community was attacked." While many in the crowds expressed outrage at the outcome of the vote, in San Francisco the Reverend G. Penny Nixon cautioned against blame, saying, "This is a movement based on love."

Frank Schubert, campaign manager of Protect Marriage, a leading group that supported the passage of Proposition 8, said, "If they want to legalize same-sex marriage, they are going to have to bring a proposal before the people of California. That's how democracy works."

NOVEMBER 16, 2008
ACROSS U.S., BIG RALLIES FOR SAME-SEX MARRIAGE
By JESSE MCKINLEY

SAN FRANCISCO – In one of the nation's largest displays of support for gay rights, tens of thousands of people in cities across the country turned out in support of same-sex marriage on Saturday, lending their voices to an issue that many gay men and lesbians consider a critical step to full equality.

The demonstrations—from a sun-splashed throng in San Francisco to a chilly crowd in Minneapolis—came 11 days after California voters narrowly passed a ballot measure, Proposition 8, that outlawed previously legal same-sex ceremonies in the state. The measure's passage has spurred protests in California and across the country, including at several Mormon temples, a reflection of that church's ardent backing of the proposition.

On Saturday, speakers painted the fight over Proposition 8 as another test of a movement that began with the riots at the Stonewall Inn in New York in 1969, survived the emergence of the AIDS crisis in the 1980s, and has since made enormous strides in societal acceptance, whether in television shows or in antidiscrimination laws.

"It's not 'Yes we can,' " said Tom Ammiano, a San Francisco city supervisor, referring to President-elect Barack Obama's campaign mantra. "It's 'Yes we will.' "

Carrying handmade signs with slogans like "No More Mr. Nice Gay" and "Straights Against Hate," big crowds filled civic centers and streets in many cities. In New York, some 4,000 people gathered at City Hall, where speakers repeatedly called same-sex marriage "the greatest civil rights battle of our generation."

"We are not going to rest at night until every citizen in every state in this country can say, 'This is the person I love,' and take their hand in marriage," said Representative Anthony D. Weiner of Brooklyn.

In Los Angeles, where wildfires had temporarily grabbed headlines from continuing protests over Proposition 8, Mayor Antonio R. Villaraigosa addressed a crowd of about 9,000 people in Spanish and English, and seemed to express confidence that the measure, which is being challenged in California courts, would be overturned.

"I've come here from the fires because I feel the wind at my back as well," said the mayor, who arrived at a downtown rally from the fire zone on a helicopter. "It's the wind of change that has swept the nation. It is the wind of optimism and hope."

About 900 protesters braved a tornado watch and menacing rain clouds in Washington to rally in front of the Capitol and on to the White House. "Gay, straight, black, white; marriage is a civil right," the marchers chanted.

In Las Vegas, the comedian Wanda Sykes surprised a crowd of more than 1,000 rallying outside a gay community center by announcing that she is gay and had wed her wife in California on Oct. 25. Ms. Sykes, who divorced her husband of seven years in 1998, had never publicly discussed her sexual orientation but said the passage of Proposition 8 had propelled her to be open about it.

"I felt like I was being attacked, personally attacked—our community was attacked," she told the crowd.

And while some speakers were obviously eager to tap crowds' current outrage, others took pains to cast the demonstrations as a peaceful, long-term, campaign over an issue that has proved remarkably and consistently divisive.

"We need to be our best selves," said the Rev. G. Penny Nixon, a gay pastor from San Mateo, Calif., who warned the San Francisco crowd against blaming "certain communities" for the election loss. "This is a movement based on love."

The protests were organized largely over the Internet, and featured few representatives of major gay rights groups that campaigned against Proposition 8, which passed with 52 percent of the vote after trailing for months in the polls. The online aspect seemed to draw a broad cross-section of people, like Nicole Toussaint, a kindergarten teacher who joined a crowd of more than 1,000 people in Minneapolis.

"I'm here to support my friends who are gay," said Ms. Toussaint, 23. "I think my generation will play a big role."

The big crowds notwithstanding, it has been a tough month for gay rights. Proposition 8 was just one of three measures on same-sex marriage passed on Nov. 4, with constitutional bans also being approved in Arizona and Florida. In Arkansas, voters passed a measure aimed at barring gay men and lesbians from adopting children.

That vote was on the minds of many of the 200 people who protested Saturday in front of the State Capitol in Little Rock. One of those, Barb L'Eplattenier, 39, a university professor, said some of her gay friends with adopted children were fearful of state action if they appeared in public. "They think their families are in danger," said Ms. L'Eplattenier, who married her partner, Sarah Scanlon, in California in July.

The protests over Proposition 8 also come even as same-sex marriages began Wednesday in Connecticut, which joined Massachusetts as the only states allowing such ceremonies. By contrast, 30 states have constitutional bans on such unions.

At a Boston rally on Saturday, Kate Leslie, an organizer, said the loss in California had certainly caught the attention of local gay men and lesbians who have had the right to marry since 2004.

"You're watching people who could be you and are part of your community being stripped of their rights,"

Ms. Leslie said. "And in some ways that's why so many people are infuriated in Massachusetts and willing to stand up for a rally."

In California, a State Supreme Court decision legalized same-sex marriage in May. As many as 18,000 couples married, some traveling from other states to tie the knot. Such marriages may be challenged in court.

David McMullin, a garden designer from Atlanta, was one of those who made the trip, marrying his partner in Oakland, Calif., in September, in part to let their two adoptive children feel part of a married family.

"We just want our kids to know we're O.K.," said Mr. McMullin, who had come to a protest in front of the Georgia State Capitol. "We have rights as people even if we don't have rights as citizens."

Supporters of the proposition have repeatedly argued that Proposition 8 was not antigay, but merely pro-marriage.

"Marriage is between a man and a woman," said Frank Schubert, the campaign manager for Protect Marriage, the leading group behind passing Proposition 8. "If they want to legalize same-sex marriage, they are going to have to bring a proposal before the people of California. That's how democracy works."

Equality California, a major gay rights group here, indicated this week that it would work to repeal Proposition 8 if legal challenges fail.

Such dry approaches seemed a million miles away, however, from the boisterous scene in front of San Francisco City Hall on Saturday, where as many as 10,000 people gathered, carrying signs, American flags and even copies of their marriage licenses.

One of those was Lawrence Dean, 57, who had married his partner, Steven Lyle, in San Francisco in July. It was the fifth time that the couple of 19 years had held a ceremony to announce their commitment, and, of course, accept wedding gifts.

"If we keep this up, maybe I won't have to again," Mr. Dean said, looking out at the protest. "I have enough pots and pans."

- -

Iowa Constitution Protects Same-Sex Marriage

In 2009 the supreme court of Iowa said that a state law limiting marriage to opposite-sex couples was unconstitutional, joining Massachusetts and Connecticut in allowing same-sex marriages. Noting that the court has a "constitutional duty to ensure equal protection of the law," Justice Mark Cady said that excluding gays and lesbians from marriage "does not substantially further any important governmental objective."

Although opponents of same-sex marriage argued that "a court decision doesn't change what's right and what's wrong," they conceded that the only way to challenge the ruling was through constitutional amendment, a daunting process in Iowa that would require a minimum of two years. The amendment process would have to be initiated by state lawmakers, an unlikely prospect given the composition of the legislature at the time. The state Senate majority leader said, "We're just going to say no to amending our Constitution and putting discrimination into our Constitution." Same-sex marriages were expected to begin in three weeks. Iowa marriages do not require state residency, fueling speculation that same-sex couples from other states may soon head to Iowa to be married.

Supporters of the ruling celebrated at a local hotel, noting the surprise that much of the country seemed to feel about Iowa's support for same-sex marriage. While one Iowan said that she was "almost ready to up and leave Iowa," gay state senator Matt McCoy said Iowans had a long history of open-mindedness and a "live and let live" attitude.

APRIL 4, 2009
IOWA COURT VOIDS GAY MARRIAGE BAN

By MONICA DAVEY

DES MOINES – Same-sex couples will be allowed to marry in Iowa by month's end, after a ruling on Friday by the Iowa Supreme Court that found unconstitutional a state law limiting marriage to a man and a woman.

The unanimous decision moved the heated battle over same-sex marriage beyond the East and West Coasts to the nation's middle. Only Massachusetts and Connecticut now allow same-sex marriages, while California permitted them for about six months before voters approved a ban in November.

"We are firmly convinced the exclusion of gay and lesbian people from the institution of civil marriage does not substantially further any important governmental objective," Justice Mark S. Cady wrote for the seven-member court, adding later, "We have a constitutional duty to ensure equal protection of the law."

Opponents of same-sex marriage pledged to fight the outcome, but acknowledged that there appeared to be no immediate way to undo it. The only avenue would be a constitutional amendment, but under Iowa law that process would take at least two years.

Members of the Iowa Family Policy Center, a group opposed to same-sex marriage, spoke with state lawmakers after the ruling in hopes of jump-starting the amendment process.

"A court decision doesn't change what's right and what's wrong," said Bryan English, a spokesman for the group.

But there was no indication that the Legislature, controlled by Democrats, would take up the matter.

Meanwhile, the ruling set off celebrations among same-sex couples, many of whom had gathered at a hotel here to await word. They wept, embraced, laughed, and wept some more.

"I think there's been a perception that it couldn't happen here," David Twombley, 67, said, moments after he learned that he and his partner could marry. The couple was among six Iowa couples to start the legal fight four years ago that culminated in Friday's decision.

"But yes, it happened, right here in Iowa," Mr. Twombley said. "There's something about that, about it happening in the heartland, that has got to accelerate this process for the whole country."

Same-sex marriages could take place in counties here starting in three weeks, when the ruling becomes final, lawyers said. There is no requirement that people seeking marriage licenses prove they live in Iowa, so the doors will be open to same-sex couples from other states.

"Go get married!" Dennis W. Johnson, a lawyer from Des Moines who had helped represent the gay and lesbian couples in the case, told the gathering at the hotel. "Live happily ever after," Mr. Johnson called out, adding, "Live the American dream."

Opponents of the decision said they believed it would awaken enormous backlash here and throughout the Midwest once people understood what had happened.

Along the streets of this city in the hours after the ruling, people expressed mixed views of the matter, though nearly all said they were surprised—happily so, in some cases, but less so for others—at what the court had concluded.

On at least one talk-radio show, residents were enraged.

"I'm almost ready to up and leave Iowa and move back to Minnesota," one woman said angrily.

Within hours of the decision, the representatives of the Iowa Family Policy Center left the Supreme Court building here, and sought out state lawmakers in the State Capitol building just down the street.

Unlike some states that have barred the marriages with voter-led ballot measures, voters here cannot directly initiate constitutional amendments. Instead, an amendment would require approval by state lawmakers during two legislative sessions, and then approval by voters at the ballot box. That means the earliest a prospective ban could take effect would be 2012.

Opponents of same-sex marriages want state lawmakers, who are a few weeks from finishing their annual legislative session, to begin the process now. But the idea seemed to have no backing among legislative leaders; both chambers here are controlled by Democrats.

"We're just going to say no to amending our Constitution and putting discrimination into our Constitution," said Michael E. Gronstal, a Democrat and State Senate majority leader, who noted that such an amendment had failed in the Senate several years ago, even before the suit that led to Friday's ruling, and would, he said, most likely fail again.

Gov. Chet Culver, also a Democrat, was more muted in his response to the ruling.

"The next responsible step is to thoroughly review this decision, which I am doing with my legal counsel and the attorney general, before reacting to what it means for Iowa," Mr. Culver said in a written statement.

Whether or not state lawmakers take up the constitutional amendment in the coming weeks, the ruling ensures the state will become a battleground over same-sex marriage.

National advocacy groups, which have been focused on a case before the California Supreme Court that seeks to overturn the ban in that state, and on Vermont, where a bill legalizing same-sex marriage is pending, have already turned their eyes to Des Moines.

"The gay marriage movement has once again used the power of the courts to push an untruth on unwilling Iowans," said Brian S. Brown, the executive director of the National Organization for Marriage, a group formed in 2007 to preserve traditional marriage. "Same-sex unions are not marriages, and Iowans should not be forced by law to treat them as such."

Leaders of Lambda Legal, which is based in New York and led—along with state and local lawyers here—the legal case before the Supreme Court, said Iowans had a long history of openmindedness, or as State Senator Matt

McCoy, a Democrat who is openly gay, described it, "a live and let live attitude."

Camilla Taylor, a senior staff lawyer for Lambda, said the Supreme Court ruling in a way was merely "vindicating quintessential Iowa values," namely, a commitment to families. That this battle was being waged in Iowa, Ms. Taylor said, would have a "transformative effect" not just on the Midwest, but elsewhere.

"The fact that it's here in some way highlights the inevitability of this all," she said.

The legal case here began in 2005, when the six same-sex couples filed suit against the county recorder here in Polk County because he would not accept their marriage license applications.

Two years later, a local judge, Robert B. Hanson, ruled in that case that a 1998 state law defining marriage as only between a man and woman was unconstitutional. The ruling, in 2007, set off a flurry of same-sex couples from all over the state, racing for the courthouse in Polk County.

The rush lasted less than a day in August 2007. Although Judge Hanson had ruled against the state law, he quickly decided to delay any additional granting of licenses, saying that the Iowa Supreme Court should have an opportunity to weigh in first.

"If gay and lesbian people must submit to different treatment without an exceedingly persuasive justification, they are deprived of the benefits of the principle of equal protection upon which the rule of law is founded," the Supreme Court said in agreeing that the 1998 law was unconstitutional.

Obama Offers Benefits to Gay Partners While Defending Antigay Law

In his most significant statement on gay issues since taking office, President Obama signed a presidential memo that granted benefits to same-sex partners of federal employees in June 2009. Benefits did not include health care, however. Obama had been under pressure to begin to fulfill his promise to "fight hard" for gay rights. Reaction in the gay community to the announcement was mixed. While Richard Socarides said that Obama had "promised the moon and done nothing," several other gay rights activists noted that Obama had privately promised to do more in the years to come.

The Defense of Marriage Act, a 1996 law that bans the recognition of same-sex marriage at the federal level, may prohibit the government from providing health care benefits to same-sex partners. The Obama administration recently defended the constitutionality of the law in a legal brief submitted to federal court. Joe Solmonese of the Human Rights Campaign, a gay advocacy group, responded with an angry letter to the Obama administration, saying, "As an American, civil rights advocate, and a human being, I hold this administration to a higher standard than this brief. In the course of the campaign, I became convinced—and I still want to believe—that you do, too." The administration said that it would like to see DOMA repealed, but that it has a duty to defend current law in court.

JUNE 17, 2009
U.S. TO EXTEND ITS JOB BENEFITS TO GAY PARTNERS
By JEFF ZELENY

President Obama will sign a presidential memorandum on Wednesday to extend benefits to same-sex partners of federal employees, administration officials said Tuesday evening, but he will stop short of pledging full health insurance coverage.

Mr. Obama, in an Oval Office announcement, is expected to offer details about which benefits will be provided. It is the most significant statement he has made on gay issues, and it comes as he faces intense criticism from several gay rights leaders over what they suggest has been a failure to live up to campaign promises in the first months of his presidency.

Mr. Obama will be weighing in for the first time on one of the most delicate social and political issues of the day: whether the government must provide benefits to same-sex partners of federal employees. While he will announce a list of benefits, officials said, they are not expected to include broad health insurance coverage, which could require legislation to achieve.

The initial reaction from some gay rights advocates was mixed.

"Extending benefits to partners of gay federal employees is terrific, but at this point he is under enormous pressure from the gay civil rights community for having promised the moon and done nothing so far," Richard Socarides, an adviser to the Clinton administration on gay issues, said Tuesday evening. "So more important now is what he says tomorrow about the future for gay people during his presidency."

The breadth and scope of the memorandum to be signed by Mr. Obama was being completed Tuesday evening, said administration officials, who spoke on the condition of anonymity to avoid upstaging the president's announcement on Wednesday.

As a presidential candidate, Mr. Obama vowed to "fight hard" for the rights of gay couples. As a senator, he sponsored legislation that would have provided health benefits to same-sex partners of federal employees.

But President Obama and his advisers have been reluctant to wade deeply into divisive issues like overturning a ban on openly gay military members or extending benefits to partners of government employees, fearful that such moves could overtake the administration's broader agenda.

He has sent private assurances, several activists have said, that he intends to do more in coming years. But some gay groups have grown impatient with the wary stance of the White House, particularly as a growing number of state legislatures have taken up the question of same-sex marriage and other issues important to gay men and lesbians.

In considering whether to extend health benefits to same-sex partners, Mr. Obama confronted divided legal opinions.

In California, two federal appeals court judges said that employees of their court were entitled to health benefits for their same-sex partners under the program that insures millions of federal workers. But the federal Office of Personnel Management has instructed insurers not to provide the benefits ordered by the judges, citing a 1996 law, the Defense of Marriage Act.

Joe Solmonese, the president of the Human Rights Campaign, wrote an angry letter to the White House on Monday about a decision by the administration to file a legal brief supporting the constitutionality of the Defense of Marriage Act.

"As an American, a civil rights advocate, and a human being, I hold this administration to a higher standard than this brief," Mr. Solmonese wrote. "In the course of your campaign, I became convinced—and I still want to believe—that you do, too."

The brief, filed in federal court last week, was in response to a lawsuit arguing that the marriage act is unconstitutional.

A White House spokesman said that it was standard practice for the administration to back laws that are challenged in court—even those it does not agree with—and that the president "wants to see a legislative repeal of the Defense of Marriage Act." Mr. Obama repeatedly backed repealing the act during his presidential campaign.

With the administration's decision to stop short of extending full health insurance benefits or calling for legislation to do so, it remained an open question how significant the presidential announcement would be, Mr. Socarides said.

But administration officials said the timing of the announcement was intended to help contain the growing furor among gay rights groups. Several gay donors withdrew their sponsorship of a Democratic National Committee fund-raising event next week, where Vice President Joseph R. Biden Jr. is scheduled to speak.

THE INTERSECTION OF RELIGION
WITH GAY AND LESBIAN ISSUES

Traditionally, various religions have thought of homosexuality as a moral failing or as a psychological disorder. A *New York Times* column on the issue published on March 28, 1971, put it this way: "Over the years homosexuals have generally felt about as comfortable in most local churches as early Christians did in the Colosseum." Mosaic law regarded homosexuality as an abomination, and it was long condemned in Judaism and Islam as contrary to the will of God. Within the Catholic Church, traditional canon law did not deem homosexuality itself evil but suggested that same-sex sexuality is unnatural (because it does not foster reproduction) and sinful (because it occurs outside of marriage). However, according to noted historian and professor John Boswell, author of *Christianity, Social Tolerance and Homosexuality,* the Christian church became actively hostile to homosexuality only in the thirteenth century, during a period characterized by rising intolerance toward Jews, Muslims, and other minorities. At this time, some Christian states went so far as to punish those accused of engaging in same-sex sexuality with stoning, mutilation, or burning at the stake. More recently, in a *Times* report of January 25, 1965, Rev. Bernard P. Donachie warned Catholics against the "nation's spiritual bloodstream being contaminated . . . by a flood of smut," and characterized homosexuality as an evil akin to legalized prostitution, free clinics for drug addicts, and mechanical devices for the elimination of babies. Similar views have long been expressed by many Protestant Christian churches.

Over the past forty years, however, several aspects of these religious attitudes and doctrines have been challenged and even altered to some extent, although the timing of these changes has varied significantly among the various denominations. A *Times* report of November 29, 1967, noted that some Episcopalian priests were arguing that homosexual acts between consenting adults should be classified as "morally neutral" at the very least and a positive good in some circumstances. The organizer of a related conference called "Project H," the Reverend Walter D. Dennis, encouraged Christians to "rethink the usual position that has turned homosexuals

into modern-day lepers" and judge all relationships on the basis of whether they "foster a permanent relationship of love." Some in attendance disagreed, reflecting the more traditional view and arguing that homosexual acts "must always be regarded as perversions because they are not part of the natural process of rearing children."

More recently, a *Times* report of November 7, 2007, discussed a similar discussion within the Islamic faith. Many Islamic clerics continue to consider homosexuality a sin, and punishments remain severe for lesbian, gay, bisexual, and transgender (LGBT) people in several predominantly Islamic countries. However, new ways of interpreting the Koran's teachings are beginning to emerge, particularly within the United States. Professor Omid Safi, an Islamic studies professor at the University of North Carolina at Chapel Hill, argues that most verses dealing with same-sex relations in the Koran are ambiguous, and gay rights advocates are promoting more holistic interpretations that emphasize the teaching of accepting everyone as equally God's creation.

The conflict regarding the relationship of faith and homosexuality continues to this day. These issues play out in ongoing struggles regarding church membership, LGBT clergy, and same-sex marriage (see the previous chapter). Further, these deeply held beliefs continue to have an influence not only within religious communities but also in the realm of secular politics.

CONGREGATION MEMBERSHIP

Lesbian, gay, bisexual, and transgender people began to come out more frequently in the wake of the Stonewall Rebellion (see the first chapter), including in their churches; however, they were not always received with open arms, often being told, either directly or indirectly, that they could continue as members as long as they did not discuss (or in some cases, practice) their sexuality. In a *Times* report of March 25, 1971, Rev. Robert W. Wood of the United Church of Christ in Newark, New Jersey, criticized churches for failing

IN FOCUS

The Sisters of Perpetual Indulgence

• •

The Sisters of Perpetual Indulgence is a bawdy street theater group that brings together religion and sexuality in a creative and satirical manner that raises money for charity. Begun in San Francisco in 1979 by four gay men originally hailing from Iowa, the Sisters use Catholic imagery and humor to combat the guilt and shame that are sometimes applied to members of the LGBT community. The Sisters typically dress in nuns' habits, adopt religious names (such as Sister Phyllis Stein [a play on *Philistine*, a term often associated with an obtuse relationship to religious values]), and follow membership practices that parallel religious orders (for example, members serve as novices for a defined period of time before being accepted as full-fledged Sisters). With houses in various cities across the United States as well as in eight other countries, the Sisters have raised more than $1 million for causes including AIDS care, refugee relief, and antiviolence initiatives.

Some Catholics have argued that the Sisters' use of religious symbols is offensive. A case in point is the Castro Crawl, held on Easter Sunday, perhaps the most sacred holy day in the Catholic Church. Begun in 1995 by the Sisters, the Crawl features a thirteen-stop pub crawl that parodies the Stations of the Cross, a multistaged commemoration of the passion of Christ during which Catholics recite set prayers. At each pub stop in the primarily gay Castro district, the Sisters call out, "We adore thee, O Christ," and participants respond, "Luvya, mean it, let's do brunch." Actors portraying Jesus, Mary, and other iconic religious figures pass out condoms as well as vanilla wafers and Jägermeister, paralleling the wafers and wine that are central to Catholic communion practices.

A controversy arose during the 1999 Crawl when San Francisco gave the Sisters permission to close one block of the majority-gay Castro district for their Easter performance. *Catholic San Francisco,* a local religious newspaper, objected, saying that the city's decision exhibited "extraordinary insensitivity to people of all faiths," asking for the performance to be postponed until after Easter. William Donohue, president of the Catholic League for Religious and Civil Rights, said of the Sisters: "I don't give a damn about their fund-raising. They're a bunch of bigots." Sister Ann R. Key stated that the group was not mocking nuns but doing the traditional work of the sisterhood by educating and ministering to the sick. Board of Supervisors president Tom Ammiano announced that the city planned to respect the separation of church and state by allowing the event to continue as scheduled. The ongoing work of the group is documented in the 2009 feature-length film *The Sisters.*

From *The New York Times*

Staggs, Bill. "Troupe Irks San Francisco Catholics." March 26, 1999.

• •

to view homosexuals as "part of the same love of which our Savior spoke" and instead communicating the message that "you can come and worship here and receive our sacrament provided you can pass for a heterosexual."

In response to these types of exclusions, Rev. Troy D. Perry established the Metropolitan Community Church (MCC), a Christian congregation in Los Angeles that explicitly identified itself as a church for gays and lesbians. Founded in 1968, the church began with roughly 350 members, 70 percent of whom were gay males, 15 percent lesbians, and the rest straight. Having had the experience of being expelled from his previous Pentecostal church for being gay, Perry set out to create a new kind of congregation where people would be welcome regardless of their sexual orientation. By 1973 the MCC had grown to include 43 congregations in nineteen states with a total membership of approximately 15,000. By 1977 the church had gone international, including congregations in urban areas throughout the United States as well as in five other countries. As of this writing, there are nearly 300 MCC congregations in twenty-two countries serving over 43,000 people.

The first gay synagogue was established in 1973, also in Los Angeles, as noted in an April 1 *Times* report published that year. Called Beth Chayim Chadasim (House of New Life), the new synagogue was formed after four Jewish homosexuals attended a talk at Perry's MCC. Shortly after its founding, the synagogue's Friday night service was attracting an average of 60 people each week and the group was preparing to seek membership in a larger body known as the Union of American Hebrew Congregations. Although Rabbi Erwin Herman expected the congregation to be accepted, he anticipated some resistance, acknowledging that a few rabbis who were asked to help start up the new congregation expressed concerns regarding the potential impact on their careers. A *Times* article published on October 25, 1977, reporting on Yom Kippur services at Congregation Beth Simchat Torah, a gay congregation of more than 350 in Manhattan, noted that participants ended the service with a petition for gay liberation: "Fulfill your promise to lift the oppressed from degradation. Remove affliction and suffering from all gay people."

In the late 1970s and early 1980s, the Catholic Church also seemed to be moving toward a more tolerant attitude regarding its gay and lesbian members. Morally neutral language began to be used in church discussions related to homosexuality, and Dignity, a prohomosexual organization for Catholics, was allowed to hold meetings and worship services in some Catholic churches. In 1986, however, the Catholic Church issued a stricter new statement about homosexuality, calling it a "disorder." Shortly thereafter, all Catholic bishops received instructions from the Vatican discouraging support for organizations that condoned homosexuality. As a result, the Archdiocese of New York revoked permission for Dignity to use church sanctuaries to hold special masses for gay Catholics, a practice that had been going on in some New York City Catholic churches since as early as 1979. After the final Saturday night service at St. Francis Xavier, more than 1,000 people marched peacefully into the streets chanting,

"We are the church." Thereafter, Dignity demonstrated outside St. Patrick's Cathedral on the first Sunday of each month to protest the decision. In the following year, a February 13, 1987, report in the *Times* noted that the Brooklyn diocese also decided to prohibit its 850 priests from using churches, hospitals, or colleges for meetings or religious services condoning homosexuality. An exception was made for Courage, a Catholic group that encouraged nonheterosexual church members to practice celibacy. Andrew Humm of the Coalition for Lesbian and Gay Rights responded, saying, "It is a very sad thing in the middle of an AIDS crisis to say to gay Catholics that we are going to be less sensitive to your needs than we were in the past."

The AIDS crisis seemed to motivate a changed attitude toward homosexuality in some predominantly black religious institutions in New York. A *Times* piece of November 18, 1991, reported that the increasing numbers of African Americans with the disease had led clergy in black mosques and churches to speak out in sermons, to start counseling and support groups, and to sponsor housing for homeless people with AIDS. As the article noted, "Until recently imams generally said that Muslims who follow the laws of God, avoiding all intoxicants and all sex outside of marriage, do not have to be concerned about AIDS. But death began to change that." Many conservative black churches, however, did not follow suit, instead continuing to preach that AIDS is a "plague upon the land because of disobedience" (see the chapter "AIDS").

By 1994 membership in the MCC had increased by leaps and bounds, amounting to more than 42,000 congregants, with churches in major cities across the nation. The largest gay church in the country was a branch of the MCC located in Dallas. Its membership of more than 1,400 rivaled the numbers that other megachurches in the region were attracting. Rev. Elder Perry explained that people in the Bible Belt were in the habit of attending church regularly, even if they were also gay. However, when a Baptist church in Austin, Texas, began an outreach program for gay people and ordained a gay deacon, the statewide executive board voted to refuse financial offerings from the church. In a March 1, 1998, report in *The Times,* a deacon from the spurned congregation said that while the action might send a message that Baptists are "bigoted," it might also publicize the fact that there are Baptist churches that welcome gays and lesbians. Other protestant denominations faced similar struggles, as when a United Methodist church court reinstated a minister who had been suspended for expelling a gay man from his congregation in 2005. Bishops from all over the country, including socially conservative regions in the South,

IN FOCUS

The Ex-Gay Movement

• •

The ex-gay movement is focused on changing the sexual orientation identity of gays and lesbians. Founded by evangelical Christians in 1973, the movement promotes abstinence from homosexual sex as a way of allowing people of faith to live consistent with their religious beliefs. Advocating "freedom from homosexuality through the power of Jesus Christ," Exodus International, offering more than 100 chapters in North America, is perhaps the most visible of all ex-gay ministries. Other religious faiths also participate in the ex-gay movement, including Courage for Catholics, Evergreen International for Mormons, and Jonah for Jews.

The religious right ran highly visible advertising campaigns in several major newspapers in the late 1990s featuring "former homosexuals" who were said to have overcome their sexuality through prayer, conversion therapy, and other services offered by ex-gay ministries. *The Times* ran such an advertisement, which featured photographs of individuals with captions such as "Wife, mother and former lesbian." The strategist of the campaign, Janet Folger, said that the campaign aimed to undermine the assumption that homosexuality is immutable and that gay people need to be protected by antidiscrimination laws. Gay rights groups successfully placed newspaper advertisements to counter the claims of the ex-gay movement, but when the nation's largest gay and lesbian church, Dallas's Cathedral of Hope, put together a similar television infomercial, it was rejected by several nationwide networks, including WGN, the Discovery Channel, Black Entertainment Television, and Odyssey, as too controversial.

Believing that such practices may foster depression or suicidal tendencies, the American Psychological Association has said that mental health professionals should not suggest that gay and lesbian clients can become straight through therapy. *The Times* has reported instances of parents forcing teens to attend ex-gay camps against their will. Commenting on one such camp sponsored by the group called Love in Action, one gay teen said, "If I do come out straight, I'll be so mentally unstable and depressed it won't matter." Gay rights groups maintain that very few "ex-gays" are able to permanently change their sexuality and that many have been scarred by trying to do so. As evidence, they cite the fact that two male cofounders of Exodus International have since left the group and held a same-sex commitment ceremony.

From *The New York Times*

Associated Press. "Psychologists Reject Gay 'Therapy.'" August 6, 2009.
Belluck, Pam. "Gay Church Sues TV Station for Rejecting an Infomercial." October 28, 1998.
Goodstein, Laurie. "The Architect of the 'Gay Conversion' Campaign." August 13, 1998.
Williams, Alex. "Gay Teenager Stirs a Storm." July 17, 2005.

• •

protested by signing a pastoral letter that said "homosexuality is not a barrier" to church membership.

In 1999 the Vatican ordered Sister Jeannine Gramick to end her twenty-year ministry to gay and lesbian Catholics and in 2000 told her to stop speaking and writing about the issue entirely. As noted in a *Times* report of May 27, 2000, she refused to do so, saying, "After finding my voice to tell my story I choose not to collaborate in my own oppression by restricting a basic human right. To me this is a matter of conscience." Majority gay and lesbian Catholic parishes continue to exist, such as Most Holy Redeemer in the Castro district of San Francisco. A *Times* report of April 29, 2002, noted that the 80 to 90 percent gay membership of this congregation was at that time served by an openly gay pastor.

Gay and Lesbian Clergy

In much the same way as LGBT people began to come out in greater numbers after the Stonewall uprising in 1969, gay members of the clergy grew more visible in religious congregations. An early example was reported in *The Times* on June 3, 1971, when thirty-six-year-old Gene Leggett was suspended from the ministry in the United Methodist Church after more than ten years of service in Dallas.

On May 2, 1972, *The Times* reported that the United Church of Christ had approved the first known ordination of an openly gay man by a 62–34 margin. Twenty-five-year-old William Johnson of San Francisco, who had been turned down by a 3–2 margin in an earlier vote, said, "I celebrate. You give me the opportunity to do the work I know I do best. God bless you." Other churches followed suit. In 1976 the General Assembly of the United Presbyterian Church said that there were no constitutional obstacles to the ordination of homosexuals. In 1977 the Episcopal Church ordained Ellen M. Barrett, the first known lesbian, to the priesthood in New York City. In a *Times* report of January 24, 1977, Bishop Paul Moore, who presided at Barrett's ordination, said that "many persons with homosexual tendencies are presently ordained in the ministry."

At the same time, other churches were continuing to exclude self-professed homosexuals from the clergy. In 1977 the Southern Baptist Convention declared homosexuality a sin, refusing to ordain or employ homosexuals in any positions in the church. Similarly, Thomas Sweetin was told that he would not be ordained despite having trained for thirteen years to become a Catholic priest. *The Times* reported on June 4, 1978, that two homosexual students had been ousted from a United Methodist seminary in the Chicago area, by a 15–10 vote of the faculty. A spokesperson for the school said, "One of the things that is looked at is what is termed fitness for ministry, in other words if the person appears to be the kind of person who should become a minister in the Methodist Church."

Intense debate continued about the inclusion of gay clergy, even in churches that were ordaining gay ministers. As Rev. Paul Mackey of the Duke Divinity School described it in a *Times* report of August 22, 1979: "The pin has been pulled and the hand grenade of ordination of homosexuals has been tossed through the open window." In 1987 the United Church of Christ ordained an out gay man who was in a long-term relationship with another man, opening the door for noncelibate gays and lesbians to serve as clergy for the first time. Despite the Episcopal Church's ordination of gay and lesbian ministers, it continued to reject admitting to the clergy homosexuals who were in committed relationships, on the grounds that active homosexuality is akin to extramarital relations, which are prohibited for heterosexuals and homosexuals alike. In 1996 the Episcopal Church charged a retired bishop with heresy for signing a statement favoring the ordination of noncelibate homosexuals.

Perhaps the most famous example of internal controversy over the service of gay and lesbian clergy gained national attention in the summer of 2003 when the Episcopal Church approved, by a 62–45 margin, its first openly gay bishop, V. Gene Robinson. Robinson was at one time in an opposite-sex marriage and had two daughters. He originally underwent therapy in the hope of "curing" his homosexuality but eventually came to the conclusion that he was unalterably gay and that this was not a problem. By 2003 Robinson had been involved in a committed relationship with a man for sixteen years and been nominated, but not selected, to become a bishop in 1998 and 1999.

Calling the Episcopal Church's selection of Robinson a "constitutional crisis," twelve conservative bishops immediately denounced the decision as a threat to church teaching that would likely lead to schism or a separation in the church, saying "With grief too deep for words, the bishops who stand before you must reject this action." Others said it was "a great day for the church," arguing that the ordination of a gay bishop would bring in new members, particularly young people. Calling the vote a "tiny sign" that the culture is "moving into a mature adulthood" regarding the treatment of gays and lesbians, Robinson said that he hoped to be able to heal some of the division and pain that was clearly evident in the church.

The vote on Robinson's candidacy had been delayed for two days while church officials investigated eleventh-hour claims of sexual impropriety. One of the accusers said that he "regretted having used the word 'harassment,'" but that he felt obliged to report his discomfort when Robinson had publicly touched his arm and upper back while talking to him at a meeting. The second accusation concerned a Web site created by a gay youth group that Robinson had helped found in 1998. Launched four years after Robinson ceased to be involved with the group, the Web site linked to other related sites, some of which were found to include pornography. Although Robinson was swiftly exonerated of all charges, some of his supporters suggested that the accusations were

Rev. V. Gene Robinsion speaks at Trinity Episcopal Church in Columbus, Ohio, in 2007. Robinson, who is openly gay, was ordained as bishop of New Hampshire in 2005, the first openly gay man ever to serve in that capacity.

*Source: Michael Houghton/*The New York Times

last-minute political maneuvers specifically designed to discredit the soon-to-be bishop.

Emotions continued to intensify within the Episcopal Church over the months leading up to the ceremony that would officially recognize Robinson as bishop. A *Times* report of November 3, 2003, noted great celebration among the 4,000 in attendance as Robinson addressed the crowd, saying, "It's not about me; it's about so many other people who find themselves at the margins. Your presence here is a welcome sign for those people to be brought into the center." One woman in attendance commented, "Especially for me as an African American woman, I am pretty sensitive to people saying you don't have a place in the church. God makes holy what people shove away, and I'm just here to celebrate that." Others disagreed. Robinson received several death threats and as a consequence wore a bulletproof vest during the ceremony. Further, when the crowd was asked whether there were any objections to his installation, a laywoman, a priest from Pittsburgh, and a bishop from Albany interrupted the ceremony to read an explicit list of what they described as

the sexual practices of gay men, saying that people "made in God's loving image would not engage in or bless or consecrate such behavior" and that doing so would "break God's heart." As the three filed silently out of the arena to join a prayer service at a neighboring evangelical church, the presiding bishop, Frank T. Griswold, thanked "our brothers and sisters in Christ for bringing their concerns before us," adding that their objections were "well known and I think have been considered."

Griswold later said that while Robinson's election did not resolve the issue of homosexuality for the church, it did "place squarely before us the question of how a community can live in the tension of disagreement." In a *Times* report of March 21, 2004, Robinson commented: "What is interesting to me about this is that people think this is going to go away. We are just not going to go away. It's like trying to put the toothpaste back into the tube." The Most Reverend Rowan Williams, the head of the Anglican Communion and a supporter of the decision, acknowledged that the church faced difficult times going forward, noting that "it is too early to say what the result" of the decision will be worldwide. Others said the warnings of disaster were overblown, recalling that the ordination of women in 1976 and the ratification of a female bishop in 1989 had not lead to a split within the church, as had been widely predicted. The first female bishop in the church, Barbara Harris, recalled that despite "the dire predictions made at the time of my election consent process," the church remained together.

Controversy over the decision continued well after Robinson's installation. Many bishops in the worldwide Anglican community strenuously objected, including leaders not only in the United States but also in several countries in Africa and Latin America. A *Times* report of November 4, 2003, noted that Archbishop Benjamin Nzimbi had announced that his Kenyan church would have nothing to do with the Episcopal Church, U.S.A., saying, "The Devil has clearly entered our church." As the discord deepened, some individual American churches aligned themselves with the Anglican Church in Uganda in 2004. By 2006 three dioceses in Pittsburgh, South Carolina, and San Joaquin, California, asked to remove themselves from the authority of the presiding bishop in the American church. Although they did not specify an alternative primate, many speculated that these churches would align with a more conservative primate in Africa. In 2007 Archbishop Peter J. Akinola of Nigeria installed Bishop Martyn Minns of Virginia as the leader of a new diocese that would take in American congregations interested in disassociating themselves from the Episcopal Church in the United States. In addition, according to a December 4, 2008, report in *The Times,* conservatives feeling alienated from the church announced they were founding a rival denomination. Bishop Robert Duncan of Pittsburgh said, "In Reformation times new structures are emerging." The Episcopal Church responded, "There is room within the Episcopal Church for people of different views, and we regret that some have felt the need to depart from the diversity of our common life in Christ."

On March 17, 2010, the Episcopal Church confirmed a lesbian bishop, the Reverend Mary D. Glasspool. A *Times* report on that day described the move as "a decision likely to increase the tension with fellow Anglican churches around the world that do not approve of homosexuality." The experience of the Episcopalian Church is only one example of the struggle occurring within many religious traditions over the issue of LGBT clergy. The most socially progressive denominations now ordain gay, lesbian, bisexual, and transgender people, regardless of whether they are sexually active or not. Some more traditional religious groups continue to bar ministry to even celibate LGBT people. Many others fall somewhere in between these two extremes. Regardless of the specific position taken, nearly every religion includes members with a range of opinions on this issue, and therefore it seems likely to remain the subject of controversy for many years to come.

RELIGIOUS BLESSING OF SAME-SEX MARRIAGE

Professor John Boswell, who was a prominent historian at Yale University up until the time of his death in 1994, offered historical evidence suggesting that some Christian churches offered blessings to same-sex couples as early as the third century. However, this practice became a prominent political issue during the 1990s, when it appeared that Hawaii would become the first state in the country to offer same-sex marriage (see the previous chapter). Because weddings in the United States are traditionally performed by a religious official, many denominations felt the need to take a stand on this often controversial topic. For example, based on a 1984 resolution declaring homosexual activity "incompatible with Christian teaching," the United Methodist Church amended its rules in 1997 to officially prohibit ministers from officiating at same-sex commitment ceremonies. The following year, Rev. Jimmy Creech performed such a rite for two women in his Omaha congregation in direct opposition to his bishop's warning not to do so. Creech said he considered the church's condemnation of same-sex marriages to be discriminatory, and at least twenty other United Methodist ministers were said to have performed such ceremonies. Creech was officially tried in a church court and eventually defrocked. The next year, Greg Dell, a United Methodist minister in Chicago, also was suspended for blessing the union of two men. After serving a yearlong suspension, Dell continued to promote the blessing of same-sex unions, finding a loophole in church rules by having them performed off church grounds without him formally presiding. The United Methodist ban on gay marriage and the underlying statement that homosexuality is incompatible with Christianity continue to cause controversy within the church but continue to be reaffirmed, most recently at a 2008 national denominational conference. Some United Methodist ministers persist in performing same-sex ceremonies in defiance of the ban, and groups have been established within the church to promote both sides of the issue. These include the Reconciling Ministries Network (which seeks to lift the ban) and the Confessing Movement (which aims to retain and perhaps further strengthen the denomination's condemnation of homosexuality).

Like the United Methodists, many denominations officially oppose same-sex marriage, but this stance is by no means universal. According to a *Times* report of 1998, more than 5,000 same-sex commitment ceremonies were being performed annually by the Metropolitan Community Church, and the Unitarian Universalist Church and other socially progressive groups were also regularly blessing these unions, even in states where same-sex marriage was not legally recognized. The Reverend Gary A. Kowalski explained that he regularly officiated over such unions because "churches and other social institutions should be in the business of encouraging long-term relationships." In the same article, Dignity representatives reported that two or three unions were being blessed a month, typically by ordained but retired Catholic priests. For active priests, such practices could bring harsh consequences, as illustrated by the case of Rev. James Callan, who was fired in 1998 for blessing same-sex partnerships in a Catholic church in Rochester, New York. When he subsequently created a breakaway church called New Faith, where the practice continued, Callan was ex-communicated.

In 2000 Reform rabbis declared that gay unions were "worthy of affirmation" through Jewish ritual, but individual rabbis were given the option of whether to officiate at such services. Representing approximately 1,800 rabbis, this group became the largest body of American clergy yet to affirm the right of its members to bless same-sex relationships. Said Rabbi Valerie Lieber in a *Times* report of March 30, 2000, "It truly means we have gone beyond a time of tolerance and acceptance to a time of embracing the souls of gay and lesbian Jews." Although many of those in attendance expressed satisfaction with the resolution's efforts to balance opposing views within the liberal Jewish community, some expressed concerns about how the decision would be perceived in Israel. Most Israelis are not religiously active; however, the largest religious group is Orthodox and its members generally support maintaining traditional biblical prohibitions against homosexuality.

In the summer of 2003, the state of Massachusetts legalized gay marriage. France, Belgium, and Germany had all adopted various forms of same-sex partnership recognition, while both Canada and Britain seemed poised to do so soon. In an apparent response to these events, and perhaps anticipating the upcoming ordination of a gay bishop in the Episcopal Church, the Vatican issued a strongly worded statement restating the position of the Catholic Church on the issue of same-sex marriage. Titled "Considerations Regarding Proposals to Give Legal Recognition to Unions Between Homosexual Persons," the document referred to support for same-sex marriage as "gravely immoral" and stated that "there are absolutely no grounds for considering homosexual unions to be in any way similar or even remotely analogous to God's plan for marriage and family." Concluding that "marriage is holy, while homosexual acts go against the natural moral law," the statement asserted that allowing gays and lesbians to adopt children "would actually mean doing violence to these children."

As the number of gay couples seeking to have their unions consecrated in a religious ceremony continued to rise, prominent religious leaders rallied in 2006 to support a constitutional amendment to ban same-sex marriage, which had the backing of President George W. Bush, an avowed born-again Christian. The group included Catholics, evangelical Protestants, conservative rabbis, and Mormons. When a proposal to block same-sex marriage in California was on the ballot in 2008, Mormons provided the lion's share of labor for a massive door-to-door volunteer effort, as well as crucial donations through a national fund-raising drive that was widely credited with securing a victory for the referendum. In the days following the election, LGBT groups organized protests outside numerous Mormon churches. Subsequent reports suggested that the Mormon Church had failed to report many nonmonetary contributions to this campaign and could face criminal prosecution and significant fines. In 2009, however, the Mormon Church somewhat mollified its critics by actively supporting a Salt Lake City ordinance banning discrimination against gays and lesbians. As with the previous subjects discussed in this chapter, it is not possible to make general statements about religious views regarding same-sex marriage. Religious groups vary widely in their views on this issue, individuals within the same denomination often express radically different beliefs, and the positions and practices of individual churches continue to evolve over time.

RELIGION AND POLITICS

Religious organizations have long played a role in secular affairs, on both the political right and left. In 1964 the Council on Religion and the Homosexual was created in San Francisco with an agenda that included equal civil rights for homosexuals. The Council's model was followed in various other major cities across the country. In the early 1970s entire denominations such as the Lutheran Church in America and the Unitarian Universalist Association issued public statements backing equal rights for homosexuals.

A *Times* report of May 18, 1974, noted that a Catholic diocese in Newark, New Jersey, came out in favor of a proposed bill to protect the civil rights of homosexuals in New York City, challenging the Brooklyn diocese, which called the measure "a menace to family life." The Newark diocese countered, "To categorically exclude some members of society from housing or employment opportunity simply because they are homosexual is just as unconstitutional and unchristian as to exclude them from such human opportunities because of their race, national origin or religion."

In 1975 the National Council of Churches, a group representing thirty Protestant and Orthodox religious bodies, endorsed full civil rights for homosexuals as well as women. Although a *Times* report of March 7, 1975, noted that the group took pains to point out that its position did not mean that homosexuals should be allowed to serve as ministers, Rev. William Johnson, the only out gay minister to have been ordained by a major Protestant denomination (see below) said, "It will be difficult for church bodies to support civil rights in the public sector and to avoid issues of discrimination in the churches."

In the late 1970s and early 1980s, a significant shift in the political landscape occurred as the Republican Party began to shift toward a platform of family values, cultivating new constituencies in conservative churches, particularly in the South. In Miami and other major cities, Southern Baptists such as Anita Bryant began high-profile campaigns against equal rights for homosexuals and women (see the chapter "Gay Civil Rights Laws"). In a *Times* report of May 31, 1977, Bryant asked, "Why does such an abomination to God as homosexuality exist? It's Satan on the move." Her organization, Save the Children, was a major player in successfully repealing a homosexual civil rights bill in Miami that year.

The Reverend Jerry Falwell founded the Moral Majority in 1979 to forward an evangelical Christian, "pro-family" agenda, which included opposition to equal rights for gays and lesbians. Together with Pat Robertson and other television evangelists, Falwell helped to generate an increasingly influential constituency within the new right of the Republican Party. While the old right of the Republican Party was largely unconcerned with social issues, the emerging new right resisted gay rights, the Equal Rights Amendment, and abortion rights. In an article devoted to this shift that was published in *The Times* on July 30, 1980, Paul Weyrich of the Free Congress explained the group's view: "Homosexuality is explicitly condemned in Scriptures, so if you're for gay rights, you're violating a specifically articulated tenet of Holy Scripture." This emerging base within the new right, which used the Bible as a foundation for political action, became known as the Christian right as well as the religious right.

In the 1980s, the religious right became a force to be reckoned with in American politics, a key player in the electoral coalitions that propelled Ronald Reagan to the presidency in 1980 and 1984 and George H. W. Bush in 1988. However, the Republican Party was governed by an often uneasy coalition of social and economic conservatives, and these tensions were visibly manifest during the 1992 election cycle. High-profile antihomosexual initiatives on the ballot in Oregon and elsewhere were seen by many as a way to draw conservative Christians to the polls to support the reelection of President Bush. When Bush was not reelected and the antihomosexual initiative failed to pass in Oregon, the chairman of the Republican Party, Craig Berkman, threatened to form a group free of the influence of the religious right, on the grounds that the initiative had actually caused many to desert the party. In a *Times* article of November 14, 1992, Lon Mabon, leader of the Oregon Citizens Alliance, a group of evangelical Christians who supported the antihomosexual initiative, said: "We are the Republican Party. The Christians delivered for President Bush; the other groups did not. If the Republican leadership had helped us, we would have won against the homosexuals in Oregon." Berkman concluded that if the party continued to adopt the social agenda of the Christian right it might become obsolete.

Despite the loss of the presidency in 1992, conservative Christian candidates won hundreds of races at the local level, including on school boards, city councils, and state legislatures. In a *Times* report of November 21, 1992, Ralph Reed, head of the Christian Coalition, explained the results from the religious right's perspective as follows: "We focused on where the real power is: in the states and in the precincts and in the neighborhoods where people live and work. On the one hand, George Bush was going down to ignominious defeat in a landslide. On the other hand, the anecdotal evidence is that at school boards and at the state legislative level we had big, tremendous victories."

As the presidential election of 1996 neared, the Republican presidential frontrunner, Sen. Bob Dole (R-KS), caused political controversy when he first accepted and then sent back a donation from the Log Cabin Republicans, a group formed to support the interests of gay Republicans. According to a *Times* report of August 27, 1995, Dole had long been trying to show that he was every bit as conservative as his opponent Phil Gramm. Dole's spokesperson said, "We won't accept contributions from groups that have a specific political agenda that's fundamentally at odds with Senator Dole's record and his views."

Shortly thereafter, conservative Christians organized a boycott of the Walt Disney Company after the organization decided to offer partner benefits to gay employees, calling the new policy "just another step in the direction of making the traditional family meaningless," as reported in *The Times* on November 29, 1995. Disney said the decision was based on the principle of "equal pay for equal work," noting that they had long offered benefits to heterosexual spouses. When the Southern Baptist Convention joined the boycott, it met with mixed reviews from members, many of whom said they did not favor a blanket condemnation of films such as *The Lion King* or cable channels such as ESPN, according to a *Times* report of June 21, 1997, titled "Baptist Rank and File Split on Disney Boycott."

While the religious right was initially successful in many of its efforts to dominate discussion in the realm of faith and politics, by the late 1990s religious groups on the left started to gain greater attention, offering an alternative view of homosexuality grounded in religious faith. A coalition called the National Religious Leadership Roundtable was formed that included Protestants, Roman Catholics, Jews, Mormons, and Muslims, all united in an effort to support gay rights. Robert Matlovich, president of Dignity and a leader of the Roundtable, explained in a *Times* report of August 24, 1999, that "you don't have to be an atheist to respond to the Religious Right." Headed by Rev. Mel White, who was a former speechwriter for Rev. Jerry Falwell, a group called Soulforce also aimed to challenge the Christian right's view of homosexuality from an alternative religious perspective. In a *Times* article published on November 10, 2000, White said that gay and lesbian Catholics had suffered greatly from the church's teaching that homosexuality was "intrinsically disordered." During this period Soulforce conducted a series of highly visible protests at a variety of major Catholic and Protestant churches across the nation.

After the attacks on September 11, 2001, religious right leaders Revs. Jerry Falwell and Pat Robertson appeared on Robertson's *700 Club* television show and suggested the attacks were at least in part caused by gay rights supporters, abortion providers, and federal courts that banned school prayer. A *Times* report of September 14, 2001, noted that Falwell had said such actions had weakened the United States and exposed the country to terrorism. Singling out those "who have tried to secularize America," Falwell added, "You helped this happen." Robertson responded, saying

"I totally concur." After receiving intense criticism from many secular and religious leaders on both the political left and right for those remarks, Falwell apologized several days later for suggesting that an angry God had allowed the attacks, calling his remarks "insensitive, uncalled for at the time and unnecessary," as reported in a *Times* piece of September 18, 2001.

Issues of homosexuality arose again during the 2004 presidential election, as many speculated that constitutional referendums against same-sex marriage would bring greater numbers of conservative Christians to the polls, thereby increasing the likelihood that President George W. Bush would win reelection. Christian leaders believed that the issue of gay marriage would not only revitalize the movement, but that it would also serve as a basis for new alliances with African American and Hispanic churchgoers, two groups that traditionally had voted for Democratic candidates. Gay rights advocates, however, were not willing to give up without a fight and noted that African Americans have always supported civil rights. Attendance at many black churches fluctuated following this period, as noted in a *Times* report of March 27, 2007, in which Dr. Kenneth L. Samuel of Atlanta said, "The church has come to a point when it has to embrace all the people Jesus embraced, and that means the people in the margins." He conceded, however, that "it really bothered my congregation when I said that as people of color who have been ostracized, marginalized, how can we turn around now and oppress other people."

A *Times* report of May 21, 2007, suggested that a new breed of evangelical Christians was emerging that might supplant the traditional religious right. Surveys suggested that younger born-again Christians were more likely to accept homosexuality and less likely to resist equal rights for gays than were older conservative Christians. Barack Obama's 2009 presidential inauguration ceremonies seemed to reflect an effort to find a balance between religious positions on the issue of LGBT rights. On the one hand Rev. Rick Warren was asked to deliver the inauguration invocation. Warren is the founder of the evangelical Saddleback megachurch and author of the highly successful *The Purpose-Driven Life*. His selection for this honor was criticized by many LGBT rights groups owing to his history of comparing homosexuality to pedophilia and incest, yet he recently stated that he supports partnership rights for same-sex couples although he does not approve of gay marriage. On the other hand, openly gay Episcopal bishop Gene Robinson was also invited to give an invocation, but at a lesser event associated with the inauguration. Regarding the invitations extended to both himself and Warren, Bishop Robinson commented in a January 13, 2009, *Times* article, "In many ways, it just proves that Barack Obama is exactly who he says he was and would be as president, which is someone who is casting a wide net that will include all Americans."

BIBLIOGRAPHY

Boswell, John. *Christianity, Social Tolerance, and Homosexuality: Gay People in Western Europe from the Beginning.* Chicago: University of Chicago Press, 1980.

———. *Same-Sex Unions in Pre-modern Europe.* New York: Villard Press, 1994.

FROM *THE NEW YORK TIMES*

Associated Press. "Homosexual Minister Is Ousted By Southwest Texas Methodists." June 3, 1971.

———. "Homosexual's Ordination Voted in the United Church of Christ." May 2, 1972.

Banerjee, Neela. "For Some Black Pastors, Accepting Gay Members Means Losing Others." March 27, 2007.

Bennetts, Leslie. "Conservatives Join on Social Concerns." July 30, 1980.

Berke, Richard L. "Dole, in a New Bow to Right, Returns a Gay Group's Money." August 27, 1995.

Blau, Eleanor. "Churches Assailed Here as Foes of Homosexuals." March 25, 1971.

Briggs, Kenneth A. "Rights Advocated for Homosexuals." March 7, 1975.

———. "Homosexuals among the Clergy." January 24, 1977.

———. "Miami Homosexual Issue Dividing Clerics." May 31, 1977.

Cropper, Carol Marie. "Baptist Group Ousts Church for Welcoming Gay People." March 1, 1998.

Dugan, George. "A Diocese Backs Homosexual Bill." May 18, 1974.

Egan, Timothy. "Oregon G.O.P. Faces Schism over Agenda of Christian Right." November 14, 1992.

Fiske, Edward B. "Episcopal Clergymen Here Call Homosexuality Morally Neutral." November 29, 1967.

George, Jason. "Up Front: Worth Noting; Now Out in the Open, Still Welcome in Church." March 21, 2004.

Goldman, Ari L. "Brooklyn Bishop Limits Church Use by Homosexuals." February 13, 1987.

Goodstein, Laurie. "Openly Gay Man Is Made a Bishop." November 3, 2003.

———. "Episcopal Split as Conservatives Form New Group." December 4, 2008.

———. "Gay Bishop Is Asked to Say Prayer at Inaugural Event." January 13, 2009.

———. "Episcopalians Confirm a Second Gay Bishop." March 17, 2010.

Janofsky, Michael. "Baptist Rank and File Split on Disney Boycott." June 21, 1997.

Lacey, Marc, and Laurie Goodstein. "African Anglican Leaders Outraged over Gay Bishop in U.S." November 4, 2003.

Lichtenstein, Grace. "Homosexuals in New York Find New Pride." October 25, 1977.

Luo, Michael, and Laurie Goodstein. "Emphasis Shifts for New Breed of Evangelicals." May 21, 2007.

MacFarquhar, Neil. "Gay Muslims Find Freedom, of a Sort, in the U.S." November 7, 2007.

Mydans, Seth. "Christian Conservatives Counting Hundreds of Gains in Local Votes." November 21, 1992.

Navarro, Mireya. "Disney's Health Policy for Gay Employees Angers Religious Right in Florida." November 29, 1995.

Niebuhr, Gustav. "Laws Aside, Some in Clergy Quietly Bless Gay 'Marriage.'" April 17, 1998.

———. "Religious Coalition Plans Gay Rights Strategy." August 24, 1999.

———. "Reform Rabbis Back Blessing of Gay Unions." March 30, 2000.

———. "Nun Defies Vatican Request for Silence on Gay Ministry." May 27, 2000.

———. "Gay Protest Planned at Bishops Gathering." November 10, 2000.

———. "After the Attacks: Finding Fault; U.S. 'Secular' Groups Set Tone for Terror Attacks, Falwell Says." September 14, 2001.

———. "A Nation Challenged: Placing Blame; Falwell Apologizes for Saying an Angry God Allowed Attacks." September 18, 2001.

Nieves, Evelyn. "At a Largely Gay Church, a Test of Faith." April 29, 2002.

Shipp, E. R., with Mireya Navarro. "Reluctantly, Black Churches Confront AIDS." November 18, 1991.

Unsigned. "Catholics Warned on 'Flood of Smut.'" January 25, 1965.

———. "Color Some of the Churches Lavender." March 28, 1971.

———. "Churches Expand for Homosexuals." April 1, 1973.

———. "Expulsion of 2 Homosexual Students by Methodist Seminary Arouses Protest in Illinois." June 4, 1978.

Vescey, George. "Homosexual Clergy Stirs Great Debate." August 22, 1979.

● ●

REVOLUTIONARY RETHINKING OF HOMOSEXUALITY IN CHRISTIANITY

Traditionally, Christians have thought of homosexuality as a sinful or disordered condition. During the Middle Ages, punishments for homosexuality in Christian states included stoning, mutilation, and burning at the stake. In a sharp break with this position, a variety of Christian churches in the 1960s began to rethink this view, arguing that homosexuality, like all sexual behavior, should not be classified as right or wrong in a blanket manner. Several prominent theologians argued during this time that the church should not brand permanent, loving unions between homosexuals as sinful.

Canon Walter D. Dennis of the Episcopal Church said that such a relationship "should be judged by the same criteria as a heterosexual marriage—that is, whether it is intended to foster a permanent relationship of love." Roman Catholic theologian Rev. Edward Schillebeecks of the Netherlands argued that not only is homosexuality not sinful, but also that "for some men, homosexuality is a moral good because it is the only manner in which they can experience sexuality."

Opponents of more tolerant attitudes toward sexuality said that they feared that relaxing attitudes in this area would weaken moral standards more generally. Rev. L. Robert Foutz of the Episcopal Church was particularly concerned about the standards governing marriage. Others agreed, arguing that same-sex marriage lacks formal commitment and legal support.

In major cities such as San Francisco, leaders within the Episcopal Church and United Church of Christ have supported new organizations that aim to secure equal rights and greater tolerance for homosexuals. These developments suggested to gay rights advocates that Christian churches were likely to modify their formal condemnation of homosexuality.

DECEMBER 3, 1967
VIEWS ON HOMOSEXUALS
By EDWARD B. FISKE

"Homosexual acts between persons who intend a permanent union in love are not sinful nor should the church consider them as such."

The author is Norman Pittenger, a leading Episcopalian theologian, and his words—if unorthodox—reflect a revolution now taking place in the Christian view of homosexuality.

The latest evidence of the revolution came last week when 90 Episcopalian priests from New York and three neighboring dioceses met at the Cathedral Church of St. John the Divine to discuss the church's approach to the homosexual.

A large majority took the position that homosexual acts, like all sexual behavior, cannot be classified as right or wrong "per se."

As Canon Walter D. Dennis of the Cathedral staff put it:

"A homosexual relationship between two consenting adults should be judged by the same criteria as a heterosexual marriage—that is, whether it is intended to foster a permanent relationship of love."

Sharp Break

On the Roman Catholic side, a prominent Dutch theologian, the Rev. Edward Schillebeecks, recently told an interviewer, "Many theologians now think we should say that, in some situations for some men, homosexuality is a moral good because it is the only manner in which they can experience sexuality."

Obviously such thinking constitutes a sharp break with longstanding religious traditions.

Mosaic law regarded *mishkav zochor* (literally "lying with a male") as an "abomination"—a view that has carried over into Talmudic law and early Christian thinking. During the Middle Ages penalties for homosexual acts in Christian states included stoning, mutilation and burning at the stake.

Protestant and Catholic doctrine, both rooted in traditional canon law teachings, assert that homosexuality itself is not evil but that homosexual acts, like other sexual acts outside marriage, are sinful.

Unlike Judaism, which condemns homosexuality as simply contrary to the will of God, Christian opposition is also based on the rational argument that it is "unnatural" because it precludes the transmission of life.

The current religious interest in homosexuality focuses on modern psychological studies of its causes, and theologians are now asking questions such as whether the anxiety of many homosexuals is inherent in their sexual preferences or the result of social ostracism.

Inevitably this also involves some new looks at old interpretations of Scripture.

In the current issue of the National Catholic Reporter, for instance, the Rev. Henri J. M. Nouwen, a Dutch psychologist, states that St. Paul condemned homosexuality not as a sexual perversion but because in his day it was "related to temple services and therefore to the adoration of false gods."

Opponents of the new church trend toward tolerance express sympathy with programs to understand and counsel homosexuals, but they fear a weakening of morality in general.

The Rev. L. Robert Foutz, a participant in the cathedral symposium, argued, for instance, that the standards of marriage might suffer if a married man who also had homosexual tendencies were to interpret the new liberality as encouragement for his homosexuality.

Others who object to a more liberalized acceptance of homosexuality are also dubious about how "fulfilling" even a lasting homosexual relationship can be and point out that a homosexual "marriage" lacks the discipline and formal commitment of legal sanctions.

While the debate goes on, however, new programs are rapidly developing. Commissions on religion and the homosexual have been established in New York and other large cities, and many churches and church organizations have counseling programs.

In San Francisco both Episcopalian and United Church of Christ leaders have endorsed organizations working for the civil rights and public understanding of homosexuals.

Although change in the Jewish position would be difficult, it seems likely that Christian churches will eventually modify their across-the-board condemnations of homosexuality.

Before doing so, however, they will have to solve the big problem: how do you distinguish between "promiscuous" and "healthy" homosexual relations?

- -

New Church Created for Homosexuals

Founded in 1968 in Los Angeles, the Metropolitan Community Church (MCC) was the first congregation to identify itself as a church for male and female homosexuals. Offering services that resemble those of Protestant revivalist churches, the 348-member church reflected the growing tolerance toward homosexuality that had begun to characterize many Christian churches. When this article was written in 1970 some 70 percent of MCC members were male homosexuals and 15 percent were lesbians.

The founding pastor of the MCC was 29-year-old Rev. Troy D. Perry, whose homosexuality led him to be forced out of his previous congregation, the Church of God of Prophecy, a Pentecostal group in Tennessee. He argued that the MCC was necessary because most Christian churches were still not willing to integrate homosexuals into their congregations. The MCC offered a variety of programs, including job counseling, dances, alcoholism groups, and coffee hours. The church planned to create new congregations in a variety of major cities including San Francisco, San Diego, and Phoenix.

The MCC challenged the traditional view that homosexuality is a sinful or disordered condition, arguing that it offers the same possibilities for love or sin as heterosexuality. Various theologians at the time had begun to argue that such a view is more consistent with the teachings of Jesus. Noting that this view had led to new church practices, Perry said that he had officiated at eighteen same-sex weddings, using the standard marriage rite of the Episcopal Church while substituting the word *spouse* for *husband* or *wife*.

Since its founding in 1968 the MCC has grown to become a large group of 250 affiliated churches in thirty countries. Since then, MCC members and clergy have been active advocates for social justice both in LGBT-sensitive areas such as AIDS awareness and in spheres such as ending poverty and trade equality.

FEBRUARY 15, 1970
HOMOSEXUALS IN LOS ANGELES, LIKE MANY ELSEWHERE, WANT RELIGION AND ESTABLISH THEIR OWN CHURCH

By EDWARD B. FISKE

Special to the New York Times

LOS ANGELES – The Rev. Troy D. Perry burst forward from his seat to a makeshift pulpit shouting, "If you love the Lord this morning, say 'Amen.'" With one voice, the congregation of more than 400 persons roared back its response.

Such is the style of worship every Sunday at the non-denominational Metropolitan Community Church, a style that resembles that of just about any Protestant church with a revivalist flavor.

The Metropolitan Community Church is no ordinary Church, however. It is the first congregation in the country to identify itself openly as a church for male and female homosexuals.

Its founding 16 months ago reflects both the growing willingness of American homosexuals to assert themselves as a distinct minority group and the emergence of a more liberal attitude toward homosexuals among religious bodies.

In recent months, regional and national church bodies, especially those connected with the United Church of Christ, have begun to call for more dialogue between homosexuals and churches and to support drives to legalize homosexual relations between consenting adults.

In 1964, following a police raid on a dance, the Council on Religion and the Homophile was formed in San Francisco to work in this field. About half a dozen such groups now exist in other cities.

In addition, officials have estimated that across the country there are as many as 100 to 200 churches that are quietly known as congenial to homosexuals. One small denomination is also reported to have an exclusively homosexual clergy and a predominantly homosexual membership.

Mr. Perry is a dark-haired 29-year-old preacher with a charismatic manner, a Pentecostalist theological orientation and no compunction at all about admitting that he is an active homosexual.

He convened the first service in his home in October, 1968, with nine friends and three persons drawn by an advertisement in a local homosexual newspaper. Since then the congregation has grown to 348 members, most of whom are in their mid-20's to mid-40's.

Seventy per cent of the members are male homosexuals, including a number of clergymen. Fifteen per cent are lesbians. The rest are relatives of members or other "straight" persons, who, in Mr. Perry's words, "like the friendly atmosphere around here."

Mr. Perry, who was forced out of the Church of God of Prophecy, a Pentecostalist group with headquarters in Cleveland, Tenn., because of his homosexuality, attributes the rapid increases in membership to at least two factors.

One is the reluctance of most mainline congregations to integrate known homosexuals fully into their programs, with the corollary attitude of most clergymen that their task is to persuade the homosexual to alter his behavior rather than to come to terms with it as part of his condition.

The second factor is the need of homosexuals to have places where they can relate to each other in a congenial and low-pressure social setting.

"In the gay bars the emphasis is too much on sex," said Fred Conwell, a 32-year-old writer and a church member from Dayton, Ohio. "There aren't many places like this, where to be friendly to someone doesn't mean you're trying to go to bed with him."

The 17-room parsonage of the Metropolitan Community Church is thus the center of a large program of activities ranging from job counseling and alcoholism groups to a forthcoming Valentine's Day dance and well-attended coffee hours before church on Sundays.

Services are held in the 385-seat Encore Theater, a Hollywood movie house that donates its facilities. But the congregation has outgrown this facility and is now seeking to purchase a church building. Plans are also under way to establish related congregations in San Francisco, San Diego, Phoenix, Ariz., and nearby Orange Country.

Members of the congregation reject that idea that homosexuality, per se, is either sinful or sick. Rather, they argue that it is a condition that offers the same possibilities for love or sin as heterosexuality.

This attitude is in sharp contrast to the long-standing Jewish and Christian teaching that homosexuality is a sinful perversion of the natural order created by God. This is still the unquestioned attitude of the overwhelming majority of churchgoers.

Recently, however, some church leaders have begun to reconsider the rigidity of this position.

At the social level, some Protestant church leaders and some Roman Catholic priests, acting unofficially, have begun to argue that holding to a heterosexual ideal is no excuse for the ostracism that church and society as a whole have imposed on homosexuals.

Some theologians have also gone beyond the civil liberties area to question whether the traditional condemnation of homosexuality is compatible with the love ethic of Jesus. One argument is that the harshness of the past position was largely the result of historical circumstances, such as the desire of the ancient Hebrews to disassociate themselves from the Canaanites, who made homosexual acts part of their polytheistic worship.

The controversial New Catechism of the Roman Catholic Church in the Netherlands asserted that homosexuality is morally neutral. Among the individuals who have taken this position is Norman Pittenger, a prominent Anglican, who wrote that homosexual acts are "good" acts "insofar as they contribute to the movement of the persons toward mutual fulfillment and fulfillment in mutuality, with all the accompanying characteristics of love."

But the vast majority of thinkers, especially Catholics and conservative Protestants, have remained firm in rejecting such thinking. Carl F. H. Hengry, an American evangelical leader, for instance, recently called for a "compassionate" view of homosexuals but declared that acceptance of their condition as beyond their control would "strip all sexual behavior of moral significance."

Mr. Perry acknowledges that tolerance toward homosexuality raises new and complex ethical problems, including those associated with "marriages" between homosexual couples.

The preacher has officiated at 18 such weddings, eight of them involving lesbians. He uses the regular marriage rite of the Episcopal Church, substituting words such as "spouse" for "husband" or "wife."

He encourages marriages on the ground that society, by its laws and practice on matters such as the renting of housing, keeps homosexuals in an insecure and unhealthy situation. "I am a great believer in homosexuals settling down like anyone else," he said.

Most clergymen of all faiths would still reject the idea of homosexual marriages, however, and even some involved in work with homosexuals prefer to devise means of "blessing" a relationship rather than performing a "wedding."

Mr. Perry himself was married to a woman at the age of 19 and fathered two children. When his homosexual tendencies "came out" at the age of 23, he said, a divorce followed. He now lives with a 21-year-old college student, whom he has not yet "married."

Many homosexuals oppose the idea of a strictly homosexual church. The Rev. Harvey Beach, a 34-year-old Methodist clergyman in Chicago who was forced out of the ministry because of his homosexuality, declared in an interview that such a congregation in his area would "isolate homosexuals who attended even more than they are now."

But members of the Metropolitan Community Church argue that they must stand as a judgment on the church in the same way that other movements, such as Christian Science, have called attention to the failure of mainline churches to express all elements of the Christian faith.

"The churches have closed their doors on a whole group of people," said the Rev. Richard Ploen, one of two unpaid assistant pastors of the church. "That's the only reason we exist."

* *

GAY MINISTERS ORDAINED IN EPISCOPAL CHURCH WHILE CATHOLIC CHURCH RECONSIDERS CELIBACY OF PRIESTS

Issues about whether homosexuals should be allowed to be ministers began to arise in several Christian churches in the 1970s. In New York City in 1977, Ellen Marie Barrett became the second out homosexual to be ordained to the priesthood in the Episcopal Church, joining the first, Rev. William Johnson, who was ordained in 1973. On the other side of the spectrum, Thomas Sweetin, who had been in training for thirteen years to become a Catholic priest, was recently told by his superiors within the Jesuit order that he would not be ordained, because of his homosexuality.

While most churches counsel compassion toward homosexuals, few had embraced ordination, and many continued to believe that homosexuality was a sinful, psychological disorder. Some Episcopal Church leaders called Barrett's ordination an "error," while others said that "homosexuality is not a question of morality," adding that many were already ordained ministers.

A movement was also afoot to reconsider whether Catholic priests should be obliged to remain celibate. Advocates noted that such practices were not mandatory until the fourth century. A survey found that 50 percent of American priests favored optional celibacy, while 80 percent of younger priests felt the same.

By the late twentieth and early twenty-first century, attitudes had changed in some denominations regarding homosexuals in the clergy. In 1993 Otis Charles, former Episcopal bishop of Utah, announced on his retirement that he was gay. The year 2004 saw the election of the first openly gay Anglican bishop, V. Gene Robinson in New Hampshire.

JANUARY 16, 1977
RELIGION'S DIFFICULT SUBJECT

Several recent events serve as reminders of the fact that in most religious groups, the issues of clerical homosexuality and celibacy have yet to be resolved.

Last week in New York City, Ellen Marie Barrett became the second avowed homosexual to be ordained to the Episcopal priesthood. The first was the Rev. William Johnson, ordained in San Francisco in 1973. Two weeks ago, Thomas Sweetin said his New York City superiors had refused him ordination to the Jesuit priesthood, after 13 years of training for it, because of his admitted homosexuality. The Rev. Albert Bartlett, vice provincial for priestly preparation for the New York Jesuit Province, said of the issue, "There is no consensus in the church about the direction we should take."

Most national church bodies now favor compassion toward homosexuals but oppose the ordination of known homosexuals in the belief that their sexual preference is either sinful or psychologically disordered or both.

Anita L. Peterson, president of Episcopal Church Women at Christ the King parish in Arvada, Colo., called Miss Barrett's ordination a moral and spiritual "error." But Bishop Paul Moore Jr. of the Episcopal Diocese of New York, who ordained Miss Barrett, said that "homosexuality . . . is not a question of morality," and that "many persons with homosexual tendencies are presently in the ordained ministry."

Celibacy was not obligatory in the Roman Catholic Church until the fourth century. In recent years there has been pressure to give priests a choice once more. One survey found that more than 50 percent of all the American priests questioned favored optional celibacy; when only younger priests were polled, the figure rose to 80 percent.

No one knows how many priests actually remain celibate. In 1975, John N. Kotre, a psychology teacher at the University of Michigan, asserted in Commonweal that "Priest and religious—in what numbers I do not know—experiment with the full gamut of sexual and genital behavior." In a book published in 1968, Donald Hayne, an American ex-priest, wrote, "There are evidences that, while the majority priests are still remaining celibate more or less contentedly, both the number of those seeking dispensation and the number of those marrying civilly without dispensation are increasing."

Struggles between Faith and Sexuality Arise at Many Churches and Synagogues

The relationship between homosexuality and religion became more complicated in the late 1980s. Several conflicts arose in a variety of churches, fueled in part by the greater visibility of gay people in American society as well as more specific moral questions such as how to respond to the AIDS crisis, which hit the homosexual community particularly hard. Many clergy began to publicly embrace their homosexuality, while some churches, such as the Roman Catholic Church, toughened their stand on the issue.

Episcopal bishop Paul Moore of New York ordained the first out lesbian priest in his church in 1977. He argued that responsible same-sex relationships would be regarded as God's will in the future, saying that "homosexuality is a condition which one does not choose; it is not a question of morality." Another Episcopal bishop, John Spong of Newark, New Jersey, argued that the church should "open its eyes to reality" by blessing relationships between homosexuals. The United Church of Christ in September 1986 ordained the Reverend James Lawer, who had been in a three-year relationship with another man. Lawler said he made no secret of his orientation during interviews for ordination, commenting, "I couldn't take the strain of having to lie about who I was. That is not freeing, and it is my belief that our faith ought to free us."

A document issued by the Vatican in October 1986 offered a much stricter view, asserting that homosexuality is an "objective disorder," forgoing the language of moral neutrality that the Catholic Church seemed to embrace just a few years earlier. As a consequence, the Vatican instructed churches to withdraw support for groups such as Dignity, a national organization of

Catholics that advocates tolerance toward and inclusion of homosexuals. Rev. John McNeill, a celibate homosexual priest, was recently dismissed for violating a Vatican directive that ordered him to stop speaking favorably about homosexual relationships. The three branches of Judaism also offer a wide range of attitudes regarding homosexuality, from condemnation to acceptance.

Many individual church and synagogue members struggled with balancing faith and sexuality. A Roman Catholic man explained that he did not wish to abandon his sexuality or his faith. Finding that his parish church had little counsel to offer him in this regard, he joined Dignity and began to attend one of its regular masses held at a Catholic church in Greenwich Village. There, he said, he "found people who loved me for what I am and accepted me." After the Vatican's 1986 stance on homosexuality, Dignity was no longer able to offer such masses.

MARCH 2, 1987
RELIGIONS CONFRONT THE ISSUE OF HOMOSEXUALITY
By JOSEPH BERGER

Many members of the clergy and lay people are struggling with the conflicts between their homosexuality and their religious lives and are forcing their religions to engage in that struggle as never before.

Though the relationship of homosexuality and religion has been controversial for years, it is growing more complicated and more visible.

Among the reasons are an increased willingness of members of the clergy to avow their homosexuality and confront their churches, and a tougher stand by some faiths, including the Roman Catholic Church.

Other factors are the increased activism of homosexual groups and the tensions between morality and compassion engendered by the crisis over AIDS, acquired immune deficiency syndrome, the deadly disease that has hit hardest among the nation's homosexuals.

As homosexual-rights groups have made their presence known, the theology underlying the issue has been thrown into flux.

Some mainstream Protestant faiths are making finer distinctions between homosexual inclination and behavior, condemning only the behavior. Others are trying to decide whether stable homosexual relationships can be considered as acceptable as stable heterosexual relationships.

The Episcopal Bishop of New York, Paul Moore, who ordained an acknowledged lesbian as a priest in 1977, has said: "Homosexuality is a condition which one does not choose; it is not a question of morality." He instructs his ministry committees not to inquire into a candidate's personal life and has said he believes responsible homosexual relationships will one day be accepted as God's will.

Within the three branches of Judaism there is also a wide range of attitudes, from condemnation of homosexual behavior to efforts to welcome practicing homosexuals. A prayer group for homosexual Jews meets regularly in Greenwich Village.

Perhaps nowhere is the struggle more impassioned than in the Roman Catholic Church. A Vatican document in October seemed to toughen traditional theology by calling homosexuality an "objective disorder"; a few years earlier the Vatican described it as "morally neutral."

The Vatican document also directed churches to withdraw support from groups like Dignity, a national organization of Catholics that condones homosexual activity. On the other hand, the church has encouraged and supported Courage, a support group for homosexuals who decide to remain celibate.

Evidence of the struggle to balance faith and sexuality is seen in the choices individuals make about whether to join homosexual groups and which kind.

The Choice of Celibacy

Vera Sabella, a 35-year-old pastoral counselor for the Archdiocese of New York, remembers having sexual feelings for other women as early as Roman Catholic grammar school. When she began acting on those feelings, she said, she drew away from her church. "I didn't think God would approve of me," she said.

About five years ago a relationship ended badly and Miss Sabella underwent a deep spiritual experience—a feeling "that the mercy of God was on me"—that led her to resist homosexual feelings and remain celibate.

She has joined Courage, which has received church sanction from John Cardinal O'Connor because it condemns homosexual behavior. Miss Sabella says her decision has given her a more peaceful and more feminine sense of self, one that she hopes may allow her to begin moving toward a relationship with a man.

Mike Bushek, however, did not want to abandon his homosexuality or his Catholic faith. He found that the parish churches he attended had little to say to him, focusing on the family life he knew he would never have. So he joined Dignity and now attends a regular Dignity mass at St. Francis Xavier's in Greenwich Village.

"I found people who loved me for what I am and accepted me, and I found a place where I feel wanted and was ministered to," said Mr. Bushek, editor of the organization's national publication.

No Masses for Dignity

After the Vatican document was issued in October, the generally liberal Bishop Francis Mugavero of Brooklyn, and bishops in Buffalo, Atlanta, Pensacola, Fla., and Vancouver, British Columbia, rescinded permission for Dignity to hold masses at diocesan churches. The Mugavero decision came within days of the Jesuit order's expulsion of the Rev. John J. McNeill, a celibate priest dismissed not for his homosexuality but for violating a Vatican directive that he not speak in support of the virtues of stable homosexual relationships.

At the same time there have been examples of increasing acceptance by religious groups and openness toward homosexuals.

In September, an association of 30 United Church of Christ congregations in the east San Francisco Bay area ordained the Rev. James A. Lawer, 42, of Berkeley, who has had a three-year relationship with another man. Mr. Lawer made no secret of his sexual life when he was interviewed for ordination.

"I couldn't take the strain of having to lie about who I was," he said. "That is not freeing, and it is my belief that our faith ought to free us."

Mr. Lawer says he knows of six other openly homosexual ministers in the United Church of Christ, which was formed out of a merger of four religious traditions that included the Congregationalists, descendants of the 17th-century New England Puritans.

And last month John Shelby Spong, the Episcopal Bishop of Newark, called on his church to "open its eyes to reality" by blessing relationships between homosexuals.

Havens of Security and Support

The mere existence of homosexual support groups like Dignity and Courage in the Catholic church, Integrity in the Episcopal church, and Lutherans Concerned reflects the growing need of religious homosexuals for havens of security and support from which they can speak with or challenge their religious bodies.

The Rev. Bernard Lynch, a director of Dignity New York, said a group of 20 to 30 homosexual priests met regularly in Manhattan, though its members have pledged not to divulge the content or location of their meetings.

Nationally, an organization of 400 homosexual priests, nuns and brothers keeps in touch through a monthly newsletter and through periodic retreats.

One Manhattan priest, who asked not to be identified, said the group tried to help many members of the clergy cope with the conflicts they might feel about their vows to abstain from sexual activity and a homosexuality they may not have known about before entering the seminary or the convent.

"We tell them, 'You don't have to leave the clergy tomorrow because of this,'" he said. "We help them find how they can move with their newly discovered sexual understanding to live according to what they've committed themselves to or to leave the priesthood and live in freedom, grace and happiness, or to find some way to live within the structure of their commitment as a gay or lesbian clergy or religious."

How prevalent homosexuality is among members of the clergy is itself a matter of wide debate. Many religious leaders say the number of homosexual members of the clergy is not disproportionately larger than in society in general—no more than 10 percent. Homosexual-rights leaders contend that 20 percent to 50 percent of the Catholic clergy is homosexual, though no official or widely accepted studies support that.

Therapy Centers for Priests

Officially, the Catholic church encourages chastity for those who feel homosexually inclined and it urges priests struggling with their homosexuality to visit one of five "houses of affirmation," residential therapy centers that treat priests, religious brothers and nuns with emotional problems.

Several homosexual priests say they have been denied jobs because they openly avowed their homosexuality or supported homosexual rights. The Rev. Robert Carter, a Manhattan Jesuit, says that after he helped start the National Gay and Lesbian Task Force in 1973, he found it impossible to obtain teaching jobs at Catholic seminaries or universities.

Father Carter, 59, who says he joined the priesthood at a time when a homosexual orientation was not considered wrong, says of his activism: "I wasn't advocating the morality of gay sex. I was concerned about the issue of justice."

Protestant denominations have long said they welcome homosexuals as members but do not accept homosexual behavior.

Divisions Among Episcopalians

The Episcopal Bishop of Eau Claire, Wis., William Watland, says homosexuality must be recognized as sinful.

"There is no such thing as a sinless human being, and we are all in need of God's grace," he said. "God forgives sin if we repent, and that's how we have to start—in repentance—and move beyond that."

But, according to William Dearneley, a spokesman for the church, there is a great deal of division among Episcopal bishops both in theology and in practice. This was evident at the 1985 General Convention when neither resolutions permitting nor resolutions barring the ordination of avowed homosexuals won approval.

By contrast, the Southern Baptist Convention, the nation's largest Protestant denomination, with 14.6 million members, does not brook homosexual activity or homosexuals in its clergy. "In view of the fact that this would not be an appropriate role for a Southern Baptist chaplain, if there were any homosexuals they would certainly keep it quiet and very much in the closet," said W. C. Fields, a spokesman for the denomination.

CATHOLIC ARCHDIOCESE PROHIBITS HOMOSEXUAL CHURCH SERVICES

The Archdiocese of New York wrote a letter of expulsion in 1987 forbidding Dignity, a group of Roman Catholic homosexuals and their supporters, from holding any additional masses in the Manhattan church where they had been meeting since 1979. The prohibition affected more than 1,000 Dignity members. After their final Saturday night service, the group marched peacefully into the streets chanting, "We are the church." Timothy Coughlin, the president of Dignity, added, "Tonight we are not leaving a church behind. Instead we are taking a church with us . . . because no one, not even a Pope or a pompous Cardinal can take away our baptismal right." The pastor of the church, Rev. Michael E. Donahue, called it "a sad day in the life of our parish community," as he apologized for the "hurt and pain, as you experience once again the alienation of our church." He added, "We love you and we will miss you."

More than fifteen priests took part in the final mass, some at peril to their own careers. Rev. John McNeill, a celibate homosexual who had been dismissed from his Jesuit order last month, asked participants to leave with dignity, "remembering that Christ, too, was expelled from his church." While one man shook his head in bewilderment, stating, "I am a Catholic, but I cannot worship in a Catholic church," another said that the expulsion made him feel as if the church he grew up in was burning to the ground.

MARCH 9, 1987
HOMOSEXUAL GROUP HOLDS ITS FINAL MASS

By ARI L. GOLDMAN

Forbidden by the Archdiocese of New York from continuing to hold masses as an organization, a group of 1,000 Roman Catholic homosexuals and their supporters gathered Saturday night for a final service at a Manhattan church and then marched peacefully into the streets chanting, "We are the church."

"Tonight we are not leaving a church behind," said Timothy Coughlin, president of the organization that sponsored the mass, Dignity New York. "Instead we are taking a church with us. Tonight, our right to be in this building does not end, because no one, not even a Pope or a pompous Cardinal, can take away our baptismal right."

The mass culminated a period of delicate and sometimes tense negotiations between the Archdiocese and the Jesuit order that runs the church, St. Francis Xavier at 30 West 16th Street. The Archdiocese had sought to end masses sponsored by Dignity because the organization condones homosexual acts, which are against church teaching.

In a farewell to the Dignity group, the pastor of the church indicated that some Jesuits had fought hard to keep the Dignity masses at the church, which has held the special services since 1979.

'Sorry for the Hurt'

"This is a sad day in the life of our parish community," said the pastor, the Rev. Michael E. Donahue. "We are sorry for the hurt and pain, as you experience once again the alienation of our church."

Father Donahue said the Dignity members continued to have the support of the parish and of many priests, brothers and nuns in religious communities. "We will do everything in our power to reopen our doors to you," he said. "We love you and we will miss you."

The letter of expulsion was signed Feb. 27 by the vicar general of the Archdiocese, Bishop Joseph T. O'Keefe, who is second in command to the Archbishop, John Cardinal O'Connor. After celebrating mass at St. Patrick's Cathedral yesterday, the Cardinal said that the decision was based on church doctrine. "There are divine laws which give us life," he said. "We don't believe that they can be changed."

"We are not throwing anybody out of the church," the Cardinal said in response to a question. Homosexuals, he said, were welcome to participate in regular parish services or in special masses sponsored by the organization Courage, which advocates celibacy for homosexuals.

An Emotional Mass

The crackdown on Dignity came just weeks after the Bishop of Brooklyn, Francis J. Mugavero, suspended Dignity masses at a church in the Park Slope section. Church officials said that the moves, like those taken recently against Dignity chapters in dioceses around the nation, were in reaction to a stern Vatican document against homosexual activity issued last October with the approval of Pope John Paul II.

The Dignity mass, which lasted for more than an hour, was heavily laden with emotion. After taking holy communion—the consecrated bread and wine that, according to Catholic doctrine, is turned into the body and blood of Jesus—one man knelt and wept at a marble statue of the Virgin Mary.

One participant man said he felt as if he were watching the church he grew up in burn to the ground. Another, shaking his head slowly, said, "I am a Catholic, but I cannot worship in a Catholic church."

At the same time, many participants said that they felt empowered by the words of the 15 priests who, at often great risks to their careers, participated in the mass. "Let us leave with dignity," said the Rev. John J. McNeill, "remembering that Christ, too, was expelled from his church."

Father McNeill, who describes himself as a celibate homosexual, was dismissed last month from the Jesuit order after speaking out in support of stable homosexual relationships.

In a speech that had people standing and cheering from the cushioned kneeling boards, Mr. Coughlin said that the eviction from St. Francis Xavier would "not make us go away."

"We are not some fringe group in the church," he said. "We are everywhere and in everything the Archdiocese does. We are your priests, your nuns, your religious brothers. We run and staff your schools, colleges and hospitals.

We are your social workers, your accountants and your janitors. And, no doubt, we even make your fancy robes, Cardinal O'Connor.

"But in spite of all this, we stand here tonight and say loudly and clearly, we are not going away. We are the church."

The crowd filed out and, carrying candles and banners, marched four blocks to the Lesbian and Gay Community Services Center at 208 West 13th Street near Seventh Avenue. Dignity will hold weekly Catholic masses there until it finds another location, possibly in a Protestant church.

DALLAS HOUSES LARGEST HOMOSEXUAL CHURCH IN THE NATION, DEFYING CITY'S CONSERVATIVE REPUTATION

Dallas, Texas, is widely thought to be a conservative city with many big churches. It is also home to the largest gay church in the nation, the Cathedral of Hope Metropolitan Community Church. Part of a network of similar churches across the country, the MCC allows members to be openly homosexual in the context of Christian worship.

Approximately 1,400 people attended two services at the Cathedral of Hope on the Sunday this *Times* article was written. Rev. Elder Troy Perry, who founded the MCC in Los Angeles in 1968, explained that faith communities of all sorts do well in the Bible Belt because "part of the culture is going to church or going to synagogue." Many of the members of the MCC in Dallas had previously attended conservative Christian churches that did not welcome open homosexuality. One MCC member said, "The Cathedral of Hope is such a wonderful name, because so many of us were without hope. Sometimes openly, and sometimes not so openly, we were told Jesus didn't love us anymore."

When this article was written in 1994, the MCC claimed more than 42,000 members nationwide. Membership diminished somewhat in the late 1980s and early 1990s owing to deaths from AIDS. During this time the Cathedral of Hope averaged three to four funeral services each week. Rev. Michael S. Piazza, the pastor of the MCC, said there was a "huge well of grief" in the church, adding "every single Sunday [there was] an announcement that somebody's died, or there's a pew that's empty where they used to sit." He noted that the losses added a special urgency to essential church teachings, saying, "We live daily with the hope that the Resurrection is true."

OCTOBER 30, 1994
BIGGEST GAY CHURCH FINDS A HOME IN DALLAS
By GUSTAV NIEBUHR

DALLAS, Oct. 23—This conservative city of big churches and Sunday morning traffic jams is home these days to the nation's largest predominantly gay and lesbian congregation.

While many churches afford homosexuals a reception lukewarm at best, the Cathedral of Hope Metropolitan Community Church boldly proclaims itself a place where one can be openly homosexual and Christian, too.

Those who attend "are experiencing the gay and lesbian side, but they want to experience the Christian side in a safe context," said the Rev. Michael S. Piazza, the senior pastor. "So we provide a sanctuary."

That sanctuary offers visitors an unusual blend of the sacred and the secular. A bas-relief cross rises 32 feet high on its white stone wall. Beneath the cross is a pink marble altar cut in the shape of a triangle, forming the well-known symbol of homosexuality. Sunlight on stained-glass windows illuminates not only an Easter lily and a dove of peace but also the Greek letter lambda, another symbol of gay and lesbian identity.

This week the church counted a total of 1,400 congregants, including a heterosexual minority, at its two Sunday morning services.

Why such a big congregation in Dallas, rather than, say, San Francisco or New York, two cities much better known for their homosexual communities? "Our churches do very, very well in the Bible Belt," said the Rev. Elder Troy D. Perry, moderator of the Universal Fellowship of Metropolitan Community Churches, the denomination to which the Cathedral of Hope belongs. "Part of the culture is going to church or going to synagogue."

Who attends the Cathedral of Hope? People like David Pfleeger, 41, who grew up attending a conservative church in Tulsa, Okla. "The Cathedral of Hope is such a wonderful name, because so many of us were without hope," said Mr. Pfleeger, a Medicaid case worker for the state. "Sometimes openly, and sometimes not so openly, we were told Jesus didn't love us anymore."

Joyce Bell, 49, the church's vice moderator, its top lay official, said it was important to her that "women are allowed to be seen and heard" there.

"Women are treated as equals, as they should be," Ms. Bell said. "And that has nothing to do with gay and straight."

The very presence of the 34,000-square-foot church offers evidence of the gradual growth of the Metropolitan Community Churches, founded 26 years ago by Mr. Perry. A Pentecostal minister who had lost his church by acknowledging that he is gay, he placed an advertisement in a magazine with a homosexual readership, inviting people to come hear him preach at his home in Los Angeles. "That first Sunday, Oct. 6, 1968, 12 people showed up in the living room of my house," he said.

The Los Angeles-based denomination now has about 42,000 members in the United States and abroad, not only in large cities but also in some small ones like Paducah, Ky. The second-largest congregation is in Fort Lauderdale, Fla.

The denomination's leaders have had to deal with the Old Testament verses commonly cited to condemn homosexuality. In the Book of Leviticus, two verses (18:22 and 20:13) say that for two men to lie together as "with a woman" is an "abomination."

Mr. Piazza, the senior pastor at the Cathedral of Hope, says the passages should be read in the context of a sexual code among early Hebrews meant to promote population growth. "Overpopulation has made that verse as irrelevant as refrigeration has made the injunction against eating pork," he said. "We really have arguments with people taking this out of context and trying to impose them on 20th-century people."

Dedicated last year, the Cathedral of Hope seats upward of 900 worshipers in upholstered pews and cost $3.5 million to build, financed mostly through an issue of bonds bought by church members.

Sunday worship draws from varying Christian traditions. A recent service opened with a procession by robed clergy, as would be seen among Episcopalians or Roman Catholics. But later the congregation clapped and sang through a gospel chorus and applauded a guest preacher's remarks.

Scott Schubert, 40-year-old chairman of the church's board, said that before attending the Cathedral of Hope, "I'd never seen a joyous worship service."

Yet within the congregation exists a "huge well of grief," the result of devastation inflicted by AIDS, Mr. Piazza said.

The Metropolitan Community Churches estimates that 5,000 members of the denomination have died of AIDS since 1982. The Cathedral of Hope, which is dedicated to victims of the disease, averages three to four funerals a week.

"AIDS is taking the heart out of this church every day," Mr. Piazza said. "You come to church, and every single Sunday there's an announcement that somebody's died, or there's a pew that's empty where they used to sit."

AIDS lends a special urgency to some essential teachings. Guiding a visitor around the sanctuary, Mr. Piazza pointed out the word "hope" inscribed in English and Spanish in two stained-glass windows. During the service, as hundreds of men and women bowed their heads, he prayed aloud, asking God to "resurrect our bodies, resurrect our souls."

"We live daily with the hope," the pastor said in an interview, "that the Resurrection is true."

METHODIST MINISTER COULD BE DEFROCKED FOR OFFICIATING AT SAME-SEX MARRIAGE

In 1998 Rev. Jimmy Creech, a United Methodist minister stood trial in a church court for officiating at a marriage between two women at his congregation. By performing the ceremony he defied an order from his bishop as well as the United Methodist Church's "Book of Discipline," which states that "ceremonies that celebrate homosexual unions shall not be conducted by our ministers and shall not be conducted in our churches." At risk of losing his credentials as a minister, Creech said he considered the church's condemnation of same-sex unions discriminatory. No major Protestant churches offered official rituals to bless same-sex unions at the time of Rev. Creech's trial. The Episcopal Church nearly passed a proposal to develop such a service in 1997.

At this time many churches had also been taking up the related issue of whether homosexuals may be ordained as ministers. In 1996 the Methodist Church took a clear stance against doing so, as did the Presbyterian Church in 1997. The Church of Christ provides discretion to regional associations, some of which have ordained gay and lesbian ministers.

Creech said that although his trial was shaping up to be a test case, he noted that it "didn't start as a strategy. It began as a couple coming to me." Rev. Jeanne Knepper, a spokesperson for Affirmations, a Methodist group for LGBT people and their supporters, said that at least 20 other Methodist pastors had been performing similar ceremonies. A leader in the more conservative, evangelical wing of the Methodist Church said that Creech's trial would be "a shot heard round the church," adding that the ceremony "was a clear violation of biblical principles, as well as the tradition of the church."

One member of Creech's church said that he was "going to drive a wedge" into the congregation. He argued that the Methodist Church is open, but that it is also governed by the "Book of Discipline," which "is not for someone to pick and choose." Creech has said that his actions were affected by having been raised in North Carolina during the civil rights movement, noting that "it was people willing in that moment to be faithful, to take a stand, to do the right thing, that ultimately brought about change in the South." Conceding that boldness of that sort could be disruptive, he concluded, "In order for there to be any kind of growth, there must be conflict."

FEBRUARY 15, 1998
PASTOR'S CHURCH TRIAL ATTESTS TO DIVISIVENESS OF GAY ISSUE
By GUSTAV NIEBUHR

OMAHA—Joining a man and a woman before God is standard duty for members of the clergy. But for performing a union of a different sort, the Rev. Jimmy Creech, a United Methodist minister here, will soon be tried in a church court.

At issue is Mr. Creech's officiation at a covenant ceremony last September uniting two women in his congregation, First United Methodist Church. The event resembled a Methodist wedding, with Scripture readings, an exchange of vows and a celebration of communion.

But it came a month after Mr. Creech's bishop told him not to do it and a year after Methodist leaders added a statement to the denomination's rule book forbidding ceremonies uniting people of the same sex.

Mr. Creech said in a recent interview that he could not, as their pastor, refuse the women's request and that he considered the church's opposition to unions of people of the same sex to be discriminatory. He could lose his ministerial credentials if convicted.

The trial, which is scheduled to begin on March 11 in a Kearney, Neb., church, will highlight a divisive pattern emerging within Protestantism, where the consensus against homosexuality has been eroding, as it has elsewhere in society.

Issues concerning homosexuality, especially the question of whether to ordain noncelibate gay men and lesbians as ministers, have touched off rancorous debates at church conventions, where opponents often cite biblical injunctions against homosexual acts. A few cases have ended up before ecclesiastical judges.

No major Protestant denomination has voted to allow the ordination of homosexuals as ministers, nor has any developed official rituals to bless same-sex unions. But the stands that denominational leaders have taken vary considerably.

In 1996, for example, the United Methodists firmly rejected a measure to allow homosexuals to be ordained.

Last year, the regional bodies of the Presbyterian Church (U.S.A.) went a step further, amending the church constitution to bar anyone sexually active outside marriage from serving as a minister, elder or deacon.

By contrast, the United Church of Christ leaves the matter up to its regional associations, a few of which have ordained openly gay men and lesbians as ministers. In 1997, priests and lay leaders at the Episcopal Church's General Convention narrowly rejected a proposal to develop liturgies for blessing same-sex unions.

"This is the polarizing issue," said Michael McClellan, an Omaha lawyer and a member of the First United Methodist Church who will be Mr. Creech's co-counsel. A retired Methodist bishop will serve as judge and other ministers as a jury.

The number of same-sex unions quietly blessed by clergy members is not known. The privacy surrounding such ceremonies has helped insure that no minister has ever been tried for performing one in the 8.5 million-member United Methodist Church, the nation's largest mainline Protestant denomination.

"This is going to be a test case," said Mr. Creech, 53, who has been suspended with pay. "This didn't start as a strategy. It began as a couple coming to me." Mr. Creech is married with a stepdaughter and has an adult son by a previous marriage.

James V. Heidinger 2d, president of Good News, an evangelical movement among Methodists, said the trial would "be a shot heard round the church." The ceremony, he said, was "a clear violation of biblical principles, as well as the tradition of the church."

Mr. Creech described his position on homosexuality and the church as a Divine calling. "I really believe this is God's history and I'm part of what God is doing," he said. "I've been invited into it and given a responsibility."

Bans on ordaining homosexuals as ministers and blessing same-sex unions, he said, reflect "a cultural prejudice that has been institutionalized in the church." In 1997, he signed a statement, titled "In All Things Charity," that called for support for ordaining gay men and lesbians and for developing ceremonies for "same-gendered couples." The statement has been signed by more than 1,300 Methodist ministers, or about 3 percent of the denomination's 37,000 ordained ministers.

The Rev. Jeanne Knepper, a spokeswoman for Affirmation: United Methodists for Gay, Lesbian, Bisexual and Transgendered Concerns, said a few signers had performed same-sex unions. "I could give you—but I won't give you—the names of 20 United Methodist pastors who have done these ceremonies," she said. Mr. Creech, she added, "is not anywhere near alone: he's the lightning rod."

Mr. Creech is charged with violating Methodism's "The Book of Discipline," its laws and administrative rules. In 1996, the denomination's policy-making body, the General Conference, added a sentence to the book's "social principles" section: "Ceremonies that celebrate homosexual unions shall not be conducted by our ministers and shall not be conducted in our churches."

That section also contains an earlier statement describing homosexuals as people of "sacred worth," but calling homosexual acts "incompatible with Christian teaching." Mr. Creech's trial will turn on whether the 1996 statement against same-sex unions is legally binding, rather than merely advisory, as Mr. Creech and his supporters contend.

The controversy has shaken members at Mr. Creech's church, a 200,000 square-foot complex atop a small hill. Financial pledges are down, as is Sunday School attendance. Some of Mr. Creech's critics have quit attending, while some supporters have picketed the offices of the Nebraska Bishop, Joel N. Martinez. Church staff members say many in the 1,900-member congregation feel caught in the middle.

Founded in 1855, the First United Methodist Church has undergone tumult before, although nothing like this. One early pastor carried a six-shooter in the pulpit. Another, considered a Southern sympathizer in the Civil War years, was run off by the congregation. In 1975, a tornado struck the church buildings.

At one time, said the Rev. Donald D. Bredthauer, the acting pastor, First United Methodist "was sort of seen as a high-steeple church," meaning socially exclusive. But he said that was no longer true for a congregation that prepared meals for people with AIDS, backed an organization that lobbies for civic improvements in poor neighborhoods, Omaha Together One Community, and supported Habitat for Humanity, which builds housing for the needy.

"We've not stopped doing our other ministries just to take care of this," Mr. Bredthauer said.

Bishop Martinez appointed Mr. Creech to the church in 1996. He had served congregations in North Carolina. But his critics said that they found out only later that Mr. Creech left his last pulpit in Raleigh, N.C., amid a bitter dispute over his support for local gay rights initiatives.

A chapter in a book, "Congregations in Conflict: The Battle Over Homosexuality" (Rutgers, 1996), by Keith Hartman, describes that experience, saying that the congregation divided mainly along generational lines, with older members largely opposing Mr. Creech.

Mr. Creech later went to work as a lobbyist for the North Carolina Council of Churches, where he became known as an opponent of the death penalty.

The rift at the First United Methodist Church began in January 1997, after Mr. Creech preached that "to be gay was in itself healthy, normal and natural." The sermon, he said, "got a pretty strong reaction."

Bob Howell, a retired insurance company executive, said he had complained to Mr. Creech that it was "the fourth sermon we had heard on the subject."

Mr. Howell said the minister "listened very well, but the word was, 'I'm going to continue down that path.'" Mr. Howell canceled his financial pledge in protest and later stopped attending.

Melvin J. Semrad, a gas and electric company executive, said he urged Mr. Creech "to slow this train down," to give skeptics a chance to adjust. And last April, Mr. Semrad said, he warned Mr. Creech that his preaching was "going to drive a wedge" into the congregation.

"We believe we are an open church," Mr. Semrad said, "but we also believe in the 'Discipline.'" The Methodist rule book, he added, "is not for someone to pick and choose."

But Deb Keeney, an administrative assistant in a local school, said that Mr. Creech was "helping us fulfill our vision" at the church.

Before he arrived, the church had drawn up a statement of purpose, called "Vision Focus," which said, in part, that members would "welcome and celebrate the diversity of God's children," including "all economic levels, races, ethnicities, sexual orientations, marital states, abilities and age levels."

Mr. Creech, Ms. Keeney said, "came to the church knowing this was the vision we had, and had no inkling there were people who did not agree with that."

But not everyone in the church had attached such weight to the statement. Frank Rathbun, a church member who is a retired natural gas company executive, said the way the statement was interpreted under Mr. Creech "turned out to be much broader than when people agreed to it."

All this might have remained within church walls had not the two women asked Mr. Creech to perform a covenant ceremony for them. He agreed last July and wrote to Bishop Martinez, who, he said, instructed him not to conduct it.

Mr. Creech said he replied to the bishop "that I felt that it was my responsibility as a pastor to do it," and that the "Book of Discipline" statement was "unjust and discriminatory." (He has not identified the women, nor have they spoken out.)

After the ceremony, more than 400 First United Methodist members wrote Bishop Martinez, saying the event challenges "the principles of our Christian faith." A Methodist minister in western Nebraska filed a formal complaint. In November, the bishop suspended Mr. Creech.

Two months later, a church investigative committee ordered a trial. Bishop Martinez issued a statement promising to expedite the process. He did not return calls seeking comment on the case. But Mr. Creech released his own statement, saying, in part, "I believe that the sin of heterosexism is no less a sin than that of racism."

His supporters have organized a group called "Support the Vision." At a recent meeting, one woman described Mr. Creech as "a beautiful man of Christ" who "was sent here for a purpose, for all of us to be tested."

But Virginia Semrad, Melvin Semrad's wife, likened Mr. Creech's relationship with the church to a marriage gone sour. "He was not known, we did not court each other long enough," she said. "I feel Jimmy Creech cannot, should not, return to his pulpit."

Although Mr. Bredthauer occupies the pastor's office, it remains largely as Mr. Creech left it. The wall behind the desk displays portraits of the Rev. Dr. Martin Luther King Jr., Mohandas K. Gandhi and Archbishop Oscar Romero of San Salvador, all victims of assassins. There is also a picture of Rosa Parks, the African-American woman who in 1955 refused to yield her seat to a white man on a segregated bus in Montgomery, Ala.

Mr. Creech, who grew up in Goldsboro, N.C., said he had been "very much affected" by the Civil Rights movement, although he had not taken part in it. "It was people willing in that moment to be faithful, to take a stand, to do the right thing, that ultimately brought about change in the South," he said.

He acknowledged that within a congregation, such boldness could be disruptive. But the sacrifice, he said, amounted simply to the loss "of artificial unity and peace."

"In order for there to be any kind of growth," he said, "there must be conflict."

- -

Catholic Church Condemns Recognition of Same-Sex Marriage

In an apparent reaction to developments in North America and Europe regarding gay civil rights, the Vatican issued a sternly worded, lengthy document addressing homosexuality, same-sex marriage, and adoption by gays and lesbians in 2003. Titled "Considerations Regarding Proposals to Give Legal Recognition to Unions between Homosexual Persons," the document called support for legislation that recognizes same-sex marriage "gravely immoral," adding, "There are absolutely no grounds for considering homosexual unions to be in any way similar or even remotely analogous to God's plan for marriage and family."

Concluding that "marriage is holy, while homosexual acts go against the natural moral law," and that allowing gays and lesbians to adopt children "would actually mean doing violence to these children," the document offered various guidelines for Catholic bishops and politicians on the issue of gay rights as they relate to family life. It was widely understood as an attempt to influence public debate. France became the first largely Roman Catholic nation to recognize homosexual unions in 2000, while Belgium began registering partnerships in 2003 and Germany grants gay couples various protections and benefits that had been reserved only for married heterosexuals. Britain allows for protections similar to Germany's, and Canada legalized gay marriage outright in 2004.

In addition to these developments, the Episcopal Church began readying to meet to discuss whether to confirm the nomination of an openly gay bishop and whether to develop a ritual to bless same-sex unions. Conservative Episcopal leaders threatened a schism.

AUGUST 1, 2003
VATICAN EXHORTS LEGISLATORS TO REJECT SAME-SEX UNIONS
By FRANK BRUNI

VATICAN CITY, July 31—Worried about the spread of laws that recognize same-sex couples, the Vatican today urged Roman Catholic lawmakers and others to fight back, calling support for such legislation "gravely immoral."

That unwavering appeal came in a strongly worded, 12-page document that was devoted entirely to homosexuality, gay marriage and adoption by gays and lesbians, issues that have stirred fervent debate recently in North America and Europe.

"There are absolutely no grounds for considering homosexual unions to be in any way similar or even remotely analogous to God's plan for marriage and family," the document said, asserting repeatedly that marriage should be reserved for heterosexual couples.

"Marriage is holy, while homosexual acts go against the natural moral law," it said.

The document, published in several languages, including English, was presented as a set of guidelines for Catholic bishops and politicians and as an attempt to sway public debate, not as a fresh, revelatory examination of Catholic theology.

It also contained an admonition for Catholic legislators in bodies that are considering laws to recognize same-sex unions or permit gays and lesbians to marry or adopt children.

"To vote in favor of a law so harmful to the common good is gravely immoral," said the document, which spelled out, on its final page, that it was being issued with the explicit approval and under the specific orders of Pope John Paul II.

Although the document had been in the works for months and reiterated positions that the pope had already made clear, it represented an especially emphatic statement of those viewpoints. It was the second time this year that the Vatican instructed Catholic politicians to oppose gay marriages, underscoring the Vatican's objections and apprehensions.

The document was released one day after President Bush announced that his administration was looking into ways to ensure that the term "marriage" would apply legally only to unions between men and women.

Republican Congressional leaders have floated the idea of a constitutional amendment to do just that.

Those developments reflected some lawmakers' concerns over an apparently growing acceptance of homosexuality, a profusion of gay characters and themes on American television, and legal entitlements in some states.

Some European governments have formally recognized same-sex unions or are moving in that direction, an example of a widening chasm between Catholic teaching and European law that the pope has frequently decried.

A law passed in France in 2000 made that country the first predominantly Roman Catholic nation to recognize homosexual unions.

Just this year, Belgium began registering gay partnerships. Germany, which also has a large Catholic population, grants gay couples protections, benefits and responsibilities traditionally reserved for married men and women.

Similar measures are being considered in Britain. Two Canadian provinces also recently legalized same-sex marriages.

Homosexuality is the dominant issue at a convention this week of the Episcopal Church USA, which is part of the worldwide Anglican Communion. The convention is deliberating whether to confirm an openly gay bishop in New Hampshire and whether to develop a blessing for same-sex unions.

Conservative Episcopalians and Anglicans have threatened a schism if the convention votes in favor of those measures. A final resolution is expected within the next week.

The practical effect of the Vatican document was uncertain, as one Vatican official acknowledged today.

"We have to preach our principle, even if we know that many people won't abide by it," said the official, who spoke on the condition of anonymity. "The Vatican is worried, because we think marriage should be between a man and a woman."

Many Catholic lawmakers in the United States and Europe have long bucked the church on a range of issues, including abortion, which the church opposes. Many of the estimated 65 million Roman Catholics in the United

States—almost one in four Americans—pick and choose which of the pope's pronouncements to obey.

"Vatican officials seem to think that they still have the same kind of credibility they once had, and they don't," said the Rev. Andrew Greeley, a prominent Catholic sociologist in the United States. "I'm not saying that's good or bad, but that's certainly what the evidence seems to show."

Father Greeley added that there was much greater acceptance of homosexuality among American Catholics today than there was a decade ago, but he said he was not certain if that acceptance extended to approval of same-sex unions.

Congress is unlikely to entertain any legislation that supports such unions, although some states are grappling with the issue. Three years ago, Vermont passed a law that recognized gay couples.

In Europe, the limits of the Vatican's influence, as well as one of the seeds of its frustration, were made clear in the pope's failed campaign to have a reference to Christianity inserted into the preamble of the current draft of a European Union constitution.

The Vatican document issued today, titled "Considerations Regarding Proposals to Give Legal Recognition to Unions Between Homosexual Persons," condemned what it called "unjust discrimination against homosexual persons."

But it maintained that the inability of same-sex couples to procreate on their own violated one of the God-given and most important aspects of marriage.

It said legal recognition for gay and lesbian couples would amount to "approval of deviant behavior, with the consequence of making it a model in present-day society."

It added that allowing children to be adopted by gays and lesbians "would actually mean doing violence to these children" because it would put them in unhealthy home environments.

. . . .

Episcopal Church Approves Its First Openly Gay Bishop

In 2003, by a 62–45 margin, the Episcopal Church approved the election of V. Gene Robinson, the church's first openly gay bishop. Immediately after the vote twelve conservative bishops denounced the decision as a threat to church teaching that would lead to schism, saying, "With grief too deep for words, the bishops who stand before you must reject this action." Others who were present praised the decision, lauding its inclusivity. Saying, "This is a great day for the church," supporters also remarked that they felt for those who were opposing Robinson, describing them as "broken-hearted."

Supporters argued that the decision would bring new members into the church, particularly young people, while opponents feared it would drive many away from the church and discourage donations. Bishop-elect Robinson called the vote a "tiny sign" of a larger movement for greater tolerance, saying that the culture is "moving into a mature adulthood" regarding the treatment of gays and lesbians. He added that he hoped to be able to heal some of the division and pain that was evident.

The presiding bishop, Frank T. Griswold, said that while Robinson's election did not resolve the issue of homosexuality for the church, it did "place squarely before us the question of how a community can live in the tension of disagreement." Most Rev. Rowan Williams, the head of the Anglican Communion and a supporter of the decision, acknowledged that the Episcopal Church faced difficult times going forward, noting that "it is too early to say what the result" of the decision will be worldwide. Others said the warnings of disaster were overblown, recalling that the ordination of women in 1976 and the ratification of a female bishop in 1989 had not led to the splits many had predicted. For example, the first female bishop in the church,

Barbara Harris, noted that despite "the dire predictions made at the time of my election consent process," the church remained together.

The decision to approve Robinson was delayed for two days while church officials investigated eleventh-hour claims of sexual impropriety. One of Robinson's accusers subsequently said that he "regretted having used the word 'harassment,'" but that he felt obliged to report his discomfort when Robinson had publicly touched his arm and upper back while talking to him at a meeting. The second accusation concerned a group that Robinson had helped found for young gay people in 1998 that had created a Web site in 2002 with links to other sites that included some pornography. Robinson had not been involved with the group since its founding in 1998. He kept a low profile while the accusations were being investigated, saying, "I prayed a lot yesterday and felt God was very nearby." Some supporters of Robinson called the accusations last-minute political maneuvers.

AUGUST 6, 2003
GAY BISHOP WINS IN EPISCOPAL VOTE; SPLIT THREATENED
By MONICA DAVEY

MINNEAPOLIS, Aug. 5—The Episcopal Church approved the election of its first openly gay bishop tonight, reaching the historic and divisive decision after rejecting accusations of sexual misconduct against him that had suddenly halted the vote on Monday.

After being called back this afternoon, 62 of 107 diocesan bishops voted to approve the bishop-elect, V. Gene Robinson. Moments later, more than 12 conservative bishops, their faces grim, marched slowly to the front of the House of Bishops to denounce the decision as an affront to church teaching that would split the denomination in two.

"The bishops who stand before you are filled with sorrow," Bishop Robert W. Duncan of the Pittsburgh Diocese said. "This body has divided itself for millions of Anglican Christians around the world, brothers and sisters who have pleaded with us to maintain the church's traditional teaching on marriage and sexuality. With grief too deep for words, the bishops who stand before you must reject this action."

Bishop Duncan, one of a group of church leaders who had fought Bishop-elect Robinson's approval for weeks, said he and his colleagues would call on the top leaders of the Anglican Communion, the 38 primates around the world, to intervene in the "pastoral emergency that has overtaken" the church.

"May God have mercy on this church," Bishop Duncan said.

Others rejoiced, praising the popular bishop-elect for his works and saying the decision was another barrier overtaken by church leaders, another widening of church doors.

"It's a great day for the church," the Rev. Sandye Wilson of the Minnesota Diocese said. "This is a church which has finally understood that men and women created in the vision of God can be the guardians of the faith—and be gay or lesbian."

People who had pressed for the choice over weeks of lobbying and days of intense pressure at this convention of hundreds of Episcopalians said they were thrilled by the outcome but also saddened by talk of a split within the church and the calls for the primates' help.

"I am also mindful of the fact that our brothers and sisters are broken-hearted," Ms. Wilson said. "And I feel for them in their pain."

Supporters say the decision will bring new people, especially young people, into the church, which has 2.3 million members in the United States. Opponents say just the reverse will occur; that people will stay away from their churches this weekend, stop giving donations and wonder what the church has come to stand for.

Bishop-elect Robinson, 56, told reporters that his approval was a "tiny sign" of a broader movement in the church and across this country in the acceptance of gays and lesbians. As a culture, he said, "I think we're seeing the moving into a mature adulthood" about the treatment of gay people.

As his longtime partner, Mark Andrew, and his grown daughter, Ella, looked on, the bishop-elect said he doubted that the approval would make much difference in Episcopalians' daily lives. While sexuality is an important issue to people, it is by no means the only one, he said.

"When they go to church on Sunday," he added, "it's going to look pretty much like last Sunday."

Still, he acknowledged the church members who left the convention in tears tonight. He said he hoped that he would be able to help heal some of the division and pain.

The presiding bishop here, Bishop Frank T. Griswold, said the decision did not "resolve the issues about homosexuality" for the church.

"What it does do," he said, "is place squarely before us the question of how a community can live in the tension of disagreement."

After the vote, the Most Rev. Rowan Williams, the archbishop of Canterbury and the titular leader of the Anglican Communion, said the church faced difficult times.

"The General Convention's decision to approve the appointment of Gene Robinson," the archbishop said, "will inevitably have a significant impact on the Anglican Communion throughout the world, and it is too early to say what the result of that will be. It will be vital to ensure that the concerns and needs of those across the Communion who are gravely concerned at this development can be heard, understood and taken into account."

As recently as noon today, church leaders said they were uncertain whether Bishop-elect Robinson could be considered today or even by the end of the convention on Friday. The bishops had planned to vote on Monday, but delayed that indefinitely when two accusations were made against him late Sunday. The bishops began investigating.

A day later, to the surprise of many here, the investigation was over. This afternoon, Bishop Gordon P. Scruton, who was assigned to investigate the accusations, told his fellow bishops that he had found "no necessity to pursue" either complaint further.

Bishop Scruton, of the Diocese of Western Massachusetts, said he had interviewed David A. Lewis, a church member in Manchester, Vt., who sent an e-mail message to bishops on Sunday night that accused Bishop-elect Robinson of harassment in November 1999 at a church conference in Holyoke, Mass.

When Bishop Scruton called Mr. Lewis on Monday, Mr. Lewis said he "regretted having used the word 'harassment' in his e-mail," Bishop Scruton said. Mr. Lewis described two conversations with Bishop-elect Robinson at the conference, Bishop Scruton said. Mr. Lewis said the bishop-elect had touched him on the arm and upper back during the talks, which were in front of other people.

Mr. Lewis said that the gestures struck him as too familiar and that they "made him feel uncomfortable," said Bishop Scruton. But he acknowledged that other people might view the exchange as normal and natural and told Bishop Scruton two times that he did not want to pursue the matter further, Bishop Scruton said.

Mr. Lewis said he sent his message on Sunday night after hearing that Bishop-elect Robinson had been approved by the House of Deputies, one of two decision-making bodies in the Episcopal Church, along with the House of Bishops. Mr. Lewis said that he "found himself late Sunday night needing to tell someone of his experience," Bishop Scruton said.

Bishop Scruton also cleared Bishop-elect Robinson of a second accusation, made late Sunday night by his opponents in the House of Bishops. Bishop Scruton said he had found that the bishop-elect had no involvement in a Web site for young gay people that also had links to a Web site that included pornography.

Bishop-elect Robinson helped found that the organization with the site, Concord Outright, meant to help gay and lesbian teenagers. Bishop Scruton said the bishop-elect had no involvement with it since 1998. The organization created its Web site last year.

Bishop-elect Robinson, who had stayed away from the convention and out of public view on the day of the investigation, reappeared this afternoon. He said he had spent his time praying and reading psalms.

"I prayed a lot yesterday and felt God was very nearby," he said.

He said that the church regularly conducted investigations in such cases and that he had even helped create some of the processes for investigation in his diocese in New Hampshire.

Although some of his supporters had called the vote a last-minute political maneuver, Bishop-elect Robinson seemed satisfied with what had occurred.

"I am proud to be in a church which works to be a safe place for all of God's children," the bishop-elect said.

He said he did not recall meeting Mr. Lewis, but acknowledged that he often touched or hugged congregants. "I am a demonstrative person," he said.

In Vermont, people who know Mr. Lewis described him as a husband, a father, a religious scholar, a lay reader at his Episcopal church and a man who told the truth when he spoke. Many neighbors said they had no reason to doubt him. Others said they could only surmise that he must have felt moved to express a private thought, even in the last possible moments of a complicated process.

Lou Midura, senior warden at Zion Episcopal and the sole person to speak officially about Mr. Lewis here today, said his friend and fellow parishioner wanted everyone to know one thing, that his message about the bishop-elect was meant to be privately conveyed to the Minneapolis meeting and not debated in the news media.

"I'm comfortable saying I know David extremely well, and his character is beyond reproach," Mr. Midura, a house builder by trade, said in the 1782 church as television news trucks lined up in the parking lot.

The investigation, which seemed so crucial on Monday, seemed to be forgotten by the time the bishops began debating before voting. The discussion was quiet and civil, and it was preceded and followed by prayer. Bishops rose from their seats around round tables to address the audience.

"He's been tried, he's been weighed, he's been measured," Bishop J. Jon Bruno of the Los Angeles Diocese said. "On the extreme, he has been found morally capable."

But as they rose to speak, Bishop-elect Robinson's opponents said he would bring to the broader church schism, pain and confusion.

"I am absolutely committed to Jesus Christ, absolutely committed to this church, absolutely committed to

this House, absolutely committed to you," Bishop Edward S. Little II of the Northern Indiana Diocese said. "If we confirm Gene Robinson as a bishop of the church, the unity of this house will be shattered forever."

Other people called the warnings overblown. Look, they said, at other controversies that were also predicted to split the church like the ordination of women in 1976 and the ratifying of a woman, Barbara Harris as bishop, in 1989. This evening, Ms. Harris, who retired from the Massachusetts Diocese, said the church had survived and would once more.

"I remember well the dire predictions made at the time of my election consent process," she said. "The communion, such as it is, a loose federation of autonomous provinces, has held."

Others, though, were left pained by so much talk of sexuality and not enough, they said, about the other weightier issues being wrestled with every day in the church—hunger, fighting the AIDS crisis in Africa and reaching out to people searching for faith.

"To my mind, this has been too much of a distraction," said Ed Cahill, 72, an alternate from the East Tennessee Diocese. In the turmoil, he said, he had a dream about a house burning down.

The church has been struggling with the issue of its stand on homosexuality for decades, he said, and its efforts to sort it out at this meeting by no means end the debate. As an alternate in the House of Deputies, Mr. Cahill did not vote on the bishop-elect. That was fortunate, he said, because he has still not made up his mind.

Al Baker contributed to this article.

* *

More Gay Couples Seeking Religious Blessings

The number of gay couples having their unions consecrated in churches and synagogues began to rise in the postmillennial era. Although such ceremonies do not bestow legal rights, many couples seek them out as a blessing by God, rather than the government. The United Church of Christ began to hold workshops for ministers who wished to consecrate gay unions, and the Episcopal Church in British Columbia developed a rite for blessing gay couples that was circulated on e-mail to ministers in other congregations. Services were often very similar to traditional marriage rites used for heterosexual couples, with the only change being use of the word *partners* in the place of *husband and wife*.

Because homosexuality remained an extremely divisive issue for many denominations, only a few offer gay couples the option of having their unions blessed. Some prohibit them, while others are in a process of determining how to deal with the issue. Said one Catholic priest who defied his church's prohibition on gay unions: "We can bless a dog, we can bless a boat, we can bless a car, but we can't say a prayer over two people who love each other and want to spend their lives together. You don't have to call it marriage; you can call it a deep and abiding friendship, but you can't bless it." Recently interviewed clergy said that the consecration of gay unions is increasing. The Metropolitan Community Church, founded to minister primarily to gays and lesbians, is the only church that keeps formal records of same-sex unions. The MCC marries about 6,000 gay couples each year.

While many people do not think of gay couples as religious, "there are lots of us that feel very connected to our faith traditions," says Steven Baines, an elder with the Disciples of Christ. In fact, some couples say that they are more interested in receiving the church's blessing than the government's. Dolores Trzcinski says that she and her partner of 25 years "never really cared about the state. We didn't care about health insurance. It was God's blessing that we wanted."

JANUARY 30, 2004
GAY COUPLES SEEK UNIONS IN GOD'S EYES
By LAURIE GOODSTEIN
Correction Appended

Jeffrey A. Manley found Jusak Y. Bernhard five years ago after posting a note in an online chat room for a Roman Catholic man looking to share his life with another Christian man.

This March, on the fifth anniversary of their first date, the two plan to exchange vows before their families and friends, in a church. They say they would not consider having the ceremony anywhere else.

"The reason we're doing this is to make God a part of the relationship," said Mr. Manley, a television editor who lives with Mr. Bernhard in Los Angeles. "We are making our union with God in public. We do see it as a sacrament."

Although 37 states have passed laws banning same-sex marriages, members of the clergy say they are seeing a growing number of religiously observant gay couples who are sidestepping the debate over legal rights and seeking to consecrate their unions in churches and synagogues.

These ceremonies bestow no legal or civil rights whatsoever. But the couples say they are seeking to have their relationships blessed not by the government, but by God.

Ministers and rabbis are responding to the demand. The United Church of Christ is holding workshops for ministers who want to learn how to handle gay unions. A rite for blessing gay couples that was developed by the Episcopal Church in New Westminster, British Columbia,

is being shared by e-mail among ministers—including non-Episcopalians—who are looking for model liturgies.

Homosexuality has become the most divisive issue of the era for many religious denominations, and only a handful have decided to permit gay blessing ceremonies. Many prohibit them, while others are struggling to determine their stance. Although most denominations that do permit the ceremonies keep no nationwide records of how many same-sex rites have been performed, members of the clergy across the country said in interviews that the ceremonies were becoming more common in their churches and synagogues.

At the United Congregational Church in Worcester, Mass., for example, the Rev. Terry Fitzgerald, senior minister, and the Rev. Mark Seifried, minister of education, said that of the 15 to 20 gay union ceremonies at their church in the last 15 years, 7 took place in 2003.

Rabbi Sharon Gladstone, who directs a center on sexual orientation issues at Hebrew Union College in Los Angeles, said, "I was ordained last year, and the first marriage I officiated at was a marriage of two women. I think that more and more rabbis are officiating, certainly in the Reform and Reconstructionist movements."

Even some members of the clergy who do not have the permission of their denominations—including Catholic priests—say they are quietly officiating at ceremonies in defiance of their church leaders.

One Catholic priest, who has violated his church's ban, said: "We can bless a dog, we can bless a boat, we can bless a car, but we can't say a prayer over two people who love each other and want to spend their lives together. You don't have to call it marriage; you can call it a deep and abiding friendship, but you can't bless it."

Although denominations that do permit these rituals formally refer to them as holy unions, same-sex blessings, covenants or commitment ceremonies, more and more of the couples and members of the clergy are simply calling them marriages. The services are often nearly identical to the marriage rites traditionally used for heterosexual couples.

"In most cases, we use the same vows and prayers, the same scriptural references," Ms. Fitzgerald said. "The only thing we change is that we say 'partners' instead of 'husband and wife.'"

Dolores M. Trzcinski, 49, and Marie T. Auger, 46, say they fulfilled a long-held dream when they walked down the aisle last year at the United Congregational Church in Worcester. They have lived together for more than 25 years.

"We never really cared about the state," said Ms. Trzcinski, a medical assistant in a doctor's office. "We didn't care about the health insurance. It was God's blessing that we wanted."

It is a perennial complaint among members of the clergy that many straight couples regard the chapel as little more than a stage set for a picture-perfect wedding. In contrast, many of the gay couples who are heading for the altar are regular worshipers who say in interviews that religion is central to their lives.

They represent an often-overlooked slice of gay America: the monogamous homebodies more likely to have met their mates at Bible study than at a bar.

"Our relationship is faith-based," said Mr. Bernhard, an actor and producer who immigrated to the United States from Indonesia as a teenager. "We truly believe, and that's what keeps us fairly strong. We do our prayers and our Bible readings together, and depend a lot on our faith to carry us through difficult times."

Steven Baines, an elder with the Disciples of Christ who has performed gay blessings, said, "Most people think gay people are these God-hating people, but there are lots of us that feel very connected to our faith traditions."

"And just like we don't want to throw away our sexuality, we don't want to throw away our faith either because it has had just as much a role in shaping our lives as our sexuality has," said Mr. Baines, who works as a senior organizer for religious affairs for People for the American Way, a liberal advocacy group in Washington.

Mr. Manley, 39, and Mr. Bernhard, 45, say they believe that God brought them together. They met weeks after Mr. Manley's evangelical study and support group began praying for him to find a partner.

On their third anniversary they filed their domestic-partnership papers with the State of California, which legally recognizes gay partnerships. They had attended a Catholic church, but became disillusioned because of its stance on homosexuality and joined an Episcopal church.

Last year, they asked each other's parents for permission to marry. Now they are selecting hymns and having premarital counseling sessions with their priest, the Rev. Canon James Newman of St. Bede's Episcopal Church in Los Angeles, where they will celebrate their union.

Father Newman says this will be the first same-sex blessing in his parish. He keeps the guidelines for such blessings in a file marked "marriage." He requires that couples go through premarital counseling, starting by filling out a psychological inventory with 165 questions. He also requires that the couples be registered as domestic partners with the state.

"People are coming to the church for its blessing," Father Newman said, "and we have a right to look at issues of fidelity, faithfulness and permanence in a way we have never done before."

Christian churches that permit gay blessing ceremonies, though sometimes with limitations, are the Unitarian Universalists, Disciples of Christ, United Church of Christ and the Metropolitan Community Churches. Among the Jewish branches, Reform and Reconstructionist rabbis have permission.

The Episcopal Church, torn over the election of an openly gay bishop in New Hampshire last year, has never formally approved same-sex unions but left the door open for dioceses that wish to allow them. The Presbyterian Church (U.S.A.) allows holy union ceremonies as long as they are not regarded as marriages.

Most of the denominations that permit gay unions keep no centralized records because most are congregational in structure, which means that each congregation is relatively autonomous. Also, because gay unions have no legal status in any state but Vermont, there are no legal papers for the clergy to file.

The only denomination that keeps records is the Metropolitan Community Churches, which was founded as a predominantly gay church and performs about 6,000 marriages for same-sex couples each year, a spokesman said.

Gay couples who would never consider attending a march or protest for gay rights are now asking for church weddings. Ms. Trzcinski and Ms. Auger, who met in the National Guard, said they had lived together discreetly since 1977, attended a Catholic church and never considered themselves part of a gay movement. Ms. Auger said she did not even know there was a movement until she asked one day what the rainbow flag stood for.

The two used to attend weddings and hold hands secretly in the pews. It was only after Vermont passed its law permitting gay unions that they began to think about their own.

"We didn't want it to be like going to a justice of the peace or anything," Ms. Trzcinski said. "We would be more concerned about breaking vows we'd promised to God than to some guy in a suit."

Correction: Feb. 6, 2004, Friday

A front-page article last Friday about gay couples who seek blessing ceremonies from their churches and synagogues referred incorrectly to Unitarian Universalism, which permits such rites. While many members honor Jesus, the faith describes itself as "noncreedal," not Christian.

CHRISTIAN CONSERVATIVES MOBILIZE AROUND OPPOSITION TO SAME-SEX MARRIAGE

Several prominent Christian conservative leaders attended a 2004 summit meeting to discuss their support of a constitutional amendment to ban same-sex marriage. Rev. Donald E. Wildmon convened the meeting, inviting about twenty-five groups, out of which fourteen attended, including James C. Dobson of Focus on the Family and Richard Land of the Southern Baptist Convention. Recalling that Christian conservatives had helped propel the Republican Party to power in Washington during the Reagan years, Wildmon had begun to feel that the influence of the religious right was waning. "Things have not gone well in the past couple of years," said Paul M. Weyrich, chairman of the Free Congress Foundation.

Once the groups came together to refocus, "the first thing that popped up was the federal marriage amendment," said Wildmon. Not only had the issue revitalized the movement, but it had also helped the religious right to create new alliances with African American and Hispanic churchgoers, two groups from whom the Republican Party had traditionally received low support. Focusing on opposing gay marriage also promised to increase financial contributions to the party, which had been dwindling since the focus shifted away from their archrival Bill Clinton when the Republicans regained control of the White House in 2000 with the election of George W. Bush.

Many conservatives felt that the wording of the then-proposed marriage amendment did not go far enough because it would have allowed state legislatures to recognize civil unions in lieu of marriage. "I don't care if you call it civil unions. I don't care if you call it domestic partnership, I don't care if you call it cantaloupe soup, if you are legally spouses at the end of the day, I am not willing to do that," said Michael P. Farris, chairman of the Home School Legal Defense Association. He and leaders of other conservative groups met with the sponsor of the amendment, Rep. Marilyn Musgrove (R-CO), to upbraid her for allowing "counterfeit marriages." Musgrove refused to change the wording, arguing that a stricter amendment would not gain congressional approval.

The group also pressured then-president Bush to support the amendment, something he had not yet done publicly. In addition, Focus on the Family sent a direct-mail appeal to 2.5 million people asking for financial support for the effort, saying "The homosexual activist movement is poised to administer a devastating and potentially fatal blow to the traditional family." They hoped to gain backing for the amendment from Washington elites such as Bush and Musgrove as well as from grassroots supporters.

FEBRUARY 8, 2004
CONSERVATIVES USING ISSUE OF GAY UNIONS AS A RALLYING TOOL
By DAVID D. KIRKPATRICK

Last spring, the Rev. Donald E. Wildmon of Tupelo, Miss., decided to hold a summit meeting of the Christian conservative movement.

Mr. Wildmon felt the movement was losing the culture war, he recalled in an interview on Friday. Since plunging into political activism nearly 30 years ago, Christian conservatives had helped Republicans take control of Washington but did not have enough to show for it, Mr. Wildmon said. At the same time, the election of Republican politicians had drained some of the motivation out of its grass-roots constituents.

So Mr. Wildmon, founder of the American Family Association and a crusader against sex and violence in the media, sent an e-mail message inviting about two dozen other prominent Christian conservatives to a meeting in Arlington, Va., last June. About 14 people turned up with no set agenda, Mr. Wildmon recalled.

"All we knew was we were going to get together and see if there were some issues of concern that we could agree on and combine our efforts," Mr. Wildmon said.

"The first thing that popped up," he said, "was the federal marriage amendment."

Mr. Wildmon's meeting gave birth to a concerted campaign for a constitutional amendment blocking gay marriage that some Christian conservative leaders say is helping revitalize their movement. It is giving them a rare opportunity to forge potential alliances with African-American and Hispanic churchgoers. And it promises to reopen the flow of financial contributions to their advocacy groups that had slowed to a trickle when Republicans took over Washington.

"Things have not gone well in the past couple of years," said Paul M. Weyrich, chairman of the Free Congress Foundation. "The movement had not been gaining members, it has not been winning battles, with the exception of the pro-life issue, and those were marginal battles. This issue has come along and it appears to be turning things around."

Soon after the meeting—in an apartment complex where Sandy Rios, president of Concerned Women for America, has a condominium—the United States Supreme Court issued a ruling overturning state sodomy laws. Then in November, a Massachusetts court ruled that gay couples had the right to marry, bringing more attention to the issue.

Despite the Arlington group's efforts, many politicians—even some conservatives and notably President Bush—have been slow to sign on, partly out of fear that amending the Constitution to police gay unions might seem intolerant or bigoted, conservative strategists and pollsters have said.

But to many at Mr. Wildmon's meeting in Arlington, the situation was urgent. "Look at our entertainment programs, listen to the music, listen to the statistics about babies born out of wedlock," Mr. Wildmon said. "Our team is not winning, not by any stretch of the imagination."

At the same time, attracting new supporters and raising money had grown much more difficult since their bête noire, Bill Clinton, left the White House, several Christian conservative activists involved in the Arlington meeting acknowledged. "Bill Clinton was a great motivator, and when he left there was a sense of 'O.K., our guy is in the

White House,'" said Gary L. Bauer, founder of the advocacy group American Values and an early ally in organizing the Arlington meeting.

But some in the movement believe opposition to gay marriage could make for even more effective direct mail—the financial lifeblood of most advocacy groups—than their other great cause, the fight against abortion. "Abortion has never been a strong direct-mailer," said Richard A. Viguerie, founder of American Target Advertising and the dean of conservative direct mail.

In the coming weeks, Mr. Viguerie said, his company expects to send out more than 10 million letters for a host of social conservative groups.

Several people at the Arlington meeting said their constituents were more concerned about gay marriage than about almost any other issue. "I have never seen anything that has energized and provoked our grass roots like this issue, including Roe v. Wade," said Richard Land, president of the Ethics and Religious Liberty Commission of the Southern Baptist Convention, which has 16 million members.

But almost as soon as the Arlington meeting began, the discussion turned to a debate over the language of an amendment. For years, the Alliance for Marriage, an ecumenical group, had pushed for a constitutional amendment to prevent courts from forcing states or the country to recognize same-sex marriages. Echoing the 1996 Defense of Marriage Act, the proposed amendment would allow state legislatures to recognize gay civil unions, a provision that had alienated many conservatives. Though the proposed amendment had been introduced in Congress last spring, the Christian Coalition was one of the few organizations in the Arlington group to support it.

Most of the others considered it far too permissive. "I don't care if you call it civil unions," Michael P. Farris, chairman of the Home School Legal Defense Association, said last week. "I don't care if you call it domestic partnership, I don't care if you call it cantaloupe soup, if you are legally spouses at the end of the day, I am not willing to do that."

Just as important, Mr. Farris said, the 81,500 homeschooling families who belong to his organization and who each pay at least $85 a year in dues were against it.

After months of internal debate, the members of the Arlington group went to Capitol Hill for a stormy meeting in November with a group of Republicans including Representative Marilyn Musgrave of Colorado, the sponsor of the Alliance for Marriage amendment. More than 20 organizations were represented, and Ms. Rios of Concerned Women for America dominated the conversation, taking Ms. Musgrave to task for proposing an amendment that would allow "counterfeit marriages," three people present recalled.

But Ms. Musgrave refused to budge, arguing that no stronger amendment could pass in Congress, much less in the states. To illustrate her point, Representative Joe Pitts of Pennsylvania reminded the group that after decades of effort, they still had not passed an amendment banning abortion.

With that, practical politics won out over principle, and consensus shifted to the Musgrave amendment, several people present said. "That is when reality set in," Mr. Wildmon said.

The group lost little time in mobilizing their forces. Many of the organizations, including Concerned Women, Mr. Wildmon's American Family Association and Focus on the Family, used their weekly radio broadcasts to emphasize the importance of an amendment. Other organizations sent bulletins to conservative Christian churches and their lay members around the country.

Meanwhile, well-known Arlington group members like James C. Dobson of Focus on the Family and Dr. Land of the Southern Baptist Convention began pressuring President Bush to speak out in favor of an amendment. As his State of the Union address approached, several of them called Karl Rove, the president's top political aide, reminding him of the importance of conservative Christian voters.

In his speech, Mr. Bush spoke sympathetically about a "constitutional process" to define marriage but gave it only conditional support.

The same day, Dr. Dobson sent a direct-mail appeal to 2.5 million people. "The homosexual activist movement is poised to administer a devastating and potentially fatal blow to the traditional family," he wrote. "And sadly, very few Christians in positions of responsibility are willing to use their influence to save it."

Last Tuesday, the Arlington Group decided to put Mr. Rove on the spot. That evening, the members gathered around a speakerphone as Dr. Land questioned Mr. Rove. Would the president support the amendment publicly and, if so, would he do it with the vigor that he showed in fighting for his Medicare bill?

Mr. Rove told them that the president was fully behind it, several people present recalled. "We were told that the president was looking for an appropriate moment for a more public announcement of his support," Dr. Land said in a telephone interview on Saturday.

Two days later, Dr. Land sat next to Senator Bill Frist, Republican of Tennessee, the majority leader, at the national prayer breakfast. "He said, the president has given his approval to the Musgrave amendment language and that is what we are going with," Dr. Land recalled. Dr. Frist could not be reached for comment.

So far, however, the president has yet to publicly fulfill Mr. Rove's private assurances. In a statement after the Massachusetts court affirmed its ruling last week, Mr. Bush called the decision "deeply troubling" but again offered only conditional support for an amendment. "If activist judges insist on redefining marriage by court order, the only alternative will be the constitutional process," he said, without using the word "amendment."

- -

LIBERALS AND CONSERVATIVE VIE FOR SUPPORT OF BLACK CHURCHES IN SAME-SEX MARRIAGE DEBATE

Groups supporting and opposing same-sex marriage began to make concerted efforts to gain backing from African American Christians in the mid-2000s. Genevieve Wood, of the conservative Family Research Council, appealed to a group of black evangelical ministers to speak out against gay marriage, and Donna Payne, of the black gay and lesbian organization known as the National Black Justice Coalition, appealed to liberal black clergy. While Payne argued that same-sex marriage was part and parcel of equal rights for all, Wood accused supporters of gay rights of "wrapping themselves in the flag of civil rights."

Neither conservatives nor gay rights advocates have traditionally had strong ties to African American churches. Many black Christians are politically liberal and socially conservative. While many oppose gay marriage, they nevertheless support equal benefits for gays on civil rights grounds. Many conservative African American ministers recoil at the connection between same-sex marriage and civil rights. "There has always been this undercurrent, from the women's movement through other movements, that the history of black people and their struggle was being opportunistically appropriated by an assortment of groups when it was convenient," said Rev. Gene Rivers. He believes the movement for gay rights to be "particularly offensive because it hits at the Book, the Bible, and the painful history of black people all at once."

Supporters of gay rights argue that discrimination of all types resonates poorly with black people. "Yes, this is different from back-of-the-bus and Jim Crow," said Payne, referring to earlier laws that enacted racial segregation, "but it's discrimination all the same." In a recent speech given at Harvard Law School, noted civil rights leader Rev. Jesse Jackson said that he supported equal rights for gays but that comparisons to the black struggle for equal rights were inapt, noting that "gays were never called three-fifths human in the Constitution. They did not require the Voting Rights Act to have the right to vote." Jackson also predicted that Republicans would fail in their attempt to make same-sex marriage a wedge issue in the 2004 presidential race. Nonetheless, several conservative black ministers have publicly applauded President Bush's recent call for a constitutional amendment to ban same-sex marriage, including a group of Baptists from Chicago who had met earlier with Wood. "If the K.K.K. opposes gay marriage, I would ride with them," said Rev. Gregory Daniels, organizer of the Chicago event.

MARCH 1, 2004
BOTH SIDES COURT BLACK CHURCHES IN THE BATTLE OVER GAY MARRIAGE

By LYNETTE CLEMETSON

WASHINGTON, Feb. 29—Speaking recently to a group of black evangelical ministers and lay people here, Genevieve Wood of the conservative Family Research Council made an impassioned plea. Black Christians, she said, must speak out against advocates of gay marriage.

"They are wrapping themselves in the flag of civil rights," said Ms. Wood, who is white, as visitors from across the country shook their heads in dismay. "I can make arguments against that. But not nearly like you all can."

As Ms. Wood has been brokering alliances to oppose gay marriage, Donna Payne, a board member with the National Black Justice Coalition, a black gay and lesbian organization formed to increase acceptance of gay rights among African-Americans, has been appealing to liberal black clergy members. Reaching out to potential supporters, like the Rev. Abena McCray of the Unity Fellowship Church in Washington, Ms. Payne argued that recognizing gay marriage was a matter of equal rights.

"We have to find ministers who will stand with us," Ms. Payne said, while going through her list of contacts. "We have to at least try to bring some balance to the discussion."

As debate escalates around same-sex marriage, advocates on both sides are busily seeking support from the same source: black clergy members. Though their pitches are polar opposites, their motives are largely the same. Each seeks the perceived moral authority and the sheen of civil rights that black religious leaders could lend to each cause.

But the aggressive outreach is rife with complications. Neither white conservatives nor gay-rights advocates have had great success in sustaining broad alliances with black churches in the past.

The fact that many black Christians are both politically liberal and socially conservative makes them frustratingly difficult to pigeonhole in a political environment in which, many pundits contend, voters are cleanly split along ideological lines. Many blacks opposed to gay marriage, for example, support equal benefits for gays as a matter of economic justice.

And the prize often generically referred to as "the black church" is actually a diverse collection of historically black denominations and congregations that covers a wide range of theological and social beliefs.

Advocates of gay marriage are appealing to those on the left end of that spectrum to show that the issue is really about civil rights. Those opposed are courting more conservative blacks as evidence that they are not bigots for suggesting the issue has nothing to do with civil rights. The resulting alliances are often used publicly to imply backing of "the church" as a whole.

Still, the battle for the soul of the black church is in full swing. President Bush's call last week for a constitutional amendment banning gay marriage has accelerated efforts.

A day after the president's remarks a group of black Baptist ministers in Chicago held a news conference applauding his stance. It was the first of several such events in coming weeks planned by black conservative clergy members as a result of the meeting with Ms. Wood.

"If the K.K.K. opposes gay marriage, I would ride with them," said the Rev. Gregory Daniels, organizer of the Chicago event, taking a far more provocative stance than the vast majority of black—or white—clergy members speaking out on the issue.

The National Black Justice Coalition, which was planning public events with black religious and civic leaders for the spring as well as an advertising campaign in black media outlets to make a case for gay marriage, is scrambling to put together a more immediate response.

"We thought we had a few months to organize," said Keith Boykin, president of the organization, which formed in December to respond to what its members said was a dangerously one-sided airing of black public opinion on the issue. "Now we have to think in terms of days. We have to step it up."

Many important players on each side of the debate already have backing from black churches. The Alliance for Marriage, the multifaith, multiethnic coalition that oversaw the drafting of the text for the constitutional amendment now before Congress, includes among its founders bishops from the African Methodist Episcopal Church and the Church of God in Christ, two historically black denominations.

The Coalition on Urban Renewal and Education, a Los Angeles-based conservative organization that works with black religious and community groups on social policy issues like school choice, arranged Ms. Wood's talk as well as meetings of clergy members with the Heritage Foundation and the White House.

In Boston three black clergy organizations—the Black Ministerial Alliance, the Boston Ten-Point Coalition and the Cambridge Black Pastors Conference—issued a joint statement against gay marriage in early February, drawing a swift rebuke from pastors supporting the unions.

At the heart of the conflict, for many, is not merely theology, but the mantle of civil rights.

"There has always been this undercurrent, from the women's movement through other movements, that the history of black people and their struggle was being opportunistically appropriated by an assortment of groups when it was convenient," said the Rev. Gene Rivers, president of the National Ten-Point Leadership Foundation, a church-based violence-prevention program. "This movement is particularly offensive because it hits at the Book, the Bible, and the painful history of black people all at once."

Blacks fighting to establish same-sex marriage are pushing their allies to be more vocal.

"Yes, this is different from back-of-the bus and Jim Crow," said Ms. Payne, who is a lesbian and a churchgoer. "But it's discrimination all the same. And when we make that case to black people, they understand."

The National Black Justice Coalition Web site lists prominent supporters including the Rev. Peter Gomes, chaplain at Harvard, the Rev. Al Sharpton, Democratic presidential candidate, and Coretta Scott King, widow of the Rev. Dr. Martin Luther King Jr.

Perhaps trying to appease both sides, the Rev. Jesse Jackson remarked briefly on the issue in a recent speech at Harvard Law School, saying that he supported "equal protection under the law" for gays. But he added that he viewed comparisons to the historical struggles of blacks as "a stretch."

"Gays were never called three-fifths human in the Constitution," he said, "They did not require the Voting Rights Act to have the right to vote."

In other remarks in Boston, Mr. Jackson vowed that Republicans would not succeed in making the debate a wedge issue in the presidential race. Some black pastors enmeshed in the issue agree.

"Ultimately black churches cannot be dictated to on this from the left, right or center," said Mr. Rivers, a Democrat who has advised President Bush on religion-based social services and who supports some benefits for same-sex couples. "Most of the same people who believe fundamentally that marriage is between a man and a woman and who will stand up and support that with conservatives voted for Al Gore in 2000 and oppose tax cuts for the rich and cutting social services in 2004."

Still others said the most significant outcome of the political ruckus could be the start of meaningful discussion in black churches, many of which have been historically resistant to tackling any topics dealing with sexuality, including H.I.V./AIDS and births out of wedlock.

"Often this kind of dialogue in black churches lags behind social debate," said Dr. Robert M. Franklin, an ethics professor at Candler School of Theology at Emory University, in Atlanta. "The value-added dimension of the political gamesmanship is that it will accelerate a much-needed conversation."

* *

METHODIST MINISTER'S DECISION TO EXCLUDE GAY MAN FROM CHURCH MEMBERSHIP IS UPHELD

A court of the United Methodist Church said that Rev. Edward Johnson acted within his rightful powers as a minister in refusing to accept an openly gay man as a member of his Virginia congregation. The court reinstated Johnson after he had been suspended earlier by a lower court for excluding the gay man from his church. Methodists all over the country, including more traditionally conservative regions, immediately questioned the decision, with calls and e-mails coming in to church headquarters in Nashville by a 2–1 margin against the ruling.

"Even people who are conservative on issues of sexuality wouldn't want to exclude homosexuals from membership in our church," said Bishop Scott J. Jones of Kansas. Several bishops from socially conservative areas signed a pastoral letter that asserted that "homosexuality is not a barrier" to church membership, in order to assure congregations that all are welcome in the church regardless of sexual orientation. While the letter conceded that ministers have broad discretion regarding church membership, it also stated that church policies should be taken into account in such decisions, including the church's clear stand on including gay members.

NOVEMBER 5, 2005
METHODIST BISHOPS PROTEST RULING IN EXCLUSION OF A GAY CONGREGANT
By NEELA BANERJEE

WASHINGTON, Nov. 4—A recent decision by the highest court of the United Methodist Church to reinstate a pastor suspended for barring a gay man from his congregation has touched off widespread alarm within the denomination and prompted the Council of Bishops, the church's elected leadership, to issue a unanimous rebuttal.

Like other mainline denominations, the United Methodist Church, the country's third-largest denomination, has been struggling with the role of gay men and lesbians in the pews and in the pulpit. The church has traditionally welcomed gay people, though it does not ordain "self-avowed practicing homosexuals."

On Monday, the Church's Judicial Council, its equivalent of the Supreme Court, ruled that the Rev. Edward Johnson had rightfully used his pastoral discretion in refusing to accept an openly gay man as a member of his church in South Hill, Va.

Many Methodists had expected an outcry over the decision from liberal congregations clustered mainly in the Northeast and the West Coast. But Methodists all over the country, including those from historically conservative regions, have voiced alarm at the decision, lay and clergy members said. Stephen Drachler, a church spokesman, said that its headquarters in Nashville had received about 400 e-mail messages on the issue and that the Council of Bishops had received about 200. About two-thirds of the messages opposed the ruling, Mr. Drachler said.

"Even people who are conservative on issues of sexuality wouldn't want to exclude homosexuals from membership in our church," said Bishop Scott J. Jones, head of two conferences, or regions, in Kansas.

In response to the ruling, the Council of Bishops published a letter on Thursday to "the people of the United Methodist Church" stating that "homosexuality is not a barrier" to membership. Those who signed it included bishops who represented socially conservative swaths of the country and African bishops.

"Gay people are angry, and they are asking, 'Are we no longer welcome in the United Methodist Church?' And that hurts to hear," said Bishop Janice Riggle Huie, head of the Texas Annual Conference, which encompasses East Texas. "This pastoral letter, we hope, will be reassuring to heterosexuals and homosexual people that they are welcome in the church."

Some supporters of Mr. Johnson said it was unlikely that ministers would respond to the ruling by asking gay members to leave.

The Rev. Dr. H. O. Thomas, Mr. Johnson's advocate before the Judicial Council, said that while the church was open to everyone, those people must also be "willing to receive the conditions of what it means to be a Christian disciple, and that includes a whole bunch of stuff, including the practice of homosexuality."

He added: "One would need to struggle against it and repent of it. Ed Johnson was drawing the line not at homosexuality but at the practice of homosexuality."

Ms. Huie said the bishops' letter did not differentiate between celibate and sexually active gay congregants. And while the letter conceded that pastors had broad discretion, the bishops argued that clergy members could not make such decisions without taking into account the policies of the church, among them the inclusion of gay members.

"Our letter says it respects a pastor's judgment," Mr. Jones said. "But he doesn't make his decisions in a vacuum."

Three American Dioceses Begin to Split from Episcopal Church

In 2006 the Pittsburgh, South Carolina, and San Joaquin, California, dioceses of the Episcopalian Church requested permission to separate themselves from the authority of the bishop of the American church, a clear sign of significant ongoing tension within the Anglican Community regarding the recent decisions to consecrate an openly gay bishop and to bless same-sex unions. "This is to say as we have long said that we are legitimately the Episcopal Church in this place and that we believe that we'll be recognized by the world as the legitimate inheritors of the Anglican trademark," said Bishop Robert Duncan of Pittsburgh. He predicted that other dioceses would follow, choosing to be associated with their more traditional understanding of the church.

The request came on the tails of a statement by the archbishop of Canterbury, the highest official in the Episcopal Church, who blamed the American church for making decisions that challenge the theology held by most of the members of the worldwide Episcopal Church. Archbishop Williams proposed that the American church would have to renounce gay bishops and same-sex unions or forego membership in the Anglican Communion.

Joan Gundersen, a church historian who is the president of Progressive Episcopalians of Pittsburgh, called the request for separation "very divisive." She predicted that it would "create tremendous pain in a diocese," saying that "many parishes include a broad spectrum of the church, and this will drive a wedge right through them."

JUNE 29, 2006
THREE DIOCESES APPEAL TO DISTANCE THEMSELVES FROM EPISCOPAL CHURCH
By NEELA BANERJEE

Signaling a widening of the fractures within the Episcopal Church over homosexuality, three theologically conservative dioceses began efforts yesterday to separate themselves from the church.

The dioceses—Pittsburgh, South Carolina and San Joaquin, Calif.—appealed to the archbishop of Canterbury to be freed from oversight by the presiding bishop of the American church and to answer to a different primate in the worldwide Anglican Communion. They did not specify a particular primate.

All three belong to a group of dioceses, the Anglican Communion Network, that rejected the Episcopal Church's consecration of an openly gay man as a bishop in 2003 and the blessing of same-sex unions.

In explaining their decisions, the dioceses indicated that they felt emboldened to push for greater distance from the Episcopal Church because of a letter issued on Tuesday by the archbishop of Canterbury, the Most Rev. Rowan Williams, faulting the American church for actions that are sharply at odds with the theology of most of the 77-million-member Anglican Communion.

In the letter, Archbishop Williams put forward a plan that could compel the Episcopal Church in the United States either to renounce gay bishops and same-sex unions or to give up full membership in the Communion.

The Rev. Robert Duncan, bishop of Pittsburgh and moderator of the Anglican Communion Network, said the letter vindicated the position of dioceses like his, bringing them a step closer to assuming officially the mantle of Anglicanism in the United States.

"This is to say as we have long said that we are legitimately the Episcopal Church in this place," Bishop Duncan said in a telephone interview, "and that we believe that we'll be recognized by the world as the legitimate inheritors of the Anglican trademark."

Ever since the Episcopal Church consented to the election in 2003 of Bishop V. Gene Robinson to lead the Diocese of New Hampshire, individual congregations have left the 2.3-million-member denomination and placed themselves under the oversight of theologically conservative prelates, largely in Africa.

Efforts by some congregations to hold on to their property have landed them in lawsuits with their dioceses. A report in 2004 commissioned by the archbishop of Canterbury cautioned against such departures.

Until the end of the Episcopal Church's triennial general convention last week, no diocese had sought to disassociate itself from the church. But with the election of Bishop Katharine Jefferts Schori of Nevada as the church's new presiding bishop on June 18, the Diocese of Fort Worth, which does not ordain women, asked the archbishop of Canterbury to be placed under a different prelate. The three dioceses that requested alternative oversight yesterday are likely to be joined by others, Bishop Duncan said.

A representative of the archbishop of Canterbury could not be reached for comment. The Episcopal Church's presiding bishop, the Rev. Frank T. Griswold, said in a statement that he found the decision by the Pittsburgh Diocese "unsurprising and altogether consistent with their implicit intention of walking apart from the Episcopal Church."

The Diocese of Pittsburgh said its request for outside oversight did not constitute a complete break with the church. Rather, the diocese planned to withdraw its consent to remain in a province of the Episcopal Church and then ask the Episcopal Church to set up a separate new province for conservative dioceses.

If the province is not created, Bishop Duncan said his diocese would remain outside an Episcopal province, but still in the church, a step, he said, that would protect it from lawsuits over property and finances.

Bishop Duncan said similar action was taken in the Diocese of Missouri in the 1950's. But Joan R. Gundersen, the president of Progressive Episcopalians of Pittsburgh and a church historian, said the church's canons would not permit such steps.

Supporters of the Episcopal Church said the announcements by the dioceses seemed to leapfrog the process spelled out by the archbishop of Canterbury. For the proposal of a two-tier Communion to be enacted, at least a half-dozen major church meetings spread out over at least the next four years would need to be held, the Rev. Canon Kenneth Kearon, secretary general of the Anglican Communion, said Tuesday.

The Episcopal presiding bishop has far less power than other Anglican primates do. But the symbolism of an American diocese's turning to another prelate as its leader was not lost on some Episcopalians.

"It's very divisive," Ms. Gundersen said. "It will create tremendous pain in a diocese. Many parishes include a broad spectrum of the church, and this will drive a wedge right through them."

Mormon Efforts Play Extraordinary Role in California's Same-Sex Marriage Ban

Eleventh-hour donations from Mormons played an extraordinary role in the passage of Proposition 8, a referendum that amended the California constitution to prohibit same-sex marriage. When the proposed amendment appeared behind in the polls less than two weeks prior to the election, Frank Schubert, the chief strategist for the amendment, issued an emergency call for donations that resulted in $5 million for the cause, including a $1 million donation from Alan C. Ashton, grandson of a former president of the Mormon Church and cofounder of the WordPerfect Corporation. Project Marriage, the main group that supported the amendment, estimated that as much as half of the $40 million raised during the campaign came from Mormons who composed between 80 and 90 percent of volunteers walking door-to-door raising support for the amendment.

"We've spoken out on other issues, we've spoken out on abortion, we've spoken out on those other kinds of things. But we don't get involved to the degree we did on this," said

Michael R. Otterson, the managing director of public affairs for the Church of Jesus Christ of Latter-day Saints. During the campaign, the Mormon leadership in Salt Lake City issued a decree to be read to congregations that urged members to become involved in supporting the amendment, saying, "The formation of families is central to the Creator's plan."

Volunteers were given two different scripts, one for those who believe that God created marriage, the other for those who believe that humans did. The first emphasized that Proposition 8 would restore marriage as God intended it; the second said that the measure emphasized marriage rather than homosexuality. Organizers said that they directed volunteers to avoid working at church, in order to maintain a separation between politics and church.

Funds raised were used to finance advertisements offering unsubstantiated claims that same-sex marriage would lead churches to lose their tax-exempt status or that people would be sued for their personal beliefs. Another ad used video of a field trip to a teacher's same-sex wedding, suggesting that the practice would be taught to small children in school. Opponents called the ads dishonest and divisive. Said Otterson, "It was a matter of standing up for what the church believes is right."

NOVEMBER 15, 2008
MORMONS TIPPED SCALE IN BAN ON GAY MARRIAGE
By JESSE MCKINLEY AND KIRK JOHNSON

SACRAMENTO – Less than two weeks before Election Day, the chief strategist behind a ballot measure outlawing same-sex marriage in California called an emergency meeting here.

"We're going to lose this campaign if we don't get more money," the strategist, Frank Schubert, recalled telling leaders of Protect Marriage, the main group behind the ban.

The campaign issued an urgent appeal, and in a matter of days, it raised more than $5 million, including a $1 million donation from Alan C. Ashton, the grandson of a former president of the Mormon Church. The money allowed the drive to intensify a sharp-elbowed advertising campaign, and support for the measure was catapulted ahead; it ultimately won with 52 percent of the vote.

As proponents of same-sex marriage across the country planned protests on Saturday against the ban, interviews with the main forces behind the ballot measure showed how close its backers believe it came to defeat— and the extraordinary role Mormons played in helping to pass it with money, institutional support and dedicated volunteers.

"We've spoken out on other issues, we've spoken out on abortion, we've spoken out on those other kinds of things," said Michael R. Otterson, the managing director of public affairs for the Church of Jesus Christ of Latter-day Saints, as the Mormons are formally called, in Salt Lake City. "But we don't get involved to the degree we did on this."

The California measure, Proposition 8, was to many Mormons a kind of firewall to be held at all costs.

"California is a huge state, often seen as a bellwether— this was seen as a very, very important test," Mr. Otterson said.

First approached by the Roman Catholic archbishop of San Francisco a few weeks after the California Supreme Court legalized same-sex marriage in May, the Mormons were the last major religious group to join the campaign, and the final spice in an unusual stew that included Catholics, evangelical Christians, conservative black and Latino pastors, and myriad smaller ethnic groups with strong religious ties.

Shortly after receiving the invitation from the San Francisco Archdiocese, the Mormon leadership in Salt Lake City issued a four-paragraph decree to be read to congregations, saying "the formation of families is central to the Creator's plan," and urging members to become involved with the cause.

"And they sure did," Mr. Schubert said.

Jeff Flint, another strategist with Protect Marriage, estimated that Mormons made up 80 percent to 90 percent of the early volunteers who walked door-to-door in election precincts.

The canvass work could be exacting and highly detailed. Many Mormon wards in California, not unlike Roman Catholic parishes, were assigned two ZIP codes to cover. Volunteers in one ward, according to training documents written by a Protect Marriage volunteer, obtained by people opposed to Proposition 8 and shown to The New York Times, had tasks ranging from "walkers," assigned to knock on doors; to "sellers," who would work with undecided voters later on; and to "closers," who would get people to the polls on Election Day.

Suggested talking points were equally precise. If initial contact indicated a prospective voter believed God created marriage, the church volunteers were instructed to emphasize that Proposition 8 would restore the definition of marriage God intended.

But if a voter indicated human beings created marriage, Script B would roll instead, emphasizing that Proposition 8 was about marriage, not about attacking gay people, and about restoring into law an earlier ban struck down by the State Supreme Court in May.

"It is not our goal in this campaign to attack the homosexual lifestyle or to convince gays and lesbians that their behavior is wrong—the less we refer to homosexuality, the better," one of the ward training documents said. "We are pro-marriage, not anti-gay."

Leaders were also acutely conscious of not crossing the line from being a church-based volunteer effort to an actual political organization.

"No work will take place at the church, including no meeting there to hand out precinct walking assignments so as to not even give the appearance of politicking at the church," one of the documents said.

By mid-October, most independent polls showed support for the proposition was growing, but it was still trailing. Opponents had brought on new media consultants in the face of the slipping poll numbers, but they were still effectively raising money, including $3.9 million at a star-studded fund-raiser held at the Beverly Hills home of Ron Burkle, the supermarket billionaire and longtime Democratic fund-raiser.

It was then that Mr. Schubert called his meeting in Sacramento. "I said, 'As good as our stuff is, it can't withstand that kind of funding,'" he recalled.

The response was a desperate e-mail message sent to 92,000 people who had registered at the group's Web site declaring a "code blue"—an urgent plea for money to save traditional marriage from "cardiac arrest." Mr. Schubert also sent an e-mail message to the three top religious members of his executive committee, representing Catholics, evangelicals and Mormons.

"I ask for your prayers that this e-mail will open the hearts and minds of the faithful to make a further sacrifice of their funds at this urgent moment so that God's precious gift of marriage is preserved," he wrote.

On Oct. 28, Mr. Ashton, the grandson of the former Mormon president David O. McKay, donated $1 million. Mr. Ashton, who made his fortune as co-founder of the WordPerfect Corporation, said he was following his personal beliefs and the direction of the church.

"I think it was just our realizing that we heard a number of stories about members of the church who had worked long hours and lobbied long and hard," he said in a telephone interview from Orem, Utah.

In the end, Protect Marriage estimates, as much as half of the nearly $40 million raised on behalf of the measure was contributed by Mormons.

Even with the Mormons' contributions and the strong support of other religious groups, Proposition 8 strategists said they had taken pains to distance themselves from what Mr. Flint called "more extreme elements" opposed to rights for gay men and lesbians.

To that end, the group that put the issue on the ballot rebuffed efforts by some groups to include a ban on domestic partnership rights, which are granted in California. Mr. Schubert cautioned his side not to stage protests and risk alienating voters when same-sex marriages began being performed in June.

"We could not have this as a battle between people of faith and the gays," Mr. Schubert said. "That was a losing formula."

But the "Yes" side also initially faced apathy from middle-of-the-road California voters who were largely unconcerned about same-sex marriage. The overall sense of the voters in the beginning of the campaign, Mr. Schubert said, was "Who cares? I'm not gay."

To counter that, advertisements for the "Yes" campaign also used hypothetical consequences of same-sex marriage, painting the specter of churches' losing tax exempt status or people "sued for personal beliefs" or objections to same-sex marriage, claims that were made with little explanation.

Another of the advertisements used video of an elementary school field trip to a teacher's same-sex wedding in San Francisco to reinforce the idea that same-sex marriage would be taught to young children.

"We bet the campaign on education," Mr. Schubert said.

The "Yes" campaign was denounced by opponents as dishonest and divisive, but the passage of Proposition 8 has led to second-guessing about the "No" campaign, too, as well as talk about a possible ballot measure to repeal the ban. Several legal challenges have been filed, and the question of the legality of the same-sex marriages performed from June to Election Day could also be settled in court.

For his part, Mr. Schubert said he is neither anti-gay—his sister is a lesbian—nor happy that some same-sex couples' marriages are now in question. But, he said, he has no regrets about his campaign.

"They had a lot going for them," Mr. Schubert said of his opponents. "And they couldn't get it done."

Mr. Otterson said it was too early to tell what the long-term implications might be for the church, but in any case, he added, none of that factored into the decision by church leaders to order a march into battle. "They felt there was only one way we could stand on such a fundamental moral issue, and they took that stand," he said. "It was a matter of standing up for what the church believes is right."

That said, the extent of the protests has taken many Mormons by surprise. On Friday, the church's leadership took the unusual step of issuing a statement calling for "respect" and "civility" in the aftermath of the vote.

"Attacks on churches and intimidation of people of faith have no place in civil discourse over controversial issues," the statement said. "People of faith have a democratic right to express their views in the public square without fear of reprisal."

Mr. Ashton described the protests by same-sex marriage advocates as off-putting. "I think that shows colors," Mr. Ashton said. "By their fruit, ye shall know them."

Jesse McKinley reported from Sacramento,
and Kirk Johnson from Salt Lake City.

- -

GAYS WITH PARTNERS ALLOWED TO BE MINISTERS IN EVANGELICAL LUTHERAN CHURCH

In 2009 the Evangelical Lutheran Church in America (ELCA) decided to allow gay men and lesbians in committed relationships to be ministers. By a 559–451 margin, delegates to the church's national assembly approved the measure, adding to its policy of allowing celibate gays and lesbians to serve as clergy. The 4.6 million–member church is the largest Lutheran denomination in the United States.

Rev. Megan Rohrer of San Francisco said the decision was the fulfillment of "a lifelong dream." When this article was written, she was serving three congregations but was not officially listed on the church's roster of clergy. Another minister, Rev. Rebecca M. M. Heber of Florida, said she would reconsider her membership in the church, stating, "I think we have stepped beyond what the word of God allows." Four hundred conservative congregations known as the Lutheran Core met in September 2009 to discuss options, including leaving for another Lutheran denomination, creating their own unified body, and protecting the "true tenets" of the church from within.

The Episcopal Church gained a great deal of visibility on issues pertaining to homosexuality and faith, owing to the ordination of two gay bishops. This move by the ELCA seemed to add some momentum toward a liberal stance on gay issues within mainline Protestantism.

Some observers said that the largely midwestern membership of the ELCA signaled greater mainstream acceptance. Earlier in 2009, however, the Presbyterian Church rejected ordaining gay ministers, and in 2008 the United Methodist Church voted against allowing noncelibate homosexuals to serve as ministers.

AUGUST 22, 2009
LUTHERAN GROUP EASES LIMITS ON GAY CLERGY
By MICHAEL LUO AND CHRISTINA CAPECCHI

After an emotional debate over the authority of Scripture and the limits of biblical inclusiveness, leaders of the country's largest Lutheran denomination voted Friday to allow gay men and lesbians in committed relationships to serve as members of the clergy.

The vote made the denomination, the Evangelical Lutheran Church in America, the latest mainline Protestant church to permit such ordinations, contributing to a halting sense of momentum on the issue within liberal Protestantism.

By a vote of 559 to 451, delegates to the denomination's national assembly in Minneapolis approved a resolution declaring that the church would find a way for people in "publicly accountable, lifelong, monogamous same-gender relationships" to serve as official ministers. (The church already allows celibate gay men and lesbians to become members of the clergy.)

Just before the vote, the Rev. Mark Hanson, the church's presiding bishop, led the packed convention center in prayer. When the two bar graphs signaling the vote's outcome popped up on the hall's big screens seconds later, there were only a few quiet gasps, as delegates had been asked to avoid making an audible scene. But around the convention hall, clusters of men and women hugged one another and wept.

"To be able to be a full member of the church is really a lifelong dream," said the Rev. Megan Rohrer of San Francisco, who is in a committed same-sex relationship and serves in three Lutheran congregations but is not officially on the church's roster of clergy members. "I don't have to have an asterisk next to my name anymore."

But the passage of the resolution now raises questions about the future of the denomination, which has 4.6 million members but has seen its ranks steadily dwindle, and whether it will see an exodus of its more conservative followers or experience some sort of schism.

"I think we have stepped beyond what the word of God allows," said the Rev. Rebecca M. M. Heber of Heathrow, Fla., who said she was going to reconsider her membership.

Conservative dissenters said they saw various options, including leaving for another Lutheran denomination or creating their own unified body.

A contingent of 400 conservative congregations that make up a group that calls itself Lutheran Core is to meet in September. Leaders of the group said their plans were not to split from the Evangelical Lutheran Church but to try to protect its "true tenets" from within.

Among so-called "mainline" Protestant denominations, distinguishable theologically from their more conservative, evangelical Protestant counterparts, both the Episcopal Church and the United Church of Christ already allow gay clergy members.

The Episcopal Church has endured the most visible public flashpoints over homosexuality, grappling in particular in the last few years with the consecration of gay bishops. It affirmed last month, however, that "any ordained ministry" was open to gay men and lesbians.

Earlier this year the Presbyterian Church (U.S.A.) rejected a measure that would have opened the door for gay ordination, but the margin was narrower than in a similar vote in 2001. The United Methodist Church voted not to change its stance barring noncelibate homosexuals from ministry last year, after an emotional debate at its general conference.

But the Evangelical Lutheran Church's heavily Midwestern membership and the fact that it is generally seen as falling squarely in the middle of the theological milieu of mainline Protestantism imbued Friday's vote with added significance, religion scholars said.

Wendy Cadge, a sociology professor at Brandeis University who has studied Evangelical Lutheran churches grappling with the issue, said, "It does show, to the extent that any mainline denominations are moving, I think they're moving slowly toward a more progressive direction."

Describing the context of Friday's vote, several religion experts likened it to the court decision last year in Iowa legalizing same-sex marriage.

"In the same sense that the Iowa court decision might have opened people's eyes, causing them to say, 'Iowa? What? Where?'" said Laura Olson, a professor of political science at Clemson University who has studied mainline Protestantism. "The E.L.C.A. isn't necessarily quite as surprising in the religious sense, but the message it's sending is, yes, not only are more Americans from a religious perspective getting behind gay rights, but these folks are not just quote unquote coastal liberals."

The denomination has struggled with the issue almost since its founding in the late 1980s with the merger of three other Lutheran denominations.

In 2001, the church convened a committee to study the issue. It eventually recommended guidelines for a denominational vote. In 2005, however, delegates voted not to change its policies.

On Friday, delegates juggled raw emotion, fatigue and opposing interpretations of Scripture.

Before the vote but sensing its outcome, the Rev. Timothy Housholder of Cottage Grove, Minn., introduced himself as a rostered pastor in the church, "at least for a few more hours," implying that he would leave the denomination and eliciting a gasp from some audience members.

"Here I stand, broken and mournful, because of this assembly and her actions," Mr. Housholder said.

The Rev. Mark Lepper of Belle Plaine, Minn., called for the inclusion of gay clergy members, saying, "Let's stop leaving people behind and let's be the family God is calling us to be."

Michael Luo reported from New York,
and Christina Capecchi from Minneapolis.

SEXUALITY AND GENDER IDENTITY IN THE WORKPLACE

· ·

Civil rights laws typically include protection against discrimination in the areas of housing, public accommodations, and employment. Given the importance of employment in the area of civil rights, this chapter is devoted to sexuality and gender identity issues in the workplace, covering issues such as exclusions of gay and lesbians in the workplace, the proposed Employment Non-Discrimination Act, and domestic partner benefits for lesbian, gay, bisexual, and transgender (LGBT) employees.

LGBT Exclusions and Challenges in the Workplace

Although a *New York Times* report of May 7, 1967, noted that members of the early gay rights advocacy group known as the Mattachine Society claimed that "homosexuals find in New York these days more opportunities for employment than they have ever known in this country anywhere," employment discrimination against gays and lesbians was rampant in the pre-Stonewall period. Despite protests by Mattachine Society members, the federal government avoided hiring known homosexuals. As David Johnson notes in his book *The Lavender Scare: The Cold War Persecution of Gays and Lesbians in the Federal Government,* many who were alleged to be homosexuals, or to have associated with known homosexuals during the McCarthy era, often resigned rather than risking further government investigation and public attention. Members of the military who were found to be gay were given less-than-honorable discharges, as noted in a *Times* report of May 30, 1965 (see "Gays in the Military"). During this period, some homosexuals who had been dismissed were able to attain reinstatement by claiming that their homosexuality was "a youthful indiscretion" or "a youthful mistake," as discussed in a *Times* report of October 18, 1964.

As reported in the *Times* on May 9, 1969, gay and lesbian challenges led several cities to alter their policies against hiring homosexuals, as was the case in New York,

when two men who had passed the civil service examination were turned down for jobs as social workers. One of the most high-profile challenges in this period occurred when a gay man was hired by the University of Minnesota library, only to be later told that the university's Board of Regents had decided to rescind the offer on the grounds that his personal conduct was not "consistent with the best interests of the University." A federal judge disagreed, saying, "What Mr. McConnell does in his private life should not be his employer's concern unless it can be shown to affect in some degree his efficiency in the performance of his duties."

A few years later a July 10, 1975, story in *The Times* said that an American Civil Liberties Union (ACLU) study found evidence of "widespread easing of job discrimination of homosexuals at Federal, state, and municipal levels." Despite this report, resistance to hiring homosexuals remained strong in some sectors. When New York City mayor Ed Koch proposed to ban discrimination against homosexuals in city hiring, unions representing police and firefighters resisted the change, as noted in a *Times* article of January 5, 1978. Also in 1978, the Florida Supreme Court heard a case about whether homosexual attorneys could be excluded from the state's bar association (and thus from practicing law) on moral grounds. The court rejected the exclusion, arguing that no "substantial connection" was shown between the ability the carry out professional behavior and homosexuality.

Some workers have also been discriminated against because of their gender identity. In 1984 a federal judge ordered Eastern Airlines to reinstate Karen Ulane, a pilot and decorated Vietnam War veteran who was born a man prior to becoming a woman through sex reassignment surgery, saying that she would not have been discharged "but for being a transsexual." While Eastern had argued that Ulane posed a safety hazard in the cockpit, the judge ruled that "it can't be said with any rationality that transsexuals cannot be good airline pilots." As noted in a *Times* report of September 1, 1984, the decision was later overturned by a higher court,

IN FOCUS

Coming Out at Work: A Harvard Business School Case Study

In 1993 Lisa Sherman was a vice president at Bell Atlantic as well as a closeted lesbian. While attending a workplace diversity seminar, she was shocked to find many colleagues whom she considered friends publicly completing an open-ended sentence that began "Gays are . . ." with words such as *pathetic, perverse,* and *immoral.* Feeling literally sick after hearing her co-workers' responses, she had to decide whether she could continue working at Bell Atlantic, and if so, whether she would directly address the negative comments she had witnessed in the seminar.

After telling the story at the 2007 Reaching Out Conference for lesbian, gay, bisexual, and transgender MBA students, she agreed to be interviewed for a case study to be written up for the Harvard Business School, marking the first time the issue of sexual orientation in the workplace would be covered in that format while using a business leader's real name. The case asks students to debate the pros and cons of four possible solutions for a leader in Sherman's position: quit, try to change the environment, meet with a superior to discuss the situation, or maintain her closeted status and continue to work without comment.

In real life, Sherman decided to talk with the CEO of Bell Atlantic, Raymond W. Smith, with whom she had established a strong relationship. After telling him what had transpired at the diversity seminar, she came out to him as a lesbian so that he could better understand the discrepancy between Bell's stated support for diversity (including sexual orientation) and the reality on the ground for employees like her. Despite Smith's positive reception, she decided to leave Bell Atlantic and eventually became executive vice president and general manager of Logo, a cable channel specializing in gay programming.

Sherman's story had a profound impact on Smith, who subsequently strengthened the company's nondiscrimination policy, offered domestic partner benefits, and testified in favor of the Employment Non-Discrimination Act (ENDA) in Congress in 1997. While he believed that his actions would slowly change the culture of the company, he also noted that there will be intolerance in any organization: "You do your best to enact policies, which can affect behavior if not what is in people's hearts. After a while, if people behave in a tolerant way, they may start to think in a tolerant way."

From *The New York Times*

Alboher, Marci. "When Intolerance Becomes Intolerable." June 2, 2008.

which said that while Ulane may have been discriminated against, Congress did not intend for the Civil Rights Act (1964) to protect transgender people.

The emergence of acquired immune deficiency syndrome (AIDS) led to many employment discrimination claims, since many employers failed to understand that it was illegal to fire workers who developed AIDS or to compel them to go on disability leave. Some employers began to require blood tests before hiring, in order to screen out applicants who were positive for human immunodeficiency virus (HIV). Attorneys argued that such cases were often the result of co-workers who mistakenly worried that they could contract the disease through casual contact with a person with AIDS. In addition, many workplace insurance programs refused to pay for the medical expenses associated with AIDS during this period. As reported in *The Times* on September 22, 1988, contrary to a recommendation of its own presidential commission, the Reagan administration balked at providing a federal policy that would protect people with AIDS against such discrimination, on the grounds that it would expose employers to possible litigation.

In 1991 the Cracker Barrel Old Country Store and Restaurant chain announced that it would not hire employees "whose sexual preference fails to demonstrate normal heterosexual values which have been the foundation of families in our society." Perhaps sensing a shift in public opinion regarding discrimination against gays and lesbians in the workplace, Cracker Barrel rescinded the policy within a month after having dismissed several employees. The controversy continued as gay rights advocates demonstrated at various Cracker Barrel locations, claiming that the company was continuing to refuse to hire gay workers. As a *Times* story of April 9, 1992, noted, the company was within its legal rights in doing so, as "no Federal law protects gay people from such discrimination, and only five states and about 100 municipalities have such statutes."

EMPLOYMENT NON-DISCRIMINATION ACT

As discussed in the second chapter, the first national bill designed to offer gays and lesbians civil rights, including protection against employment discrimination, was proposed in 1974. To date no such bill has been approved by Congress; however, thirteen states and numerous cities and counties have passed such laws, in addition to laws that protect transgender people from gender identity discrimination. As noted in a *Times* piece published on March 28, 1993, titled "Gay Rights Hurt by Lack of Uniform Protections," "the vast majority of complaints stem from allegations of discrimination in employment." Of seven states surveyed, over 75 percent of civil rights cases filed involved employment discrimination claims.

In 1994 the first federal bill specifically dedicated to providing employment protections to gays and lesbians was introduced in Congress. Popularly known as the Employment Non-Discrimination Act (ENDA), the proposed bill was designed to protect against employment discrimination because of sexuality, similar to the way that the 1964 Civil Rights Act does so on the basis of sex and race. In an editorial of June 26, 1994, that commemorated the twenty-fifth anniversary of the beginning of the modern gay rights movement at the Stonewall Inn in New York City, *The Times*

Rep. Barney Frank (D-MA), left, and Sen. Ted Kennedy (D-MA) talk to the media after meeting with President Clinton about the Employment Non-Discrimination Act in 1997. The legislation, originally introduced in 1994, was designed to offer protections against discrimination in the workplace. The legislation has been introduced multiple times but has never passed both the House and Senate.

Source: Reuters/Luc Novovitch

endorsed ENDA as part and parcel of a just society. The bill failed to pass in 1994 and again in 1995, despite gaining President Bill Clinton's official backing in the latter year. In a third attempt, ENDA missed passage in the Senate by a single vote on the same day that the Senate resoundingly passed the Defense of Marriage Act, a law that made it illegal for the federal government to recognize same-sex marriages, as noted in a *Times* report of September 11, 1996.

By 2003 the nation's largest private employer, Wal-Mart Stores, expanded its nondiscrimination policy to include LGBT employees. This development was seen as a major turning point in the struggle for equal rights at work for gays and lesbians, due in part to Wal-Mart's long-standing reputation of taking care not to offend customers with conservative viewpoints. In 2007 ENDA gained a bipartisan majority in the House for the first time, although it was not passed by the Senate. Controversy arose in the House when transgender

IN FOCUS

The Fair Employment Mark

• •

Although the Employment Non-Discrimination Act (ENDA) was introduced in 1994, it has yet to pass Congress. Over 85 percent of Fortune 500 companies have adopted policies that protect gay and lesbian employees from discrimination based on sexual orientation. In addition, several major corporations, including AT&T, IBM, and General Mills, have indicated that they would be pleased to follow ENDA when it is passed. Professor Ian Ayres of the Yale Law School and Professor Jennifer Gerarda Brown of the Quinnipiac University School of Law have devised a way for companies to opt in to the provisions of ENDA in advance of its passage. Rather than waiting for Congress to pass ENDA, they have advised interested corporations to adopt a do-it-yourself strategy that they call the "Fair Employment mark."

Companies that formally commit to the terms of ENDA through a licensing agreement are allowed to use the Fair Employment mark (*FE* inside a circle), which makes visible to consumers their commitment to equal treatment regardless of sexual orientation, allowing supporters of gay rights to purchase products made by corporations that share their values. Ayres and Brown have argued that the mark might also help recruit better talent to companies that adopt it. The Fair Employment mark is similar to the UL mark of the Underwriters Laboratories, which signals an electronic product is safe, or the Orthodox Union's mark, indicating that a product is kosher.

Ayres and Brown have pitched the Fair Employment mark to organizations such as Microsoft and Goldman Sachs, advocating the mark as a creative incremental strategy that would foster greater equality in the workplace. To date no major company has signed on to the agreement.

From *The New York Times*

Shea, Christopher. "The Fair Employment Mark." December 11, 2005.

• •

workers were removed from the bill's coverage in order to gain passage. While several gay rights advocacy groups questioned the exclusion of transgender people from the bill, Speaker of the House Nancy Pelosi (D-CA) defended the strategy, saying "History teaches us that progress on civil rights is never easy. It is often marked by small and difficult steps." Even if ENDA had passed both houses of Congress, it was widely assumed that President George W. Bush would have likely vetoed the bill.

DOMESTIC PARTNER BENEFITS

Many observers have speculated that if ENDA were to pass Congress in the near future, President Barack Obama would be likely to sign such a bill. Such predictions have been fueled by Obama's willingness to extend some domestic partner benefits to gay and lesbian federal workers. During the 1990s a number of major corporations began to offer domestic partner benefits to their gay and lesbian employees. William Rubenstein, director of the ACLU National Lesbian and Gay Rights Project, argued that without domestic partner benefits, compensation packages for straight and gay employees would be unequal. In a *Times* piece of June 21, 1992, he commented, "It's as if a job posting said, 'Lesbians and gay men: $30,000; heterosexuals: $40,000.'" Relatedly, a study discussed in a December 4, 1994, *Times* piece found more generally that both "gay men and lesbians earn less on average than similarly qualified heterosexual men and women."

On June 28, 1992, *The Times* reported that major corporations such as Levi Strauss and MCA had begun offering such benefits not only as a matter of fairness but also as a recruitment and retention tool. Local governments also began to offer domestic partner benefits during this time, as evidenced by a *Times* article of September 18, 1996, that documented the city of Denver's decision to do so, calling it "an action that will echo far beyond this city." Less than a year later, a *Times* piece of April 27, 1997, noted that "few workers are taking advantage" of increasingly available domestic partner plans, well below the 3–4 percent rate that had been expected. Elizabeth Birch, executive director of the Human Rights Campaign, said that this may be due to the fact that gay workers have to pay taxes on such benefits. Unlike for heterosexual employees who receive health benefits for their spouses tax-free, such health care benefits accrue to gay and lesbian employees as additional income for which they must pay federal and state taxes. Despite this, employers are allowed to treat health insurance payments as tax deductions regardless of the sexual orientation of employees claiming health benefits for their partners. Birch also speculated that some gay workers might not claim domestic partner benefits because of a reluctance to be out at work.

Running against the grain of offering equal benefits to gay and lesbian employees, the Exxon Mobil Corporation took the unusual step of rescinding a policy that guaranteed health care benefits to gay employees in 1999. As reported in *The Times* on December 7, 1999, the only other company known to have made a similar change is Perot Systems, whose chairman, Ross Perot, decided to stop offering such benefits. By 2008, 83 percent of the Fortune 100 companies offered domestic partner benefits to gay and lesbian employees and 18 percent of the Fortune 100 included transgender-inclusive health insurance benefits for medical treatments related to gender identity.

President Obama said that he would "fight hard" for the rights of gay couples during his presidential campaign, fueling speculation that he might be willing to extend partner benefits. Shortly after he took office, a *Times* report of March 13, 2009, noted that two federal judges had said that employees of their court were entitled to health care benefits for their same-sex partners. On June 17, 2009, *The Times* reported that the Obama administration planned to offer some limited benefits such as family leave to gay and lesbian partners, stopping short of full health care benefits. Reaction in the gay community to the announcement was mixed. Richard Socarides, an advisor to the Clinton administration on gay issues, said that Obama had "promised the moon and done nothing." In a June 18, 2009, *Times* piece, several activists noted that Obama had privately promised to do more in the years to come, while Obama himself noted

that the measure was "only one step." The Obama administration subsequently added language to the federal jobs Web site that explicitly bans employment discrimination based on gender identity, as noted in a *Times* piece of January 6, 2010. Time will tell whether the Obama administration will offer full domestic partner benefits to federal employees and whether the passage of ENDA is as imminent as many pundits have suggested.

BIBLIOGRAPHY

Ayres, Ian, and Jennifer Gerarda Brown. *Straightforward: How to Mobilize Heterosexual Support for Gay Rights.* Princeton, NJ: Princeton University Press, 2005.

Currah, Paisley, Richard Juang, and Shannon Price Mintor. *Transgender Rights.* Minneapolis: University of Minnesota, 2006.

Johnson, David K. *The Lavender Scare: The Cold War Persecution of Gays and Lesbians in the Federal Government.* University of Chicago Press, 2004.

Unsigned. Degrees of Inequality: A National Study Examining Workplace Climate for LGBT Employees. Washington DC: Human Rights Campaign Foundation, 2009.

FROM *THE NEW YORK TIMES*

Associated Press. "Pilot Loses Ruling Over Sex Change." September 1, 1984.

Brooke, James. "Denver Extends Health Coverage to Partners of Gay City Employees." September 18, 1996.

Franklin, Ben A. "Ex-Homosexual Got U.S. Job Back." October 18, 1964.

Kihss, Peter. "A.C.L.U. Study Finds Wide Easing of Job Bias against Homosexuals." July 10, 1975.

Kilbourn, Peter T. "Gay Rights Groups Take Aim at Restaurant Chain That's Hot on Wall Street." April 9, 1992.

Knowlton, Brian. "U.S. Job Site Bans Bias over Gender Identity." January 6, 2010.

Lambert, Bruce. "Federal Policy Against Discrimination Is Sought for AIDS." September 22, 1988.

Noble, Barbara Presley. "At Work; Legal Victories for Gay Workers." June 21, 1992.

———. "At Work; Linking Gay Rights and Unionism." December 4, 1994.

Oppel, Richard A. "Exxon to Stop Giving Benefits to Partners of Gay Workers." December 7, 1999.

Pear, Robert. "Obama on Spot over a Benefit to Gay Couples." March 13, 2009.

Ranzal, Edward. "Homosexual Hiring Stirs Union Study." January 5, 1978.

Rutenberg, Jim. "Outcry on Federal Same-Sex Benefits." June 18, 2009.

Sack, Kevin. "Gay Rights Hurt by Lack of Uniform Protections." March 28, 1993.

Schmitt, Eric. "Senators Reject Both Job-Bias Ban and Gay Marriage." September 11, 1996.

Schumach, Murray. "On the Third Sex." May 7, 1967.

United Press International. "Homosexuals Stage Protest in Capital." May 29, 1965.

Unsigned. "City Lifts Job Curb for Homosexuals." May 9, 1969.

——. "After Stonewall: Pride and Prejudice." June 26, 1994.

Whitaker, Barbara. "Partner Benefits Have a Surprising Lack of Takers." April 27, 1997.

Zeleny, Jeff. "U.S. to Extend Its Job Benefits to Gay Partners." June 17, 2009.

Federal Court Says Homosexual Employees Should Be Judged on Qualifications, Not Identity

In September 1970 a federal judge ruled that the University of Minnesota could not refuse to hire James McConnell simply because he is an out homosexual. McConnell was offered a position as head cataloger by the university's library in April 1970, but the offer was rescinded by the Board of Regents on the grounds that his "personal conduct, as represented in the public and university news media, is not consistent with the best interests of the university." McConnell and his partner, Jack Baker, had made national news when they applied for a marriage license in Hennepin County, also in Minnesota.

One of the regents argued that McConnell's public stances indicated that he would break the law by committing sodomy. In response, the judge said that "a homosexual is a human being," adding, "What Mr. McConnell does in his private life should not be his employer's concern unless it can be shown to affect in some degree his efficiency in the performance of his duties." Said McConnell: "I've seen a lot of gay society, and they're no different from straight people except for their sexual preferences. So we should have the same rights." The university appealed the decision.

James McConnell and Jack Baker would continue to be active in the gay rights movement, later becoming the first homosexual couple to establish a legal relationship via adult adoption. As of this writing they are still together, living in Minnesota where Baker is retired from his law practice and McConnell works for the Hennepin County Library system.

SEPTEMBER 20, 1970
HOMOSEXUAL WINS A SUIT OVER HIRING
Special to the New York Times

MINNEAPOLIS, Sept. 19—Declaring that "a homosexual is a human being," a Federal judge has ruled that the University of Minnesota may not refuse to hire someone merely because he is an avowed homosexual.

The decision was handed down by District Judge Philip Neville, and the university is appealing to the United States Court of Appeals for the Eighth Circuit.

Meanwhile, the principal in the case, James McConnell, who was offered a job by a university librarian in April but was rejected by the university's Board of Regents in July, is living in a university-area apartment with Jack Baker, a law student.

The controversy over Mr. McConnell's appointment started when he and Mr. Baker applied for a marriage license. The application was turned down by the court clerk on the advice of the Hennepin County (Minneapolis) attorney.

The regents then disapproved the job application on the ground that "Mr. McConnell's personal conduct, as represented in the public and university news media, is not consistent with the best interests of the university."

One regent, John Yngve, testified at Mr. McConnell's court hearing in August that by seeking a marriage license, Mr. McConnell had signaled his intention to break the law by committing sodomy.

Judge Neville disagreed. He said other court decisions on homosexuality, while never precisely facing this issue, had distinguished between "a sexual propensity for persons of one's own sex and the commission of homosexual criminal acts."

"What Mr. McConnell does in his private life should not be his employer's concern unless it can be shown to affect in some degree his efficiency in the performance of his duties," Judge Neville said.

Since the judge noted that Mr. McConnell was "otherwise qualified" and since the university did not challenge his qualifications in the lawsuit, the court's ruling is tantamount to an order to hire Mr. McConnell.

An Order to Hire

The job is being kept open until the university's appeal is heard.

Mr. McConnell said in an interview that he faced economic hardship. "I had some money saved," he said, "but I'm getting to the end of my funds this month."

He had moved from Kansas City, Mo., in expectation of being hired as head cataloguer at the university's St. Paul campus library.

He said he had "no regret" about making his proclivities public except for "the frustration of not being able to do a useful job."

"I didn't train for years to come up here and sit on my backside," he said, "I want to work."

Mr. Baker is also unemployed but the two do not share their savings.

"It's not that we don't feel married," said Mr. McConnell. "We believe there should be an equality in the relationship between marriage partners. We feel a husband and wife should handle their finances the way we do."

"I've seen a lot of gay society and they're no different from straight people except for their sexual preferences. So we should have the same rights," he said.

- -

Florida Finds Homosexuals Morally Fit for the Practice of Law

In a landmark 1978 decision, the Florida Supreme Court found that Robert Eimers could not be denied entry to the state bar because of homosexuality. The court ruled that homosexuality by itself does not amount to a lack of "good moral character," noting that it is a well established principle that "government may not discriminate constitutionally by reason of status alone." Decided on a 6–1 margin, the case is thought to be the first in the nation to address a homosexual's right to practice law.

A spokesperson for the American Bar Association said that sexuality rarely comes up in bar admissions, and when it does, applicants typically evade the question. However, Eimers's attorney countered that "the situation is not too unusual," speculating that someone probably outed her client in a private letter to the state Board of Bar Examiners. When asked at a special hearing if he was gay, Eimers honestly replied in the affirmative. A divided Board then asked the state supreme court for guidance on the matter. The court said that in order for the Board to exclude someone from membership on moral grounds, a "substantial connection" would have to be shown between the ability the carry out professional behavior and the behavior in question, "otherwise the bar will be virtually unfettered in its power to censor the private morals of Florida bar members."

Noting that the court's ruling meant that homosexuals should be considered in good moral standing unless proven otherwise, Eimers's attorney added that "what happened in Florida in the past is that applicants simply lie about it if the question comes up because of blackmail or extortion. Too much was at stake, and they were not willing to risk their careers to come out of the closet."

MARCH 21, 1978
FLORIDA HIGH COURT UPHOLDS RIGHT OF HOMOSEXUALS TO PRACTICE LAW

By JON NORDHEIMER

Special to the New York Times

MIAMI, March 20—The Florida Supreme Court ruled today that a homosexual could not be denied admission to the state bar because of sexual preference.

In a 6-to-1 landmark ruling, the court declared that acknowledgement of a homosexual preference by an applicant was not in itself a failure to meet the "good moral character" standard for admission.

The decision was believed to be the first in the United States concerning a homosexual's right to practice law. The matter has not been the subject of controversy in legal circles since state bars apparently have not systematically excluded homosexuals.

Sources in the American Bar Association headquarters in Chicago said that applicants were not routinely questioned about sexual orientation by bar examiners in individual states. If the subject was raised under any pretext, they said, applicants have apparently been able to evade the issue and gain admission.

Background of Case

"The subject is rarely addressed during application procedures in most states," sad an A.B.A. spokesman.

The Florida case arose in 1976, when Robert F. Eimers, then a resident of California, applied for admission to the Florida Bar. He had passed the Florida Bar examination but was summoned to Florida for a special hearing before the State Board of Bar Examiners. In that interview, he was asked if he was a homosexual. Mr. Eimers' response was affirmative.

"The situation was not too unusual," said Terry De Meo, a lawyer for the American Civil Liberties Union, who is representing Mr. Eimers. "Apparently, someone in California wrote the Board of Examiners as a form of blackmail against Mr. Eimers."

The 12-member board deadlocked on whether to admit Mr. Eimers and asked the Florida Supreme Court for guidance.

Broad Principle Seen

The court ruled today that a declaration of homosexuality could not block the admission of Mr. Eimers if he had been found to be qualified in all other respects, as he had.

However, the court indicated that its ruling might go against an applicant when evidence established that the applicant engaged in homosexual acts beyond his admission that he was a homosexual.

"This case stands for a broad antidiscrimination principle—that government may not discriminate constitutionally by reason of status alone," said Bruce Winick, general counsel of the Florida Civil Liberties Union. "The court decision in favor of Mr. Eimers means that a person's status cannot be considered sufficient reason to disqualify any person from government benefits, privilege, license or employment."

In 1976, an A.B.A. subcommittee asked bar associations across the country whether sexual orientation was weighed in applications for admission. No state bar acknowledged that such information was sought from an applicant. To a questionnaire sent to the state bar associations and those of the American territories, asking "Do you have a policy, formal or informal, relating to the admission of gays?" 45 state bar associations responded in the negative, while at least six, including Florida, made no response.

A spokesman for the New York Bar Association said that it had no official stand on the matter, and that its policy-making body, the House of Delegates, had not adopted any resolution on the admission of homosexuals.

Says Applicants Lied

"What happened in Florida in the past is that applicants simply lie about it if the question comes up because of blackmail or extortion," said Miss De Meo. "Too much was at stake, and they were not willing to risk careers to come out of the closet."

Today's ruling, she said, essentially stated that a homosexual should be considered in good moral standing unless it could be demonstrated otherwise. By that measure, heterosexuals would face the same test of character before bar examiners, she said.

However, the court specified that any disciplining of bar members because of personal moral standards should take place only when there was "a substantial connection" between private behavior and the ability to carry out professional responsibilities.

"Otherwise," the court stated, "the bar will be virtually unfettered in its power to censor the private morals of Florida bar members regardless of any nexus between the behavior and the ability to responsibly perform as an attorney."

FEDERAL JUDGE ORDERS TRANSSEXUAL PILOT REINSTATED

In 1980 a federal judge ordered Eastern Airlines to reinstate Karen Ulane, a pilot and decorated Vietnam War veteran who was born a man prior to becoming a woman through sex reassignment surgery, saying that she would not have been discharged "but for being a transsexual." The decision was based on the Civil Rights Act of 1964, which is most known for protecting the rights of blacks in the area of employment, housing, and public accommodations such as motels and theaters. Arguing that "it can't be said with any rationality that transsexuals cannot be good airline pilots," he concluded that the "American public is a lot smarter than the bigots gave them credit for being."

Eastern defended the firing by saying that Ulane posed a safety hazard in the cockpit and that she had concealed her transsexuality while taking female hormones in preparation for surgery. Nevertheless, Eastern's own witnesses acknowledged that Ulane was one of their better pilots and that it was her sex change that made her unacceptable as an employee. In a stinging oral opinion, the judge noted that Eastern did not act similarly when it discovered instances of concealed alcoholism in thirty of its pilots. He added that "ignorance, prejudice, discrimination and hatred have throughout history been justified by saying, 'I don't know. We can't take a chance.'" While Ulane stated that she is ready to start work "tomorrow," and that she feels she is now "the person who I was meant to be," Eastern appealed the ruling.

An appeals court eventually found that the Civil Rights Act did not protect transsexuals. Although Ulane was given a sizable cash settlement from Eastern Airlines, she was not rehired. She died in 1989 in Illinois when the twin-propeller chartered plane she was flying crashed, killing her and two others.

DECEMBER 29, 1983
JUDGE TELLS EASTERN AIRLINES TO REHIRE TRANSSEXUAL PILOT
By E.R. SHIPP

CHICAGO, Dec. 28—A Federal district judge ordered Eastern Airlines today to reinstate a pilot who underwent a sex change in 1980.

"But for being a transsexual and for having the operation and assuming a life style of a woman, the plaintiff would not have been discharged," said the judge, John F. Grady. The pilot, who flew for the airline as Kenneth Ulane for 12 years, is now known as Karen F. Ulane.

In an oral opinion, Judge Grady said that Eastern was guilty of sex discrimination and that the justifications it offered for not reinstating Miss Ulane were "a pretext and a sham of the first order."

Eastern's main argument was that, despite a lack of evidence to support its view, it believed Miss Ulane's presence in the cockpit posed safety hazards.

Judge Grady responded, "Ignorance, prejudice, discrimination and hatred have throughout history been justified by saying, 'I don't know. We can't take a chance.' "

'Image Problem' Cited

He said that more than legitimate concerns for safety, Eastern feared that "it had a real image problem with a transsexual in the cockpit."

Eastern had also argued that Miss Ulane, while still a man, had concealed the fact that she was taking female hormones. But Judge Grady noted that Eastern had not complained when it learned that 30 pilots had concealed alcoholism.

Judge Grady, who based his decision on the Civil Rights Act of 1964, said Miss Ulane's case was reminiscent of what happened when blacks asserted their rights in the 1950's and 1960's. At that time, he said, "bigots" cited a litany of dire consequences that could result from accepting blacks in the mainstream of society.

"The American public is a lot smarter than the bigots gave them credit for being," he said. "Some transsexuals, just as some tall people and left-handers and fat people and Irishmen, are not good pilots. It can't be said with any rationality that transsexuals cannot be good airline pilots."

Appeal of Ruling Planned

Eastern plans to appeal what it called Judge Grady's "novel view of the law" in holding that transsexuals are protected under the Civil Rights Act.

In Miami, James R. Ashlock, a spokesman for Eastern, said, "Eastern remains confident that its position in this case is correct under the law."

Kenneth Ulane joined Eastern Airlines in 1968. He had previously been an Army pilot and had been decorated for valor in connection with the combat missions he flew in Vietnam, according to lawyers in the case. He was twice married and divorced and has a 16-year-old child.

The decision to go ahead with the sex change, performed in April 1980, followed years of consultations with doctors, Miss Ulane said today.

U.S. Certified Her to Fly

"I did consider all the ramifications as far as my job, and, of course, had to weigh that against what I thought would be the positive outcome of the surgery itself," she said. "I feel I am the person who I was meant to be before."

In January 1981, after what one lawyer called "a rigorous battery of psychological and physical tests," the Federal Aviation Administration certified Miss Ulane as fit to fly.

"In terms of sexual discrimination, Karen Ulane was kind of a perfect control group," said Fay Clayton, one of her lawyers. "As a male pilot, Eastern's own witnesses acknowledged that she was one of their better pilots. When she changed her sex, she was all of a sudden not acceptable. Eastern was willing to retain one sex in their employ, but not willing to retain the other."

Mr. Ashlock said two of Eastern's 4,200 pilots were women.

Judge Grady has ordered Eastern to reinstate Miss Ulane with back pay and full seniority but held his order in abeyance pending appeal.

"I'm ready to start tomorrow," Miss Ulane said.

AIDS JOB DISCRIMINATION CASES SHIFT FROM FIRING TO BLOOD SCREENING AND INSURANCE CLAIMS

In the mid-1980s many employers came to understand that it was illegal to fire employees because they had developed AIDS, as the disease was understood to be a disability. Given this reality, other kinds of employment discrimination cases related to AIDS began to arise. For example, some firms required preemployment blood tests to screen out those with AIDS antibodies. Mark Senak, a lawyer at the Gay Men's Health Crisis, said that these tests are "getting to be like the yellow star of the 1930's" a reference to the symbol that Jews were forced to wear to identify themselves under Nazi rule. He added that such testing "brands people and sets them apart, preventing them from getting jobs or insurance. Using the results of the test as a condition of employment is illegal discrimination." Some employers put workers with AIDS on involuntary disability leave, which also is illegal if employees are able to work.

Mitchell Karp, a lawyer with the AIDS Discrimination Unit of the New York City Commission on Civil Rights, argued that "a panic by co-workers" often induces such discriminatory practices, despite the fact that AIDS cannot be spread through casual contact. Both Karp and Senak argued that better education about the disease would lessen workplace discrimination. Few of these cases ever made it to court, because many of those afflicted with the disease were reluctant to accept the visibility and publicity associated with them. In addition, many died before their case could be heard. Numerous attorneys representing such workers sought out-of-court settlements, but according to Senak, "It's often difficult for a person to go back to work at a place where he was publicly humiliated."

Some cases were more complicated than others. For example, can a waiter who has Kaposi's sarcoma lesions on his face be fired because it scares the customers? According to Karp, the case would hinge on whether physical appearance is substantially related to the work being done, or what is known in the law as a bona fide occupational qualification (BFOQ). Senak argued that insurance claims were "the biggest area of discrimination right now," as insurance companies often resisted paying sizable medical expenses related to AIDS on the grounds that it is a preexisting condition. He said that his strategy was to convince insurance companies that it would cost them as much to prove that the claimant had or should have known he had AIDS than it would to simply pay off the claim.

APRIL 15, 1986
BUSINESS AND THE LAW; AIDS AND JOB DISCRIMINATION
By TAMAR LEWIN

The epidemic of Acquired Immune Deficiency Syndrome that has killed nearly 10,000 people in five years has spawned a new wave of employment discrimination claims.

Few AIDS cases have gone to court, in part because many people with the disease are reluctant to face the publicity that comes with filing a lawsuit, and in part because the legal process is so slow, and AIDS so deadly, that AIDS victims know they may die before their case is heard. Then, too, in New York and California, where most AIDS victims live, administrative agencies offer help that may make a formal lawsuit unnecessary.

Lawyers familiar with AIDS discrimination say that, over the last two years, most major employers have come to accept that it is illegal to dismiss a worker who develops AIDS. "There has been a lot of education on that point and even the most hard-line management lawyers are now advising their clients that AIDS is a disability, and workers may not be dismissed because of a disability," said Arthur S. Leonard, who teaches labor law at the New York Law School. But the problem still arises from time to time. "We had stopped getting calls from people who had been fired because they got AIDS, but only yesterday, I heard from someone who worked in a law firm who said it had happened to him," Mark Senak, a lawyer at the Gay Men's Health Crisis, said last week. "But it's rarer."

Mr. Senak and others in the field say there are now many other forms of job discrimination against AIDS victims. Some employers have refused to hire those whom they believe to be at high risk of developing the disease. Others are requiring pre-employment blood tests to try to screen out those who have AIDS antibodies in their bloodstream.

"The blood test for HTLV-3 virus is getting to be like the yellow star in the 1930's," Mr. Senak said. "It brands people and sets them apart, preventing them from getting jobs or insurance. Using the results of the test as a condition of employment is illegal discrimination, but I think some employers are doing it."

Still other employers put workers with AIDS on involuntary disability leave, paying full salary and benefits, but refusing to allow them to work. Most lawyers say this is illegal, if the employee is capable of working. In a pending California case, the Fair Employment and Housing Department is pressing the claims of a former Raytheon Company employee who was forbidden to return to work after being diagnosed as having AIDS in late 1983. The employee, John Chadbourne, died last year, but the department is still seeking both damages for his family and a ban on such discrimination.

Mitchell Karp, a staff lawyer with the AIDS Discrimination Unit of the New York City Commission on Human Rights, said much of the job discrimination springs from fears of contagion. "It's often a panic by co-workers that leads the employer to try to get a worker with AIDS out of the office," he added. "What's really needed is more education about the fact that AIDS cannot be spread through casual workplace contact."

Mr. Senak, too, stressed that better education about AIDS would end much of the discrimination.

"We had a rash of calls from women whose employers asked them to take a blood test because they had platonic gay friends," he said. "That didn't make much sense. When we get a complaint, I call the offending party, and explain the error of their ways and we usually work out a settlement. It's often difficult for a person to go back to work at a place where he was publicly humiliated. And it's generally not professional people who have trouble. It's the file clerks who get trashed, and they can easily change jobs."

Mr. Karp says his agency gets more complaints from people who are discriminated against because they are perceived to have AIDS than from those who actually have the disease. "Most of them don't want to file a legal complaint because they fear that doing so will isolate them and make more people think they have AIDS," he added.

A broadly written New York law specifically forbids discrimination against those who are perceived to have a disability, as well as those who really are handicapped.

But some of the other legal questions surrounding AIDS are less clear-cut.

"If a waiter or a salesperson develops facial disfigurement from the Kaposi's sarcoma lesions that many AIDS patients get, most restaurants and stores don't want him to keep working because it scares the customers," Mr. Senak said. "That's a complicated question and there's not much case law in the area. The reality of it is that, by the time the disfigurement is that severe, most people are probably going to die within four or five months, so getting a financial settlement is usually more practical than getting the job back."

Adds Mr. Karp: "The legal question is whether physical appearance is a bona fide occupational qualification, and when you get into esthetics, it's uncharted territory. It has to be decided case by case."

The insurance questions, too, are difficult. Many AIDS victims find that when they begin to have medical claims—and medical costs for an AIDS patient range from $45,000 to $140,000—their insurers refuse to pay out, arguing that the claims are not covered because the policyholder had AIDS as a pre-existing condition at the time the insurance went into effect.

"Insurance is the biggest area of discrimination right now," Mr. Senak said. "We try to convince the insurers that they will have to prove that the person knew or should have known he had AIDS when the coverage began, and that it will cost them as much to prove that as to just pay the claims."

CRACKER BARREL RESTAURANT DISMISSES GAY AND LESBIAN EMPLOYEES

The Lebanon, Tennessee–based Cracker Barrel Old Country Store and Restaurant chain rescinded a policy against employing homosexuals after dismissing at least nine gay employees in 1991. A company memo had been issued stating that Cracker Barrel was founded on "traditional American values," and that employing people "whose sexual preference fails to demonstrate normal heterosexual values which have been the foundation of families in our society" was inconsistent with the "perceived values of our customer base." After talks with the National Gay and Lesbian Task Force, Cracker Barrel rethought the policy, calling it "a well-intentioned over-reaction to the perceived values of our customers and their comfort levels." In response, the National Gay and Lesbian Task Force asked, "How can discrimination ever be well-intentioned?"

Several of those who had been dismissed said that they were unaware of the policy shift. Cheryl Summerville, a thirty-two-year-old lesbian who previously worked as a cook for Cracker Barrel had been told by managers that the policy was not really aimed at her, but rather at "effeminate men and women who have masculine traits who might be working as waiters and waitresses." Wylie Petty was dismissed after working at a Cracker Barrel restaurant in Georgia for more than a year and a half, even though he told his managers that he was gay two weeks after having been hired. He said that he didn't regret coming out, "because I never would have had a true friend there if I hadn't been honest. But now I know what it is like to be discriminated against."

Attorneys sympathetic to gay rights said there was little that could be done about these firings because most states and localities still did not have laws in place that prohibit employment discrimination on the basis of sexuality. At the time of the 1991 firings, only Massachusetts, Wisconsin, and eighty cities and counties protected gays and lesbians from being fired because of their identity. Calling Cracker Barrel's actions "outrageous and incredible," William Rubenstein, director of the Lesbian and Gay Rights Project of the American Civil Liberties Union, conceded that "it would be very difficult to challenge these discharges" in areas without such protections.

After years of lobbying by civil rights groups, Cracker Barrel agreed to add sexual orientation to the company's nondiscrimination policy after a shareholder vote in 2002. The company, however, still has a lackluster record in workplace equality, according to the Human Rights Campaign. In HRC's 2009 Corporate Equality Index, Cracker Barrel achieved the lowest score in the food and beverage industry, 15 out of a possible score of 100.

FEBRUARY 28, 1991
COMPANY OUSTS GAY WORKERS, THEN RECONSIDERS
By RONALD SMOTHERS
Special to the New York Times

DOUGLASVILLE, Ga., Feb. 27—The sign on the door of the Cracker Barrel Country Store and Restaurant said, "Now Hiring," and added that the company was a place that "gives you everything you need to cook up a great future."

But earlier this year the chain of restaurants, based in Lebanon, Tenn., adopted a hiring policy that belied the meaning of the sign. It said it would no longer employ homosexuals, and at least nine gay employees were dismissed.

Dan Evins, chairman of the company, was quoted today in The Tennessean in Nashville as saying the policy had been rescinded. But workers who had been dismissed, like Cheryl Summerville, said they had heard nothing about that.

Ms. Summerville, a 32-year-old lesbian who worked here as a cook for more than three years, said sympathetic managers had advised her to be quiet about her sexual preferences, stay in the kitchen and wait for things to blow over.

"They said they didn't really want to fire me," she said, "because the policy was really aimed at effeminate men and women who have masculine traits who might be working as waiters or waitresses.

"But I said I couldn't let them fire other people and keep me because it would just be a matter of time before the policy caught up with me, too."

First Time to See Discrimination

About 200 miles south, in Tifton, Ga., Wylie Petty, 21, had been a waiter at the Cracker Barrel off Interstate 75 until last week, when he was dismissed for being gay.

"I told them I was gay two weeks after I was hired a year and half ago," Mr. Petty said. "I don't regret that because I never would have had a true friend there if I hadn't been honest. But now I know what it is like to be discriminated against."

Lynn Cothren, chairman of the Atlanta chapter of Queer Nation, a gay rights group, said nine Cracker Barrel employees had notified his organization of their dismissal.

While the National Gay and Lesbian Task Force strongly protested Cracker Barrel's policy since learning of it from gay managers at the company, civil liberties lawyers said there was little they could do in most states to stop such hiring practices. Only two states, Massachusetts and Wisconsin, and about 80 cities and counties specifically prohibit discrimination in hiring based on sexual preference, they said.

"It's outrageous and incredible," said William Rubenstein, director of the Lesbian and Gay Rights Project for the American Civil Liberties Union, "but it's fair to say that as a general matter it would be very difficult to challenge these discharges other than in one of those places where there is a law specifically prohibiting it."

Little Support for Policy

Even groups like the Family Research Council and Morality in Media, which espouse the traditional family values that Cracker Barrel's management said it was defending, had little to say in support of the company's initial policy.

Carrie Howard, a spokesman for the Washington-based council, said the council was more concerned about legislative efforts to change the definition of families. Joseph Reilly, president of Morality in Media, which is based in New York, said, "It was prudent to rescind the policy, and it would have been even more prudent to never have instituted it."

Cracker Barrel, which had sales of $200 million last year, has about 100 locations in the Southeast. Each is a wooden, barnlike building usually just off an interstate highway. One section is outfitted like a traditional country store, complete with pot-bellied stove; the other section, housing the restaurant, has a large stone fireplace with wrought-iron hooks and hanging kettles.

The company employs 9,000 to 10,000 people, according to the National Restaurant News, a trade publication.

In announcing earlier this year that homosexual employees would be dismissed, a company memorandum said Cracker Barrel was founded on a "concept of traditional American values." Continued employment of those "whose sexual preference fails to demonstrate normal heterosexual values which have been the foundation of families in our society" appears inconsistent with those values and the "perceived values of our customer base," it said.

Repeated efforts to reach Mr. Evins today for comment on what prompted the decision and how the policy was put into effect were unsuccessful. He did not respond to several telephone messages and requests for an interview.

'Well-Intentioned Over-Reaction'

Robert Bray, a spokesman for the gay and lesbian task force, said that on Feb. 22, after talks with representatives of the group, Cracker Barrel said it had rethought the hiring policy and was rescinding it.

A company statement said: "In the past, we have always responded to the values and wishes of our customers. Our recent position on the employment of homosexuals in a limited number of stores may have been a well-intentioned over-reaction to the perceived values of our customers and their comfort levels with these individuals."

But Mr. Bray said retraction amounted to a "further defaming of the gay community."

"How can discrimination ever be well-intentioned?" he asked.

Today, outside the Cracker Barrel in this small town 20 miles west of Atlanta, customers generally disagreed with the policy of dismissing gay workers, though one man, who refused to give his name, said he and others who he considered "average customers" of the chain "don't feel comfortable about homosexuals."

But Clarice Thompson, who lives in adjacent Carroll County, said the dismissal of homosexuals seemed outmoded and out of step with the times.

"It's so open now and everybody is out of the closet," she said. "Customers don't care as long as they aren't insulting. And some of the heterosexual ones are more insulting, if you ask me."

Growing Numbers of Businesses Offer Domestic Partner Benefits

Although some companies such as Lotus Development Corporation have long had policies in place that forbid discrimination in the workplace against gays and lesbians, most did not offer equal benefits to gay and lesbian partners or "spousal equivalents." In 1992 Lotus started offering domestic partner benefits after two years of negotiations that began when one of its employees filled in her lesbian partner's name on a benefit request form. According to Ed Mickens, editor of a publication on gay and lesbian employment issues, "If employees don't say something, it won't happen."

Several other high-profile companies began to offer domestic partner benefits in the 1990s, including Levi Strauss and MCA. In addition to equalizing packages for gay and lesbian employees, domestic partner benefits also serve as a valuable recruiting tool for these companies. A Lotus spokesperson said, "We assume that there are gay men and lesbians among the best people available. If offering benefits gives us an edge, we want that." Critics note that unlike heterosexual spouses, same-sex couples must pay taxes on the benefits, which can amount to thousands of dollars each year.

Lotus's insurer was initially concerned about the costs of including domestic partners in the company's plan, primarily because of the incidence of AIDS in gay populations. Research showed that the costs associated with treating AIDS were comparable to those of treating heart disease and less than the expenses associated with treating several forms of cancer, while other studies revealed no differences between same-sex and heterosexual health care costs. On the basis of this information, Lotus's insurer decided to include gay and lesbian partners in its health care offerings.

A lawyer in San Francisco who wrote a guidebook on domestic partnership policy for the National Center for Lesbian Rights in San Francisco concluded that the lesson of the Lotus example is: "One or two people with a strong sense of what's right can make an enormous difference."

JUNE 28, 1992
AT WORK; BENEFITS FOR DOMESTIC PARTNERS

By BARBARA PRESLEY NOBLE

The day in 1987 that Margie Bleichman sat down to fill out forms required of new employees at the Lotus Development Corporation, she was fairly certain benefits were not extended to "spousal equivalents" like her female partner. "I put my partner's name down to see what would happen," said Ms. Bleichman, a software engineer at the Cambridge, Mass.-based software company. "I was politely told that the insurance company wouldn't allow it."

Of course, even as a new employee, Ms. Bleichman wasn't unaware of the irony that Lotus had a longstanding policy forbidding workplace discrimination, including that against gay men and lesbians. So a year or so later, when she and other gay employees began to think about asking for domestic partner benefits, they went straight to the heart of the matter.

"We decided to meet to make benefits more equitable for gay employees," she said. Last September, after more than two years of negotiating and, as Ms. Bleichman put it, "not quite nagging," Lotus agreed to offer benefits to same-sex partners.

Gay and lesbian activism is at its most visible every year during Gay Pride Week, which ends today with marches in New York and other cities. But that activism—in pinstripes instead of leather or flannel—is becoming evident in corporate America as gay employees lobby for workplace change.

As Ms. Bleichman is the first to point out, the move by Lotus was a tribute to the company's flexibility and sense of fair play. But it was also an example of how serendipitously change comes to the corporation: a convergence of policy, open-minded managers and, mostly, employees willing to gavotte straight out to the end of a limb.

"If employees don't say something, it won't happen," said Ed Mickens, editor of Working It Out, a New York-based newsletter on gay and lesbian employment issues.

Since last fall, Lotus, once seemingly in permanent recumbence upon the high-technology cutting edge, has been perched on the social cutting edge, with companies like Levi Strauss and, as of July 1, MCA. Some three dozen companies recognize, formally and informally, the concerns of gay and lesbian employees. And the employees, who naturally enough reflect the diversity of the gay population, from the in-your-face activists of Queer Nation to closeted Republican fundraisers, have transposed their experiences into the steam for change. A questionnaire, for example, now used for sensitivity training—posing for heterosexuals the type of questions often asked of gay people—will be familiar to anyone who remembers consciousness-raising groups in the lesbian counterculture of the 1970's.

"One or two people with a strong sense of what's right can make an enormous difference," said Patti Roberts, a lawyer in San Francisco who is revising the domestic partner benefits handbook the Lotus group used as guidance. The revision will be published in the fall by the National Center for Lesbian Rights in San Francisco.

Ms. Bleichman's involvement with the Lotus Extended Benefits Group, as it came to be called, was a natural extension of her experience with gay and lesbian community activities: "I know it sounds funny in the corporate context, but this is grass-roots organizing." When the group—of the original core, Ms. Bleichman and Polly Laurelchild are still at Lotus—began meeting in early 1989, it spent two months devising a proposal. One immediate goal was the replacement of the word "spouse" in company handbooks with the phrase "spouse equivalent" or "domestic partner." On the more cosmic issue of benefits, the group proposed partner criteria—stricter, as it turned out, than those eventually adopted.

Knowing that even at a modern, meritocratic high-tech company, upper echelons speak to the C.E.O. and the C.E.O. only to God, the group sought out sympathetic middle management to carry its message. "We wanted to stress that the policy should be extended for fairness, but that it would come back to the company in positive ways," Ms. Bleichman said. "More prospective employees would look to the company as a good place to work."

The group's proposal was in synch with Lotus's general workplace philosophy. "One of our operating principles is to value diversity and encourage it," said Bryan E. Simmons, a Lotus spokesman. "We assume that there are gay men and lesbians among the best people available. If offering benefits gives us an edge, we want that."

The benefit negotiations, everyone agrees, were amicable, but stuttered to a halt when the insurance company that provides medical coverage above the limit set by Lotus's own self-insured policy balked. (Lotus declined to name the insurer.) The company required "some educating," for example, on costs. The discussions "danced," as Ms. Bleichman put it, around certain topics, like catastrophic illness: "We kept saying, 'Is it AIDS?' Nobody would say the word 'AIDS.'"

Lotus and the group researched and found a comparison of the average costs of treating various diseases: heart disease, $50,000 to $70,000; cancer, $30,000 to $100,000; AIDS, $50,000 to $70,000. "It's a terrible way to think about it," Ms. Bleichman said. "But you have to address their concerns. It did give this free-floating anxiety a name and a cost."

That comparison, assurances that the company would be vigilant about fraud and a study that found no difference between same-sex and heterosexual partners in health-care costs persuaded Lotus's insurer to accede.

Ms. Bleichman regrets that the final program does not include the group's original proposal to cover unmarried straight domestic partners, which Lotus rejected because heterosexuals may marry. And the benefit's Internal Revenue Service status as taxable income makes taking advantage of it a true cost-benefit calculus. Since the negotiations began, her partner has gotten benefits on her own, making Ms. Bleichman's participation moot. But even as a semi-disinterested observer, she savors her role in what may eventually be a workplace revolution.

Clinton Supports ENDA, Becomes First Sitting President to Support Civil Rights for Gays

President Clinton announced in October 1995 that he would support a bill, commonly known as the Employment Non-Discrimination Act (ENDA), that would prohibit discrimination against gay and lesbian employees. It was the first time that a sitting president had endorsed a major civil rights proposal for gays and lesbians. Noting that employees could be fired in forty-one states because of their sexual orientation, Clinton stated that "those who face this kind of job discrimination have no legal recourse," adding, "this is wrong." The Republican majority in Congress was expected to resist the measure, leading openly gay representative Barney Frank (D-MA) to conclude, "We won't even get hearings on it."

The bill exempted the armed forces and small businesses with fewer than fifteen employees, as well as religious institutions and schools. It also did not include provisions for domestic partner benefits and prohibited affirmative action on the basis of sexual orientation. Clinton administration spokesperson George Stephanopoulos said that the bill "is about the simple bedrock judgment that you shouldn't discriminate against people because of who they are, and we think the public will support that."

Opponents of the bill claimed not to be surprised, stating that the Clinton administration had "been relentlessly pursuing the homosexual agenda within the Federal Government and the military. And this would extend it to the private sector with grave consequences." One gay rights advocate countered that "while others continue to be engaged in the politics of division, I feel that he's staking out some moral high ground."

Some form of ENDA has been introduced in every session of Congress except the 109th. In 2010 three versions were in committee, two in the House and one in the Senate. Although many observers expected it to pass in this session of Congress, it stalled at the end of 2010.

OCTOBER 20, 1995
CLINTON BACKS BILL TO PROTECT HOMOSEXUALS FROM JOB BIAS
By STEVEN A. HOLMES

WASHINGTON, Oct. 19—Two years after being politically wounded by the issue of homosexuals in the military, President Clinton has decided to back a bill outlawing job discrimination against homosexuals, White House officials said today.

In a letter sent today to Senator Edward M. Kennedy, Democrat of Massachusetts and a chief sponsor of the anti-discrimination legislation in the Senate, Mr. Clinton noted that in 41 states it is legal for a person to be dismissed from a job because of sexual orientation.

"Those who face this kind of job discrimination have no legal recourse, in either state or Federal courts," Mr. Clinton wrote. "This is wrong."

Gay rights leaders who have been lobbying the White House for Mr. Clinton's endorsement of the bill conceded that his backing would have little immediate practical effect because the Republican Congress was dead set against the measure, which would apply to public and private employment.

"We won't even get hearings on it," said Representative Barney Frank, Democrat of Massachusetts, one of three openly gay members of Congress.

Still, Mr. Clinton's endorsement is the first by a sitting President involving a major piece of legislation to secure equal rights for homosexuals. And it is likely to guarantee that gay rights will become an issue in next year's Presidential campaign.

"I'm sure Pat Robertson and Pat Buchanan will try to make hay of this," said George Stephanopoulos, a senior adviser to Mr. Clinton. "But the President believes it's the right thing to do, and I believe that most Americans agree that discrimination is wrong for whatever reason."

The bill, the Employment Non-Discrimination Act, would extend to sexual orientation the same Federal protection against bias in hiring, promotions or dismissals that currently exists on the basis of race, sex, religion, color or national origin. But to try to gather more support and trump critics' argument that they are seeking "special rights" for homosexuals, the drafters of the bill carved out several exemptions.

The measure would not cover the armed forces, businesses with fewer than 15 employees and religious institutions, including sectarian schools. The measure would not require businesses to provide health or other benefits to domestic partners of employees, and it would prohibit employers from giving anyone preference in hiring or promotion because of sexual orientation.

If enacted, the measure would cover Congress. It would cover heterosexuals as well because it would prohibit discrimination as a result of sexual orientation.

Even with the exemptions, social conservatives have condemned the bill, and they criticized Mr. Clinton today for his endorsement.

"I'm not surprised," said Robert H. Knight, director of cultural studies at the Family Research Council, a conservative advocacy group. "He's tried to give them everything they've wanted. This seems to be the one issue area where the Clinton Administration doesn't flip-flop. They have been relentlessly pursuing the homosexual agenda within the Federal Government and the military. And this would extend it to the private sector with grave consequences."

Gay rights leaders were thrilled with Mr. Clinton's endorsement despite the dim prospects for the bill in Congress.

"I feel that it's an excellent move, and it's in keeping with his broader message of healing the country," said Elizabeth Birch, executive director of the Human Rights Campaign, the country's largest gay rights organization. "While others continue to be engaged in the politics of division, I feel that he's staking out some moral high ground."

Though Mr. Stephanopoulos concedes that the bill will have rough sledding in Congress, he said he believed that the Administration would attract more support for the goal of ending discrimination against homosexuals in the workplace than it did in trying to lift the ban in the military.

"Part of the power of the argument that the military had was that the military is different," he said. "It has special problems of morale and discipline that require different standards. We didn't agree with the argument, but we understood it, and the President had to act in a way that was consistent with maintaining morale and discipline. But this bill is about the simple bedrock judgment that you shouldn't discriminate against people because of who they are, and we think the public will support that."

Backers of the measure say public opinion polls consistently show that a large majority of Americans do not favor discrimination against homosexuals. The advocates say the polls also indicate that most Americans do not know that in most states, homosexuals have no protections against being dismissed.

"The right wing says what these people want is special rights," Mr. Frank said. "And people are prepared to believe that we are asking for special rights because they assume we already have the protections we are asking for, and so we must be asking for something more."

WAL-MART POLICY SIGNALS MAINSTREAM ACCEPTANCE OF GAYS AND LESBIANS

In an indication of how far corporate America has come in accepting openly gay people into the workforce, Wal-Mart Stores in 2003 expanded its anti-discrimination policy to include gay and lesbian employees. The policy did not include domestic partner benefits, but it did include sensitivity training for all employees. Wal-Mart's vice president of corporate communications, Mona Williams, commented on the policy change: "It's the right thing to do for our employees. We want all of our associates to feel they are valued and treated with respect—no exceptions. And it's the right thing to do for our business."

The policy change was seen as an especially important victory for advocates of gay and lesbian rights because Wal-Mart has been careful not to alienate customers with conservative views, for instance, by refusing to sell CDs with explicit lyrics or racy magazines. Wal-Mart said that the policy change was a response to gay employees, rather than outside pressure from investors. Both had been asking for changes in the policy.

Wal-Mart is the country's largest private employer.

JULY 2, 2003
WAL-MART SETS A NEW POLICY THAT PROTECTS GAY WORKERS
By SARAH KERSHAW

SEATTLE, July 1—Wal-Mart Stores, the nation's largest private employer, has expanded its antidiscrimination policy to protect gay and lesbian employees, company officials said today.

The decision to include gay employees under rules that prohibit workplace discrimination was hailed by gay rights groups, already buoyed by a Supreme Court ruling last week that struck down a Texas sodomy law, as a sign of how far corporate America has come in accepting gay employees.

The decision was first disclosed today by a Seattle gay rights foundation that had invested in Wal-Mart and then lobbied the company for two years to change its policy. The group, Pride Foundation, which along with several

investment management firms holding stock in Wal-Mart had met as shareholders with company officials to discuss the policy, received a letter last week from Wal-Mart outlining the new employee protections. Wal-Mart officials confirmed the policy change today.

"It's the right thing to do for our employees," Mona Williams, Wal-Mart's vice president for communications, said in a telephone interview. "We want all of our associates to feel they are valued and treated with respect—no exceptions. And it's the right thing to do for our business."

Ms. Williams said the company was sending out a letter today to its 3,500 stores and that store managers would then convey the policy change to the company's more than 1 million employees. She said that while investors like Pride

Foundation had a role in the decision, the most important factor was a letter to senior management officials about six weeks ago from several gay Wal-Mart employees, saying that unless the company changed its policy the employees would "continue to feel excluded."

Wal-Mart has been careful not to alienate its customers who might hold conservative views. In recent months, the company has decided to stop selling three men's magazines it said were too racy and to partially obscure the covers of four women's magazines on sale in checkout lines. The company said customers felt the magazine cover headlines were too provocative and planned to use U-shaped blinders to cover them.

Wal-Mart has also refused to sell CD's with labels warning of explicit lyrics.

Ms. Williams said she saw no conflict between the decision to limit the distribution of entertainment products based on content and the decision to protect gay employees.

"In each case, we sit down and think through the individual decisions," she said. "Putting in the blinders was the right thing to do. In this case, once again, we talked about it and decided it was the right thing to do."

With Wal-Mart making the policy change, 9 of the 10 largest Fortune 500 companies now have rules barring discrimination against gay employees, according to the Human Rights Campaign, a gay rights group in Washington, D.C., that monitors discrimination policies and laws.

The exception is the Exxon Mobil Corporation, which was created in 1999 after Exxon acquired Mobil, and then revoked a Mobil policy that provided medical benefits to partners of gay employees, as well as a policy that included sexual orientation as a category of prohibited discrimination.

Wal-Mart said it had no plans to extend medical benefits to unmarried couples, but gay rights groups that have pressed for coverage for domestic partners said they would continue to lobby the company to do so.

Among the Fortune 500 companies, 197 provide domestic partners with medical coverage, including several of the major airlines and the Big Three automakers, and 318 have antidiscrimination policies that extend protection to gay employees, according to the Human Rights Campaign.

With Wal-Mart now joining the ranks of companies with protections for gay employees, and in light of last week's Supreme Court ruling, gay rights groups said they expected many corporations, and possibly state governments, to follow suit.

"A major argument against equal benefits, against fair treatment of employees, has been taken away," said Kevin Cathcart, executive director of the Lambda Legal Defense and Education Fund, referring to the Supreme Court ruling on Lawrence v. Texas. "And so even within corporations it's a very different dialogue today, a very different dialogue."

There is no federal law prohibiting discrimination in the workplace on the basis of sexual orientation, but 13 states, the District of Columbia and several hundred towns, cities or counties have such legal protections in place for public and private employees, according to the latest information from the Human Rights Campaign.

As outlined in the letter to Pride Foundation, Wal-Mart's new policy states, "We affirm our commitment and pledge our support to equal opportunity employment for all qualified persons, regardless of race, color, religion, gender, national origin, age, disability or status as a veteran or sexual orientation."

It goes on to say that managers and supervisors "shall recruit, hire, train and promote in all job positions" based on those principles and "ensure that all personnel actions" are taken based on those principles.

The company said that it also revised its policy on harassment and inappropriate conduct to include sexual orientation and that the new written policy would encourage employees to report discriminatory behavior to management.

As the nation's largest private employer and one whose stores are not unionized, Wal-Mart has long been the target of organized labor, and some of its labor practices have been challenged in lawsuits. One lawsuit, filed in San Francisco, accused the company of favoring men over women in promotions and pay.

In addition, the company faces more than 40 lawsuits accusing the company of pressuring or forcing employees to work unpaid hours.

While Wal-Mart attributed the discrimination policy change to the letter from its gay employees, it had been under pressure from several investors, including the Seattle group and three other management investment firms with stock in the company.

They are all members of the Equality Project, a non-profit group in New York that monitors corporate policies on sexual orientation and lobbies for protections for gay employees.

Under Securities and Exchange Commission regulations, any stockholder with $2,000 or more in shares can introduce a "shareholder resolution" on an array of company policy issues, including antidiscrimination rules. The resolutions are not binding, and the shareholders have no influence over "ordinary business," including benefits and wages, according to S.E.C. officials.

The Seattle group and the other investors began discussions with Wal-Mart in August 2001, when several members of the groups went to the company headquarters in Bentonville, Ark., to try to persuade officials to change the policy, several group members said. As investors in General Electric and McDonald's, the Seattle group had already pressured the companies, through shareholder resolutions, and both companies have since extended workplace protections to gay employees.

Wal-Mart initially said it would study the issue, said Zan McColloch-Lussier, campaign director for Pride Foundation. But in a conference call in the spring of 2002, Mr. McColloch-Lussier recalled, company officials told the group, "Thanks, you've educated us, but we're not going to change our policies, we'll do management training."

More letters and telephone calls were exchanged, and then last Friday a letter came announcing the policy change.

Arthur D. Ally, president of the Timothy Plan, a religious-based investment group that had pressured the company about the magazines, said today that he would not sell Wal-Mart stock because of the revised antidiscrimination policy but would object to certain sensitivity training programs like "taking every employee in an organization and indoctrinating them in the homosexual agenda."

It was unclear today exactly how Wal-Mart planned to train employees, but Ms. Williams said that a computer-based training program would include discussion of sexual orientation.

House Approves ENDA, First Gay Civil Rights Bill to Pass House of Congress

In November 2007, by a vote of 235–184, the House of Representatives approved a bill that would grant employment protections to gays, lesbians, and bisexuals, marking the first time in U.S. history that a house of Congress had approved a civil rights bill for this population. Rep. Steny Hoyer (D-MD) called the vote "historic" and "momentous." The Employment Non-Discrimination Act (ENDA) would make it illegal for an employer "to fail or refuse to hire or to discharge any individual, or otherwise discriminate against any individual with respect to compensation, terms, conditions or privileges of employment of the individual, because of such individual's actual or perceived sexual orientation."

Supporters, including Sen. Susan Collins (R-ME), believed that there was a good chance that ENDA would also pass in the Senate. She said that "there is growing support in the Senate for strengthening federal laws to protect American workers from discrimination based on sexual orientation." Opponents of the bill said that it would lead to unnecessary lawsuits. President Bush threatened to veto an earlier version of the bill, and if the Senate were to pass this bill, he was expected to veto it.

Thirty-five Republicans joined 200 Democrats in voting for the bill, while 25 Democrats and 159 Republicans voted against it. Several of the Democrats who voted against the bill did so on the grounds that it was not inclusive enough, arguing that the current version does not protect transgender employees by outlawing discrimination based on gender identity. Language that would have protected transgender employees was removed in order to gain the votes necessary for passage. Defending this strategy, Speaker Nancy Pelosi (D-CA) said, "History teaches us that progress on civil rights is never easy. It is often marked by small and difficult steps."

Several gay rights advocacy groups questioned the exclusion of transgender people.

This version of ENDA would die in the Senate. The 2010 version of the bill that was before committees in the House and Senate did include protections for gender expression but did not gain passage.

NOVEMBER 8, 2007
HOUSE APPROVES BROAD PROTECTIONS FOR GAY WORKERS
By DAVID M. HERSZENHORN

WASHINGTON, Nov. 7—The House on Wednesday approved a bill granting broad protections against discrimination in the workplace for gay men, lesbians and bisexuals, a measure that supporters praised as the most important civil rights legislation since the Americans with Disabilities Act of 1990 but that opponents said would result in unnecessary lawsuits.

The bill, the Employment Nondiscrimination Act, is the latest version of legislation that Democrats have pursued since 1974. Representatives Edward I. Koch and Bella Abzug of New York then sought to protect gay men and lesbians with a measure they introduced on the fifth anniversary of the Stonewall Rebellion, the brawl between gay men and police officers at a bar in Greenwich Village that is widely viewed as the start of the American gay rights movement.

"On this proud day of the 110th Congress, we will chart a new direction for civil rights," said Representative Kathy Castor, a Florida Democrat and a gay rights advocate, in a speech before the vote. "On this proud day, the Congress will act to ensure that all Americans are granted equal rights in the work place."

Senator Edward M. Kennedy, a Massachusetts Democrat and a longtime supporter of gay rights legislation, said he would move swiftly to introduce a similar measure in the Senate. Some Senate Republicans said that, if worded carefully, it would have a good chance of passing, perhaps early next year.

Senator Susan Collins, Republican of Maine, has said that she would be the lead co-sponsor of the Senate bill. Ms. Collins, in a statement, said that the House vote "provides important momentum" and that "there is growing support in the Senate for strengthening federal laws to protect American workers from discrimination based on sexual orientation."

President Bush threatened to veto an earlier version of the bill, but a White House spokesman, Tony Fratto, said the administration would need to review recent changes before making a final decision. Few Democrats expect Mr. Bush to change his mind.

The House bill would make it illegal for an employer "to fail or refuse to hire or to discharge any individual, or otherwise discriminate against any individual with respect to the compensation, terms, conditions or privileges of employment of the individual, because of such individual's actual or perceived sexual orientation."

While 19 states and Washington, D.C., have laws barring discrimination based on sexual orientation, and many cities offer similar protections, federal law offers no such shield, though it does bar discrimination based on race, religion, ethnicity, sex, age, disability and pregnancy.

In the House on Wednesday, 35 Republicans joined 200 Democrats voting for the bill, which was approved 235 to 184, perhaps reflecting polls showing that a plurality of Americans believe homosexuality should be accepted as an alternative lifestyle, though a majority still oppose same-sex marriage. Voting against the bill were 25 Democrats and 159 Republicans.

Among the Democrats opposed, many said the bill should have also outlawed discrimination based on gender identity.

And while the Democrats fell far short of the votes that would be needed to override a presidential veto, many of them, including the majority leader, Representative Steny H. Hoyer of Maryland, spoke about the vote in exuberant tones, calling it "historic" and "momentous."

For more than 30 years, outlawing discrimination based on sexual orientation has been a cause of liberal Democrats, who have fought many partisan battles with Republicans but have always come up short. In 1996, the Senate came within one vote of passing a bill; the House did not vote on the bill that year.

The twist this year is that the measure has emerged as an example of Speaker Nancy Pelosi's pragmatism in trying to make headway on leading issues by granting concessions, even at the risk of angering her party's base.

To ensure passage of the bill, Ms. Pelosi and other Democrats, including Representative Barney Frank of Massachusetts, who is openly gay, removed language granting protections to transsexual and transgender individuals by barring discrimination based on sexual identity, a move that infuriated gay rights groups.

The Democrats also carved out a blanket exemption for religious groups, drawing the ire of civil liberties advocates who argued that church-run hospitals, for instance, should not be permitted to discriminate against gay employees. The civil liberties groups wanted a narrow exemption for religious employers.

On the House floor, Ms. Pelosi acknowledged challenges. "History teaches us that progress on civil rights is never easy," she said. "It is often marked by small and difficult steps."

Ms. Pelosi did maintain the support of the Human Rights Campaign, the largest gay rights group in the country, even though it was disappointed that gender identity protections were not included in the bill.

"Today's vote in the House sends a powerful message about equality to the country, and it's a significant step forward for our community," said Joe Solmonese, the group's president.

Others were not so upbeat. "What should have been one of the most triumphant days in our movement's history is not," said Matt Foreman, the executive director of the National Gay and Lesbian Task Force. "It's one of very mixed reactions."

But many longtime supporters of the legislation cheered its passage. "It's wonderful," said Mr. Koch, a former mayor of New York City. "Even though it is a vote that was delayed too long."

Much of the debate Wednesday was taken up by Republicans complaining, somewhat oddly, that they could not hold a vote on a Democratic amendment to restore gender identity language.

Democrats suggested that these Republicans were not hoping to protect transsexuals from discrimination but to restore provisions to the bill that would have made it easier to rally opposition.

Representative Doc Hastings of Washington, who led the Republican effort to get a vote on the amendment, said he opposed the overall bill in part because many states already had similar laws and because he viewed it as intrusive. "I do not think it is the place of the federal government to legislate how each and every place of business operates," Mr. Hastings said.

Other opponents said the law would result in spurious lawsuits.

"It would be impossible for employers to operate a business without having to worry about being accused of discriminating against someone based on their 'perceived' sexual orientation," said Representative Ginny Brown-Waite, Republican of Florida, who raised two fingers on each hand to flash quotation marks over her head as she said "perceived."

Mr. Kennedy, who is chairman of the Health, Education, Labor and Pensions Committee, issued a statement praising the House vote. He could introduce a measure identical to the House bill or a new version, which might restore language about gender identity.

INDEX

Photographs are indicated by italic page numbers.